Principles of Criminology

Principles of Criminology

BY

EDWIN H. SUTHERLAND

PROFESSOR OF SOCIOLOGY
INDIANA UNIVERSITY

THIRD EDITION, REVISED AND RESET

Lippincott Sociology Texts—Floyd N. House, Editor

J. B. LIPPINCOTT COMPANY

CHICAGO   PHILADELPHIA   NEW YORK

PREFACE

A SCIENCE OF CRIMINOLOGY is greatly needed at present both for satisfactory understanding and for adequate control. The existing criminology is inadequate: it has consisted of obviously unsound theories of criminal behavior, of scattered and unintegrated factual information, and unwarranted application of that knowledge to practical problems. The present edition of this book is designed to show some development of criminology toward science.

Two fundamental modifications have been made in this edition. First, the theory of criminal behavior is brought into the foreground. Previously this theory was stated in scattered passages and was not developed. It now appears in the first chapter and may be used as the point of departure and perhaps as the principle of integration in the whole study. Obviously this theory is not the last word on the subject; in fact, it is stated thus openly in the expectation that it will be criticized and will thus lead to the development of a more satisfactory theory of criminal behavior. Second, a chapter on behavior systems in crime is presented with the hope that it may prove to be useful in orienting and directing research work in criminology. It may supplement the scattered individual case studies and the superficial statistical studies, and assist in the development of a systematic body of knowledge regarding crime.

In addition to these fundamental modifications, the modifications in this revision are of two kinds. First, the scattered statistical and other factual information has been brought up to date as far as practicable. On most points it has been possible to secure relatively recent information. On some relatively unimportant points it has been necessary to use the earlier facts because new facts were not available and could have been secured only by extensive studies. Second, some chapters have been completely rewritten, and portions of all other chapters have been rewritten. This has involved clarification of statements in some cases, but in many cases has involved a reorganization of thought and the introduction of the results of new studies.

EDWIN H. SUTHERLAND

CONTENTS

Principles of Criminology

Chapter One

A THEORY OF CRIMINOLOGY

CRIMINOLOGY. Criminology is the body of knowledge regarding crime as a social phenomenon. It includes within its scope the processes of making laws, of breaking laws, and of reacting toward the breaking of laws. These processes are three aspects of a somewhat unified sequence of interactions. Certain acts which are regarded as undesirable are defined by the political society as crimes. In spite of this definition some people persist in the behavior and thus commit crimes; the political society reacts by punishment or other treatment, or by prevention. This sequence of interactions is the object-matter of criminology.

Criminology is sometimes defined more narrowly than this to include only the information regarding the causes of crime, and the term "penology" is then applied to the body of knowledge regarding the treatment of criminals. The broader definition is justified in etymology and is preferable to the narrower definition both because it is desirable to have one term to refer to the unified sequence of interactions and because the term "penology" is obviously inappropriate as a name for the knowledge regarding policies of treatment, many of which are not now penal in character.

The objective of criminology is the development of a body of general and verified principles and of other types of knowledge regarding this process of law, crime, and treatment or prevention. This knowledge will contribute to the development of other social studies and through these other social studies it will contribute to efficiency in general social control. In addition, criminology is concerned with the immediate application of knowledge to programs of social control of crime. This concern with practical programs is justified, in part, as experimentation which may be valuable

1

because of its immediate results but at any rate will be valuable in the long run because of the increased knowledge which results from it. If practical programs wait until theoretical knowledge is complete, they will wait for eternity, for theoretical knowledge is increased most significantly in the efforts at social control. John Dewey has described the relationship between knowledge and control thus:

It is a complete error to suppose that efforts at social control depend upon the prior existence of a social science. The reverse is the case. The building up of a social science, that is, of a body of knowledge in which facts are ascertained in their significant relations, is dependent upon putting social planning into effect. . . . Physical science did not develop because inquirers had piled up a mass of facts about observed phenomena. It came into being when men intentionally experimented, on the basis of ideas and hypotheses, with observed phenomena to modify them and disclose new observations. This process is self-corrective and self-developing. Imperfect and even wrong hypotheses, when acted upon, brought to light significant phenomena which made improved ideas and improved experimentations possible. The change from a passive and accumulative attitude into an active and productive one is the secret revealed by the progress of physical inquiry. Men obtained knowledge of natural energies by trying deliberately to control the conditions of their operation. The result was knowledge, and then control on a larger scale by the application of what was learned.[1]

While experimentation may increase theoretical knowledge and thereby contribute to ultimate improvements in policies, it is unnecessarily wasteful unless it be directed by the best organized and critical thought available. The average citizen is confronted by a confusing and conflicting complex of popular beliefs and programs in regard to crime. Some of these are traditions from eighteenth-century philosophy; some are promulgations of special interest groups; and some are blind emotional reactions. Organized and critical thinking in this field is therefore peculiarly difficult and also peculiarly necessary.

It is therefore desirable to begin this study with a tentative

---

[1] John Dewey, "Social Science and Social Control," *New Rep.*, 67:276–277, July 29, 1931. Reprinted by permission.

theory of criminology and to keep this theory in mind throughout the entire study. The principles of this theory should be regarded as tentative and hypothetical and should be tested by the factual information which is presented in the later chapters and by all other factual information and theories which are applicable.

CONSIDERATIONS IN A THEORY OF CRIMINAL BEHAVIOR. Three general considerations should be kept in mind in the construction of a theory of criminology. First, the other theories of criminology should be considered. The various theories of criminology differ principally in the points which they emphasize. These theories may be classified regarding the points of emphasis in two principal groups, namely, individual differences and situational or cultural processes. The individual differences may be inherited or acquired, and may include anatomical and physiological deviations, feeblemindedness, psychopathy, and minor mental and emotional deviations. The situational and cultural processes may place emphasis on small groups such as family and neighborhood, on general institutions such as the economic and political systems, or on general cultural processes such as differential association, cultural conflicts, and social disorganization. All of these must be considered and most of them included in a final organization of thought regarding criminal behavior.

Second, the execution of a crime requires desire for the results to be secured by the crime, lack or weakness of internal inhibitions, lack or weakness of external inhibitions (including accessibility of the object, public opinion or group opinion regarding the behavior, and the danger of detection and punishment), and technical ability to execute the crime. A theory of criminal behavior should take all of these into account. Many of the theories have been concerned only with the desires and inhibitions of the person who commits the crime.

Third, delinquency is adventitious when considered as a specific act of a specific person. No one can explain why a coin comes up "heads" on a particular toss. It is described as due to chance. Chance does not mean that no causes are operating, but that the causes are so complicated that they cannot be analyzed. Similarly, a specific criminal act may be the result of a complex of causes which cannot be analyzed. This does not mean that it is similar to the flipping of a coin with only two alternatives and those of equal likelihood. Rather it is like rolling loaded dice, with high probability but not certainty. It is not possible to explain adequately why one person commits a specific crime while another, with traits, experiences, and social situation almost identical, does not. The plot of a recent motion picture is based on a comparison of two boys engaged in theft. When discovered, one ran more rapidly, escaped, and became a priest; the other ran less rapidly, was caught and committed to a reformatory, and became a gangster. In other circumstances, the one who ran more rapidly might have become the gangster and the one who ran less rapidly the priest. It is such combinations of factors which make it impossible to explain each individual act adequately, because it is never possible to include all of these unique combinations in a generalization. On that account attention should be concentrated on systematic criminal behavior, either in the form of criminal careers or organized criminal practices. By this statement of the problem it may be possible to discover the processes which are general and uniform and to arrive at an adequate theory of such behavior. If a theory can be developed that is adequate for systematic criminal behavior it will be easier to explain specific acts in relation to this framework.

A THEORY OF CRIMINAL BEHAVIOR. This tentative theory of criminal behavior is stated in the form of the seven following propositions.

First, *the processes which result in systematic criminal behavior are fundamentally the same in form as the processes which result in systematic lawful behavior.* If criminality were specifically determined by inheritance, the laws and principles of inheritance would be the same for criminal behavior and for lawful behavior. The same is true of imitation or any other genetic process in the development of behavior. Criminal behavior differs from lawful behavior in the standards by which it is judged but not in the principles of the genetic processes.

Second, *systematic criminal behavior is determined in a process of association with those who commit crimes, just as systematic lawful behavior is determined in a process of association with those who are law-abiding.* Any person can learn any pattern of behavior which he is able to execute. He inevitably assimilates such behavior from the surrounding culture. The pattern of behavior may cause him to suffer death, physical injury, loss of friendship, or loss of money, but it may nevertheless be followed with joy provided he has learned that it is the thing to do. Since criminal behavior is thus developed in association with criminals it means that crime is the cause of crime. In the same manner war is the cause of war, and the Southern practice of dropping the "r" is the cause of the Southern practice of dropping the "r." This proposition, stated negatively, is that a person does not participate in systematic criminal behavior by inheritance. No individual inherits tendencies which inevitably make him criminal or inevitably make him law-abiding. Also, the person who is not already trained in crime does not invent systematic criminal behavior. While personality certainly includes an element of inventiveness, a person does not invent a system of criminal behavior unless he has had training in that kind of behavior, just as a person does not make systematic mechanical inventions unless he has had training in mechanics.

Third, *differential association is the specific causal process in the development of systematic criminal behavior.* The principles of the process of association by which criminal behavior develops are the same as the principles of the process by which lawful behavior develops, but the contents of the patterns presented in association differ. For that reason it is called differential association. The association which is of primary importance in criminal behavior is association with persons who engage in systematic criminal behavior. A person who has never heard of professional shoplifting may meet a professional shoplifter in his hotel, may become acquainted with and like him, learn from him the techniques, values, and codes of shoplifting, and under this tutelage may become a professional shoplifter. He could not become a professional shoplifter by reading newspapers, magazines, or books. The impersonal agencies of communication exert some influence but are important principally in determining receptivity to the patterns of criminal behavior when they are presented in personal association, and in producing incidental offenses. These patterns are presented through the impersonal agencies of communication to everyone in our culture. Every child capable of learning inevitably assimilates knowledge regarding property rights and thefts in the simpler situations. It is probably for this reason that everyone is somewhat criminal. College students, with a few exceptions doubtless due to poor memories, report an average of eight thefts or series of thefts during their lifetimes; a series of thefts in this case may include scores of incidents, such as stealing fruit from neighbors' trees from the age of seven to twelve. These thefts were reported equally for males and females, and continued in most cases to the age at which the reports were made. In the later years they generally took the form of theft of books from the library, of equipment from the gymnasium or laboratory, or of souvenirs from hotels and restaurants. Students do not regard such thefts as especially reprehensible; they regard them as amusing. Similarly, boys in the delinquent areas of cities do not regard thefts of automobiles or the burglary of stores as reprehensible, and business or professional men do not regard their frauds and tricky manipulations as reprehensible. A person engages in those criminal acts which are prevalent in his own groups, and he assimilates them in association with the members of the groups.

Fourth, *the chance that a person will participate in systematic criminal behavior is determined roughly by the frequency and consistency of his contacts with the patterns of criminal behavior.* If a person could come into contact only with lawful behavior he would inevitably be completely law-abiding. If he could come into contact only with criminal behavior (which is impossible, since no group could exist if all of its behavior were criminal) he would inevitably be completely criminal. The actual condition is between these extremes. The ratio of criminal acts to lawful acts by a person is roughly the same as the ratio of the contacts with the criminal and with the lawful behavior of others. It is true, of course, that a single critical experience may be the turning point in a career. But these critical experiences are generally based on a long series of former experiences and they produce their effects generally because they change the person's associations. One of these critical experiences that is most important in determining criminal careers is the first public appearance as a criminal. A boy who is arrested and convicted is thereby publicly defined as a criminal. Thereafter his associations with lawful people are restricted and he is thrown into association with other delinquents. On the other hand a person who is consistently criminal is not defined as law-abiding by a single lawful act. Every person is expected to be law-abiding, and lawful behavior is taken for granted because the lawful culture is dominant, more extensive, and more pervasive than the criminal culture.

Fifth, *individual differences among people in respect to personal characteristics or social situations cause crime only as they affect differential association or frequency and consistency of contacts with criminal patterns.* Poverty in the home may force a family to reside in a low-rent area where delinquency rates are high and thereby facilitate association with delinquents. Parents who insist that their boy return home immediately after school and who are able to enforce this regulation may prevent the boy from coming into frequent contact with delinquents even though the family resides in a high delinquency area. A child who is not wanted at home may be emotionally upset, but the significant thing is that this condition may drive him away from the home and he may therefore come into contact with delinquents. A boy who is timid may be kept from association with rough delinquents. It is not necessary to assume a generic difference between persons by reason of which some are generally receptive to criminality and others not receptive. Such an assumption would be far-fetched and un-justified. There may be receptivity at a particular moment to a particular stimulation, but the elements are so complex that no generalization regarding such receptivity is possible. The closest approach to a generalization is to say that this specific receptivity is determined principally by the frequency and consistency of pre-vious contacts with patterns of delinquency and that beyond this the delinquent behavior is adventitious.

Sixth, *cultural conflict is the underlying cause of differential association and therefore of systematic criminal behavior.* Differen-tial association is possible because society is composed of various groups with varied cultures. These differences in culture are found in respect to many values and are generally regarded as desirable. They exist, also, with reference to the values which the laws are designed to protect, and in that form are generally regarded as undesirable. This criminal culture is as real as lawful culture and is much more prevalent than in usually believed. It is not confined to the hoodlums in slums or to professional criminals. Prisoners frequently state and undoubtedly believe that they are no worse than the majority of people on the outside. The more intricate manipulations of business and professional men may be kept within the letter of the law as interpreted but be identical in logic and effects with the criminal behavior which results in imprisonment. These practices, even if they do not result in public condemnation as crimes, are a part of the criminal culture. The more the cultural patterns conflict, the more unpredictable is the behavior of a par-ticular person. It was possible to predict with almost complete certainty how a person reared in a Chinese village fifty years ago would behave because there was only one way for him to behave. The attempts to explain the behavior of a particular person in a modern city have been rather unproductive because the influences are in conflict and any particular influence may be very evanescent.

Seventh, *social disorganization is the basic cause of systematic criminal behavior.* The origin and the persistence of culture conflicts relating to the values expressed in the law and of differential association which is based on the cultural conflicts are due to social disorganization. Cultural conflict is a specific aspect of social disorganization and in that sense the two concepts are names for smaller and larger aspects of the same thing. But social disorganization is important in another sense. Since the law-abiding culture is dominant and more extensive, it could overcome systematic crime if organized for that purpose. But society is organized around individual and small group interests on most points. A law-abiding person is more interested in his own immediate personal projects than in abstract social welfare or justice. In this sense society permits crime to persist in systematic form. Consequently systematic crime persists not only because of differential association but also because of the reaction of the general society toward such crime. When a society or a smaller group develops a unified interest in crimes which touch its fundamental and common values, it generally succeeds in eliminating or at least greatly reducing crime. This occurred, for instance, when baseball players in the world series took bribes for throwing away a game they could have won. This affected so many people in a manner which they regarded as vital, and they reacted in such evident opposition, that the crime, so far as is known, has never been repeated. Also, when many wealthy people were kidnaped and held for ransom at the end of the prohibition period, our society reorganized the legal and administrative system in violation of the slogans and myth of state sovereignty and such kidnapings practically ceased. However, in previous times when poor and helpless people were the victims of kidnapings, as in the slave trade, impressment of sailors, shanghaiing of sailors by crimps, and unjustifiable arrests, it took generations and in some cases centuries for society to become sufficiently aware and interested to stop kidnapings in those forms. When a gang starts in a disorganized district of a city it keeps growing and other gangs develop. But when a delinquent gang started on a business street adjacent to Hyde Park, a good residential district in Chicago, the residents became concerned, formed an organization, and decided that the best way to protect themselves was by providing a club house and recreational facilities for the delinquents. This practically eliminated the gangs. Therefore, whether systematic delinquency does or does not develop is determined not only by associations that people make with the criminals, but also by the reactions of the rest of society toward systematic criminal behavior. If the society is organized with reference to the values expressed in the law, the crime is eliminated; if it is not organized, crime persists and develops. The opposition of the society may take the form of punishment, of reformation, or of prevention.

The general theory which has been presented may be summarized in the following statements: Systematic criminal behavior is due immediately to differential association in a situation in which cultural conflicts exist, and ultimately to the social disorganization in that situation. A specific or incidental crime of a particular person is due generally to the same process, but it is not possible to include all cases because of the adventitious character of delinquency when regarded as specific or incidental acts.

Chapter Two

CRIMINAL LAW AND CRIMINOLOGY

THE CONVENTIONAL DEFINITION OF CRIMINAL LAW AND OF CRIME. Crime is defined legally as a violation of law. The criminal law is defined conventionally as a body of specific rules regarding human conduct which have been promulgated by political authority, which apply uniformly to all members of the classes to which the rules refer, and which are enforced by punishment administered by the state. The characteristics of these rules regarding human conduct are, therefore, politicality, specificity, uniformity, and penal sanction. These rules are found in the constitutions, treaties, common law, enactments by the legislatures of the state and of its subdivisions, and in judicial and administrative regulations. A violation of the criminal law as thus defined requires both an overt act and a culpable intent. A crime is dealt with as an injury to the state rather than to a private citizen and in this respect differs from a tort or civil injury, for which the injured party may attempt to secure damages.

This definition, to be sure, constitutes a neat system of thought, but it has been criticized by the authorities in jurisprudence and elsewhere and it is evidently not an adequate definition, even from the legal point of view.

WHAT IS THE CRIMINAL LAW? Criminal law, in the first place, is not merely a collection of written proscriptions. The agency of enforcement of law is the court, and thus it is the court rather than the legislature which determines what the law is. The techniques used by the court in interpreting and applying the statutes and the body of ideals held by the court are a part of the law in action, as truly as are the written statutes. The importance of these general views is made very evident when a problem of selecting a justice of the supreme court confronts the nation. The nature of the federal law is determined to a considerable extent by the proportion of liberals and conservatives on the supreme bench. Thus back of the supreme court and also of inferior courts is public opinion. Also, between the courts and the legislature are intermediate agencies, such as the police, which affect the enforcement of the law. Many statutes are never enforced, others only on rare occasions. These agencies, also, are affected by public opinion, so that Pound has concluded that law in action is determined chiefly by public opinion.[1] Consequently the law does not consist in the statutes alone and may change while the statutes remain constant.

Politicality is regarded almost universally at present as a necessary element in criminal law. The rules of the trade union, the church, or the family are not regarded as criminal law, and violations of these rules are not regarded as crimes. The differentiation of these groups and the political state in this respect, though arbitrary, causes little difficulty until attention is turned to other cultural groups, where patriarchal power, private self-help, popular justice, and other forerunners of legislative justice may be found. Among the gypsies at present there is no territorial organization and no written law, but there are customs, taboos, and a semi-judicial council which makes definite decisions regarding the propriety of behavior of members of the group and may impose penalties. These councils have no political authority in the territory in which they happen to be operating, but they perform the same function within the gypsy group that courts perform in the political order.[2] Similarly, the Chinese immigrants in Chicago have established an unofficial court which has no political authority but which in practice exercises the functions of an authorized court in controversies among the Chinese people, just as did the guild and the family council in their home country.[3] Thus, the element of politicality is arbitrary and is not sharply defined. These earlier systems of law, together with the present relation between public opinion and legal precepts, raise the question, Why should not the rules of any group or agency be regarded as the law and violations of these rules as crimes?

---

[1] Roscoe Pound, *Criminal Justice in America,* New York, 1930, p. 120.
[2] Irving Brown, "Children of the Earth," *Survey,* 59:9, October 1, 1927.
[3] Chu Chai, "Administration of Law among the Chinese in Chicago," *Jour. Crim. Law and Criminol.,* 22:806–818, March, 1932.

Specificity is included as an element in the definition of criminal law because of the contrast in this respect between criminal law and civil law. The civil law is general. The German civil code, for instance, provided that whoever intentionally injured another in a manner contrary to the common standards of right conduct was bound to indemnify him.[4] The criminal law, on the other hand, generally gives a strict definition of a specific act. Some laws, to be sure, are more general, as the laws in regard to nuisances, conspiracy, disorderly conduct, use of the mails to defraud, and official misfeasance. The criminal law, however, contains no general provision that any act which, when done with culpable intent, injures the public can be prosecuted as a punishable offense.[5] Consequently it frequently happens that one thing is prohibited by law while another thing which is very similar in nature and effects is not prohibited and is not illegal.

Uniformity or regularity is included in the conventional definition of criminal law because law attempts to provide even-handed justice without respect to persons. This ideal, however, has varied widely in practice. Rigid rule and judicial discretion have alternated in importance. Rigid rule treats all persons in the class to which the law refers exactly alike, while judicial discretion takes cognizance of varying elements in the situations of the members of the class and thus approaches closer to individualization. Equity, also, developed as a method of doing justice in particular situations where iron regularity would not do justice. As precedents in equity have accumulated, the decisions tend to become uniform, and thus similar to law. In line with the present tendency toward judicial discretion, authority has been conferred by legislative assemblies upon many administrative bodies to make regulations applicable to particular situations.

Coercion is one of the elements in the orthodox definition of law, and the method of coercion is threat or application of punishment.

---

[4] Ernst Freund, "Classification and Definition of Crimes," *Jour. Crim. Law and Criminol.*, 5:807–808, March, 1915.

[5] A German law of June 28, 1935, seems to be an exception to this generalization. It provides: "Whoever commits an action which the law declares to be punishable or which is deserving of punishment according to the fundamental idea of a penal law and the sound perception of the people, shall be punished. If no determinate penal law is directly applicable to the action, it shall be punished according to the law, the basic idea of which fits it best." Lawrence Preuss, "Punishment by Analogy in National Socialist Penal Law," *Jour. Crim. Law and Criminol.*, 26:847, March, 1936.

A law which does not provide a penalty that will cause suffering is regarded as quite impotent and in fact as no law at all.[6] In view of the difficulty of defining criminal law in primitive society, the suggestion has been made that the penal sanction is the only essential element in the definition of criminal law, and that wherever proscriptions are enforced by a penal sanction there criminal law exists. It is evident, however, that the punitive aspect of criminal law is on the wane at present. In the juvenile court and to a smaller extent in the criminal courts, the tendency is to use methods which have been found to be effective, regardless of whether they are coercive and punitive or not. Oliphant has made this suggestion:

It would be very interesting to see some legislature try the following. Suppose it wants to stop the killing of certain game at certain times. Let the legislature, instead of enacting a prohibition with penalties, simply recite the cogent and persuasive reasons why the game in question should not be killed and end with an appropriate exhortation so that the whole would appeal to the reason of thoughtful and fair-minded people. Such a measure, calculated to inform and crystallize group opinion, might be, in some carefully chosen situations, quite as effective as legislation of the present character which, uncritically following the ancient models, is universally peremptory in form but not always so in effect.[7]

The coercion of the law differs from that of the lynching mob in that it is applied decently by representatives of the state in such manner that it may win the approval of the cool judgment of impartial observers.

The conventional idea has been that a crime from the legal point of view must include both an overt act and a culpable intent or *mens rea*. A behavioristic school in jurisprudence, however, insists that the intent can be determined only by the circumstances of the act and that a translation of these circumstances into mental terms confuses rather than clarifies the procedure. They contend that the

---

[6] In the Courts of Honor a verdict was reached and one party declared guilty but no punishment inflicted. The disgrace of a declaration of guilt was the only penalty.

[7] Herman Oliphant, "The Public and the Law," *Amer. Bar Assoc. Jour.*, 18:791, December, 1932.

doctrine of *mens rea* should be greatly modified or even abandoned.[8]

Finally, the conventional view is that a crime is an offense against the state, while in contrast a tort in violation of civil law is an offense against an individual. In practice, however, the general public is actively interested in a very small proportion of the crimes which result in arrest, and the victim in many cases is interested primarily in securing restitution. Prosecutors complain because victims refuse to act as complaining witnesses after restitution has been made and prosecution is generally ineffective without the assistance of the complaining witness. The criminal law, thus, acts as a collecting agency for victims of crime. The suggestion has been made that these victims should use the civil rather than the criminal law.[9]

For many centuries the philosophers of jurisprudence have been attempting by deductive reasoning to determine the principle back of the specific laws. Divine will, the will of the sovereign, nature, reason, history, public opinion, and other principles were presented.[10] Jerome Frank has attempted to explain by a quasi-psychoanalytic method the effort to secure exactness, certainty, and predictability in the law as due to the persisting childish need for an authoritative father, and he suggests that the solution of the conflict between the wish for certainty and the impossibility of securing certainty is to get rid of the need for the father authority.[11] Pound has stated that a final answer to the question, "What is law?" is impossible because law is a living, changing thing, which may at one time be based on sovereign will and at another time on juristic science, which may at one time be uniform and at another time give much room for judicial discretion, which may at one time be

---

[8] Albert Levitt, "The Origin of the Doctrine of *Mens Rea*," *Ill. Law Rev.*, 17:117–137, June, 1922; Albert Levitt, "Extent and Function of the Doctrine of *Mens Rea*," *Ill. Law Rev.*, 17:578–595, April, 1923; O. W. Holmes, *The Common Law*, Boston, 1881, Ch. 2; F. B. Sayre, "Mens Rea," *Harv. Law Rev.*, 45:974–1026, April, 1932.

[9] C. L. B. Lawndes, "Civil Liability Created by Criminal Legislation," *Minn. Law Rev.*, 16:361–377, March, 1932; M. Solberg, "Civil Remedies and Mercenary Crime," in E. D. McDougall (Editor), *Crime for Profit*, pp. 193–204.

[10] John W. Burgess, *The Sanctity of Law*, Boston, 1927; Roscoe Pound, *Interpretations of Legal History*, New York, 1923; Roscoe Pound, *Law and Morals*, Chapel Hill, N. C., 1926; Morris H. Cohen, *Law and the Social Order*, New York, 1933.

[11] Jerome Frank, *Law and the Modern Mind*, New York, 1930.

very specific in its proscriptions and at another time much more general.[12]

NATURE OF CRIMINAL LAW FROM THE GENETIC POINT OF VIEW. Many theories of the origin of the criminal law as an agency of social control have been developed. First, in the classical theory the criminal law was regarded as originating in torts, or wrongs to individuals. According to this theory, all wrongs produced efforts at self-redress in the injured parties and were therefore treated as injuries to particular individuals; and later, by a series of transitions, the group took charge of the treatment, and the wrongs came to be regarded as injuries to the group or to the state. These transitions included a requirement that the avenger announce his intention of seeking revenge; a requirement that the avenger secure the consent of the group before taking vengeance; the regulation of the amount of injury that could be done to the wrong-doer by the injured party; the limitation of time and place in which vengeance could be secured; public investigation of the merits of the case in connection with the requirements mentioned previously or independently of these; and participation of some members of the group in the efforts of the injured party to secure self-redress. There can be no doubt that some crimes did originate in torts and became crimes through one or more of the steps described. The theory is inadequate, however, as a general or universal explanation of the criminal law. It assumes the priority of the individual to the group and this is not justified, for it is certain that in early societies some wrongs were regarded as wrongs against the group. Such wrongs were regarded as dangerous to the group directly, as in treason and in violations of the hunting rules, or indirectly, as in sacrilege and witchcraft which might bring down the wrath of the gods upon the group.[13] Furthermore, even so far as crimes did originate from torts the process is not adequately described. It is at this point, in part, that some of the other theories are concentrated.

A second theory is that the criminal law originated in the rational processes of a unified society. When wrongs occurred the society took thought and made a regulation to prevent a repetition of such wrongs. It is obvious that some criminal laws are made in that

---

[12] Roscoe Pound, *Interpretations of Legal History*, New York, 1923, Ch. 3.

[13] S. R. Steinmetz, *Ethnologische Studien zur ersten Entwicklung der Strafe*, Leiden, 1894, Vol. II, pp. 327-348; H. Oppenheimer, *The Rationale of Punishment*, London, 1913, pp. 66-91.

manner, and the general program of professional students is directed toward the development of this procedure for criminal laws in general. But the theory is obviously inadequate as a general description of how the criminal law has developed.

A third theory is that the criminal law originated in and is a crystallization of the mores. Customs developed with little or no rational analysis and after persisting for a time developed a body of ethical and philosophical thought. Infraction of such customs produced antagonistic reactions of the group, which were expressed in the form of criminal law with penal sanctions. This statement is a fairly accurate description of primitive law and of modern common law, but is not an accurate description of many of the modern statutes which deal with railways, factories, automobiles, and radio. It should be noted, however, that even in the laws dealing with these modern inventions the general values are, for the most part, taken over from the mores of the time, although the specific practices had not previously become customary.

A fourth theory is that criminal law originated in conflict of interests of different groups. When an interest group secures the enactment of a law it secures the assistance of the state in a conflict with a rival interest group; the opposition of the rival group thus becomes criminal. According to this theory, wrongful acts are characteristic of all classes in present-day society; the upper classes are subtle in their wrongdoing, the underprivileged classes are direct. The upper classes are politically important and they prohibit the wrongful acts of the underprivileged classes, but the laws are defined and implemented in such manner that the wrongful and subtle acts of the upper classes do not come within their scope. In this theory the criminal law originates in the conflict of groups and in the inconsistency of the mores. Like the other theories it correctly describes a part of the process of lawmaking but fails of accuracy regarding other aspects of the law.

A fifth theory is that the enactment of a statute is an expression of emotion. Something occurs which upsets a group and it rushes to the legislature to secure a prohibition of such acts. Professor Park said in one of his lectures, "We are always in America passing laws. We might as well get up and dance. The laws are largely to relieve emotion, and the legislatures are quite aware of that fact."

For one or more of the reasons described, laws are being utilized in America with increasing frequency. The number of statutes in a selected group of states increased approximately 40 per cent from 1900 to 1930, and the same trend appears in regard to football rules, bridge rules, trade union rules, and probably almost all other rules.[14] There is probably a somewhat general disorganization which throws this burden upon the rule-makers. Laws have accumulated because the mores have been weak and inconsistent; and because the laws have not had the support of the mores they are relatively ineffective as a means of control. When the mores are adequate, laws are unnecessary; when the mores are inadequate, the laws are ineffective.

Evidently the theories of the origin of the criminal law are in conflict with one another, and no positive conclusion can be reached. Research as to the social aspects of the criminal law is greatly needed. While the medical profession is constantly engaged in research work as to the origin of diseases and the effects of treatment, the legal profession engages in practically no research work of an analogous kind; it confines its research work almost entirely to a study of what the law *is*. One of the small number of exceptions to this is found in the excellent analysis by Jerome Hall of the development of the law of theft in modern society.[15] If more studies of this nature were available, it might be possible to develop a realistic interpretation of the criminal law.

THE RELATIVITY OF CRIME. Crime is relative from the legal point of view and also from the social point of view. It has had a constantly changing content. Many of the early crimes were primarily religious offenses, and these remained important until recent times; now few religious offenses are included in the penal codes. It was a crime in Iceland in the Viking age for a person to write verses about another, even if the sentiment was complimentary, if the verses exceeded four strophes in length. A Prussian law of 1784 prohibited mothers and nurses from taking children under two years of age into their beds. The English villain in the fourteenth century was not allowed to send his son to school, and no one lower than a freeholder was permitted by law to keep a dog. The following have at different times been crimes: printing a book, professing the medical doctrine of circulation of the blood, driving with reins, sale of coin to foreigners, having gold in the house, buying goods

---

[14] *Recent Social Trends in the United States,* New York, 1933, Vol. II, pp. 1115–1122.

[15] Jerome Hall, *Theft, Law, and Society,* Boston, 1935.

on the way to market or in the market for the purpose of selling them at a higher price, writing a check for less than $1.00. On the other hand, many of our present laws were not known to earlier generations—quarantine laws, traffic laws, sanitation laws, factory laws.

Laws differ, also, from one jurisdiction to another at a particular time. A state law of Indiana in 1938 required the owner of an automobile to paste on the windshield his certificate of ownership, while, according to newspaper reports, some of the adjoining states prohibited the pasting of anything on the windshield which might obstruct vision.

In a particular jurisdiction at a particular time there are wide variations in the interpretation and implementation of the law. Fraudulent statements on a bottle of patent medicine are prohibited, while fraudulent statements in a newspaper or over the radio regarding the same medicine are not specifically included in the law. In general, the criminal law is not implemented to punish the somewhat subtle kinds of fraud. The status of the wrongdoer and the attitudes of the influential part of the public toward his actions are highly important in determining whether his actions are or are not crimes. Thus crime and not-crime are not two distinct types of behavior but constitute a continuum.

NATURE OF CRIME FROM THE SOCIAL POINT OF VIEW. The statement that we would have no crime if we had no laws and that we could eliminate all crime merely by abolishing all laws is logomachy. It is true that if the laws against stealing were repealed, stealing would not, in a legal sense, be a crime, but it would still be stealing and the public would react to it by lynch law and public disgrace. The name of the behavior would be changed but the behavior would remain essentially the same. Because of this, efforts have been made to include within the definition of crime a description of the nature of the acts which the law prohibits and thus to define crime in social rather than legal terms. Garofalo developed a concept of the natural crime and defined it as a violation of the prevalent sentiments of pity and probity.[16] Radcliffe-Brown has defined crime as a violation of usage which gives rise to the exercise of the penal sanction. Thomas has defined crime from the point of view of social psychology as an action which is antagonistic

---

[16] R. Garofalo, *Criminology*, Boston, 1914, p. 59.

to the solidarity of that group which the individual considers as his own.[17] Crime may be considered, in the light of the discussion in the preceding sections, to involve three elements: a value which is appreciated by a group or a part of a group which is politically important; isolation of or cultural conflict in another part of this group so that its members do not appreciate the value or appreciate it less highly and consequently tend to endanger it; and a pugnacious resort to coercion decently applied by those who appreciate the value to those who disregard the value. When a crime is committed, these relationships are involved. Crime *is* this set of relationships when viewed from the point of view of the group rather than of the individual. This conception of the social nature of crime, as well as the preceding definitions, is suggestive and may be developed into a fundamental definition, but at present certainly lacks precision.

CLASSIFICATION OF CRIMES. Since crime is not a homogeneous type of behavior, efforts have been made to classify crimes. They are frequently classified in respect to atrocity as felonies and misdemeanors. The more serious are called felonies and are usually punishable by death or by confinement in a state prison; the less serious are called misdemeanors and are usually punishable by confinement in a local prison or by fines. As a classification of crimes this is not very useful, as was pointed out long ago by Sir James Stephen, and it is difficult to make a clear-cut distinction between the classes. Though one may agree that murders, as a class, are more serious offenses than permitting weeds to grow on a vacant lot in violation of a municipal ordinance, yet the effects of permitting the weeds to grow, in a particular case, may be more serious because of the hay fever produced by the pollen and the resulting incapacity of, say, ten people affected by it than one murder would be. The fact that many things which are classed as felonies in one state are classed as misdemeanors in near-by states shows how difficult it is to make a real distinction between them. Queen reports an investigation which shows that of 110 offenses in the laws of eleven states in 1918, 39 were punishable in some states as misdemeanors, in other states as felonies, from which he draws the conclusion that there is no inherent distinction between a felony

---

[17] W. I. Thomas and F. Znaniecki, *The Polish Peasant*, New York, 1927, Vol. II, pp. 1753–1755.

and a misdemeanor.[18] The distinction even within one state is often vague. This principle of classification is not used in the reports on prisoners by the Bureau of the Census.

The greatest objection to the classification of crimes as felonies and misdemeanors is that it is used, also, as a classification of criminals. The individual who commits a felony is a felon; the individual who commits a misdemeanor is a misdemeanant. It is assumed that misdemeanants are less dangerous than felons. But it is quite fallacious to judge the danger to the group from one act, for an individual may commit a misdemeanor one week, a felony the second week, and a misdemeanor the third. The acts do not represent changes in his character or changes in the danger to the group. Queen found that there were few respects in which those judged to be felons were different from those judged to be misdemeanants and many respects in which the two groups overlapped.[19] It is evident, for instance, that some misdemeanants are more dangerous and more costly than some felons. Sixty-three per cent of the persons sentenced to county jails and houses of correction in Massachusetts in 1936 had served terms previously in penal institutions, as contrasted with 75 per cent of those in the state prison; and their average number of previous commitments was five, as contrasted with three in the case of those in the state prison. Moreover, the definition is influenced by various other considerations. Since 1852, when a felony was first defined in Massachusetts as a crime punishable by confinement in the state prison, four changes have been made in the laws of that state, determining the conditions under which a sentence is served in state prison rather than in a jail or house of correction. These changes, which also changed crimes from felonies to misdemeanors or the reverse, were not made because of alterations in views regarding the atrocity of crimes but for purely administrative reasons, generally to relieve the congestion of the state prison.[20] Consequently there seems to be good reason to demand an entire abandonment of this classification.

Bonger has classified crimes by the motives of the offenders as economic crimes, sexual crimes, political crimes, and miscellaneous

---

[18] S. A. Queen, *The Passing of the County Jail*, Menasha, Wis., 1920, pp. 75–82.

[19] *Ibid.*, pp. 87–94.

[20] W. F. Spalding, "The Legislative History of a 'State Prison' Sentence as a Test of 'Felony' and 'Infamous Punishment' and the Practical Results in Massachusetts," *Mass. Law Quart.*, 7:91–108, January, 1922.

crimes (with vengeance as the principal motive).[21] But no crime can be reduced to one motive. A desire for excitement or vengeance may be very important in such crimes as burglary, which Bonger classified as economic crime. The classification is clearly inadequate.

Crimes are frequently classified for statistical purposes as crimes against the person, crimes against property, and crimes against public decency, public order, and public justice. Most recorded crimes are crimes against public order or public morality, such as disorderly conduct and drunkenness; next in frequency come the crimes of dishonesty without violence. Of the persons committed to local, state, or federal penal and reformatory institutions in 1933, 46 per cent were convicted of drunkenness or disorderly conduct or vagrancy, 16 per cent of crimes of dishonesty without violence. The crimes which are regarded as most serious are relatively few, according to this criterion. Homicide constituted 0.8 per cent, rape 0.2 per cent, burglary 1.3 per cent, and robbery 1.7 per cent, a total for these serious offenses of 4.0 per cent of all crimes for which persons were committed to institutions in 1933. It is probable that if all cases of fraud could be recorded, fraud would rank close to drunkenness and disorderly conduct in frequency.

An attempt was made by police officials to secure a uniform classification of crimes for statistical purposes,[22] and some effort has been made to classify crimes for purposes of codification of criminal laws.[23] Each of these classifications has value for its own purposes, but neither of them serves adequately for theoretical analysis.

In a classification of crimes for theoretical purposes each class should be a sociological entity, differentiated from the other classes by variations in causal processes. Professional crime, for instance, would be a class, or more likely a combination of classes, differentiated from other crimes by the regularity of this behavior, the development of techniques, and the association among offenders and the consequent development of a group culture. Within this class might be included some cases of murder, arson, burglary,

---

[21] W. A. Bonger, *Criminality and Economic Conditions,* Boston, 1916, pp. 536–537.

[22] *Uniform Crime Reporting: A Complete Manual for Police,* New York, 1929.

[23] John W. MacDonald, "The Classification of Crimes," *Cornell Law Quart.,* 19:524–563, June, 1933; Ernst Freund, "Classification and Definition of Crimes," *Jour. Crim. Law and Criminol.,* 5:807–826, March, 1915.

robbery, and theft, but not all of the cases in any of those legal categories. Jerome Hall has made an excellent beginning of the analysis of theft from this point of view.[24] It is not worth while at present to attempt a complete classification of crimes from this point of view. Such a classification should grow out of research work rather than of *a priori* speculation.

THE NATURE OF THE CRIMINAL. Who is a criminal? The most simple answer is: A person who commits a crime. This answer merely raises other questions. For how long is a person who commits a crime a criminal? Is it during the time he is committing the crime, until he has "paid the penalty," or during the remainder of his life? This question is perhaps unimportant and it is difficult to answer only because we use the word "criminal" to stigmatize the one who violates the law. In public thought the word "criminal" is generally applied only to those who are ostracized by society. It is in this sense that Tarde states that criminals are social excrement.

The criminal is . . . no more a social product than he is a natural product; he is—forgive me the word—a social excrement. . . . When the natures of these people happen to change it is always a serious symptom. If a society excretes excellent elements which it does not know how to utilize,—the Protestants under Louis XIV, the "aristocrats" under the Terror,—it is dangerously ill, rather like a man suffering from diabetes, and for a reason which is at bottom analogous.[25]

A second question is: What is the nature of the persons who commit crimes? It is highly probable that every person who is capable of self-direction commits crimes. Some people commit crimes frequently, others infrequently; some commit more serious crimes with a definitely antisocial sentiment, others with no antisocial sentiment whatever; some commit crimes with glee, others with apology, and others without awareness that they are committing crimes. Even regarding the criminals confined in prisons, it is not safe to generalize.

Moreover, even the most confirmed and professional criminal probably performs a larger number of acts which are in themselves

---

[24] Jerome Hall, *Theft, Law, and Society,* Boston, 1935.
[25] G. Tarde, *Penal Philosophy,* Boston, 1912, p. 222. Reprinted by permission of Little, Brown & Company, publishers.

law-abiding than he performs criminal acts. He is characterized by a portion of his acts just as is the non-criminal. Probably the term "criminal" should be abandoned completely or at least until the social type can be more clearly defined. Some of the legal distinctions between crimes correspond roughly to traits of personality and of character. Murderers are, as a class, different from robbers, and embezzlers from burglars. These legal distinctions, however, are not satisfactory for theoretical or administrative purposes. The principle of classification of criminals, as well as the general concept of the criminal, needs to be clarified.

POSSIBILITY OF A SCIENCE OF CRIMINOLOGY. Criminology at present is clearly not a science but it has hopes of becoming a science. The argument has been made, however, that criminology cannot possibly become a science. According to this argument, general propositions of universal validity are the essence of science; such propositions can be made only regarding stable and homogeneous units; crime is not a stable and homogeneous unit but varies from one jurisdiction or age to another; therefore universal propositions cannot be made regarding crime, and scientific studies of criminal behavior are therefore impossible.

The emphasis on universal propositions might be regarded by some students as exaggerated, but all will agree on the value of such universal propositions when they can be secured and the desirability of organizing a study so that such propositions may be reached. Furthermore, this criticism neglects the possibility of selecting areas and types of crimes in which definitions are essentially uniform, or at least of taking into account variations in definitions. To some extent it is possible for the criminologist by selection of criminal cases to re-define crime for his own purposes. But in general the difficulties of the legal definitions of crime should be recognized.

Sellin implicity acknowledges the validity of the criticism described above and proceeds to re-define crime as a violation of any conduct norm whatever. He argues that a solid basis for a science of criminology cannot be found unless the arbitrary definitions of the legislatures are replaced by definitions drawn up by scientists and for scientific purposes.[26] Even if this is done, it is not possible to escape the evaluations of behavior which are made by groups.

---

[26] Thorsten Sellin, *Culture Conflict and Crime,* Social Science Research Council, New York, 1938.

Courage, for instance, cannot be defined as a fixed aspect of behavior, for behavior which is called courageous in one situation is called cowardly in another, and the difference in the names applied to the behavior makes the behavior different. Physiologically acts can be defined apart from group evaluations, sociologically they cannot be. In this respect crime is like all other social phenomena, and the possibility of a science of criminal behavior is similar to the possibility of a science of any other behavior. Social science has no stable unit, for all social sciences are dealing with phenomena which involve group evaluations. Consequently the methodological problems are by no means solved when crime is redefined as a violation of any conduct norm.

A universal explanation of crime, if it should be found, would be extremely broad and would not be especially enlightening or valuable for purposes of control. In medicine progress is being made principally by defining and explaining particular diseases. Similarly in criminology the significant explanations will probably relate not to crime as a whole, but to particular types or classes of crimes, each class being defined in terms of universal elements. When types or classes of crimes are conceived in this way, it is probable that some classes will lie entirely within the legislative definitions of crimes, and others will lie in part inside and in part outside of those definitions. Obviously, the legal definitions should not confine the work of the criminologist, and he should be completely free to push across the barriers of legal definitions whenever he sees behavior outside the legal field which resembles the behavior within.

Some students, admitting the criticisms outlined above, have abandoned the effort to make criminology a science and place their emphasis on the study of social control. A study of the sequence of lawmaking, lawbreaking, and reactions to lawbreaking from the point of view of the efficiency of the law as a method of control is a useful objective in a criminology of this nature.

THE PROBLEM OF CRIME. The seriousness of the social problem of crime hardly needs to be described. The general public is, by definition, always the victim of crime. The general public suffers losses from crime either directly as in treason or theft and destruction of public property, or indirectly in the form of the expense of maintaining the police and the courts and in the form of uneasiness or even terror because of the prevalence of crime. In this sense every individual in the state is a victim of crime. In addition, some individuals are victims of crime in a more specific sense. The victims of crime may lose anything that has value. Life and money are perhaps basic values, because they contribute to the satisfaction of many wishes. Approximately ten thousand persons a year are victims of homicides, of which perhaps one-third are felonious homicides not due to negligence. The financial losses from fraudulent stock and bond issues and from fraudulent business transactions of other types are probably many times as great as the financial losses from burglary, robbery, and ordinary larceny. One chain store has about five hundred burglaries and robberies a year, with a total loss of about $100,000 a year. The same chain store had one embezzlement which caused a loss of more than $600,000. The loss of status in the community is frequently a result of crime. The victim of rape, especially, suffers this loss, and the loss is immensely magnified by the continued publicity given to it in the newspapers. Also the loss of status may be suffered by persons not ordinarily considered to be the victims, as the relatives of the prostitute or of the murderer or embezzler. The victim is sometimes immediately aware of the loss he suffers, but the realization is frequently delayed. The child who is employed in violation of the child-labor law, for instance, may not have an immediate realization of the loss he suffers by this crime and, in fact, may never realize the relation of his childhood labor to his subsequent career.

In crimes of personal violence the victims and the offenders are generally of the same social group, and have residences not far apart. Negroes murder Negroes, Italians murder Italians, and Chinese murder Chinese. These crimes of personal violence are generally committed against persons with whom the offenders have personal dealings. They develop out of conversation, romantic relations, and business transactions, and are committed against friends or acquaintances.[27] Intoxication is involved in many cases of homicide. The estimate has been made that 40 per cent of the murdered victims are intoxicated at the time they are murdered.[28]

Crimes against property are generally committed against strangers. They may be either direct and personal attacks, as in

[27] J. V. DePorte and Elizabeth Parkhurst, "Homicide in New York State: A Statistical Study of the Victims and Criminals in 37 Counties in 1921–1930," *Human Biology,* 7:47–73, February, 1935.

[28] Theron W. Kilmer, "Alcoholism, Its Relation to Police Work and Jurisprudence," *Correction* (N. Y. Department of Correction), Vol. 3, No. 8, pp. 11–12, August, 1933.

robbery or burglary, or may be much more general and public, as in fraudulent stock and bond sales or fraudulent advertisements. In modern society these general and impersonal crimes have become much more serious in their effects than have the direct and personal attacks; although the impersonal crimes generally represent no antagonism toward the victims, they do represent a ruthless and reckless pursuit of interests at variance with the interests of the victim.

Estimates have been made that the total financial cost of crime, both direct and indirect, is ten or fifteen billion dollars a year. These estimates are completely worthless. In the first place, they are principally guesses; and in the second place, they are based on unwarranted assumptions. They start with the question, How much would be saved if no crimes were committed and no precautions had to be taken against future crimes? This hypothetical situation could not exist if everything else except crime remained constant. In order to bring about a crimeless state of society it is possible that the annual expenditure would need to be greater than the expenditure for crime at present.[29]

It is urged by some persons that crime makes certain contributions to society which offset this loss to some extent. One suggested contribution is that it promotes the solidarity of the group, just as does war.[30] While it is true that the group is welded together by certain spectacular crimes of murder or rape, it is probable that many other crimes promote dissension, suspicions, and divisions in society. Moreover, the solidarity which is aroused in this manner is generally rather futile, for it is an emotional expression which drives criminals into organized groups. In this respect crime, like war, may have some effect in producing group solidarity, but the values can be produced better in other ways.

Again, it is urged that we must have crime in order to prevent morality from going to an extreme. If under an existing régime all criminals were eliminated, the standards would be set a little higher. If those at the bottom who violated the new standards were eliminated, the standards would be set still higher. Thus the group would become more and more strict in its morality until the situa-

---

[29] E. R. Hawkins and Willard Waller, "The Cost of Crime," *Jour. Crim. Law and Criminol.*, 26:679–694, January, 1936.

[30] G. H. Mead, "The Psychology of Punitive Justice," *Amer. Jour. Sociol.*, 23:577–602, March, 1918; A. C. Hall, *Crime in Its Relation to Social Progress*, New York, 1902, pp. 1–10.

tion became impossible. This argument, also, is not entirely convincing. At least, many primitive groups retained essentially the same standards with practically no violations for long periods of time.

The real function of crime is to act as a notification of maladjustments. Just as pain is a notification to an organism that something is wrong, so crime is a notification of a social maladjustment, especially when crime becomes prevalent. Crime is a symptom of social disorganization and probably can be reduced appreciably only by changes in the social organization.

SUGGESTED READINGS

Cairns, Huntington, *Law and the Social Sciences,* New York, 1935.

Cohen, Morris H., *Law and the Social Order,* New York, 1933.

Frank, Jerome, *Law and the Modern Mind,* New York, 1930.

Frank, Jerome, "Realistic Reflections on Law as a Constructive Social Force," *Proc. Natl. Conf. Social Work,* 1933, pp. 326–332.

Freund, Ernst, "Classification and Definition of Crimes," *Jour. Crim. Law and Criminol.,* 5:807–826, March, 1915.

Garofalo, R., *Criminology,* Tr. by R. W. Millar, Boston, 1914, Chs. 1–2.

Gotein, H., *Primitive Ordeal and Modern Law.*

Gutmann, Bruno, *Das Recht der Dschagga.*

Hall, Jerome, *Theft, Law, and Society,* Boston, 1935.

Hawkins, E. R., and Waller, Willard, "The Cost of Crime," *Jour. Crim. Law and Criminol.,* 26:679–694, January, 1936.

Hobhouse, L. T., *Morals in Evolution,* New York, 1919, Ch. 3.

Hogbin, H. Ian, *Law and Order in Polynesia,* New York, 1934.

Llewellyn, K. N., "Law Observance versus Law Enforcement," *Proc. Natl. Conf. Social Work,* 1928, pp. 127–136.

Lowie, R. H., *Primitive Society,* New York, 1920, Ch. 14.

MacDonald, John W., "The Classification of Crimes," *Cornell Law Quart.,* 19:524–563, June, 1933.

Mead, G. H., "The Psychology of Punitive Justice," *Amer. Jour. Sociol.,* 23:577–602, March, 1918.

Michael, J., and Adler, M. J., *Crime, Law, and Social Science,* New York, 1933.

Oliphant, Herman, "The Public and the Law," *Amer. Bar Assoc. Jour.,* 18:787–793, December, 1932.

Oppenheimer, H., *The Rationale of Punishment,* London, 1913, pp. 66–91.

Pound, Roscoe, *Criminal Justice in America,* New York, 1930.

Pound, Roscoe, *Law and Morals,* 2nd ed., Chapel Hill, N. C., 1926.

Queen, S. A., *The Passing of the County Jail,* Menasha, Wis., 1920, Chs. 3–4.

Recent Social Trends in the United States, New York, 1933, Vol. II, pp. 1115–1123.

Sellin, Thorsten, *Culture Conflict and Crime,* Social Science Research Council, New York, 1938.

Simpson, S. P., and Others, "The Cost of Crime," *Natl. Com. on Law Obs. and Enf.,* Washington, D. C., 1931, No. 12.

Spalding, W. F., "The Legislative History of a 'State Prison' Sentence as a Test of 'Felony' and 'Infamous Punishment,' and the Practical Results in Massachusetts," *Mass. Law Quart.,* 7:91–108, January, 1922.

Stephen, J. F., *A History of the Criminal Law of England,* 3 Vols., London, 1883, Vol. II, Ch. 17, and pp. 192–196.

Sumner, Wm. G., *Folkways,* Boston, 1906.

Tulin, L. A., "The Rôle of Penalties in Criminal Law," *Yale Law Rev.,* 37:1048–1069, June, 1928.

Specific references to the standard textbooks in criminology are not included in the suggested readings because of their ready accessibility. In general the following textbooks should be consulted on each chapter:

Aschaffenburg, G., *Crime and Its Repression,* Tr. by A. Albrecht, Boston, 1913.

Cantor, N. F., *Crime, Criminals, and Criminal Justice,* New York, 1932.

Gillin, J. L., *Criminology and Penology,* New York, 1926. Rev. ed. 1935.

Tannenbaum, Frank, *Crime and the Community,* Cincinnati, 1938.

Chapter Three

INDEXES OF CRIME

GENERAL DIFFICULTIES IN STATISTICS OF CRIME. The statistics
of crimes and criminals are known as the most unreliable and most
difficult of all statistics. First, the laws which define crimes change.
Second, the number of crimes actually committed cannot possibly
be enumerated. This is true of many of the major crimes and even
more true of the minor crimes. Third, any record of crimes, such as
arrests, convictions, or commitments to prison, can be used as an
index of crimes committed only on the assumption that this index
maintains a constant ratio to the crimes committed. This assumption is a large one, for the recorded crimes are affected by police
policies, court policies, and public opinion. Sellin has stated:

The value of a crime rate for index purposes decreases as the distance from the crime itself in terms of procedure increases.[1]

That is, the police statistics are more reliable for this purpose than
court statistics, and court statistics more reliable than prison statistics, for the further removed the index is from the crime the greater
is the possible number of procedures that may affect the index. It
is probable that arrests for serious crimes are less than 10 per cent
of the serious crimes actually committed in large cities. Out of
1,000 consecutive burglaries and robberies of chain grocery stores
in Chicago in 1930–1931, only two resulted directly in arrests.
Fourth, the only criminal statistics available for the entire United
States are prison statistics, and these certainly are not in constant

---

[1] Thorsten Sellin, "The Basis of a Crime Index," *Jour. Crim. Law and
Criminol.*, 22:346, September, 1931. For a general discussion of the difficulties
and defects in the several indexes of crime, see Thorsten Sellin, *Crime and the
Depression*, New York, 1937, Ch. 4.

ratio to the crimes committed, because of variations in the use of fines, probation, and other alternatives to imprisonment. Fifth, the statistics of crimes must, for the purposes of comparison, be stated in proportion to the population or to some other base. The population figures should be corrected for variations in age, sex, racial, composition, and urban-rural composition, and much of this information is available only in the years in which decennial enumerations of the population are made. Moreover, in many cases it is necessary to have other information. For instance, the convictions of violations of motor vehicle laws in Michigan increased from 1,566 in 1912–1913 to 27,794 in 1931–1932. In the meantime the number of cars registered in Michigan increased from 54,366 to 1,230,980. This shows a lower rate of violation, in ratio to the number of cars, in 1931–1932 than in 1912–1913. But prosecutions in the earlier period more frequently involved bicycles and horse-drawn vehicles than in the later period, and these are not included in the enumeration. The difficulty of securing an adequate base for computing a rate is therefore evident.

CRIMES KNOWN TO THE POLICE. The crimes which are reported to the police are designated "crimes known to the police." These refer only to the more serious crimes. These records are the best index of the number of crimes committed, provided the police department uses honesty and clerical efficiency in its reports. In certain respects they agree with judicial and penal statistics, and in certain respects they disagree. The English reports on criminal statistics have since 1857 included both the crimes known to the police and the prosecutions, as indexes of crimes. These two indexes were fairly consistent until about the end of the World War, but have been diverging since that time. Finland reports crimes known to the police, prosecutions, and convictions. For different types of crimes the percentages of prosecutions vary widely, from 22.8 per cent of crimes against the public security to 97.8 per cent of crimes connected with alcohol. Also the percentages of convictions vary, although less widely, for those prosecuted for the different types of crimes, from 79.7 per cent of those prosecuted for crimes against property to 97.8 per cent of those prosecuted for crimes against the public security.[2] These variations indicate that if crimes known to the police are a good index, then prosecutions and convictions are not—at least for purposes of comparison of types of crimes.

---

[2] Finland, *Criminal Statistics,* 1936, pp. 11–13.

These variations in the crime indexes are due in part to the circumstances under which crimes become known to the police; crimes against property will become known to the police generally by complaint of the victim, while crimes connected with alcohol will become known generally by observation of an intoxicated person. In any case, the number of crimes known to the police is certainly much less than the number actually committed. Sellin reports that the number of cases of shoplifting known to three Philadelphia department stores was greater than the total number of thefts of all kinds in the entire city which were known to the police.[3] This may be due to the failure of victims to complain or to the inefficiency and dishonesty of the police. The police of some cities do conceal crimes known to them in order to protect their city's reputation.

The Department of Justice of the United States publishes a quarterly bulletin on crime statistics, and for an index uses crimes known to the police in about 2,000 cities. These statistics have been available only since 1929. The number of robberies per 1,000 population decreased from 1930 to 1936, while burglaries moved slightly upward from 1930 to 1933 and then downward slightly from 1934 to 1936.[4]

TRENDS IN CRIME. Opposition to law has been a tradition in the United States. Popular rebellions against laws constitute an almost continuous series from the early colonial period to the prohibition controversy, and the violations of many of the early laws were quite as general as were the violations of the national prohibition law. The manufacture of nails and of other commodities in violation of English law, the sale of firearms and of liquor to Indians, smuggling and other violations of laws regulating commerce, Shay's Rebellion in 1787, the whiskey insurrection in 1794, trading with the enemy during the War of 1812, riots against the Catholics, the Irish, and the Mormons, the Dorr Rebellion in 1841–1842, trading in slaves, harboring fugitive slaves, Negro disfranchisement, violation of anti-trust laws, violation of banking laws,

---

[3] Sellin, *loc. cit.*, p. 69.

[4] *Uniform Crime Reports,* Vol. VIII, No. 4, p. 191. On the value of crimes known to the police as an index of crime see S. B. Warner, "Report on Criminal Statistics," *Natl. Com. on Law Obs. and Enf.*, No. 3; S. B. Warner, "Crimes Known to the Police—An Index of Crime," *Harv. Law Rev.*, 45:307–334, December, 1931; Thorsten Sellin, "The Basis of a Crime Index," *Jour. Crim. Law and Criminol.*, 22:335–356, September, 1931; Audrey M. Davies, "Criminal Statistics and the National Commission's Report," *Jour. Crim. Law and Criminol.*, 22:357–374, September, 1931.

and violation of prohibition laws are some of these popular rebellions. These violations of law cannot be measured statistically and it is not possible to determine from the descriptions whether the number of violations in such cases has increased.

Gehlke has collected and organized the principal available statistics for the purpose of determining what they show regarding the trend in crime rates from 1900 to 1930. The general conclusion is that, when traffic offenses and drunkenness are excluded, these statistics show a slight upward trend during this period, with no sudden surge that could be called a crime wave.[5] An analysis of Canadian criminal statistics indicates that the crime rate there has increased, but that if urbanization had remained constant the crime rate would have remained constant, also.[6]

POST-WAR CRIME WAVES.   A general opinion prevails that crimes increase after every war and that the post-war increase in crime rates was due to the war. This is unsatisfactory as an explanation of the crime rates in the United States most obviously because the rate was steadily upward before the war. In general, however, the statistics of several post-war periods in European countries agree with the belief that crime rates increase after wars. The crime rates in several European countries increased enormously after the World War,[7] but it is not clear that the increase was a direct effect of the war rather than a direct effect of the inflation of the currency and of the general economic distress. Abbott analyzed the prison statistics of the United States for the period 1860–1870 and concluded that some increase in crime after the Civil War is indicated by them.[8] Carroll D. Wright made a very careful analysis of the judicial statistics of Massachusetts and concluded that the number of sentences imposed decreased in every county of the state during the period of the Civil War, and then increased rapidly after the end of the war, reaching in 1873 a point approximately three times as high as in 1860, after which there was until 1879 a decrease which, however, did not return quite to the level of 1860. His more detailed study showed that the increase in convictions was made up

---

[5] Recent Social Trends in the United States, New York, 1933, Vol. II, pp. 1123–1135.

[6] R. E. Watts, "The Influence of Population Density on Crime," Jour. Amer. Stat. Assoc., 26:11–20, March, 1931.

[7] Franz Exner, Krieg und Kriminalität in Oesterreich, Vienna, 1927; M. Liepmann, Krieg und Kriminalität in Deutschland, New Haven, 1930.

[8] Edith Abbott, "The Civil War and the Crime Wave of 1860–1870," Social Serv. Rev., 1:212–234, June, 1927.

almost entirely of offenses connected with intoxicating liquors and that it was due not to an increase in intoxication but to a strong sentiment for prohibition during this period and to various modifications in the law. Sentences for "high crimes" did not increase during this period as rapidly as the population.[9] In general, therefore, his study did not support the belief that crimes increase in a post-war period but that the procedures in dealing with crimes change.

HOMICIDE STATISTICS. The coroner keeps a record of known homicides and the Bureau of the Census tabulates these and reports them annually for all states and cities in the registration area. This area since 1933 has contained the entire population of the United States. Table I shows number of deaths by homicide per hun-

TABLE I

AVERAGE ANNUAL NUMBER OF HOMICIDES PER 100,000 POPULATION

Years	Entire Registration Area	Registration Area of 1900
1900–04	2.4	1.2
1905–09	5.6	3.1
1910–14	6.7	4.1
1915–19	7.2	4.0
1920–24	8.1	4.4
1925–29	8.7	4.9
1930–34	9.1	4.7
1935	8.3	3.6

dred thousand population in the entire registration area and in those states which were in the registration area in 1900. The original registration area was composed almost entirely of New England states, to which have been added many Southern and Western states to compose the present registration area. The states that have been added have distinctly higher homicide rates than the original states. The only figures that are significant for the purpose of determining the trend, therefore, are those in the original registration area. Moreover, the reports for the period 1900–1904 were declared by the Director of the Census to be "incorrect and absolutely misleading." These inaccuracies were not completely corrected until shortly before 1910. Consequently, the trend in the original area during the period 1910–1934, for which the figures

9 Massachusetts, *Report of Bureau of Statistics of Labor*, 1880, pp. 123–195.

are accurate, is from 4.1 to 4.7. This, of course, is a very decided increase in percentage terms but it is not so great as the uninterpreted figures indicate. Moreover, even if homicides have increased, it does not necessarily follow that murder and felonious manslaughter, as ordinarily understood, have increased. These homicides include justifiable and excusable homicides, such as killing in self-defense, killing a prisoner who is trying to escape, and similar acts. In Chicago the justifiable and excusable homicides ranged between 10 and 17 per cent during the period 1914–1919, but increased to 30 per cent in 1931. In Detroit they increased from 14 per cent in 1919 to 41 per cent in 1930. Also, the principal increase in homicides has probably been due to homicides by negligence, especially in the form of automobile killings. The number of homicides by negligence is at present about equal to the number of other criminal homicides. Thus, there is little reason to believe that murder and manslaughter as usually understood have increased appreciably in the United States. No judgment regarding other crimes, however, should be based on homicides, for homicides are in a class by themselves, except that they are closely related to assaults.

The homicide rate in the United States is, however, much higher than in many European countries. In 1931 the average rate in 31 American cities was 10.8 per 100,000 population, while it was 0.3 in Amsterdam, 0.6 in Liverpool, 1.8 in Berlin, 1.9 in Prague, 2.7 in Vienna, 3.3 in Brussels, and 4.4 in Rome.[10] A considerable part of the difference, here also, is probably due to the greater frequency of excusable and justifiable homicides and of homicides due to automobiles in the United States. Wide differences within the United States are found. In 1935 Chicago had the highest rate of any American city with more than a million population, having nearly twice as high a rate as Philadelphia or New York. The rate in Chicago, however, is about one-fourth the rate in Birmingham and one-fifth the rate in Atlanta.

BANK BURGLARIES AND ROBBERIES. The American Bankers Association since 1894 has had a protective department, through which member-banks and some other banks report burglaries and hold-ups to a detective agency employed by the Association. There was a change of detective agencies in 1909 and the records of the

---

[10] Frederick Hoffman, "The Homicide Record for 1931," *Spectator*, Vol. CXXVIII, No. 13, pp. 4–5, 12–13, March 31, 1932.

agency that had been employed previously were declared to be worthless by the agency which has been employed since 1909. The number of burglaries per 10,000 members of the Association ranged in general between 15 and 25 per year during the period 1909 to 1919, and then jumped to about 100 per year during the period 1920–1922, after which they decreased again to about 25 per year. This represented a real crime wave and was concentrated in the Central Western states. Almost as many burglaries occurred in the states of Illinois, Iowa, Indiana, Kansas, Missouri, and Oklahoma in the period 1919–1922 as had been committed against all the member-banks in the Association during the eighteen years ended in 1917. During these four years 6.5 per cent of the member-banks in these states had burglaries, while in the same period only 0.4 per cent of the member-banks in New England had burglaries.

An equally significant change is evident in bank robberies or hold-ups. The number of hold-ups per 10,000 members was approximately 5 per year during the period from 1909 to 1914, when it jumped to 18, and increased rather steadily to 41 in 1922 and to 75 in 1924, after which it decreased to about 50. This represents a very decided increase in bank robberies after the World War.

EMBEZZLEMENT. The available statistics indicate that embezzlement has increased at approximately the same rate as burglary or as crimes against property in general. The number of prosecutions in Ohio is shown in Table II.

TABLE II

NUMBER OF PROSECUTIONS FOR SPECIFIED OFFENSES IN OHIO PER 100,000 POPULATION IN 1900–1904 AND IN 1925–1929, AND INDEX OF CHANGE

CRIME	PROSECUTIONS PER 100,000 POPULATION		INDEX NUMBER	
	1900–1904	1925–1929	1900–1904	1925–1929
Embezzlement	3.9	10.1	100	259
All property crimes.......	64.3	158.1	100	246
Burglary	17.4	36.0	100	207
Robbery	6.2	19.5	100	315

This table shows that prosecutions for robbery increased more than prosecutions for embezzlement, and that prosecutions for burglary and for all crimes against property increased less. The number of persons arrested for burglary or robbery of post offices increased from 132 in 1878 to 410 in 1912, while the number of members of the post office force who were arrested for theft from the post office increased from 166 to 337.[11] This shows that the outside burglaries and robberies increased somewhat less than the thefts by post office employees. The number of convictions under the national bank law for embezzlement and related offenses increased from 42 in 1915 to 51 in 1922, to 86 in 1923, to 107 in 1930, and to 241 in 1931. It is highly probable that the increase in the number of convictions in 1930 and 1931 was due not so much to increased frequency of embezzlements in those years as to the discovery in those years of embezzlements which had been consummated in earlier years. The probability of discovery of past defalcations was increased because many banks and other concerns went into the hands of receivers or merged with other concerns, because work assignments were changed with the decrease in the number of employees, and because of other changes during the financial depression.

The statistics of embezzlement are highly important from the point of view of a theory of crime, for embezzlers are customarily in positions of finanical responsibility and must be bonded by a fidelity company before they secure their positions. The prior records of these employees must be excellent in order to secure the positions and for that reason the embezzlers are persons who have characteristically had no record of crime prior to their employment in positions of responsibility and who become criminals in these circumstances. Undoubtedly individual differences between employees may be found, but the persons who occupy positions of financial trust are seldom psychopathic, feebleminded, residents of deteriorated slum areas, or in other ways personally or situationally pathological. They are a product of more general influences. Since this type of crime has been increasing as rapidly as the crimes committed by persons reared in slums, the conclusion may be that certain influences are producing an approximately identical effect on the residents of slums and of other areas, and that the slum dwellers react to this influence by robbery, burglary, and larceny, while the residents of other areas react by embezzlement and fraud.

THE PERVASIVE NATURE OF CRIMINALITY. Crime is much more pervasive than the ordinary statistics of crime indicate, and an

---

[11] Similar statistics for years later than 1912 are not published.

entirely incorrect impression regarding criminality is formed if conclusions are limited to these statistics. Many types of offenses are
widespread but seldom result in prosecution. Some of these offenses
are crimes in the strictly legal sense, but prosecution is avoided
because of the political or financial importance of the parties concerned, because of the apparent triviality of the crimes, because
of the difficulty of securing evidence sufficient for conviction, or for
other reasons. Some of the offenses are not crimes in the strictly
legal sense, for the parties concerned have cleverly obeyed the letter
of the law while violating the spirit of the law. Some of the offenses
are not even a violation of the spirit of the law, for the parties concerned have been able by bribery and other means to prevent the
enactment of laws to prohibit wrongful and injurious practices.
The people in this last group, however, are not different in attitudes
and their behavior is not different in effects from the other groups.
In general, underlying these failures to prosecute is the lack of a
developed social feeling and ethical code in the groups concerned
and, to some extent, in the general public. The danger from robbery or kidnaping is clearly realized, for they involve direct sensory
processes and are based on social relations which have existed for
many centuries. Theft by fraudulent advertisements and pros-
pectuses is a recent development, and affects persons who may be
thousands of miles away from the thief. Codes of behavior have
not been developed in regard to this behavior. These white-collar
criminaloids,[12] however, are by far the most dangerous to society
of any type of criminals from the point of view of effects on private
property and social institutions.

The comptroller of the currency reported that approximately
three-fourths of the national banks examined in a particular quarter
were found to be violating the national banking laws. Dishonesty
was found in 50.4 per cent of the national bank failures during the
period 1865–1899, and in 61.4 per cent during the period 1900–
1919. The highest rate of dishonesty in bank failures was found in
the New England banks in the period before 1900, where it was
76.5 per cent, but after 1900 this decreased to 58.3 per cent, which
was slightly less than the average in the United States.[13] These

---

[12] E. A. Ross, *Sin and Society*, Boston, 1907, Ch. 1.

[13] These statistics were included in the annual reports of the Comptroller of
the Currency and of the Department of the Treasury until 1923, when they
were discontinued. See, also, Thos. P. Kane, *The Romance and Tragedy of
Banking*, New York, 1922, pp. 320–321 and 368.

violations of law were not the principal reasons for the bank failures in more than 10 per cent of the cases, for they were generally technical violations.

The statistics of crime in European countries show a general tendency for crimes of violence to decrease and crimes of fraud to increase.[14] It is probable that the tendency is even more pronounced in America, but neither the trend nor the present extent of fraud can be determined by available statistics. It is probable, also, that fraud is the most prevalent crime in America. Insull, after his flight from America to escape prosecution for fraud and embezzlement, is quoted as saying that he could not understand why people in the United States hated him so much, for he had done only what all other business men had been doing. Misleading balance sheets which public accountants have been able to invent and develop, wash sales by which the value of a security is fraudulently determined, concessions in rent by real estate dealers for the purpose of fraudulently increasing the sales price of property, excessive and misleading claims made by the manufacturers, vendors, and advertisers of patent medicines, toothpaste, cosmetics, and many other articles, transfer of deteriorated securities from the banker's own possession to the trust funds under his direction, and a considerable part of present-day salesmanship and of advertising illustrate this kind of criminality. These things represent either active fraud with the intent to deceive the prospective purchaser or else misrepresentation by silence. Expert techniques of concealment have developed in many occupations for the purpose of preventing the purchaser from learning the defects of the commodity. Not many farmers would sell hogs with the knowledge that the hogs were infected with cholera and would die within a few days, and those farmers who did this would be regarded as dishonest, even if the misrepresentation consisted merely in silence regarding the danger. On the other hand, not many brokers or bankers would hesitate to sell securities which, by advance information, they had learned would soon be worthless, and the few who did refrain from immediate sale would be regarded as foolish. The physical disease of the hogs is more readily appreciated than the financial disease of the securities, and the effects are likely to be more definitely recognized. Defects in commodities are frequently concealed and labels often misrepresent.

[14] C. Tovo-Rota, "Sur une loi de développement de la criminalité," *6 Cong. Intern. d'Anthr. Crim.*, Turin, 1908, p. 167.

Shirting which is of inferior quality is filled with clay in order that the defects may be concealed until the sale is consummated. This is essentially the same principle that was used by the old horse-trader in concealing the blemishes in the horses. The label "Made in Japan" or "Made in Great Britain" carries with it no assurance that the commodity was made there. If the label on a bottle of whiskey implies or states that the whiskey was made in Scotland the chance that it was made there is exceedingly slight. The distilleries of America are fighting strenuously against proposed laws for the enforcement of honesty in labels. These cases of misrepresentation and fraud have not been subject to prosecution in most cases, for the courts have operated on the principle *caveat emptor,* which has meant that the purchaser must protect himself against ordinary dishonesty and could appeal to the courts for protection only against extraordinary dishonesty. President Roosevelt in 1933 insisted that the principle be reversed and *caveat vendor* be substituted, especially in regard to securities.

An immense amount of fraud is involved in insurance, both on the part of the insured and the insurers. Murders are committed, houses burned, automobiles destroyed, and sickness or injury feigned in order that insurance may be collected. The fraud in personal injury cases is unusually extensive, and has developed principally under the stimulation of lawyers who are known as "ambulance chasers" and generally work on contingent fees. The fraud in these cases seldom results in prosecution, although murder and arson may be occasion for prosecution of those crimes as such. The insurance company is seldom free to prosecute for fraud, for it seldom has clean hands. The insurance company adopts the usual policy that "business is business" and sentiment must be eliminated, and makes a settlement at the lowest possible figure rather than at the figure which the nature of the loss justifies. For this purpose the claim agents, the lawyers, and the physicians for the insurance company frequently practice misrepresentation. Physicians for the company, for instance, frequently minimize the extent of injuries, in the expectation that the physician on the other side will magnify them. Also, in many cases the claim agent collects an additional sum for settlement and divides this with the attorney for the injured party.

Fraud is unusually prevalent in the legal profession, though official statistics are not available as proof. Popular feeling inclines to the belief that a lawyer cannot be successful if completely honest, and that almost any law firm will take any case within its field of specialization for a sufficient fee, no matter how extreme the dishonesty required for representing the interests of the client. A suggestion was made in 1933 that the profession of law should be socialized, somewhat as efforts have been made to develop socialized medicine. This suggestion was based on the statement that the legal profession is so overcrowded that more than half of the lawyers are driven by competition to unethical practices. Disbarment proceedings have increased in the last generation, due to the organization of bar associations and their activity in prosecuting unethical legal practices, but the proceedings against lawyers are generally successful only in extremely flagrant cases. The profession of law would almost disappear if all lawyers who practice fraud and misrepresentation by misstatement and by concealment of the whole truth were disbarred.

Fraudulent reports of property and income for tax purposes are general. The person who reported his personal property honestly would generally be regarded as a freak, for the only method by which a person can avoid paying more than his share of the taxes is by accepting the common level of dishonesty. Most citizens would probably prefer to make honest reports, if they were assured that others would do the same. Dishonesty in reporting incomes has become more dangerous, and the general method is to cover the dishonesty by transfer of property to relatives or by other subterfuges.

Many churches and denominational colleges have misapplied funds, under the direction of boards of trustees composed of clergy, lawyers, and business men. Gifts for endowment have been used for current expenses, gifts for missions have been used for pastors' salaries, and in other ways funds have been misapplied.

These frauds are sometimes committed under the drive of necessity, but frequently are an expression of a desire to beat a competitor for the sake of the game. This gaming interest is very general and is found in all types of cultures, but has been immensely developed in modern life and has been accompanied by an efflorescence of bizarre forms, such as flag-pole sitting, gum chewing, hog calling, and marathon dancing. The extraordinary development of fraud in modern life has been an aspect of the drive for profits, which in itself has been regarded as one of the primary virtues and which for that reason has appeared to remove somewhat the taint from sharp practices. Persons practicing fraud have ordinarily felt no pangs of conscience, for the effects of fraudulent behavior have not become apparent in individual victims known to the defrauders but have been impersonal and diffuse. If the effects were discernible in particular persons known to the defrauders and if the practices were not purified by attachment to the virtuous search for profits, many business and commercial practices would be clearly recognizable as crimes.

Bribery is another extremely prevalent crime for which arrests are seldom made. This involves both bribery of public officials and of private persons. Bribery of public officials is a crime both for the bribe-taker and the bribe-giver. Bribery of private persons is not a crime, from the legal point of view, but is closely akin to it in effects and attitudes. Both public and private bribery may be in the form of a direct exchange of money, but is much more frequently a concealed and indirect method of putting a person under obligation to return a service.

In many cities and states an immense amount of bribery occurs in connection with the purchase of supplies, the making of contracts, the enforcement of regulations, and the enactment of legislation. It is involved when coal is purchased, when school books are purchased, when roads or buildings are constructed, when land is purchased for public purposes, when franchises are granted to railroads, bus companies, steamship companies, and other public utility companies, and on hundreds of other occasions. Agents of book publishing companies have testified regarding their methods of bribing school boards, and many public investigations have shown the wide prevalence of bribery of public officials. In some cities and states any purchase of commodities which is strictly honest is an oversight. Much of the wealth of public officials is secured from these bribes, and it has come from the most important of the financial and commercial concerns as well as from the agencies of the underworld. Enforcement of regulations regarding insurance, banking, factories, housing, building construction, streets, garbage, public utilities, weights and measures, and most other important functions is a matter of bargaining between the agents of the state and the agencies subject to the law. The process, once started, grows and involves firms which were previously honest. The honest firm is forced to bribe the inspector in order to protect itself against arbitrary and persecutory enforcement of laws, but the inspector's expectation of securing bribes has grown out of bribes given previously by other concerns. Campaign contributions may protect a firm against demands for petty graft and be effective in protecting agencies and interests against laws which may decrease profits. Bribery is not the only method used to prevent the enactment of legislation which might change quasi-criminal acts into definite criminal acts. Dishonest propaganda is a method frequently used. During 1933 and 1934 the investment bankers engaged in much propaganda of this nature for the purpose of emasculating the national securities bill of 1933. This law made a person or firm selling securities financially responsible for the honesty of the statements made in connection with the sale, and this destroyed a privilege which investment bankers had previously enjoyed. Consequently they made every possible effort, including much misrepresentation regarding the true situation, in order to maintain this special privilege which had proved to be highly injurious to the investing public.[15]

Bribery is extremely prevalent, also, in private business. Buyers for department stores, hotels, factories, railways, and almost all other concerns which make purchases on a large scale accept and sometimes demand bribes. Persons acquainted with these fields report that direct and indirect methods of bribery in these relationships are widespread.[16] Agents of general credit bureaus and of credit bureaus of special trade associations have reported that they are frequently approached with offers of bribes if information which tends to lower their rating is concealed or if their credit rating is raised.

In 1939 one of the judges in a high court of the federal government resigned, under charges that he had accepted more than a half million dollars in thinly concealed bribes from important national business concerns which had cases in court before him. These business concerns were no more reluctant than the professional thief to "fix" their cases.

Aiding and abetting criminals is itself a crime and involves a gradation from definitely illegal to definitely legal acts. The number of persons and agencies which aid and abet criminals is very great. Many saloons, gambling places, and houses of prostitution not only

---

[15] Bernard Flexner, "The Fight on the Securities Act," *Atlantic Mo.*, 153:232–250, February, 1934.
[16] Robert Littell, "Arrival of Buyer," *Harpers*, 167:739–748, November, 1933.

violate the laws which are intended to regulate their behavior, but also shelter and protect professional criminals and occasional criminals. Cigar stores and pool-rooms are sometimes the arsenals of gunmen, though the proprietors may not themselves engage in crimes of violence. Some lawyers are regularly retained to advise professional criminals and to protect the professional criminals in case of arrest, and are an essential part of any criminal organization. A very large part of the perjury by witnesses in trials grows out of the suggestions and instructions of lawyers. Reputable business concerns frequently purchase the proceeds of thefts with a clear realization of the source of the commodities. The manufacturers and distributors of guns, especially machine-guns, of silencers, and of material for bombs are important assistants of gangsters. All large cities and most of the smaller cities have persons who make a business of "fixing" cases for professional thieves. The police, bailiffs, clerks, prosecutors, and judges frequently co-operate with these "fixers," either for direct money payments or under orders from political leaders who control appointments and elections.

The police constantly break the laws. The laws of arrest are rigidly limited, but the police exercise their authority with little reference to these limitations and in violation of law. Hopkins refers to illegal arrests as kidnapings, and in this sense the number of kidnapings by the police is thousands of times as great as the number of kidnapings by burglars and robbers. The courts, similarly, are not immune from criminal contagion, and this is true especially of the lower courts, as the Seabury investigation has shown in New York City and as other evidence shows is equally true in other large cities.

Thus criminality and quasi-criminality are found in most occupations and are very prevalent. The people of the business world are probably more criminalistic in this sense than are the people of the slums. The crimes of the slums are direct physical actions—a blow, a physical grasping and carrying away of the property of others. The victim identifies the criminal definitely or indefinitely as a particular individual or group of individuals. The crimes of the business world, on the other hand, are indirect, devious, anonymous, and impersonal. A vague resentment against the entire system is felt, but when particular individuals cannot be identified, the antagonism is futile. The perpetrators thus do not feel the resentment of their victims and the criminal practices continue and spread.

THE MORAL HOLIDAY. Certain occasions are defined in traditions and culture as moral holidays. Hallowe'en, New Year's Eve, election nights, spring celebrations, and important football victories are occasions of this nature. Crimes are committed on these occasions by persons who would ordinarily not commit such crimes, and may take the form of destruction of property and of assaults. These crimes are committed primarily in a spirit of exuberance, which is, on some of these occasions, the persistence of a tension developed in a hot contest. There is much evidence that the delinquency of boys in the deteriorated areas is an extension of this attitude through the entire year.

Strikes are in certain respects like these moral holidays. There is a gathering of persons with a common interest, an attitude during the early period of the strike which is much like that of a picnic, and an exuberance which is like that of the spring celebration. Assaults and destruction of property occur on these occasions, just as on other moral holidays. The violation of law, however, is much more purposive in the strike than in these other emotional outbursts. Factory workers, skilled tradesmen, and farmers, without much differentiation, violate the laws on such occasions.

These moral holidays are so generally recognized that prosecutions and impositions of penalties for lawlessness seldom result.

CONCENTRATION OF CRIMES. In the preceding sections crimes have been considered as varying chronologically and occupationally. It is possible to secure some evidence, also, of geographical variations in crime rates. Crimes are not distributed evenly over a nation or a community but are concentrated. In general the places of crimes are close to the residences of the criminals. This is especially true in regard to crimes against the person, for the offender and the victim are usually of the same race, the same economic class, and also of the same neighborhood. Petty crimes against property are similarly concentrated near the places of residence of criminals, but the more serious crimes against property are committed some distance from the places of residence of criminals.[17]

Crimes of petty theft are concentrated in cities. The burglaries of chain stores, in which the average loss in money and goods is less than one hundred dollars, may be regarded as near the upper limits of petty theft. The percentages of stores which are burglar-

---

[17] R. Clyde White, "A Study of Residence and Place of Offense of Felons in Indianapolis," *Social Forces,* 10:498–509, May, 1932.

ized or robbed decrease regularly from the center of Chicago toward the city limits, and the decrease continues thence steadily for 125 miles beyond the city limits except in one zone where the rate increases slightly due to the presence of a medium-sized city. Similar results were found for the metropolitan area of Detroit.[18] Bank burglaries, on the other hand, are more frequent just beyond the city limits than within the city limits, and do not decrease as rapidly as do the burglaries of chain stores, due to the fact that burglaries and robberies of banks are confined somewhat more to professional criminals.

STATISTICS OF CRIMINALS. Efforts have been made to develop statistics which will reveal the social and personal characteristics of criminals. These are generally confined to the records of the police and the prisons. The selective nature of arrest and of imprisonment makes these statistics an inadequate source of information regarding the characteristics of criminals, but it is difficult to develop statistics regarding criminals who are not recorded in some manner. Apparently, therefore, the best that can be done at present is to recognize the bias in the statistics of arrests or of prisons and attempt to secure statistics in other ways regarding the classes which are not adequately represented.

A second problem regarding the statistics of criminals is the reliability of the information which is recorded. The statistics of criminals are generally based on the unverified statements of the criminals. Although Jack Black has testified that when he was committed to prison he lied in regard to every point on which he was questioned, as a matter of principle, it is probable that the data which are recorded are fairly reliable except on items which have considerable significance from the point of view of the prospective action of the parole board. The statistics of criminals have generally been confined to items such as age, sex, nativity, education, and general occupational class and there is seldom any reason why the offenders should lie on these points. Moreover, if they do lie, they are consistent in their lying, for a comparison of several records of identical individuals, taken independently and with intervals of time, shows that the distributions of characteristics, such as ages, are almost identical on the different records.[19] If the inquiry goes

[18] Stuart Lottier, "Distribution of Criminal Offenses in Metropolitan Regions," *Jour. Crim. Law and Criminol.*, 29:37–50, May, 1938.
[19] Edwin H. Sutherland and C. C. Van Vechten, Jr., "The Reliability of Criminal Statistics," *Proc. Amer. Prison Assoc.*, 1933, pp. 315–322.

beyond these formal items, honest information can generally be secured if the relationship between the offender and the interviewer is friendly and congenial, although even then the information may be unreliable because of errors of memory and of interpretation.

Many specialized statistical studies have been made during the last generation by means of tests, questionnaires, and standardized schedules. These devices are still in a primitive stage, the units are not adequately defined, and they are confined to the characteristics at a particular time and have little value in showing the process by which criminality develops. They are, however, of value for the purpose for which they are used, namely, describing in standardized manner the static characteristics. In connection with such studies efforts are being made to rank crimes with respect to their seriousness.[20]

INTERNATIONAL CRIMINAL STATISTICS. Considerable interest has developed in European countries during the last generation in a program for the international codification of criminal laws and for the development of international statistics of crime and criminals. Comparisons of different countries in respect to crimes and criminals should be of decided value in securing an understanding of criminality, because these statistics should show the wider variations which may be concealed within a particular country. On the other hand, it is extremely difficult to differentiate between criminality and the procedures used in dealing with criminals when international comparisons are made, and the international statistics are on that account under suspicion. The situation therefore is that international comparisons would be extremely valuable, but comparisons on the basis of present statistics are unreliable. The essential problem is to develop units that can be used for international comparisons.[21] Several interesting studies have been made recently on the basis of international statistics of crime.[22]

---

[20] J. H. Gersuch, "A Scale of Seriousness of Crimes," *Jour. Crim. Law and Criminol.*, 29:245–252, July, 1938.

[21] E. Hacker, "Die Methoden der International Kriminalstatistik," *Deutsches Stat. Zentralblat.*, 24:65–70, May, 1932; Stephane Rzepkiewicz, "Observations sur la possibilité des comparaisons des statistiques criminelles des divers pays," *Bull. de l'Inst. Intern. de Stat.*, 23:569–577, No. 2, 1930.

[22] See, especially, Verkko, Veli, *Verbrechen wider das Leben und Körperverletzungsverbrechen über die Bestimmung ihrer Entwicklungsrichtung und Stufe,* Trans. from the Finnish, 1931, Helsinki, 1937; Verkko, Veli, *Väkivaltarikollisuuden Riippuvaisuus Kansanluonteesta ja Muista Etnillisistä,* Helsinki, 1936; E. Hacker, "Internationalkriminalistik," *Monats. für Kriminalpsychologie und Strafr.,* 22:269–278, March, 1932, and 25:1–22, January, 1935.

SUGGESTED READINGS

Adams, J. T., "Our Lawless Heritage," *Atlantic Mo.*, 142:732–740, December, 1928.

Brearley, H. C., *Homicide in the United States*, Chapel Hill, N. C., 1932.

Canada, Bureau of Statistics, Judicial Statistics Branch, *Annual Reports on Statistics of Criminals and Other Offenders*, Ottawa.

Dodd, W. E., "Our Ingrowing Habit of Lawlessness," *Century Mag.*, 116:691–698, October, 1928.

Flynn, J. T., *Graft in Business*, New York, 1931.

Flynn, J. T., "How Whitney Went Broke," *New Rep.*, 95:266–268, July 13, 1938.

Gehlke, C. E., "Development of Criminal Statistics in the Past Decade," *Proc. Amer. Prison Assoc.*, 1931, pp. 176–190.

Hartshorne, H., and May, M. A., *Studies in the Nature of Character*, New York, 1928–1930, 3 Vols.

Littell, Robert, "Arrival of Buyer," *Harpers*, 167:739–748, November, 1933.

Marshall, Leon C., *Comparative Criminal Statistics, Six States, 1931*, Baltimore, 1932.

Marshall, Leon C., *Unlocking the Treasuries of the Trial Courts*, Baltimore, 1933.

Massachusetts, Department of Correction, *Annual Reports*.

New York, Commissioner of Correction, *Report on Crime Statistics, 1930*, Albany, New York, 1931.

Olson, W. C., *Problem Tendencies in Children*, Minneapolis, 1930.

Phelps, H. A., "Frequency of Crime and Punishment," *Jour. Crim. Law and Criminol.*, 19:165–180, August, 1928.

Recent Social Trends in the United States, New York, 1933, Vol. II, pp. 1123–1135.

Robinson, L. N., *History and Organization of Criminal Statistics in the United States*, Boston, 1911.

Robinson, L. N., "History of Criminal Statistics, 1908–1933," *Jour. Crim. Law and Criminol.*, 24:125–139, May, 1933.

Sellin, Thorsten, "The Basis of a Crime Index," *Jour. Crim. Law and Criminol.*, 22:335–356, September, 1931.

Truesdell, L. E., "The Problem of Collecting and Standardizing Statistics of Crime in Forty-eight Sovereign States," *Proc. Amer. Stat. Assoc.*, March, 1928.

U. S. Attorney General, *Annual Reports,* Washington, D. C.

U. S. Bureau of the Census, *Annual Reports on Prisoners in State and Federal Prisons and Reformatories,* Washington, D. C.

U. S. Bureau of the Census, *Children under Institutional Care 1923,* Washington, D. C., 1927.

U. S. Bureau of the Census, *County and City Jails, 1933,* Washington, D. C., 1935.

U. S. Children's Bureau, *Annual Reports on Juvenile Court Statistics.*

U. S. Department of Justice, *Uniform Crime Reports,* Quarterly Bulletins.

Warner, S. B., "Report on Criminal Statistics," *Natl. Com. on Law. Obs. and Enf.,* Washington, D. C., 1931, No. 3.

Watts, R. E., "The Influence of Population Density on Crime," *Jour. Amer. Stat. Assoc.,* 26:11–20, March, 1931.

White, R. Clyde, "A Study of Residence and Place of Offense of Felons in Indianapolis," *Social Forces,* 10:498–509, May, 1932.

Willbach, Harry, "The Trend of Crime in New York City," *Jour. Crim. Law and Criminol.,* 29:62–75, May, 1938.

Chapter Four

CAUSES OF CRIME: GENERAL

CONTROL OF BEHAVIOR can be adequate and satisfactory only if it is based on a knowledge of the factors or processes by which the behavior is produced. The experience of the physical sciences has made that quite positive. This truth has not been realized or applied adequately in relation to crime, though for several generations consistent efforts have been made to develop explanations of crime.

THE PRINCIPAL SCHOOLS OF CRIMINOLOGY. During the medieval and early modern periods many unorganized and ephemeral explanations of crimes were stated and accepted. Probably the principal explanation during this time was that crime was due to innate depravity and the instigation of the devil. The English indictment used as late as the nineteenth century not only accused the defendant of violating the law, but also of "being prompted and instigated by the devil and not having the fear of God before his eyes." And the Supreme Court of North Carolina as late as 1862 declared:

To know the right and still the wrong pursue proceeds from a perverse will brought about by the seductions of the evil one.[1]

During the period when this explanation was used most frequently the conception of natural causation was not developed even with reference to such things as disease, and, of course, was not developed with reference to crime. Little interest was manifested in motives, intentions, circumstances, or other immediate factors in the causation of crime. Punishments were arbitrary and unequal, with the general principle of heaping tortures on criminals in accordance

[1] Quoted by H. Shepard, *Jour. Crim. Law and Criminol.*, 13:486, February, 1923.

with the divine example, and of relying on divine interposition as the sole method of reformation.

Out of that situation developed the classical school of criminal law and criminology. This school had its basis in hedonistic psychology. Jeremy Bentham[2] made applications of that psychology to legislation and Beccaria[3] made applications of it to penology. According to this psychology, the pleasures anticipated from a particular act may be balanced against the pains anticipated from the same act, or the algebraic sum of pleasures and pains from one act may be balanced against the algebraic sum of pleasures and pains from another act. The actor was assumed to have a free will and to make his choice with reference to the hedonistic calculation alone. This was regarded as the final and complete explanation of the causes of crime and no need for further investigation of causation could be imagined.

Beccaria in 1764 made the principal application of this doctrine to penology. His objective was to make punishment less arbitrary and severe than it had been. He contended that all persons who violated a specific law should receive identical punishment regardless of age, sanity, wealth, position, or circumstance. This was justified on the ground that the rights of individuals could be preserved only by treating all individuals alike, and also on the ground that the punishment must be definitely determined in advance in order that it might be taken into account in the calculation of pains and pleasures that would result from violation of the law. According to this school the penalty should be just severe enough so that the pains would exceed the pleasures derived from violation of the law. This extreme idea of equality was soon modified at two points; children and lunatics were exempted from punishment on the ground that they were unable to calculate pleasures and pains intelligently, and the penalties were fixed within narrow limits rather than absolutely so that a small amount of judicial discretion was possible. With these modifications this classical doctrine became the backbone of the body of the law and has so persisted in popular thought and judicial decisions to the present day.

The psychology underlying this theory is now generally questioned. It is highly intellectualistic. It assumes a freedom of the will which gives no room for further investigation or for efforts

---

[2] Jeremy Bentham, *Principles of Legislation.*
[3] Cesare Beccaria, *Crime and Punishment.*

to prevent crime. The system of thought was essentially pre-scientific and metaphysical; the method was armchair speculation with no careful analysis of factual data.

The first scientific school of thought was called the "geographical" or "cartographic" and was very similar to the later school, which has been called "ecological." The leaders of this school were concerned primarily with the distribution of crimes in certain areas, both geographical and social. They were interested in crime as a necessary expression of the social conditions. Quetelet and A. M. Guerry were the leaders of this approach in France, and they had a large number of followers in that country and in England and Germany. The school flourished from about 1830 to 1880. Not only did the adherents of this method analyze the distribution of general crime rates but they made special studies of juvenile delinquency and of professional crime which are comparable with those of the present generation and much superior to anything in the interval between 1880 and the present. This period in the history of criminological theory was practically unknown to the present generation of criminologists until it was "re-discovered" by Lindesmith and Levin. They have listed a very large number of factual studies by this method.[4]

A second scientific school of criminology was economic determinism. This school was concerned with crime only as a by-product, but it conducted many factual studies, principally by the statistical methods, and provided much material regarding the variations in crime rates in association with variations in economic conditions. The conclusions which were derived from these factual studies were generally in agreement with the preconceptions of the students who were using this approach and were regarded as supporting the socialist program. Nevertheless, this school may properly be called scientific, for it began with a general hypothesis and collected factual data in a manner which enabled others to repeat the work and verify their conclusions.

Another system of thought began with the writings of Lombroso in 1876.[5] He and his followers, known as the Italian or positive school, insisted on the importance of studying the criminal. This

[4] Alfred Lindesmith and Yale Levin, "The Lombrosian Myth in Criminology," *Amer. Jour. Sociol.*, 42:653–671, March, 1937; Yale Levin and Alfred Lindesmith, "English Ecology and Criminology of the Past Century," *Jour. Crim. Law and Criminol.*, 27:801–816, March, 1937.

[5] C. Lombroso, *L'uomo delinquente*, 1876.

was in opposition to the armchair speculation of the classical school, upon which the legal systems of Europe had been based; it was not directed against the geographical or the economic schools, for Lombroso was apparently unacquainted with the rich literature that had been produced by those schools. Their system of thought attracted immediate attention, and the geographical method was soon forgotten and the economic emphasis was withdrawn. In fact, therefore, they shifted the emphasis from crime as a social phenomenon to crime as an individual phenomenon. They made no lasting contribution to an understanding of the criminal and delayed for fifty years the continuation of work which was in progress when they appeared on the scene. Even in the study of the individual criminal they had a poor technique and were obsessed by preconceived notions of the character of the criminal. Their principal argument was that criminals constitute a born type. There are so many variations of this doctrine that, strictly speaking, it is not correct to refer to it as a doctrine of the positive school; strictly speaking, also, there is no such thing as *a* positive school, for the members of this Italian group have many variations in their theories. Lombroso in his first edition insisted that all criminals are born criminals and that they can be recognized by physical stigmata. In later editions he gradually retracted this theory, and introduced social and psychological factors, but still insisted that a considerable proportion of criminals are born criminals and that other criminals approach this type. Garofalo, Ferri, and other followers of Lombroso made additional modifications. The theory in its earlier and more clear-cut form may be summarized as follows: (a) Criminals are by birth a distinct type. (b) This type can be recognized by stigmata or anomalies, such as asymmetrical cranium, long lower jaw, flattened nose, scanty beard, low sensitivity to pain.[6] If a person has five or more such stigmata, he is of the complete criminal type; from three to five indicate an incomplete criminal type; and less than three do not indicate criminal type. (c) These stigmata show that the criminal is either a reversion to the savage type—an atavism—or else is degenerate and especially of the epileptoid type. (d) Because of his nature, the typical criminal cannot refrain from crime unless the circumstances of his life are unusually favorable. One who is not a typical criminal may commit crime because of unusually unfavor-

---

[6] This notion runs far back in history. See C. Bernaldo de Quiros, *Modern Theories of Criminality*, Boston, 1911, pp. 4–5.

able circumstances. Some of the followers of Lombroso maintained not only that there is a born criminal type in general, but also that there are special types, such as thieves, murderers, and sex offenders, who can be recognized by physical stigmata.

After much debate over this theory between Lombroso and his followers and the adherents of the French school, who claimed that crime is primarily the result of imitation, it was suggested in 1899 by Lombroso that his opponents select one hundred criminals and one hundred persons who were not criminals and make comparative measurements to determine whether there was a criminal type. The challenge was accepted and a committee appointed for this purpose, but the committee was unable to agree on procedure and the work was not performed. One of the English prison officials, Dr. Griffiths, began such a study of the inmates of his own institution for the purpose of comparison with the non-criminal population. By changes in administration, Dr. Goring succeeded to this task and, with the help of other prison physicians and of Karl Pearson, studied more than three thousand consecutive entrants to English convict prisons during a period of about eight years. He made very careful measurements of various physical traits which Lombroso had contended were characteristic of criminals. Goring's conclusion is stated as follows:

We have exhaustively compared, with regard to many physical characters, different kinds of criminals with each other, and criminals, as a class, with the law-abiding public. . . . Our results nowhere confirm the evidence [of a physical criminal type], nor justify the allegation of criminal anthropologists. They challenge their evidence at almost every point. In fact, both with regard to measurements and the presence of physical anomalies in criminals, our statistics present a startling conformity with similar statistics of the law-abiding class. Our inevitable conclusion must be that there is no such thing as a physical criminal type.[7]

Goring reported that he found about the same difference in cranial measurements between the graduates of Cambridge and the graduates of Oxford as between the criminals and law-abiding people.

A great deal of credence has been given to this theory of a physi-

[7] Charles Goring, *The English Convict*, London, 1913, p. 173.

cal criminal type by people who visit courts or prisons occasionally. The appearance of prisoners, of course, is strange, but it is due partly to facial expression, haircut, dress, and other things more or less easily modifiable. Warden Osborne reports that while he was spending a week in Auburn prison as a voluntary prisoner, dressed in prison garb, some friends came through the buildings with the intention of seeing him. Though they looked directly at him, they failed to recognize him, so much was his appearance changed. Goring has proved quite conclusively that as a class criminals are not different anatomically from other people.

The only thing that Goring found characteristic of the criminals studied was that they were from one to two inches shorter than other people of the same occupational groups and weighed from three to seven and a half pounds less. He concluded, also, that they were mentally inferior, although he did not base this conclusion on mental tests. Some members of the positive school contended that Goring really proved their hypothesis that criminals constitute a distinct type. This contention has some justification, but the type he found on the basis of inadequate data and methods was a mental rather than a physical type. In spite of the apparently conclusive nature of Goring's findings regarding physical type, investigations along the same line have been continued in several European countries and even in the United States.

PRESENT THEORIES OF CRIME. The controversy between the schools of Tarde[8] and Lombroso resulted in a somewhat general acceptance of the "multiple factor" theory of criminality. This theory includes all kinds of factors, both individual and social, within the total explanation. A multiple factor theory is undoubtedly closer to the facts than the earlier theories, but since the quantitative and qualitative relations between the several factors are not known, it is unsatisfactory for purposes of understanding, of control, and of prevention. On that account continued efforts have been made to discover a somewhat unified process in which the factors are involved. This has, to some extent, resulted merely in the selection of one or more factors for emphasis, while to some extent it has resulted in a variety of points of view from which the various facts are observed. Considerable attention has been paid by some writers to climatic or seasonal variations in crime rates, without

---

[8] G. Tarde, *Penal Philosophy*, Boston, 1912.

resulting in a general theory of crime. Also, considerable attention has been devoted to certain physiological factors, such as the Lombrosian stigmata of degeneracy, body build, and endocrine glands, though these also are seldom regarded as a general theory of criminality. Others have emphasized family relations, neighborhood, economic conditions, disintegration of religious orthodoxy, political corruption, and many other factors.

These theories and emphases may be classified in the following manner: (a) biological, (b) personality, (c) primary social groups, (d) broader social processes. The biological or constitutional theories are characteristically in conflict with the other three which are social and which are, characteristically, supplementary rather than conflicting. *The* theory of criminality which may be derived finally will probably weave these various elements into an integrated and compact system of thought.

The approach from the point of view of the physiological organism may emphasize heredity, endocrine glands, anatomical structure, or inherited mental traits. In general the approach from this point of view reaches a conclusion that sterilization is the most effective method of reducing crime.

The approach from the point of view of personality cannot be sharply differentiated from the biological theories. Just outside of this group is Goddard's theory[9] that feeblemindedness, inherited as a Mendelian unit, causes crime for the reason that the feebleminded person is unable to appreciate the meaning of law or foresee the consequences of his acts. Kelley makes a combination of intellect and emotions and states that crime is caused by the lack of balance between intellectual and emotional capacities; a weak intellect can direct and control the persons whose emotions are weak, but is inadequate if the emotional drives are strong.[10] He states that the institutions for the feebleminded contain many persons who are quiet and placid and never cause the least trouble. Patrizi has stated a monogenetic theory of criminality to the effect that crime results from a short-circuiting of the emotional drives; in honest people the egoistic drives are directed and inhibited by social, moral, and civic sentiments, but in criminals these egoistic drives are expressed directly without passing over the circuit which contains these higher

---

[9] H. H. Goddard, *Feeblemindedness,* New York, 1914.
[10] Truman Kelley, "Mental Aspects of Delinquency," *Univ. of Tex. Bull.,* No. 1713, March 1, 1917, p. 39.

sentiments.[11] Some psychoanalysts explain crime as due to unsettled mental conflicts, which are generally sexual in origin.[12] Certain other psychiatrists have explained crime as due to an inferiority complex, or as due to a lack of agreement between a person's conception of himself and the conception others have of him.

This approach from the point of view of personality is not necessarily in conflict with the approaches from the points of view of primary groups and social processes. Those who make this approach state that behavior is the reaction of a person to a situation and that, therefore, both the person and the situation must be taken into account. They add that the situation which is important is the situation as defined and interpreted by the person, and thus all the influences can be discovered by a study of the person.

These theories which approach the explanation of crime from the point of view of personality have a decided advantage in the concreteness and specificity of the data. In spite of this they have no appearance of agreeing with each other. The difficulty is that this sets an almost impossible task for itself in asking, "Why did this particular person act in this particular manner?" It seems probable that in a situation where all the influences point consistently in one direction, all persons will act in the same manner. In actual life we have no situation of this nature, for the influences are conflicting. The more conflicting these influences are, the more completely does the behavior of the individual become unpredictable, incalculable, and unexplainable, for it will be determined by a series of subtle and attenuated influences.

Though the students who make the approach from the point of view of personality disagree regarding the specific contents of their theories, they agree in general in their therapeutic program. They attempt to change the individual while the groups to which he belongs remain constant. They recognize the desirability of changing the groups but have no facilities for doing this. It is probably for this reason that the results of individual case work have been very meager.

The approach from the point of view of the primary group may be entirely in harmony with the approach from the point of view of

---

[11] M. L. Patrizi, *Monogenesi psicologica del delitto;* M. L. Patrizi, *Dopo Lombroso,* 1916; M. L. Patrizi, *Addizioni al Dopo Lombroso,* 1930.

[12] Franz Alexander, "Mental Hygiene and Criminology," *Mental Hygiene,* 14:853–882, October, 1930.

personality. The primary group is chosen as the point of attack because the problem is less difficult than the problem of the behavior of a particular individual and also because the therapeutic program is different. This emphasis among sociologists was derived largely from Cooley's theory that personality is determined in primary groups and among psychiatrists from the Freudian and Adlerian theories of family tensions and complexes. In this general class of theories, however, there are many differences in emphasis. Some place the emphasis upon the neighborhood and others upon the home; among those who emphasize the home, some emphasize the œdipus complex, others the family patterns, others parental neglect. Family case work agencies have recognized the family as the unit of work, and have not often gone beyond the family in their therapeutic programs, though they have encouraged settlements, churches, clubs, and other agencies to attempt to modify the neighborhood.

In general the primary group approach to the problem of delinquency has concentrated on the families and neighborhoods in the slum areas, and has not taken cognizance of the immense amount of criminality in the modern commercial and industrial transactions, which generally takes the form of fraud. The persons who commit these crimes do not have juvenile court records and few of them have appeared in adult courts. It may be said that their criminal behavior in imitation of current business practices is due to intimate personal groups to which they belong in the business world. Such groups, however, are not primary in the sense in which the family and neighborhood are, for they come later in life and are much more completely departmentalized. Undoubtedly many of the traditions of sharp practice come to the recruit in the business world through these groups, but they are transmitted, also, by many impersonal agencies.

The broader social processes are taken as the point of departure in the third group of theories. Some of these theories insist that crime is due to the loopholes in the punitive system, through which guilty persons escape detection, conviction, or punishment, and they bend all their efforts to increase the celerity, certainty, and severity of punishment. Others insist that the efficiency and honesty of the police and the courts have deteriorated for the same reason that crime has increased and that the underlying processes must be discovered and modified in order to purify the police and courts and prevent crime. It is believed by those who accept this theory that the nature and organization of the family and neighborhood, also, are determined by natural processes, and that just as individual case work has not been highly successful because the individual is so enmeshed in primary groups that he cannot be changed while his groups remain constant, so also the primary groups are the product of natural processes and these groups cannot be changed without changing these processes. Those who take this point of view are likely, also, to be pessimistic about the possibility of rational control of these processes and to believe that at best leadership can be effective only at times when serious crises occur. The soviet régime was introduced in Russia, and the New Deal in America, in such crises, and neither could have been introduced five years earlier by any organization of arguments or interests. This theory therefore is inclined to emphasize the economic organization, but has been stated also in terms of cultural lag, mobility, and social disorganization. The principal difficulty in this theory is that the data have not been specific, and *a priori* conceptions play an unusually important role. Perhaps the greatest significance of the theory may be as a framework for more specific studies of primary groups and of personality.

METHODS OF DETERMINING CAUSES OF CRIME. The explanations of crime have been derived from two general types of methods. The first is the exploratory, common-sense method by which people become acquainted with a community, a business, politics, or religion. This method is used by the historian and by all social scientists. It consists of the collection and arrangement of all data that are believed to be significant. It is not one of the methods of science outlined in the textbooks on logic. It is impressionistic and deals with general tendencies rather than with specific interpretations. Because of this it is possible to take into account a great variety of conditions which are eliminated in the more specific studies. One of the most important of these omissions in criminology is the immense amount of fraud in modern social life which cannot be presented statistically and which seldom results in arrest or imprisonment, but which, nevertheless, is either vaguely or clearly in violation of law and is similar to the other crimes in its social effects and in the attitudes with which it is perpetrated.

The second general method is confined principally to studies of persons who are arrested or convicted of crimes or to the statistics of such arrests or convictions. These methods tend to be atomistic, breaking up the whole analysis of crime into units and dealing with these units one at a time. These more specific methods may be divided as follows:

1. *Statistics of crimes.* One of the methods is the correlation between arrests or convictions and physical or social variables. Bonger has presented an immense mass of materials to prove that there is a close correlation between crime rates and economic conditions.[13] Others have used the same method in an effort to determine the significance of seasons, of unemployment, of congestion of population. One of the difficulties of this method has been the lack of reliable crime rates. Another difficulty is that it merely locates causes in a general way. It may determine, for instance, that more crimes are committed against the person in hot weather than in cold weather, but it does not tell whether this is due to the direct effect of temperature upon temper, or to a greater frequency of contacts between people in hot weather than in cold weather, or to a greater frequency of intoxication in hot weather, or to something else. Consequently this method may be of value in preliminary studies but does not locate causes with sufficient precision to be final.[14]

2. *Statistics of traits and conditions of criminals.* A second statistical method is the comparison of the frequency of one or more traits or conditions of criminals and of non-criminals. Thus mental tests have been used to determine the relative frequency of feeblemindedness in criminals and in non-criminals. Or an enumeration is made of the criminals who come from homes broken by death, divorce, and desertion of one or both parents in comparison with the number of law-abiding persons who come from such homes. Similarly, color, sex, age, nativity, alcoholism of self or of parents, education, and other factors are studied. In the course of these studies many traits and conditions are compared, but in general each one is abstracted from the others. No pretense is made of studying any criminal as a unit, and no effort is made to determine the cause of the criminality of a particular person by this method. Goring states the reason for this method in the following paragraph.

---

[13] W. A. Bonger, *Criminality and Economic Conditions*, Boston, 1916, pp. 1–246.
[14] Some of the results of this method are shown in Chapter Three.

Our science, recognizing the protean nature of any one human soul, the mutability and interchangeableness of all human influences, does not attempt to "reckon with" the *individual*. Its methods sketch the broader outline, the cruder features of a portrait of human beings *in the mass*. In more technical language, we seek to estimate the final resultant value and direction of certain universal influences and tendencies which, invisible and intangible in their action upon individuals, by the study of individuals can never be measured or appraised; but which, by their operation and interaction over a wide field and in the hearts of all people, lead in the long run to inevitable results; and become not only tangible and visible but capable of the finest definition and measurement.[15]

Valuable information may be secured in this way. Goring disproved Lombroso's theory by the use of this method. It seems to be possible to measure the importance of feeblemindedness and presumably any other trait or condition that can be stated in quantitative terms for the criminal and non-criminal populations.

But there are several difficulties and inadequacies in this method: (a) There is practically no information accessible regarding criminals, as such. The only information generally available is concerning prisoners. Prisoners are a selected group of criminals and an enumeration of traits or conditions of prisoners would, presumably, yield results different from an enumeration of the same traits or conditions of all criminals. This is a difficulty that confronts any method of studying criminals, but it is more distinctly a limitation of this method than of some of the others because this method depends on mass information. (b) The data regarding prisoners are doubtful in many respects. Such evident things as color, sex, and age can be determined with a fair degree of accuracy, but it is impossible to determine other things, such as nativity, home conditions, or the character of parents, without intensive investigations in the communities in which the prisoners lived prior to confinement. (c) If this method is used it is necessary to make comparisons with the general population and also with specialized occupational, racial, sex, age, and other groups from which the prisoners come. But standards for the entire population and especially for particular groups are lacking for most of the important traits. Because of

---

[15] Charles Goring, *The English Convict*, London, 1913, p. 364, note.

this it has been customary for those who used this method to enumerate their cases and then, without knowing how prevalent the same traits were in the general population, assert that the enumerated traits were the principal causes of crime. This is exactly Lombroso's defect, but it has been imitated by many investigators of the present day. For instance, it is frequently reported that a specified part of the criminal population is found, on examination, to be psychopathic, and that this trait is therefore extremely important in the causation of crime. But no one knows how large a percentage of the general population would also be found, by the same tests, to be psychopathic. In addition, many of the standards that we have for the general population are unreliable. It was frequently asserted that the feebleminded person was from forty to fifty times as likely to be a criminal as the person who was not feebleminded, but the general application of army tests revealed a much larger proportion of the population feebleminded, as judged by mental tests. This made it clear that the former judgment had immensely exaggerated the probability of criminality of feebleminded persons. (d) It is possible to secure measurements of only a few traits or conditions and therefore this method cannot locate the causes of crime precisely. It does not explain the mechanisms by which criminality is produced. We may find, for instance, that the male is ten times as criminalistic, judged by commitments to prison, as the female. But males are also five times as likely to be killed by lightning. Is this a sex difference, or a result of differences in occupations, or the general method of life, or something else? If we find that there is a close correlation between the criminality of juveniles and the alcoholism of their parents, we want to know whether this connection is due to a constitutional defect that is responsible both for the alcoholism of the parent and the delinquency of the child, or whether the child is delinquent because the parent spends money for alcohol that ought to be used to secure necessities for the child, or because the discipline in the home is irregular or brutal, or because the status of the family is lowered. Goring's total positive conclusion from his statistical study was that the criminal is physically and mentally inferior. Even if this is true, it does not explain why the inferior person is more likely to commit crime. His correlations are, therefore, merely the beginning of an explanation, locating the field in which to look for an explanation rather than furnishing the explanation. This method seems incapable of carrying the explanation beyond the rather external factors. As Thomas has stated: "Taken in themselves, statistics are nothing more than symptoms of unknown causal processes."[16] The mechanisms involved in the delinquency can be understood only by prying into the situation by methods that do not abstract the traits or conditions, but see them in relation to the rest of the situation. It is for that reason that Healy gave this advice:

We strongly counsel against reckoning up the total dynamic value of any cause apparently making for delinquency by regarding it as an isolated fact.[17]

(e) The statistical enumeration of traits and conditions tells us that certain of these are important and perhaps measures the importance in mathematical terms. It may tell us how much more frequently children from homes broken by divorce, desertion, or death become delinquent than children from homes not so broken. But we need to know more than that: why some children from broken homes do not become delinquent, and why some children from homes not broken do become delinquent. We need to know not only why feebleminded persons become criminals more frequently than normal persons (if they do), but also why some feebleminded persons do not become delinquent and why some normal persons do become delinquent. That is, we should have information that will enable us to state that a person with such and such a nature or such and such attitudes in such and such a situation will always become delinquent. Perhaps it will never be possible to construct such laws, but it is certain that the statistics of traits of criminals will not be sufficient in themselves. The method must be supplemented by other methods.

3. *Individual case study.* By the individual case study method the criminal rather than the trait or condition is regarded as the unit. The traits and conditions of one criminal are all studied together. It is not necessary to abstain from statistics in this method.

---

16 W. I. Thomas, *The Unadjusted Girl*, Boston, 1923, p. 244. Reprinted by permission of Little, Brown & Company, publishers.

17 Wm. Healy, *The Individual Delinquent*, Boston, 1915, p. 282. Reprinted by permission of Little, Brown & Company, publishers. A useful form has been employed by E. A. Doll by which to show at a glance the relation between several traits of prisoners. See New Jersey, *State Prison Report*, 1919, pp. 62 ff.; E. A. Doll, "The Study of Multiple Criminal Factors," *Jour. Crim. Law and Criminol.*, 11:33–46, May, 1920.

Statistics must be used, if a general view of causation is to be secured and if the results are to be stated precisely, just as is true of any other field in which there is a combination of phenomena. The methods differ, not in that one is statistical and the other one not statistical, but in that the individual is the unit in one, and the abstracted trait or condition is the unit in the other. The same traits may be studied in each method. If the importance of the home environment is determined by a comparison of the grades or indices of the homes of criminals and of non-criminals, it is not the individual case method. If the importance of the home environment is determined by a consideration of the home in relation to the rest of the situation, it is the individual case method. The comparison might be expressed better, however, if it is recalled that the purpose of the comparison of home-indices of criminals and non-criminals is to determine the importance of home conditions of specified kinds in producing delinquency; while the purpose of the individual case study is to determine how and why certain types of homes produce delinquency—how they produce delinquency, rather than how frequently they produce delinquency.

In his study of juvenile delinquents in Chicago, Healy considered the following items: family history, developmental history, environment (including home and neighborhood), mental and moral development, physical measurements, medical examination, mental tests, psychological analysis, and description of delinquencies.[18] Under these heads he has a list of items covering nine pages in his book. In the more recent studies made for the Judge Baker Foundation in Boston, Healy has included under the head of psychological studies the following: psychological examination, mental balance, and personality traits. It is evident, also, that the more recent studies have been based much more on field inquiries than were the previous studies and that the relation of the delinquent to his groups has been emphasized.

On the basis of such studies of the traits and situations of the delinquent, an effort is made to select the ones that seem to be instrumental in producing the delinquency. In the earlier studies by Healy, one primary and one secondary cause was selected for each case. In the later studies Healy has not attempted to do that, but gives a list of "probable direct causes" in connection with a descrip-

---

[18] Healy, *op. cit.*, pp. 53–63.

tion of the personality and background of the delinquent. The following may serve as an illustration:

(1) Bad companions, a delinquent group. (2) Lack of good parental management, parents sickly, etc. (3) Dearth of good recreational opportunities in neighborhood. (4) Treatment under the law: (a) continuance of crowd associations through sending boy and companions to same institution, (b) return of boy on parole to old associations.[19]

The method used in determining the significant causal factors varies. Adler has maintained that for this purpose the important things to study are the behavioristic tendencies manifested in the past behavior of the delinquent rather than his mental processes.[20] Healy, on the other hand, has insisted that it is necessary to determine the mental antecedents of the delinquency, including such things as mental dissatisfactions, irritative mental reactions to environmental conditions, obsessional imagery, adolescent mental instabilities and impulsions, mental conflicts, worries or repressions, antisocial grudges, mental peculiarities or aberrations, and mental defects.[21] For this purpose he reports that the delinquent's own story is of primary importance, though this does not mean that the story must be accepted as a correct explanation of the delinquency.

This individual case study method is criticized by opponents as follows: (a) Explanations are too much subject to the individual whim or prejudice of the investigator. Consequently there is danger of making much of factors that are really insignificant and neglecting factors that are very significant. The Whittier State School in California published in its Manual three case studies and stated their judgments as to the probable causes of delinquency in each. Miss Bronner, in a review of the Manual, stated that she did not agree with the Whittier authorities as to the probable cause in any one of the three cases.[22] This seems to indicate that one sees in the materials of an individual case those things which fit into his own pre-existing scheme of explanation of delinquency. The same thing is true of any statistical method of abstracted traits or conditions. And the check in both cases is the judgment of other investigators

---

[19] Judge Baker Foundation, *Case Studies*, series 1, No. 8, p. 29a.
[20] H. M. Adler, "A Psychiatric Contribution to the Study of Delinquency," *Jour. Crim. Law and Criminol.*, 8:66, May, 1917.
[21] Healy, *op. cit.*, pp. 28 and 32.
[22] Augusta F. Bronner, *Mental Hygiene*, 6:868–869, October, 1922.

and the control that is secured by means of the knowledge. (b) Most of the agencies that are making case studies are part of an administrative system dealing with delinquents and their studies must result in advice regarding procedure. Consequently there is a probability that the items which can be modified will be selected as causes, or that considerations of practicability in dealing with the offender will determine the explanation. In addition there is a tendency to introduce as a part of the causation any physical or other defect that may need to be corrected, even if it is not a significant part of the causation.

4. *Study of the criminal "in the open."* Another method of explanation of crime is by association with criminals "in the open." It is asserted by those who have had intimate contacts with criminals "in the open" that criminals are not "natural" in police stations, courts, and prisons and that they must be studied in their everyday life outside of institutions if they are to be understood.[23] By this is meant that the investigator must associate with them as one of them, seeing their lives and conditions as the criminals themselves see them.

There is no doubt of the desirability of securing information in this way, but it is clearly limited by considerations of practicability. Few individuals could acquire the technique to pass as criminals; it would be necessary to engage in crime with the others if they retained a position once secured. One individual could not build upon the work of another to a very great extent. Moreover, even if these difficulties were overcome, it would still be impossible to secure information regarding the origin of most of the attitudes of the criminals, for few of them would permit interrogations regarding their earlier lives or would volunteer information regarding the factors that had made them criminals. Nevertheless the more information we can secure in this way, the less likely we are to be led astray by the other methods. So far as it can contribute, it is very valuable.

5. *Therapeutic method.* It is possible to test hypotheses regarding the causes of delinquency by changing the behavior of individuals or of groups, under controlled conditions. This is somewhat like the experimental method in the physical and biological

---

[23] Josiah Flynt Willard, *Tramping with Tramps,* New York, 1899; Josiah Flynt Willard, *My Life,* New York, 1908; Max Kauffmann, *Psychologie des Verbrechens,* Berlin, 1912.

sciences, although the control is necessarily much less complete in social situations.

GENERAL METHODOLOGICAL PROBLEMS. In addition to the specific problems of method which have been discussed, one more general methodological problem arises frequently. This problem is concerned with the nature of scientific explanation. Two contrasted positions have been taken in regard to it. One is the argument that science consists of continuous additions to knowledge. For instance, it is found in statistical studies that males have a higher rate of imprisonment than females, Negroes a higher rate than whites, young adults a higher rate than the middle aged, city residents a higher rate than rural residents, and the lower economic classes a higher rate than the upper economic classes. It is believed that the accumulation of such comparisons will gradually narrow the area of ignorance, or enlarge the area of knowledge, until we finally have, merely by this process of addition, an understanding of crime. Some attempts have been made to combine these several factors into an organic system, so that the probability that a young adult Negro male of low economic status who lives in a city will become a criminal can be determined, in comparison with the probability that some other person who varies in one or all of the characteristics listed will become a criminal. In this method, the legal definition of crime is accepted, and the multiple factor theory is the starting point, but otherwise no hypotheses are formulated; it is usually an attempt to explain crime in general.

The general methodology which is contrasted with this may be illustrated in the study of drug addiction by Lindesmith. The procedure he followed consists of the following steps: first, a rough definition of the entity to be explained is formulated; second, a rough statement of a hypothetical explanation of the entity is formulated; third, one case is studied in the light of the hypothesis, to determine whether the factual data in that case fit the hypothesis; if they do not fit, it is necessary either to re-formulate the hypothesis or else to re-define the entity so that the case is excluded; fourth, by a continuation of this procedure of examination of cases, re-definition of the entity, and re-formulation of hypotheses, a universal relationship may be reached. The negative case is the essential point in the procedure, that is, one which calls for a re-definition of the entity or a re-formulation of the hypothesis. Investigation should continue until no more negative cases can be discovered.

Practical certainty may be reached after a small number of cases have been examined—perhaps ten or fifteen. Studies of conceptual segments of criminality in this manner should result in a series of general propositions regarding those segments, and from such general propositions a general body of theory may be developed.[24]

SUGGESTED READINGS

Bernaldo de Quiros, C., *Modern Theories of Criminality*, Tr. by Alfonso de Salvio, Boston, 1911.

Bridges, J. W., and Bridges, K. M. B., "A Psychological Study of Juvenile Delinquency by Group Methods," *Genet. Psychol. Monog.*, 1926, No. 1, pp. 411–506.

Burgess, E. W. "The Study of the Delinquent as a Person," *Amer. Jour. Sociol.*, 28:657–680, May, 1923.

Ferri, E., *Criminal Sociology*, Tr. by J. I. Kelly and John Lisle, Boston, 1917.

Filter, R. O., "Experimental Study of Character Traits," *Jour. Appl. Psychol.*, 5:297–317, December, 1921.

Garofalo, R., *Criminology*, Tr. by R. W. Millar, Boston, 1914.

Goring, Charles, *The English Convict*, London, 1913.

Gruhle, Hans W., "The Task of Criminal Psychology," *Jour. Crim. Law and Criminol.*, 22:506–516, November, 1931.

Harper, F. V., and Reinhardt, J. M., "Four Relationship States of a Group of Delinquent Boys," *Jour. Crim. Law and Criminol.*, 12:379–392, November, 1930.

Levin, Yale, and Lindesmith, Alfred, "English Ecology and Criminology of the Past Century," *Jour. Crim. Law and Criminol.*, 27:801–816, March, 1937.

Lindesmith, Alfred R., "A Sociological Theory of Drug Addiction," *Amer. Jour. Sociol.*, 43:593–609, January, 1938.

Lindesmith, Alfred R., and Levin, Yale, "The Lombrosian Myth in Criminology," *Amer. Jour. Sociol.*, 42:653–671, March, 1937.

Lombroso, C., *Crime, Its Causes and Remedies*, Tr. by H. P. Horton, Boston, 1911.

Reckless, W. C., "A Sociological Clinic for the Study of Juvenile Delinquency," *Pub. Amer. Sociol. Soc.*, 22:187–194, 1928.

---

[24] Alfred R. Lindesmith, "A Sociological Theory of Drug Addiction," *Amer. Jour. Sociol.*, 43:593–609, January, 1938. The general study, of which this article is an abstract, is *The Nature of Opiate Addiction*, Dissertation, 1938, manuscript, University of Chicago Library.

Rohden, F. von, "Methoden der Kriminalbiologie," *Handbuch der Biologischen Arbeitsmethoden,* Vol. IV, No. 12, pp. 581–829, 1933.

Sellin, Thorsten, *Culture Conflict and Crime,* Social Science Research Council, New York, 1938.

Shaw, Clifford R., "Case Study Method," *Pub. Amer. Sociol. Soc.,* 21:149–157, 1927.

Tarde, G., *Penal Philosophy,* Tr. by R. Howell, Boston, 1912.

Thomas, W. I. and Dorothy S., *The Child in America,* New York, 1928.

Chapter Five

CRIME AND SOCIAL PROCESSES

THE PURPOSE of the present chapter is to present the general historical background of present-day crime in terms of the social processes by which the criminality has developed. This is, for the most
part, in the nature of hypothesis rather than demonstrated fact.
Furthermore, criminality is considered in this chapter somewhat
more broadly than in the following chapters in which specific research studies are analyzed. Much criminality is not prosecuted, and
this lack of prosecution is biased in favor of the crimes of the well-
to-do classes. This is partly because the well-to-do classes are socially
and politically powerful and can protect themselves against prosecution, and partly because the mores have not become so definitely
formed regarding the fraudulent crimes of this class as against the
more direct and immediate crimes which have been in existence for
centuries. These acts, however, are properly regarded as crimes and
are probably much more prevalent and much more injurious to
society than the robberies, burglaries, kidnapings, and murders
which are direct and personal.

SOCIAL DISORGANIZATION. In preliterate and peasant societies
the influences surrounding a person were steady, uniform, harmonious, and consistent. China until recently exemplified this situation
perfectly except in a few of the coast cities. The individual was
surrounded by all of his relatives and this larger family determined
his career and his ambitions. His principal satisfactions were found
in co-operation with that group, which was considered as extending
beyond his own life into the distant future. Within this group he
had perfect individual security, for the group cared for him in case
of sickness, accident, old age, insanity, or other emergency and this
care involved no stigma or disgrace whatsoever. This large family,
moreover, was supported by the surrounding community which also

69

was harmonious in its traditional culture. In that situation the behavior of the individual was almost completely predictable, for he
had only one pattern to follow and only extraordinary emergencies
could induce him to invent a new mode of behavior. The local
group had little contact with outsiders, since the community was a
self-supporting and self-contained society. Within this group almost
no crimes were committed, and the occasional crimes were chiefly
confined to crimes committed by non-residents upon the members
of the group, or crimes committed by members of the group upon
non-members. The standards of the outside political society meant
little within this group and national loyalty was not significant.[1]

At present such uniformity is nowhere evident in Western civilization, though the village communities are the closest approach to
it. A child is confronted with various cultures even within his own
home, for no parent can act consistently in modern life even within
his own home; the parent changes from day to day with stimulations, successes, moods, contents of books he has read or lectures
he has heard. A great deal of behavior is in the nature of playing a
role and when the roles are conflicting the behavior is inconsistent.
Groups outside of the home have standards which are extremely
different from those within the home. Dewey has described the conflicts within a community thus:

It is not easy to exaggerate the extent to which we now pass from one
kind of nurture to another as we go from business to church, from
science to the newspaper, from business to art, from companionship to
politics, from home to school. An individual is now subjected to many
conflicting schemes of education. Hence habits are divided against
one another, personality is disrupted, the scheme of conduct is confused
and disintegrated.[2]

This is a state of disorganization or un-organization, in the sense
that the influences are not uniform and harmonious. The processes
by which this condition has developed are mobility, competition,
and conflict. These processes have been accompanied by an individualistic ideology which has been logically and intellectually
harmonious with a criminalistic ideology.

---

[1] Ching-Yueh Yen, "Crime in Relation to Social Change in China," *Amer.
Jour. Sociol.*, 40:298–308, November, 1934.
[2] John Dewey, *Human Nature and Conduct*, New York, 1930, p. 130. Reprinted by permission of Henry Holt and Company, publishers.

One starting point of this process of disorganization was the colonization of America, which threw the Old World out of economic balance. This was followed by the break-up of the feudal system, in which the ownership of land had been limited and in which the fixed social classes had mutual duties to each other. Experimental science developed and mechanical inventions resulted. The industrial revolution and the democratic revolutions ushered in a system of capitalism, competition, and democracy. With the development of machinery, the production of wealth passed from the control of the consumer to the control of the capitalist, the laborer followed his work from the home to the factory, and thus the city developed around the factory and the market place. The traditional restrictions on economic activity were irksome as world commerce began to develop, and rebellion against these restrictions resulted in a system of relatively free competition, with an accompanying individualistic ideology according to which social welfare is best attained if every person works only for his own selfish interests. The new condition of mobility was not compatible with political absolutism, and this resulted in democratic revolutions with accompanying individualistic ideologies of natural and inalienable rights and the slogan "the least government the best."

This sequence of events necessarily resulted in an immense increase in crime. In the first place the large family and the homogeneous neighborhood, which had been the principal agencies of social control, disintegrated, primarily as the result of mobility. They were replaced by the small family, consisting of parents and children, detached from other relatives, and by a neighborhood in which the mores were not homogeneous, and the behavior of one person was a matter of relative indifference to other persons. Thus the agencies by which control had been secured in almost all earlier societies were greatly weakened.

Second, at the same time the problem of control was greatly intensified by the extension of the boundaries of frequent and effective interaction from the local community to the nation or even to the whole earth in the form of commerce, travel, newspapers, picture shows, and radio. When interaction was confined to the local community the spontaneous and sentimental influences controlled behavior, for the effect of the behavior of a person was immediately apparent to himself and to others. When interaction extended beyond the area of personal observation and intimate association, and the effects of behavior did not become immediately discernible, the problem of control was greatly intensified. It is probable that the family and neighborhood, even if retained in their original strength, would have been relatively impotent to control their members in their activities with outsiders, for the early community and the present village community have been generally effective only in intra-community relations. A certain national loyalty had developed in the earlier period in connection with the doctrine of the divinity of royalty, but apparently the common people did not take this doctrine as seriously as did royalty and when the belief in the doctrine disintegrated, no substitute was found.

Also, the attitudes and ideology which developed with the industrial and democratic revolutions were favorable to weak governments and antagonistic toward all efforts at control. Economic and political individualism was useful at the time of revolt against the fixed status and restrictions of the feudal system and against the absolutism of the political system. But individualism is not a positive principle of social organization, and when the revolutions were ended, the usefulness of the negative principle was ended. Since that time it has constantly hampered social organization and has encouraged the individual to disregard social welfare in the interest of his selfish satisfactions.[3] The only duties are observance of law and contracts, and this means the letter rather than the spirit of the law and contracts. Public welfare need not be considered, for it will be best realized if each person works for his own selfish interest. On that principle the natural resources of the United States have been depleted, government officials corrupted by bribery, and wage-earning and agricultural classes exploited, with the result that the common people have little satisfaction with present achievements and no security for the future, and both the common people and the people who have economic and political advantages and privileges have no inspiration from association in work for the larger social welfare. The criminal and the grafter, also, believe that

---

[3] H. W. Anderson, "Introduction to Report on Causes of Crime," *Natl. Com. on Law Obs. and Enf.*, No. 13, Vol. I, p. xxxi.

Trigant Burrow has argued that the identification of ethical feeling and egotistic advantage is a characteristic of human nature. The argument might be made, however, that this identification, if not confined to the modern culture, has been greatly magnified by the current individualism. See "Crime and the Social Reaction of Right and Wrong," *Jour. Crim. Law and Criminol.*, 24: 685–699, November, 1933.

social welfare need not be an object of consideration and that they may get what they can by whatever methods they can. It is difficult to imagine a respectable philosophy which would be more in harmony with and conducive to criminality than this philosophy of individualism. Is it possible for the leaders in a society to adopt a policy of self-interest in opposition to social welfare without having criminals adopt a policy of self-interest in opposition to social welfare?

Since competition drives participants toward the limits of achievement either because of the pleasure of beating competitors or because of the desire for the material rewards of superior achievement, impediments to or restrictions on competition are galling. The participant rebels against restrictions on his own behavior and therefore attempts to make and keep the government weak. But as competition developed, it became apparent that competitive advantages could be secured by governmental privileges. Industries secured tariffs, franchises, patents, and other special privileges, and for the same reason they prevented or attempted to prevent banking laws, child-labor laws, and workmen's compensation laws. Driven by competition they resorted to bribery, either overtly or in the form of campaign contributions and personal kindliness. Thus government has been made ineffective in the control of behavior in the area of wider interaction. This has created among the dispossessed an impression that the rules and the referees in the economic world are not fair.

Finally, the ambition for luxury standards of life and for easy money became effective for all social classes, since the fixed barriers which previously restricted these privileges to the nobility had been removed. After the disappearance of the nobility business men constituted the élite and wealth became respected above all other attainments; necessarily, poverty became a disgrace. Wealth was therefore identified with worth, and worth was made known to the public by conspicuous consumption. The ambition for luxury standards of life, developed by competitive consumption and by competitive salesmanship, spread to all classes and the simple life was no longer satisfying. These expanded wants therefore tended to become stronger than the inhibitions. Also, it became apparent at an early period in the capitalist system that great wealth was not secured by manual labor but by social manipulation which did not necessarily increase the nation's wealth. This might be in the form of farsighted appreciation of future developments, but might be in the form of bribery or fraud, and was generally speculative in nature. In earlier years wild speculation in real estate and in later years wild speculation on the stock market were expressions of this desire for easy money. Crime is frequently a similar speculative expression of the desire for easy money.

In summary, it may be said that the industrial and democratic revolutions started social processes which produced general criminality in three ways: (1) The need of control was greatly increased because the area of social interaction was widened immensely from the local community to the entire earth, people were driven hard against restrictions by the pressure of competition, wealth became the principal distinction, ambitions for a luxury standard of life and for easy money were characteristic of all social classes, the basic wants and general security were neglected or cared for only by charity, and a competitive ideology of individual rights and individual services rather than duties and social welfare was an excellent background for the criminal. (2) The old agencies of control in the local community and the institutional control, as in the authority of the church, were eliminated or greatly weakened. (3) The law as an agency of control in the wider area was kept relatively weak and restricted by the dominant business group, due at first to the principle that the least government is the best and later to direct and indirect bribery for the sake of special privileges, and a consistent and important public opinion has not developed. In view of these conditions universal criminality might be expected.

The nations of the Occident have not become equally criminalistic, for they have not become equally mobile, equally competitive, equally capitalistic, or equally individualistic. The industrial and democratic revolutions produced their consequences with fewer inhibitions or counteracting influences in the United States than in any other country, and for that reason the rates of the so-called serious crimes and also of bribery and business fraud are highest here. The immigrants since the first colonization have been most heterogeneous, and as each new group of immigrants has been excluded from intimate association with the earlier generations, it has become acquainted only with the public life of America.[4] The Revolution produced a sudden break with traditions of the Old

---

[4] Edwin H. Sutherland, "Social Process in Behavior Problems," *Pub. Amer. Sociol. Soc.*, 26:55–61, 1932.

World, and the democratic and industrial revolutions therefore began with almost no background of counteracting traditions. England, on the other hand, has retained fairly definite class lines and a fairly homogeneous population, with little immigration, in comparison with the United States. Canada has had many immigrants but they have come principally from two countries and, furthermore, Canada had no democratic revolution to produce a distinct break with traditions as did the United States. The industrial revolution in China is now producing the same consequences that it has in Western countries, though the change from familism to individualism is much more abrupt.[5]

TENDENCIES TOWARD REORGANIZATION. The individualistic system in business and politics has been modified in the last generation or two in its material aspects. Free competition was ruining individuals and they were driven into corporate activities. Huge corporations, huge banks, chain stores, chain theaters, chain newspapers, and radio broadcasting companies have developed. Also, trade associations, trade unions, chambers of commerce, and many other associations have been formed. To an increasing extent the behavior and opportunities of individuals are determined and defined by these corporations and associations. Thus the general development has been from feudalism and absolutism to individualism, and from individualism to corporate and associated activities. But the transition from individualism has been confined principally to material effects. Corporations and associations have no more interest in social welfare than did the competing individuals who preceded them. The ideology of individualism still remains in a world of corporate activity. This may be seen in the frequency with which the directors and officers of corporations are traitors to their stockholders, in the controversies between associations for financial advantages, and in many other ways.

Three tendencies toward social reorganization, aside from the corporate activities above described, may be discovered in the modern world. A certain type of uniformity of thought and of interest is secured by newspapers, radio, theaters, and public education. This interest, however, is restricted in scope or is concerned with ephemeral incidents. Its importance, however, may be indicated in relation to bribery of baseball players. When in 1919

---

[5] Ching-Yueh Yen, "Crime in Relation to Social Change in China," *Amer. Jour. Sociol.*, 40: 298–308, November, 1934.

Arnold Rothstein, the notorious gambler and gangster, bribed some of the baseball players in the world series to "throw" the game, a tremendous pressure for punishment of the players was exerted. The players were dismissed, and in some states laws were enacted which made the penalty for giving bribes in athletic contests more severe than the penalty for robbery with a gun. On this point the public or that part of it which counted in baseball presented a united front. In an ordinary burglary, on the other hand, the attitude of the public is one of indifference, for burglary involves property which is private, while baseball is a public matter. Bribery of a member of the president's cabinet provoked less popular antagonism than the bribery of these baseball players. It is possible that baseball may become the nucleus around which public morality may be unified, as has been claimed of cricket in England. But in general the public interests, like the newspapers which largely create them, are fluctuating, unstable, and concerned with unimportant things. Dewey says regarding the uniformity of thought produced in this manner:

We think and feel alike but only for a month or a season. Then comes some other sensational event or personage to exercise a hypnotizing uniformity of response. At a given time, taken in cross-section, conformity is the rule. In a time span, taken longitudinally, instability and flux dominate.[6]

A second tendency toward uniformity of thought and feeling is seen in the artificial efforts to develop nationalism in Europe at present, as in the Nazi régime in Germany, fascism in Italy, sovietism in Russia, and dictatorships in other countries. These, as also the New Deal in the United States, are gropings toward social organization to replace the individualism which has broken down or is breaking down economically, legally, and politically. This disorganization will certainly be terminated by reorganization of some sort, and then a definite reduction in crime may be expected. It is probable that at some future time the eighteenth and nineteenth centuries will be designated as the period of the world's most extreme social disorganization between a solidly organized society

---

[6] John Dewey, "Individualism, Old and New," *New Rep.*, 62:14, February 19, 1930. Reprinted by permission.

in the feudal period and a solidly organized society toward which we seem to be developing.

A third tendency toward reorganization of society may be found in the development of scientific activities and intellectual honesty. The number of scientific people in modern society is, of course, not large, but the results of science have permeated all society to a greater or lesser extent. This factor has been one, though probably not the most important, reason for the decay of some of the old institutions. The first effect of intellectual honesty was to produce decay in the principles of social organization which were incompatible with intellectual honesty. Intellectual honesty provides, also, a principle on which reorganization may develop.[7]

MOBILITY AND CONFLICT. The universal and most significant element in the process of social disorganization is mobility. Mobility of persons and of commodities inevitably widens the area within which control becomes necessary and at the same time inevitably weakens the local agencies of control in the communities into which migrants go. This is true, however, only in so far as mobility means change of social situation. Change in geographical location need not mean change in social situation. This conclusion regarding the inevitability and universality of the effects of mobility has not been based on sufficient evidence to justify a final conclusion regarding its significance or validity. It is possible that the whole process could be described in terms of Ogburn's concept of cultural lag. According to this concept, crime has been prevalent because the immaterial culture does not develop as rapidly as the material culture.[8] Certain students of law, on the other hand, have insisted that the prevalence of crime is due to the fact that the law has been extended much more rapidly than the general mores, and that when the law is not thus supported by general mores it is relatively impotent and is violated frequently.[9] In general, it is desirable to make comparative studies of crime in different cultures for the purpose of securing more precise evidence regarding the processes

---

[7] P. W. Bridgman, "The Struggle for Intellectual Integrity," *Harpers*, 168:18–25, December, 1933.

[8] W. F. Ogburn, *Social Change*, New York, 1923, Part IV.

[9] K. N. Llewellyn, "Law Observance versus Law Enforcement," *Proc. Natl. Conf. Social Work*, 1928, pp. 127–136; Jerome Frank, "Realistic Reflections on Law as a Constructive Social Force," *Proc. Natl. Conf. Social Work*, 1933, pp. 326–332; Herman Oliphant, "The Public and the Law," *Amer. Bar Assoc. Jour.*, 18:787–791, December, 1932.

in relation to criminality, in order that the processes which are universal in their significance may be identified.

A few studies have been made in this country which throw some light on mobility and conflict. These studies are concerned with direct effects of mobility and conflict and therefore fail significantly to measure the full importance of these processes, for the effects of the processes are principally indirect and are diffused over a period of time and over a wide area. The data are presented, however, as illustrations of the first efforts to study these processes.

McKenzie found a correlation of 0.39 between juvenile delinquency and mobility by wards in Columbus,[10] and Sullenger found a correlation of 0.34 in a similar study in Omaha.[11] Carpenter concluded that a criminal group studied in Buffalo was much more migratory than a control group in the same city.[12] Stuart, in a study in Berkeley, found that delinquents lived in areas which had high rates of mobility, but that they personally were less mobile than the average family.[13] Prison reports show that the rate of commitments to prisons in Iowa has been more than twice as high for natives of the four principal states surrounding Iowa as for natives of Iowa, in proportion to the population of each group living in Iowa. The rate of commitment to prisons in Connecticut in 1910 was four times as great for persons born in New York State as for persons born in Connecticut in proportion to the population of each group living in Connecticut. On the other hand, Joly found in France in 1889 that the natives of some departments had higher rate in other departments than in their home departments, and natives of other departments had higher rates at home than they did when in other parts of France; the conclusion seems to be that the comparative crime rate at home and abroad depends on the customary behavior in the two departments: those who go from a department with a high crime rate to a department with a low crime rate become less criminal, while those who go from a department with a low crime rate to a department with a high crime rate

---

[10] R. D. McKenzie, "The Neighborhood," Amer. Jour. Sociol., 28:166, September, 1921.

[11] T. E. Sullenger, Social Determinants in Juvenile Delinquency, New York, 1936, p. 179.

[12] Niles Carpenter and William M. Haenszel, "Migratoriness and Criminality in Buffalo," Social Forces, 9:254–255, December, 1930.

[13] Johannes Stuart, "Mobility and Delinquency," Amer. Jour. Orthopsych., 6:486–493, October, 1936.

become more criminal.[14] In the United States occasional studies
have indicated that crimes are unusually frequent in cities with a
large non-resident population, such as the seaports and resort towns,
and in occupations which are migratory, such as carnivals and
circuses and the old river boats. Hotels suffer loss by theft roughly
in proportion to the transiency of their guests. One city hotel serving transients suffers a loss by theft of about 25,000 towels a year,
and another hotel lost by theft within two years one-fifth of the
pictures which had been hung on the walls at the time it opened.[15]
These statistics give some understanding of the reason why the word
"traveler" in medieval England was used in popular discourse to
designate the thief. Such statistics, however, are entirely inadequate
as illustrations of the significance of mobility, for the important
point is that mobility has affected all persons in modern society and
not merely those who happen to be non-residents at the time of
a crime.

Conflict of cultures has to some extent been studied from the
statistical point of view, though these statistics, also, are extremely
inadequate as a measure of the conflict. The immigrant population,
having reached maturity in the Old World environment, has a
relatively low crime rate when the immigrants settle in America,
but some studies show that the second generation has a much higher
crime rate than their parents or the native-born of native parentage,
apparently because of the conflict within their experience between
the Old World culture and the American culture. Beynon has
shown some specific ways in which this occurs through conflicts of
cultures.[16] Also, some studies, though not all, have resulted in the
conclusion that the native-born children with one parent native-
born and the other foreign-born have a higher rate than native-born
children with both parents foreign-born or both parents native-
born, and this also seems to be due to the greater conflict of cultures
in those cases. Psychiatrists and psychoanalysts, also, find these
conflicts within the home to be highly significant from the point of
view of behavior problems. Levy has reported that differences in

[14] Henri Joly, *La France criminelle*, Paris, 1889, pp. 45–46.
[15] N. S. Hayner, "Hotel Life and Personality," *Amer. Jour. Sociol.*, 33:792,
March, 1928; Margaret A. Barnes, "How We Behave Away from Home,"
Amer. Mag., 111:23, March, 1931; Allison Gray, "The Queer Things Guests
Leave and Take," *Amer. Mag.*, 97:135–138, January, 1924.
[16] E. D. Beynon, "Crime and Custom of the Hungarians of Detroit," *Jour.
Crim. Law and Criminol.*, 25:755–774, January, 1935.

language, manners, methods of discipline, and ideals represented by the parents are important factors in the maladjustment of children.[17] Evelyn Crook has found that 86 per cent of the delinquent girls who were studied resided on racial or language frontiers, where two or more racial or language groups came in contact, and only 14 per cent resided in the interior of a racial or language group. The exact proportion of children residing on frontiers of this kind, which one should know in order to construct a rate of delinquency, is not available, but it is certainly much less than 86 per cent.[18] Delinquency might equally well be studied in relation to cultural conflicts produced by social changes other than those which have been mentioned.

The effects of mobility and culture conflict become more apparent when an isolated country is suddenly brought by mobility into contact with the rest of the world. This happened in China within the last fifty years, and has been accompanied by remarkable changes in criminality in that country. The old social relations and standards of behavior which had been quite adequate for control while the country was relatively isolated have proved very inadequate in the last generation when many foreigners have lived in China and when Chinese have gone to foreign countries, and when in addition the cultures of other communities have been introduced into China through impersonal means.[19]

Sellin has summarized the principal studies in regard to culture conflict, in a general theoretical setting, and has outlined projects for research in this field. Concentration of research work on the projects suggested should yield results that would test this theory of culture conflict.[20] It is likely that such studies would show that culture conflict is significant principally, as suggested in Chapter One, either through differential association or through social disorganization in the control of behavior.

[17] John Levy, "Conflict of Cultures and Children's Maladjustments," *Mental Hygiene,* 17:41–50, January, 1933. See, also, Louis Wirth, "Culture Conflicts and Delinquency," *Social Forces,* 9:484–492, June, 1931; Maurice Price, "The Concept of Culture Conflict," *Social Forces,* 9:164–167, December, 1930; A. B. Luria, *The Nature of Human Conflicts,* New York, 1932.

[18] Evelyn B. Crook, "Cultural Marginality in Sexual Delinquency," *Amer. Jour. Sociol.,* 39:493–500, January, 1934.

[19] Ching-Yueh Yen, "Crime in Relation to Social Change in China," *Amer. Jour. Sociol.,* 40:298–308, November, 1934.

[20] Thorsten Sellin, *Culture Conflict and Crime,* New York, 1938.

SUGGESTED READINGS

Anderson, H. W., "Introduction to Report on Causes of Crime," *Natl. Com. on Law Obs. and Enf.,* No. 13, Vol. I, pp. xv-lxxxi.

Carpenter, N., and Haenszel, W. M., "Migratoriness and Criminality in Buffalo," *Social Forces,* 9:254–255, December, 1930.

Crook, Evelyn B., "Cultural Marginality in Sexual Delinquency," *Amer. Jour. Sociol.,* 39:493–500, January, 1934.

Dewey, John, "Individualism, Old and New," *New Rep.,* 61:239–241, 294–296; 62:13–16, 184–188, January–April, 1930.

Frank, Jerome, "Realistic Reflections on Law as a Constructive Social Force," *Proc. Natl. Conf. Social Work,* 1933, pp. 326–332.

Hayner, N. S., "Hotel Life and Personality," *Amer. Jour. Sociol.,* 33:784–795, March, 1928.

Levy, John, "Conflict of Cultures and Children's Maladjustments," *Mental Hygiene,* 17:41–50, January, 1933.

Llewellyn, K. N., "Law Observance versus Law Enforcement," *Proc. Natl. Conf. Social Work,* 1928, pp. 127–136.

Lottier, Stuart, "Regions of Criminal Mobility," *Jour. Crim. Law and Criminol.,* 28:657–673, January, 1938.

Luria, A. B., *The Nature of Human Conflicts,* New York, 1932.

McDougall, William, "Crime in America," *Forum,* 77:518–523, April, 1927.

McKenzie, R. D., *The Neighborhood,* Chicago, 1923.

Ogburn, W. F., *Social Change,* New York, 1923, Part IV.

Oliphant, Herman, "The Public and the Law," *Amer. Bar Assoc. Jour.,* 18:787–793, December, 1932.

Price, Maurice, "The Concept of Culture Conflict," *Social Forces,* 9:164–167, December, 1930.

Sombart, W., *The Quintessence of Capitalism,* New York, 1915.

Weber, Max, *General Economic History,* New York, 1927.

Wirth, Louis, "Culture Conflicts and Delinquency," *Social Forces,* 9:484–492, June, 1931.

Yen, Ching-Yueh, "Crime in Relation to Social Change in China," *Amer. Jour. Sociol.,* 40:298–308, November, 1934.

Chapter Six

PHYSICAL AND PHYSIOLOGICAL FACTORS
IN CRIMINALITY

THIS CHAPTER is concerned with the relation of physical and physiological conditions and traits to criminality, and the data are confined to criminals who are arrested or prosecuted. These traits and
conditions are taken as a point of departure for the discussion, and
the fact that they appear in this chapter does not necessarily mean
that they are believed to be important causes of crime or that any
associations they may have with criminality are explained by
physical or physiological processes rather than by social processes.

SEASONAL VARIATIONS. Statistical studies show very uniformly
that crimes against property reach a maximum in winter months,
and crimes against the person and against morals in the summer
months.[1] While the general conclusion is substantiated by a large
number of statistical studies, the difference in rates is not great for
certain types of offenses. Attempts have been made to explain the
seasonal variations by the direct action of temperature or humidity
upon motives and inhibitions, and also by the length of the period
of daylight or of darkness. The basic differences can probably best
be explained in social terms, for crimes against property reach a
maximum in winter months when the cost of living increases, and
crimes against the person and against morals reach a maximum in
the summer months when the contacts between persons are most
frequent and the consumption of alcohol in group relationships is
greatest. This does not explain all of the variations in the rates; for
instance, burglaries increase decidedly in the winter, while robbery
increases very slightly. It is possible that some of the variations are

---

[1] For statistics of crimes known to the police in the United States see *Uniform Crime Reports,* Vol. VI, No. 4, pp. 22–25; and the fourth quarterly
reports in subsequent years. For a summary of European studies on this point
see G. Aschaffenburg, *Crime and Its Repression,* pp. 16–30.

influenced directly by climatic conditions. Some of the departures from the uniform tendencies are due to local social conditions. Schmid found that homicides reach a maximum in Seattle during the winter months, and explained that this was due to the influx of migratory laborers during the late autumn.[2]

HEREDITY. For many years the discussion of the causes of crime was concentrated on the controversy between heredity and environment. It is desirable to consider these concepts, although the controversy has long been considered to be futile.

Lombroso and his followers, especially during the early period of their school, considered that the typical criminal was a born criminal. They did not attempt to describe the mechanism by which criminality was inherited but merely referred to inborn criminality as an atavism, which is no explanation at all. Moreover, their principal evidence that criminality was atavistic was the resemblance of the criminal to the savage, and the savage who was hypothecated for this comparison was very different from the actual savage. Consequently Lombroso had no significant proof or explanation of the inheritance of criminality.

Family trees have been used extensively by certain scholars in the effort to prove that criminality is inherited. It has been reported that out of about 1,200 descendants of the Jukes family who were studied by Dugdale and Estabrook, 140 were criminals, of whom 7 were convicted of murder, 60 of theft, and 50 of prostitution.[3] The Kallikak family had among its members 3 convicted of felonies, 24 of confirmed alcoholism, and 33 of sexual immorality (mostly prostitution) out of 480 descendants from an illegitimate mating of a Revolutionary soldier and a feebleminded woman, while there were no known criminals among the offspring of the same soldier and a normal wife. In the Zero family, with about 800 descendants in six generations, 7 were convicted of murder, 76 of other serious offenses, and 181 of prostitution.

The fact that a trait appears frequently in successive generations does not prove that it is inherited. The use of the fork in eating has been a characteristic trait in many families for several gener-

---

[2] C. F. Schmid, "A Study of Homicides in Seattle," *Social Forces*, 4: 745–756, June, 1926.

[3] Estabrook found that criminality was decreasing in the Jukes family; 11 per cent of the members of the family were criminals when studied by Dugdale, 6 per cent when studied by Estabrook thirty years later. See A. H. Estabrook, *The Jukes in 1915*, Washington, 1916.

ations but this does not prove an inherited tendency to use a fork. Every child in the families described above is subject to the influences of environment as well as of heredity, and the environment has customarily been conducive to crime. The children from these families who were adopted by other families were in most cases removed from their parental homes late in childhood. Dahlström has shown that in a family of criminals whose records for four generations were known, six children removed from the family before the age of seven became respectable members of society, and two removed after the age of seven became criminals.[4] Moreover, the comparison of the somewhat criminalistic Jukes family with the famous Jonathan Edwards family has become decidedly unconvincing regarding the effect of heredity since it has been discovered that some of the earlier members of the Edwards family had criminal records. Elizabeth Tuthill, the grandmother of Jonathan Edwards, was divorced on the ground of adultery and other immoralities; her sister murdered her own son, and her brother murdered his sister. If criminality be inherited, the Jonathan Edwards family should have produced many criminals.

Others have tried to prove that criminality not only appears in successive generations but also appears in accordance with the Mendelian ratios. Carl Rath, in a study of family histories of 98 inmates of a penal institution in Sieburg, Germany, concluded that the offspring were criminal in a ratio which is fairly close to the Mendelian ratio.[5] Aside from the fact that the investigations of Goring, Estabrook, and others show no approach to the Mendelian ratios in the criminality of successive generations, and that the number of cases studied by Rath is very small, there is the further difficulty that since criminality is assumed to be a recessive trait, the only way the trait (duplex, simplex, nulliplex) of an ancestor who does not have a criminal record can be determined is by assumption from the criminal record of the offspring. Therefore he and others like him use the criminality of the offspring to determine the nature of the parent and then use the nature of the parent to explain the criminality of the offspring. This is a necessary difficulty, apparently, in dealing with human beings, whose breeding and life con-

---

[4] Sigürd Dahlström, "Is the Young Criminal a Continuation of the Neglected Child?" *Jour. Delinq.*, 12:97–121, June, 1928. See, also, Sigürd Dahlström, "Arv og Milieu," *Tidss. for den norske Laegeforening*, No. 24, 1928, and No. 12, 1929.

[5] Carl Rath, *Ueber die Vererbung von Dispositionen zum Verbrechen*.

ditions cannot be controlled for a sufficient length of time to determine whether a strain is "pure," as can be done in experiments with plants and insects.

Goring attempted to prove by elaborate correlations that the criminal diathesis or criminalistic tendency is inherited and that environmental conditions are of slight importance. He found that criminality, measured by imprisonment, of fathers and sons was correlated by a coefficient of +.60, which is very nearly the same as the coefficient for stature, span, length of forearm, eye color, diathesis of tuberculosis, insane diathesis, and hereditary deafness; and that brothers had a coefficient of correlation for criminality of +.45, which is approximately the same as for physical traits.[6] Goring realized that such correlations might be the result of either heredity or environment or both, and he attempted to eliminate the factor of environment, on the hypothesis that if the influence of environmenal factors is found to be very low, heredity will, by elimination, be the explanation. In order to do this he divided environmental factors into contagion and force of circumstances, and his argument regarding them is as follows: (a) The resemblance of fathers and sons regarding criminality is not due to contagion, first, because the coefficient of correlation is no higher in crimes of stealing, in which fathers are examples for their sons, than in sex crimes, which fathers ordinarily attempt to conceal from their sons and in which therefore they are not examples; second, because children taken away from the influence of parents at an early age, by imprisonment, become confirmed criminals to a greater extent than those taken at a later age. (b) This resemblance is not due to the force of circumstances, such as poverty, standard of living, or ignorance, because, after the influence of defective intelligence is eliminated by the use of partial correlations, the correlation between criminality and force of circumstances is negligible.

The argument and methods that Goring used are open to criticism at a great many points, but, without multiplying criticisms, the following essential defects are found in his argument: (a) He attempts to determine the importance of the residual element, heredity, by eliminating the factor of environment; in order to do this accurately it would be necessary to measure completely the influence of environment. (b) He considers only eight environ-

[6] Charles Goring, *The English Convict*, London, 1913, p. 369.

mental factors, and it is possible that the coefficient of correlation between criminality and each of these might be very low even though environment as a whole was extremely important. (c) He restricts parental contagion entirely to the teaching of a technique of a particular crime, such as stealing. As a matter of fact it is not so much the transmission of a definite technique of crime that is important as the transmission or contagion of a general attitude toward law and authority. Again and again cases occur in which the sex delinquency of the parents tends to produce stealing in the offspring. (d) The removal of the child from the home to prison at an early age does not remove the child from a criminalistic to a non-criminalistic environment, as Goring assumes. (e) He assumes that mental ability, as judged by acquaintances, is not at all affected by environment; consequently his method results in finding inherited mental ability to be much more important than it is in fact.[7] And since he is using the method of elimination, the more he under-rates the force of circumstances, or environment, the more he over-rates heredity in this way. (f) He restricts his study to male convicts, though he mentions the fact that the ratio of sisters to brothers in respect to imprisonment is 6 to 102. If criminal diathesis is inherited to the same extent that physical traits, such as the color of the eyes, are inherited, it must affect females to the same extent as males unless it is sex linked. Since, according to Goring, the diathesis consists entirely of physical and mental inferiority, there is little reason to believe that it is sex linked. On the basis of these defects in his argument, his whole conclusion may be doubted. This does not, however, justify a conclusion that "heredity has nothing to do with crime."

Another method of measuring the relation of heredity to criminality is the study of twins. Lange made a study of thirty pairs of twins of the same sex, in which one of each pair was a criminal. Thirteen of these were identical twins and seventeen were fraternal twins. Identical twins are the product of a single embryo, and therefore have an identical heredity, while fraternal twins are the product of two eggs fertilized by two sperms and are therefore related in exactly the same manner as ordinary brothers. Lange

---

[7] F. N. Freeman, K. J. Holzinger, and Others, "The Influence of Environment on the Intelligence," *Yearbook of Natl. Soc. for Study of Educ.*, Vol. XXVII, Part 1, pp. 103–217, 1928; Barbara S. Burke, "Relative Influence of Nature and Nurture," *ibid.*, pp. 219–316.

found that in cases in which one of the twins had a prison record, 77 per cent of the identical twins, and only 12 per cent of the fraternal twins, had prison records. All cases in which the sexes were mixed were excluded, as well as those in which the age was not sufficiently advanced to make it possible for both brothers to become criminals.[8] This study has been accepted by some students as conclusive proof of the inheritance of criminality. Several reasons for doubting the conclusion appear, however. First, the method of selection of cases is not clearly described. Some of the cases were secured from Bavarian prisons, others from the German Psychiatric Institute. No statement is made regarding the number secured from each of these sources or the proportion of identical and fraternal twins secured from each source. It is conceivable that the identical twins may have been secured entirely from the Psychiatric Institute and that the inheritance of psychopathy rather than of criminality may be in some way involved in the conclusions. Second, the classification of twins as identical or fraternal is not clearly defined and in any case is open to suspicion, since the only certain method of determining this is by observation at the time of the birth process. Measurements were used in some cases, but apparently the evidence that twins were identical consisted principally of statements by acquaintances that the twins were indistinguishable in childhood. Also, in the detailed descriptions of the thirteen identical cases, the evidence that the twinship is of the identical type is not entirely consistent. Third, nearly half of the identical twins reported in the general literature on twins are of the "mirror image" type. This is illustrated by the right-handedness of one and the left-handedness of the other of the pair. Thus identical twins have physical differences even though the heredity is identical, and these physical differences may be highly significant in social situations. Fourth, the inheritance of criminality is not proved even if the identical twins are definitely proved to be more nearly alike than fraternal twins in regard to criminal records. The parents had no criminal records in eight of the ten cases in which both members of identical twinships had criminal records, and no criminality of other ancestors was described. Consequently this study merely shows that identical twins resemble each other in criminality more than fraternal twins do, but there are practically no criminal ancestors from whom the

---

[8] Johannes Lange, *Verbrechen als Schicksal*, Leipzig, 1929; translated by Charlotte Haldane under the title *Crime and Destiny*, New York, 1930.

criminality might be inherited. It is possible that either of two other conditions may explain the difference in the criminality of identical twins and fraternal twins. (a) The division of vital powers may produce abnormalities in identical twins, so that the criminal behavior results from the abnormalities caused by the division of the embryo. (b) The identical twins in general came from homes in which economic distress, illegitimacy, and drunkenness are reported. No evidence is reported regarding the homes of fraternal twins and consequently no assertion can be made regarding their homes, but it is at least conceivable that a difference between the two types of twins may exist in this respect. Fifth, the environments of identical twins who are reared together are more nearly alike than the environments of fraternal twins who are reared together, for the reactions of other persons toward identical twins will be more nearly similar than toward fraternal twins, because of the difficulty of distinguishing identical twins. These reactions of other persons are the most important part of the social environment. Newman, in a study of more than one hundred pairs of identical twins, has found that identical twins reared in the same type of environments had no significant divergence in character, while significant divergence in the characters of identical twins reared apart and in different types of environments occurred.[9] Sixth, subsequent studies by methods similar to Lange's have reduced very greatly the difference which he found. While Lange found the percentage of concordance to be 6.4 times as high in identical twins as in fraternal twins, the aggregate of three other studies has an analogous ratio of 1.4, which shows only slightly greater resemblance among identical twins in respect to criminality.[10]

When one speaks of the inheritance of criminality, just what does he consider is inherited? It cannot be criminality as such, for crime is defined in terms of laws and thus far no adequate definition of criminality in social terms has been stated. Goring maintained that the inherited element is not criminality, as such, but defective intelligence, but he does not explain how this produces crime. Karl Pearson, in the introduction to Goring's study, asserted that the

---

[9] H. H. Newman, *Evolution, Genetics and Eugenics*, Chicago, 1932, pp. 476–490.
[10] A. M. Legras, *Psychose en Criminaliteit bei Tweelingen*, Utrecht, 1932; F. Stumpfl, *Die Ursprünge des Verbrechens, dargestellt am Lebenslauf von Zwillingen*, Leipzig, 1936; Heinrich Kranz, *Lebensschicksale Krimineller Zwillinge*, Berlin, 1936.

inherited element in criminality is "defectiveness of the social instinct," but he does not attempt to define the social instinct or prove that this is the inherited element in crime. Davenport refers to "hereditary criminal instincts," but all the cases he presents involve feeblemindedness, chorea, migraine, or epilepsy which appear in successive generations.[11]

The concept of heredity is vague and requires an assumption of a "normal environment"[12] and that assumption cannot safely be made regarding social traits. Human beings have, by heredity, something or some set of things which make them or enable them to be different from sunflowers or amoebas, frogs or oysters. They have many specifically predetermined reactions, such as sneezing or the change in the size of the pupil of the eye with variations in the intensity of light. And in addition heredity in some way seems to affect mental ability, temperament, and affectivity, though there is no evidence that these are inherited in accordance with Mendel's law. Mental ability and instincts seem to be related to the central nervous system, though not uninfluenced by the rest of the organism; temperament and affectivity seems to be rather more closely connected with other parts of the organism, the consensus at present turning in the direction of the endocrine system for an explanation of the differences in energy, limen of stimulation, and other traits included under the name "temperament."

There is no reason to suppose that these more general traits or the significant social reactions are specifically predetermined. They are inherited, if at all, as vague tendencies that may be directed in specific ways by contacts with others. Cooley explains this as follows:

Roughly speaking ... the heredity of other animals is a mechanism like that of a hand-organ: it is made to play a few tunes; you can play

---

[11] C. H. Davenport, *Heredity in Relation to Eugenics,* New York, 1911, pp. 85 ff.

[12] Stockard found that by increasing the amount of magnesium chloride in the water in which the eggs of fundulus were hatched he could produce a fish with a single median eye. C. R. Stockard, "The Development of Artificially Produced Cyclopean Fish," *Jour. Exper. Zoöl.,* 6:285–337, 1909. In the normal sea-water this fish always has two eyes, and this two-eyed system would be described as inherited. But it is inherited only as long as the environment remains "normal," and in the "abnormal" environment, with an added amount of magnesium chloride, the one-eyed system is "inherited," the germ plasm being the same in both cases.

those tunes at once, with little or no training; and you can never play any others. The heredity of man, on the other hand, is a mechanism more like that of a piano: it is not made to play particular tunes; you can do nothing at all on it without training; but a trained player can draw from it an infinite variety of music.[13]

Consequently there is no evidence that there can be such a thing as a born criminal. No one has such an heredity that he must inevitably be a criminal regardless of the situations in which he is placed or the influences which play upon him. A phlegmatic temperament, which we might assume is inherited, may keep a person from becoming a criminal in one environment, and make him a criminal in another environment. In one environment the individual with an average intelligence becomes a criminal, and in another the individual with a dull intelligence. Both the individual trait and the situation must be included in the statement of the causation; neither one works alone to produce crime. Every person is a "potential criminal," but it requires contacts and direction of tendencies to make either a criminal or a law-abiding person. The behavior of some of the tribes in India makes it clear that individual abnormalities are not required in criminal behavior, for there every member of the tribe has engaged in crimes; they must, however, have individual traits which enable them to understand and follow the patterns which are traditional.

ANATOMICAL AND PHYSIOLOGICAL FACTORS. Lombroso insisted that criminals were characteristically different from non-criminals in certain physical characteristics, and especially in the shape of the cranium. Goring disputed Lombroso's conclusion after making careful measurements of prisoners and comparing them with measurements of non-criminals, and came to the conclusion that criminals are shorter in stature and lighter in weight than non-criminals but in other respects are not physically different. In several European centers efforts are still being made to discover physical differences between criminals and non-criminals. Kretschmer's classification of types of body-builds among psychotic patients has been utilized in the study of criminals, but thus far a difference between criminals and non-criminals has not been conclusively

---

[13] C. H. Cooley, *Human Nature and the Social Order,* New York, 1917, p. 19. Reprinted by permission of Charles Scribner's Sons, publishers.

demonstrated.[14] Vervaeck in Belgium has maintained that criminals and other abnormal classes are differentiated from the normal population by a height which is less than the "grand stretch," or the distance from fingertip to fingertip when the arms are outstretched. The hypothesis is that the arms of apes and savages are abnormally long in comparison with the height and therefore the arms of criminals must be abnormally long. He has no standardized "grand stretch" for the normal population and therefore his whole procedure is based on assumption. Moreover, Goring and Baer made comparative measurements of the "grand stretch" in the criminal and the non-criminal population and found no significant difference.

Hooton has published a preliminary report of an extensive study of criminals, with the finding that the physical characteristics of criminals are statistically different from those of non-criminals, and that the physical characteristics of criminals in one offense category, such as murder, are different from those of criminals in the other principal offense categories. He reaches the general conclusion that "the primary cause of crime is biological inferiority."[15] The findings and the conclusion cannot be appraised adequately until the final report is published. Several questions are raised regarding the procedure. The first of these questions is in regard to the adequacy of the samples of the non-criminal population. For comparison with the native-born white criminals of native parentage he uses about 150 Nashville firemen and 150 Boston out-patients, militiamen, and patrons of a bath house. For comparison with Italian-American criminals he uses 29 Italian-Americans apparently located in the same places in Boston. A second question is whether he has criteria of physical inferiority which are independent of this study. He obviously makes ethical evaluations of physical characteristics but gives no explanation of his evaluations. Is dark hair biologically inferior to blond hair? And if so, is the proof to be

---

[14] S. Blinkov, "Zur Frage nach dem Korperbau des Verbrechens," *Monats. f. Krim. Psych.*, 20:212–216, 1929; G. J. Mohr and R. H. Grundlach, "Relation between Physique and Performance," *Jour. Exper. Psychol.*, 10:117–157, 1927; G. J. Mohr, "Incidence and Test Performance of Kretschmer Types among Convicts," *Arch. of Neur. and Psych.*, 18:485–488, 1927; M. Riedl, "Ueber Beziehungen von Geistig-Körperlischen Constitution zur Kriminalität und änderen Defekten," *Monats. f. Krim. Psych.*, 23:473–484, August, 1932; F. von Rohden, "Korperbau Untersuchungen an Geisteskranken und Gesunden Verbrechern," *Arch. f. Psych. und Nervenkr.*, 77:77–151, 1926.

[15] E. A. Hooton, *Crime and the Man*, Cambridge, 1939, p. 130.

found in its greater frequency among murderers or in its greater proximity to the hair color of simian ancestors? If the proof of inferiority is found in the rate of imprisonment associated with it, then the male is biologically inferior to the female, for males are committed to prison ten times as frequently in proportion to numbers as are females. If Hooton's policy were adopted, the males should be weeded out of the population because of this greater crime rate. In general, so many variables are associated with crime that a statistical association of one of them with crime does not in any sense justify a conclusion that it is the primary cause of crime.

PHYSICAL DEFECTS AND ABNORMALITIES. Physical defects such as blindness, deafness, and lameness are sometimes regarded as important in relation to criminality. These physical defects may be due to heredity, as in cataract of the eye, to antenatal conditions, to difficulties in the birth process, and to postnatal conditions. Attempted abortions, overwork, shock, or sickness of the mother during the period of pregnancy, infection of the embryo during the birth process by the germs of syphilis or gonorrhea, premature birth, instrumental delivery, prolonged labor, undernourishment, accidents, and diseases are some of the specific causes of these defects.

No general statistical comparison of the frequency of these defects in the criminal and the non-criminal population has been made. The Massachusetts Census of 1905 reported the number of defectives of these types in the general population and also among juvenile and adult offenders. This comparison shows exactly the same number of blind persons per 10,000 population among offenders and the total population of the state, but a considerable excess of lameness and deafness among the delinquents. The number of lame, deformed, and maimed was 39 per 10,000 population of the state, while among the offenders it was 150; the number of deaf or dumb was 19 in the general population and 31 among offenders. The definitions of these defects, however, were not standardized and the difference shown in this Census is not' beyond suspicion. The optometrists have reported wide differences between the delinquents and school children in respect to defective vision, and explain that the children with defective vision are more likely to become delinquent than other children, both because of the physical irritation caused by the defective vision and also because their difficulties in connection with reading drive them into truancy and gang activities. It has been reported, also, that 44 per cent of a criminal group had "flap ears" as compared with 23 per cent in a non-criminal group. This difference was explained as due to the ignorance or neglect of parents; children who are neglected are permitted to sleep with one ear twisted under the head. They become delinquent for the same reason that they develop "flap ears," namely, the ignorance and neglect of the parents.[16]

Though these defects have not been shown to be significant from the statistical point of view they are unquestionably significant in some cases and this significance depends largely on the reactions of other persons toward the defects. The child with enlarged tonsils who consistently holds his mouth open, the child with crossed eyes, and the child who stutters or lisps meet ridicule and suffer loss of social status. Unless special elements of strength are found in these persons or the circumstances are in other respects unusually favorable, the character is likely to be affected by this treatment. Both the person with the physical defects and other persons are likely to find the defects irritating, and for the person with the defect the sequence of irritation, retardation in work, dissatisfaction with school or work, truancy, association with delinquents, and a general view of one's self as an outcast may result. Victor Nelson has presented a different explanation of the excessive number of these defects among criminals, as follows:

I have wondered a great deal about the connection between crime and physical ugliness or deformity. That there is such a connection I have no faintest doubt. The physically unattractive man is naturally handicapped in the competition for women and sexual satisfaction. To compensate for this he desires money with which to bribe or impress the woman he desires. Unable to get it quickly enough by legitimate means, he steals it. If this is true of the thief, how much more so is it true of the raper and the murderer.[17]

Sexual satisfaction is probably too narrow an interpretation of the social difficulties of the deformed, to which they react by crime. There are, however, other counteracting elements in connection with

---

[16] T. W. Kilmer, "A Study of the Human Ear from the Standpoint of Identification and Criminology," *Correction* (New York State Department of Correction), Vol. II, p. 12, November, 1932.

[17] Victor Nelson, *Prison Days and Nights,* Boston, 1933, p. 135. Reprinted by permission of Little, Brown & Company, publishers.

these defects. Of these the most important among the blind, the deaf, and the lame are the difficulties in motility.[18]

Undernourishment, disease, and poor health are sometimes reported to be found among criminals in excessive proportions, while in other investigations no significant difference is found. Goring reported that he found prisoners to be slightly undersized and underweight and this was the only significant physical difference he could find. Healy reported that physical ailments were a major factor in 4 per cent of his cases of juvenile delinquency and a minor factor in 23.3 per cent.[19] While there is no reason to minimize the importance of good health, it is apparent that the connection between crime and physical ailments is not close or necessary. Many criminals are quite healthy and free from ailments, and many non-criminals are extremely defective from the physical point of view. Even if a difference could be demonstrated, the criminality would probably not be an immediate and direct effect of the physical ailment but of the social and economic consequences of the defect.

Among the things which should be included, though perhaps not a physical defect, is excess of physical vigor. This may lead to restlessness and a difficulty of doing things in the assigned way, and so may lead to delinquency. It is frequently as difficult for such persons to adjust to the situations in which they are placed as for those with a decided lack of vigor. This excessive vigor sometimes appears in the form of hypersexualism in girls.

Healy has shown that underdevelopment and overdevelopment at the age of adolescence are related to delinquency. Of 823 cases of juvenile recidivists, 13.5 per cent had some such anomaly in development as one of the probable causes of delinquency; moreover, 73 per cent of the delinquent girls were overdeveloped for their ages, while of the boys 52 per cent were below normal.[20]

The girl who reaches physical maturity at a very early age before her experiences have passed those of childhood is decidedly handicapped. The boy who reaches the physical development of manhood before he attains the years of manhood is in a particularly irritating situation; chronological age is the main factor in determin-

---

[18] See Hans von Hentig, "Die kriminellen Tendenzen der Blinden," *Schweiz. Zsch. f. Strafrecht,* Vol. XL, Part I, 1927.

[19] Wm. Healy, *The Individual Delinquent,* Boston, 1915, p. 130; compare Wm. Healy and Augusta Bronner, *Delinquents and Criminals,* New York, 1926, pp. 44–46.

[20] Healy, *op. cit.,* pp. 145 and 236.

ing his relations with parents and teachers, but physical size is the main factor in determining his relations with strangers; he may pass as a young man of twenty-two when only thirteen years of age. The result is a very irritating conflict in expectations and conditions.[21] Lack of adjustment is due also to underdevelopment in general or in sex characteristics. A boy who continues to look childish long after other boys of his age look like men is in a difficult position. Or the one who has developed the primary sex characteristics, while his voice or other secondary sex characteristics remain like those of children, is in a position of irritation where he cannot secure a status that is known to be proper at that age.

Other physiological abnormalities which are less evident to casual observations are regarded as important. The endocrine or ductless glands have received much attention from this point of view. The endocrinologists are not agreed regarding the importance of these glands in relation to personality and their conclusions range from a denial that they have any demonstrated relation to personality to a conclusion that they are the primary determiners of personality. The evidence is sufficient at any rate to justify continued study of criminals from this point of view.[22]

AGE. Age appears to be either directly or indirectly one of the important factors with respect to the frequency and types of crimes. The crime rate is about five times as great for persons twenty to twenty-four years of age as for those over fifty, and the rate of serious crimes is about fifteen times as great. The age of maximum criminality lies clearly in the young-adult period of life.[23] This maximum is not clearly defined, for delinquency or criminality increases from the age of ten to about nineteen, where it remains nearly constant until the age of twenty-seven, after which it de-

---

[21] Judge Baker Foundation, *Case Studies*, Series 1, Nos. 2–3. This is a discussion of a group of overdeveloped boys.

[22] The following are some of the more extreme exponents of the determination of personality by endocrine glands: Louis Berman, *The Glands Regulating Personality*, New York, 1921; I. G. Cobb, *The Glands of Destiny*, New York, 1928; Max Schlapp and Edward H. Smith, *The New Criminology*, New York, 1928; Adolf Lens, *Grundriss der Kriminalbiologie;* Mariano Ruiz-Funes, *Criminalidad y Endocrinologia*, 1928.

[23] The incidence of problem cases in the Toronto schools shows no distinct trend with increasing age, either for boys or girls. See W. E. Blatz and E. A. Botts, "Behavior of Public School Children," *Pedagog. Sem.*, 34:556–582, December, 1927. Similarly, Lockhart found no significant difference between children and adults in his tests of attitudes toward certain laws. E. G. Lockhart, "The Attitudes of Children toward Certain Laws," *Relig. Educ.*, 25:144–149, February, 1930.

creases sharply with advancing age. The juvenile court statistics show the number of delinquents increasing steadily until the age of sixteen, and the boys' court statistics show the same process continued to the age of eighteen or nineteen. Thus there is no sharp break at the age of puberty, though this is often assumed to be a period of personal disorganization. The statistics of police departments and of prisons show a very decided decrease beginning shortly before the age of thirty.

The age of maximum criminality varies somewhat with the types of crimes. The age of maximum arrests for the serious crimes against property is about nineteen. The median age of those committed to prisons and reformatories in 1936 was twenty-four years for burglary and robbery, thirty for homicide and forgery, and thirty-six for fraud and embezzlement. The median age for drunkenness, disorderly conduct, and vagrancy is high, for these offenses are to a greater extent characteristic of persons in middle age and old age.

Though the crime rate for old age is low in comparison with the young-adult period, it has some characteristic features, of which the most important is sex crimes. Bowers found in Indiana that two-thirds of 175 cases of rape recorded were committed by men over fifty years of age. Aschaffenburg states that while men over seventy years of age commit grand larceny in the ratio of 1 to 150 as compared with men aged eighteen to twenty-one, they commit sex offenses in the ratio of 1 to 4.[24] Bresler found that the smallest proportion of first offenders was in the age group from thirty to forty, that the proportion increased steadily from 46 per cent in the group from thirty to forty to 67 per cent in the group seventy years of age and over, and concluded that a person not previously convicted is more likely to violate the laws in old age than in middle age.[25] The statistics of prisons in Finland show that the rate of commitment of females during the ages of thirty-five to forty-five is higher than during the preceding or subsequent ages. American prison statistics do not show this increase in criminality of women at the time of the menopause.

The assertion is sometimes made that adult criminals begin their careers as juvenile delinquents. There can be no doubt that adult

---

[24] G. Aschaffenburg, *Crime and Its Repression*, Boston, 1913, p. 154.
[25] J. Bresler, "Greisenalter und Kriminalität," *Juristisch-Psychiatrische Grenzfragen*, Vol. V, Nos. 2–3, p. 7.

criminals do commit delinquencies in childhood, but then all other people commit delinquencies in childhood. There is evidence that a comparatively small proportion of persons who are arrested in adult or young-adult life had juvenile court records. The Massachusetts Commission on Probation found that of the young men between the ages of seventeen and twenty who had court appearances in Massachusetts during the period 1924 to 1930 only 20 per cent had previously appeared as delinquents in the juvenile court. Consequently it is evident that so far as official records are concerned, a very large proportion of first appearances occur after adolescence. Similarly the Massachusetts prison reports for 1936 show that 74 per cent of the offenders sentenced to the state prison and the state reformatories for young adults had not previously been in institutions for delinquent children.

Habitual criminals, on the other hand, more frequently than other adult criminals, had juvenile court records in their childhood. Something like a process of maturation appears in these cases. Delinquencies begin at an early age and increase in frequency and seriousness. Delinquencies start as a recreational incident and become an integrated pattern of life. Criminal maturity is reached in early middle age, about thirty or thirty-five. Some criminals then abandon their crimes abruptly, others adopt less strenuous types of crimes, others engage in quasi-criminal activities in connection with politics, gambling, prostitution, and the liquor business, while others become vagrants. This process, however, is only roughly characteristic of the careers, and exceptions may be found regarding the age of beginning criminality and the age at leaving the profession. Especially, the burglars and robbers abandon those careers at a relatively early age, the pickpockets and confidence men at a much later age. According to the gossip of the underworld a man ninety years of age is picking pockets today. having started during the Civil War at the age of sixteen.

The assertion has been made frequently that the average age of criminals has been decreasing during the last two or three generations. The statistics of prisoners do not show much change in this respect. The mean age of criminals admitted to the Michigan State Prison at Jackson decreased only from thirty-two and four-tenths in 1900 to thirty-one and five-tenths in 1930, and the modal age of prisoners admitted to the state prison of Missouri increased from twenty-three years in 1894 to twenty-four in 1924. The distribution of convictions by age groups in Canada shows no distinct trend in the period 1891 to 1929. For a century and a half the prison authorities have been calling attention to the fact that most of the prisoners convicted of serious crimes are young adults. Alexander Smith reported that the median age of fifty-two robbers hanged in England in the period 1710–1719 was twenty-six years, while the median age of persons killed while committing crimes (generally robbery, burglary, or auto theft) in Chicago in 1930–1933 was twenty-five years. A reduction in the average age of criminals would be expected for *a priori* reasons, for the average age in other professions has decreased. Furthermore, the evidence indicates that in areas of high delinquency rates the first official record occurs at an earlier age than in areas of low delinquency rates.

These variations in crime rates are not adequately explained by relating them to variations in age. Various explanations have been suggested, not all of which are concerned with the same aspect of the relationship between age and crime. One explanation is that the variations in crimes are due to variations in physical strength or other characteristics of the physiological system. Children and middle-aged persons refrain from robbery and burglary for the same reason they do not play professional baseball. A second explanation adds to the preceding explanation the recklessness which is often characteristic of young adults. Their period of experience has been too short to develop forethought commensurate with their physical strength. The age of greatest frequency of robbery is approximately the same as the age of greatest frequency of automobile accidents per thousand licensed drivers, just under twenty years. A third explanation is inheritance. Goring concluded from his analysis of age statistics of criminals that those persons who are predisposed to crime become criminals as soon as they are exposed to criminal influences, just as those who are susceptible to scarlet fever or enteric fever acquire those diseases as soon as they are brought in contact with them.[26] This explanation has raised one special question. If those with the strongest innate tendencies toward crime become criminals at the earliest age and those with weaker innate tendencies become criminals at a later age, we should expect a steadily increasing rate of crime with advancing age because of the addition of recruits with weaker tendencies to the confirmed crim-

---

[26] Goring, *op. cit.*, pp. 201–214.

inals who started earlier. As a matter of fact the maximum rate is found before the age of thirty, which indicates either that many of those who started crime at an early age do not persist in crime or else that the explanation in terms of inheritance is not satisfactory. Finally an explanation in terms of social relations has been advanced. Those children who live in an area where the delinquency rates are high begin to commit serious crimes at the age of fourteen to sixteen, after a period of training in less serious crimes. The children who are reared in more favorable situations do not commit crimes of a serious nature until they leave home and come in contact with criminal examples in rooming houses and other situations. In both cases experience with penalties for crimes leads to abandonment of criminal careers in early middle age unless the crimes are of the type for which the penalties are not severe, in which case criminal careers continue longer. The crimes of the older group are due to the loss of morale which comes with unemployment, family separations, and similar social changes.

These statistics of the age of criminals are probably biased to some extent. Because of sympathy the police are less likely to arrest a child than an adult for the same overt crime. This tends to reduce the recorded criminality of childhood and youth. Similarly, older criminals are more careful in their crimes than are the young adults and more frequently escape arrest. Also, crimes of fraud which are directed by older men established in business or the professions seldom result in arrest. The excessive rate of young adults is therefore exaggerated somewhat in the official records.

SEX. Statistical studies indicate that sex is an extremely important factor in crime. The Toledo schools have five times as many problem boys as problem girls, and the Toronto schools twice as many.[27] A questionnaire study of two thousand school children resulted in the conclusion that girls have a stronger sense of honor than boys.[28] Twenty times as many males as females in proportion to the total population of each sex were committed to state prisons and reformatories in 1936, and fourteen times as many males as females were committed to all types of penal and reformatory insti-

---

[27] W. E. McClure, "Characteristics of Problem Children," *Jour. Juv. Res.*, 13:124–140, April, 1929; W. E. Blatz and E. A. Botts, "Behavior of Public School Children," *Pedagog. Sem.*, 34:556–582, December, 1927.

[28] Robert Clark, "A Direct Study of the Child's Sentiment of Honor," *Inter. Jour. of Ethics*, 42:454–461, July, 1932.

tutions in 1933.[29] In respect to the rate of commitment to state
prisons and reformatories the sexes are most nearly alike in early
age and become progressively different. In the age period from
fifteen to seventeen, thirteen times as many males as females are
received, while in the age period from sixty to sixty-four, twenty-six
times as many males are received.

The proportions of the sexes vary widely for different crimes.
More than fifty times as many males as females are arrested for
burglary, twenty-two times as many males as females for robbery,
and about ten times as many for homicide, assault, larceny, forgery,
and embezzlement. On the other hand, the females have a higher
rate for sex offenses, and for certain specific offenses against property. In a Chicago department store 70 per cent of all persons
apprehended by the store officers as shoplifters were females; of
those above the age of sixteen 82 per cent were females, while
boys and girls under sixteen were apprehended in almost equal
numbers.

The proportion of the sexes is more nearly equal in cities than
in smaller towns. In 1936 males were arrested in Massachusetts
towns of less than fifteen thousand population twenty times as frequently as females for offenses against the person, but only twelve
times as frequently in cities above fifteen thousand; for offenses
against property the ratio was 34 to 1 in towns as compared with
12 to 1 in cities, and for offenses against public order (consisting
principally of drunkenness and violation of traffic regulations) the
ratio was 26 to 1 in towns and 13 to 1 in cities. The proportion
of the sexes varies also in the different divisions of the United
States, being most nearly equal in the Southern states, where the
Negro females show a close resemblance to Negro males.

Females committed to state and federal prisons and reformatories
in 1936 had a lower rate of recidivism than did male prisoners; 34.2
per cent of the females and 57.6 per cent of the male prisoners were
recidivists. In the jails and workhouses in 1933, however, 61 per
cent of the female prisoners were recidivists and only 58 per cent of

---

[29] The sex ratio of convictions in different countries varies from 1:3 in
Belgium to 1:22.5 in Finland, but in all countries reported the rate for males
is considerably higher than for females. The variations among countries are
probably due to differences in the jurisdictions of the courts and to practices
in regard to treatment of prostitutes. See Ervin Hacker, "Der Anschauungsun-
terricht im Strafrecht und in der Gefängniskunde," *Blätter f. Gefäng.*, 63:323,
1932.

the male prisoners. The high rate of recidivism of females in jails and workhouses is explained by the large number of professional prostitutes incarcerated in these institutions.

It is possible that the sexes are tending to approach equality in crime rates, but the evidence is not sufficient to justify a positive conclusion. In 1907–1914 12 per cent of the arraignments in the Children's Court of New York City were girls, and in 1920–1930 it was 29 per cent. This change involved a decrease in the rate of arraignment of boys and an increase in the rate of arraignment of girls. On the other hand, the girl delinquency cases in 28 juvenile courts decreased from 17 per cent of all delinquency cases in 1929 to 15 per cent in 1937.

These several variations in the ratio of female to male delinquents indicate that the ratio is not determined by sex differences as such, but is affected by many social elements, such as conditions of life and training, codes of behavior, and ideals. Radzinowicz has found in an intensive analysis of Polish statistics that the sex ratio has a range of from 8.6 to 56.6 in forty-two groups based on age, civil status, provinces, urban or rural localities, and religion.[30]

The statistics of crime are somewhat selective in relation to sex. Females are arrested in much larger numbers than males for sex offenses, though the sexes are generally involved in equal numbers in sex offenses. This bias is due to the professional nature of the female sex offender, but it is a bias nevertheless. For other offenses, the tendencies are conflicting. Females probably receive more sympathetic treatment than males from police and courts, but they have greater difficulty in escaping from the scene of a crime.

SUGGESTED READINGS

Bingham, Anne T., "Determinants of Sex Delinquency in Adolescent Girls," *Jour. Crim. Law and Criminol.*, 13:494–586, February, 1923.

Buschan, G. H. T., *Geschlecht und Verbrechen*, Berlin, 1908.

Castellanos, Israel, *La delincuencia femenina en Cuba*, Havana, 1929.

Goring, Charles, *The English Convict*, London, 1913.

Lange, Johannes, *Crime and Destiny*, New York, 1930.

Lockhart, E. G., *Attitudes of Children toward Law*, Iowa City, 1930.

---

[30] L. Radzinowicz, "Variability of the Sex-Ratio of Criminality," *Sociol. Rev.*, 29:1–27, January, 1937.

Radzinowicz, L., "Variability of the Sex-Ratio of Criminality," *Sociol. Rev.*, 29:1–27, January, 1937.

Schroeder, Paul L., "Criminal Behavior in the Later Period of Life," *Amer. Jour. Psychiat.*, 92:815–824, January, 1936.

Thomas, W. I. and Dorothy S., *The Child in America*, New York, 1928, Ch. 11.

Uniform Crime Reports, Quart. Bull., Vol. III, No. 4, pp. 14–15.

Vorwahl, H., *Psychologie der Vorpubertät*, Berlin, 1929.

Chapter Seven

PSYCHOPATHY AND CRIME

THE LOMBROSIAN THEORY that criminals constitute a distinct physical type was continued in America as a Neo-Lombrosian theory, which maintained the same logic and substituted psycho-pathological type for physical type. This Neo-Lombrosian theory declares criminals to be psychopathic, and when one psychopathy proves to be inadequate as an explanation of crime, it merely retreats to another psychopathy. Some psychiatrists have found the explanation of crime in mental defectiveness, others in dementia praecox, others in psychopathic personality, and others in a composite group of psychopathies. The psychiatrists in the Illinois Reformatory at Pontiac classified 99.5 per cent of the incoming inmates during the period 1919–1929 as mentally pathological, 0.4 as having no demonstrable abnormality, and reported that 0.1 per cent were unclassified. In contrast, 82.3 per cent of all persons who were convicted or who plead guilty in the Court of General Sessions, New York City, in 1932–1935 were reported to be normal.[1]

The mental pathologies have been classified in many ways. One of the simpler classifications includes three groups, namely, mental defect or feeblemindedness, psychosis or insanity, and neuropathic conditions, which include epilepsy, post-encephalitic personality, psychopathic personality, and the psychoneuroses.

MENTAL DEFECT. Mental defect has been used by a few authors almost as a specific explanation of crime. Their theory includes these propositions: first, almost all criminals are feebleminded; second, feebleminded persons commit crimes, in the absence of special inhibiting conditions, because they do not have sufficient intelligence

---

[1] Walter Bromberg and Charles B. Thompson, "The Relation of Psychosis, Mental Defect and Personality Types to Crime," *Jour. Crim. Law and Criminol.*, 28:1–22, May, 1937.

to appreciate the reasons for laws and the consequences of violations of law; third, feeblemindedness is inherited as a unit character
in accordance with Mendel's law of heredity; fourth, a policy of
sterilization or segregation of the feebleminded is the only effective
method of preventing crime and of dealing with criminals.

This statement of the theory does not include the many exceptions made by various authors, and perhaps is unfair even to Harry
H. Goddard, who was in the early period the most extreme adherent
of this theory. He stated in 1919:

Every investigation of the mentality of criminals, misdemeanants,
delinquents, and other antisocial groups has proven beyond the possibility of contradiction that nearly all persons in these classes, and in
some cases all, are of low mentality. . . . It is no longer to be denied
that the greatest single cause of delinquency and crime is lowgrade
mentality, much of it within the limits of feeblemindedness.[2]

And in another connection, he said that the feeblemindedness of a
delinquent *fully* explained the delinquency.[3]

An attempt was made in 1928 and 1929 to assemble the results
of all mental tests of criminals and determine what conclusions were
justified.[4] The following conclusions were derived from an analysis
of approximately 350 reports of this nature, which included tests of
approximately 175,000 criminals and delinquents. First, the proportion of delinquents diagnosed feebleminded decreased from more
than 50 per cent in the average study made in the period 1910–1914
to 20 per cent in the period 1925–1928. This decrease was due
primarily to alterations in the methods of scoring the tests. Second,
wide variations in the results of tests given within the last decade
are found, and these variations are much more likely to reflect the
methods of the testers than the intelligence of the criminals. Third,
when allowance is made for the selection involved in arrest, conviction, and imprisonment, the distribution of intelligence scores of
delinquents is very similar to the distribution of intelligence scores
of the general population. Zeleny, after equating the procedures

---

[2] H. H. Goddard, *Human Efficiency and Levels of Intelligence*, Princeton,
1920, pp. 73–74. Reprinted by permission of Princeton University Press, publishers.

[3] H. H. Goddard, *Juvenile Delinquency*, New York, 1921, p. 22.

[4] Edwin H. Sutherland, "Mental Deficiency and Crime," Ch. XV in Kimball
Young (Editor), *Social Attitudes*, 1931, pp. 357–375.

of different testers, concluded that the ratio of delinquents and general population in respect to mental deficiency was about 1.2 to 1.[5] This ratio shows a slight excess of mental deficiency among the delinquents, but it certainly does not justify the conclusions of the early testers. Fourth, the studies of groups of feebleminded persons in the community do not show an excess of delinquency among them, as compared with the normal population. Fifth, feebleminded prisoners have about the same disciplinary records in prisons as other prisoners. Sixth, feebleminded offenders are successful on parole about as frequently as other parolees. Seventh, feebleminded offenders become recidivists with about the same frequency as other offenders. Eighth, persons convicted of sex crimes are more likely to be feebleminded than persons convicted of other crimes. Therefore, this analysis shows that the relationship between crime and feeblemindedness is, in general, comparatively slight. Certainly it is a much less important factor than age or sex. This does not, however, mean that it may not be a very important factor in individual cases.

The most extensive survey of the literature on the general relation between morality and intellect was made by Miss Chassell. Her conclusion is that the relation is positive but low, with correlations usually between 0.10 and 0.39. The only significant point of difference from the survey described above is on the fourth point, for she reports that feebleminded groups in the community have an unusually large number of delinquencies.[6]

The proposition that feeblemindedness is inherited as a unit character has now been generally abandoned, and the extent to which and manner in which feeblemindedness is inherited are open questions. Intelligence as measured by tests has been proved to be modifiable as is shown both by the re-testing of identical individuals and by comparisons of foster children with siblings raised in different environments.[7]

---

[5] L. D. Zeleny, "Feeblemindedness and Criminal Conduct," *Amer. Jour. Sociol.*, 38:564–578, January, 1933.

[6] Clara F. Chassell, *The Relation between Morality and Intellect*, Teachers College, Contributions to Education, No. 607, p. 133, New York, 1935.

[7] Frank N. Freeman, K. J. Holzinger, and Others, "The Influence of Environment on Intelligence," *Yearbook of Natl. Soc. for Study of Educ.*, Vol. XXVII, Part 1, 1928; Frank N. Freeman, "What We Call Intelligence," *Survey*, 66:17–19, April, 1930; Helen Gildea and Constance Macoubrey, "Factors Affecting the Constancy of the Intelligence Quotients of Problem Children," *Smith Col. Stud. in Social Work*, 3:229–248, March, 1933.

PSYCHOSES. Though insanity has been studied for many generations, much disagreement still prevails regarding definitions, classifications, causes, methods of diagnosis, extent in the general population, and frequency in the criminal population. It is not one disease but a large number of diseases, differing from each other as much as bronchitis differs from tuberculosis. Paresis is a fairly well-established disease with clear symptoms and demonstrable origin, but dementia praecox is extremely indefinite both in regard to symptoms and origin. Some claim that all these diseases are inherited in accordance with Mendel's law; others claim that those of exogenous origin, such as alcoholic insanity or paresis, do not follow Mendel's law but that all the others do; others claim that almost all of the mental disorders are psychogenic in origin and are similar to war neuroses, which were a method of escaping from the intolerable conditions of war; others claim that all these disorders are the result of focal infections and that if they are inherited it is not directly but by an inheritance of a susceptibility to focal infections and a susceptibility of the nervous system to the poisons from the focal infections; others claim that they are the result of disorders in the endocrine system; and others that they are the result of race poisons. Myerson sums up the situation in this way:

The insane have normal descendants; normal folks have insane descendants in a perfectly bewildering and inexplicable fashion. When all the facts are gathered in an impartial manner this is the one phenomenon that stands out. It is likely, in my opinion, that we are dealing with a disease of the germ-plasm and injury inflicted upon it, which is thereupon transmitted for a long or a short time through one or more generations according to the severity of the injury.[8]

New light has been thrown on the origin of psychoses in the studies by Dunham and Faris of the residences of psychotic patients received in the public and private hospitals of Illinois. They found that the previous places of residence clustered around the center of the city and decreased in frequency toward the city limits. Moreover, they found that the different psychoses did not follow the

[8] A. Myerson, "Inheritance of Mental Disease," *Second Internatl. Cong. of Eugenics*, 1921, Vol. 1, p. 225. Reprinted by permission. See, also, E. A. Strecker, "The Non-Specificity of Mental Disease," *Mental Hygiene*, 7: 277–306, April, 1923.

same pattern of distribution, but were related in some cases either to selection or to the manner of life.[9]

Psychiatric examinations of criminals on admission to state prisons generally show not more than 5 per cent to be psychotic, and in many institutions less than 1 per cent. This variation may be due to the traits of the criminals, but is certainly affected somewhat by the preconceptions of the psychiatrists. The proportion of psychotic persons in the general population is not known but is probably less than the proportion of psychotic persons in prisons. Many psychotic persons do not commit crimes. The number of law-abiding psychotic persons at large in the community probably amounts to hundreds of thousands. A study of the records of 55 unselected patients in the Psychiatric Institute of the Illinois Research Hospital indicated that 11 had been arrested for offenses shortly before they were referred to the Institute, that 13 others had been "behavior problems" in their communities, but that the other 31 had no known delinquencies in connection with the onset of the psychosis.[10] A similar study of 1,262 patients in the Eloise State Hospital in Michigan showed that 21.1 per cent had records of definite crimes, and an additional 4.4 per cent had records of threatened or attempted crimes, making a total of 25.5 per cent for whom such behavior was recorded; of these 126 had the recorded behavior before the recognized onset of mental disease, 197 after the onset.[11] Many famous persons have been psychotic. The law-abiding behavior of these persons is explained partly by the types of psychoses, partly by the fact that their characters and inclinations were law-abiding prior to the onset of the psychosis and persisted after the mental disturbance occurred.

Offenders admitted to houses of correction and to jails have a slightly higher rate of psychoses than those admitted to state prisons. Even so, the rate is seldom higher than 5 per cent of the admissions and in many studies is reported to be about 2 per cent. The offenders in these institutions often have alcoholic psychoses, from which they may quickly recover, or dementia praecox, which has reduced them to a state of vagrancy.

---

[9] R. E. L. Faris and H. W. Dunham, *Mental Disorders in Urban Areas: An Ecological Study of Schizophrenia and Other Psychoses,* Chicago, 1939.

[10] Lena Heath, *Some Cases of Delinquency in Psychopathic Patients,* Unpublished manuscript, 1934.

[11] Milton H. Erickson, "Criminality in a Group of Male Psychiatric Patients," *Mental Hygiene,* 22:459–476, July, 1938.

Psychoses produce crimes in various ways. To some extent crimes result from definite delusions or hallucinations. A voice may repeat a command to kill and the voice may finally be obeyed. Industrial inefficiency may result from the psychosis and this may lead to vagrancy, drunkenness, and petty theft. The psychosis may produce social tensions and conflicts. Or it may reduce inhibitions on sex tendencies.

The diagnosis of epilepsy is made frequently in some prisons, and seldom in others. The range is from less than 1 per cent in most prisons to more than 10 per cent in others. The lack of standardization is shown by the decrease from 19 per cent among the admissions to Elmira Reformatory in 1919 to 0.81 per cent in 1929. Little is known, however, regarding the proportion of epileptic persons who commit crimes or the comparative proportions of criminal and non-criminal persons who are epileptic.

POST-ENCEPHALITIC PERSONALITY. Epidemic encephalitis or encephalitis lethargica is relatively recent as a known disease. This disease produces lesions in the central nervous system and after-effects in the form of behavior problems, especially if the patient is a child. The primary effect is lethargy, retardation, and irritability. Quarrels, thefts, truancy, and other disorders of behavior are reported frequently. There is, however, little evidence regarding the proportion of cases of this disease in which behavior disorders appear and continue beyond the period of the primary sickness. It has been believed by certain psychiatrists that subsequent behavior disorders are almost universal and they have suggested that many other delinquents may have become disorganized as a result of the disease, though the disease was not recognized as such. If this be true, it is possible that many other children may have had the disease, not recognized as such, and have had no *sequelæ* in the form of behavior problems. In general, however, the evidence at present indicates a more specific relation of delinquency to encephalitis than to any other form of psychopathology.

This disease is regarded as very significant because it is taken as evidence that injuries to the neural system produce delinquency. As a matter of fact, however, the explanation is not simple. There is the direct physiological explanation that the lesions in the central nervous system produce irritability and reduce efficiency and inhibitions, and consequently the child acts impulsively. These effects persist beyond the acute stage of the disease because of habit formation. A second explanation is that the inferiority resulting from the lesions in the central nervous system lowers the status of the child, and the criticisms of parents and teachers when the child does not do as well as previously drive the child desperate. When the child is placed in a group of other post-encephalitic children, from whom less is expected, the feeling of inferiority is overcome and the behavior improves.[12] Another explanation is that the encephalitic patient who manifests subsequent behavior difficulties is generally a member of a family which manifests other abnormalities, such as psychosis, drunkenness, and extreme poverty. In fact, the explanation of the behavior disorders following this disease is not certain, though the injury to the nervous system is evidently a direct and primary cause, and it is probable that the behavior is affected through the emotions rather than through intellectual deterioration.[13]

Chorea is sometimes reported as significant in relation to delinquency. Ebaugh found that delinquency accompanied chorea in 21.2 per cent of a group of thirty-two children studied, and that the behavior symptoms were somewhat similar to those found in post-encephalitic children.[14]

PSYCHOPATHIC PERSONALITY. The psychopathic personality is definitely different from the psychotic person. The psychopathic personality manifests abnormalities in emotional life but not the break with reality which characterizes the psychotic. Psychopathic personalities are generally classified in three groups, the egocentric, the inadequate, and the vagabond. The egocentric person has a generalized tendency to self-reference, and a lack of social feeling. He is characterized by defiance, refusal to submit to authority, and aggressive attitudes of superiority. The inadequate reacts by dependence, helplessness, and often by sulking. The vagabond resorts to flight, which may take the form of vagabondage in the literal sense; alcoholism and drug addiction are often interpreted as symbolic methods of flight. Other classifications are: schizoid, paranoid,

---

[12] For a description of an interesting experiment in the re-education of post-encephalitic children, see Earl D. Bond and Kenneth E. Appel, *The Treatment of Behavior Disorders Following Encephalitis*, New York, 1931. Earl D. Bond and L. H. Smith, "Post-encephalitic Behavior Disorders," *Amer. Jour. Psychiat.*, 92:17–31, July, 1935.

[13] M. Molitch, "Chronic Post-Encephalitic Behavior Problems," *Amer. Jour. Psychiat.*, 91:843–861, January, 1935.

[14] Franklin G. Ebaugh, "Neuropsychiatric Aspects of Chorea in Children," *Jour. Amer. Med. Assoc.*, 87:1083, October 2, 1926.

cyclothymic, sexual, drug addict, constitutionally inferior, and epileptoid.

Many psychiatrists have used this concept in the analysis of criminals. Two conclusions may be derived from a comparison of the reports of psychiatric examinations of prisoners: The first is that the proportion of prisoners diagnosed as psychopathic personalities varies widely from one institution to another. Reports from most of the New York and Massachusetts institutions show about 10 per cent of the incoming criminals to be psychopathic personalities, while reports from Illinois institutions generally show more than 75 per cent to be psychopathic personalities, and in fact 88.3 per cent of all offenders admitted to the Illinois Reformatory during the period 1919–1929 were so diagnosed. This variation is clearly due to the difference in the preconceptions of the psychiatrists rather than to a difference in the criminals. The second conclusion is that there is a somewhat general tendency toward increase in the proportions of prisoners reported to be psychopathic personalities. This seems to be a result of the belief of the psychiatrists that criminals must be mentally abnormal. The theory that crime is due to lack of mental ability gave way to the theory that it is due to emotional maladjustments.

The method of diagnosis of psychopathic personality is not at all standardized or objective. Wallin gave warning in 1922 against the emphasis of this concept:

The inexorable logic of facts has brought a sharper limitation of the concept of the feebleminded than the most conservative of us conceived possible a few years ago. It will probably only be possible through a similar inescapable logic of inexorable facts to set a reasonable limitation to the category of psychopathy, which has attained sudden popularity as a result of the limitation of the feebleminded group. Since no one has been able to supply a scientifically adequate pathognomy of a nosological entity corresponding to a psychopath, would it not be prudent merely to refer for practical purposes to the emotionally unstable or ill-balanced and volitionally weak delinquent who is neither feebleminded nor insane, as a "defective delinquent" without making any assumptions regarding a "disease entity" called psychopathy, which may prove to be mythical? [15]

---

[15] W. E. Wallin, "An Investigation of Children Assigned to Special Public School Classes," *Jour. Abn. Psychol.*, 17:34, April, 1922.

The origin of psychopathic personality, whatever it may mean, has not been determined. It seems to appear most frequently in children from homes with little supervision, with inconsistency of discipline, foster parents, and other broken homes. The organization of attitudes which is described by the term is apparently formed rather early in life and is manifested in many different types of situations. The psychoanalysts, however, have a somewhat characteristic description of these mechanisms. The psychopathic personality is described as one in which there is mental conflict, with an adjusted portion striving against the unadjusted portion of the personality. When this person becomes a criminal he does so because of this unconscious striving, which takes the form of a desire for punishment to remove the guilt-feeling. The offender commits a crime in order to be eligible for punishment and then by unconsciously motivated errors reveals the crime to the authorities in order to secure the punishment. The same conflict is found in the neurotic person but the conflict remains within the person so that others are not injured by it.

OTHER PERSONALITY DEVIATIONS. Emotional instability and other traits of personality have been studied by psychologists independently of the concept of psychopathy. Scores of tests, rating scales, and other devices for measuring these traits have been used. Studies have been made of instincts, emotions, moods, temperaments, moral judgments, ethical discriminations, as well as of such specific tendencies as aggressiveness, caution, conformity, conscientiousness, deception, honesty, self-assurance, social resistance, trustworthiness, and many others. Thomas has stated that if these tests had really measured the things they were intended to measure our knowledge of and control over human nature would be nearly complete, but that as a matter of fact the units are not adequately defined, the tests do not measure the things they purport to measure, and the results have not been validated by reference to other data.[16] When attempts are made to compare groups, they cannot be differentiated sharply. It is reported that child guidance clinics estimated in a specific experiment that one-third of the children regarded by teachers as normal should receive the attention of such clinics.[17] Delinquent groups, nevertheless, are generally differentiated

---

[16] W. I. and Dorothy S. Thomas, *The Child in America*, New York, 1928, Ch. 9.

[17] C. M. Louttit, *Clinical Psychology*, New York, 1936, p. 263.

from non-delinquent groups by these tests, and it is likely that studies of these characteristics may be more enlightening than the intelligence tests have been.

These tests have almost universally shown a large number of personality deviations among delinquents and criminals. Bromberg and Thompson found, in addition to 17.7 per cent who were definitely psychopathic, 65.1 per cent who had personality deviations such as aggressiveness, emotional instability, and shiftlessness, in their report on psychiatric examinations of all offenders who were convicted or pleaded guilty in the Court of General Sessions, New York City, in 1932–1935.[18] More significant, perhaps, are the comparisons with non-delinquents. Miss Covert found excitability to be characteristic of 37 per cent of the delinquent boys and 7 per cent of the public school boys tested.[19] Healy and Bronner report that of 105 delinquents 68 were more active and restless than their non-delinquent siblings who were selected for comparison, and only 11 were less active and restless; also that 46 of these delinquents were extraordinarily hyperactive and restless, and none of the 105 siblings were so hyperactive.[20] Moreover, Healy and Bronner report that the most significant difference they found between the delinquents and their non-delinquent siblings was the deep emotional disturbances; 91 per cent of the delinquents and 13 per cent of the non-delinquents had such emotional disturbances.[21] This difference is very striking, but the study should be repeated under the control of persons who are not convinced in advance that delinquents are differentiated from non-delinquents principally by deep emotional disturbances, and with much more searching inquiry regarding the non-delinquents.[22] Moreover, in studies of this nature it is

---

[18] Bromberg and Thompson, loc. cit., p. 13.

[19] Mildred S. Covert, "Excitability in Delinquent Boys," Jour. Delinq., 5: 224–239, November, 1920.

[20] Wm. Healy and Augusta F. Bronner, New Light on Delinquency, New Haven, 1936, p. 63. See, also, A. T. Childers, "Hyper-Activity in Children Having Behavior Disorders," Amer. Jour. Orthopsych., 5:227–243, July, 1935.

[21] Op. cit., p. 122. See, also, A. Courthial, "Emotional Differences of Delinquent and Non-Delinquent Girls of Normal Intelligence," Arch. of Psychol., No. 133, 1931.

[22] Healy and Bronner report that of the 105 in the control group only 21 "had ever been so much as mildly delinquent" (op. cit., p. 54). Over a period of several years 98 per cent of the students in my University classes have reported that they were at least mildly delinquent in childhood, engaging in petty pilfering and in some cases in very serious thefts. While there is undoubtedly a great difference between the delinquent group and the control group in the study described, the statement that only 21 were found who were even mildly delinquent throws doubt on the adequacy of the investigation of the control

difficult to distinguish between the deviations which result from the delinquency and the deviations from which the delinquency results. The individual who engages for some time in delinquency is ostracized, criticized, and punished; in many cases he will have deep emotional disturbances growing out of the reactions of others toward his delinquency. In so far as the emotional disturbance antedates the delinquency, it is likely to be due to the acquisition of incompatible codes through associations which are made essentially by chance,[23] or else to be a part of the total reaction to the situation. It has been found, for instance, that emotionally unstable teachers have a larger proportion of unstable children than do stable teachers.[24] It is quite likely that emotionally unstable children will manifest more overt behavior problems than emotionally stable children in schools, but the discovery of the emotional instability does not aid much in understanding or control.

ALCOHOL AND INTOXICATION. Excessive drinking of intoxicating liquors is sometimes interpreted as a symptom of psychopathy. While there is much reason to question the validity of this belief, alcohol is included in this chapter on psychopathy as a matter of convenience. Intoxication has been recognized as a social problem for many decades. Approximately two-thirds of the arrests in a year prior to prohibition were occasioned by intoxication and were charged either as drunkenness, disorderly conduct, or vagrancy, and more than one-half of all persons committed to all types of prisons were committed for intoxication. This proportion was reduced to about one-third in the period immediately after the adoption of national prohibition but increased thereafter nearly to the previous proportion.[25] Though these cases number more than half of all cases, they certainly cause considerably less than half of the expense of these agencies, for they are generally handled summarily.

Probably a relatively small proportion of the serious crimes result directly from intoxication. A few homicides are committed as the result of drunken quarrels; a few rapes and a few robberies and

---

group, not only in respect to their delinquency but also in respect to their emotional disturbances and other characteristics.

[23] Pauline V. Young, *Pilgrims of Russian-Town*, Chicago, 1932, pp. 198–216.

[24] P. L. Boynton, Harriet Dugger, and Masal Turner, "The Emotional Stability of Teachers and Pupils," *Jour. of Delinq.*, 18:223–232, October, 1934.

[25] In this computation of arrests, the citations for violation of traffic regulations are not included. The estimate is based on the statistics for the state of Massachusetts and for ten cities.

burglaries are committed by persons whose inhibitions are not working in the habitual manner because of intoxication. The indirect effects of the excessive consumption of alcohol are much more serious than the direct effects. These indirect effects are manifested primarily in the non-support of families and in a general deterioration of family life. Healy reported that in 31 per cent of a thousand cases of juvenile delinquency in one of his series one or both parents drank to excess, in another series 26.5 per cent, and in his Boston series 51 per cent.[26] Healy found that the delinquency of children was more frequently related to their habits of using tea, coffee, and tobacco, than to habits of using alcohol or drugs. He assigned tea, coffee, and tobacco as a major factor in no case in the series of one thousand, but did assign tea or coffee as a minor factor in forty-three cases and tobacco in sixty cases.[27] Tea, coffee, and tobacco produce nervousness in young children, which is injurious to efficiency in schools and places of work and is conducive to friction at home and elsewhere. There is no evidence that an appreciable effect is produced by these commodities in adult life.

Efforts have been made to determine whether alcoholization of parents produces a physiological effect on the progeny. The experimental work on animals is not conclusive; and even if it were, it would not be conclusive so far as criminality is concerned. Apparently the most important relation between alcohol and crime is social and economic. The wealthy person who can use alcohol in his own home may be injured somewhat physiologically but he is not rendered criminal, as is the poor person whose deterioration is evident to the public. The loss of efficiency, of self-respect, and of social-respect tends to turn the poor person who drinks excessively into a vagrant and disorderly person. Because of the lack of control which comes with excessive drinking, recidivism is promoted. Moreover, there has been for a long time a distinct relationship between alcohol and respect for law. Before prohibition the saloon openly violated the law, and the huge brewing and distilling companies corrupted the legislature, the police departments, and the courts and by their campaign contributions controlled the political parties. During national prohibition those who were producing, distributing, or drinking alcohol did the same thing, and in addition some of the most respected members of American society and some of the

---

[26] Judge Baker Foundation, *Case Studies,* Series 1, Nos. 2–3, p. 5a.
[27] Wm. Healy, *The Individual Delinquent,* Boston, 1915, p. 138.

influential newspapers openly scoffed at and advocated violation of the law. Whether respect for law in general, if there be any such generalized respect, was greater during the period of national prohibition or prior to it cannot be determined, but in both systems respect for law was distinctly decreased by the practices connected with alcohol.

NARCOTIC DRUGS. Drug addiction, like alcoholic intoxication, is often regarded as a symptom of psychopathy and for that reason is included in this chapter, although the interpretation is not clearly justified. Lindesmith has shown conclusively that drug addiction cannot be explained as due to psychopathy; though some addicts are psychopathic, many "normal" persons, especially in earlier years, became addicts through medical prescriptions and patent medicines.[28]

Opium and cocaine and their derivatives and a few other habit-forming drugs have been frequently discussed as causes of crime. The general tendency in recent years is to conclude that these drugs have very slight direct effects on criminality. Drug addiction is likely to cause serious deterioration in persons who are socially or personally maladjusted, but comparatively slight deterioration in persons who are personally and socially well adjusted. Though the effects of the drugs differ, in general the aggressive impulses are inhibited rather than stimulated by the drugs, so that criminals are made less dangerous on that account. The deterioration makes the addicts economically inefficient, and petty thefts are frequently committed as a means of securing a supply of drugs. Consequently drug addicts are frequently arrested and frequently committed to institutions, where the demand for the drugs increases the disciplinary problems to a considerable extent.

Among the criminals who have been studied the drug habit is generally acquired during the ages twenty to twenty-nine. Sandoz was able to determine the histories of sixty persons addicted to morphine. Of these, forty-two had never been arrested before addiction to drugs, and after addiction had an average number of arrests of 8.2 each; the other eighteen persons had on the average 2.8 arrests each prior to addiction and 8.3 after addiction. For the

---

[28] A. R. Lindesmith, *The Nature of Opiate Addiction*, MSS. in University of Chicago Library; abridgement under same title, privately distributed, 1937; A. R. Lindesmith, "A Sociological Theory of Drug Addiction," *Amer. Jour. Sociol.*, 43:593–609, January, 1938.

group as a whole the average number of arrests prior to addiction was 0.8 each, after addiction 8.2 each, of which 5.5 were for offenses other than violation of the drug law.[29]

CONCLUSION REGARDING CRIME AND PSYCHOPATHY. The Neo-Lombrosian theory that crime is an expression of psychopathy is no more justified than was the Lombrosian theory that criminals constitute a distinct physical type. Encephalitis is apparently more closely related to behavior difficulties in children than any other psychopathic or neuropathic condition, and even here the relationship is not definitely determined either in quantitative terms or in terms of the processes by which the association develops. Feeblemindedness has proved to be relatively unimportant as a general factor. Psychopathic personality is a vague concept and its relation to criminality is unknown either in quantitative or qualitative terms.

The methods of diagnosis of the psychoses and of psychopathic personality are not standardized and the diagnoses are not reliable. The large proportion of criminals found to be psychopathic is explained by this lack of standardization and by the preconception that criminality must be due to psychopathy. This preconception is shown in extreme form in the editorial in the *Journal of the American Medical Association,* which was approved by the sub-committee on the medical aspects of crime, to the effect that a diagnosis of mental disease is "permissible even when the criminal has shown no evidence of mental disease other than his criminal behavior."[30] A diagnosis of mental pathology assumes a criterion of the normal, and the normal in regard to thoughts, feelings, and sentiments is not stated in objective terms but is determined by the psychiatrist's preconceptions.

The contention that all professional criminals are psychopathic is likely to be true in one sense. A career of professional crime means not only a change in objective behavior but also a change in loyalties, moral standards, values, sentiments, and feelings, just as a change from teaching to business or from preaching to law means an analogous change in both objective and subjective processes. If the values of the general law-abiding population are assumed to be normal, then the values of the professional criminals are necessarily

---

[29] C. E. Sandoz, "Report on Morphinism to the Municipal Court of Boston," *Jour. Crim. Law and Criminol.,* 13:43, May, 1922.

[30] *Jour. Amer. Med. Assoc.,* August 2, 1930, quoted by M. Ploscowe, "Report on Causes of Crime," *Natl. Com. on Law Obs. and Enf.,* No. 13, Vol. I, p. 57.

abnormal, and since these values are subjective, this is mental abnormality. This, however, is principally logomachy and does not assist in understanding the criminal.

Psychiatrists are, to some extent, abandoning their diagnoses and classifications and trying to understand the processes at work in the development of crime and delinquency rather than to determine the quantitative importance of any particular psychopathy or of all psychopathies. In so far as they turn their attention to the study of these processes they find, first, that many of the so-called psychopathies are results rather than causes of criminal behavior; and second, that social processes and relations generally underlie the psychopathies. McDougall has reached the conclusion that crime and some of the psychopathies are natural consequences of the weakening of the traditions due to the conflicts of moral standards and the detachment of persons from community life.

Where traditions are diverse and shapeless, and where each man's place in his community is undefined and temporary, there men are thrown back on themselves and are perpetually called upon to make moral decisions; and, in the absence of clear guidance and sanction from community opinion, this is too great a task for most of us. The decisions are never made; and, in the moral sense, such men live from hand to mouth. Thus they become the seat of unresolved moral conflicts, which in so many cases result in neurotic disorders.[31]

The question is asked, Why do people differ in their behavior when they live in the same objective environment? Not all boys in a deteriorated area become gangsters and not all cashiers become embezzlers. Why does one person become a criminal and another in much the same objective situation not become a criminal? One answer to this question is that the gross psychopathy of the criminal individual is the explanation of his criminality. This hypothesis does not serve adequately as a general explanation of burglars and robbers and is far more inadequate when applied to fraud, bribery, and embezzlement. The tendency has been, therefore, to look for more subtle processes of a psychopathic nature, on the assumption that since crime is abnormal social behavior the criminal must be abnormal mentally. It is probable that differences of this nature

---

[31] William McDougall, "Crime in America," *Forum,* 77:520–521, April, 1927. Reprinted by permission.

may be discovered, but certainly nothing significant has been demonstrated yet. It is possible that the significant traits of individuals are not the gross pathologies but very subtle processes. Also it is possible that the important differentiating elements are coincidents. A person happens to read an advertisement at a particular time, secures a particular position, and in that connection becomes a criminal. If he had read the paper ten minutes later another person would have secured the position and the first person would not have become a criminal, at least in that particular situation. This coincidental theory of differences in individual behavior is not suggested as a total explanation of criminality but it is a partial alternative to the hypothesis that criminals must be psychopathic.

SUGGESTED READINGS

Adler, H. M., "A Behavioristic Study of the Delinquent," *Amer. Assoc. for Study of Feeblemindedness, Annual Report,* Vol. XLVI, pp. 39–56, 1922.

Alexander, Franz, and Staub, Hugo, *The Criminal, the Judge and the Public,* New York, 1931.

Ball, R. J., "The General Emotionality of the Prisoner," *Jour. Appl. Psychol.,* 15:436–461, October, 1931.

Ball, R. J., "Introversion and Extroversion in a Group of Convicts," *Jour. Abn. and Social Psychol.,* 26:422–428, January, 1932.

Channing, Alice, "Alcoholism among Parents of Juvenile Delinquents," *Social Serv. Rev.,* 1:357–383, September, 1927.

Chassell, Clara F., *The Relation between Morality and Intellect,* Teachers College, Contribution to Education, No. 607, New York, 1934.

Courthial, A., "Emotional Differences of Delinquent and Non-Delinquent Girls of Normal Intelligence," *Arch. of Psychol.,* No. 133, 1931.

Fairbanks, Ruth E., "The Subnormal Child Seventeen Years After," *Mental Hygiene,* 17:177–217, April, 1933.

Glueck, Eleanor T., "Mental Retardation and Juvenile Delinquency," *Mental Hygiene,* 19:549–572, October, 1935.

Grimberg, L. E., *Emotion and Delinquency,* New York, 1928.

Hawthorne, J. W., "A Group Test for the Measurement of Cruelty-Compassion," *Jour. Social Psychol.,* 3:189–216, May, 1932.

Hayes, M. M., and Bowery, L. E., "Marihuana," *Jour. Crim. Law and Criminol.*, 23:1086–1098, March, 1933.

Healy, William, *Mental Conflicts and Misconduct*, Boston, 1917.

Healy, William, *The Individual Delinquent*, Boston, 1915.

Healy, William, and Bronner, Augusta F., *New Light on Delinquency*, New Haven, 1936.

Holsopple, J. Q., "The Social Adjustment of Delinquents Who Are Unable to Inhibit Old Automatic Perceptual Responses," *Jour. Social Psychol.*, 3:91–96, February, 1932.

Kahn, Eugen, *Psychopathic Personalities*, New Haven, 1931.

Karpman, B., *Case Studies in the Psychopathology of Crime*, Washington, 1933.

Kolb, L., "Drug Addiction in Its Relation to Crime," *Mental Hygiene*, 9:74–89, January, 1925.

Levy, John, "A Quantitative Study of the Relationship between Intelligence and Economic Status as Factors in the Etiology of Children's Behavior Problems," *Amer. Jour. Orthopsych.*, 1:152–162, January, 1931.

Lindesmith, A. R., "A Sociological Theory of Drug Addiction," *Amer. Jour. Sociol.*, 43:593–609, January, 1938.

Owen, Mary B., "The Intelligence of the Institutionalized Juvenile Delinquent," *Jour. Juv. Research*, 21:199–205, October, 1937.

Partridge, G. E., "Psychopathic Personalities among Boys in a Training School for Delinquents," *Amer. Jour. Psychiat.*, 8:159–186, 1928.

Raven, A., "A Contribution towards a Psychological Conception of Insanity and Its Relation to Crime," *Sociol. Rev.*, 20:274–292, October, 1928.

Rosanoff, A. J., "A Theory of Personality Based Mainly on Psychiatric Experience," *Psychol. Bull.*, 17:281–299, September, 1920.

Sullivan, W. C., *Crime and Insanity*, London, 1924.

Sutherland, Edwin H., "Mental Deficiency and Crime," in Kimball Young (Editor), *Social Attitudes*, New York, 1931, pp. 357–375.

Terry, C. E., and Pellens, Mildred, *The Opium Problem*, New York, 1928.

Willemse, W. A., *Constitution-Types and Delinquency*, London, 1932.

Willoughby, R. R., "A Scale of Emotional Maturity," *Jour. Social Psychol.*, 3:3–36, February, 1932.

Chapter Eight

CRIME IN RELATION TO RACE AND NATIVITY

RACE. Statistical records show that in proportion to adult population Negroes are arrested, convicted, and committed to prisons a little less than three times as frequently as are native white persons. Arrests during 1937, as recorded by the Federal Bureau of Investigation, were 1,395.0 for Negroes and 514.2 for native white persons, per 100,000 adult population, or a ratio of 2.7 to 1. In 1933 2.7 times as many Negroes as native white persons were committed to federal and state prisons, and 2.9 times as many to jails and houses of correction. This is a slight decrease from 1923 and 1910 in the relative rate of commitment of Negroes. These rates differ in the various sections of a city in a manner similar to the variations of rates of white persons. Also, they differ in the several sections of the United States, being relatively high in the Northern and Western states. The ratios are not constant for all types of crimes. While 2.7 times as many Negroes were arrested in 1937 as native white men in proportion to adult population for all offenses, 7.5 times as many were arrested for assault, 5.3 times as many for homicide, 3.7 times as many for robbery, 3.5 times as many for larceny, 3.2 times as many for burglary, and 2.4 times as many for rape. These ratios, as well as similar ratios based on prison commitments, indicate that Negroes are most likely, in comparison with native white persons, to commit homicides and assault, and least likely to commit rape.

The difference between Negro women and white women in the rate of arrests for 1937 was greater than the difference between Negro men and white men. Negro men were arrested 2.7 times as frequently as white men, but Negro women were arrested 5.4 times as frequently as white women. White men were arrested 16 times as frequently as white women, but Negro men were arrested only 8 times as frequently as Negro women. Such differences indicate that the crime rate is not closely, if at all, related to racial biology.

Indian men were arrested in 1937 2.6 times as frequently as white men in proportion to adult population, and Indian women 4.6 times as frequently as white women. The Indian women, like the Negro women, approached closer to the crime rate of men of the same race than did the white women. But Mexican men had an arrest rate 3.7 times as high as white men, and Mexican women 2.4 times as high as white women. And Chinese and Japanese men had an arrest rate in 1937 only 1.4 times as high as white men, and Japanese and Chinese women only 0.6 times as high as white women. The rates of commitment to penal institutions are similar to these arrest rates in this respect. In general, these variations in the comparative crime rates of the sexes constitute one of the great difficulties in an interpretation based on hereditary or constitutional traits. The explanation can be made more easily in terms of the traditional position of the women in the several races.

These statistics probably reflect a bias against all of the minority races but especially against the Negro. The assertion has been made frequently that this bias is not as important in the South as in the North so far as it affects arrests and convictions, but this statement cannot be proved or disproved. The Chicago Commission on Race Relations in 1922 made an effort to determine the comparative criminality of Negroes and whites in Chicago and abandoned the effort on the ground that the statistics were completely unreliable as indexes of crime rates. Sometimes the number of arrests of Negroes is exaggerated because of clerical errors. An investigation by the Urban League shows that the number of arrests of Negroes as published in the reports of the municipal court of Minneapolis for 1923–1925 was 65 per cent greater than the unpublished records of individual arrests justified.[1] Testimony before the Seabury Commission in New York City indicated that policemen on certain assignments were expected to make a specified number of arrests per month and if in a particular month they were short on this quota "they used to go to Harlem and in Harlem they go to any colored house or colored apartment and they make any arrests at

---

[1] Maurine Boie, "An Analysis of Crime Statistics for Minneapolis," *Opportunity*, 6:171–173, June, 1928, quoted by Thorsten Sellin, "The Negro Criminal," *Annals of Amer. Acad. of Pol. and Social Sci.*, 140:52, November, 1928.

all, just because they thought colored people had less chance in court." Sellin has made an excellent analysis of the unreliability of the statistics regarding Negro crime rates, which summarizes this evidence.[2] On the other hand the records of robberies and a few other serious crimes committed in Negro districts in certain cities indicate that these districts are much more criminal than the average residential district.

Even if the statistics are completely reliable, they involve a comparison of groups which differ economically, educationally, and socially, as well as racially. The leaders of the Negroes have pointed to the following facts: Only one of the 200 graduates from the Salem, N. C., high school has a criminal court record; not one of the 800 graduates of Atlanta University or of the 130 graduates of Water's Normal Institute has been arrested or convicted; only one of about 3,500 graduates from Fisk University has been imprisoned.[3] In Mound Bayou, Mississippi, a town entirely Negro, there has been almost no crime of a serious kind in 30 years. This argument is clearly valid. The difference in crime rates cannot be assumed to be due to racial differences as such. The significance of race as a biological factor could be determined only by comparing Negroes of a specified economic and cultural status with native white persons of the same status.

The explanation of racial variations in crime rates in terms of the direct effects of race-biology can be discarded, in view of the general evidence against the direct inheritance of criminality and also in view of the variations in the crime rates within any one race. This does not mean that race can be discarded entirely in the explanation of crime. Race may conceivably be a factor in crime in either of two ways: first, by the inheritance of differential characteristics which, while not in themselves criminal tendencies, determine the social and economic level of the race in competition with other races and thus indirectly affect the crime rates; second, by the experiences of the race, including (a) confinement of a race to a given status by barriers imposed by other races, (b) the role of a race in the society as defined in interaction with other races, and (c) conflicts in the patterns of behavior which

---

[2] Thorsten Sellin, "The Negro Criminal," *Annals of Amer. Acad. of Pol. and Social Sci.*, 140:52–64, November, 1928.

[3] B. T. Washington, *The Story of the Negro*, New York, 1907, Vol. II, pp. 371 ff.

impinge on the race and the persistence of the resulting reactions by force of tradition.

IMMIGRATION. The relation of immigration to crime in the United States is a problem of first-rate importance from the point of view of a theory of criminality and of legislative and administrative policies. Many research studies have been conducted on this problem. These studies have yielded certain statistical conclusions, and other less definite conclusions. The statistical conclusions are supported by a large mass of data, but the data are relatively unreliable as indexes of crime. The statistics, however, agree in general with the opinions of persons who are intimately acquainted with the immigrant groups.

First, mobility generally increases criminality. This seems to be true of migration between countries and also of migration within a country. It is probable that immigrants to America have higher rates of serious crimes than their brothers at home have. Statistical evidence on this point is not available in a general form, for the definitions of crime and the methods of recording crimes differ so widely among the nations that international comparisons may not safely be made. The conclusion stated above is based on a relatively small number of specific studies, such as Thomas and Znaniecki, *The Polish Peasant in Europe and America,* and Young, *The Pilgrims of Russian-Town.*

Second, immigrants in general contribute less than their quota to the criminal population of the United States when correction is made for variations in the age composition of the immigrant population. The arrest rate per 100,000 adult population in 1937 was 514.2 for native white and 212.1 for foreign white. The native white population had a higher arrest rate in each age group and for all except three types of crime, and in those three types the rates were almost identical. The number of native white persons committed to all types of prisons in 1933 was 536.5, and for foreign white 402.4 per 100,000 adult population. Similar conclusions have been reached in all of the later studies, although the opposite conclusion was reached in the earlier studies.[4]

---

[4] Alida C. Bowler, "Report on Crime and the Foreign Born," *Natl. Com. on Law Obs. and Enf.,* No. 10, 1932; "Immigration and Crime," *U. S. Immigration Commission,* 1910, Vol. XXXVI; Chicago City Council, *Report of Committee on Crime,* 1915, pp. 51–56; Joseph M. Gilman, "Statistics and the Immigration Problem," *Amer. Jour. Sociol.,* 30:29–48, July, 1924; Edwin H. Sutherland, "Is There Undue Crime among Immigrants?" *Proc. Natl. Conf. Social Work,* 1927, pp. 572–579; H. H. Laughlin, "Analysis of America's Mod-

Taft has raised questions regarding the trustworthiness of the statistical data in view of the fact that the immigrants are affected by poverty, mobility, and most of the other crimogenic conditions. The rational argument that these conditions *must* increase crime is set over against the relatively unreliable statistics of crime.[5] There is no necessary conflict here, however. The explanation seems to be as follows: Immigrants developed respect for law in their home countries. In their homogeneous and stable groups they were controlled during their formative years by the traditions which had come down to them through the generations, and by their primary groups they were welded together into a general community unity. These habits, ideals, and codes persist after they reach America so that they are not so criminalistic as persons reared in the social disorganization of the American city. They are, nevertheless, affected by the mobility and the separation from their communities, for their crime rates are probably higher than the rates in their home countries. Thus their own crime rates are raised by their immigration, but the crime rates of America are not raised. In line with this explanation is the fact that immigrants who arrive in the United States in childhood have a higher rate of imprisonment than immigrants who arrive in adult ages.

The several immigrant groups differ widely among themselves in the general rate of arrest and of imprisonment. The rate of imprisonment to all types of prisons in 1910 and 1923 was five times as high for persons of Irish nativity as for persons of German nativity, and in 1933 was over three times as high. National groups differ widely also in the comparative frequency of different crimes. Some immigrant groups have high rates for drunkenness and other misdemeanors and low rates for felonies, while other groups have high rates for felonies and low rates for misdemeaners. Persons of Italian nativity were committed to state prisons for major offenses in 1933 three times as frequently as persons of

ern Melting Pot," *Hearings before Com. on Immig. and Natur., House of Rep., 67th Cong.,* November 21, 1922; William F. Ogburn, "Factors in the Variation of Crime among Cities," *Jour. Amer. Stat. Assoc.,* 30:12–34, March, 1935.

Of these references the first is the most comprehensive but has two defects which were unavoidable: first, the crime rates for 1929 and 1930 were computed from population estimates derived from the 1920 census, since the report for 1930 was not available at the time of publication; second, the change in national boundaries resulting from the World War has made the statistics of nativity of the foreign-born very unreliable.

[5] D. R. Taft, "Does Immigration Increase Crime?" *Social Forces,* 12:69–77, October, 1933.

Irish nativity, while they were committed to jails and work-houses only two-thirds as frequently. This difference is due principally to differences in their drinking habits. The Finnish immigrants, who had the highest rate of commitments of any immigrant group, suffered 85 per cent of their commitments in 1923 for drunkenness, violation of liquor laws, and disorderly conduct, while in contrast the Greeks had only 39 per cent of their commitments for these offenses. Of German immigrants committed to federal and state prisons in 1932-1936 4.5 per cent were committed for homicide, 3.6 per cent for assault, and 14.3 per cent for burglary, while of Italian immigrants the percentages were 10.7, 9.4, and 7.1; that is, the Italians had twice the proportion of homicides and assaults, and half the proportion of burglaries. Thus certain crimes or groups of crimes are characteristic of certain national groups. These same types of crimes are, usually, characteristic of the home countries, also. The Italian immigrants have an extraordinarily high rate of conviction for homicide, and also Italy has had the highest rate of homicide of any of the nations in western Europe. Italians have a low rate of arrest for drunkenness, and drunkenness is comparatively absent in Italy. Thus the traditions of the home country are transplanted to America and determine the relative positions of the immigrant groups with reference to the types of crimes. Laughlin attempted to explain the low crime rate of the foreign-born as due to the weeding out of the criminals by immigration officials, and for their efficiency in doing this congratulated the officials. This selection certainly keeps the crime rate of immigrants lower than it would otherwise be. But if this explanation is accepted, the immigration officials should be congratulated for weeding out the inebriates from among the Greeks and Italians but berated for their failure to weed out the murderers and robbers, and they should be congratulated for their success in weeding out the murderers and robbers from among the Irish and Finnish immigrants but berated for their failure to weed out the inebriates. The important factor in the differential crime rates of the several national groups is the strength and consistency of the traditions which they assimilated in their home countries. These traditions, also, explain the differences in the sex ratios among the criminals in the several immigrant groups. In proportion to the population of each sex, Swedish men are committed to prison fifty times as frequently as Swedish women, while Irish men are committed only twelve times as frequently as Irish women. This is primarily a reflection of the differences in the drinking habits of the sexes in these two national groups. Furthermore, the Italian women have a high murder rate in comparison with women of other nativity groups.

The second generation of immigrants has been generally believed to be more criminalistic than their foreign-born parents and also more criminalistic than the native whites of native parentage. Recent statistics indicate that this belief is not generally true at the present time. Ogburn found that crimes known to the police have a negative correlation with the number of second generation immigrants in three groups of cities, and that the negative association persists when other factors are held constant; the coefficients of correlation in the three groups of cities range between —0.34 and —0.54.[6] The Bureau of the Census, in its *Report on Federal and State Prisons* for 1933, presented a table regarding nativity of prisoners in twenty-six states in which reports regarding nativity were complete enough for comparison. In seventeen of these states the second generation immigrants had a rate of commitment lower than the native white of native parentage, while in the other nine states their rate of commitment was higher. Taft has made an analysis of this table, with corrections for variations in age distribution, and has concluded that the states in which the second generation have lower rates are those in which the older immigration is predominant, and the states in which they have higher rates are those in which the newer immigration is predominant.[7] This report shows, also, that the second generation of immigrants had higher rates of commitment than their foreign-born parents in all except one of these twenty-six states, and that offspring of mixed parentage had lower rates of commitment than offspring of foreign parentage in seventeen states and higher in nine states.

These statistical studies indicate that the second generation of immigrants sometimes has lower commitment rates and sometimes has higher commitment rates, but they do not carry the explanation of the difference very far. Certain more specialized studies in

[6] William F. Ogburn, "Factors in the Variation of Crime among Cities," *Jour. Amer. Statis. Assoc.*, 30:21–24, March, 1935.
[7] D. R. Taft, "Nationality and Crime," *Amer. Sociol. Rev.*, 1:724–736, October, 1936.

areas in which the second generation had higher crime rates than their parents indicate that the delinquency rates of the second generation are comparatively low when the immigrant group first settles in a community, and that they increase as contacts with the surrounding culture multiply. The rate remains low in those foreign colonies which are comparatively isolated from the surrounding culture. The rate is low in the heart of the colony but increases on the borderlines where the group comes into contact with other groups. Moreover, the rates are comparatively low in the immigrant groups which have moved away from the areas of deterioration into better residential areas. These findings point to a conclusion that the high rate of the second generation of immigrants is due to the contacts with delinquency in America and to the conflict of standards.[8]

The second generation appears to approach the native-born of native parentage in regard to the kinds of crimes committed. In 1910 the Immigration Commission stated its findings on this point as follows:

The movement of the second generation crime is away from the crimes peculiar to immigrants and toward those of the American of native parentage. Sometimes this movement has carried second generation criminality even beyond that of the native-born of native parentage.[9]

This may be illustrated by the following comparison of the Irish immigrants of the first and second generations and the native whites of native parentage with reference to a few crimes of which they were convicted in the New York Court of General Sessions in 1908-1909,[10] as given in Table III. The tendency is very distinct, though it is not found for all crimes and all nationalities. The same tendency appears, also, in a comparison of the first and second generations of Italian immigrants with reference to crimes

---

[8] Ross argues that the high crime rate of the second generation is due to the low social and economic position, just at is the crime rate of any other group in the same position, and that it is not due to isolation from American culture and the breakdown of the old native culture. Harold Ross, "Crime and the Native Born Sons of European Immigrants," *Jour. Crim. Law and Criminol.,* 28:202-209, July, 1937.

[9] U. S. Immigration Commission, *Report on Immigration and Crime,* 1910, Vol. XXXVI, p. 14; see, also, pp. 14–16 and 67–86.

[10] *Ibid.,* p. 14.

TABLE III

RATE OF CONVICTION OF SPECIFIED GROUPS

OFFENSE	IRISH		NATIVE WHITE OF NATIVE PARENTAGE
	Immigrants	2nd Generation	
Homicide	2.3	1.0	0.5
Rape	0.0	0.3	0.7
Gaming	1.2	2.7	3.6

of personal violence in Massachusetts, as shown in Table IV.[11] This tendency has been analyzed with great detail for the State of New Jersey by Stofflet.[12]

TABLE IV

FREQUENCY OF COMMITMENTS TO STATE PRISON AND STATE REFORMATORY OF MASSACHUSETTS FOR MURDER, MANSLAUGHTER, AND ASSAULT, IN SPECIFIED GROUPS, 1914–1922, PER 100,000 IN EACH GROUP IN 1915

Nativity and Parentage	Number Committed for Specified Offenses
Born in Italy..	192
Native-born, one or both parents born in Italy.............	24
Native-born, of native parentage........................	24
Native-born, one or both parents born in any foreign country.	22

This seems to show that the tendency to commit crimes of personal violence which is seen so clearly in the Italian immigrants is a matter of tradition—a tradition that is not passed on to the second generation.

Immigration has affected the behavior of the native stock, also. This result has been produced in at least three ways. Immigrants have displaced the native stock in many occupations and the displaced workers have to some extent turned to crime as a means of livelihood. Second, immigration has promoted urbanization, and crime rates are higher in cities than in the country. Third, and most important, immigration has increased the variety of patterns of behavior. The population of the area to which immigrants go is not homogeneous but is a mixture of various national groups,

[11] Computed from reports of Massachusetts Department of Correction, 1914–1922; population was secured from the Massachusetts State Census of 1915; the Census report of 1920 does not give the necessary information for that year; the Italians of all ages are included, and native-born, both white and colored, of all ages.

[12] E. H. Stofflet, "A Study of National and Cultural Differences in Criminal Tendency," Arch. of Psych., No. 185, 1935.

with many cultures, standards, and modes of behavior. In contrast with European cities the American cities have a very difficult problem of control. While the principal European cities have from 1 to 6 per cent of their populations foreign-born, the principal Northern and Western cities in the United States have from 10 to 30 per cent foreign-born. While the foreign-born do not commit more crimes than the native-born of the same age and sex, the native-born probably commit more crimes than they would commit if the immigrants were not in the vicinity. This, however, is only one side of the picture. The variations in codes of behavior promote variations of other kinds, including inventions and progress, and are a condition of development as well as of delinquency.

SUGGESTED READINGS

Beach, Walter C., "Oriental Crime in California," *Stanford Univ. Pub., Hist., Econ., and Pol. Sci.*, Vol. III, No. 3, 1932.

Bowler, Alida C., "Report on Crime and the Foreign Born," *Natl. Com. on Law Obs. and Enf.*, No. 10, Washington, 1932.

Brinton, Hugh P., "Negroes Who Run Afoul of the Law," *Social Forces*, 11:96–101, October, 1932.

Chicago Commission on Race Relations, *A Study of Race Relations and a Race Riot*, Chicago, 1922.

Frazier, E. Franklin, *The Negro Family in Chicago*, Chicago, 1931.

Hacker, Ervin, "Criminality and Immigration," *Jour. Crim. Law and Criminol.*, 20:429–438, November, 1929.

Hayner, Norman S., "Social Factors in Oriental Crime," *Amer. Jour. Sociol.*, 43:908–919, May, 1938.

Johnson, Charles S., *The Negro in American Civilization*, New York, 1930.

McCord, C. H., *The American Negro as a Dependent, Defective, and Delinquent*, Nashville, 1914.

Ogburn, William F., "Factors in the Variation of Crime among Cities," *Jour. Amer. Statis. Assoc.*, 30:12–34, March, 1935.

Park, R. E., and Miller, H. A., *Old World Traits Transplanted*, New York, 1921, Ch. 4.

Reid, Ira De A., "Notes on the Negro's Relation to Work and Law Observance," *Natl. Com. on Law Obs. and Enf.*, No. 13, Vol. 1, pp. 219-256, Washington, 1932.

Reuter, E. B., *The American Race Problem*, New York, 1927.

Ross, Harold, "Crime and the Native Born Sons of European Immigrants," *Jour. Crim. Law and Criminol.*, 28:202–209, July, 1937.

Sellin, Thorsten, *Culture Conflict and Crime,* Social Science Research Council, Bulletin 41, New York, 1938.

Sellin, Thorsten, "The Negro Criminal," *Annals of Amer. Acad. of Pol. and Soc. Sci.*, 140:52–64, November, 1928.

Shaw, Clifford R., and McKay, Henry D., "Report on Social Factors in Juvenile Delinquency," *Natl. Com. on Law Obs. and Enf.*, No. 13, Vol. II, Washington, 1932.

Smith, W. C., "The Second Generation Oriental in America," *Institute of Pacific Relations,* 1927.

Stofflet, E. H., "A Study of National and Cultural Differences in Criminal Tendency," *Arch. of Psych.*, No. 185, 1935.

Sutherland, Edwin H., "Is There Undue Crime among Immigrants?" *Proc. Natl. Conf. Social Work,* 1927, pp. 572-579.

Taft, D. R., "Does Immigration Increase Crime?" *Social Forces,* 12:69-77, October, 1933.

Taft, D. R., "Nationality and Crime," *Amer. Sociol. Rev.*, 1:724-736, October, 1936.

Thomas, W. I., and Znaniecki, F., *The Polish Peasant,* New York, 1927.

Woofter, T. J., *Negro Problems in American Cities,* Garden City, N. Y., 1928.

Chapter Nine

CULTURE AREAS AND CRIME

REGIONALISM. Crime rates vary in different portions of a nation. Ferri has shown that the rate of convictions for homicides per million population varies widely in different provinces in each of the principal European countries. In Italy twenty-seven provinces had rates of less than fifty, while thirteen provinces had rates of more than two hundred. Convictions of homicide in Sardinia were more than fourteen times as frequent in proportion to population as in Lombardy.[1] Aschaffenberg found the offenses against the person were much higher in East Prussia, Bavaria, and the Palatinate in 1912 than in the other German provinces. He found also that convictions for larceny were much higher in the provinces adjoining the Russian frontier than elsewhere in Germany, while resistance to or attacks on officers were most frequent in seaports and in manufacturing districts. The number of indictable crimes known to the police in England in 1927 per million population was highest in the counties containing and adjacent to London, next in the counties containing the principal seaports, next in the manufacturing counties in the central part of England, and lowest in the agricultural and mining counties. This same distribution was found in 1893, except that the southwestern agricultural counties, which had a low general rate for indictable offenses, had the highest rate of any section of the country for offenses against morals.[2] At an earlier period, according to Pike, the counties in England in which crime was most prevalent were those adjoining Scotland, and this continued until the final amalgamation of the countries.

---

[1] E. Ferri, *L'omicidio nell' antropologia criminale*, Torino, 1895, pp. 241–325; A. Niceforo, *La delinquenzia en Sardegna*.
[2] Rates for 1927 computed from Report on Criminal Statistics. See Great Britain, *Criminal Statistics for 1893*, p. 91.

In France Joly found the same variations in the 86 departments that are reported for other countries. In addition, he described an analysis of the internal migration in relation to crime rates. He found, for instance, that the Corsicans were prosecuted less often in the rest of France than in their native department. Corsica had next to the highest rate of the 86 departments, when considered as prosecutions in Corsica of persons born in Corsica; it dropped to sixty-fifth position when considered as prosecutions of persons born in Corsica regardless of whether the prosecutions were in Corsica or in other departments. Similarly the department which was next to the lowest in its rate at home rose to the thirty-sixth rank when prosecutions away from home were included. Some departments retained the same rank in the two methods of computing rates, but others showed these very significant changes.[3]

The several divisions of the United States have similar variations in crime rates. Homicides known to the police in 1937 ranged from 1.3 per 100,000 population in New England to 22.7 in the East South Central states; robberies known to the police ranged from 19.4 in New England to 105.6 in the South Atlantic States. The lowest rate for each type of serious crime known to the police was found either in New England or the Middle Atlantic states. The highest rates for robbery and burglary were found in the South Atlantic division, for homicide and assault in the East South Central division, and for larceny and auto theft in the Pacific division. In general, these divisions hold their ranks for both large and small cities.

Lottier has analyzed these sectional crime rates with a refined method. He finds a center of concentration for murder in the Southeastern states, with somewhat regular gradients to the north and west, that is, the rates decrease somewhat consistently from this center. Also, he found a center of concentration for robbery in the Middle Central states, with an axis running from Tennessee and Kentucky to Colorado, and with decreasing rates on either side of this axis. These two types of offenses show definite regional concentration, but the crimes against property do not show such marked concentration, probably because they are not based on the total property values in the states in question.[4]

---

[3] Henri Joly, *La France criminelle*, Paris, 1889, pp. 45–46.
[4] Stuart Lottier, "Distribution of Criminal Offenses in Sectional Regions," *Jour. Crim. Law and Criminol.*, 29:329–344, September, 1938.

Certain types of towns, also, have high crime rates. Lombroso reported that in every province in Italy certain villages had acquired reputations for special crimes; one was noted for murder, another for robbery, and another for swindling. Artena, for instance, had thirty times as many highway robberies as the average community in Italy,[5] and had been noted as a home of robbers since the twelfth century. Similarly, certain types of towns in America have been noted for high crime rates for longer or shorter periods. Frontier towns, river towns, and resort towns are somewhat outstanding in this respect. Mining towns generally have higher rates than agricultural towns of the same size, and the mining counties of a state generally have higher rates than the agricultural counties.[6]

Such broad comparisons of crime rates have been made in many countries over a long period of time. Lindesmith and Levin have described the earlier studies which had previously been practically unknown in this generation.[7] These studies have raised problems in a form in which it is possible to do specific research work,[8] and various attempts have been made to explain the differences. Aschaffenburg believed that the explanation of the differences in rates of crimes against the person in different provinces in Germany were related to the consumption of alcohol, while larceny was related to poverty, and crimes against public officials to the heterogeneity of population. Niceforo concluded that the differences in the crime rates in Sardinia were due to differences in racial origin of the population. Beurle found a distinctly lower crime rate in the Austrian provinces inhabited by persons of German origin than in the other provinces.[9] The high crime rates in the Southern states are generally interpreted as due to the large number of Negroes, but it is evident that homicides, at least, cannot be explained so simply, for the death rate by homicide for white persons in the

---

[5] C. Lombroso, *Crime, Its Causes and Remedies*, Boston, 1911, p. 23.

[6] Helen L. Yoke, "Crime in West Virginia," *Sociol. and Soc. Research*, 16:267–273, January, 1932; Mary Phleger and E. A. Taylor, "An Ecological Study of Juvenile Delinquency and Dependency in Athens County, Ohio," *Pub. Amer. Sociol. Soc.*, 26:144–149, 1932.

[7] Alfred Lindesmith and Yale Levin, "The Lombrosian Myth in Criminology," *Amer. Jour. Sociol.*, 42:653–671, March, 1937; Alfred Lindesmith and Yale Levin, "English Ecology and Criminology of the Past Century," *Jour. Crim. Law and Criminol.*, 27:801–816, March, 1937.

[8] For a general criticism of the ecological method, see Milla Aïssa Alihan, *Social Ecology: A Critical Analysis*, New York, 1938.

[9] Beurle, "Einige Erlebnisse der Oesterreichischen Kriminalstatistik," *Zeits. S. W.*, 8:325, quoted in Aschaffenburg, *op. cit.*, p. 39.

South is approximately five times as high as in New England. A general code favorable to homicide is more prevalent among whites in the South than in other sections of the United States.[10] The number of variables is too great to justify a generalization at the present time, but it is evident that standards of behavior may become general in wide areas and be transmitted as a tradition over many generations. An illustration of these traditions in exaggerated form is provided by the criminal tribes in India.

The Bhamptas are a tribe who give an infinity of trouble. Their home is in the Decan; but there is no limit to their field of operations. They work all over India, travelling even to Assam; and no railway is exempt from the Bhampta pest. . . . The Bhampta is a marvellously skilful pickpocket and railway thief. He frequents fairs, landing-places, bazaars, temples—any place, in fact, where there is a crowd. He is always on the lookout for his prey. . . . The Bhamptas are trained to crime from their earliest childhood, so it is not wonderful that they should become very expert. The children are initiated into the profession of their life by lessons in the pilfering of shoes, cocoa-nuts, and any odds and ends that they may come across. If they are slow or stupid they are encouraged to improve by the application of a stick. The boys soon become adept. . . . Adults generally work in small gangs of three or four. One of them stealthily removes an ornament from some one in the crowd, or adroitly picks a pocket, or, jostling the victim, boldly snatches his bag or satchel, and instantly passes his booty to one of his accomplices, who in turn passes it on to another; and in an incredibly short space of time the stolen property is far away. . . . Again a Bhampta sees a well-to-do person in the street. He makes a great show of brutally beating a small boy. The boy screams and yells and rushes for protection to the prosperous-looking stranger, who shields the child and expostulates with the Bhampta. The latter in apparent anger snatches away the boy from his protector, while the young rascal, who has been well trained, kicks and struggles for all that he is worth. The sympathizer has had enough of it, and is glad to let the youngster go. Later on he realizes that his purse has disappeared.[11]

---

[10] H. C. Brearley, *Homicide in the United States,* Chapel Hill, N. C., 1932.
[11] Edmund C. Cox, *Police and Crime in India,* London, 1911, pp. 234–237. See also, Paul F. Cressey, "The Criminal Tribes of India," *Sociol. and Soc. Res.,* 20:503–511; 21:18–25, July-September, 1936.

RURAL-URBAN DISTRIBUTION. The number of serious crimes increases with the size of the community. The number of auto thefts known to the police per 100,000 population in 1937 increased from 93.6 in communities of under 10,000 population to 263.4 in communities of over 250,000. The same trend occurred in each type of crime, with slight variations upward or downward from the trend, and it has occurred in each year since these statistics have been available. The deviation from this trend which appears most frequently is that the rate for cities of over 250,000 population is less than for cities of 100,000 to 250,000. Homicides and rapes known to the police show less consistency than other types of crimes, perhaps because the number of cases is smaller.

Similar tendencies have been reported generally for European countries.[12] However, in recent years, as has been pointed out by several statisticians, the crime rates are lower for the large cities in certain countries than for the small towns.[13] Watts has concluded from a careful analysis of Canadian statistics that crimes have increased during the past fifty years in Canada in proportion to the increase in density of population.[14]

In certain respects the number of crimes decreases as the distance from the large city increases. Burglaries or robberies were committed against 59.6 per cent of the stores belonging to a chain in the city of Chicago in the years 1931 and 1932, while only 29.8 per cent, or exactly one-half the proportion, were burglarized or robbed in the suburban area within 25 miles from the center of Chicago in the same period. Moreover, the proportion of stores burglarized or robbed decreased by 25-mile zones steadily until it reached 6.2 per cent in the zone 100-125 miles away from the city. If the suburban cities above 20,000 population are eliminated, the trend remains the same. Similarly, while 57.9 per cent of the stores in a chain of drug stores were burglarized or robbed in Chicago in 1927-1932, only 21.4 per cent of the stores in this chain in the suburban area within 100 miles of the city were burglarized or robbed. The banks in Chicago, East St. Louis and Wich-

---

[12] Alexander von Oettingen, *Moralstatistik,* Erlangen, 1882, p. 494; P. Sorokin and C. C. Zimmerman, *Principles of Rural-urban Sociology,* New York, 1929, Ch. 16.

[13] Hans von Hentig, "Der kriminelle Aspekt von Stadt und Land," *Monats. f. Krim. Psych.,* 23:435–436, July, 1932.

[14] R. E. Watts, "The Influence of Population Density on Crime," *Jour. Amer. Statis. Assoc.,* 26:11–20, March, 1931.

ita are less frequently burglarized or robbed than banks outside those cities but within 25 miles of the center of the city, but the rate of burglaries and robberies of banks decreases as the distance from the city increases. Thus in the period 1924-1929 19.5 per cent of the suburban banks within 25 miles of the center of Chicago were burglarized or robbed, while only 5.6 per cent of those 75 to 100 miles away were burglarized or robbed.

Lottier, in a more extensive analysis of the distribution of crimes, found that murders, assaults, rapes, and robberies known to the police in 1932–1933 decreased consistently in the commutation area of Detroit to a distance of twenty miles from the city hall, but that burglaries, auto thefts, and larcenies did not show a consistent decrease. Also he found the same crimes against the person decreasing in the entire metropolitan area of Detroit within a radius of two hundred miles, but again the crimes against property showed no such consistent decrease. He suggested that the difference in the two types of crimes may be due to the fact that crimes against the person were calculated in proportion to the number of persons, but crimes against property were not calculated in proportion to the amount of property. He found that the burglaries of stores in a chain of grocery stores decreased steadily by zones from 1.87 burglaries per store in the first five-mile zone to .07 per store in the zone 45–55 miles from the city hall, rising in the next zone to .44 per store.[15]

In view of the close association between urbanization and crime, it is to be expected that as transportation and communication have developed the rural districts have become more nearly like the urban districts and that the difference in crime rates between urban and rural districts must have decreased. In Sweden the conviction rate in rural districts steadily approached the conviction rate in city districts from 1879 to 1935. The same trend is found in France, but the opposite trend is found in Finland. An analysis of the conviction rate in Iowa for the period 1865–1925 shows that the rural rate has been consistently lower than the urban rate but has not shown any significant tendency to approach the urban rate. Consequently this expected trend is found, but is not consistent in all countries.[16]

---

[15] Stuart Lottier, "Distribution of Criminal Offenses in Metropolitan Regions," *Jour. Crim. Law and Criminol.*, 29:37–50, May, 1938.
[16] Thomas P. Monahan, *The Trend in Rural and Urban Crime*, Mss., 1937,

The proportion of male and female arrests is more nearly equal in cities than in smaller towns. Males were arrested in 1932 in Massachusetts towns of less than fifteen thousand twenty-six times as frequently as females, in proportion to the population of each, for offenses against the person, but only twelve times as frequently in cities above fifteen thousand; somewhat similar ratios were found for other types of offenses.

The excessive criminality of the city may be due either to selective migration from the country of those most likely to commit crime, or to the influence of the city life upon its residents. Both of these processes certainly occur, but the comparative importance of the two processes has not been determined. Kinberg has shown that in Sweden about half of the vagrants were born in the country, and half in the towns, but that the persons who became vagrants migrated from country to towns four times as frequently as the general population did, and migrated from towns to country less than half as frequently as the general population did.[17] Tönnies concluded from a careful study of criminal statistics in Schleswig-Holstein that

The closer a crime approaches the nature of swindling or cheating and the more regularly it is practised as a means of livelihood, the greater the probability that the criminal is born in the city. On the other hand, when the crime is casual and motivated by passion, the criminal is likely to have been born in the country.[18]

However, the personal relations in the small community are decidedly more effective as agencies of control than are the impersonal and anonymous relations in the city, and the consistent decrease in crime rates with size of community can be explained most satisfactorily in these terms.

No evident bias or selective principle in rural-urban distribution is apparent in the statistics of crimes known to the police or of crimes recorded by commercial agencies. On the other hand, ar-

---

based principally on the data in Charles N. Burrows, "Criminal Statistics in Iowa," *Univ. of Iowa Studies,* Iowa City, 1930, and Hans H. Burchardt, "Kriminalität in Stadt und Land," *Abh. d. Krim. Inst. Univ. Berlin,* 4 Folge, 4 Bd., 1 Heft, Berlin, 1936.

[17] O. Kinberg, "On So-Called Vagrancy," *Jour. Crim. Law and Criminol.,* 24:552–583, September, 1933.

[18] Ferdinand Tönnies, "Verbrechertum in Schleswig-Holstein," *Archiv. f. Soc. Wiss.,* 58:608–628, 1927.

rests, convictions, and commitments to institutions are likely to be affected by the type of community. Detection is probably easier in the small community because of personal acquaintance which leads to recognition, but the police staff is usually not so expert in the small community as in the city. Sympathy probably plays a larger part in court procedure in the small community, but corruption counterbalances this in the city court. When conviction occurs in a rural community, imprisonment is much more likely to be used than in the urban community. Thus the statistics represent a rather complex group of selective principles.

Though there is in general less crime in rural than in urban districts, recent years have witnessed some instances of very strenuous resistance to the enforcement of laws, such as the opposition in Iowa to the testing of cattle for tuberculosis, which resulted in calling out the national guard. Wars between competing dairy organizations have involved the same violent tactics that are used in city strikes.

THE NEIGHBORHOOD. It has been evident for many decades that juvenile delinquents were much more numerous in some neighborhoods than in others. Shaw and his collaborators have amplified this information and organized it in relation to the general pattern of the American city. By an analysis of twelve series of statistics of juvenile delinquents in Chicago they reached the following conclusions: First, the rates of delinquency vary widely in different neighborhoods. No boys are arrested in some areas, while in others more than one-fifth of the boys are arrested in one year. This variation has been found in each of fifteen cities which have been studied in this manner. Second, the rates are generally highest near the center of the city and decrease with the distance from the center of the city. Also, the rates are high near large industrial or commercial sub-centers of the city and decrease with distance from those sub-centers. Third, the areas which have high rates of truancy also have high rates for all juvenile court cases, for all boys' court cases, and for all adult commitments to the county jail. The areas which have high rates for boy delinquencies also have high rates for girl delinquencies. Fourth, the areas which had high rates in 1930 had high rates, also, in 1900, although in the meantime the national composition of the population of the area had changed almost completely. When Germans and Swedes occupied an area near the center of the city their children had high rates of delinquency; when they were replaced by Polish, Italian, or other national groups, the juvenile delinquency rates in the area were essentially the same. Fifth, the delinquency rate of a particular national group such as German or Polish shows the same general tendency as the delinquency rate for the entire population, namely, to be high in the areas near the center of the city and low toward the outskirts of the city. The juvenile delinquency rate of Negroes on the South Side of Chicago decreases regularly by square mile areas from 19.4 per cent in the area adjoining the center of the city to 3.5 per cent in the area five miles from the center of the city.[19]

This study has been criticized somewhat from the point of view of the reliability and organization of the data, but the conclusions are substantiated by studies in other localities by other authors. The question which has been raised most persistently, perhaps, is whether the arrests or juvenile court appearances do not give a biased measure of delinquencies because of the poverty of the families in the areas which are reported as having the highest delinquency rates. Wealth and social position, to be sure, do provide a certain degree of immunity against arrest. Also, certain national or religious groups maintain welfare agencies which take problem cases that would otherwise be referred to the police or to the juvenile court, while other national and religious groups have no agencies of this nature.[20] Even when allowance is made for these variables, the concentration seems to remain, and this concentration is in accordance with the experiences of people who suffer from delinquencies.

Though this concentration near the industrial and commercial centers is demonstrated in an adequate sample of American cities, it is not evident that the centers of concentration are the same in European and Asiatic cities. In fact, a study of residences of criminals in Peiping indicates a concentration at the gates of the city rather than in the center of the city, and much the same distribution is reported in the older European cities, although special studies of residences of delinquents have not been made in this manner. Also, in some smaller cities in America the residences of

---

[19] Clifford R. Shaw, *Delinquency Areas*, Chicago, 1929; Clifford R. Shaw and Henry D. McKay, "Report on Social Factors in Juvenile Delinquency," *Natl. Com. on Law Obs. and Enf.*, No. 13, Vol. II.

[20] Sophia M. Robison, *Can Delinquency Be Measured?* New York, 1936.

delinquents are adjacent to the railway tracks or to the "dumps" on the outskirts of the town.

Two interpretations of the concentration of delinquents near the business and industrial centers of cities have been presented. The first is in terms of social disorganization in the neighborhood. The areas of concentration in American cities and especially in Chicago, where the problem has been studied most intensively, are areas of physical deterioration, congested population, decreasing population, economic dependency, rented homes, foreign and Negro population, adult criminality, and few institutions supported by the local residents. Lawlessness has become traditional; adult criminals are frequently seen and have much prestige. Gangs have continued to exist, with changing personnel, for fifty years in some of these areas. At a particular time the gang may have a senior, junior, and midget branch. The techniques, codes, and standards are transmitted from older to younger offenders. Junking, which is one of the early manifestations of theft, is encouraged or at least condoned by the parents, as is also theft from trucks and freight cars. Delinquencies begin here at an early age, and maturity in crime is reached at an early age. Boys fourteen or fifteen years of age steal automobiles and commit robberies with sawed-off shotguns, while in other areas delinquents of the same age are committing petty thefts of which the boys in the first area would be heartily ashamed. They not only acquire skill in the execution of crimes, but also prepare for avoidance or mitigation of penalties. They know the techniques of "fixing," of intimidating witnesses, of telling plausible stories in court, of appeals to sympathy. Consequently the pressures toward delinquency there are strong and constant.

At the same time the inhibiting influences are few and weak. Parent-teacher associations do not exist nor do other community organizations which are supported principally by the people of the neighborhood. The school, the settlement, and the church are supported by people who reside elsewhere, and these agencies are for the most part formal and external to the life of the neighborhood. Contact with outside society comes principally through the movies, the newspaper, the factory, the store, and the political machine. The areas of high delinquency rates are the ones which are generally described as "in the vest pocket" of the political leaders, for there is a striking similarity between delinquency maps and maps which show majorities for straight party candidates in elections.

The residents of these neighborhoods probably know much better than do the members of the upper classes the details of the graft and dishonesty of the political machine which controls the city. Thus the American culture which they see is a culture of competition, grasping greed, deceit, graft, and immorality. They see practically nothing of the culture of co-operation, decency, and good taste, in which the boy in the older American home is immersed from infancy. Thus they come in contact with the disorganized and lawless neighborhood, and the dishonest public culture of America, but are isolated from the culture of the primary groups of the native American population.[21]

The second interpretation has been favored by psychiatrists. The argument is made that the areas in which delinquency rates are high are low-rent areas, and that a population segregated on the basis of rent-paying ability involves a selection of the constitutionally inferior. They interpret the concentration of delinquents therefore in terms of segregation or selective migration. As a matter of fact those who reside in the areas of high delinquency rates at a particular time are of three types: recent immigrants, remnants of the earlier residential group, and failures in the better residential districts who have been forced to move back into the cheaper rent areas. A small study in Minneapolis indicates that persons who committed suicide or secured divorces in that city in 1925 had in 1920 lived about the average distance from the center of the city, but during the succeeding five years had moved inward slightly toward the center of the city while the general population had moved slightly outward from the center of the city. Taft found in Danville, Illinois, that though the residences of adult criminals were concentrated near the center of the city, very few of them had been reared in that area and that most of them had been reared in families in which other members, also, were delinquent.[22] This, however, may mean merely that they had been reared in the delinquency areas of other cities.

In opposition to this interpretation of delinquency areas in terms of segregation, the most important evidence is Shaw's finding that the delinquency rate remained practically constant over a thirty-

[21] Edwin H. Sutherland, "Social Process in Behavior Problems," *Pub. Amer. Sociol. Soc.*, 26:55–61, August, 1932.

[22] D. R. Taft, "Testing the Selective Influence of Areas of Delinquency," *Amer. Jour. Sociol.*, 38:699–712, March, 1933.

year period in spite of an almost complete change in the national composition of the population. This indicates that the delinquency rate is a function of the area rather than of the type of people who reside there. Moreover, Mrs. Young has shown that when the Moloccans first settled in Los Angeles, only 5 per cent of their children appeared in the juvenile court; five years later 46 per cent, and after another decade 83 per cent of their children appeared in the juvenile court.[23] The stock in this case remained constant but the opportunities for assimilation of the culture of the American city increased, and in their neighborhood this meant assimilation of delinquency and crime. Similarly it has been reported that when a national group, such as the Greeks or Mexicans, first settles in an area of deterioration, the children do not play with the children of other residents and do not become delinquent, but as contacts develop in five to ten years the delinquency rates increase.

The location of the delinquency area near the commercial or industrial centers is evidently related to the rents in those areas. Rents are low because accommodations are poor, and the accommodations are not improved because of the expectation that the commercial and industrial activities will expand and the near-by areas will be annexed to the business sections. Consequently they are areas of deterioration, for there is little expectation of permanence or provision for the future as residence sections. When immigrants arrive they settle in these districts where the rents are low, and as soon as they accumulate a sufficiency they move outward to better residential districts. The Negroes and Italians have dispersed less than other national or racial groups and on that account are likely to continue longer as problems in delinquency.

The areas of high delinquency, however, contain many boys who are not delinquent. In an intensive study in an area with a relatively high rate less than half of the boys could be identified as past or present delinquents, and almost half were engaged in school work or occupations and showed no sympathy whatever for the delinquent boys. It is difficult to explain why some of the boys in the neighborhood do not become delinquent. One factor is the limitation on contact with delinquents, even in the most delinquent areas. A delinquent area is practically never solidly delinquent;

---

[23] Pauline V. Young, "Urbanization as a Factor in Juvenile Delinquency," *Pub. Amer. Sociol. Soc.*, 24:162–166, 1930; Pauline V. Young, *The Pilgrims of Russian-Town*, Chicago, 1932.

rather there are certain streets or parts of streets on which at a particular time the delinquents reside, and on other streets the children may associate with each other in relative isolation from the delinquents. Sometimes one or more national groups within a general residential area are isolated from the rest of the population, or a few members of one such group may be isolated within a larger area of another nationality. Also, some children are kept from frequent or intimate contact with delinquents because of their retiring, quiet, and unaggressive dispositions. Others are kept from such associations by careful and capable parents or siblings. Some of the children may refrain from delinquency because they have formed attachments at school with teachers, or at other agencies with other leaders; and their interests have been developed and their lives organized around lawful activities, so that association with delinquents is not attractive to them. Finally, whether contacts and association with delinquents develop or contacts and association with lawful agencies is often a matter of sheer chance. The consistency of the pressures in one direction is obviously significant. In Honolulu practically no delinquents were found in the heart of the Japanese colony, but in near-by areas where the population was a mixture of various nationalities many Japanese boys were delinquent.[24] Similarly, in Seattle the delinquency rate in the Japanese colony, which is in a very deteriorated area, is lower than in the best residential areas.

Another influence that may be significant is punishment. This, however, operates both for and against delinquency. All children are somewhat delinquent; some are caught and punished, and thus publicly defined as delinquents; the probable effect of this is to fix their behavior in delinquent channels. Others who are equally delinquent are not publicly defined as delinquents, and it is comparatively easy for them to slip away from delinquent behavior if it has not developed far. On the other hand, it is probable that the careers of the delinquents in some areas have not been attractive to all children in the vicinity. It is reported that of the young adults in the so-called Forty-Two Gang in Chicago, approximately one-third have been killed by the police or by private parties, one-third are in penal or reformatory institutions, and almost all the others are engaged in vicious or illegal behavior. Certainly

---

[24] Andrew W. Lind, "Some Ecological Patterns of Community Disorganization in Honolulu," *Amer. Jour. Sociol.*, 36:206–220, September, 1930.

some of the boys in the vicinity will avoid delinquency because of the outcomes of the older boys.

While the centers of delinquency are, as has been indicated, primarily the areas of transition, studies in New York City indicate that the delinquency rates are high in many areas which are isolated by such physical barriers as streams, hills, and water fronts. The New York Crime Commission reported in 1930 that "at least half of New York's delinquency areas are areas of isolation."[25] These areas of isolation also may be in transition from one type of occupancy to another, and the distinction thus far has not been made entirely clear.

THE GANG. Among the influences in a neighborhood the mutual stimulation of children in association is one of the most important. Breckinridge and Abbott, Healy, Shaw, and others have shown that delinquencies are generally committed by two or more children acting together. Shaw and McKay found by a study of the juvenile court records in Chicago that 88.2 per cent of the boys had been engaged in delinquencies in company with others, and that 93.1 per cent of those engaged in stealing had been in company with others.[26] The number of participants known to the juvenile court was two in 33.0 per cent of the cases, three in 30.9 per cent, four in 11.8 per cent, and more than four in 13.3 per cent.[27] In the more delinquent areas the boys are organized for purposes of theft in definite working groups, which they call "cliques," in which the labor is definitely divided. One boy drives the car and is known as the "wheel man," a second carries the gun and perhaps he may have, also, the duty of crashing the window of the store, while a third has the principal responsibility for entering the store. The assignment of tasks, of course, varies with the type of theft but the "wheel man" is likely to have a somewhat permanent assignment.

The term "gang" is generally used for a somewhat larger and less definite group. The definition of the gang is not clear. Inquiries among university students indicate that more than two-thirds of the men had been for longer or shorter periods during childhood members of groups which were called gangs, and that approximately

---

[25] New York Crime Commission, *Crime and the Community*, Albany, 1930, p. 122.
[26] Shaw and McKay, *op. cit.*, pp. 193–199.
[27] *Ibid.*, p. 197.

one-third of the women had had such memberships. Most of these groups were described as harmless in their activities, though inclined to mild rowdyism, and the name "gang" was applied largely in a spirit of bravado. These are essentially different from the gangs in the delinquency areas. Frequently all the boys who live on one street, or the boys of one national stock in a neighborhood, belong together for purposes of fights and are known by a common name. Frequently a portion of the boys in a neighborhood of about the same age and with somewhat similar attitudes toward delinquency or toward play have a common meeting place on a corner and engage in many common activities without any other formal organization. A stranger would not be permitted to associate with this group and certain boys in the neighborhood might be ostracized, but otherwise the group is inclusive. Some gangs are much more formally organized, with names, leaders, passwords, and slogans, and may persist with changing personnel for several decades.

A gang in this sense is a means of disseminating techniques of delinquencies, of training in delinquency, of protecting its members engaged in delinquency, and of maintaining continuity in delinquency. It is not necessary that there be bad boys inducing good boys to commit offenses. It is generally a mutual stimulation, as a result of which each of the boys commits delinquencies which he would not commit alone. The following selections show the traits of some of these gangs and something of their methods and importance.

Healy gives a history of a gang of fifteen members with which he came into contact. All of these have been delinquent in somewhat serious ways, involving court actions in most cases and commitments to institutions in many. Only four members of this gang of fifteen have turned out well, of whom two joined the navy, one continued to live in the neighborhood but quarrelled with the gang and had nothing further to do with it. Only one of the boys came from a distinctly criminalistic home and at least half of them came from good or fair homes; only two of twelve that were given mental tests had intelligence quotients lower than 80. It seemed impossible for the boy who had been a member of the gang and remained in the neighborhood not to do as the rest of them did.[28]

---

[28] Judge Baker Foundation, *Case Studies*, Series I, Nos. 2–3.

A group of high-school boys, living in the university section of a city, most of them children of members of the faculty, organized a gang and called it "Bevo Bums." Membership in the inner circle of the organization was secured only by stealing an article worth more than a dollar, and the theft had to occur in the daytime and in the presence of one of the members of the inner circle. There were fifteen or twenty members in the gang, of whom about half were in the inner circle. The nature of the gang was finally discovered; three of the members were sent to the state reformatory, and the others put on probation. Some of the members are still delinquents, but most of them are getting along quite well.[29]

For the first ten years of my life I lived on Fourteenth Place, had only one companion; was much interested in school work; made good grades and had great respect and admiration for my parents. Then we moved about three blocks away and the leader of a gang of Irish boys took me under his wing though I was Bohemian by parentage. During the course of this friendship I learned all the lessons this gang could teach me in making myself a nuisance to the community: making kerosene-soaked soot-bags for smearing clothes; breaking windows; organizing assaults and gang fights, especially on the Jews; organizing raids on back-porches and stores. The result was that I lost interest in school, my grades dropped, I began to play truant, I became sullen and disrespectful at home. I preferred the approval of this gang to the approval of my parents. Then my parents moved to a suburb where I found entirely different sentiments prevailing. With the other children of the suburb, I began to be interested again in school work, in organized athletics, in Boy Scout work and took much greater pride in my behavior at home. Every man in the gang which I left is now a "gun-toter," every one has a police record and most of them have served prison terms. The gang has the reputation of being one of the toughest in the city at present. I have no doubt that I would have continued to behave like the rest of them if we had continued to live there.[30]

It is not possible to determine the extent to which the gang produces the criminality. Many gangs are merely organizations of persons who are, as separate persons, criminalistically inclined. But the gang does, also, force recalcitrant members into crime.

---

[29] *Manuscript.*
[30] *Manuscript.*

A boy who had been seriously delinquent wrote in an account: "If the others steal and you don't steal they call you a 'scare-crow.' This name means 'yellow'; and the boy that doesn't steal, just to show that he isn't afraid, goes and steals."[31]

It is quite clear that not all gangs are criminal gangs. The gang has probably been overemphasized as a factor in crime, in view of the large number of gangs that exist without criminal records. To be left out of groups may be just as productive of delinquency as to be included in them, as the following case illustrates:

I grew up in a small town. Among the boys with whom I associated there were very distinct groups. The difference in the groups was largely a matter of age, athletic ability or general scholastic ability. There were always some boys who for some reason, either lack of athletic ability or being "dumb" in school, could not become affiliated with any group. Practically every one of the boys who belonged to no group, who were ostracized, so to speak, was taken before the authorities for delinquencies before they were sixteen years of age. Later some of them committed more serious offenses.[32]

NEIGHBORHOOD INSTITUTIONS. Individuals and institutions of moral consequence in the neighborhood may be productive of delinquency. The following case shows one individual turning many children in the direction of delinquency.

In one neighborhood in Boston there was a modern Fagan, called "The Lobster" by the children in the neighborhood. He lived in a "rickety, disreputable dwelling, facing the alley, in which was a running sewer, infested with rats and vermin. . . . For many years his ramshackle house has been the rendezvous for the boys and girls of the surrounding neighborhood, and he had displayed an aptitude that might well be termed genius, in discovering and developing the peculiar weakness of the individual child, and then twisting and further distorting that trait, till the child was prepared to enter upon a career of juvenile delinquency. With fiendish precision and ingenuity he had planned his illicit laboratory, carefully planting and fostering

[31] Judge Baker Foundation, *Case Studies*, Series I, No. I, p. 39a.
[32] *Manuscript.*

various vices and apportioning that iniquity to the individual child that best suited its characteristics. Therefore, in his gang were juvenile offenders of all types and kinds, and in proportion as they flourished and prospered, so his finances increased, as he permitted them to keep but a fraction of their peculations and ill acquired booty."[33]

The "fence," the junk-man, and other persons who are willing to purchase stolen commodities are often engaged in stimulating delinquencies. Sometimes the person who influences the standards of the children may be another child. Miss Claghorn reports that general sex immorality developed among the children in one district in New York State as a result of the arrival of a few children from one of the state homes on placement in this community. The following account was written by a middle-aged student recently regarding his own childhood. It shows the effect of one new arrival in the community upon the lives of the juvenile inhabitants.

I lived near the edge of a town of about 15,000 population. My father was a lawyer. My chief companions were boys of about my own age, one being the son of a Methodist preacher, one the son of a Baptist preacher, and one the son of the fireman at the Tuberculosis Sanitarium. The son of the Methodist preacher knew much more about the world than the rest of us did. He told us a great deal about sex matters and about Jesse James. Under his guidance we built a cave, secured some detective stories, and had what we regarded as a regular den of iniquity in the cave. Eventually, with the help of a few others, we constituted a small gang which threw rocks at the street cars, broke windows in empty houses, shot pigeons belonging to other boys, stole fruit from orchards and candy from stores and flipped the trains. We did not learn all of these things from the son of the Methodist minister; he undoubtedly learned much from the rest of us. We worked out our plans together. But our delinquent tendencies started soon after he arrived in the neighborhood and ceased soon after his father was called to another church.[34]

Injurious institutions may be located in the neighborhood without desire on the part of the members of that neighborhood. This is especially true of houses of prostitution, and the Negroes are

---

[33] Drucker and Hexter, *Children Astray*, Cambridge, 1923, p. 77.
[34] *Manuscript.*

the ones who suffer principally from such vice districts. The Chicago Commission on Race Relations in its report of 1922 stated:

The chief of police [of Chicago] in 1912 warned prostitutes that so long as they confined their residence to districts west of Wabash Avenue and east of Wentworth Avenue, they would not be disturbed. This area contained at that time the largest group of Negroes in the city, with most of their churches, Sunday Schools and societies. . . . That many Negroes live near vice districts is not due to their choice, nor to low moral standards, but to three causes: (1) Negroes are unwelcome in desirable white residence localities; (2) small incomes compel them to live in the least expensive places regardless of surroundings; while premises rented for immoral purposes bring notoriously high rentals, they make the neighborhood undesirable and the rent of other living quarters there abnormally low; and (3) Negroes lack sufficient influence and power to protest effectively against the encroachments of vice.[35]

Such institutions are likely to produce delinquency not only because of the sex standards involved, but also because the district of vice is frequently the district of professional criminals. They have their "hang-outs" and headquarters in such sections, and thus set general standards that are likely to infect the people of the neighborhood, quite apart from the sexual vice. Pool-rooms, also, are likely to be thick in such sections and to be the general rendezvous of criminals and near-criminals, where standards are set which the youth of the district can hardly resist. Also, the presence of such institutions lowers the status of the people; they have less to lose if convicted of crime; their role is necessarily one of inferiority; their self-respect consequently is lowered and crime often results.

School-stores, while relatively harmless to the adults, contribute immensely in some sections to the delinquency of the children. Many of these stores have small gambling devices, and pornographic pictures and literature. By thus causing confusion of standards they frequently undermine the morale of the juvenile part of the community.

Many of the places of recreation contribute, also, to the delinquency of the children of the neighborhood. It has been a commonplace that most of the delinquencies of children occur in the search

---

[35] Chicago Commission on Race Relations, *A Study of Race Relations and a Race Riot,* Chicago, 1922, pp. 343–344.

for recreation. The general situation, as pointed out most clearly by Jane Addams,[36] is as follows: The only recreations generally available are those furnished by commercial concerns. These concerns are interested primarily in securing a profit, and consequently offer whatever recreation produces the largest profit, regardless of the welfare of the patrons. From the point of view of the manager the recreations are what the public demands. The recreations, if of a socially undesirable character, are particularly dangerous, due to the fact that people generally lower their inhibitions during recreation; a different code generally prevails in places of recreation than in the home or business or school. The result is that many of the neighborhood dance-halls, pool-rooms, school-stores, motion picture shows, and other recreational institutions are injurious to many juveniles. Perhaps these institutions are particularly important in connection with truancy. In the country a truant goes to the woods or the river and spends a comparatively harmless day away from school. But in the city the truant must keep out of sight and that forces him into the places of commercial recreation.

On the other hand the absence of places of recreation, either public or commercial, is perhaps more important than the presence of injurious commercial institutions. Thurston found in his study of the relation between delinquency and spare time in Cleveland that 75 per cent of the delinquents studied had conduct difficulties related to spare-time activities and that these affected the delinquencies in four principal ways. Delinquencies are suggested by spare-time activities, are means of securing money for recreations, are prerequisites to entrance into certain play groups, and are logically akin to acts which are not treated as delinquent. He found, also, that delinquents had a much narrower range of recreational activities than non-delinquents and that they spent much more time in desultory pursuits. While most of the delinquents had formed their recreational habits casually or surreptitiously, 70 per cent of the persons who had developed into "wholesome citizens" reported that their recreations during school years were suggested or guided by parents, teachers, or relatives. Delinquency flourishes in neighborhoods where institutions for wholesome recreations are absent.[37]

---

[36] Jane Addams, *The Spirit of Youth and the City Streets*, New York, 1926.
[37] H. W. Thurston, *Delinquency and Spare Time*, New York, 1918, pp. 114-118.

SUGGESTED READINGS

Addams, Jane, *The Spirit of Youth and the City Streets*, New York, 1926.

Adler, Herman, Cahn, Frances, and Stuart, Johannes, *The Incidence of Delinquency in Berkeley 1928–1932*, Berkeley, 1934.

Aschaffenburg, G., *Crime and Its Repression*, Tr. by A. Albrecht, Boston, 1913, pp. 36–51.

Breckinridge, S. P., and Abbott, Edith, *The Delinquent Child and the Home*, New York, 1912.

Carpenter, Niles, "Urban Expansion and Neighborhood Change," *Social Forces*, 9:80–84, October, 1930.

Claghorn, Kate H., "Juvenile Delinquency in Rural New York," *U. S. Children's Bureau*, No. 32, 1918.

Elmer, M. C., "Maladjustment of Youth in Relation to Density of Population," *Pub. Amer. Sociol. Soc.*, 20:138–140, 1926.

Frazier, E. Franklin, *The Negro Family in Chicago*, Chicago, 1931.

Goldmark, Pauline, *West Side Studies*, Vol. I, Part I, "Boyhood and Lawlessness," New York, 1914.

Green, E. R., "The Use of Census Tracts in Analyzing the Population of a Metropolitan Community," *Jour. Amer. Stat. Assoc.*, 27:147–153, March, 1933.

Halpern, Irving W., Stanilaus, John N., and Botein, Bernard, *The Slum and Crime: A Statistical Study of the Distribution of Juvenile Delinquents in the Boroughs of Manhattan and Brooklyn, New York City*, New York, 1934.

Hayner, N. S., "Delinquency Areas in the Puget Sound Region," *Amer. Jour. Sociol.*, 39:314–328, November, 1933.

Landesco, John, "Crime and the Failure of Institutions in Chicago's Immigrant Areas," *Jour. Crim. Law and Criminol.*, 23:238–248, July, 1932.

Levin, Yale, and Lindesmith, Alfred, "English Ecology and Criminology of the Past Century," *Jour. Crim. Law and Criminol.*, 27:801–816, March, 1937.

Lind, Andrew W., "Some Ecological Patterns of Community Disorganization in Honolulu," *Amer. Jour. Sociol.*, 36:206–220, September, 1930.

Lindesmith, Alfred, and Levin, Yale, "The Lombrosian Myth in Criminology," *Amer. Jour. Sociol.*, 42:653–671, March, 1937.

Longmoor, E. S., and Young, Erle F., "Ecological Interrelationships of Juvenile Delinquency, Dependency, and Population Mobility," *Amer. Jour. Sociol.*, 41:598–610, March, 1936.

Lottier, Stuart, "Distribution of Criminal Offenses in Metropolitan Regions," *Jour. Crim. Law and Criminol.*, 29:37–50, May, 1938.

Lottier, Stuart, "Distribution of Criminal Offenses in Sectional Regions," *Jour. Crim. Law and Criminol.*, 29:329–344, September, 1938.

McGill, Helen G., "The Oriental Delinquent in the Vancouver Juvenile Court," *Sociol. and Soc. Research*, 22:428–438, May, 1938.

Perrigo, L. I., "The Community Background of Denver Criminality," *Social Forces*, 17:232–239, December, 1938.

Reckless, W. C., *Vice in Chicago*, Chicago, 1933.

Shaw, Clifford R., and McKay, Henry D., "Report on Social Factors in Juvenile Delinquency," *Natl. Com. on Law Obs. and Enf.*, No. 13, Vol. II.

Sheldon, H. D., "Problems in the Statistical Study of Juvenile Delinquency," *Metron*, 12:201–223, 1934.

Shulman, Harry M., *Youthful Offenders*, New York State Crime Commission, Albany, 1931.

Sorokin, P., and Zimmerman, C. C., *Principles of Rural-urban Sociology*, New York, 1929, Ch. 16.

Sutherland, Edwin H., *Report on an Ecological Survey of Crime and Delinquency in Bloomington, Indiana*, Indianapolis, 1937.

Taft, D. R., "Testing the Selective Influence of Areas of Delinquency," *Amer. Jour. Sociol.*, 38:699–712, March, 1933.

Thrasher, Frederic, *The Gang*, Chicago, 1937.

White, R. Clyde, "A Study of Residences and Place of Offense of Felons in Indianapolis," *Social Forces*, 10:498–509, May, 1932.

White, R. Clyde, "Delinquency Areas in Indianapolis," *Ind. Bull. Char. and Corr.*, No. 222, June, 1936, pp. 161–166.

Woods, R. A., *The City Wilderness*, Boston, 1898.

Young, Pauline V., *The Pilgrims of Russian-Town*, Chicago, 1932.

Chapter Ten

THE HOME AND FAMILY IN RELATION TO CRIME

THE FAMILY AS AN AGENCY OF CONTROL. The family is potentially a most effective agency of control. It has exclusive contact with the child during the period of greatest dependency and greatest plasticity, and continued intimate contact over a subsequent period of several years. No child is so rigidly fixed at birth that it must inevitably become a delinquent or that it must inevitably be law-abiding. The homes which are close to either extreme in efficiency produce children whose behavior can be predicted with a high degree of precision.

Even in the homes which are regarded as most efficient, trial and error is the usual method in child training. There is no real science of child rearing, and such knowledge as is developed is not available to or utilized by many families. The task of child training was comparatively simple in early society but has become extremely difficult in modern life. First, the number of home regulations has increased. The congestion of population, together with the regulation of life by the clock, make it necessary that children keep quiet at home in order that neighbors may not be disturbed. The protection of furniture, pictures, and windowpanes calls for additional regulations. The germ theory of disease and public standards of hygiene result in additional regulations within the home. Second, the persons in charge of the training of the child cannot be consistent in modern life. In preliterate life both parents were reared in the same simple, harmonious culture, as were also the grandparents, the other relatives, and the neighbors. The result was a steady and harmonious pressure upon the child which formed his character without difficulty and without conflicts. This is impossible in modern society. Parents are in conflict with each other because they have been reared in different environments, have read different books and magazines, have heard different lectures and seen different picture shows that have a bearing on child training. Parents are in conflict with grandparents, with school teachers, and with motion picture actors. Moreover, parents are in conflict, probably more than previously, for the affection of the child. In this situation the simple, harmonious pressure of consistent authorities is impossible. It is not even possible for one parent to be consistent with himself, for his policies vary with his state of fatigue, worry, hurry, and with the books he has read or the lectures he has heard, since he does not have the support of a consistent culture to keep his policies stable. Furthermore, obedience in the home depends largely upon the prestige of the parents, and this is affected not only by the consistency of the demands made by them upon a child but also by their status in the community. The poverty, the physical features, the competitive ability and comparative attainments, the language, the social status of the parents in comparison with other persons with whom the child is acquainted, may destroy the prestige of the parents and give the child a conception that he is able to determine his own behavior better than are his parents. Consequently it is very difficult in modern life to secure the obedience of a child even in homes which are above the average.

The home cannot be isolated from the general community in which it is situated and it cannot be appraised without reference to the culture in which it exists. The home of an immigrant may have served well in the old country, where it was supported by the community, but it may fail dismally when torn from its setting and transplanted to the United States. The home is customarily appraised by setting a "normal" standard of efficiency for homes and concluding that the home is the cause of delinquency if the delinquent comes from a home below this normal and that it is not the cause of delinquency if the delinquent comes from a home above this normal.

MEASURING THE IMPORTANCE OF THE HOME. Four methods have been used in the effort to determine the importance of the home as a factor in delinquency. One of these is the score-card method and is illustrated by the Whittier scale, which has a maximum grade of five on each of five items: necessities, neatness, size, parental conditions, and parental supervision. The median score of 162 delinquents on this scale was 14, while the median score of

50 non-delinquents in a control group was 22, out of a total of 25 points.[1] After a short period of use, this score-card and others designed for the same purpose seem to have disappeared, and they are certainly open to criticisms as to the comparative weighting of different items.[2]

A second method of measuring the importance of the home is a rating procedure. This is somewhat like the score card but is less mechanical. This method was used by Miss Fernald in studying the economic status, the moral standards, and the parental supervision of the childhood homes of delinquent women in New York State. These homes were rated as "very poor," "poor," "fair," "good," or "very good." The ratings for the three items combined are given in Table V, and refer to 92 delinquent women in Bedford Reformatory whose stories were verified by field investigations, and 420 delinquent women in all institutions studied, of whose stories 328 were not verified by field investigations.[3]

TABLE V

DISTRIBUTION OF RATINGS OF CHILDHOOD HOMES OF DELINQUENT
WOMEN IN NEW YORK STATE

Ratings	92 Bedford Delinquents	420 Delinquents, All Groups
	Per cent	*Per cent*
Very poor	10.9	8.3
Poor	51.1	38.1
Fair	31.5	47.1
Good	6.5	6.0
Very good	0.0	0.5

This shows 62 per cent of the homes judged to be poor or very poor; incidentally a comparison of the two columns shows how unreliable the unverified statements of prisoners are. These ratings are subject to many of the difficulties of the grading system mentioned previously, and the homes of non-delinquents have not been similarly rated. Consequently this method has not yielded a real

---

[1] J. H. Williams, "The Whittier Scale for Grading Home Conditions," *Jour. Delinq.*, 1:273–286, November, 1916; J. H. Williams, *The Intelligence of the Delinquent Boy*, pp. 167–173.

[2] W. W. Clark, "Home Conditions and Native Intelligence," *Jour. Delinq.*, 7:20–21, January, 1922; Judge Baker Foundation, *Case Studies*, Series 1, No. 9, p. 9a; National Committee for Mental Hygiene, *Report of the Mental Hygiene Survey of Cincinnati*, 1922, pp. 21–22.

[3] Mabel R. Fernald, Mary H. S. Hayes, and Almena Dawley, *A Study of Women Delinquents in New York State*, New York, 1920, p. 216.

conclusion regarding the importance of the home as a factor in delinquency.

A third method is to evaluate the influence of the home by a general study of the entire case. Healy judged that the home conditions were the major factor in delinquency in 19 per cent of the cases studied in Chicago and a minor factor in 23 per cent, and that they constituted 22 per cent of the entire number of major and minor factors.[4] This first series was not studied intensively, however, and it is extremely probable that similar figures for a second series of one thousand recidivists studied in Chicago would, if major and minor factors had been selected, have shown a much higher proportion of homes listed. This conclusion is based on a comparison of the conditions listed, without selection of important factors, which shows 23 per cent of the delinquents from homes having "extreme lack of parental control" in the first series, and 46 per cent in the second series.[5] This method is commendable, at any rate, because it does not attempt to isolate the home from all other factors, but considers it in relation to the rest of the influences. A home that would be rated as "good" by standardized criteria may be instrumental in producing delinquency in a boy who is not adapted to the home. There are many types of such lack of adaptation, but one that often appears is the case of the overgrown boys in "good" homes, who are irritated by the attempts of parents to exercise the same control over them that they would exercise over other boys of the same age but much smaller size. The result is that such boys are often delinquent at home and entirely law-abiding when they get away from home.[6]

A fourth method is the comparison by areas of delinquency rates and home conditions. Sheldon used this method in an analysis of the delinquency rates in Cleveland from 1928 to 1931. He found a correlation of $-.70$ between delinquency rates and home ownership by areas, and a partial correlation of $-.53$.[7]

TYPES OF HOMES AND OF FAMILY RELATIONS. Children who get into the juvenile courts come, in more than fair proportion, from homes that would be ranked as poor or very poor, but none of the

---

[4] William Healy, The Individual Delinquent, Boston, 1915, pp. 130–131, 134.
[5] William Healy and Augusta F. Bronner, "Youthful Offenders," Amer. Jour. Sociol., 22:50, July, 1916.
[6] Judge Baker Foundation, Case Studies, Series 1, Nos. 2–3.
[7] Henry D. Sheldon, "Problems in the Statistical Study of Juvenile Delinquency," Metron, 12:201–223, 1934.

children in some homes of this kind, and not all of the children in other homes, get into the juvenile court, while on the other hand some delinquent children come from homes that are ranked as good or very good. The homes from which delinquent children come most frequently are characterized by one or more of the following conditions: (a) other members of the family criminalistic, immoral, or alcoholic, (b) parents separated, (c) crowded housing conditions, (d) lack of parental control through ignorance, blindness or other sensory defect, or absence of one or both parents, (e) parental neglect, (f) home uncongeniality, (g) irritation at home, (h) severity and harshness of parents, (i) poverty.[8]

Another arrangement of family situations which tend to produce maladjustments of children is suggested by Blanche Weill [9] under four main heads: (a) poor personal relations, such as domination by one member, favoritism, oversolicitude, overseverity, neglect, jealousy, step-parent, interfering relative; (b) physical or mental disabilities of parent or other member of the family, such as blindness, deafness, invalidism, feeblemindedness, psychosis, or neurosis; (c) social or moral maladjustments, such as racial or religious differences, differences in conventions or standards, foster home, institution home, broken home, or an immoral situation in the home; (d) economic pressures, such as unemployment, insufficient income, mother working out.

CRIMINALITY IN THE HOME. Criminal acts of other members of the family are one of the important reasons why a particular child becomes delinquent. Burt concluded from his study in England that vice and crime were present five times as frequently in the homes from which delinquents came as in the homes of non-delinquents. The Gluecks report that 84.8 per cent of the offenders released from the Massachusetts Reformatory had been reared in homes in which there were other criminal members; also they found that 86.7 per cent of the juvenile delinquents and 80.7 per cent of the women delinquents whom they studied were from such homes. The other studies do not show criminality of other members of the family in such a large proportion of the families. Sullenger, for instance, found criminal records in other members of the family for 39.8 per cent of the delinquents studied in Omaha and for 32 per cent of those studied in Columbia, Missouri.

---

[8] Healy, op. cit., pp. 130–131, 134, 149, 286–293.
[9] Behavior of Young Children of the Same Family, Cambridge, 1928, p. 23.

These influences are in some respects cumulative. The New York Crime Commission, in a study of 251 truants, six to eight years after the record of truancy, found that 43 per cent of those who had no other charge than truancy came from families which had criminal records, that 50 per cent of those who had subsequent records of juvenile delinquency came from such families, and that 66 per cent of those subsequently charged with misdemeanors and 83 per cent of those subsequently charged with felonies were reared in such families.

Thus the homes in which delinquents are reared are in an extraordinary degree situations in which patterns of delinquency are present. These patterns do not generally result in exact copies by the children, for the parents are most frequently alcoholic, while the children steal. Rather it is the contact with the police and the courts, and the attitudes toward those agencies, which are likely to be most significant.

THE BROKEN HOME. The home broken by death, divorce, or desertion has generally been believed to be an important reason for delinquency of the children. This belief is found even in preliterate tribes, for the Ama-Xosa, a Bantu tribe in southern Africa, have a proverb, "If the old bird dies, the eggs are addled." The reports of juvenile courts and the special investigations, generally based on court records, show a somewhat wide range of broken homes among delinquents. The range is generally from 30 to 60 per cent, but the percentages tend to cluster around 40 per cent. The report of the Children Bureau on juvenile courts for 1931 showed that 37 per cent of the delinquent boys and 53 per cent of the delinquent girls were from such broken homes.

Such statistics are meaningless except in comparison with similar percentages for the non-delinquent children or for the total population. Shideler estimated that about 25 per cent of the children of the United States were reared in broken homes, and concluded that the ratio of broken homes among delinquents and the general child population is about two to one.[10] Burt arrived at about the same proportion in comparing a delinquent group with a control group in England. On the other hand, Slawson found a ratio of 1.5 to 1 in comparing the institutions for delinquents in New York State with the public school in New York City which had children

[10] E. H. Shideler, "Family Disintegration and the Delinquent Boy in the United States," *Jour. Crim. Law and Criminol.*, 8:715, January, 1918.

of the lowest social status.[11] The most careful comparison of homes in this respect has been made by Shaw and McKay. They show that the situation is more complex than is ordinarily recognized in the investigations, for, first, the percentage of broken homes of school children varies in the different national and racial groups from 16.3 for Jewish children to 46.0 for Negro children, and, second, that the percentage of broken homes increases with the age of the children from 26.2 at age ten to 38.9 at age sixteen. When delinquent boys are compared with equal numbers of school boys of the same age and national composition 42.5 per cent of the delinquent boys come from broken homes and 36.1 of the school boys, or a ratio of 1.18 to 1. This indicates that the broken home is relatively insignificant in relation to delinquency.[12] A study of delinquent girls in Chicago by identical methods yields the conclusion that 66.8 per cent of the delinquent girls and 44.8 per cent of the non-delinquent girls are from broken homes, or a ratio of 1.49 to 1, which is more significant.[13] It is possible that the difference in these two studies may be explained by the smaller number of cases in the second study, which made it necessary to limit the study to the national groups which had the largest number of girl delinquents, or by the greater effect of the broken home upon girls than upon boys. If the latter is the correct explanation it may mean that the supervision of both parents is necessary for girls more than for boys, or that there is an attachment between the girl and the missing parent (generally the father) which, when broken, is more likely to result in the delinquency of girls than of boys, or that the economic position resulting from the loss of one parent affects the girl more seriously than the boy.

Thus the evidence in general indicates that the break in the home is less important than was previously believed. Moreover, Sherman found that only about 25 per cent of the children in broken homes present problems, from the standpoint of the clinic, while 75 per cent do not present problems. Hirsch reported that the proportion of siblings who are delinquent in cases from broken homes is about the same as the proportion in cases from unbroken homes. And Campbell found that neither school achievement nor conduct was

---

[11] John Slawson, *The Delinquent Boy*, Boston, 1926, pp. 354, 366.

[12] Clifford R. Shaw and Henry D. McKay, *Social Factors in Juvenile Delinquency*, pp. 261–284.

[13] Margaret Hodgkiss, "The Influence of Broken Homes and Working Mothers," *Smith Col. Stud. in Social Work*, 3:259–274, March, 1933.

affected appreciably by a break in the home after the immediate stress had passed.[14]

According to the rather scanty evidence, delinquency is less likely to result from a break due to death than from a break due to desertion, divorce, or separation. The discord, immorality, and lack of discipline may be more significant as causes of delinquency than the subsequent break. Miss Elliott found that 67 per cent of the broken homes of delinquent girls had records of immoralities of one or both parents, as compared with 44 per cent of the unbroken homes of delinquent girls.[15] Miss Lumpkin found that 82 per cent of the broken homes and 61 per cent of the unbroken homes of delinquent girls were socially defective in the sense of being alcoholic, sexually irregular, or involving mental or physical disabilities. Two-thirds of all of the socially defective homes were broken homes.[16]

DISCIPLINE AND TRAINING. Burt has concluded that the most important difference between the situations of delinquent and non-delinquent children was in the home discipline. Defective discipline was present 6.9 times as frequently in the homes of delinquents as of non-delinquents. It appeared in the following forms: parental indifference to discipline; physical, intellectual, or moral weakness of parent which made discipline weak; lack of discipline due to absence of parent; disagreement about the control of the child; and overstrict discipline. Discipline was four times as important as poverty in the home in relation to delinquency. Glueck found unsound disciplinary methods in the homes of 70 per cent of the delinquent children and 64 per cent of the childhood homes of delinquent women.

The home discipline fails most frequently because of indifference and neglect. In many homes no effort is made to train or control the children. As soon as the children become physically able they are thrown on their own resources to direct their behavior. As a result they are brought into contact with persons outside the home

14 Baruch Sherman, "The Behavior of Children from Broken Homes," *Amer. Jour. Orthopsych.*, 5:11–18, January, 1935; N. D. M. Hirsch, *Dynamic Causes of Juvenile Crime*, Cambridge, 1937; Marian Campbell, "The Effect of Broken Home upon the Child in School," *Jour. Educ. Soc.*, 5:274–281, January, 1932.

15 Mabel A. Elliott, *Correctional Education and the Delinquent Girl*, Harrisburg, 1928, pp. 26–28.

16 Katharine D. Lumpkin, "Factors in the Commitment of Correctional School Girls in Wisconsin," *Amer. Jour. Sociol.*, 37:225–226, September, 1931.

and it is largely due to the community patterns if they become delinquent. This neglect of training by the parents is frequently accompanied by vicious and criminal behavior of the parents.

Inconsistency in disciplinary efforts is a second form of the inadequacy of the home. Miss Bingham, speaking of the homes of 500 delinquent girls in Waverly House, explained:

> From infancy on, not only are they yelled at, jerked about and hit, but even these would-be deterrents from wrongdoing are not consistently employed, An act may be severely dealt with at one time which at another may be allowed to pass without notice, or punishment out of all proportion to the delinquency may be impulsively inflicted and the effect entirely offset by an equally impulsively given threat. From early childhood these girls are conscious of injustice in their family relations, a state of things which in some natures lays strong foundations for the development of a grudge attitude and an anti-social point of view. . . . There is rarely found intelligent, sympathetic parental supervision of recreation and of friends.[17]

Miss Sheffield writes:

> The father, although a sober man, was habitually ugly and abusive at home, giving way to a violent temper and beating the children. They were much afraid of him, as was also his wife. . . . When the latter learned of her daughter's pregnancy, she appeared indifferent except to the possibility of her husband's finding it out. Overworked, with numerous children, the wife kept an untidy home, and made no attempt to cope with her husband or to control her boys and girls. The latter quarrelled among themselves. The girl in question said that her father was sometimes kind to the others, never to her, and that she therefore avoided him at all times. She could recall no show of affection from either parent during her whole childhood. . . . In such a family the father, who should have exemplified to his children the social approvals and disapprovals which their conduct would meet outside the family group, failed in his function as a representative to them of the community. Parental anger had for them no significance because it was incalculable, immoderate, prompted not by social sentiments but by nerves. Missing on the one hand the in-

---

[17] Anne T. Bingham, "Determinants of Sex Delinquency in Adolescent Girls," *Jour. Crim. Law and Criminol.*, 13:509, February, 1923.

timations of a fostering parental concern and on the other the incipient signs of social demurring, the children developed no fineness of response. They might be described as socially hard of hearing. . . . When it came to the girl's love affairs, her sex impulses showed themselves with as little subtlety as had her father's anger. Her flirtations might be described as crass. What else could be expected of a young person who had never been initiated into that common social language of quiet looks, gestures, intonations, through which most persons learn to sense the feelings of others, and to express their own various shades of approval and disapproval? The worker who knows this girl well speaks of her as being markedly "obtuse to public opinion." In the home of a foster mother she would hang around listening to conversations that did not concern her, and could not seem to comprehend the fact that she was not wanted. She was entirely untroubled and unashamed at the prospect of bearing a child out of wedlock and for a long time could not seem to grasp the fact that with such a child her standing was different from that of a married woman.[18]

The immigrant family has an extremely difficult task. Parental control frequently breaks down because of ignorance regarding conditions in American cities and because the children may outstrip the parents in securing knowledge on this subject. The result is that the children may look on their parents with contempt. The following cases illustrate how this occurs:

A boy thirteen years of age, son of Russian immigrants, had become a truant, a drug peddler, and a notorious criminal. A social worker asked the mother of the boy whether she had tried to make the home attractive for the boy. The mother replied:

"I did, I did. . . . I did everything I could to keep them home, and let them turn the house upside down. But they refused to bring their friends to the house. They said they were ashamed of us because we were greenhorns and couldn't speak like American people. . . . I did all I could to learn how to speak English—I even went to night school—but the language wouldn't come to me—maybe I'm too old, and—you can't imagine how awful it is when parents and children do not speak the same language." [19]

[18] Ada E. Sheffield, "Clue Aspects in Social Case Work," *Survey,* 47:241–243, November 12, 1921. Reprinted by permission.
[19] S. Drucker and M. B. Hexter, *Children Astray,* p. 74. Reprinted by permission of Harvard University Press, publishers.

Six boys robbed and, apparently without any motive, killed a truck gardener who was driving into Chicago. Two of the boys were under seventeen years of age, another under nineteen, and two between the ages of twenty-one and twenty-four. The general family situations are described thus:

"All but one of them had been born in the old country and brought to America when quite young; the parents were laboring people without education or privilege; the fathers were absorbed in the dreary grind of earning food and shelter for their large families in this new land where work is none too plentiful and where there are so many problems for the immigrant; the mothers were absorbed in the care of their younger children. One mother said, 'I have had fourteen children and have had no life outside my kitchen. You see how it is. How could I see where my boy was going?' All of the mothers admitted that they asked no questions about the work their boys were doing nor the conditions under which it was done, whether they found the work congenial or distasteful. The only question was, 'How much money on Saturday?' The father of two of the boys said, less than a week before the day set for the execution, 'I don't care what they do with them; they may hang them or shoot them; it is nothing to me.' On being asked how he, the father, could speak so brutally of his own sons, he answered with a shrug of his shoulders, 'Neither of those boys brought home a penny.'

"In one of the other homes where eleven people lived in two dark, unsanitary, rear basement rooms, the old father, a rag picker by profession, recounting the circumstances of the crime, told how the other boys had urged his son Philip to go out with them on the night of the murder. The boy left the house saying he would return soon. In the morning the old father, coming from the bedroom into the kitchen, 'looked all around on the floor, but Philip was not there,' an unconscious commentary upon Philip's sleeping accommodations. The mother of the youngest child, crying over the tub as she bent to the family washing, said that he had 'always been a good boy at home.' . . . When asked where her boy had spent his evening, she replied, 'Maybe at the corner over there; how should I know? He never tells me.' "[20]

As a result of such home conditions in immigrant families the children are often thrown upon their own resources or the resources

---

[20] From Louise H. Bowen, *Safeguards for City Youth,* pp. 108–109. By permission of The Macmillan Company, publishers.

of the very disorganized communities in which they live. Thomas and Znaniecki state that because the immigrants do not have the support of the larger family and of the community as they did in the home country they cannot control their children.[21]

GENERAL PROCESSES. From the preceding analysis of home conditions in relation to delinquency three principal processes appear. First, a child may assimilate within the home by observation of parents or other relatives the attitudes, codes, and behavior patterns of delinquency. He then becomes delinquent because he has learned delinquency at home. Second, a child may be driven from the home by unpleasant experiences and situations or withdraw from it because of the absence of pleasant experiences, and thus cease to be a functioning member of an integrated group. He may run away from home, or remain relatively isolated from the family even though he continues to eat his meals and to sleep in the home. He does not on this account necessarily become a delinquent. The important element is that this isolation from the family is likely to increase his association with delinquency, which is the primary factor in delinquency. Third, the home may fail to train the child to deal with community situations in a law-abiding manner. This failure may be due either to complete neglect of training or to over-protection. In either case he fails to develop inhibitions against delinquency, which are supposed to be developed in the family life.

Most of the factors which have been found in the preceding analysis can be interpreted in relation to the second and third of the processes which have been outlined. The fact that the mother works away from home, that the father is dead, that the housing facilities are very inadequate, that the parents are unconcerned with the behavior of the child or are extremely harsh in their discipline—all of these may fall within the framework of the second and third processes. And in both of those processes the active factor is the assimilation of delinquency from association with delinquents. These two processes are important because they increase the probability that a child will come into intimate contact with delinquents and will be attracted by delinquent behavior. If the family is in a community in which there is no pattern of theft, the children do not steal, no matter how much neglected or how unhappy they may be at home. There are isolated regions in which the parents neglect

[21] *The Polish Peasant*, Vol. I, p. 711.

and abuse their children, are in dire poverty, are frequently intoxicated, and in many respects are vicious; in spite of such home conditions the children of the community may engage in practically no theft.

A fourth process may operate, although it is probably not very important. This is the persistence in the general community of habits of disobedience formed in the home. This is frequently presented as an important factor in delinquency, either in commonsense terms of the failure of the child to develop habits of obedience or in psychiatric terms of the grudge against any authority. Both of these views assume that there is a generalized attitude toward authority. That is questionable, for disobedience develops in a large proportion of the children in the modern home, due to the impossible demands made on them and to the inconsistency in the enforcement of home regulations. It is difficult to determine the extent to which such transference occurs. Children who are very disobedient at home are frequently well behaved in the home of a neighbor or in school. It is possible to conclude on the basis of very scanty evidence that there is no respect for authority of a generalized nature, but that respect for authority is built up in each situation.

Another process is frequently suggested, namely tensions and emotional disturbances in the home. The psychiatrists and psychoanalysts have recently brought this theory into prominence. The psychoanalysts have emphasized the oedipus complex as the principal source of delinquency. This complex consists of hatred of the father because of rivalry for the affections of the mother; because the father is the authority in the home, the boy transfers hatred of authority when he becomes active in the outside community. To persons who are not psychoanalysts this appears to be an unjustified extension of subtle symbolism. However, this does not deny the existence and importance of tensions in the home. Favoritism, rejections, insecurity, harshness, rigidity, irritation, and many other conditions within the home affect many children. This view has resulted in the proposition: "The problem child is a child with problems." The question regarding this interpretation of delinquency is, How do these emotional disturbances produce delinquency? Obviously, they may produce delinquency through the second and third processes described above, that is, either through isolation from the family or failure of the family to train and guide the child so that the child may be protected against contacts with attractive delinquents. Emotional disturbances at home may drive the child away from home and into contact with delinquents. Slawson found that 54 per cent of the delinquents he studied had run away from home, as compared with 4 per cent of the school children on a low economic level.[22] A girl who finds no affection at home may find affection in illicit relations with boys. But a child does not necessarily become delinquent because he is unhappy. That is, it is probable that the tensions and emotional disturbances are important within the framework of the processes described previously rather than as independent processes.

DELINQUENT AND NON-DELINQUENT SIBLINGS. It might be expected that all children in the homes in which the processes described above are operating would become delinquent. As a matter of fact, many of the children in such homes are not delinquent. Healy and Bronner have reported three series of juvenile delinquents of both sexes in regard to this.[23] Each of these series consists of one thousand juvenile delinquents and each shows the proportion of siblings who were delinquent and the proportion who were not delinquent. For instance, in 372 two-child families in which one child was delinquent, the other child was delinquent in 20 per cent of the families, and the character was not known in 2 per cent. In 333 six-child families in which one child was delinquent, 12 per cent of the siblings were known delinquents, 82 per cent non-delinquents, and 6 per cent unknown. This shows a relatively small proportion of the siblings delinquent, and indicates that the home as such is not a completely determining factor in behavior. It is probable, however, that some of the siblings were too young to be involved in delinquencies and the proportion delinquent might be increased if the figures were restricted to children above the age of ten years.[24] Moreover, the home changes greatly in some cases by reason of the death of a parent, a change in economic status, formation or discontinuance of habits of alcoholism by parents, or

---

[22] John Slawson, *op. cit.*, p. 256.

[23] William Healy and Augusta F. Bronner, *Delinquents and Criminals*, New York, 1926, p. 104.

[24] How little it is possible to depend on published series of case studies for information of this kind may be illustrated by the fact that only 3.6 per cent of the siblings old enough to be delinquent in the Judge Baker Case Studies were reported as delinquent; 61.5 per cent of such siblings were reported delinquent by S. Drucker and M. B. Hexter, in *Children Astray*, Cambridge, 1923.

other conditions; thus the home of one child is not the same as the home of another child in the same family.[25] Fourth, parental affection and supervision vary considerably in a home at a particular time for the different children, so that a child may not, on that account, have the same home as his brother.[26] Finally, many of the reasons why an individual becomes a delinquent or refrains from delinquency are adventitious. It is not necessary to believe that every turning point in the life of an individual is a choice directed by a deep-seated and fundamental trait of personality. Many a choice is made because someone else made another choice a few minutes earlier or a few minutes later than he might otherwise have done. Such adventitious factors are probably of little importance in a consistent and highly organized culture, but in the complex and pluralistic culture of modern life they may assume great importance.

ORDER OF BIRTH IN RELATION TO CRIME. Many studies have been made of the relation of order of birth to achievement, intellectual ability, psychopathy, aggressiveness, and other traits of personality and of behavior. The earlier studies generally showed inferiority of the first-born child, but the later studies have reduced this difference, due principally to an improvement in the statistical procedures. The result is that it is now doubtful whether order of birth has any association with traits of personality or behavior. Two explanations have been offered for the difference which has been found or has been assumed. One of these is biological and is to the effect that the first-born child is inferior because of the greater difficulty of his birth process or because of the sexual immaturity of the parents. The other explanation is in terms of social relations and includes undeveloped skill of parents in training the child, oversolicitude of parents because of the newness of the experience, and conflict for the child in passing from a favored position as an only child to a subordinate position when a second child is born.

Recently studies of delinquents have been made from this same point of view, though most of the studies have been confined to very small numbers of cases. Levy in New York and Goodenough and Leahy in Minneapolis have found the first-born child delin-

---

[25] For an illustration, see Clifford R. Shaw, *The Jack-Roller*.
[26] For an illustration, see Clifford R. Shaw, *The Natural History of a Delinquent Career*.

quent in a disproportionately large number of cases,[27] while Rosenow has questioned the validity of the conclusion from the statistical point of view.[28] Miss Parsley studied 361 delinquent girls in comparison with an equal number of non-delinquent girls of the same ages and nationalities, and found no significant difference in regard to the proportions of first-born, but did find that a significantly smaller proportion of the non-delinquents were youngest children. This indicates that the youngest child is less likely to become delinquent, and this conclusion applies equally to the native white and the Polish groups, but no significant difference was found in the Negro cases. In general, there are variations of such size and types that a conclusion on the significance of ordinal position seems unjustified.

Sletto has made an investigation of a different nature on this topic. He compared 1,145 juvenile delinquents in Minneapolis with an equal number of school children matched for age, sex, and sibling position. His conclusion was that the order of birth, when taken in connection with the sex distribution of siblings, is statistically significant in relation to juvenile delinquency. The delinquency ratio of the older boys was greater than that of younger boys, and of older girls greater than that of younger girls in comparison with school children of the same sex, age, and sibling position. Moreover it was found that girls who have brothers and no sisters have a higher delinquency ratio than girls who have sisters and no brothers. Apparently a girl with no sibs of the same sex is likely to approach the delinquency standards of the brothers. A boy who has sisters and no brothers does not show a consistent tendency of an analogous kind.[29] Sletto's study, in general, justifies a conclusion that social relations are affected by the ordinal position and that the social relations are important as factors in delinquency.

The "only child" is generally supposed to be extraordinarily prone to delinquency. The studies which have been made do not yield a

---

[27] John Levy, "A Quantitative Study of Behavior Problems in Relation to Family Constellation," *Amer. Jour. Psychiat.*, 10:654, 1931; Florence Goodenough and Alice Leahy, "The Effect of Certain Family Relationships upon the Development of Personality," *Pedagog. Sem.*, 34:69, March, 1927; Mannie Parsley, "The Influence of Ordinal Position and Size of Family," *Smith Col. Stud. in Social Work*, 3:274–283, March, 1933.

[28] Curt Rosenow and Anne P. Whyte, "The Ordinal Position of Problem Children," *Amer. Jour. Orthopsych.*, 1:430–434, July, 1931.

[29] R. F. Sletto, "Sibling Position and Juvenile Delinquency," *Amer. Jour. Sociol.*, 39:657–669, March, 1934.

conclusive general answer. To cite only a few of the studies, Bohannon,[30] Burt,[31] Slawson,[32] and Parsley[33] found a disproportionate
amount of delinquency among "only children," while Levy,[34]
Goodenough and Leahy,[35] and Ward[36] did not find this dispropor-
tion. Those who believe that the only child is especially likely to
become delinquent explain that this is due to the oversolicitude and
the lack of opportunity to develop adjustments to equals during
early age.

On the other hand, it is frequently asserted that the child in the
large family is more likely to become delinquent than the child
in the small family. Slawson,[37] Blatz and Botts,[38] and Levy[39] have
found slight tendencies for problem children to come in disproportionate numbers from large families. In so far as this conclusion is
reached, it is interpreted as due to the poverty and the immigrant
stock of these families rather than as due to the number of children
in itself.

INSTITUTIONAL AND FOSTER CHILDREN. Miss Bingham found
that of 500 delinquent girls in Waverly House in New York City,
100 had been in orphanages or other child-caring institutions for
periods ranging from one to twelve years.[40] Slawson found that
13.3 per cent of the delinquents studied by him had been at one
time in an orphan asylum, as compared with 1.8 per cent of an
unselected group of New York City school children.[41] Thais reports
that of 84 foster children who had reached the age of eighteen who
had never been in orphanages, only 18 per cent had not made
satisfactory adjustments, while of 96 children of the same kind who

---

[30] E. W. Bohannon, "The Only Child in a Family," *Pedagog. Sem.*, 5:306–
310, 1898.

[31] Cyril Burt, *The Young Delinquent*, London, 1925, pp. 91–92.

[32] John Slawson, *op. cit.*, pp. 398–409.

[33] Mannie Parsley, "The Influence of Ordinal Position and Size of Family,"
Smith Col. Stud. in Social Work, 3:278–279, March, 1933.

[34] John Levy, "A Quantitative Study in Behavior Problems in Relation to
Family Constellation," *Amer. Jour. Psychiat.*, 10:654, 1931.

[35] Florence Goodenough and Alice Leahy, "The Effect of Certain Family
Relationships upon the Development of Personality," *Pedagog. Sem.*, 34:69,
March, 1927.

[36] Anne Ward, "The Only Child," *Smith Col. Stud. in Social Work*, 1:41–65
January, 1930.

[37] John Slawson, *op. cit.*, pp. 398–409.

[38] W. E. Blatz and E. A. Botts, "Behavior of Public School Children,"
Pedagog. Sem., 34:556–582, December, 1927.

[39] John Levy, *op. cit.*, p. 651.

[40] Anne T. Bingham, "Determinants of Sex Delinquency in Adolescent Girls,"
Jour. Crim. Law and Criminol., 13:505, February, 1923.

[41] John Slawson, *op. cit.*, p. 379.

had been in orphanages for five years or more 34 per cent had not made satisfactory adjustments.[42] This difference, however, may be attributed to the fact that those who spent this much time in orphanages were not taken into private homes at as early an age. The institutional child does not acquire the feeling of security and self-esteem which comes from membership in a strong primary group, and at the same time is thrown with few inhibitions into association with delinquents and patterns of delinquency.[43]

Foster children are often believed to be more inclined toward delinquency than are other children. The truth of this belief cannot be determined, for there is no good comparison of the two groups on this point and it would be extremely difficult to select adequate samples for such comparisons. Armstrong reports that 27.5 per cent of a group of runaway boys had step-parents, as compared with 12.8 per cent of all children before the same clinic in 1929.[44] The belief in the criminal tendency of foster children is based, probably, on occasional observations of foster children who become delinquent and on *a priori* beliefs. The one solid fact which points to a conclusion is that children who are placed in a home at an early age adjust more satisfactorily than those placed at a later age.[45] Those who are placed at an early age are more nearly in the same environment as the ordinary children, but even these children are likely to be somewhat differentiated from other children.

MARITAL STATUS. The marital status of the adult person appears to have considerable significance in relation to crime. In 1923 the rate of commitment to prisons and reformatories per 100,000 population of the same marital status, was lowest for the married, next to the lowest for widowed, next for the single, and highest for the divorced. These ranks, however, are affected in part by age. Divorced persons have the highest commitment rate at each age, and this is true for each of the sexes. Divorced males twenty to twenty-four years of age have a rate of commitment 6.2 times as high as single males of the same age and 6.7 times as high as married males of the same age, while divorced females of that age have a rate 10.4 times as high as single females and 9.3 times as high as married females of the same age. Married males have a

---

[42] Sophie V. Thais, *How Foster Children Turn Out*, Albany, 1924, p. 151.
[43] Alberta S. Guibord, "The Handicap of the Dependent Child," *Survey*, 44:614–616, August 16, 1920.
[44] Clairette P. Armstrong, *660 Runaway Boys*, Boston, 1932, p. 73.
[45] Thais, *op. cit.*, p. 114.

lower commitment rate than single males in all age groups except fifteen to nineteen; the rate is only slightly lower in the age twenty to twenty-four, but is significantly lower in later ages. For females, however, the married women have a higher commitment rate at each age except twenty-five to thirty-four but the difference is not very great except in the age group fifteen to nineteen. These statistics, which are based on commitments to prisons in the United States, are in substantial agreement with the German statistics based on convictions. Prinzing found that in 1883–1892 married men had fewer convictions than unmarried men at each age except eighteen to twenty-one and twenty-one to twenty-five and for each of the principal crimes, while married women had a higher rate of convictions than unmarried women at each age and for most of the principal crimes. More recently Krille has reported that married women have a lower crime rate in Germany than unmarried women until the age of forty.[46] The statistics from European countries generally show that divorced persons have a considerably higher rate of crimes than married or single persons. It has been found, also, that married persons succeed on parole better than persons of any other marital class, and that those who are compatibly married succeed better than those incompatibly married.[47] Gillin made a study of 172 prisoners in comparison with their non-criminal brothers and found that the prisoners had the following characteristics more frequently than their brothers: single or divorced; did not have harmonious relations with wife; did not come from same nationality, religion, educational, or economic status as wife.[48] It is not possible, however, to conclude from these statistics that marital status is a direct causative factor. One may judge *a priori* that it has some influence in the direction indicated, but both the marital status and the criminality are probably affected by other variables in the situation.

SUGGESTED READINGS

Ackerson, L., *Children's Behavior Problems*, Chicago, 1931.
Armstrong, Clairette P., *Six Hundred and Sixty Runaway Boys*, Boston, 1932.

---

[46] Hans Krille, *Weibliche Kriminalität und Ehe.*
[47] Sheldon and Eleanor T. Glueck, *Five Hundred Criminal Careers*, New York, 1930, p. 269.
[48] John L. Gillin, "Backgrounds of Prisoners in the Wisconsin State Prison and of Their Brothers," *Amer. Sociol. Rev.*, 2:204–212, April, 1937.

Blatz, W. E., and Botts, E. A., "Behavior of Public School Children," *Pedagog. Sem.*, 34:556–582, December, 1927.

Breckinridge, S. P., and Abbott, E., *The Delinquent Child and the Home,* New York, 1912.

Burt, Cyril, *The Young Delinquent,* London, 1925.

Campbell, Marian W., "The Effect of the Broken Home upon the Child in School," *Jour. Educ. Sociol.*, 5:274–281, January, 1932.

Glueck, Sheldon and Eleanor T., *Five Hundred Criminal Careers,* New York, 1930.

Goodenough, Florence, and Leahy, Alice, "The Effect of Certain Family Relationships upon the Development of Personality," *Pedagog. Sem.*, 34:69, March, 1927.

Haggerty, M. E., "The Incidence of Undesirable Behavior in Public School Children," *Jour. Educ. Res.*, 12:102–122, September, 1925.

Healy, William, *The Individual Delinquent,* Boston, 1915.

Healy, William, and Bronner, Augusta F., *New Light on Delinquency,* New Haven, 1936.

Hodgkiss, Margaret, "The Influence of Broken Homes and Working Mothers," *Smith Col. Stud. in Social Work,* 3:259–274, March, 1933.

Levy, John, "A Quantitative Study of Behavior Problems in Relation to Family Constellations," *Amer. Jour. Psychiat.*, 10:637–654, 1931.

Parsley, Mannie, "The Influence of Ordinal Position and Size of Family," *Smith Col. Stud. in Social Work,* 3:274–283, March, 1933.

Rosenow, Curt, and Whyte, Anne P., "The Ordinal Position of Problem Children," *Amer. Jour. Orthopsych.*, 1:430–434, July, 1931.

Shaw, Clifford R., and McKay, Henry D., "Report on Social Factors in Juvenile Delinquency," Natl. Com on Law Obs. and Enf., No. 13, Vol. II, Ch. 9.

Slawson, John, *The Delinquent Boy,* Boston, 1926.

Sletto, R. F., "Sibling Position and Juvenile Delinquency," *Amer. Jour. Sociol.*, 39:657–669, March, 1934.

Thais, Sophie V., *How Foster Children Turn Out,* Albany, 1924.

Thomas, W. I., and Znaniecki, F., *The Polish Peasant,* New York, 1927.

Ward, Anne, "The Only Child," *Smith Col. Stud. in Social Work,* 1:41–65, 1930.

Weill, Blanche, *Behavior of Young Children of the Same Family,* Cambridge, 1928.

White House Conference, *The Delinquent Child,* New York, 1932.

Chapter Eleven

OTHER INSTITUTIONS IN RELATION TO CRIME

ECONOMIC AND OCCUPATIONAL CONDITIONS. The effect of economic and occupational conditions may be considered from three points of view: first, the economic status of the parents of juvenile delinquents; second, the economic status of the offenders themselves; and third, the general effects of the economic system.

The evidence regarding the effect of economic status of parents upon behavior of their children is not unanimous but indicates that juvenile delinquents probably come in undue proportions from the homes of the lower economic classes. Breckinridge and Abbott in their study of juvenile delinquency in Chicago found that 44.7 per cent came from homes that were very poor from the economic standpoint, and 34.3 per cent from homes that were poor, a total of 79.0 per cent.[1] Fernald found that 41.4 per cent of the women delinquents studied in New York State had been reared in very poor homes, and 45.0 per cent in poor homes, a total of 86.4 per cent.[2] The families of one-fourth of the delinquents in Connecticut were registered with charitable societies, and of 45 per cent in Omaha.[3] These studies, however, do not provide comparisons with the total population, and the significance of poverty is therefore not revealed.

The following are a few of the studies in which comparisons have been made between offenders and other groups in respect to economic status. Slawson found no significant relation between

---

[1] S. P. Breckinridge and E. Abbott, *The Delinquent Child and the Home*, New York, 1912, pp. 70–72.

[2] Mabel R. Fernald, Mary H. S. Hayes, and Almena Dawley, *A Study of Women Delinquents in New York State*, New York, 1920, p. 210.

[3] W. B. Bailey, "Children before the Courts in Connecticut," *U. S. Children's Bureau*, No. 43, p. 80; E. T. Sullenger, *Social Determinants of Juvenile Delinquents*, New York, 1936, p. 191.

delinquency and the number of rooms per family in a comparison of delinquent and non-delinquent groups of approximately the same economic status in New York City.[4] Mrs. Robison has reported that the delinquency rate was found to be as high in New York City among children in families with incomes more than $50 per week as in families with incomes of less than $25 per week.[5] Sorenson found no important difference in economic groups regarding the proportion of children who were problems at school in Minneapolis.[6] It is significant that the last two studies were not confined to juvenile court cases.

The studies have generally shown a distinct difference between economic groups. Caldwell reports that judged by the Barr occupational rating scale 33.4 per cent of the parents of boy delinquents and 52.7 per cent of the parents of girl delinquents studied in Wisconsin institutions were unskilled, compared with 11.8 per cent of the employed population of the state, and that 32.7 per cent of the parents of boy delinquents and 19.4 per cent of the parents of girl delinquents were semi-skilled in comparison with 39.6 per cent of the employed population of the state.[7] Thomas reports that the average score of 205 delinquents in Detroit on the Sims socioeconomic rating scale was 10.5 and of 375 non-delinquents was 14.5.[8] Gillin found that more prisoners had full-time jobs before the age of fourteen than did their non-criminal brothers.[9] Sheldon found coefficients of 0.69, 0.75, and —0.58 between unemployment and delinquency by census areas in Cleveland.[10] Shaw and McKay report that the areas in which delinquency rates are high are also areas in which dependency rates are high. The coefficient of correlation by square mile areas between delinquency rates and rates of financial aid to families by the United Charities and the Jewish Charities was +.74, between delinquency cases and de-

[4] John Slawson, *The Delinquent Boy,* Boston, 1926, pp. 418–424.

[5] Sophia M. Robison, "The Apparent Effect of the Factors of Race and Nationality on the Registration of Behavior as Delinquent in New York City in 1930," *Pub. Amer. Sociol. Soc.,* Vol. XXVII, pp. 37–44, 1933.

[6] Herbert Sorenson, *Some Factors in School Organization,* Dissertation, Univ. of Minn., 1928.

[7] M. G. Caldwell, "The Economic Status of Families of Delinquent Boys in Wisconsin," *Amer. Jour. Sociol.,* 37:233, September, 1931.

[8] C. Thomas, "Results of the Sims Socio-Economic Rating Scale," *Amer. Jour. Orthopsych.,* 1:527–539, October, 1931.

[9] John L. Gillin, "Backgrounds of Prisoners in the Wisconsin State Prison and of Their Brothers," *Amer. Sociol. Rev.,* 2:204–212, April, 1937.

[10] Henry D. Sheldon, "Problems in the Statistical Study of Juvenile Delinquency," *Metron,* 12:201–223, 1934.

pendency cases in the juvenile court was +.82, and between delinquency cases and mothers' pension cases was +.63.[11] The homes of 26.7 per cent of the white delinquents in Washington were congested, as compared with 5.5 per cent of the homes of white school children.[12]

Though association between delinquency and poverty is generally found in these studies, the interpretations differ. The argument is made that delinquency of children and poverty are associated because both are produced by the same underlying causes. Drunkenness of parents is asserted to be a factor underlying both the low economic status of the family and the delinquency of the children. Levy has concluded by methods of correlation that intelligence is much more important than economic conditions in problems of children.[13] Goring reached essentially the same conclusion in his study of English prisoners.

Poverty, at any rate in the modern city, generally means segregation in low-rent areas, where people are isolated from many of the cultural influences and forced into contact with many of the degrading influences, and in this respect is very different from poverty in a small town or on the frontier. In the city poverty generally means a low social status, with little to lose, little to respect, little to be proud of, little to sustain the efforts at self-advancement. It means bad housing conditions, lack of sanitation, and lack of attractive community institutions. It may mean that both parents are away from home during most of the waking period of the children, and are burdened with fatigue and irritation while they are home. It generally means that the child is withdrawn from school at the earliest permitted age, to enter mechanical and unskilled labor which is not interesting or remunerative and which offers few opportunities for advancement. It is surprising in view of these conditions that any of the poor people remain law-abiding.

Some studies have been made of the effect of occupations upon the children engaged in them. Occupations of children are, according to these studies, conducive to delinquency. About 38 per cent

[11] Clifford R. Shaw and Henry D. McKay, "Report on Social Factors in Juvenile Delinquency," *Natl. Com. on Law Obs. and Enf.*, No. 13, Vol. II, pp. 74–79.

[12] *The Relation between Housing and Delinquency*, Fed. Emerg. Adm. of Pub. Works, Housing Division, Research Bull., No. 1, Washington, D. C., 1936.

[13] John Levy, "A Quantitative Study of the Relationships between Intelligence and Economic Status as Factors in the Etiology of Children's Behavior Problems," *Amer. Jour. Orthopsych.*, 1:152–162, January, 1931.

of the delinquents in the Manhattan Children's Court in 1916 had been employed prior to court proceedings, while only about 10 per cent of the children in Manhattan in general were employed. The working boys committed more serious offenses and had a higher rate of recidivism, for 43 per cent of the working boys were recidivists, as compared with 28 per cent of the boys who were not working.[14] The Commission on Woman and Child Wage-earners concluded that the proportion of working children who become delinquent is about four times as great as the proportion of children not working. The ratio is even higher than this in several cities for boys engaged in street trades.[15] The newspapers probably more than any other agency in this way contribute to modern criminality, for newsboys have exceptionally high rates of delinquency.[16] The work of the servant girl is conducive to sexual immorality and finally to prostitution, and much the same is true of waitresses.[17]

The statistics of juvenile delinquents which have been presented in the preceding paragraphs are likely to be somewhat biased, for it is highly probable that of two children, one poor and the other well-to-do, apprehended in the same offense, the poor child would be arrested and referred to the juvenile court for action, while the other would be referred to his parents and no official record made. This is true, especially, of the less serious offenses, but intimate acquaintance with the poorer sections of a city generally convinces one that the delinquencies there are more numerous and more serious than in the higher rent areas.

The effect of economic and occupational conditions upon the criminality of adults has been studied principally by comparing the distribution of previous occupations among prisoners and in the general population. Such comparisons shows a disproportionately large representation in prisons from the unskilled and semi-skilled occupations, but the statistics are relatively unreliable and justifiable comparisons are difficult. Furthermore, it is probable that

---

[14] Ruth McIntyre, "Child Labor and Juvenile Delinquency," *Jour. Delinq.*, 3:95–114, May, 1918.

[15] United States, "Report on Woman and Child Wage-earners," *Juvenile Delinquency and Its Relation to Employment*, 1910, Vol. VIII, p. 37; Nettie P. McGill, "Children in Street Work," U. S. Children's Bureau, Pub. 182, 1928, p. 3.

[16] Louise H. Bowen, *Safeguards for City Youths*, New York, 1914, p. 218.

[17] W. I. Thomas, *The Unadjusted Girl*, Boston, 1923, p. 118; Frances Donovan, *The Woman Who Waits*, Boston, 1920; "Child Labor: Facts and Figures," *U. S. Children's Bureau*, Pub. 197, 1930, pp. 34–35.

arrests, convictions, and commitments to prisons are distinctly biased against the unskilled and semi-skilled classes because of their inability to resist arrest and conviction.

The occupation is significant in relation to the type of crime committed. An unskilled laborer will not have many opportunities to commit embezzlement, but bankers, brokers, and lawyers will have such opportunities. This is exactly what is found in the distribution of the charges on which any occupational group is convicted. Of the physicians committed to Sing Sing Prison in 1923–1927 31 per cent were convicted of homicide, probably committed in connection with abortions. Similarly, 84 per cent of the preachers who were committed during this period were convicted of sexual offenses, which was greatly in excess of the proportion of sexual offenses in any other occupational group.[18]

The effect of business cycles on crime rates, regardless of the age of the offenders, has been studied by statistical methods for several decades. This information has been analyzed by Bonger, Van Kan, von Mayr, Roesner, Sellin, and others.[19] Bonger believes that these studies justify a conclusion that the economic organization is the fundamental explanation of crime, while the others draw more limited conclusions, especially that there is a significant association between poverty and crimes against property and between prosperity and alcoholism. Dorothy Thomas found a negative correlation of .25 between economic prosperity and all indictable crimes in Great Britain for the period 1857–1913, with a positive correlation of .34 between prosecutions for drunkenness and prosperity.[20] Ogburn found a negative correlation of .35 between convictions in the courts of record in New York State and the business cycle in the period 1870–1920.[21] Phelps found a positive correlation of .33 between poverty and crime in Rhode Island in the period

---

[18] Lewis E. Lawes, *Life and Death in Sing Sing*, Garden City, N. Y., 1928, p. 43. See, also, on this topic in general, S. Türkel, "Criminografia de las profesiones," *Rev. de Crim., Psiq., y Med. Leg.*, 19:703–713, November, 1932.

[19] W. A. Bonger, *Criminality and Economic Conditions*, Boston, 1916; Joseph Van Kan, *Les causes economiques de la criminalité*, Paris, 1903; Georg von Mayr, *Statistik und Gesellschaftslehre*, Vol. III, Tübingen, 1917; Ernst Roesner, *Der Einfluss von Wirtschaftslage, Alkohol und Jahreszeit auf die Kriminalität*, Berlin, 1931; Thorsten Sellin, *Crime in the Depression*, New York, 1937, Chs. 2–3.

[20] Dorothy S. Thomas, *Social Consequences of the Business Cycle*, New York, 1925, pp. 143–144.

[21] W. F. Ogburn, "Business Fluctuations as Social Forces," *Jour. Social Forces*, 1:73–78, January, 1923.

1898–1926.[22] In general these correlations are large enough and consistent enough to indicate that serious crimes increase in periods of depression, and that drunkenness increases in prosperity.

One of the most intensive investigations of the relation of crime to business conditions in America was made by Miss Winslow for the Wickersham Commission on the basis of the statistics of Massachusetts for the period of 1885–1926. This shows a very distinct upward trend of vagrancy and theft in periods of depression, but comparatively little effect on other crimes.[23]

The effect of depression upon crime is seen in its most exaggerated form in the European countries during the war and post-war years. Theft increased immensely during these years of hardship. Women had a higher rate of conviction of theft in Austria during the post-war years than men had prior to the war,[24] which means that their theft rate increased more than ten times. Sellin has analyzed the available information on crime in depressions and concludes that it yields few significant conclusions.[25]

Ogburn has approached the question of economic factors with a different method. He has attempted to explain the variations in crime rates in 62 cities by determining what other variables are associated with variations in crime rates. He finds that a cluster of economic factors shows a fairly high correlation with crime rates.[26]

This whole body of information regarding economic conditions and crime yields the following conclusions, if we assume that the indexes of crime are reliable: First, there are significant but not large associations between juvenile and adult delinquency rates and poverty in homes, in residential areas, and in cities. Second, crimes against property increase, although with no high degree of consistency, in periods of depression, while alcoholism increases in periods of prosperity. Third, child labor, especially in street trades,

---

[22] H. A. Phelps, "Cycles of Crime," *Jour. Crim. Law and Criminol.*, 20:107–121, May, 1929.

[23] Emma A. Winslow, "Relationships between Employment and Crime Fluctuations as Shown by Massachusetts Statistics," *Natl. Com. on Law Obs. and Enf.*, No. 13, Vol. I, pp. 173–333.

[24] Franz Exner, *Krieg und Kriminalität in Oesterreich*, Vienna, 1927, p. 155. See, also, M. Liepmann, *Krieg und Kriminalität in Deutschland*, New Haven, 1930; E. Hacker, "Soziale Kapilarität und Kriminalität," *Monats. f. Krim. Biol.*, 28:355–364, August, 1937.

[25] Sellin, *op. cit.*

[26] W. F. Ogburn, "Factors in the Variation of Crime among Cities," *Jour. Amer. Stat. Assoc.*, 30:12–34, March, 1935.

results in a disproportionately high delinquency rate. Even if these conclusions are regarded as valid, it is difficult to derive from them an explanation of crime. The higher crime rates may be due to lack of satisfaction of physical needs, to excessive leisure time, to loss of social status, to greater opportunity for contact with delinquents, or to reductions in the opportunities for constructive participation in social life. Also, it is evident that crimes which were committed in a period of prosperity may not appear until a period of depression. Persons in positions of financial responsibility embezzled funds during 1926–1929 with the expectation of making profits in the market from which to replace the stolen funds. When the crash came in 1929 many embezzlers could not repay, though thousands of others, doubtless, had already replaced the funds they had stolen and were not discovered.

The reliability of the indexes of crime has been questioned repeatedly. When this is taken into consideration, the conclusions regarding economic conditions and crime become highly doubtful. First, the administrative processes are more favorable to persons in economic comfort than to those in poverty, so that if two persons on different economic levels are equally guilty of the same offense the one on the lower level is more likely to be arrested, convicted, and committed to an institution. Second, the laws are written, administered, and implemented primarily with reference to the types of crimes committed by people of lower economic levels. An immense number of cases of fraud by persons on the upper economic levels does not enter into the statistical indexes of crime, although they are logically and in their social consequences in the class of larcenies.

For that reason the economic system is sometimes charged with the stimulation of crime because of its highly individualistic nature, even though the crimes with which the police and courts deal are concentrated in economic classes which are unable to defend themselves. The ideal of the capitalistic system, as described by its earlier defenders, is that action directed solely by self-interest, within the limits of the laws, will result in the greatest social welfare. Consequently in economic transactions no one should consider the social effects of his behavior so long as he does not violate the laws. The self, as conceived in this argument, moreover, was a narrow self, with practically no social implications, and the laws were held in little respect except in so far as they were for the protection of the capitalistic system itself, together, of course, with the protection of life.

The capitalistic system in this ideal state long ago disappeared, if it ever existed. The number of restrictions on free competition has been constantly increasing, largely at the insistence of competing economic groups. Tariffs, patents, copyrights, franchises, and similar privileges were among the first of the restrictions upon free competition. Each group pressed for similar restrictions upon other groups for its own welfare. Furthermore, competition is much less in terms of efficiency in production and distribution and much more in terms of efficiency in advertising and salesmanship, and these activities are so highly colored that they raise serious questions of fraud. The result is a series of public conflicts between groups, organized for group interest. Legislative lobbies, support of grafting politicians, and subsidizing of newspapers to perpetrate their frauds become important means of competition. The result is that modern society has become one of conflict and disorganization which is publicly displayed. Everyone seems to be working, without concern for the general social welfare, to get what he can in any way he can. With this background crime is encouraged. The criminal, like the business man, does what he can to get money, with little respect for the laws.

GOVERNMENT AND POLITICS. A prominent theory is that crime is due to the lack of enforcement of laws, and the solution of the problem of crime is pressure upon the police and courts to enfore the laws strictly. Strict enforcement of laws would certainly reduce crime, but strict enforcement of laws is extremely difficult because the agencies of justice have been demoralized by exactly the same influences which have produced crime.

A few centuries ago government had prestige because it was based on the divine right of the sovereign. The prestige secured from that source persisted after the doctrine was abandoned, and this prestige was supported by a certain degree of practical efficiency in simple situations. As situations became more complex and less stable, governmental agencies frequently proved to be inefficient. General opposition to strong government developed because of the necessity of breaking away from the regulations which had persisted from the feudal period, because of the democratic fear of absolutism, and because of the new problems of the frontiers. In spite of this distrust, the widening area of social interaction and the deadly effects of competition drove many groups to appeal to government for assistance. Many laws have been passed for the purpose of controlling behavior in these impersonal situations but the legislation has not been supported by a cohesive body of opinion and sentiment. The result has been the anomalous condition of a great amount of legislation and little respect for legislation. Each group rebels against the legislation forced upon it by other groups, and each group attempts to secure legislation to regulate other groups. It is easy to break laws derived from a source that no one respects greatly and it is easy to manipulate policies in the interest of one's own group when few people have an intense interest in the larger group.

The result is a general disrespect for law and disrespect for those who make and enforce laws. This is seen not only in the fact that people break laws but also in the attitudes of those who do not break laws. Legislative bodies, considered as corporate bodies rather than as individuals, are generally considered with contempt, suspicion, and distrust. Hardly one novel dealing with legislatures has been written in the United States during the last four generations which has not presented these bodies as corrupt, boss-ridden, inefficient, and lacking in scientific methods and procedure. Similarly, the police are generally regarded as brutal, corrupt, and inefficient. The public attitude toward the courts is perhaps a little more favorable but inclines toward ridicule of the higher courts for corporate inefficiency, and still greater ridicule and contempt for the lower courts for the additional defects of dishonesty, individual inefficiency, and squalid surroundings. The lack of respect was illustrated recently when a club woman who was the complaining witness in a case of burglary notified the policeman that she could not be in court at the hour set for trial because she had an appointment for tea with a prominent visitor, and, in fact, she did not attend the trial. The same lack of respect for law is seen in the failure to pay taxes. In Chicago more than a half million automobiles were in May still using the license plates of the previous year although new plates were required by law in January. Similarly, income taxes and real estate taxes are evaded by outright neglect or by subterfuge and the officers in most cases are fearful of arousing public antagonism and do not enforce payment. For the same reason many laws are not enforced at all or are enforced only sporadically. These include not only the laws regarding gambling, prostitution, and liquor, but many laws regarding automobiles, building regulations, and business practices. There may in other circumstances be some fear of detection and punishment but little inner opposition to lawbreaking by one's self or others as long as one is not himself affected and his immediate associates do not object. Aside from the fear of punishment one would generally prefer to be caught breaking almost any of the laws except those regarding the most serious felonies rather than eating peas on his knife, and in certain groups even the felonies are less serious than breaches of etiquette. The public attitude seems to be that one should use his own discretion as to obeying the laws, and in fact a prominent newspaper in 1923 gave that advice regarding the prohibition law. Thus there has developed a code of selective obedience of law. Some crimes are taboo in certain circles, but the crimes that are taboo in one circle may not be in another circle.

When one is caught, the problem is to "fix" things. This occurs very commonly in the so-called law-abiding groups in relation to traffic violations, gambling, smuggling, liquor, and certain other crimes. In other circles it occurs in relation to shoplifting, picking pockets, robbery, burglary, and murder. There is a prevalent belief among prisoners that their own cases could have been "fixed" if they had had sufficient money. According to that belief the only reason for being arrested or convicted is poverty. It is probable that no part of the population is better acquainted with the corruption and graft in the legislative, judicial, and police systems, so far as they exist, than are the professional criminals and near-criminals.

The principal cities and states are under the control of political machines, and these are sometimes bipartisan and continue their control regardless of the party in power. The political party is an agency for predatory control. It can retain its position only by rendering services to one special group or another, or to the general society. It must serve the general society, but service to the general society is a means to its own welfare. In the first place, the ordinary individual does not want to be bothered with political activity and does not have the initiative to get the government to act. He wants to permit someone else to do the work, and the politician steps in and meets this need. In the second place, ordinary citizens who do have initiative and force in relation to government generally have an individual interest to promote; it may be a financial return to themselves, a crank's utopian scheme, or a fanatic's hostility to existing practices. It is necessary to have some person or group to weigh these many demands against each other and work out compromises that will give some satisfaction to the discontented groups. The politicians, being essentially unmoral, calculate these demands in terms of returns to their own welfare. These calculations do produce a balancing of extremes, and this is a service to the general society. In the third place, the politician is generally a personal friend and benefactor of the people in his immedate district. He renders many services to them in a warm-hearted manner and without antagonizing them. Even though his benefactions may come from the public treasury, he acts as a personal friend in the midst of a huge impersonal society.

Among the services which the political machine renders and from which the politicians are most likely to derive their own direct financial gains, those which are rendered to persons who violate the law or who wish to prevent the enactment of laws injurious to them are very important. It is these services which are generally regarded as corruption. The first of these services, which is generally known as political corruption, is protection of law-violators. The political machine provides immunity for prostitution, gambling, and violation of liquor laws. This, in fact, is so important that the leaders in these vices are generally either themselves in positions of importance in the local political machine or else are the heaviest contributors to the party treasury in return for their immunity. Consequently an individual policeman is completely unable to take action regarding these violations of law; and furthermore, the chief of police is equally impotent, for he himself is under the control either directly or indirectly of the same machine. This immunity, moreover, is extended to the organized vices even when it becomes evident that this means protection of groups which are engaging in bank robberies, kidnapings, and other serious crimes, as was the case in many of the organized bootlegging groups during the period of national prohibition. Similarly, immunity may be granted to individuals or organized groups which have little or no connection with the liquor business and which engage exclusively in serious crimes. The dealers in stolen automobiles are seldom arrested, even when information is given to the police, and at least in some of these cases the dealers have political connections. Equally important is the immunity granted to huge and respectable business concerns to violate the laws regarding fire hazards, safety devices, obstruction of sidewalks, and other dangers and inconveniences. Certainly a large part of the campaign contributions come from those who expect immunity in the violation of the law, and not all of the persons who expect immunity belong to the underworld.

A second form of the support on which the political machine relies is protection against injurious legislation. Many industries, of which perhaps the public utilities are the most important in recent years, make huge contributions for campaign purposes in order that they may have the good will of those who regulate the legislatures and may thus prevent the enactment of legislation that these industries regard as injurious. This is a form of bribery only slightly concealed.

A third form of corruption is through contracts for public works and the franchises which are granted to public utilities and other concerns. Every public contract is regarded as an opportunity for money-making by those who are engaged in it. Politicians get rich by letting these contracts for buildings, parks, pavements, and purchase of coal. This, also, is a form of embezzlement, generally known as graft. It is a means of enriching the politicians either as individuals or as a machine. The extent to which persons in important political positions become wealthy after securing office is evidence of the extent of this collusion with private contractors to rob the public treasury.

A fourth form of political corruption is the patronage system. In some organizations each candidate for an elective office, including the governor of the state, is required to agree in advance that the appointive offices will be filled by the organization. A patronage secretary or a patronage committee may be publicly recognized as in charge of this function. In Indiana the principal opposition to a state patronage secretary comes from the township and county politicians, who insist that patronage is the function of the local organization rather than of the state organization. It is important to the organization, whether national, state, or local, that it control the patronage, for it is through patronage that many of its services are rendered to individuals and groups. First, it may thus reward its members who have rendered services in elections. The governor of a Central Western state was criticized by members of his own party because he retained two persons of the opposite party who had held office during the previous administration. The governor explained that these two appointments were temporary until successors could be found, but his party colleagues insisted, "To us the only thing N.R.A. means is 'No Republicans around.' " The result is that a large proportion of offices are filled by inferior persons whose principal loyalty is to the political machine and whose salaries frequently are an incidental part of their incomes. Second, through control of patronage the organization can control the activities of the officeholders. Third, as a specific form of the second value, the organization can thus grant immunity, in return for campaign contributions, to the agencies which violate the law or are in other ways injuring the community. One of the members of the patronage committee in Illinois a few years ago was the president of one of the principal banks of the state and he had membership on that committee because the banks, utility companies, insurance companies, and similar concerns were interested in the selection of bank examiners, public utility commissioners, and other similar officers, who would be friendly and could be controlled. Thus the banks, utilities, manufacturing concerns, and railroads co-operate with houses of prostitution, gamblers, and saloons to pervert and corrupt the government. Patronage is the most obvious indication of the fact that the political organization is interested primarily in its own welfare, and only secondarily in the welfare of the state.

Finally, fraud in voting is an important method of insuring the control of the political machine. In a recount of votes in Chicago in 1933, fraud was discovered in 29 per cent of the ballot boxes and in some wards in every box. In Kansas City 275 election officials and other party workers have been indicted for fraud in connection with the election of 1936.

As a result of these influences which corrupt politics, the honest operation of the police and of the courts is limited. An honest official must make many compromises with the party machine if he is to get along at all, for the system has been operating for many decades and no person can change it very much. An aroused public sentiment sometimes produces temporary improvement, but the improvement is often in the form of greater severity of punishment of petty offenders. It is highly probable that reforms will be temporary and sporadic and enforcement of criminal law ineffectual until the more general situations which produce political corruption are changed.

NEWSPAPERS AND CRIME. The American newspapers have been generally and severely criticized for the part they play in relation to crime. The following charges are made against them: First, they promote crime by the constant advertising of crime, by glorifying the criminal leaders and acting as press agents for them, by a jocular method of presenting crime news which takes away the dignity of the court proceedings, and by providing advance information to the public, including the criminals, regarding the plans of the police and prosecutors. Second, they interfere with justice by "trial by newspaper" and by distortion of news. Third, they produce a public panic in regard to crime which makes consistent and sober procedure difficult. Fourth, they interfere with the right of innocent individuals to decent privacy. Fifth, they become agencies of corruption by the employment of children under morally injurious conditions, of gunmen in circulation wars, and of racketeering reporters.

The desirability of publishing crime news is not here in question. Rather it is the amount and style of the crime news. The English newspapers publish crime news in the form of brief factual statements. The American crime news is much more colorful and detailed, so that the crimes are presented vividly and not distastefully to the reader. Because nothing is said about the millions of persons who lead a consistently law-abiding life, the impression is created that crime is the customary mode of life. Thomas, speaking of the yellow journal, says:

It is a positive agent of vice and crime. The condition of morality, as well as of mental life, in a community depends on the prevailing copies. A people is profoundly influenced by whatever is persistently brought to its attention. A good illustration of this is the fact that an article of commerce—a food, a luxury, a medicine, or a stimulant —can always be sold in immense quantities if it be persistently and largely advertised. In the same way the yellow journal by an advertisement of crime, vice, and vulgarity, on a scale unexampled in commercial advertising, and in a way that amounts to approval and even applause, becomes one of the forces making for immorality.[27]

[27] W. I. Thomas, "The Psychology of the Yellow Journal," *Amer. Mag.*, 65:496, March, 1908. Reprinted by permission.

The effect of this constant presentation of crime news to the public can certainly not be demonstrated in ordinary cases. Presumably the effect in ordinary cases differs only in degree from the effect in the extraordinary cases, such as the following. Not long after the newspapers were filled with vivid stories of the Hickman case in California, Hotelling committed a somewhat similar crime in Michigan and when asked regarding it stated that he could not get the Hickman case out of his mind. Holmes states that an epidemic of similar cases occurred and in some of the other cases the accused persons claimed that the idea was suggested by the Hickman case.[28] Martin Durkin, with a long record of crimes, including the killing of a policeman, was captured in St. Louis and was being returned to Chicago. The newspapers had been filled with news regarding the case. When Durkin reached the station in Chicago he found flashlights, reporters, moving-picture machines, and an immense crowd to greet him. The crowd was not only interested but was distinctly sympathetic, for they shouted, "We're for you, Marty!" When the motion pictures were shown later in the theaters, the crowds cheered the pictures of Durkin and hissed and booed at those of the police until the Mayor prohibited the showing of the pictures. The situation was definitely dangerous and all the information on which the public had formed its impression had come to it through the newspapers. The newspapers tried to change the public attitudes by writing in disparaging terms about Durkin but the public sympathy could not be changed that easily.[29] Again in 1932 the newspapers created a near-riot. A man was murdered by his wife. The details were of the usual sordid type, but the striking appearance and mannerisms of the wife gave the reporters an opportunity for a story, and for days the papers were crammed with details. Then the funeral of the murdered man was announced, with the information that the widow would attend the funeral. The streets adjoining the undertaker's chapel were well filled an hour and a half before the hour of the services, and were jammed to capacity a half hour before the time. As the services were about to begin the spectators crashed into the chapel, swarming between the casket and the minister. After some effort sufficient quiet was secured to start the services, but the continued

---

[28] Joseph L. Holmes, "Crime and the Press," *Jour. Crim. Law and Criminol.*, 20:258, August, 1929.
[29] R. M. Lovett, "Chicago," *New Rep.*, 50:243–246, April 20, 1927.

pressure of the crowd outside made it necessary to bring the services to a speedy close. As the services ended a plate-glass window was crashed in by the pressure of the mob, chairs were overturned, and the police were helpless. The streets along which the procession was conducted were crowded for many blocks, with people filling the sidewalks, the windows, and even the roofs of houses. At the cemetery crowds swarmed over the graves and pushed until those in the front ranks could keep from falling into the open grave only by holding to the coffin. Policemen were shouting and pushing in the effort to keep the spectators back and later to make a path for the widow to start back to jail. If the story of this murder had been confined to the usual factual statement which appears in cases of this kind, there would have been no public interest. The interest which did develop was not based on antagonism against the murder; it was morbid curiosity, created by lurid stories. It served absolutely no useful purposes and could not have occurred in a community in which good taste and morality restrained the newspapers and the public.

Bingay, the editorial director of the *Detroit Free Press,* stated in 1933 that press agents are as useful to criminals as to movie stars or politicians, that the newspapers act without salary as press agents for the criminal leaders, build up their reputations and increase their power with other criminals, with the police and courts, with the politicians and the public. A reporter applied the name "Purple Gang" to a relatively unimportant group in Detroit which up to that time had had no name. The name was used by others, and these gangsters were built up by the label into criminal giants. Their reputation was made by the newspapers. Consequently when a member of this group went to a business man with a racketeering proposition and announced himself as a member of the Purple Gang, the business man was afraid to kick him out as he might otherwise have done. In Chicago the newspapers announced that Murray Humphries would be the successor to Capone. The successor was by no means determined, but the announcement in the newspapers helped Humphries secure this position as much as a similar announcement would help an aspirant for a political position. Furthermore, the newspaper accounts contribute considerably to the self-esteem of certain criminals, for these professional criminals are generally avid readers of the newspapers. When a newspaper carries the story that a certain criminal is the worst, or the best, or the most dangerous, or some other superlative appellation, it is one of the few consolations this criminal will have, in case of conviction, while he is in prison.

Newspapers frequently carry advance information to the criminals regarding the plans of the police and the prosecutors. During 1933 one of the Chicago newspapers contained an announcement with big headlines that twenty police squads were watching two buildings, the addresses of which were printed in the article, because of information that a notorious criminal who was being hunted used these places as hangouts. The announcement would certainly destroy completely the efficiency of the police work. Such items appear frequently. Though they are sometimes a camouflage of the real plans of the police, they are frequently secured from subordinates by bargains, bribery, or threats. One of the ransom notes in the Peter Levine kidnaping case threatened the death of the child if information were given to police or newspapers. A reporter for a New York City paper secured verification of the kidnaping story by representing himself over the telephone to be an agent of the kidnapers, and his paper printed the story. The dead body of the child was found later. Federal agents have threatened reporters with arrest for obstructing justice in kidnaping cases because the reporters persisted in interfering with the investigations.

The effect of crime news is to throw the public into a panic. Newspapers learned in 1917 that it was dangerous to publish colorful stories about an epidemic of disease and they customarily keep such information entirely out of their columns, especially when a convention or fair is imminent or in progress. They refuse to publish information regarding the financial condition of a bank for fear that a panic which might produce public injury will ensue. The newspapers in England deal with crime news as they do with sickness and financial dangers, that is, quietly and factually. The American newspapers, on the other hand, have not realized the dangers of panics of this nature and continue to make the crime stories as colorful as possible.

Aside from the effect of colorful crime stories in producing crime and throwing the public into a panic, the newspapers seriously interfere with the course of justice by what has been called "trial by newspaper." Prior to the trial, the reporters present such evidence as they have, which is likely to be partisan information, again and again, until the public accepts the implied verdict of the newspaper and thereafter cannot easily be shaken in its opinion. A fair trial under such circumstances becomes almost impossible, especially in communities where the judges are elected and where they are afraid of arousing public antagonism. It is quite certain that many persons are convicted under such circumstances who are actually innocent, or are punished very severely who would otherwise be given much less severe penalties. The number of cases which attract this detailed and continued attention is probably not large. Any case may be selected for this presentation because some detail is sufficiently striking to make a good story. A man was killed in a drunken brawl; the murderer had previously had a good reputation but was not prominent in any way. The case would probably have passed with the customary procedure as a manslaughter case with imprisonment for, perhaps, three years except that a reporter happened to learn that the murderer had the nickname "Banjo Ben." That trivial point made a good story of it. It was written up at length and repeated frequently. Consequently this offered an opportunity for the prosecutor to build up publicity for the next election. The offender was convicted of murder and sentenced to prison for one hundred and ninety-nine years. Reporters did everything possible to violate the rules of the court in the Lindbergh kidnaping case. These rules were made in order to secure a dignified and unbiased trial, and the newspapers interferred with justice by their violations. Many members of the bar believe that the reporters should have been severely punished for their behavior, and that this would have been legitimate.

In the spectacular crimes life is made almost unbearable for victims, witnesses, and officials by the reporters. Such persons claim that they have a right to privacy and that their right is invaded. The notorious behavior of reporters in connection with the Lindberghs is an illustration.

The newspapers, furthermore, are sometimes agencies of corruption. The newspaper circulation war in Chicago, which began in 1900 when two Hearst papers started publication in competition with the other papers and lasted for several years, resulted in the employment of armed guards by both sides, in the killing of more than a score of persons, and the injury of hundreds. Among the guards employed in this war were several persons who later became "public enemies." They had learned that violence, including murder, is safe if one is backed by a strong organization with money and influence. A few editors have been closely associated with gangsters, and several reporters have used their newspaper influence to assist gangsters. An important police official made the following statement:

I firmly believe that newspapers are responsible for a lot of crime. Out of the newspaper alleys come many gamblers, pimps, sex perverts and a big share of the gangsters. There is no better breeding ground in the world for gangsters than a newspaper alley. Besides that the newspaper circulation department violates every child labor law and statute and many city ordinances that are enforced on other private citizens. They haul their papers through the streets at fifty miles an hour, endangering the life and property of the whole city, but you never heard of one of them being arrested.

The primary reason why the newspapers conduct themselves in this fashion is that they are business concerns, operated for the purpose of profits. Their primary interest is circulation, and public welfare is secondary. The studies of newspaper presentation of crimes, however, provide no evidence that the percentage of space in the papers devoted to crime news has increased or that the emphasis upon crimes has changed.[30]

The newspapers defend their method of presenting crime news, first, on the ground that it is what the public wants. Though there is truth in this argument, it does not take into consideration that the newspapers themselves have to a considerable extent created the wants. At present some of the papers present crime news in the comic strips which are read by the youngest children. Second, they argue that the only way to solve the crime problem is by arousing the inert public and the inert public officials by this means. The difficulty is that action under such circumstances is not likely to be calm and consistent. Expressions of public opposition to crime unquestionably assist in deterring people from crime, but the newspaper expressions are based largely on unusual and extraordinary cases which make good stories. This, however, does not deny the very great contribution that the newspapers make by the factual information regarding crime and regarding official corruption, and by the support of desirable policies. Crime news, as well as other

[30] Frank Harris, *The Presentation of Crime in the Newspapers*, Hanover, 1932.

methods of portraying crimes, has been defended on the ground
that it satisfies a deep-seated compulsion toward criminality and is
thus something like a sublimation of the criminal tendencies. Bar
associations have criticized the newspapers for the anti-social behavior which has been described. Recently a joint committee of
the bar, the press, and the radio outlined a code of ethics in regard
to publicity.[31]

Some of the earlier novels, such as Ainsworth's and Bulwer-
Lytton's, glorified criminals. Mayhew offers some evidence of the
effect of this from statements of criminals, for many persons desired to be followers of Jack Shepard and the other romantic criminals. In somewhat the same way two generations ago the Jesse
James stories and the Diamond Dick novels and others known as
"dime novels" thrilled the youth of the country. Though this function has now for the most part been assumed by the motion pictures,
the "wood pulp" magazines are continuing it. These magazines,
however, are seldom read by the pre-adolescents. The erotic literature in these magazines is perhaps the most deleterious because of
the continued direction of attention toward sex and the continued
presence of sex imagery. There is little evidence that any of this
literature is of primary importance in the development of juvenile
delinquency, and probably it is not highly important except in
occasional cases in adult criminality.[32]

THE MOTION PICTURES. The motion pictures are unquestionably
an extremely important agency in determining the ideas and behavior of people, and especially of children. Blumer has interpreted
this effect as due to the vivid visual imagery, together with the de-
cisiveness and unambiguity of the films. On account of this effect
the pictures are likely to be accepted as correct and authoritative.
Children impersonate the actors in their play and in other ways
imitate them in overt behavior. They daydream about the scenes
which are depicted. The emotions are affected, including fight and
terror, sorrow and pathos, and excitement and passion. The pictures provide people with schemes of life, with ideas of rights and
privileges, and standards of behavior.[33]

---

[31] Paul Bellamy, Stuart Perry, Newton D. Baker, "Cooperation between
Press, Radio, and Bar," *Jour. Crim. Law and Criminol.*, 28:641–656, January,
1938.
[32] S. Sighele, *Littérature et criminalité*, Paris, 1908, pp. 165 ff. Sighele
maintains that Goethe's *Werther* produced many suicides.
[33] Herbert Blumer, *Movies and Conduct*, New York, 1933.

In view of this significant effect produced by the pictures on conduct, the content of the pictures is highly important. When the content is analyzed it is found to be very distorted. Almost everyone in the pictures is wealthy and formal dress is featured. Crime and sex are the themes in more than three-fourths of the films which were analyzed. People are animated by goals of easy money and sex, and seldom by the goals of social achievement. The criminal and prostitute are often glorified and seldom receive official punishment in the pictures. Children play as gangsters after seeing the pictures and are influenced in other ways. Within a month after "The Wild Boys of the Road" was presented as a motion picture in Evanston, Illinois, during the Christmas holidays of 1933, fourteen children ran away from home. Four of these were apprehended by the police and three of the four stated that the freedom depicted in the picture had appealed to them. One of these was a girl fifteen years of age and she was dressed in almost identically the same fashion as the girl who had taken the feminine lead in the picture.

Blumer and Hauser summarize the effects of the motion pictures on delinquency thus:

It seems clear that the motion pictures were a factor of importance in the delinquent or criminal careers of about 10 per cent of the male and 25 per cent of the female offenders studied. . . . Several important indirect influences disposing or leading persons to delinquency or crime are discernible in the experiences of male offenders. Through the display of crime techniques and criminal patterns of behavior; by arousing desires for easy money and luxury, and by suggesting questionable methods for their achievement; by inducing a spirit of bravado, toughness, and adventurousness; by arousing intense sexual desires; by invoking daydreaming of criminal rôles, motion pictures may create attitudes and furnish techniques conducive, quite unwittingly, to delinquent or criminal behavior. One may detect in the case of delinquent girls and young women influences similar to those spoken of in the case of young men. Motion pictures may play a major or minor rôle in female delinquency and crime by arousing sexual passion, by instilling the desire to live a gay, wild, fast life, by evoking longings for luxury and smart appearance, and by suggesting to some girls questionable methods of easily attaining them; by the display of modes of beautification and love techniques; by

the depiction of various forms of crime readily imitated by girls
and young women; and by competing with home and school for an
important place in the life of the girls.[34]

This conclusion does not deny certain beneficial influences that
movies have and does not deny that other social influences are significant in determining sensitivity to the criminal and sexual patterns presented by the pictures. In fact the general tendency seems
to be that the children who reside in areas where delinquency rates
are high are influenced more significantly by the crime and sex
pictures than are those who live in areas of low delinquency rates.
This, in general, is what would be expected on a priori grounds.
All children, however, are susceptible to the influence of the motion
pictures much more than are adults. Upon people who already have
a fairly stable scheme of life, as adults and as children in good
residential areas do, the influence of the motion pictures is less
harmful than upon people whose habits are less definitely formed
and whose environment is more distinctly limited.

The motion-picture houses have at intervals attempted to stimulate attendance by various devices. One of the most harmful of
these methods was the "Opportunity Night," but they had, also,
bank nights, bathing girl contests, and Kiddies' Barrels of Fun,
some of which introduced the burlesque standards into the family
theater and others violated the child labor laws.[35]

As a result of the report of the Payne Fund study of motion
pictures and of campaigns by religious organizations in 1934 new
methods of censorship were developed. While this has reduced the
"smut" in the films it has also given an opportunity for partisan
censorship of pictures regarding economic and political issues.

THE RADIO. The development of the radio programs is motivated by the same competitive goals that control the newspapers
and picture shows. Any program which attracts attention and
creates a demand for a product is presented, no matter how injurious its social effect may be. Thus certain food-producing manufacturers recently developed crime stories for the children's hours
and have thus brought crime into the early childhood and into the

[34] From Herbert Blumer and Philip M. Hauser, Movies, Delinquency and Crime, New York, 1933, pp. 198-199. By permission of The Macmillan Company, publishers.
[35] F. Zeta Youmans, "Opportunity Night," Survey, 58:485-488, September 1, 1927.

home. This, however, aroused a storm of protest from parents and some, at least, of these programs have been changed.[36] These programs have not been continued long enough to produce significant effects, but they are a part of the accumulation of crime models and crime patterns which has flooded the country.

RELIGION. There is no specific evidence regarding the effect of religion, as such, on crime. Certain external expressions of religion are found to be slightly related to crime. Persons who have membership in churches are committed to prison slightly less than persons who are not members, but the relationship is not entirely consistent.[37] Those who attended church regularly prior to the crimes of which they were convicted succeeded on probation or parole more frequently than those whose attendance had not been regular. Compulsory church attendance, however, has produced negativistic reactions as a rule,[38] so that it is presumably not the church attendance as such but the group relationships of those who attend church which are influential in this respect. In America the Baptists and the Catholics have the highest rate of commitment to those prisons which report religious affiliations. This is apparently explained by the fact that most of the Negroes are Baptists and most of the recent immigrants are Catholics. Similarly, an intensive analysis of the differences in crime rates of the several denominations in Hungary resulted in the conclusions that these differences were due not to the differences in the creeds but to the differences in the economic, educational, and family status of the members, to the differences in places of residence, and to the differences in age and sex.[39] Ogburn found a negative correlation of 0.25 between crime rates and church membership in 66 cities, but this correlation became insignificant when certain other variables were held constant.[40] Efforts to determine the comparative crime rates of the Jews have been relatively unproductive.[41]

[36] Arthur Mann, "The Children's Hour of Crime," *Scribners,* 93:313–315, May, 1933.

[37] John R. Miner, "Church Membership and Commitment to Prisons," *Human Biol.,* 3:429–436, September, 1931.

[38] John L. Ernst, "An Analysis of the Religious and Ethical Habits of a Group of Convicts," *Univ. of Pittsburg Bull.,* 27:47–53, November 15, 1930.

[39] Ervin Hacker, *Der Einfluss der Konfession auf die Kriminalität in Ungarn,* Miskolc, 1930.

[40] W. F. Ogburn, "Factors in the Variation of Crime among Cities," *Jour. Amer. Stat. Assoc.,* 30:24–25, March, 1935.

[41] Liebman Hersh, "Delinquency among Jews," *Jour. Crim. Law and Criminol.,* 27:515–538, 857–873, November, 1936, and April, 1937. This study refers to Poland.

EDUCATION. On the basis of the very inadequate and unreliable statistics which are available, the conclusion is that crime decreases with the amount of formal education. In 1923 4.6 per cent of the general population between the ages of fifteen and thirty-five were illiterate, while 10.7 of all prisoners within these ages were illiterate. Per 100,000 population twenty-one years of age and over and of the same educational status, the number of commitments of illiterates was 42.8, of persons whose last school was the elementary school was 31.4, of those who attended high school 17.5, and of those who attended college 14.3. Thus in proportion to their numbers about three times as many illiterate persons as persons who had attended college were committed to prison. Those who committed embezzlement, forgery, and fraud had the greatest amount of education, those who committed rape, homicide, and assault the smallest amount of education. In certain states, at least, the proportion of illiterates among prisoners is decreasing.

These differences do not prove that formal education, in itself, deters from crime, for the formal education may merely reflect the economic status or the intelligence, and either of these may be the direct and significant influence in causing or deterring from crime.

The schools have been criticized severely by certain persons because the difference in criminality between the educated and uneducated is not greater than it is. The failure of the schools to prevent crime to a greater extent may be due to lack of facilities, lack of preparation of teachers, lack of point of view, lack of individualization, and to overcrowding. The curriculum has not been developed in many schools to meet modern needs or the abilities of the child. The work of the school has not been extended sufficiently beyond the walls of the school into the homes and neighborhoods. The general public has not been willing to pay taxes sufficient to prepare children adequately for adult life. The social sciences, which are perhaps most important in preparing people for adult life, have not been sufficiently developed for purposes of education of children.[42]

WAR SERVICE. The war is frequently said to be an important and direct cause of criminality. This is explained as due to the

[42] Carl Murchison argued some years ago that college-trained persons committed a disproportionately large number of crimes and explained that this was due to the development of social sciences in the schools and colleges in place of the basic sciences. See "College Men Behind Prison Walls," *School and Society,* 13:633–640, June 4, 1921.

disorganization produced in young men who were removed from the home environment and placed in an environment of ruthlessness and hate; especially it is asserted that the government taught them to shoot and they have continued this since the war as murderers and robbers. The report on prisoners for 1923 gives the only general statistical information available on this point. This report does not show the proportion of ex-service men who have become criminals, in comparison with those who did not have war service. It shows merely that when ex-service men are committed to prison, they are most likely, in comparison with those who have not had war service, to be committed for fraud, embezzlement, and nonsupport and least likely to be imprisoned for homicide, violating liquor laws, carrying concealed weapons, rape, burglarly, and assault. Robbery is the only offense of the more violent type for which ex-service men have more than their expected proportion of commitments. This, of course, does not prove that ex-service men are not disproportionately criminal, for they may exceed the men who have not had war service in every type of crime, but only that when they are imprisoned they, in comparison with persons who were not in war service, are more likely to be convicted of the less violent crimes.

SUGGESTED READINGS

Alexander, Holmes M., "I Hold Office," *Harpers*, 167:414–424, September, 1933.

Bent, Silas, *Ballyhoo*, New York, 1927.

Bingay, Malcolm W., "Newspapers' Responsibility in Law Enforcement," *Proc. Inter. Assoc. of Chiefs of Police*, pp. 101–109, 1933.

Blumer, Herbert, *Movies and Conduct*, New York, 1933.

Blumer, Herbert, and Hauser, Philip M., *Movies, Delinquency and Crime*, New York, 1933.

Bonger, W. A., *Criminality and Economic Conditions*, Tr. by H. P. Horton, Boston, 1916.

Breckinridge, S. P., and Abbott, E., *The Delinquent Child and the Home*, New York, 1912.

Caldwell, C. N. (Editor), "The Crisis of Democracy," *Annals of Amer. Acad. of Pol. and Social Sci.*, No. 169, September, 1933.

Conyngton, Mary, "Relation between Occupation and Criminality of Women," *Report on Condition of Woman and Child Wage-Earners,* Vol. XV, Washington, D. C., 1910.

"Corruption," *Encyc. Soc. Sciences.*

Harris, Frank, *The Presentation of Crime in the Newspapers,* Hanover, N. H., 1932.

Holmes, Joseph L., "Crime and the Press," *Jour. Crim. Law and Criminol.,* 20:6–59, 246–293, May and August, 1929.

Jones, Vernon, "Relation of Economic Depression to Delinquency, Crime and Drunkenness in Massachusetts," *Jour. Social Psychol.,* 3:259–282, August, 1932.

Kent, F. R., *Political Behavior,* New York, 1928.

Kent, F. R., *The Great Game of Politics,* Garden City, N. Y., 1930.

Merriam, C. E., *Chicago, A More Intimate View of Urban Politics,* New York, 1929.

Motion Picture Research Council, *Report,* New York, 1933.

Overcracker, Louise, and West, Victor J., *Money in Elections,* New York, 1933.

Park, R. E., "The Natural History of the Newspaper," *Amer. Jour. Sociol.,* 29:273–289, November, 1923.

Ploscowe, M., "Some Causative Factors in Criminality," *Natl. Com. on Law Obs. and Enf.,* No. 13, Vol. I, Washington, 1932.

Salter, J. T., *Boss Rule,* New York, 1935.

Seldes, George, *Lords of the Press,* New York, 1938.

Sellin, Thorsten, *Crime in the Depression,* New York, 1937.

Sprague, Jesse R., *High Pressure: What It Is Doing to My Town and My Neighbors,* New York, 1938.

Steffens, Lincoln, *Autobiography,* New York, 1931.

Tannenbaum, Frank, *Crime and the Community,* Boston, 1938, Chs. V-VI.

Thomas, Dorothy S., *Social Aspects of the Business Cycle,* New York, 1925.

Watts, H. M., "The Fourth Estate and Court Procedure as a Public Show," *Jour. Crim. Law and Criminol.,* 19:15–29, May, 1928.

Winslow, Emma A., "Relationships between Employment and Crime Fluctuations as Shown by the Massachusetts Statistics," *Natl. Com. on Laws Obs. and Enf.,* No. 13, Vol. I, pp. 173–333.

Zink, Harold, *City Bosses in the United States,* Durham, N. C., 1930.

Chapter Twelve

PROCESSES IN CRIMINAL BEHAVIOR

IN THE LIFE HISTORY of the criminal, in the interaction between criminals and the public, and in the interaction among criminals all of the processes seen in other social life may be discovered. Some of these processes have greater significance than others for the understanding of crime. One of the significant processes in the life history of the criminal is maturation. Segregation, conflict, and the competitive development of techniques of crime and of protection against crime appear in the interaction between criminals and the public. Fashion, organization, and professionalization appear in the interaction among criminals. These processes are discussed briefly in this chapter as illustrations rather than as a complete analysis of the topic.

MATURATION. A process which may be called "maturation" appears in the life history of persisting criminals. This means merely that criminality in such persons grows in a somewhat consistent course. It does not mean that an individual who starts on this course must follow it to the end, or that he may not begin at some other point than that at which most other criminals begin. Like other terms borrowed by the social sciences from biology, the term "maturation" is misleading but it is used in the absence of a better term.

A person's criminal age is determined by the point he has reached in this process of maturation. The process describes the development of criminality, with reference first to the general attitudes toward criminality, and second, to the techniques used in criminal behavior. A boy who is reared in an area of high delinquency reaches criminal maturity at a very early age, perhaps by twelve or fourteen. He has reached criminal maturity because criminality has become an integrated part of his personality and no crisis upsets him. He makes plans for the execution of delinquencies, but quite as carefully considers how to secure immunity in case he is caught. Furthermore, in case his precautions in these respects are inadequate, he takes imprisonment philosophically as a part of his life, just as a newsboy who has made what provision he could against the rain takes the rain as a part of his life. The embezzler, on the other hand, may be four times as old as this delinquent but he has made no provision for immunity in case of detection, and he has no philosophy to support him in his trial and punishment. His character is not integrated and from the point of view of criminality he is immature.

The development of criminal methods in relation to chronological age varies in different crimes. Life histories of persons who in young adult life become robbers and burglars[1] show that criminality proceeds from trivial to serious, from occasional to frequent, from sport to business, from emotionally balanced criminality to the desperado complex, and from crimes committed by isolated individuals or by very loosely organized groups to crimes committed by rather tightly organized groups. This process in crimes of violence reaches its height when the offender is about nineteen years of age and then remains constant for five or ten years, when it either changes into crimes which require less agility and daring, or into the quasi-criminal behavior connected with politics, gambling, liquor, and prostitution, or is abandoned entirely. Glueck reports in his study of five hundred graduates of the Massachusetts Reformatory that 25 per cent of those 21–25 years of age at the beginning of the second five-year period after release were drunkards, while of those 36 years or over at this time 62 per cent were drunkards; the proportion who committed crimes against property decreased from 3½ per cent to 11 per cent.[2] The non-violent crimes of a professional nature are continued, however, to an older age.

The process in the life history of embezzlers is decidedly different. Persons who are placed in positions of financial responsibility must have previous histories of rectitude in order to pass the examination

---

[1] See Clifford R. Shaw, *The Jack-Roller*, Chicago, 1930; Clifford R. Shaw, *The Natural History of a Delinquent Career*, Chicago, 1931; Hutchins Hapgood, *The Autobiography of a Thief*, New York, 1903; Stephen Burroughs, *Memoirs of the Notorious Stephen Burroughs of New Hampshire*, New York, 1924.

[2] Sheldon and Eleanor T. Glueck, *Later Criminal Careers*, New York, 1937, p. 109.

of fidelity companies. They become criminals after they secure these business positions. The evidence so far accumulated does not indicate whether the embezzlements are committed principally by employees who have held positions of financial responsibility for many years or by recent recruits. Occasionally embezzlers snatch a large sum of money and abscond. The usual procedure is that they abstract small sums, ordinarily for speculation or other gambling, for the maintenance of an extra-marital establishment, or for extravagant living. The first intention is to repay the money which has been taken, and undoubtedly many persons do make these repayments and are not discovered. Often the defalcations increase in frequency and in amounts, so that repayment becomes impossible. These crimes are generally committed individually, but occasionally two or more persons are in collusion. The discovery of an embezzlement generally prevents further employment in positions of financial responsibility. Embezzlers are scorned by professional criminals but are regarded by prison officers as model prisoners. A comparatively small proportion of them become recidivists.

The life history of the chronic alcoholic is different from that of the embezzler or of the bandit. The development of drinking habits has not been studied intensively, but the available information indicates that alcoholism seldom becomes chronic until middle age. Thereafter its progress is associated either as cause or effect with deterioration in efficiency and with detachment from former associates.

Similarly, the life history of other types of criminals might be described. The legal crime is probably not the best principle to use in these descriptions. After a sufficient number have been defined and described, the types which appear can be differentiated from each other with little reference to the legal crime.

A few statistical studies have been made from the point of view of the sequential relations between crimes. Grassberger made a study of the arrest records of habitual criminals in New York City which shows that the habitual criminal during his lifetime spreads his crimes over almost the entire field of illegality and is not confined to a single specialty. This study, however, does not show the sequence of types of crimes.[3] Riddle made a study of juvenile

[3] Roland Grassberger, "Gewerbs– und Berufsverbrechertum in den Vereinigten Staaten von Amerika," *Kriminologische Abhandlungen,* Vienna, No. 8, 1933.

thieves from the point of view of sequence of offenses, and concluded that the aggressiveness used in stealing increased with mental age.[4] Burkey found that boys of normal intelligence were more likely to begin with sex offenses, and that both the normal and the subnormal who begin with stealing are likely to continue that offense rather than turn to some other offense.[5] Several studies of the sequential relations between truancy and theft have been made, with no positive conclusion. Also, the assertion has been made frequently that problem children become delinquent children, and delinquent children become criminal adults. While there is some possibility that this is true, it has not been adequately demonstrated.[6]

Glueck has treated this process of maturation from a different point of view. He regards maturation as the underlying influence in reform. According to his conclusions the criminals became law-abiding as they matured chronologically; this process of reformation practically stopped at the age of thirty-five; further, he concluded that those who passed the age of thirty-five and had not reformed were much more frequently mental deviates. Thus his proposition is that age has a beneficent effect on those who are not mental deviates, so that they reform before the age of thirty-five; age has no such effect on the mental deviates and they continue in crime thereafter.[7] He reaches this conclusion, however, by two very questionable methods: first, a definition of mental deviate so broad that it could be made to include all persons whatsoever; second, a comparison of persons of a given age-span in the first follow-up period with another group of persons of the same age-span in the second follow-up period, and from this drawing conclusions regarding the effect of age.[8]

SEGREGATION. Segregation may be observed in the interaction

---

[4] E. M. Riddle, "Stealing as a Form of Aggressive Behavior," *Jour. Abn. Psychol.*, 22:157–169, July, 1927.

[5] Ruth E. Burkey, "A Statistical Study of the Sequence of Successive Delinquencies," *Jour. Juv. Res.*, 16:133–144, April, 1932.

[6] See Nathan Bodin, "Do Problem Children Become Delinquent Children?" *Jour. Crim. Law and Criminol.*, November, 1936. Bodin reports that 92.5 per cent of the problem cases in the Bureau of Research and Guidance in the Berkeley School had developed records of delinquency within the subsequent eight years. It should be noted, however, that slightly more than half of the children had juvenile court records prior to their reference to the Bureau.

[7] Sheldon and Eleanor T. Glueck, *Later Criminal Careers*, New York, 1937, Chs. X–XI.

[8] *Ibid.*, p. 395.

between criminals and the public. The extent to which segregation occurs is determined largely by the hatred the group has for the criminal. The sex offender was completely ostracized in many communities two generations ago, much less completely now. The person with a prison record is still completely ostracized in certain communities but he may become a political leader in other communities. Thus segregation as a process does not apply universally to all criminals in all groups.

There is, however, a general portion of American society which may be called the underworld. Admission to this underworld is secured generally by personal introductions and can be secured only by those who are regarded as not dangerous to the criminals, quasi-criminals, and politicians who compose the underworld. This underworld has a general suspicion of respectable society, moves for the most part in different circles, and has its own meeting places. Criminal slang has developed and persisted in this underworld. Words have been carried for two or three centuries and are known to a large part of the underworld though they are not known outside of that area of social life.

In some of the earlier societies the criminals lived entirely apart from law-abiding society, in remote regions from which they might issue to make raids upon travelers or householders. Today most of the criminals live in the midst of society, in certain areas of the cities, where they are protected by collusion with predatory politicians and have developed a symbiotic relation with many kinds of business men.

PROGRESSIVE CONFLICT. Criminals and the protective agents are engaged in continuous conflict. In this conflict each side tends to drive the other side to greater violence unless the conflict becomes stabilized, on a recognized level, as it has been in England. In England the police and the criminals both go without guns and the danger of death is practically eliminated. In the American city, on the other hand, there has been progressive armament of both sides and progressive rapidity of shooting. Each side adopts the slogan "Shoot and shoot first." Each side feels that it is dangerous to give the other side a chance. This affects not only the police but also that part of the general public which is repeatedly victimized by criminals. The result is an increasing death rate on both sides. The number of policemen murdered annually in the course of duty increased in New York City from 1.8 per 10,000 members of the staff in 1906–1910 to 4.1 in 1926–1930, and in Chicago from 5.1 to 18.2 in the same years. The number of policemen murdered in Chicago in the course of duty increased from 47 in 1919–1925 to 62 in 1926–1931, while the number of criminals killed in connection with their crimes increased in the same years from 190 to 314. Approximately one-third of these criminals were killed by private citizens, and two-thirds by the police. The number killed by policemen increased only 58 per cent while the number killed by citizens increased 125 per cent during this period. In general there tends to be progressive interaction in violence. When the police treat criminals violently, the criminals react violently when they have an opportuntiy. This spurs the police to greater violence, which again produces more violence by the criminals. It is not evident and perhaps makes no difference which side is responsible for the beginning of this process. The result was not foreseen by either side and seems to be a relatively inevitable outcome of the process.

In the absence of settled traditions, this process of progressive conflict begins with arrest, which is interpreted as defining a person as an enemy of society, and which calls forth hostile reactions from representatives of society prior to and regardless of proof of guilt. It is not surprising that the arrested person reacts by further hostility. Thus, in certain areas where arrests are frequent a tradition of hostility is developed and is assimilated by many persons who have had no personal experiences with the procedures of arrest. From this stage hostilities progress until the offender may in middle age or in old age abandon the conflict and confine himself to the vices.

COMPETITIVE DEVELOPMENT OF TECHNIQUES OF CRIME AND OF PROTECTION AGAINST CRIME. Both criminals and protective officers appropriate the inventions of modern science so far as these are useful to them. In early days both proceeded on foot or horseback, then both used bicycles, and now automobiles, with the occasional use of an airplane. In the early days both used clubs as weapons, and now both use guns and machine-guns, with an occasional survival of the knife among some national and racial groups. Both use bullet-proof vests and armored cars. Both on some occasions use tear-gas bombs, and both may be equipped with gas masks. Kidnapers use adhesive tape, which was practically unknown forty years ago even to physicians, to bind the eyes, mouth, and hands of victims.

When the police develop an invention for the detection or identification of criminals, the criminals utilize a device to protect themselves. When the police began to use the fingerprint technique, criminals began to wear gloves and to wipe surfaces that had been touched by them. The police utilize the radio to notify squad cars of the location of a crime that is being committed and to direct those cars in the pursuit of criminals. The well-equipped burglars carry their own short-wave radio sets with them, tune them in while they are at work, and are informed of an alarm as quickly as are the police. The police are trying to perfect selective devices for radio calls which will restrict the calls to police cars, but it may be expected that if this difficulty develops the criminals will devise methods of overcoming it.

The history of the safe furnishes one of the best illustrations of this alternation of progress in the techniques of protection and of crime. The safe seventy years ago was locked with a key. Professional safe-burglars learned how to pick these locks, and then the combination lock was invented. The criminals rigged a lever by means of which the whole spindle of the combination could be pulled out of the safe. When correction was made to prevent this, the burglars drilled holes in the safe and inserted gunpowder or dynamite. Then the manufacturers made the safe drill-proof, and the burglars secured harder drills with more powerful leverage. The manufacturers used harder materials for the safe and therefore the burglars turned to nitroglycerine, which could be inserted in minute crevices around the door where powder and dynamite would not enter. The safe-makers then developed doors which fitted so perfectly that a small piece of paper would prevent the door from locking, and this made it impossible to insert even nitroglycerine in the cracks. The burglars then adopted the oxyacetylene torch and turned it against the safe, and the manufacturers devised a compound which was proof against the torch. Somewhere in this process the burglars began to kidnap bankers and compel them to open the safe, regarding this as easier than mechanical methods of opening safes. To prevent this the time-lock was invented so that the banker could not open his own safe until the appointed hour. The safe-makers also experimented with safes which would release gas if the safe were tampered with. The burglars then went equipped with gas masks. This process of alternations of techniques has given first one side and then the other the advantage. When the protective devices were ahead, some safe-burglars turned to other types of crimes. As the criminal technique was perfected it was adopted by others and the number of safe-burglars increased.

The tendency during the last generation has been to substitute robbery for burglary, for a criminal gang can reach a bank by automobile, can rush into the bank completely armed, make a raid in a few minutes, and rush away. The search for devices to prevent this type of crime is under way. Secret push-buttons to call guards have been developed. Also, secret push-buttons to release tear gas at the same time having been utilized. Efforts are being made to secure automatic photographs of the scene in order that the robbers may be identified. In general the protective devices in the larger banks, both against burglary and robbery, are so well developed that the criminals prefer to make attacks on the smaller banks which cannot afford such expensive equipment, although the prospective gains in these banks are less than in the impregnable banks. If the smaller banks improve their protective devices, the criminals will direct their attacks against other business or commercial concerns which do not have adequate protection. Thus, there is a selection and development of techniques of crimes and a selection of types of crimes in relation to the protective devices, and similarly there is a development of protective devices in relation to the methods used by criminals.

FASHIONS IN CRIME. Certain types of crimes have disappeared almost entirely. This has generally been due to changes in the situation, other than the protective devices. Piracy has practically disappeared, and its disappearance was due to the development of steam ships which were too large and fast for attack by pirates. The development of the steamship did not occur, however, as a protection against piracy. Train robberies, of the type in which a train was stopped and the mail car and the passengers were robbed, have been discontinued. Cattle stealing in the form of driving away a herd of cattle has ceased, but for it has been substituted the loading of two or three cows into a truck and delivering them in the city. The general situation may change and cause the disappearance of a crime. In this sense there is a rational element involved in the frequency of the crimes.

In addition, however, the type and method of crime vary in ways which much resemble fashion in other affairs. A criminal makes an attack on a gambling place and within a short time dozens of other gambling places are attacked. Some criminal selects a hotel for robbery and quickly dozens of other hotels are robbed. A pickpocket secures a thousand dollars in a certain railway station, and the other pickpockets flock to that station. A criminal makes an unusually successful gain by a method which was not customary. Other criminals try the method.

ORGANIZATION OF CRIMINALS. Organization develops in the interaction of criminals. This organization may be a formal association with recognized leadership, understandings, agreements, and division of labor, or it may be informal similarity and reciprocity of interests and attitudes. A group which has been formed for legitimate purposes may change into a criminal group, or individual criminals may organize an association for illegitimate purposes. The criminal tribes of India, the bandits of China, the brigands of southeastern Europe, the smugglers in America and in many European countries in earlier times, the Ku Klux Klan and the lynching mobs, guerilla warfare and feuds were earlier forms of organized crime. The James gang in Missouri and the criminal organizations in Italy were produced by wars and political differences and survived as organized criminals. The Chinese Tongs in America are primarily business associations but on occasions direct their activities along criminal lines.

Aside from these earlier forms of organized crime, the organization of criminals appears at present in the following forms: First, criminals form a working group, known as a mob or troupe, with understandings, division of labor, and sometimes with recognized leadership. The number of criminals in the mob is determined by the requirements of the work, but is generally restricted to two, three, four, or five members. Second, the underworld is bound together by a common hostility toward the law, and consequently the members co-operate in assisting and protecting each other. Third, within certain areas syndicates control gambling, prostitution, and illicit sale of liquor. Fourth, co-operation develops between each of the above mentioned types of criminal organizations and the agencies whose legal business is enforcement of law. Large and strong criminal organizations cannot develop if the government is strongly organized. The strong criminal organizations in the past have generally been found during an interregnum, or on the borderline between conflicting states, or in inaccessible territory remote from the seat of government. The disorganization of the present American governments, however, is different from the early types of governmental disorganization. Modern law-enforcement agencies co-operate with criminal organizations because they are under the control of politicians who are either criminals in the usual sense of the word, grafters and bribe-takers (specialized forms of criminals), or have sympathetic relations because of common membership in the underworld.

Small groups, organized for the execution of a particular type of crime, have existed for centuries. These groups during the Elizabethan period have been described with some detail.[9] Similar groups exist today for purposes of bank burglary, kidnaping, post-office robbery, shoplifting, confidence games, picking pockets, and stealing automobiles. Frequently these groups co-operate with each other. A group of automobile thieves on the West Side in Chicago and another group on the South Side developed an exchange of information which enabled one group to steal cars from the neighborhood in which the other group lived.

Organization involves, also, the development of arrangements for the disposal of stolen goods. A "fence" or receiver of stolen goods is frequently consulted in advance of a crime, and a theft may be executed for the purpose of securing specific commodities desired by the "fence." Somewhat permanent relations are established between a group and a particular "fence." "Fences," likewise, are organized in a network which sometimes covers the principal cities of America.

Protection against arrest and conviction is a necessary part of organized crime. The precautions that the individual criminal may take in order to escape detection are merely the beginning. Additional protection is secured by finding traitors among law-enforcement officers. The techniques of fixing crimes are much more important than the techniques of executing crimes. Fortunately for the criminals, the political machine in the ordinary city stands ready to protect criminals if proper compensation in money or services is made. Since this political machine controls appointments and elections it controls the police and the courts and its orders must be obeyed. The fixing of cases involves, first, various methods of inducing victims not to testify and not to press the prosecution. These methods include persuasion, restitution of

---

[9] A. V. Judges, *The Elizabethan Underworld*, London, 1930.

stolen property, frequently with additional compensation, intimidation, tricks, and murder. The police are frequently the agents of the criminals in persuading victims to accept restitution. They inform the victim that a criminal trial will cause him great inconvenience and expense, and may be continued for many months. At the end of the time the victim has no prospect of recovering his stolen goods. Sometimes the criminals themselves make the contact with the victim and present the same arguments, together with an offer of restitution. Second, the police are induced not to make complaint or, if the complaint has been made, not to testify truthfully. This result may be secured by direct bribery or by political orders. Third, the prosecuting attorney may be induced not to prosecute, or if prosecution is inevitable, to see that the evidence is presented badly so that the case against the offenders is not clear. In the modern court, the prosecutor has immense power in this respect. Immunity is secured in this manner in many cases, generally through the orders of the political leader, though the prosecutor generally secures financial compensation for his assistance either directly or indirectly. Fourth, the court may be induced not to convict. Immunity is less frequently secured at this stage, for the court is public and the judge or jury is subject to much criticism for open protection of the criminal. It is possible, however, for the judge to impose sentence for the sake of the public and then to modify the sentence in his chambers, or for him to commit an offender to a workhouse and then, within a short time, recall him and change the sentence to a small fine. Fifth, officers in institutions of the more corrupt kind may be induced to release the offender immediately, for a suitable payment, but carry him on the books as an inmate of the institution until the end of his sentence. If this is too dangerous, they can at least give the criminal a comfortable position in the institution and recommend an early release on parole. It is probable, however, that there is less fixing of cases with the parole board, about which the newspapers have made so many criticisms, than at any other point in the whole judicial and penal procedure.

These cases of fixing as a part of organized crime are not glaring to the casual observer, for the organized criminals are a comparatively small part of the entire number who are arrested and prosecuted. The police, the prosecutor, and the judge can be severe with the friendless and unorganized criminals, who have no money and no political connections, and thus the favors granted to organized criminals are not apparent.

The process of organization, therefore, involves association of a small group of criminals for the execution of a certain type of crimes, together with the development of plans by which detection may be avoided, and the development of a fund of money and political connections by means of which immunity or relative immunity may be secured in case of detection. In order that immunity may be secured in this manner it is necessary that the political machine be kept intact, and this requires, among other things, large campaign contributions from respectable as well as disreputable businesses. These campaign contributions, however, are made in order that laws may not be passed or may not be enforced against the businesses which make the contributions. Thus organized crime begins with a small working group of three or four members, but it involves the political machine, and disreputable and respectable businesses. It is not necessary, from the point of view of the concept of organized crime, that the organization should extend this far. It could properly be called organized if it involved no collusion beyond the working group.

The most widespread organization of lawlessness is in connection with the vices. Relatively few people demand that burglars, pickpockets, and confidence men engage in crime, but many persons demand opportunities for illicit sexual intercourse, gambling, and consumption of alcohol. Probably the principal public demand comes from the underworld rather than respectable society, but at any rate the demand is insistent. This provides a basis for extensive organization which involves the places of vice, the patrons, the real estate dealers, the manufacturers of commodities used in the vices, the police and courts, the politicians, and sometimes a much wider public.

Organization of the vices in American cities has existed for several decades, at least. Laws designed to regulate the liquor traffic have been violated rather systematically in most American cities for at least a century. This consistent violation was possible only because the police did not try to enforce the laws. The non-enforcement of laws naturally involved a service to the saloons and the saloons were compelled to make a return, which was done in the form of campaign contributions, graft, and other financial and political services. In fact the liquor interests and the political machine have been almost identical in many cities.

During the period of national prohibition the difficulties of enforcement were very great, to be sure, but the efforts at enforcement were frequently insincere. For a considerable part of the period of national prohibition the leading American manufacturer of intoxicating drinks was in charge of the enforcement of the law against the illicit manufacture and sale of intoxicating drinks. With comparative immunity from prosecution, with a somewhat widespread public demand for alcohol, and with huge profits, the supply was forthcoming. Almost from the first the manufacture, distribution, and sale was in the hands of groups of people rather than of isolated individuals. These groups at first were generally based on neighborhood or national lines and reflected homogeneity of culture. These groups came into competition and by violent warfare were forced into larger units, and these larger units were again forced into huge syndicates. The process was exactly the same as in legitimate business, though the methods inclined somewhat more to violence and less to fraud than in legitimate business. While the organized syndicate was using warnings, destruction of property, and murder as means of preventing competition, the police, acting under orders of political leaders, were harassing any dealers or manufacturers who attempted to enter the liquor business. The organization was never secure, however, for subordinates were rebellious and ambitious, and since the entire business was illegal, control depended finally upon violence.

The process in the organization of gambling has been somewhat similar to that in liquor. Gambling has existed in violation of law but with protection by officers of the law for many decades. The assistance of the officers of the law was secured by payments to them as individuals, or payments to the controlling officers, or by financial and political services to the politicians who controlled the higher officers. These arrangements were generally confined to particular gambling places, and formal organization did not go much beyond that relationship with the officers of the law. This, however, was changed during the period of national prohibition. The liquor syndicate began to develop gambling as an organized business, depending especially upon slot machines. The number of the machines in a particular area was greatly increased, and the area under the control of the syndicate was increased, so that both intensive and extensive developments occurred. This, also, required collusion of the public officers and of the politicians and, as in the case of alcohol, this was easily secured. Competition developed as the profits from this business became apparent, but competition was restrained both by the assistance of the police and by the destruction of property and life.

Prostitution involved somewhat more organization than gambling did in the early period. Houses of prostitution were segregated in many cities to a much greater extent than were the gambling places. Individual houses and the area as a whole were protected by the police, who, however, harassed competitors. Vice drives shortly before the war broke up these segregated districts, which had never had a monopoly on prostitution. As early as that, also, girls were transported from place to place for purposes of prostitution and were held against their will in places of prostitution. The federal law against the white slave traffic was directed at this development of the business but has never had much effect. The principal organization of the business of prostitution came, as did the organization of gambling, when it passed into the hands of the liquor syndicates. The organization which took over the payment of protection money for the liquor business could equally well make collections and payments for gambling and prostitution. Consequently most houses of prostitution in the cities passed into the control of the syndicate, and those prostitutes who attempted to ply their business outside of protected houses were harassed by the police, while those in the protected houses were secure. Thus the prostitutes were forced very generally into the organization.

Many of the trade unions were captured by representatives of criminal syndicates. The syndicate developed protective organizations, which were based essentially on threat of violence if the person did not join. These organizations at first were in the weaker groups, but they spread to the groups which already had trade unions or trade associations, and have frequently involved both the trade union and the employers' association. These associations secured gains from the racketeering practice, even though the racketeer became wealthy at this.

There is sufficient evidence that many liquor gangs engaged in other types of crime. If the income from the liquor, gambling, and prostitution business was less than was needed at a particular time, a group of the regular staff of the organization would rob a bank or a hotel, or commit some other profitable crime. Since they had the support of the politicians and thus of the police and the courts for their organized traffic in liquor, gambling, and prostitution, they were relatively immune even in cases of robbery. Kidnaping developed to some extent in the later period of national prohibition, but it appears that kidnaping was to a very slight extent in the hands of the liquor syndicates.

PROFESSIONALIZATION. The term "professional" when applied to a criminal refers to the following things: the pursuit of crime as a regular, day-by-day occupation, the development of skilled techniques and careful planning in that occupation, and status among criminals. The professional criminal is differentiated from the occasional criminal, the amateur criminal, the unskilled and careless criminal. The term "profession" does not carry with it the ideal of public service which is supposed to be characteristic of the legitimate professions, but the professional criminal argues that the ideal of public service is no more developed in the legal profession than in the criminal profession.

Certain types of crimes can be committed without previous experience in crime. Murder by shooting, for instance, may be committed by a person who had no previous experience in murder, even if he did have experience in shooting. Most crimes, however, require training. Boys in a delinquency area are taught how to commit thefts of various kinds. The boy who moves into an area at, say, the age of ten years without previous experience in stealing has to learn many things in order to keep out of difficulty. The other boys will show him how to steal articles from a department store, how to steal from a truck, how to steal an automobile. These are techniques which must be learned. Among these skilled techniques connected with stealing is the method of driving an automobile, which is known as "whipping" the corners. This training, however, extends somewhat beyond the execution of the crime. It includes also knowledge of methods of behavior in case one is caught, knowledge of when to cry and when not to cry, what types of lies to tell the police or the court. This, however, is on a relatively crude and low plane, as is also the work of the older burglars and robbers. Violence, force, bribery, intimidation, and similar methods are used and they are, after all, very crude.

The professional with status, on the other hand, has a much

more highly skilled occupation. The old safe-breaker stood at the head of the criminal professions, for his skill was unusually great and his plans had to be made with unusual care. There is, in addition, a group of thieves whose occupation requires skill in social manipulation. These include picking pockets, shoplifting, and confidence games. The crime of picking pockets requires manual skill, to be sure, but in addition it requires the proper diversion of attention at the crucial moment. Shoplifting may be of the casual amateur kind, but there is also a highly skilled technique, which requires that the thief give to the clerks in the store the impression that he is a respectable customer so that they dare not stop him for fear of insulting a regular customer. The confidence games are based essentially on salesmanship and generally involve a willingness on the part of the victim to engage in an illegitimate profit.

Professionalization extends beyond the execution of the crime, however. It involves the prior location of "spots," and the prior preparation for escaping punishment in case of detection in crime. Arrangements have been made in advance for bail, legal service, and fixing the case. It is in these advance arrangements quite as much as in the technique of executing the crime that professionalization is found.

THE CRIMINAL CODE. In connection with organization and professionalization codes of behavior develop among criminals. The codes are not the same for all types of crimes or all types of criminals. There are, however, two very general laws. One is not to inform on another criminal, the other is to make an honest division of the loot with the companions or partners in crime. "Do not squeal" and "Do not burn your partner" are the basic commandments of the criminals. Unquestionably these commandments are violated frequently among criminals, but on the other hand it is surprising how much pain many criminals will suffer at the hands of the police in the third degree rather than inform on other criminals. These commandments are enforced by direct and violent punishment in criminal groups. They are perhaps obeyed most strictly by professional criminals and least strictly by the occasional and amateur criminals.

In certain criminal groups "toughness" must be displayed in dealing with the public. This is in part based on the segregation of criminals and of criminal behavior. Just as the business man acts on the principle that "business is business," so these criminals act on the principle "crime is crime." There is no place for sentiment in either case. In addition, however, there is a considerable amount of bravado involved in the displays. A group of young criminals make a successful daylight robbery of a store across the street from a police station and as they drive away in their automobile, they shoot several times through the window of the police station. A young criminal is angered at the way the police have treated his brother and he sets fire to a police automobile which is parked in front of the police station. Automobile thieves make a special effort to steal police automobiles. A criminal who is on trial in a courtroom filled with people and with policemen and bailiffs standing around secures a gun and tries to shoot his way out of the courtroom. Such acts are expressions of bravado. They give the criminal status in his group and a thrill. The professional criminals, however, are not likely to engage in such exploits. The professional pickpockets, for instance, do not pick the pockets of policemen though they could easily do so. This would simply antagonize the police and the professional criminal wants to reduce antagonism.

The criminals of the crude type, also, display feelings in other ways. It is fashionable for robbers to punish the man who has no money or very little money when he is searched. Similarly burglars may destroy property in a store if they find no money. One of the burglary insurance companies has suggested to its clients that they should always leave a small sum of money accessible in the till so that burglars will not destroy property. These expressions of resentment may be spontaneous, but they seem to some extent to vary in fashion-like manner. It is probable that newspapers describe these expressions of resentment, other criminals read these accounts, and imitate the procedure.

IMPORTANCE OF CRIMINAL PROCESSES. Efforts are frequently made to explain why a particular person committed a particular crime in the particular situation and manner. Because of the large number of variables this is an extremely difficult if not impossible problem. The problem is simplified if uniformities in criminal behavior can be defined and described and efforts then made to explain these uniformities. The processes which have been discussed above are illustrations of this effort to define and describe some of the uniformities in criminal behavior.

SUGGESTED READINGS

Asbury, Herbert, *Barbary Coast,* Garden City, 1933.

Asbury, Herbert, *The French Quarter,* New York, 1935.

Asbury, Herbert, *The Gangs of New York,* New York, 1928.

Asbury, Herbert, *Sucker's Progress,* New York, 1938.

Ashton-Wolfe, H., *The Underworld,* London, 1929.

Black, Jack, "A Burglar Looks at Laws and Codes," *Harpers,* 160:306–313, February, 1930.

Bolitho, W., "The Gangster Trauma," *Survey,* 63:661–665, March 1, 1930.

Bolitho, W., "The National History of Graft," *Survey,* 64:138–140, 170–176, May 1, 1930.

Bolitho, W., "The Psychosis of the Gang," *Survey,* 63:501–506, February 1, 1930.

Bulger, J. E., "Automobile Thefts," *Jour. Crim. Law and Criminol.,* 23:806–810, January, 1933.

Burroughs, Stephen, *Memoirs of the Notorious Stephen Burroughs of New Hampshire,* New York, 1924.

Byrnes, T. F., *Professional Criminals of America,* New York, 1886.

Clarke, Donald H., *In the Reign of Rothstein,* New York, 1929.

Duffus, R. L., "The Function of the Racketeer," *New Rep.,* 58:166–168, March 27, 1929.

Encyclopedia of Social Sciences, articles on "Brigandage," "Camorra," "Carbonari," "Comitadji," "Feud," "Gangs," "Guerilla Warfare," "Lawlessness," "Mafia," "Mercenary Troops," "Outlawry," "Piracy," "Racketeering," "Secret Societies," with bibliography in each article.

Gunthorpe, *Criminal Tribes of Bombay, Berar, and the Central Provinces.*

Hapgood, Hutchins, *Autobiography of a Thief,* New York, 1903.

Hoover, J. Edgar, "Bankruptcy Frauds," *Jour. Crim. Law and Criminol.,* 23:1073–1080, March, 1933.

Hoover, J. Edgar, "White Slave Traffic," *Jour. Crim. Law and Criminol.,* 24:475–482, July, 1933.

Hostetter, G. L., "Gangsterized Industry," *Survey,* 59:16–17, January, 1933.

Joly, Henri, *Le crime, étude sociale,* Paris, 1888.

Judges, A. V., *The Elizabethan Underworld,* London, 1930.

Kennedy, M., *Criminal Tribes of the Bombay Presidency,* Bombay, 1908.

Landesco, John, *Organized Crime in Chicago,* Part III of the *Illinois Crime Survey,* Chicago, 1929.

Lewis, Alfred H., *The Apaches of New York,* New York, 1912.

Lynch, D. T., *Criminals and Politicians,* New York, 1932.

McCarthy, Katherine C., "Racketeering: A Contribution to a Bibliography," *Jour. Crim. Law and Criminol.,* 22:578–586, November, 1931.

Moore, Langdon W., *His Own Story of His Eventful Life,* Boston, 1893.

Nelson, Victor, *Prison Days and Nights,* Boston, 1933.

New York Legislature, *Joint Commission on the Government of the City of New York* (Hofstadter and Seabury Committee), 5 Vols. in 2, New York, 1933.

New York Legislature, *Report and Proceedings of the Senate Committee on the Police Department of the City of New York* (Lexow Committee), Albany, 1895, 5 Vols. See especially pp. 5311–5388.

Parkhurst, Charles H., *Our Fight with Tammany,* New York, 1895.

Reckless, W. C., *Vice in Chicago,* Chicago, 1933.

Sanders, R. C., "Syndicated Bank Robbery," *Jour. Crim. Law and Criminol.,* 23:797–805, January, 1933.

Shaw, Clifford R., *The Jack-Roller,* Chicago, 1930.

Shaw, Clifford R., *The Natural History of a Delinquent Career,* Chicago, 1931.

Shaw, Clifford R., and McKay, Henry D., "Report on Social Factors in Juvenile Delinquency," *Natl. Com. on Law Obs. and Enf.,* No. 13, Vol. II, 1932.

Steffens, Lincoln, *Autobiography,* New York, 1931.

Sullivan, E. D., *Chicago Surrenders,* New York, 1930.

Sullivan, E. D., *Rattling the Cup on Chicago,* New York, 1929.

Tannenbaum, Frank, *Crime and the Community,* Boston, 1938, Chs. 2–7.

Thomas, Norman, and Blanchard, Paul, *What's the Matter with New York?* New York, 1932.

Thrasher, F. M., *The Gang,* Chicago, 1927.

Verrill, A. H., *Smugglers and Smuggling,* New York, 1924.

Wermert, G., *Die Insel Sicilien,* Berlin, 1905, Ch. 28.

Wulffen, E., *Gauern- und Verbrecher-Typen,* Berlin, 1910.

Chapter Thirteen

BEHAVIOR SYSTEMS IN CRIME

INTRODUCTION. Most of the scientific work in criminology has been directed at the explanation of crime in general. Crime in general consists of a great variety of criminal acts. These acts have very little in common except the fact that they are all violations of law. They differ among themselves in the motives and characteristics of the offenders, the characteristics of the victims, the situations in which they occur, the techniques which are used, the damages which result, and the reactions of the victims and of the public. Consequently it is not likely that a general explanation of all crimes will be sufficiently specific or precise to aid greatly in understanding or controlling crime. In order to make progress in the explanation of crime it is desirable to break crime into more homogeneous units. In this respect crime is like disease. Some general theories of disease have been stated and are useful. The germ theory of disease is a very useful general theory, but even this theory does not apply to all diseases. Progress in the explanation of disease is being made principally by the studies of specific diseases. Similarly, it is desirable to concentrate research work in criminology on specific crimes.

What, for purposes of theoretical explanation, is a specific crime? Evidently it is not a crime as legally defined, for almost any one of the legally defined crimes involves a great variety of casual processes. Jerome Hall has shown this excellently in the field of larceny from the point of view of control, and has suggested a classification of larcenies into sociological units.[1] Such a sociological unit or entity may be called a behavior system.

THE BEHAVIOR SYSTEM IN CRIME. The behavior system in

---

[1] Jerome Hall, *Theft, Law, and Society,* Boston, 1935.

crime may be described by its three principal characteristics. First, a behavior system in crime is not merely an aggregation of individual criminal acts. It is an integrated unit, which includes, in addition to the individual acts, the codes, traditions, *esprit de corps*, social relationships among the direct participants, and indirect participation of many other persons. It is thus essentially a groupway of life. Behavior systems in crime may be illustrated by professional theft, circus grifting, drug addiction, racketeering, fraudulent advertising, and manipulation of corporate securities as practised by Insull, the Van Sweringens, and many others.

Second, the behavior which occurs in a behavior system is not unique to any particular individual. It is common behavior. It operates in the same manner in a large number of persons and therefore it should be possible to find causal factors and processes which are not unique to the particular individual.

Third, while common and joint participation in the system is the essential characteristic of a behavior system, it can frequently be identified by the feeling of identification of those who participate in it. If the participants feel that they belong together for this purpose, they do belong together. A professional confidence man and a professional forger would feel that they belonged together, even though they used different technique, because they have many common interests and standards and can therefore participate in the same system. On the other hand an embezzler would not identify himself with an automobile thief. If these two should meet they would have no common reactions or sentiments growing out of their crimes except such as were common to practically all other persons who violate the laws. Ultimately a behavior system should be defined as a way of life which grows out of a unified causal process. A behavior system in this respect would be similar to a disease, which is differentiated from other diseases by the causal process common to it regardless of the person in whom it occurs.

If a behavior system can be isolated, the problem is to explain that system as a unit. This is similar to an attempt to explain baseball in America. This does not consist primarily of explaining why a particular person becomes a baseball player, and in fact the explanation of why a particular person becomes a ball player merely assumes the existence and persistence of baseball as a system. By taking the behavior system as a problem it is possible to avoid some of the methodological difficulties which arise when the act of a specific person is taken as the problem.

Moreover, by taking the behavior system as the problem it is possible to break away from the legal limitations that have often impeded scientific work in criminology. A sociological unit need not be confined to the legal proscriptions. It can be studied wherever it exists, whether as crime or not crime, and generalizations should apply throughout the system. In this way the criminologist can define his own units and does not need to accept the decisions of courts and legislatures.

KIDNAPING. Kidnaping is discussed here as an illustration of a legal entity which is not a sociological entity. As a legal entity kidnaping consists of taking possession of the body of another person, against his will, by force or fraud and in violation of the law. Kidnaping appears in at least ten forms which are socially distinct and which generally involve different causal processes. First, kidnaping was the basis of the slave trade, and all those who participated in the slave trade and in slavery were accessory to kidnaping. Second, impressment was a form of kidnaping in which a sailor was forced to leave a ship in which he had a legal right to be, to board another ship and work there as a sailor. Third, sailors were shanghaiied by force and compelled to work as sailors in ships. They received wages, but commissions for the crimps who had kidnaped them were deducted from their wages. Fourth, girls were kidnaped and used for prostitution. This aroused attention in the period before the World War under the name of white slavery. Probably few bona fide cases occurred, and at any rate the law which was enacted has been used extensively by "gold diggers" as a means of blackmailing their paramours. Fifth, underworld leaders were kidnaped by underworld criminals and held for ransom, especially during the prohibition period. Since the underworld leaders were not able to appeal to the law for support and did not wish to advertise their inability to protect themselves, these kidnapings aroused little public attention. Sixth, kidnaping of wealthy persons in the upperworld by members of the underworld for purposes of ransom developed extensively about 1930, so that newspapers announced a new crime in the making. While kidnaping of wealthy and respectable persons for ransom had occurred occasionally in the

United States prior to this date, its prevalence increased at that time. But kidnaping for ransom was not new, and kidnaping for other purposes was not new. The only thing that was new was the importance of the victims. Seventh, offenders took possession of victims in connection with other crimes, such as robbery, as a means of security for themselves. This was temporary and the victim was released as soon as the offender was secure. Eighth, illegal arrest is a form of kidnaping. If a policeman takes possession of a person under conditions not authorized by law, he is committing the legal crime of kidnaping. In this sense, policemen have kidnaped many times as frequently as all other offenders combined. A special form of this has appeared in connection with strikes, when special police have taken pickets, reporters, students, and others to the state line and pushed them across, with instructions not to return. Ninth, children have been kidnaped by lonesome and probably psychopathic women in lieu of other methods of securing children of their own. Tenth, a parent has kidnaped his own children who have been assigned by the court to the other parent in divorce proceedings, or under other circumstances. Doubtless other minor forms of kidnaping could be found by a relatively slight effort, but these ten are a sufficient number to show that kidnaping is not an entity in the causal sense.

These ten forms are, to be sure, somewhat interrelated. The first six forms mentioned (slave trade, impressment, shanghaiing, white slavery, underworld ransom cases, and upperworld ransom cases) all have financial returns as the objective, while the last four do not have this objective. Moreover, the six which have financial gain as the objective may be divided into two groups: those in which there is a large demand for victims with a small price per victim, and those in which there is a restricted demand with a high price per victim; the latter cases are those in which ransom is used. Also, they can be divided into kidnapings with respectable and important offenders and lowly, unimportant victims; and kidnapings with underworld offenders and important victims. The only form of kidnaping that has aroused great public antagonism is that in which the victims are important and respectable; the much more extensive kidnapings in which the victims were unimportant or not respectable continued for centuries before enough opposition developed to stop the practices. Consequently the existence and continuance of one form of kidnaping involves quite different factors than another form.[2]

PROFESSIONAL THEFT AS A BEHAVIOR SYSTEM. Professional theft is presented as an illustration of a behavior system which can be defined and explained as a unit.

The principal, but not the only, rackets used by professional thieves are confidence games, shoplifting, and pocket-picking. Not all persons who commit these specific crimes are professional thieves. Professional thieves make a regular business of theft. They use techniques which have been devolped over a period of centuries and transmitted to them through traditions and personal association. They have codes of behavior, *esprit de corps,* and consensus. They have a high status among other thieves and in the political and criminal underworld in general. They have differential association in the sense that they associate with each other and not, on the same basis, with outsiders, and also in the sense that they select their colleagues. Because of this differential association they develop a common language or argot which is relatively unknown to persons not in the profession. And they have organization. A thief is a professional when he has these six characteristics: regular work at theft, technical skill, consensus, status, differential association, and organization. The amateur thief is not a professional; neither is the consistently dishonest bondsalesman. The case is not quite so clear for the professional burglar or robber, for there the principal differential is the nature of the technique and the identification. The techniques of the professional thief are much the same as those of the salesman and the actor; they consist of methods of manipulating the interests, attention, and behavior of the victim. The professional thief depends on cleverness and wits, while the robber or burglar resorts more frequently to force or threat of force. Professional thieves have their groupways of behavior for the principal situations which confront them in their criminal activities. Consequently professional theft is a behavior system and a sociological entity.

The principal genetic question regarding professional theft is, How does it originate and how is it perpetuated in our culture?

---

[2] The following references on kidnaping are restricted principally to the recent literature on kidnaping for ransom. Herbert Asbury, *Barbary Coast,* New York, 1933, pp. 199–231; Justine Mansfield, *True Tales of Kidnapings,* New York, 1932; Melvin Purvis, *American Agent,* Garden City, pp. 70–97, 117–174, 221–242; E. D. Sullivan, *The Snatch Racket,* New York, 1932.

A secondary question is, How does a particular person get into this professional group?

The motives of professional thieves are much the same as the motives of other occupational groups: they wish to make money in safety. These desires require no specific explanation. The specific problem is, How do professional thieves remain secure in their violations of the law? Many professional thieves have conducted their illegal activities for a normal lifetime and never been locked up longer than a few days at a time; others have had one or two terms over a period of twenty or thirty years.

Security in professional theft is attained in three ways. First, the thieves select rackets that involve a minimum of danger. The confidence game is relatively safe because the victim generally agrees to participate in a dishonest transaction and when he finds that he is the victim he cannot make complaint without disgracing himself. Shoplifting is relatively safe because stores do not wish to run the risk of accusing legitimate customers of stealing, and the professional shoplifter makes it a point to look and act like a legitimate customer. Picking pockets is relatively safe because the legal rules of evidence require direct evidence that the thief puts his hand in the pocket and withdraws money, and that evidence is seldom secured. Second, the professional thieves develop clever and skilled techniques for executing the crimes which they select. They do this through tradition, tutelage, and general association. Third, they make arrangements to fix those cases in which they may be caught. Because of the importance of "the fix" in the profession of theft it will be discussed in more detail.

The professional thief expects to fix every case in which he may be caught. He generally does not fix the case himself but employs a professional fixer, for in a larger city one man generally does all of the fixing for all of the professional thieves. Whether the fixing is done by the thieves themselves or by their fixer, it is generally accomplished by the direct or indirect payment of money. First, a promise is made to the victim that his stolen property will be returned, sometimes with a bonus, if he will refuse to push the prosecution or to testify in a way that would damage the thief. A large proportion of the cases are fixed in this manner, for the victim is generally more interested in the return of his stolen property than he is in seeing that justice is done to the thieves. Second, the police, prosecutor, bailiff, or judge may be bribed. The policeman may advise the victim to take his money back and not be bothered with a long trial; or he may give evidence which conflicts with that of the victim or other witnesses; or he may render other services. The prosecutor may refuse to push the prosecution or, if he is compelled to do so, he may make a very weak effort to bring out evidence which is damaging to the thief. As a last resort, the judge may be bribed to render decisions in favor of the thief, or he may impose minor penalties. It is not necessary that everyone of these officeholders act dishonestly. The only thing necessary is to find one of them who will twist or pervert evidence or decisions. Most of the cases are fixed before they reach the higher courts. They can be fixed more easily in municipal courts than in federal courts. But a federal judge who presided at an important trial of confidence men has recently been indicted for accepting indirect bribes from persons and firms whose cases were heard in his court.

The profession of theft, then, exists in modern society because victims are more interested in getting their property back than in abstract justice, because officeholders are under the control of a political machine or have predatory personal interests. Also, professional theft exists because business concerns are willing to purchase stolen commodities, and because lawyers are willing to defend professional thieves by every clever argument and device available. Professional theft exists not only because persons are willing to steal, but also because the rest of society does not present a solid front against theft. In other words, society is disorganized with reference to theft.

The entrance of a particular person into the professional group is of secondary importance, for the explanation of theft as a profession cannot be found in the life-history of one of the members of the profession. Rather it is necessary to understand the profession in order to explain the individual thief. For admission into the profession is not merely an act of will of a person who decides that he would like to be a professional thief. He can no more become a professional thief in that manner than he can become a professional ballplayer. Others must permit him to become a professional thief, just as they must permit a person to become a professional ballplayer. Members of the profession make their entrance by a process of mutual selection.

No one can acquire all of the skills and work safely in co-operation with others without training and tutelage. Tutelage can be given only by those already in the profession. Consequently one gets into the profession by acceptance. The neophyte is instructed verbally regarding the principles of the racket and regarding the simple part he is given to play in it. He performs these minor tasks under the supervision of the professional thieves. If he does these tasks satisfactorily his responsibilities may be increased until he is finally given the same tasks as regular members of the profession. Not only is he instructed in the execution of the crime, but also in the codes of behavior; and he is made acquainted with other thieves, with the fixer, and the fences. This personal acquaintance is necessary for a safe career in the underworld.

Professional thieves do not extend this tutelage to everyone who would like to join them. They extend their assistance, of course, only to those with whom they come in contact in a friendly manner; that is, to fellow-lodgers in hotels, rooming-houses, or jails, and to waiters, cashiers, and taxicab drivers. The thieves get acquainted with most of these people in a legitimate manner, and confidence develops. They like a certain prospect, and he likes them. They may suggest that he join them, but more frequently he asks to join them because he wants more money than he can make at legitimate work and because their life looks attractive. Doubtless thousands of others with whom they do not come in contact in this manner have the abilities required for professional theft, but they do not happen to meet. Thus entrance into the profession is by selection. The selection is impersonal in the sense that a person must be in a position where he will come in contact with professional thieves in order to develop personal acquaintance. The selection is also personal in the sense that the thieves must be attracted to the prospect, and he must be attracted to them. He has a veto on joining the profession, but just as certainly they have a veto on him joining it.[3]

---

[3] Roger Benton, *Where Do I Go from Here?* New York, 1936; Hutchins Hapgood, *Autobiography of a Thief,* New York, 1903; Will Irwin, *Confessions of a Con Man,* New York, 1909; A. V. Judges, *The Elizabethan Underworld,* London, 1930; John Landesco, "The Criminal Underworld of Chicago in the Eighties and Nineties," *Jour. Crim. Law and Criminol.,* 25:341–357, 928–940, September, 1934–March, 1935; Charles E. Merriam, *Chicago,* New York, 1929, Ch. 2; J. F. Norfleet, *The Amazing Experiences of an Intrepid Texas Rancher,* Rev. Ed., Sugar Land, Tex., 1927; John J. O'Connor, *Broadway Racketeers,* New York, 1928; Edwin H. Sutherland, *The Professional Thief,* Chicago, 1937; Philip S. Van Cise, *Fighting the Underworld,* Boston, 1936.

CIRCUS GRIFTING. Circus grifting is a second behavior system in crime, which will be described as an illustration of this method of analysis. It consists principally of sure-thing gambling, as seen in the shell-game, three-card monte, the eight-dice cloth, the cologne joint, and the spindle. In order that circus grifting may be conducted satisfactorily and safely, four elements are necessary: grifters, victims, a dishonest circus management, and dishonest public officials. The behavior system is a combination of these four elements.

Circus grifters come from two principal sources. They may have been grifting previously in state fairs, resort communities, or carnivals, with methods somewhat similar to those used in the circus. Or they may have been living in the community in which the circus is playing, have been employed for a day as a shill or assistant in one of the games, have proved efficient, and have been taken along with the circus and trained in other details of the game. It is reported that a large proportion of the circus grifters originated in Indiana, where several circuses make their winter headquarters.

The circus grifters form a relatively cohesive group. They have a saying, "Once a circus grifter, always a circus grifter." The gambling games played in the circus are played elsewhere, but seldom with the same abandon. Many people who play one of these games elsewhere do not succeed in the circus, and many who are very successful in the circus are inefficient when they try to operate the same games elsewhere. The grifters in a particular circus are a somewhat exclusive group while the circus is on the road; the performers do not associate with them. In the early days the grifters rode in the "privilege car" of the circus train. This car was lined with steel to protect the occupants from attacks by angered residents of the community in which the gambling games had been operated. Also the grifters from all circuses associate during the winter season, for many of them spend the winter, or as much of it as their funds permit, in Hot Springs. The grifter in one circus will know the principal grifters in all of the other circuses. This exclusive association is a product of the necessity for training and tutelage in the operation of the gambling games.

Victims are available in practically every community. The general interest in gambling is the basis, but to this are added, first, the general atmosphere of make-believe and celebration connected with the circus, and second, the techniques used in appealing to spectators. One of these techniques is the example of the shill, who appears to be another spectator, but is actually an assistant in the game, and who plays and wins frequently. Another technique is an apparent opportunity for dishonesty; one of the shills raises one of the shells while the operator's back is turned and enables the other spectators to see the pea under the shell, or he bends the corner of the card in the monte game so that the spectator knows which card to guess. Since this dishonesty seems to make the gamble absolutely certain, many spectators then try it, and lose. The suggestions and insistence of the operator and of other assistants who seem to be spectators are factors. Finally, the general method is to induce a spectator to make a start, even without paying, and he is then ashamed to stop after a loss or two.

Dishonest public officials can be found in a large proportion of the communities in which circuses appear. Gambling is at least winked at in most communities, and the officials feel that some gambling in connection with the celebration at the time of a circus can be condoned, especially in return for tickets or money.

Dishonest circus managers are, or at least have been, abundant. The circus thirty years or more ago generally depended on the return from grifting for a substantial part of its income. The circus manager employed a "privilege man" who had charge of all of the grifting, and who paid to the circus a percentage of everything taken in on all of the games. Many of the circus managers started as grifters, and were sympathetic toward the grifters.

These four elements are therefore the necessary characteristics of this behavior system. Circus grifting was authorized and flourished in practically all of the circuses in 1880, in all except Ringlings in 1900, and in all except the largest circuses in 1930. In other words, circus grifting is decreasing. The circus grifters explain that this decrease is not due to a reduction in the number of potential grifters, or in the number of potential victims, or in the number of dishonest public officials. They insist that the decrease is due entirely to the changed attitude of circus managers. Moreover, the changed attitude of the circus manager is not due to an increase in honest motives, but to a change in the economic relationships. In the earlier days the grifting circus could change its name and thus conceal its identity before returning to a community which had been angered by the gambling games on the last trip. As the circus increased in size, its name came to be an asset from the point of view of advertising and could not be changed without loss of prestige and therefore loss of income. The loss from the change of name would be greater than the gain from grifting, and therefore grifting was reluctantly abandoned. It is for that reason that grifting is now found only in the smaller circuses.

The principal question is, Why did the circus ever authorize and participate in grifting? The most immediate answer is that this was a specific manifestation of generally dishonest tendencies. Many circuses in early days were fences for stolen horses. Its employees have been notorious for thefts from clotheslines. The circus management has frequently dealt dishonestly with its employees, holding out a part of the wages, overcharging on expenses. The circus has been unfair in its competition with the other circuses. The men who put up posters in the early decades were necessarily sluggers who could fight with the bill plasterers of rival circuses. Many of the attractions have been frauds. The "garmagunt" with three heads and eight legs was made of sole leather. The Siamese twins were two separate persons with a flesh-colored belt holding them together during the time they were on exhibition. The "horse with its tail where its head ought to be" was discovered, after payment of ten cents, to be a horse with its tail toward the manger. The exhibit "for men only" proved to be a pair of suspenders. The emu eggs sold by the attendant to farmers for $1.50 each proved to be goose eggs. The man who sold balloons hired an assistant to go through the circus grounds and, with his mouth full of tacks, blow them at the balloons which had been purchased so that resales could be made. Hundreds of incidents of this nature are recounted in the histories of the circus.

This general dishonesty, in which the circus grifting was embedded, was a product of four conditions. First, the circus was a mobile organization. It seldom remained longer than one day in a community, and there were no permanent ties, duties, responsibilities, or relationships. The circus was regarded as queer by the community, and the community was regarded as queer by the circus people. Second, the community was hostile toward the circus in several respects. In some places the circus or any other exhibit was prohibited. The opposition was partly on the ground of morals. It was believed that the circus would corrupt the young people. In some communities it was customary for the preachers to agree to preach anti-circus sermons in all churches on the Sunday preceding the circus. To counteract this Barnum advertised moral lectures as a part of the circus program, but the lectures bulked larger in the advertisements than they did in the program. The opposition was also on economic grounds. It was believed that the circus took away from the community money which should be spent in the community. Third, the people of the community frequently were dishonest in their dealings with the circus. The head of the department of streets in one city on the night before the appearance of the circus substituted old, worn-out manhole covers for the ones then in use, so that many of these covers would be broken by the heavy wagons in the circus parade. He then presented to the circus a bill for damages each year until the circus became suspicious and discovered the truth. A woman whose home was adjacent to the circus grounds claimed damages of fifty dollars because her laundry on the clothesline was spotted by flies attracted by the circus. The circus promised to give a free ticket to each child in an orphanage and to enough attendants to take care of the children; when the children arrived each one had an adult attendant. Thus the circus has been confronted with continuous efforts to impose upon it. Fourth, on the basis of this mobility, opposition, and community impositions, the circus population have undoubtedly been selected. It is not a random assortment of the population of the country, but rather is selected for that type of life. They have had a hard, unsociable life, and they have been hard, unsociable people. Out of this has grown the general dishonesty and grifting. It is reported that the English circus, which is much less mobile than the American circus, has very little dishonesty.[4]

CONCLUSION. Professional theft and circus grifting have been described in some detail as illustrations of the point of view and methods which are suggested. Neither of these topics has been investigated exhaustively and the interpretations are therefore tentative and hypothetical. More intensive studies are needed of these

---

[4] Bert J. Chipman, *Hey Rube!* Hollywood, 1933; C. R. Cooper, *Circus Day*, New York, 1925; E. C. May, *The Circus from Rome to Ringling*, New York, 1932; Gil Robinson, *Old Wagon Show Days*, Cincinnati, 1925; R. E. Sherwood, *Hold Yer Hosses*, New York, 1932; E. H. Smith, "Grift, An Account Based on Statement by Hoke Hammond," *Collier's*, 69:11–12, 20–21, April 8, 1922; M. R. Werner, *Barnum*, New York, 1930.

two behavior systems and of other behavior systems in crime before general propositions can be developed.

It is not understood that the entire area of crime can be covered in this manner. Rather it is understood that certain crimes cluster in systems, are organized, are combined with other behavior in such manner as to form systems, and that certain other crimes stand somewhat isolated and outside of systems. These behavior systems may be understood more readily than the isolated crimes, and therefore may yield general propositions that apply to a considerable part of criminal behavior. Later the less systematic criminal behavior can be interpreted and related to the more general propositions.

Chapter Fourteen

THE POLICE SYSTEM

THE CRIMINAL LAW and its violations have been discussed in the preceding chapters. We now pass to the reactions of society toward those who violate the laws and to the agencies organized for the direction of these reactions. The police system is the first of these agencies. Two problems concerning the police are fundamental. The first is to understand the police, the second to improve the efficiency of the police.

IMPORTANCE OF THE POLICE. The police are in a strategic position with reference to the causation and prevention of crime and to the treatment of criminals. They are frequently personified as "the law." Respect for law probably depends more upon the behavior of the police than of any other representative of the state. All of the other agencies of justice depend upon the police. Furthermore, the police system is important from the point of view of numbers and costs. Approximately three hundred thousand persons are included in the civil and private police forces and the annual expenditures for this system are approximately a half billion dollars.

COMPOSITION OF THE POLICE. The term "police" refers primarily to those civil agents whose principal duty is the enforcement of law and order, and secondarily to the specialized public inspectors and examiners and to private guards, detectives, vigilance committees, and watchmen, many of whom have public commissions as police.

Each governmental unit, under the American constitution, may have its own police force. The city has a uniformed police, plain clothes police, and many special examiners and inspectors, while the small town has a marshal and the township has a constable. The county may have an organized and uniformed police force, or, more frequently, a sheriff and deputies. A few states have a regular uniformed police force, some additional states have only a traffic police force, and all states have specialized inspectors, such as game wardens, factory inspectors, or bank examiners. The state militia may be called out for police duty in emergencies. To some extent the police work of the federal government is centralized in the Bureau of Investigation of the Department of Justice, but each federal department may have agents for enforcement of its laws, including laws regarding the currency, liquor, narcotic drugs, internal revenue, customs, immigration, naturalization, post office, the public domain, food and drugs, plant quarantine, meat inspection, conservation, and interstate commerce. The army and navy may perform police duties in emergencies.

Private police were found on the frontiers and in the early cities. They have not by any means disappeared in the modern cities. In fact they are tending to increase in some areas, largely because of a belief that the public police are not efficient. Many railroad systems employ policemen who are commissioned as constables, sheriffs, or municipal police. The Pennsylvania Railroad Company spends approximately a million dollars a year for police work. In Pennsylvania an industrial police force, known as the "coal and iron police," has been commissioned by the state but paid from private sources and used principally in connection with strikes. Gifford Pinchot testified that about two-thirds of this force were thugs, gunmen, and professional trouble makers. This police force was prohibited in Pennsylvania by an act of 1935. Many rural communities have had vigilance committees for the protection of horses, chickens, and other possessions. State bankers' associations have been instrumental in developing vigilance associations for the protection of banks in California, Illinois, Indiana, Iowa, Kansas, Michigan, Minnesota, and Wisconsin. In a survey of Indiana it was found in 1930 that the number of private police was almost as large as the number of public police, there being 1,600 members of vigilance committees and 313 private railway police as against 2,250 municipal and county police. Private detective agencies are employed for the protection of race tracks, exhibitions, conventions, department stores, jewelry stores, banks, and other places of business. The lawlessness of the agents of the more prominent of these private agencies has been demonstrated several times. Commercial agencies in Chicago, disgusted with the scandals in the municipal police department, developed a group of crime-fighters, known as the Secret Six, to which a police detail was assigned. This group ended its existence in 1933 with a scandal involving its investigators and other agents.

THE FUNCTION OF THE POLICE. The function of the police is the enforcement of law and order. The Continental idea is that the police should have wide grants of power and should include within their scope a great variety of administrative functions and have authority to make and enforce specific regulations within this broad field. The English idea has been that the work of the police should be narrowly circumscribed and that within this narrow field the authority of the police should be carefully restricted. The American conception has been similar to that of England, but the trend has been toward the Continental system. Many administrative tasks are being imposed upon the police. Some of these are concerned primarily with public order, as in the direction of traffic (including installation and maintenance of traffic lights and signals, designation of one-way streets and of zones), granting permits or licenses for taxicabs, taxi-drivers, and taxi-stands, parades, and similar activities, restraining crowds at fires, and aiding in emergencies. Other tasks are more specifically concerned with the enforcement of laws, and include licensing of amusement parks, dance halls, theaters, concealed weapons, property for advertising purposes, auctioneers, places for handling explosives, and also of inspecting motion pictures, weights and measures, and a great variety of other places and activities. The laws which require licensing and inspection are increasing rapidly, and in many places the enforcement of these laws is imposed upon the police. Suggestions have been made that the regular police should confine their activities to the enforcement of laws against serious crimes, and that separate organizations should be developed for dealing with "morals," traffic, and licensing and inspection. In fact, the tendency seems to be toward concentration rather than dispersion of police authority.

THE LAW OF ARREST. In the common law, the power of arrest resided almost equally in the police and the ordinary citizen. The legal right of arrest was as follows: Arrests could be made on warrants, or written orders of the court, by anyone authorized to serve them. Arrests could be made without such warrants on two conditions: (a) that a crime was known to have been committed, and (b) that the crime was committed in the presence of the person making the arrest, or, in case the crime was a felony and was not committed in the presence of the arresting officer, he had good reason to suspect that the person arrested was guilty. That is, a person committing a misdemeanor could not be arrested, except on warrant, by anyone, police officer or other, not present when the offense was being committed; a person suspected of having committed a felony might be arrested by one who was not present when the felony was committed, provided he had positive knowledge that a felony had been committed by someone and had good reason to suspect that this was the guilty person. This is the general law of arrest, which has been modified somewhat by statutes. Even with the modifications the law is frequently violated in making arrests. Most police departments, for instance, have rules that authorize policemen to make arrests on suspicion quite in opposition to the law. Doubtless thousands of illegal arrests are made by policemen in the "drag-net raids." A professor in a state institution of a neighboring state who was visiting in Chicago in 1933 was arrested by two detectives on a down-town street early in the evening as he was looking in a store window and he was held incommunicado for twenty hours. About the same time a girl eighteen years of age was held in jail by the police, and the method of arrest and detention violated eleven laws. A rather difficult situation exists. The police are criticized for not arresting persons who violate the law, but if they make illegal arrests the cases are dismissed whenever the defendant has adequate legal defense. Persons charged with carrying concealed weapons are very often dismissed on the ground that the officer had no reasonable ground for making an arrest; the fact that concealed weapons were found in the search subsequent to the arrest is of no legal importance, for the evidence was secured illegally and therefore might not be introduced in the court. In many other respects the law of arrest is inadequate.[1]

---

[1] J. B. Waite, "Some Inadequacies in the Law of Arrest," *Mich. Law Rev.*, 29:448–468, February, 1931; J. B. Waite, "Public Police and the Arrest of Felons," *Mich. Law Rev.*, 31:749–767, April, 1933; H. L. Wilgus, "Arrest without a Warrant," *Mich. Law Rev.*, 22:541–577, 673–709, 798–822, April–June, 1924; Jerome Hall, "Legal and Social Aspects of Arrest without a Warrant," *Harvard Law Rev.*, 49:566–592, April, 1936; Jerome Hall, "The Law of Arrest in Relation to Contemporary Social Problems," *Univ. of Chicago Law Rev.*, 3:345–375, April, 1936. For a different approach to this problem, see E. J. Hopkins, *Our Lawless Police*, New York, 1931, Ch. 5.

The American policeman is in an impossible position in that he must use more power than the law permits if he is to do his work efficiently. He can safely exceed his legal authority only when he deals with people who are helpless. When he thus exceeds his authority he makes enemies. The policeman must exercise judicial functions. He must know whether a certain act violates the law, whether it is a felony or misdemeanor, and the conditions under which a case can be proved if the law has been violated. He must determine whether the violation should be treated by warning or arrest, for the police cannot arrest everyone who violates a law. The courts would find it impossible to do their work if the police brought all cases into court, and the police would be in court so much of the time that the force would need to be enlarged very greatly. Consequently the police decide, and settle more cases than they take into court. These cases are, to be sure, trivial affairs— disputes between landlords and tenants or between neighbors, petty thefts, breaking windows, and such acts. A settlement is reached immediately and cheaply. The European plan of depending upon the policemen to use discretion is the sensible one, but for this reason it is important that, if the limits of discretion are widened by law, the persons who serve as policemen should be able to use discretion wisely.

CRITICISMS OF THE POLICE. At this time when strenuous efforts are being made in several departments to build up the respect for the police and the morale of the police, it is rather ungracious to dwell on the inefficiency of the police. But an understanding of the situation with reference to crime makes it necessary to state the situation as it generally prevails, and this means criticism. The criticisms of the rural police may be considered separately from those of the organized city police.

Four principal criticisms have been urged against the rural police, such as sheriff, marshal, and constable: (a) They are not professionals, and therefore are not able to cope successfully with the criminals of the present time. In addition, these officers are generally limited by law to one term or to two terms and consequently do not remain in office long enough to use the experience they secure. (b) These officers are limited by law to their territorial jurisdiction and this prevents them from effective pursuit of criminals. (c) The three types of police within a county are not co-ordinated; the marshal confines his efforts to his own municipality, the constable to his own township, and they are not an integral part of the sheriff's force. (d) These rural officers are usually paid by fees—fifty cents for making an arrest, fifty cents for discharging a person from jail, and similar fees for other services. The reasons for this fee system are: first, many of these officers devote only a part of their time to public work and by the fee system they can be paid "by the piece"; second, it is designed to stimulate the officer to increase his output; third, it is regarded as economical for the community, since the guilty party can be compelled to pay the costs of the case, which include these fees. But this fee system is thoroughly bad. Officers are induced to make unjustifiable arrests in order to get the fees; particularly notorious instances of this are reported in speed traps and in some of the Southern communities where Negroes are usually the victims. Even when this practice is not used, the prisoners and the public are likely to suspect that it is being used, and this lowers respect for law.

The general criticism of the city police is that they are inefficient. They do not compare favorably with police in other countries. This inefficiency takes two principal forms. The first is somewhat similar to that of the rural police. The city police force is not carefully selected, well trained, well organized, and well managed for the performance of its very difficult task of enforcing law and order. This criticism is generally admitted by everyone intimately acquainted with the situation. The second criticism is that the police force of the average city is systematically lawless. This does not mean that every policemen is lawless but that as a system it operates in a lawless manner.

The lawlessness of the police is expressed in several forms. Graft is the first of these forms of lawlessness. One of the most revealing investigations of a city police system that has been made was that of the Lexow Committee in New York City in 1894–1895,[2] and the most revealing part of the testimony before that committee was given by Max F. Schmittberger, a captain in the police department. His testimony, better than any other part of the evidence, shows that graft was characteristic of the police system rather than

[2] New York Legislature, *Report and Proceedings of the Senate Committee Appointed to Investigate the Police Department of the City of New York* (Lexow Committee), Albany, 1895, Vol. V, pp. 5311–5388. For a brief description of this investigation and of the history of Captain Schmittberger, see Lincoln Steffens, *Autobiography*, New York, 1931, pp. 221–230.

of isolated patrolmen. A decade and a half later Theodore A. Bingham, ex-commissioner of police of New York City, stated that he could have made a million dollars in bribe money during the first year in office. The Seabury Committee a generation later found the same situation persisting. The places of gambling, prostitution, and drinking in Chicago were closed tight for a week after the inauguration of a recent mayor of the city, and were then reopened. This temporary closing has been interpreted as pressure for payment of tribute, but regardless of the interpretation it is eloquent proof that the police can drive these agencies out of existence if they wish and if they are permitted by higher authorities to do so. But it is a mistake to believe that graft is restricted to the regulations of "morals." The Lexow Committee found in 1894–1895 that the same system of bribery was used by commission merchants, contractors, pushcart vendors, and bootblacks who wanted to use the public sidewalks or streets for private business. In Chicago the efforts to secure adequate regulation of taxicab companies were in vain until the discovery was made that the head of the police bureau supposed to regulate taxicabs and seven other policemen who were members of this bureau had been asked by the taxicab companies to become the original incorporators of an insurance subsidiary which was wholly owned by the taxicab companies. Thus they were closely affiliated in business with the taxi companies which they were supposed to regulate. Similarly in 1932 the Seabury Committee reported that the bribery of public officers was the method used in securing special privileges regarding building zone ordinances, bus franchises, waterfront leases, condemnation cases, weights and measures, taxi regulations, and many other things.[3] It is evident that bribery, graft, and corruption are not confined to the police department and in so far as found in the police department, are not confined to prostitution, gambling, and liquor. On the contrary, they may develop wherever business concerns or individuals see an opportunity for gain by bribery and wherever the police see an opportunity to force contributions from such concerns or individuals.

---

[3] New York Legislature, *Joint Committee on the Government of the City of New York*, 5 Vols. in two, New York City, 1932. This report has been summarized, interpreted, and amplified in several unofficial books, of which the following are the most important: W. B. Northrup and J. B. Northrup, *The Insolence of Office*, New York, 1932; Raymond Moley, *Tribunes of the People*, New Haven, 1932; Norman Thomas and Paul Blanchard, *What's the Matter with New York?* New York, 1932.

A second aspect of the lawlessness of the police is the large number of illegal and unnecessary arrests. This is, to some extent, a form of extortion and graft. The method of enforcement of graft is arrest. The Chief Justice of the Municipal Court in an important American city stated in 1932 in a semi-public address:

> The only gambling places raided are those which are not in the syndicate. If the court imposes a heavy fine on the proprietors of gambling places the only effect is to drive them into the syndicate, for it is cheaper to pay for police protection than to pay heavy fines.

The same method is used in extorting money from completely innocent persons. This is found in traffic cases in many places, whe.e it may be a means of enriching either the arresting officer or his office. One of the most astonishing revelations of the Seabury Committee was that the vice squad, operating in connection with lawyers, bondsman, and the prosecutor in the women's court, was systematically exploiting innocent women on charges of prostitution.[4] In many places pressure is placed on the patrolmen and the specialized squads to secure their quota of arrests because a large number of arrests gives an appearance of efficiency. Probably most of the illegal arrests are designed to protect society. The arrest of drunk persons, of vagrants, and of the disorderly, with unofficial release after several hours, is generally illegal in the form it takes and is a philanthropic but inefficient way of protecting the community. Somewhat related to these lawless arrests is the summary method of extradition frequently used by the police. A criminal who had escaped from the Indiana state prison was captured in Chicago and was taken by the Chicago police to the state line and pushed across into the arms of the Indiana police.

A third form of lawlessness is the collusion with professional criminals. Much evidence of this was found by the Chicago City Council on Crime in 1915 and several members of the police department were convicted, disappeared, or committed suicide. A Texas rancher named J. F. Norfleet, who had been swindled out of $45,000 in 1919 by a group of confidence men, pursued them for three years through Florida, California, Colorado, New York, and other states. His efforts were seriously hampered by the police in many cities,

---

[4] New York Legislature, *Joint Committee on the Government of the City of New York* (Hofstadter Committee), New York City, 1932, Vol. II, p. 86.

especially in Florida and California, and some of these interfering policemen were convicted as a result.[5] When the district attorney in Denver attempted to secure evidence against a ring of confidence men in 1922 he called in the state troopers to make arrests, and kept his prisoners confined in the basement of a church until the raid was complete, for he was afraid to let any of the city police learn of his plans.[6] A professional thief has reported that professional thieves in general work on the assumption that any case of theft by them in any American city can be "fixed" and that an arrest is merely a temporary discomfort from which no great inconvenience results. This does not involve the entire police system in the sense in which graft connected with gambling or liquor does, but is more specifically confined to the members of the squad which has the assignment of dealing with pickpockets and confidence men. Positions on this squad are regarded as highly desirable because of the opportunities they furnish, and the supervising officers are unquestionably aware of the collusion.

A fourth form of lawlessness is brutality. Violence which is not legally justified is unquestionably used at the time of arrest or between the arrest and the hearing. Inspector Williams of the New York City police force stated, "There is more law in the end of a policeman's night stick than in a decision of the Supreme Court," and Captain Willemse has published a defense of illegal violence.[7] Such violence is generally denied by police officials in their public statements, as might be expected, but in confidential conversations the policeman will ask, "If you caught one member of a kidnaping gang and had no information regarding the other members of the gang, would you not be inclined to use violence in forcing him to reveal the identities of the other members?" It is not likely that violence is used frequently on the organized gangsters in those occupations which are systematically protected by the police or on the professional thieves, unless such criminals attack the police. The most injurious aspect of police violence is that it tends to alienate the public.[8]

---

[5] J. F. Norfleet, *The Amazing Experiences of an Intrepid Texas Rancher*, Rev. Ed., Sugar Land, Tex., 1927, pp. 71, 81–83, 92–98, 142–144, 158, 178, 198–220, 235, 243–247, 270, 297; Philip S. Van Cise, *Fighting the Underworld*, Boston, 1936.

[6] J. F. Norfleet, *op. cit.*, pp. 314 ff.

[7] Cornelius W. Willemse, *Behind the Green Lights*, New York, 1931.

[8] August Vollmer and Others, "Report on Police," *Natl. Com. on Law Obs. and Enf.*, No. 14, Washington, 1931, p. 45; Ernest J. Hopkins, *Our Lawless*

DIFFICULTIES OF POLICE WORK. While the public is making criticisms of the police such as those outlined above, the police are making equally cogent criticisms of the public. The first and most important of the impediments to efficient police work is that the police force is under the control of corrupt politicians who do not wish and will not permit the enforcement of law and order. For this the public is responsible. Vollmer writes:

Recently the gamblers were driven out of Detroit by the commissioner. These gamblers were strong enough politically to oust this commissioner from office despite the fact that he was recognized by police chiefs as one of the strongest and ablest police executives in America. For a number of years Kansas City, Mo., was controlled by a vice ring and no interference with their enterprises was tolerated.[9]

Appointments of commissioners and superintendents, and advancement of policemen from one rank to another are controlled largely by politicians. The politicians therefore control the fundamental policies of the police department. If the police department as a system is inefficient or corrupt, it may be traced first to the politicians and then to the public. Nominally the police department is organized and operates for the welfare of society; actually it is controlled for the welfare of the politicians. The politicians in the ordinary American city secure their incomes by plunder and graft, and keep their control by the distribution of patronage. Turner reported in 1907 that one-half of the precinct captains in Chicago were proprietors of questionable saloons, and at least six others were dealers in prostitution.[10] At present they represent different occupations but are not different in character. The politicians, being in control and being criminal or semi-criminal in their own behavior, naturally protect other criminals.

A second criticism is that the public has retained an antiquated system of criminal law and of criminal procedure, which all students report to be inadequate both in urban and rural communities. The

---

Police, New York, 1931; E. H. Lavine, The Third Degree, New York, 1930; Herbert Best, "Why the Police Fail," Harpers, 166:204–210, January, 1933; Raymond Moley, Tribunes of the People, pp. 193–203.

[9] Z. Chafee and Others, "Lawlessness in Law Enforcement," Natl. Com. on Law Obs. and Enf., No. 11, 1931, p. 45.

[10] G. K. Turner, "The City of Chicago," McClure's Mag., 28:575–592, April, 1907.

efforts of the police to control crime are frustrated, for criminals who are arrested escape conviction because of this system. Moreover, the same politicians who control the police also control the courts. The law of arrest is entirely inadequate at the present time. The police, according to law, are expected to enforce all laws, but some laws are unenforceable. The police are not taken into consideration when laws are passed and have no official voice in the determination of legislative policies. Many of the rules of evidence are not adapted to modern conditions.

A third criticism is that the duties of the police are enormously and frequently increased without proportionate increases in staff. The police must devote much time to the regulation of traffic, parades, inspection and licensing of various activities and agencies, and other tasks that are only remotely related to the repression and prevention of crime.

A fourth criticism is that the police are hampered by an anti-quated system of local boundaries. In the area within fifty miles of the center of Chicago more than four hundred independent police forces are operating, with no central control or organization except incidental co-operative efforts. Criminals are not restricted by these boundaries but police forces are. The result is a system of duplicating and conflicting efforts which is necessarily inefficient.

Fifth, the public is not willing to assist in the maintenance of law and order. The task is assigned to the police, and the public then withdraws. It is extremely difficult for the policeman to secure assistance from passersby in the pursuit of a criminal or the detection of crime. Some of these members of the public are afraid of reprisals by criminals, others have no interest. In the same spirit they are not willing to make sacrifices in other respects in order to assist the police to work more efficiently. The police believe, for instance, that a universal registration system would facilitate efficient work by the police. The ordinary American interprets this as an imposition on his personal liberty, though he makes no objection to submitting his fingerprints when he opens an account in the postal savings bank.

The sixth criticism of the public is that it has failed to recognize that the control of crime in modern life is extremely difficult and that it can be secured only by continuous patient effort. The development of modern means of transportation, the resulting mobility of peoples, and the contact of a great variety of races and nationalities in the American city have immensely increased the difficulties of control. The population of the European city is almost entirely native-born, but many American cities have 25 per cent of their population foreign-born. Negroes are almost unknown in European cities, but many American cities have from 10 to 50 per cent of the population colored. As mobility increases in European countries, the police forces there are finding the problem increasingly difficult. People in a city are anonymous. Two generations ago criminals wore masks, but today the criminal seldom wears a mask because he is a stranger and it is difficult to identify a stranger. The crowd on the city streets facilitates escape. A professional burglar has stated that one block and around the corner in a city is as good as twenty miles in the country. The automobile, also, greatly facilitates escape. The very number of crimes impedes the solution of any of them. A murder occurs in Chicago, on the average, almost every day. A specialized homicide squad therefore has little time for study of a particular murder but must rush from one case to another. In England, on the other hand, where less than one-half as many murders occur, a specialized force can concentrate on one murder until it is solved. This difference would probably not be so significant if it were not for the public pressure to solve spectacular crimes. For this pressure the newspapers are almost exclusively to blame, and they, more than any other agency, make it impossible for the police department to develop a policy of consistent work. The newspapers have learned that the public can be thrown into a panic by colorful publicity regarding the weakness of a bank or the spread of an epidemic disease. They have not learned the disastrous effects of colorful publicity regarding crime.[11]

Finally, the public is responsible for the failure to select policemen carefully, to provide adequate training, to furnish adequate salaries and conditions of employment, and to make possible continuous policies. The average term of office of the chief official of police departments in cities of a half million population or more is only slightly more than two years, while in London it has been about fifteen years. The Commissioner of Police in Chicago has his office about one mile from police headquarters and spends his time principally in conferences with political visitors, having little time for the direction of police work. The methods of selection of the police are

---

[11] Malcolm W. Bingay, "Newspapers' Responsibility in Law Enforcement," *Proc. Intern. Assoc. of Chiefs of Police,* 1933, pp. 101–209.

not adequate to keep morons and criminals out of the force. The mental tests of policemen have made it evident that many persons of low intelligence secure positions in police work.[12] Police work is very attractive to certain types of criminals. Of the 1,200 applicants for positions in the sheriff's department in Los Angeles County from 1927 to 1929 9 per cent had criminal records, of which at least two-thirds were for very serious crimes.[13] Doubtless many criminals secure positions in police departments. Also, the staff is inadequate. New York City or Chicago has less than half as many policemen per thousand population as Rome, Brussels, or Berlin, only slightly more than half as many as Paris or Vienna, and about three-fourths as many as London. Wages and salaries are comparatively low. In 1934 the median salary of patrolmen was $2,175 and the median salary of the controlling officer was $3,107. There is no force of experts and trained technicians available for specialized service in the cases of unusual difficulty.

In general, therefore, the police are inefficient, but the inefficiency is due to the fact that the public permits corrupt politicians to control the police policies and fails to provide the conditions which are essential to efficiency in the repression and prevention of crime. The social conflicts and social disorganization which produce a high crime rate also produce a police system which cannot deal effectively with crime under existing conditions. It cannot properly be said that the public wants the police to repress and prevent crime.

TRENDS AND A PROGRAM FOR IMPROVEMENT OF POLICE WORK. Plans for the improvement of the police system have been developed by various persons and agencies. This program includes freedom from corrupt politics, stability of organization, larger territorial organization, improvements of personnel, systems of assignments, equipment and scientific techniques, the development of preventive police work, cordial relations between police and public, and the general development of police morale and of police work as a profession. These elements in the program will be discussed, together with the trends toward the realization of the program.

[12] Grace M. Fernald and Ellen B. Sullivan, "Personnel Work with the Los Angeles Police Department," *Jour. Delinq.*, 10:252–267, January, 1926; M. A. Merrill, "Intelligence of Policemen," *Jour. Personnel Res.*, 5:511–515, April, 1927; L. L. Thurstone, "The Intelligence of Policemen," *Jour. Personnel Res.*, 1:64–74, June, 1922; August Vollmer and Others, "Report on Police," *Natl. Com. on Law Obs. and Enf.*, No. 14, p. 58–61.

[13] Bureau of Efficiency of the County of Los Angeles, *Survey of the Sheriff's Department of the County of Los Angeles*, 1929, p. 44.

A large proportion of the policemen are average citizens, no more brutal and no more dishonest than any other group of average citizens. Moreover they would like to do their work efficiently, as the average citizen would like to have them. But they are held in a system which prevents them from doing efficient work. The politicians, the public suspicion and hatred, and the public panics developed and expressed by the newspapers drive them into behavior of which they are ashamed but from which they do not find a way of escape. An occasional reform administration does not assist them or the public very much, because the police expect the regular system to be re-established at the next election and they are unwilling to sacrifice their future by co-operation with the reform administration. Nevertheless, they would probably co-operate very sincerely in a permanent program in which they had confidence.

POLITICS. The fundamental requirement for efficient police work is freedom from corrupt politics. The other parts of a program for the improvement of the police system are likely to be largely futile unless the impediments caused by corrupt politics are reduced, but the development of the other parts of this program may have an indirect influence in producing freedom from politics.

Freedom from corrupt politics does not, of course, mean freedom from all outside control. A police department cannot be a completely self-governing organization. Moreover, freedom from corrupt politics does not mean freedom from pressures of various kinds. It may be expected that people will always continue to put pressure on the police department for special privileges, and for leniency in dealing with their friends. If the police are free to deal on their merits with these inevitable pressures, efficiency need not be decreased thereby. Freedom from corrupt politics does mean freedom from the political control which is characteristic of most American cities. The political party in the typical city is an end in itself. It has no principles and no policy of social welfare. Its fundamental interest is to pay its political debts and win the next election. Elections come and go but the party machine remains relatively intact.

Indications of the waning of this type of municipal politics are faintly apparent. The strength of party affiliations is decreasing as we leave behind us the Civil War with its heritage of party loyalty. Party affiliations in the city, however, are maintained principally by the machine, with personal service to the constituents generally at the expense of the public, with direct bribery, and patronage. Civil service measures have made some inroads on patronage as compared with fifty years ago. Campaign contributions by wealthy persons are made in order to secure special privileges from the party managers. The autobiography of Lincoln Steffens, the biography of Frank L. Smith,[14] and an abundance of other evidence show that political corruption frequently emanates from large business concerns. The interest of business men in securing special privileges is likely to decrease because the pressure for business expansion will decrease as the rate of increase of population approaches zero, and also because all business concerns pay for these special privileges in high taxes and high crime rates although the privileges go to a relatively small number of interests. Business men are likely to revolt against this corruption of government for special privilege.

Second, the police system may secure a measure of freedom from politics even if politics remains corrupt. The executive officer of the police department is customarily appointed and removed by the mayor. This method prevails, nominally, in order to prevent police oppression and to promote police efficiency. As a matter of fact it has not produced these results and it has made the police system subservient to machine politics. Vollmer has suggested that the executive officer of the police department should be selected by civil service and given permanent tenure, subject to removal for cause, and this method is being used with good results in a few cities. Furthermore, the police are inactive and uninfluential in politics in comparison with fifty years ago. Also, since graft has been centralized and syndicated the police secure little of the proceeds, but they get most of the criticism. This is an intolerable position, especially in view of the developing pride in police work as a profession, and tends to produce a revolt of the police against the politicians. At the same time suggestions and even demands are made that the police should have a direct voice in legislative and executive policies. They are expected to enforce laws which they believe are unenforceable, and they demand that their voice should be heard before such legislation is enacted. Also, the police to some extent are developing programs for increasing their influence with the public. These tendencies are not entirely encouraging, but on the other hand they are not entirely hopeless. It is possible that the police may be able to work free from political control and regain the

---

[14] Lincoln Steffens, *Autobiography*, New York, 1931; C. H. Wooddy, *The Case of Frank L. Smith*, Chicago, 1931.

confidence of the public and take pride in their achievements. That it can be done has been illustrated in a few cities, in many of the state police systems, and in some of the federal forces.

STABILITY OF ORGANIZATION. The fundamental organization of the police system is modified frequently. A board of commissioners, a single commission, appointment of the municipal police commissioners by the state governor, election of commissioners, and other mechanical changes in police organization have been made. These frequent changes in the organization are one of the reasons for inefficiency. In the seventy-five years of New York's experience nine fundamental changes in organization have been made and in fifty years of police experience in Cincinnati ten changes have been made,[15] while in the ninety-one years in which London has had an organized police force there has been only one change in the fundamental machinery of control. These changes in American police systems have not been consistent efforts to reach an ideal but have been mere makeshifts and patchwork due to the popular clamor for a change.

REGIONAL AND STATE POLICE. One reason for the inefficiency of rural and urban police is the large number of small territorial units, each with its own police force. One of the fundamental elements of a program of police work is the amalgamation and co-ordination of these forces. Three tendencies are apparent in this field. One is to develop a regular uniformed county police or else to place all of the constables and marshals of the county under the direction of the sheriff, so that at least within the county the police force will be organized, placed on a civil service basis, and become somewhat professional. A second trend is the development of a single police system for an entire metropolitan area. The large number and great variety of police forces in the area of a great city and its suburbs makes efficiency impossible. Co-operative efforts between the police forces in the metropolitan area of Chicago have been developed, while in Cincinnati an organization which includes counties in Ohio, Kentucky, and Indiana has been devolped. These organizations are merely co-operative, and each force retains its independent existence. A more complete organization of these forces is regarded as desirable. There are some prospects that new regional units of government may be set up in the future. If this can be

---

[15] R. B. Fosdick, *American Police Systems,* New York, 1920, pp. 111–113.

done it will have, among other things, the advantage of bringing the suburban residents who have business interests in the city into the elections.

The development of the state police is already well under way. In 1934 forty-seven state police systems were found in thirty-eight states, of which eleven were regular state police systems, nine highway police systems with general powers over crimes, twenty highway police systems with powers restricted to regulation of traffic, four were state sheriffs, and three governor's reserves. The number of members on the forces of Connecticut, Massachusetts, New Jersey, New York, Pennsylvania, and West Virginia increased from 921 in 1920 to 1,753 in 1930, and the number of arrests increased from 29,268 to 126,822.

The state police work almost entirely outside of the large cities and are intended primarily for protection of rural communities and for the co-ordination of the work of the various local units. In Connecticut only 15 per cent of the arrests by the state police are in towns of more than twenty-five hundred population. The principal opposition to the extension of state police has come from the trade unions, which fear that the state police will be used as strike-breakers in mining communities and in other rural parts of the state. The state police of Pennsylvania has been on strike duty on the average only one day a year, but this has varied widely, being as high as 30 per cent in some years. Unquestionably the state police have on some occasions prevented strikers from legal activities.[16] but in this respect are no different from municipal police and are certainly superior to deputized strike-breakers furnished by private detective agencies who have records as gunmen, who have no permanent residence in the state, and who have no reputation to maintain.[17]

Related to this development of regional and state police forces is the tendency to increase the participation of the federal government in the administration of justice. At present the federal agencies participate only in so far as crimes involve interstate relations or federal activities. These federal activities have been enlarged recently with excellent effect by bringing kidnaping and extortion under federal jurisdiction in 1932, and bank robbery in 1934. The

---

[16] S. Adele Shaw, "Closed Towns," Survey, 43:58 ff., November 8, 1919; see, also, Survey, 43:372, January 3, 1920.

[17] On the activities of the iron and coal police in Pennsylvania and the general character of its members see Congressional Record, February 1, 1928, pp. 2406–2408.

Federal Bureau of Investigation claims that bank robberies have decreased 75 per cent since 1934. Professional criminals are not restrained by state boundaries, and in fact make efforts to get across state boundaries in order to secure temporary immunity from state agencies. The extent of the interstate relations of crime is illustrated in the following extract from a radio address on January 10, 1934, by Homer S. Cummings, the attorney-general of the United States:

The Urschel kidnaping occurred in the State of Oklahoma, the victim was held captive in a remote rural section of Texas, the ransom money was paid in Missouri, a portion of the ransom money was exchanged in Minnesota, another portion was hidden in Texas, one of the guilty parties was located in Colorado, and the others in Tennessee, Minnesota, Texas, and Illinois.

Because of this mobility of professional criminals the local agencies are seriously handicapped and a larger organization of police activities is needed. Furthermore, there is no logical reason why all serious crimes should not be defined by federal laws, as is done in Canada, and it is at least an open question whether much of the administrative work might not be transferred to the federal government to advantage. Certainly methods of co-operation between local and federal agencies in the police field can be promoted.

PERSONNEL PROBLEMS. The efficiency of the police system depends upon a careful selection of policemen and adequate training, discipline, and remuneration. In most cities at present policemen are selected by civil service, though a few cities still have a large turnover on each change of administration. Even when civil service exists it is far from adequate. An extensive literature has developed on the selection of policemen, and standards are at least being formed in the literature and are used in a few cities.[18]

Police training, likewise, has developed almost entirely within the last fifty years. In a questionnaire study of cities of over ten thousand population, it was found that about 20 per cent now possess some method of school training, although not more than sixteen, or 4 per cent of the entire number, of these schools were regarded as

---

[18] See August Vollmer, *op. cit.*, Ch. 3; L. J. O'Rourke, "The Use of Scientific Tests in the Selection and Promotion of Police," *Annals of Amer. Acad. of Pol. and Social Sci.*, 146:147–159, November, 1929; M. S. Viteles, "Psychological Methods in the Selection of Policemen in Europe," *Annals of Amer. Acad. of Pol. and Social Sci.*, 146:160–165, November, 1929.

having decent minimum requirements. In New York City there is a Police Academy in which eight hours of classwork per day for ninety days are required, and in New York State there are zone schools for the training of police officers in the smaller cities and towns. In at least ten cities or states police training is being developed by co-operation between a university and a city or state police department.[19] Students of August Vollmer have been outstanding in the development of this training, as illustrated by Chief O. W. Wilson of Wichita, Kansas. The Federal Bureau of Investigation organized a National Police Academy in 1935. This ordinarily has a session of twelve weeks, and in each session representatives from thirty-five to forty city, county, or state police departments are accepted for training, generally in technical aspects of police work.

ASSIGNMENTS. The assignment of police to specific tasks and the organization of work is another problem to which some attention has been given. Vollmer has developed a program for statistical and ecological studies of crimes as a basis of assignments. If the records of the police department indicate that robberies are concentrated in certain areas, at certain hours, and on certain days of the week, it is possible to concentrate the police force at those places and times so that the work of repression will be more efficient. This method has been used formally in a few cities, largely under Vollmer's influence, and it is used informally in many other cities. In many police departments spot maps are now hanging on the walls, while the tabulation of crimes by hours is a regular part of the revised annual reports. In addition, the neighborhood patrolman is tending to disappear and specialized squads are increasing in number. In Chicago in 1930 out of a force of 5,080 patrolmen only 250 were available for patrol duty in an average eight-hour shift. The word "patrolman" is becoming little more than a designation of rank and no longer describes a type of work. The small number assigned to regular patrol duty is explained in part by the large number assigned to courts, public buildings, baseball parks, parades, and to act as guards of private houses and places of business. In part it is due to the larger number assigned to special squads. The most important of these squads is the traffic squad. The number of members in the traffic division in New York City increased from 511 in 1905 to

---

[19] George B. Vold, *Survey of Police Training*, Minneapolis, 1937.

2,960 in 1930, or from 5.9 per cent to 15.9 per cent of the total police force. In addition New York City has pickpocket squads, gunman squads, mendicant squads, narcotic squads, an aviation police squad, and other squads and divisions. When one of these squads is given authority, the neighborhood patrolman may be expected to withdraw entirely from the enforcement of that law. This is especially true in regard to "morals." The owner of a house of prostitution in Chicago stated that the prostitute is careful when the squad car comes down the street but the patrolman is merely another prospective patron. Police authorities, however, believe that the neighborhood patrolman is a necessary unit in police work and should not entirely disappear.

EQUIPMENT. The equipment of the police department has often been inadequate in comparison with the equipment of professional criminals. A patrolmen on foot is expected to catch a bandit in an automobile. The equipment of the police department in larger cities has been steadily improving, and includes motorcycles, automobiles, armored cars, machine guns, tear-gas bombs, and airplanes. In many of the medium-sized cities the equipment is still extremely inadequate, but that this is not the primary defect in police work is shown by the statement of Bruce Smith that by and large American police departments are the best equipped of all police departments in the world.

One of the most striking developments in the equipment of police departments is in the means of communication. Thirty years ago the most important problem in communication was the method by which a central police station could communicate with the patrolman on the beat. The flash and gong signals were regarded as important innovations at that time. In the meantime the teletype or telephone-typewriter has been developed for communication between stations, and the police radio for communication between stations and also between a station and cars equipped with receiving sets. The police radio began in Dallas in 1922 and in 1931 was operating in fifty-nine cities, one township, two counties, and three state police systems. By 1937 more than 2,000 stations were licensed for police radio communication. The police airplanes have been equipped with receiving sets and efforts have been made, thus far unsuccessfully, to develop receiving sets for patrolmen on foot. The police radio has immensely increased the efficiency of the police.

The first teletype system in police work was used in 1925. By

1931 it was in use in five state police systems and in twenty cities not included in those states. A message can be sent by teletype from New York City to 35 master stations and thereby to 532 local police stations in New York, New Jersey, and Pennsylvania, and announcement has been made that Connecticut, Rhode Island, and Massachusetts will soon be linked with this unit. This method, also, has greatly increased the efficiency of the police work.

SCIENTIFIC TECHNIQUES. About 25 per cent of the arrests in the more serious crimes are made at the time of the commission of the crime. In the others, efforts are made to detect and identify the guilty party. This work is done in part by the regular patrolmen, in part by detectives in plain clothes. The plain-clothes detective is supposed to be a specialist, with unusual ability. As a matter of fact these positions are probably secured by purchase or political favoritism more frequently than other positions because of the opportunities they offer for graft. Train states, "The ordinary chauffeur is probably a brighter man than the average detective," and mental tests of policemen in Cleveland showed that the detectives had the lowest average score of any rank in the department. The regular patrolmen are frequently jealous of the detectives because the detectives appropriate all of the publicity. The method which is most frequently used is the stool-pigeon. In this case the police put pressure upon some criminal who is in their power and compel him, under threat of arrest for some crime he is known to have committed, to give information regarding the gossip of the underworld. Thus the spies and traitors of the criminal class are the real sources of information.

The essential thing about detective work is continuous and intelligent work on a particular case. It is at this point, especially, that the detective system in the American city is a failure. In Chicago during the spring and summer of 1933, a blond young woman assisted by two gunmen committed more than fifty robberies in the north and northwest parts of the city. The woman made herself conspicuous by slapping and cursing the victims. The police did not succeed in identifying or apprehending this gang until several months had passed. It is inconceivable that a trained force of detectives, concentrating on this group, could not have caught them more quickly.

In some cities and other centers scientific methods of crime detection are being developed and used. The federal officers, some of the state police, and some of the municipal police have made good use of these. The Bertillon system of physical measurements, started by Bertillon in France in 1883, was first used in America in 1893, and was regarded at the time as a great invention for purposes of identification. It has proved, however, to be difficult and expensive in operation and has been replaced by an organized system of fingerprints. The federal government has developed a central clearing house in Washington which in 1938 had more than eight million records; 52.4 per cent of the records received in 1937 were identified from previous records. The number of co-operating agencies increased from 543 in 1920 to 11,000 in 1937. In addition many states have developed state bureaus of identification. Three states had such bureaus in 1914, none were added until after 1920, but the number had increased to twenty-four at the end of 1934. Thus a network of local, state, and federal bureaus is developing, by means of which the previous criminal records of persons arrested or convicted may be determined. Many police departments still fail to contribute their records to this system, and especially is this true in misdemeanor cases.

In addition to fingerprints a great variety of techniques for the study of the traces of crimes has been developed. Many of these are being used in the larger police departments, though they are generally regarded as useful in a very small proportion of the cases. These include the identification of arms and bullets, identification of clothes, hair, teeth, automobile tires, and many other objects. The techniques of physics and chemistry have been applied to the detection of crime with remarkable success in this small number of cases. The "lie detector" and other devices for determining the truth of testimony are proving to have some value, though they are still definitely in the experimental stage. The Federal Bureau of Investigation has developed these methods further than any other center in America.

Another method of identification is known as the *modus operandi* system, which was devised by Major Atcherley of the English constabulary. This method is based on the principle that a criminal is likely to use the same technique repeatedly, and that an analysis and record of the technique used in every serious crime will provide means of identification in a particular crime. Some burglars always enter through basement windows, some through doors, some through second-story windows; some always steal silver, some jewelry, some clothing, some money; some come in the afternoon, some in the evening, some in the early morning. The California State Bureau of Identification has developed this method in a formal manner, and many municipal departments make at least informal use of the method.

The police departments in some of the European countries are greatly assisted in their work by the system of registration of inhabitants. In many cities this includes a requirement that the inhabitant report to the police within a specified time after he arrives in a city. European detectives would generally be rather helpless if they did not have this information to assist them. In Argentina the inhabitant is required to carry a registration card which serves to identify him. The police associations in this country have urged the adoption of some universal system of registration. As a matter of fact, fingerprints are recorded in some places for a fairly large proportion of the male citizens, including the army and navy, United States civil service and some state and municipal civil service positions, depositors in the postal savings banks, illiterate depositors in many other banks, and employees of some of the larger corporations. More than a million fingerprints of civilians are now in a special file in Washington. Also in maternity hospitals the fingerprints of the mother and the footprint of the baby are usually taken. The result is that a very large number of prints identifying individuals are already recorded but are not centralized or organized. Moreover, a very large proportion of the inhabitants of the country are recorded in some manner—in registers for election purposes, gas and electric light companies, the post office, directories of telephone companies and of cities—and when the individual or family changes residence this is recorded by the same agencies, and also by trucking companies. If this information were organized in a central registration system, it would cause little inconvenience to the average citizen and might be of great assistance in dealing with criminals. One reason for the very large number of arrests on suspicion at the present time is the fact that the individual has no method of identification. There is a question whether in the present anonymous city life, some organized method of registration for purposes of identification is not essential. The objection which is usually raised against this system is that it is undemocratic, but it may be pointed out that Switzerland, which is a close approach to the ideal democracy, has a system of this nature. A recent poll of public opinion in the United States found 62 per cent of those voting to be in favor of universal registration.

PREVENTIVE POLICE.   Arthur Woods made the statement:

The preventive policeman is the policeman of the future. However faithfully he does it he can no longer fully justify himself by simply "pounding the beat." . . . Police forces must try to keep crime from claiming its victims as Boards of Health try to keep plague and pestilence away.[20]

Vollmer, also, has emphasized the preventive work of the police. In 1930 thirteen cities reported that they had crime prevention bureaus. On examination these proved to be in most cases another name for women police.[21] The concept of preventive police work has not been clearly defined. It seems to include a great variety of methods, including "hounding the hoodlums," attacks on criminal hangouts, frequent patrolling, warning residents and business concerns to keep doors and windows locked, friendly acquaintance with the residents on the beat, friendly relations with boys' gangs, organization of recreational activities in areas where delinquency rates are high, concentrated and co-operative efforts to influence boys who are getting into trouble, and social service work with families or individuals in distress.

Some of this preventive work evidently can be done to advantage by women. In 1933 800 policewomen were carrying on their duties in about 200 communities. In 377 cities from which reports were secured in 1934 there were 484 policewomen out of a total of 88,985 employees of police departments.

On the other hand, much of the preventive work of the police must be done by the regular male policemen, and must become a part of the regular police program. This preventive work by the regular staff has been well developed in Rochester, New York, and in Berkeley. Efforts are made to build up friendly relations with the schools, and in case conferences with the various social agencies which are interested in programs for individuals who are inclined toward delinquency.[22]

[20] Arthur Woods, *Crime Prevention*, Princeton, 1918, p. 123. Reprinted by permission of Princeton University Press, publishers.
[21] Hubert R. Gallagher, *Crime Prevention as a Municipal Function*, Syracuse, 1930. For description of the preventive work of several police departments and a general program, see Pauline V. Young, *Social Treatment in Probation and Delinquency*, New York, 1937, Ch. 13.
[22] August Vollmer, "Predelinquency," *Jour. Crim. Law and Criminol.*, 14:282–283, August, 1923.

THE POLICE AND THE PUBLIC. The police of the United States have been severely criticized and this criticism has seldom been discriminating. The honest police who are trying to do their work efficiently have been hurt and are smarting under this criticism. One of the reactions it has produced is an organized effort to develop friendly understanding by the public. This tension seems to be developing, also, in England, where the friendly relations have been famous for many decades.[23] An article by H. A. Tripp has the thesis that the maintenance of friendly relations with the public is at present the most severe test of police efficiency.[24] The Royal Commission on Police Powers and Procedure in Great Britain in 1929 was much concerned with charges that the police had been questioning arrested persons illegally, and attempted to develop methods that would reduce the small amount of irritation that was being provoked by the existing procedures. The criterion was that the behavior of the police must under no circumstances arouse public antagonism.

The problem in America is much more difficult because the background of friendly relations does not exist. In certain cities the police department is making a systematic effort to create confidence and respect. In Rochester, New York, the police selected three members of the staff for full-time work in speaking to school assemblies, churches, welfare clubs, and other organizations. The International Association of Chiefs of Police has an active committee on publicity which is attempting to develop friendly understanding, and counteract injurious and erroneous statements regarding the police. There is no doubt that the police departments have reached the stage of propaganda, which is perhaps necessary in the complex life of the present day. Many police departments are giving instructions that the policemen must be polite and courteous, though this rule seems to apply primarily to traffic policemen. Occasional rewards are given to the most courteous policemen.

It is probable, however, that a friendly understanding will require more than politeness and speeches before clubs. Methods must be improved. One of the things that produces much irritation is arrest of a person who is completely responsible and who could be

---

[23] See S. Fowler Wright, *Police and Public,* London, 1929, 2nd ed. This is an attack on the English police for being overbearing, especially in the large number of regulations.

[24] H. A. Tripp, "Police and Public: A New Test of Police Quality," *Police Jour.,* 1:529–539, October, 1928.

depended upon to appear in court. The summons is being used as a substitute for arrest in many cases. In Boston the proportion of court actions initiated by summonses increased from 9.5 per cent in 1910 to 33.1 per cent in 1930. This increase is due principally to the increase in the proportion of traffic offenses rather than to the extension of the method of summons for other offenses. In many European countries summonses are used in an increasing proportion of non-traffic offenses. In England the percentage of prosecutions for all indictable offenses initiated by summons increased from 8 in 1893 to 25 in 1927. It is probable that summonses could be used to advantage in a much larger proportion of cases in this country. It must be admitted, however, that the experience with summonses for traffic violations in many cities in America has not been such as to make the police inclined to extend their use. An announcement was made by the Chief Justice of the Municipal Court of Chicago in 1931 that 10,000 persons who had been given tickets for violating traffic regulations had failed to appear, and that these persons would be arrested unless they appeared. When after many warnings and much difficulty they were finally induced to appear in court, the judges ordinarily released them with a warning, or some politician "fixed" the case. The police have a feeling that a person who is arrested for an offense at least gets that much punishment.

POLICE MORALE. Police morale must be created or developed. The police have had a certain morale for a generation or more, but it has been a pride in physical courage. It must come to be a pride in police work as a useful profession contributing to social welfare. It probably cannot be developed except as a by-product of efficient work and friendly relations with the public. Efforts are being made to develop police work as a profession. The chiefs, detectives, and others have formed associations and are attending conferences. The leaders in these associations are doing much to develop an honorable pride in their calling. Writings like those of Vollmer, Woods, and others are having the same effect. Fingerprint experts are holding technical conferences. These meetings tend to develop an *esprit de corps* that gives considerable reason for confidence in the future. In no other part of the entire field of criminal justice or of municipal administration is as much enthusiasm shown in regard to the possibility of developing scientific and professional methods as in the police field.

SUGGESTED READINGS

Best, Herbert, "Why the Police Fail," *Harpers,* 166:204–210, January, 1933.

Brereton, G. H., "Police Training: Its Needs and Problems," *Jour. Crim. and Criminol.,* 26: 247–254, July, 1935.

Cahalane, Cornelius F., *The Policeman,* New York, 1929.

Chafee, Z., and Others, "Report on Lawlessness in Law Enforcement," *Natl. Com. on Law Obs. and Enf.,* No. 11, Washington, 1931.

Chicago Citizens' Police Committee, *Chicago Police Problems,* Chicago, 1931.

Culver, Dorothy C., "Training of Police: A Bibliography," *Jour. Crim. Law and Criminol.,* 26:444–448, September, 1935.

Fosdick, R. B., *American Police Systems,* New York, 1920.

Fosdick, R. B., *European Police Systems,* New York, 1915.

Hall, Jerome, "The Law of Arrest in Relation to Contemporary Social Problems," *Univ. of Chi. Law Rev.,* 3:345–375, April, 1936.

Harrison, Leonard V., *Police Administration in Boston,* Cambridge, 1934.

Hopkins, E. J., *Our Lawless Police,* New York, 1931.

Hutzel, Eleonore L., *The Policewoman's Handbook,* New York, 1933.

Key, V. O., "Police Graft," *Amer. Jour. Sociol.,* 40:624–636, March, 1935.

Langeluttig, A., "Federal Police," *Annals of Amer. Acad. of Pol. and Social Sci.,* 146:41–54, November, 1929.

Larson, J. A., *Lying and Its Detection,* Chicago, 1932.

Lavine, E. H., *The Third Degree,* New York, 1930.

New York Legislature, *Report and Proceedings of the Senate Committee to Investigate the Police Department of the City of New York* (Lexow Committee), Albany, 1895, Vol. V. pp. 5311–5388.

New York Legislature, *Report of Joint Committee on the Government of the City of New York* (Hofstadter and Seabury Committee), 5 Vols. in 2, New York, 1932.

Seagle, William, "The American National Police: Dangers of Federal Crime Control," *Harpers,* 169:751–761, November, 1934.

Sellin, Thorsten (Editor), "The Police and the Crime Problem," *Annals of Amer. Acad. of Pol. and Social Sci.,* 146:1–268, November, 1929.

Shalloo, J. P., "Private Police," *Amer. Acad. of Pol. and Social Sci.,* Monograph No. 1, 1933.

Smith, Bruce, *Rural Crime Control,* New York, 1933.

Van Houten, M. C., "The International Coöperation of Criminal Police, Its History and Aims," *Police Jour.,* 3:482–497, October, 1930.

Vold, George B., *Survey of Police Training,* Minneapolis, 1937.

Vollmer, August, "Police Progress in the Past Twenty-Five Years," *Jour. Crim. Law and Criminol.,* 24:161–175, May, 1933.

Vollmer, August, and Others, "Report on Lawlessness in Law Enforcement," *Natl. Com. on Law Obs. and Enf.,* No. 14, Washington, 1931.

Vollmer, August, and Parker, Alfred E., *Crime and State Police,* Berkeley, 1935.

Waite, J. B., "Public Policy and the Arrest of Felons," *Mich. Law Rev.,* 31:749–767, April, 1933.

Willemse, Cornelius W., *Behind the Green Lights,* New York, 1931.

Woods, Arthur, *Crime Prevention,* Princeton, 1918.

Woods, Arthur, *Policeman and Public,* New Haven, 1919.

Chapter *Fifteen*

DETENTION BEFORE TRIAL

PROCEDURE AFTER ARREST. When a person is charged with a crime it is important that he should be available for trial. Since he may be innocent the method used in securing his presence at the trial should involve a minimum of hardship upon him. He may be summoned or notified to appear in court at a specified time or he may be arrested. The procedure after arrest may take any of the following courses: (a) He may be taken immediately to court and tried. (b) He may be held in the police station for a few hours or a few days and then released without trial. (c) He may secure a release on a writ of *habeas corpus*. (d) He may secure a release on bail with financial security for his return. (e) He may secure a release on his own recognizance or promise to return for the hearing. (f) He may be detained under supervision in some private home or hotel. (g) He may be detained in a police station or jail until the court is in session and ready to hear his case.

Persons are frequently released by the police without court appearance. This method is used especially in cases of intoxication and is known as the Golden Rule disposition. In Detroit in 1930 25,549 persons were arrested for intoxication, of whom 21,267 were released by the police without prosecution. In addition 28,742 persons were arrested on other charges, of whom 2,754 were released by the police, and 24,414 more were arrested for investigation or on suspicion and were released by the police without being charged with an offense. This makes a total of 62 per cent of the arrests (not including city traffic cases) which resulted in release by the police without court appearance. Reports from other cities indicate that the percentage in Detroit is not unusual, although it is probably above the average in such releases. These arrests are made without warrants and from a strictly legal point of view either the arrests or the releases are, with a few exceptions, unjustified. From a practical point of view it is probable that most of these arrests represent the selection of the best method available at the time. Intoxicated persons are arrested and detained in the police lockup until they are sober. This is a protection to them and to the public. If these persons were taken to court they would either be dismissed or fined, and since most of them would be unable to pay fines they would be committed to a house of correction for a short period. None of these methods is of great value in solving the problem of intoxication, but the police method of release probably makes as great a contribution as the alternative methods and is much cheaper. It is evident, however, that intoxication is a serious social problem at present and that more constructive methods should be made available for the solution of the problem. Some of the other releases are probably much like those which occur in cases of intoxication. On the other hand, many of the arrests are entirely unjustified from any social point of view. Some of these are a means of forcing gambling places and houses of prostitution into a syndicate, some are penalties for failing to bribe the arresting officer, and some are merely a device used by the officer or the department to make a good record.

Some persons, after arrest, secure a release from detention by a writ of *habeas corpus*. This writ makes it necessary for the police to bring the arrested person before a court immediately for a hearing to determine the power and jurisdiction of the police. This is not for the purpose of determining the guilt of the defendant. In some cases this writ is issued immediately after arrest. Some professional criminals have attorneys constantly prepared to secure a writ of *habeas corpus* and sometimes the attorney arrives at the police station with the writ before the police arrive with the prisoner. The police, in order to prevent this and for other reasons, frequently hold prisoners incommunicado, shifting them frequently from one station to another. It is reported that a series of fifteen outlying station houses in Detroit constituted a "loop" and that prisoners were shifted from one to another of these stations for a period of a week or ten days and then released.[1]

A third method of release before trial is on bail with financial security. The right to bail is guaranteed in the constitutions of

---

[1] E. J. Hopkins, *Our Lawless Police*, New York, 1931, p. 126.

thirty-five of the states in all cases except capital charges. In early English law a person charged with a crime could be released if a friend would act as the keeper of the prisoner and thus act as surety for his appearance in court. The person who acted as surety was then liable for the punishment if the prisoner was not delivered. Later the surety pledged his property, which generally consisted of his house or land, but still remained essentially the keeper of the prisoner. The real estate of friends is still used as security in small towns and to some extent in cities, but in the city many defendants have no friends who own property available for bail. Consequently professional bondsmen and corporate surety companies have been called on by many defendants to provide surety. In New York City from 40 to 50 per cent of the criminal bonds are provided by surety companies, but in other cities these companies secure less of this business. Arrangements for bail are generally made with a police officer for minor charges, with a magistrate if the charge is serious. The security for minor charges is generally cash and is fixed at an amount approximately equal to the fine customarily imposed for such offenses. Persons who furnish cash bail frequently forfeit it rather than return to court and pay the fine. This is tacitly accepted by police and court as a satisfactory solution of the difficulty. Cash bail is used in about 40 per cent of the arrests, but is confined largely to traffic cases. The usual bond for a person charged with burglary is $5,000 and for robbery with a gun $10,000. Surety companies generally charge a fee of 2 per cent of the bond and in New York are limited by law to 3 per cent of the bond. The Municipal Court of Chicago has a maximum fee of 10 per cent of the first $100 of the bond and 5 per cent for each additional hundred dollars, but the usual fee for a bond of $5,000 for burglary is $100.

This system of financial security for persons charged with crimes has been criticized on several points. The principal criticism is that the police department and court have inadequate facilities for determining whether financial security is needed, how much security is needed, and how adequate the security which is offered may be. The amount required is therefore generally determined by the charge against the defendant rather than by his character and responsibility. This bears heavily on the poor and makes bail practically prohibitive for them. In effect, therefore, a poor person of excellent character and responsibility charged with a crime of which he is completely innocent has no alternative to detention in an institution. This hardship cannot be defended by the argument that poor persons should not commit crimes, for many of them are actually innocent. On the other hand, the financial security has little value if the defendant is not responsible and is not willing to return to court. Since the court has no facilities for investigating the security which is offered and since professional bondsmen as a group are closely allied with the underworld, the security is generally inadequate. Moley has described a professional bondsman in St. Louis who was security for bonds aggregating $670,295, although his real property was worth not more than $20,000 and the encumbrances against this property were greater than its assessed valuation, and in addition he had been arrested twelve times. In spite of this the courts continued to accept him as surety for persons charged with crimes.[2] This is perhaps an exaggerated case so far as amounts are concerned, but is not exaggerated so far as the principle is concerned. The bondsman sometimes does not even own the property he schedules. If one court refuses to accept the property as security, the bondsman "peddles" it to other courts until he finds one which will accept it. From 8 to 10 per cent of the bonds were forfeited in Chicago in 1928 and about 2 per cent of the amounts forfeited were collected. The defendant therefore generally appeared, but when he did not appear the financial security meant almost nothing. This situation in Chicago has been changed. The number of bonds forfeited decreased from 500 in 1928 to 6 in 1937.

A second criticism of the bail system is that it involves collusion between the police, the courts, and the professional bondsmen. The occasional offender asks the police how he can secure bail, and the police suggest a bondsman or inform a runner for a bondsman that the defendant has no bondsman. Fees are then divided with officers of the police and courts. The bondsman also acts as "fixer" for professional criminals. He is generally intimate with the underworld and with the political machine, and can make contacts with the corrupted portions of the police department and of the court. This strategic position gives the professional bondsman an advantage which enables him to charge high fees although he runs little risk, since collections are seldom made on forfeited bonds. Also,

---

[2] Raymond Moley, *Our Criminal Courts,* New York, 1930, pp. 49–50.

this system permits the professional criminal to continue his crime immediately so that he may secure funds to pay the bondsman.

A third and less important criticism is that the court sometimes violates the requirement that bail must be reasonable. When this occurs, it is generally a spectacular gesture of a judge who is seeking publicity. A judge in Chicago fixed the total bail for three persons charged with robbery at more than a million dollars.

Several suggestions for reform of the bail system have been made. First, one bureau should have complete control of all the work of granting bail, recommending forfeitures, and collecting forfeited bonds in a city. This organization has been arranged in several cities with varying degrees of success. It results in better inspection of securities so that the bonds can always be kept within the value of the securities listed, and it prevents bondsmen from "peddling" bonds from one court to another. It appears to have no effect on other aspects of the bail problem.[3] Second, this bureau or a section of this bureau should be responsible for investigating the character of the defendant for the purpose of determining whether release should be granted without financial security, for heavy security, or under no conditions at all. Under present constitutional provisions an outright refusal of bail is not permissible in the United States but is permissible in England. Third, it should be made a crime to jump bail.

In addition to the releases without trial, the releases by *habeas corpus,* and the releases on financial surety, some defendants are released on their own recognizances and without financial security. This method is used in Chicago in about 5 per cent of the charges, and is generally confined to minor charges and to persons who are known to be responsible. The practice could be extended to advantage if methods of appraising character and responsibility were devised.

TYPES OF DETENTION INSTITUTIONS. Many persons are detained in institutions awaiting trial. These institutions are of the following types: (a) the station under the control of the city police department, in which offenders are practically never held as punishment, and in which few are held for trial more than a few days; (b) the municipal jail or lockup in the small town, which is generally under the control of the police department or marshal and

---

[3] "Detroit Court Solves the Bail Problem," *Jour. Amer. Jud. Soc.,* 16:143–149, February, 1933.

which resembles the city police station except that offenders are more frequently held there in lieu of payment of fines ordered by the court; (c) the county jail, which is usually under the control of the sheriff and which is generally used both for those awaiting trial and those serving sentences; (d) specialized detention institutions for women and children.

Persons accused of crimes are customarily detained awaiting a hearing or trial in the police station or lockup. If the court has final jurisdiction, it fixes the penalty; if the court does not have final jurisdiction, it fixes bail or commits the defendant to the county jail awaiting disposition by a grand jury or a higher court.

NUMBER OF INSTITUTIONS AND OF INMATES. Approximately 14,000 institutions for detention of prisoners before trial have been listed in the United States, of which 3,000 are county jails and 11,000 village and city lockups. Approximately 3,000,000 persons were committed to these institutions in 1930,[4] of which, however, many were committed more than once during the year. Most of those committed to city and village lockups are detained for a few hours only, but the period of detention of those held in county jails for grand jury action or, after that, for trial in the criminal courts is very much longer. The average time spent in the county jail awaiting trial on federal charges ranges from 12 days in Georgia to 56 days in Wyoming. The survey of the Cook County jail made by the Chicago Community Trust showed that of 587 persons held in jail awaiting trial on December 1, 1920, 50 per cent were held for more than two months and 8.3 per cent more than six months before final action was taken.[5] Moreover of those so detained 36 per cent were discharged before, during, or after trial, without conviction. A rough estimate may be made that at least half of those detained in lockups awaiting trial are not convicted and that a third of those detained in county jails awaiting trial are not convicted.

NECESSITY OF DECENT TREATMENT DURING DETENTION. The

---

[4] This estimate is based on the enumeration reported by H. H. Hart, "Penal Institutions, Probation, and Parole," *Natl. Com. on Law Obs. and Enf.*, No. 9, p. 329. To his enumeration were added estimated numbers committed to county jails awaiting trials and to lockups in villages with population less than 500, and in cities which did not report. Another estimate is that 1,000,000 persons are held in jail pending trial in a year, but this estimate seems to be limited to county jails.

[5] Chicago Community Trust, *Reports Comprising the Survey of the Cook County Jail*, Chicago, 1922, p. 196.

suggestion has been made that the hardships involved in arrest and detention should not be reduced, for since a large proportion of guilty persons escape conviction they should at least suffer this amount of discomfort as a deterrent to others. The difficulty about this is that the hardships are imposed upon innocent as well as guilty persons, and no one has argued that people can be kept innocent by punishing the innocent. Even if they are actually guilty it is probably good policy to treat them, so far as practicable, on the presumption of innocence. The rule of presumption of innocence until guilt is proved, strictly speaking, refers only to the preponderance of evidence in a trial in court. The rule of evidence is that the defendant is assumed to be innocent rather than guilty, and the evidence must then be sufficient to convict. But the rule is, with limitations required by practical considerations, good social policy in other situations. Of course, if the rule were made absolute there would be no justification for arrest or for detention until after conviction. For practical reasons it is necessary that the state apprehend and detain persons suspected of crime, and thus impose hardships upon persons who may be innocent. This is something like confiscation of property for public purposes or drafting men for the army in time of war, and the hardships should be reduced to the minimum consistent with the public purpose. Furthermore, especially for first offenders, the arrested person is in a very impressionable condition and sympathetic treatment and understanding will have great effect at this point, just as unnecessary and unwarranted hardships will be very damaging. In general, therefore, those who are detained awaiting trial should be treated decently and honorably, at least as well as those drafted for army purposes. The place of detention should be something like a hotel, secure against escape, and should be not much less comfortable than a second-class hotel.

EVILS IN JAILS. In general the physical conditions in the county and city jails are decidedly worse than the conditions in state prisons in which criminals are confined after conviction of serious offenses. Those who are presumed to be innocent, many of whom are actually innocent, and almost all of whom are detained because of poverty only, are treated much worse than are persons already convicted of serious crimes. Criticisms of these conditions have been made for nearly a century by native and foreign observers. The president of the International Prison Congress in 1907 said that nothing as bad as the American jails had been known in the history of the world except the prisons of Turkey in the thirteenth century. The federal government inspects county jails for the purpose of selecting the jails in which federal prisoners may be detained. In an inspection of 2,067 jails only 15 rated 80 or over, where 100 was the perfect rating, and 1,668 rated below 60.[6] State surveys generally show the same conditions. The criticisms most frequently made are the following: filth, vermin, fire hazard, inadequate food, inadequate plumbing, inadequate lighting and ventilation, lack of segregation of person with infectious diseases, universal idleness, supervision of women prisoners by male attendants, lack of provision for rehabilitation (medical care, education, religion), special privileges for favored prisoners (sometimes including a key to the prison door), and inadequate security against escape. Fishman, who was inspector of jails for the federal government for some time, defined the jail thus:

Jail: An unbelievably filthy institution in which are confined men and women serving sentences for misdemeanors and crimes, and men and women not under sentence who are simply awaiting trial. With few exceptions, having no segregation of the unconvicted from the convicted, the well from the diseased, the youngest and most impressionable from the most degraded and hardened. Usually swarming with bedbugs, roaches, lice, and other vermin; has an odor of disinfectant and filth which is appalling; supports in complete idleness countless thousands of able-bodied men and women, and generally affords ample time and opportunity to assure inmates a complete course in every kind of viciousness and crime. A melting pot in which the worst elements of the raw material in the criminal world are brought forth blended and turned out in absolute perfection.[7]

The fundamental criticism of the jail is that it permits association of convicted and unconvicted prisoners. Approximately half of the inmates of county jails are awaiting trial and most of the others are serving sentences imposed after conviction. The effect of this association with convicted prisoners is bad, first, because it leads the person accused of crime to think of himself as a criminal;

---

[6] Nina Kinsella, "County Jails and the Federal Government," *Proc. Amer. Prison Assoc.*, 1932, pp. 365–375.
[7] Joseph F. Fishman, *Crucibles of Crime*, New York, 1923, pp. 13–14.

second, contacts with those convicted of crime often cause moral deterioration. A person with considerable experience as a criminal wrote:

I entered jail an amateur in crime and stayed there a little over three months. In that time I learned more of the devious methods which crooks use against society than I had ever dreamed of knowing. . . . I mingled daily with men grown old in the underworld; I assimilated just as much of their vices as my immature nature would hold. I learned the language of the crooks. The tales told were strong with the flavor of adventure. They fascinated me and I looked up to the old crooks as men to be envied. . . . They came to be heroes, as it were, out of the great book of adventure.[8]

And Josiah Flynt thus described the jail in which he was held during his youth while awaiting trial for the theft of a horse and buggy:

From morning till night the "old hands" in crime were exchanging stories of their exploits, while the younger prisoners sat about them with open mouths and eyes of wonder, greedily taking in every syllable. I listened just as intently as anybody, and was hugely impressed with what I heard and saw. The seriousness of my offense advanced me somewhat in the scale of youthful prisoners and at times I was allowed to join a "private confab" supposed to be only for the long initiated and thoroughly tried offenders.[9]

The attitude of the public and the physical conditions and treatment in the jail show the prisoner that he is regarded as an enemy of society; he therefore tends to look upon himself as an enemy of society. His feelings are expressed sympathetically by the convicted criminals of the group, who are able to secure prestige and leadership for that reason. The result is that the moral tone of the jails is generally distinctly low.

There are only two invariable topics of conversation—sex and the chance of getting out. Filthy talk and filthy practices are common

---

[8] W. Scott, *Seventeen Years in the Underworld*, Cincinnati, 1916, pp. 24–25. Reprinted by permission of The Abingdon Press, publishers.
[9] Josiah Flynt Willard, *My Life*, New York, 1908, p. 82.

in the crowded cells and bull-pens. Homo-sexual vice is not uncommon and is laughed at. It seems to excite no horror and scarcely any reprobation. Young boys are corrupted and forced. Dope can be had by any one who can pay for it. Even those who are not "fiends" often get it and use it to find temporary relief from the unbearable irritation and the depression of jail life. Not infrequently newcomers are set upon, mauled and robbed of what little money or other valuables they may have, sometimes stripped of shoes, shirts, and other articles of clothing.[10]

It is possible to exaggerate the importance of the convicted criminals, however. It is not clear that detention in a city police station in which no convicted prisoners are held is any less injurious than detention in a county jail in company with convicted prisoners. Detention means association with criminality even if it does not mean association with criminals.

Some exceptional jails have conditions which are good in practically every respect, and many have conditions which are good in certain respects. It is possible, though by no means certain, that there is a slight trend toward better physical conditions in jails.

EXPLANATION OF EVILS OF JAILS. The bad conditions in jails have existed for many decades and have become a tradition. Howard's investigations during the later part of the eighteenth century and Mrs. Fry's work during the early part of the nineteenth century were investigations of jails similar to our police stations, for the prisons in those periods were used primarily for detention prior to trial. The conditions in these English jails were certainly worse than in present American jails. The criticisms of the jails in America which were made three-quarters of a century ago, and a half century ago, and a quarter of a century ago, all sound very similar.[11] This persistence of bad conditions may be explained partially by inertia and the expense of improvements. But this is not a sufficient explanation; there is some popular sympathy with the existing conditions. This is accounted for in two ways: First, accusation is

---

[10] Chicago Community Trust, *Reports Comprising the Survey of the Cook County Jail*, pp. 35–36.

[11] New Jersey, *Report of Prison Inquiry Commission*, Trenton, 1917, Vol. II, pp. 321–325; E. C. Wines and T. W. Dwight, *Report on the Prisons and Reformatories of the United States and Canada*, New York, Assembly Doc. No. 5, 1867, Vol. II, pp. 314–336; Joseph F. Fishman, *Crucibles of Crime*, New York, 1923.

taken as equivalent to proof. The person who is arrested and detained for trial is associated in the mind of the public with the persons already convicted of crime. Because of a popular feeling that life should be made unpleasant for those convicted of crime those who are accused but not convicted are made to suffer in the same ways. But, why does the public fail to make the distinction between those awaiting trial and those serving sentences? Second, only the poor are held in jail for trial. Persons who are politically important do not get into jail before trial; they secure bail. The poor, whether guilty or not, are unable to change the situation; those who have been in jail try to conceal this fact rather than advertize it. The general public is not in touch with the situation, looks down upon those who get into jail, and does not suffer the hardships in person that would lead to insistence on modification. The attitude of the public is, in general, one of indifference. The public makes no objection when jail authorities permit important prisoners to have their liberty, wandering around the institution or the community "on honor." No matter how jails are operated, the public is complacent. Perhaps the situation will be improved in this country as in England, where Bernard Shaw has said that the day of improvement was at hand because in a short time every honest man would have spent some time in jail and would know what jails meant.

PROGRAM FOR IMPROVEMENT OF JAILS. A program for the improvement of methods of detention involves improvement in the physical conditions of jails, but it involves much more than that. The following are some of the important items: (a) The fundamental modification necessary for better conditions is publicity. This is the only way to break down the isolation of the public. The public must be made acquainted with the situation, if not by direct experiences in the jails, at least by descriptions and analyses of effects. The principal part of this publicity should be descriptions of the improved methods used in some communities, the reasons for the improvements, and the advantages which result.

(b) The number of arrests should be reduced. It has been indicated previously that 60 per cent of the arrests in certain cities result in release without prosecution. In addition, between a third and a half of the persons who are prosecuted are dismissed without conviction. It is not possible to determine what proportion of the dismissals results from inefficiency of the courts, but it is probable that both the courts and the police share responsibility. The summons may be substituted for arrest in many cases. Summonses are used now almost exclusively for violations of traffic regulations.

(c) The courts should dispose of cases more rapidly. The shorter the period of detention of the average prisoner, the smaller is the number detained at a particular time. The survey of the Cook County jail reported that the jail would contain only 29 people at one time if the average period of detention were one day, 200 if it were one week, 887 if it were one month, and 10,642 if it were one year. Experiences in several courts have demonstrated that speedier justice is possible without injury to defendants, and this will shorten the period of detention in jail.

(d) The jails and lockups should be improved. Even if the number of persons committed and the length of the period of detention be reduced greatly, it will still be desirable to improve the places of detention. The conditions of health and safety should be greatly improved. This is not at all an easy thing to accomplish because the arrested persons include many who are intoxicated at the time of arrest, or are habitual drunkards and vagrants, or are diseased, or are ignorant of the conditions of hygiene. But institutions can be made fireproof, sanitary plumbing can be installed, facilities for bathing can be made available, diseased persons can be segregated, organized activities can be provided. Some jails provide opportunity for voluntary but paid employment, recreational activities, reading, organized educational classes, and picture shows. The complete and practically universal idleness of the jail and lockup should be eliminated. The convicted prisoners should be removed to other institutions. Indiana has a state farm for misdemeanants which has taken most of the convicted misdemeanants out of the county jails. Certain counties have provided farm work for convicted prisoners and these are housed separately from the prisoners awaiting trial. The jails and lockups should be inspected by the state, and the inspectors should have authority to close the jails and lockups which do not meet requirements. The states of Indiana, New York, New Jersey, Minnesota, and Oklahoma now have regular state supervision of jails and lockups, and certain other states inspect jails and lockups "on complaint."[12] The Department of Correction in New York State publishes reports of these inspections. It has closed

---

[12] H. H. Hart, "Special Report on Police Jails and Village Lockups," *Natl. Com. on Law Obs. and Enf.*, No. 9, pp. 331–332.

more than 60 village lockups. The inspectors of county jails in South Carolina have used a score card by which each jail is given a mathematical grade on permanent plant, sheriff's management, and the work of the county commissioners in connection with the jail; these grades are published annually and assist the counties in visualizing their jail conditions. Hart states that this scoring system "has exercised a powerful influence upon sheriffs, jailers and county officials in favor of cleanliness, sanitation, good order and discipline."[13]

In order that the standards mentioned may be attained it will, in many cases, be necessary that the territorial area for a particular institution of detention be enlarged. The lockup is necessarily a local institution for temporary detention, but if detention continues more than a day or two the prisoner should be removed to an institution with the standards and facilities described. The county is too small a unit to maintain a jail of this nature, especially if the convicted prisoners and the responsible unconvicted prisoners are removed. In New York only 30 per cent of the county jails had more than ten prisoners awaiting trial on June 30, 1931, and nearly 14 per cent had no prisoners at all awaiting trial on that particular day. Very much the same condition was found in special surveys in other states in earlier years—8 per cent of the county jails in Indiana, 16 per cent in Illinois, and 29 per cent in California had fewer than ten inmates each awaiting trial. Counties should combine, or the state should establish jail districts, or probably the best of all, the state should own and operate the places of detention in which persons are held awaiting trial for longer than two or three days. It is clear that an institution which contains only two or three persons at a time cannot provide a system of employment, recreation, or medical care, and that the per capita expense of maintenance of a small institution is much larger than of a large institution. No recent statistics on this point are available, but statistics for Michigan in 1918 show that the daily per capita cost is in inverse ratio to the size of the institution, ranging from $1.04 in institutions in which the days of detention (the number of prisoners multiplied by the number of days each was detained) was more than 10,000 to $23.49 in institutions in which the days of detention were less than 100. In one county one man was held in jail

---

[13] H. H. Hart, "Prison Conditions in the South," *Proc. Amer. Prison Assoc.*, 1919, p. 206.

one day during the year 1918 at a cost to the county of $1,072. Moreover, if these larger units were organized, specialized institutions for special classes could be established. This has already started in the detention homes for children and women, but can be developed outside of the large cities only by state management of these places of detention. The Chicago Community Trust recommended for Cook County, as a substitute for a single immense jail, a number of cottages for specialized classes. Hart recommended a skyscraper jail with different floors for the various classes.

(e) The dependents of those detained in jail awaiting trial should be cared for by the state or other governmental unit in charge of the jail. If the state finds it necessary to detain in an institution a person against whom a charge of crime is made, the duty of providing for those dependent upon the detained person follows logically as a corollary. Whether the person is subsequently found guilty should make no difference in the care during the period of detention before trial.

(f) Those who are acquitted should be indemnified for financial losses suffered as the result of the detention.[14] Such a system has prevailed for a long time in some of the European countries. By act of 1911 Massachusetts authorized indemnification, in case of acquittal or discharge, for financial losses if the detention awaiting trial exceeded six months. But there is no reason for such a long minimum period. Indemnification should logically be justified for any period of detention whatever, but because of the heavy clerical expense and the small amounts of indemnification for very short periods, a minimum of one week might be fixed. The general arguments regarding indemnification are as follows: First, when private property is taken for public use the owner is compensated; likewise when the state requires an individual to give his time or services to the state, he is compensated. The person detained for trial is deprived of his liberty for the sake of public welfare; if the trial shows that this detention was not justified, he should be compensated for the loss which he has suffered for the sake of public welfare. Second, the principle involved in indemnification is the same as that of workmen's compensation laws: spread the loss on the public

---

[14] The arguments and facts regarding indemnification have been taken principally from the following articles: E. M. Borchard, "European Systems of State Indemnification for Errors of Criminal Justice," *Jour. Crim. Law and Criminol.*, 3:686–706, January, 1913; E. M. Borchard, *State Indemnity for Errors of Criminal Justice*, U. S. Senate Doc. 974, 62d Cong., 3d Sess.

rather than impose it on one individual. Some objections are advanced against indemnification: First, the case is not similar to the taking of private property for public purposes, since the state is enriched by the private property and is not enriched by detaining a person for trial. But this argument is unsound for the reason that the state does not compensate the person who is deprived of his property because the state was enriched but because the individual suffered a loss at the hands of the state. A second objection is that there is no liability unless there is fault. But this argument has been upset by the workmen's compensation laws; the state has ruled that an employer, though he is not at fault, must compensate a workman for injuries. A third objection is that an individual who is arrested unjustly can sue for damages. But this is not an adequate remedy because in a large proportion of cases the policeman who makes the arrest has no property that can be attached, because the antagonism of the police force would result in additional injury to the one bringing the suit, and because the lawyer would get a large share of the damages allowed.

If indemnification is authorized by the state, it should certainly be limited to financial losses only, with a maximum fixed by the state (say $5,000) and with a brief statute of limitations (say six months). It should be granted only to those whose conduct in the matter is uncensurable. There should be no indemnification, for instance, if the person has refused to testify, has attempted to escape, or was drunk at the scene of the crime. Aside from the remedy for loss that this would provide, it would be desirable because it would tend to prevent needless arrests, would tend to speed up the courts, and would tend to create a public opinion favorable to greater efficiency in police departments and courts in general.

THE JUVENILE DETENTION HOME. Children within the juvenile court age are generally permitted to remain at home after complaint is made against them; a summons is issued for the parents to bring the children to court at the appointed time. But it is frequently necessary to detain children because of the serious nature of the offense, the condition of the home, or the possibility that the child will try to escape from the jurisdiction of the court.

The jail is frequently used as a place of detention for juveniles. But the laws in a large portion of the states place restrictions on the use of jails for juveniles. Twelve states and some counties in two other states have an absolute prohibition against the detention of children of juvenile court age in jails or police stations under any circumstances; nineteen other states have the same prohibition except that the age limit is a little lower than the juvenile court age limit; five other states prohibit the detention of children in jails or police stations except in a small number of specified conditions, such as "if the child has committed a felony." In addition thirteen states provide that if children are, for any reason, detained in jail they must be kept apart from adults.[15] But in general practice these laws are frequently violated, especially in districts that do not have specially organized juvenile courts. A study of 118,772 children detained in various ways in the fiscal year 1929–1930 showed that nearly 15 per cent of them were detained in jails and police stations; 65 per cent in public detention homes; and the others scattered in private orphanages, in shelters and homes, in boarding homes, in hospitals and sanitoria, and in almshouses.[16] The almshouses and hospitals should be eliminated as places of detention, except in so far as hospitals may be utilized because of sickness. Various arguments have been presented regarding the comparative values of public detention homes, private orphanages and shelters, and private boarding homes. An inspection of these institutions in thirty-eight states in 1929–1930 resulted in the conclusion that any one of these types may be very injurious and any one of them may be very satisfactory. The best agencies found anywhere were private shelters, but some of the private shelters were appraised as entirely unsuitable.

DETENTION OF WITNESSES. The material witness who is detained in a city or county jail awaiting trial has received little consideration until recently. The newspapers recently reported a case of a person who was knocked down and robbed; he could not furnish financial security for his appearance at the trial and he was therefore detained in jail for three months as a material witness while the person accused of the crime was released on bail. During the fiscal year 1930–1931 383 men and 94 women were detained in county jails in New York State as witnesses. This was slightly less than 1 per cent of the total number of persons admitted to these institutions and is therefore a small number in comparison

---

[15] S. P. Breckinridge and Helen R. Jeter, "A Summary of Juvenile Court Legislation in the United States," *U. S. Children's Bur.*, No. 70, pp. 29–30.
[16] Florence M. Warner, *Juvenile Detention in the United States*, Chicago, 1933.

with the number serving sentences or the number awaiting trial. It is, however, important that the performance of the task of testifying for purposes of public justice should not impose a hardship on these persons. They, like the persons accused of the crimes, are held at the demand of the state and should likewise not be detained unless the necessity is definite, and if detained should be treated in a decent manner. The American Law Institute has proposed that if a witness is unable within three days to secure financial sureties he be examined in the presence of the defendant and his deposition be authorized for use in the trial, in case he is not available at the time of the trial. In addition, other specific proposals have been made for speeding up court action, and for compulsory attendance and bail for defense witnesses as well as for the people's witnesses.

SUGGESTED READINGS

"Administration of Bail," *Yale Law Jour.*, 41:293–300, December, 1931.

Beeley, A. L., *The Bail System in Chicago*, Chicago, 1927.

Borchard, E. M., *Convicting the Innocent*, New Haven, 1932.

Chicago Community Trust, *Reports Comprising the Survey of the Cook County Jail*, Chicago, 1922.

"Detroit Solves Bail Problem," *Jour. Amer. Jud. Soc.*, 16:143–149, February, 1933.

DeVine, Russell B., "What Price Jails: A Critical Survey of a Depression-proof Industry," *Proc. Amer. Prison Assoc.*, 1935, pp. 302–313.

Fishman, Joseph F., *Crucibles of Crime*, New York, 1923.

Hart, H. H., "Special Report on Police Jails and Village Lockups," *Natl. Com. on Law Obs. and Enf.*, No. 9, pp. 327–344.

Hoffer, F. W., Mann, D. M., and House, F. N., *The Jails of Virginia*, New York, 1933.

Hopkins, E. J., *Our Lawless Police*, New York, 1931.

Kinsella, Nina, "County Jails and the Federal Government," *Proc. Amer. Prison Assoc.*, 1932, pp. 365–375.

Kinsella, Nina, "The County Jails," *Proc. Amer. Prison Assoc.*, 1935, pp. 283–289.

Lavine, E. H., *The Third Degree*, New York, 1930, Ch. 17.

Lewis, O. F., *The Development of American Prisons and Prison Customs, 1776–1845*, Albany, 1922, Ch. 22.

McGee, Richard A., "The Care and Treatment of the Untried Prisoner," *Proc. Amer. Prison Assoc.*, 1937, pp. 321–332.

Missouri Association for Criminal Justice, *The Missouri Crime Survey*, pp. 189–218.

Moley, Raymond, *Our Criminal Courts*, New York, 1930, Ch. 3.

Queen, S. A., *The Passing of the County Jail*, Menasha, Wis., 1920, Ch. 1.

Warner, Florence M., *Juvenile Detention in the United States*, Chicago, 1933.

Chapter Sixteen

THE CRIMINAL COURT

POPULAR DISSATISFACTION WITH THE CRIMINAL COURT. The American system of criminal justice has been criticized for a long time, but the criticisms have become much more general and severe during the present generation and have been voiced by acknowledged leaders of the judiciary. Taft in 1909 said that "the administration of criminal law is a disgrace to our civilization." In England, where our criminal law originated, many reforms in criminal law were made between 1820 and 1890, but in America little change occurred. Little effort has been made by law schools, lawyers, or judges to improve the criminal law. The more competent lawyers and judges have generally been interested in civil law, and the lawyers who enter the criminal field have not been interested in changes which would make criminal law more efficient from the point of view of social welfare.

Pound in 1906 published an excellent analysis of the causes of this popular discontent with the criminal law, in which the causes are shown to inhere in part in any legal system, in part in the American judicial organization and procedure, and in part in the environment of the judicial administration.[1]

The principal criticisms of the administration of the criminal law are: it frequently produces injustice rather than justice; it is corrupt; it is not organized on principles of businesslike efficiency; it does not base its procedure on available scientific knowledge; it does not maintain the dignity which is necessary for respect. In general the criticism is that the criminal court is not an efficient system for the administration of justice. The courts are not efficiently

---

[1] Roscoe Pound, "Causes of Popular Dissatisfaction with the Administration of Justice," *Report Amer. Bar Assoc.,* 29:395–417, 1906. This analysis is elaborated in Roscoe Pound, *Criminal Justice in America,* New York, 1930.

organized either as a system of courts or as a part of an integrated system of justice. Even within a particular court the procedure does not result in justice, for special privileges are given to those who can employ clever lawyers or who have political backing, and in other cases the decisions are based on snap judgments. From the point of view of the guilty criminal who has money or influence enough to secure special privileges, the criminal court is an excellent institution. From the point of view of the general public, these defects result in distrust of the court, disrespect for law, great financial cost, failure to convict many who are guilty, and great hardship upon all persons who must be involved in court procedure either as defendants, witnesses, or jurors.

ORGANIZATION OF THE COURTS. The organization of the criminal courts is roughly as follows: (a) Justices of the peace, police magistrates, and other inferior courts serve the dual purpose of preliminary hearing in felony cases and final decision, subject to appeal, in minor cases. Almost all criminal cases are finally settled in these inferior courts. (b) County, district, or circuit courts, known as trial courts, render final decision, subject to appeal, in serious cases. The county is usually taken as the unit, even when the circuit includes several counties. In the city these courts are in session every day, but in most rural districts they are in session in a particular county only a few days during the year. (c) Specialized branches of one of the above mentioned courts, such as traffic courts, morals courts, or domestic relations courts, have been organized to deal with specified types of offenses. (d) Appellate courts and supreme courts take cases on appeal from lower courts and have original jurisdiction in a restricted field.

Each of these courts is customarily a separate unit, except in a few places where organization has been developed. The justices of the peace in a particular city generally act without reference to each other or to other courts, except to consider the possibility of reversal of decisions by higher courts. The work is not organized or co-ordinated. But court work is a big business and requires organization as certainly as does a big commercial enterprise.

Certain trends toward organization are evident. In 1905 the legislature of Illinois authorized a municipal court in Chicago to take the place of scattered and unco-ordinated justices of the peace and of police courts. The chief justice of this court has wide powers in regard to assignment of judges and of cases, and in regard to organization of work. Detroit in 1921 developed a somewhat similar organization, and other cities have done the same. The federal courts were similarly unified in 1922, with William H. Taft as chief justice.

Another trend toward organization of the court work is found in the development of state judicial councils. Nineteen states in 1933 had judicial councils. The authority and activities of these councils vary but are rather narrowly confined to the collection of statistics and to suggestions for new legislation. As a matter of fact they probably exert an influence which goes far beyond their authorized scope. They are producing some changes in procedure and in administration which are resulting in better organization. Also, in some states associations of judges and of prosecuting attorneys have been formed, and these associations hold conferences in which common problems are discussed.

A further suggestion has been made that all the work of criminal justice should be integrated. The police, the courts, the prisons, the probation and parole boards, and perhaps other related agencies would, according to this plan, be brought together under one director. At present they are distinct units, in accordance with the theory that judicial and executive branches should be separate, and consequently they are frequently working at cross purposes.

THE PROSECUTOR. The prosecutor is the most important person in the judicial system under present conditions. Baker has given an interesting description of a typical day's work of a prosecutor in a city of medium size, showing the immense power of this officer and the conditions under which he works.[2] The prosecutor determines whether a particular case shall be prosecuted. He determines whether a compromise shall be accepted, which generally means a plea of guilt of a lesser offense in return for a recommendation for mitigation of penalty. He is responsible for the organization and presentation of evidence before the court, and upon his efficiency in doing this the decision of the court depends. He is generally very influential in regard to the disposition of cases, suggesting to the judge or jury the appropriate penalty. In fact, he is almost an absolute ruler of the whole judicial process.

---

[2] N. F. Baker, "The Prosecutor—Initiation of Prosecution," *Jour. Crim. Law and Criminol.*, 23:770–796, January, 1933. See, also, N. F. Baker and E. H. DeLong, "The Prosecutor and His Office," *Jour. Crim. Law and Criminol.*, 23:926–963; 24:1025–1065; 25:358–400, 884–901; 26:821–846, March, 1933 to March, 1936.

At the same time this prosecutor is generally elected and, as is true of other elected officers, he secures his position primarily as a favor of the political machine. Explicitly or implicitly this means subservience to the wishes of the politicians, and it means also distraction of attention from his official business for the sake of political activities; he must be careful not to antagonize any large organized group. Also, his record must show a large proportion of convictions in cases which go to trial. It is customary in elections for the prosecutor to present statistics on this point, and James A. Reed includes in his statement for *Who's Who* that as public prosecutor in Kansas City he secured 285 convictions in 287 cases that went to trial.

The assistant prosecutors, also, secure their positions in many cases because they have been active in political organizations, although in some communities the bar association urges and assists the voters to make selections on the basis of efficiency. The assistant prosecutors are generally inexperienced in this work at the time they are appointed and are dismissed when the administration changes. Responsibility for their work is generally not definitely located and their work is usually not well organized. In the inferior courts the assistant prosecutors generally make little preparation and even when the case comes into court they pay little attention, except in spectacular cases. The Wickersham Report makes this statement regarding the work of the prosecutor:

Taking the country as a whole, the features which chiefly operate to make the present-day criminal justice in the States ineffective are: Want of adequate system and organization in the office of the average prosecutor, decentralization of prosecution whereas law and order have come to be much more than local concern, diffusion of responsibility, the intimate relation of prosecution to politics, and in many jurisdictions no provision for a prosecutor commensurate with the task of prosecution under the conditions of today. . . . The system of prosecutors elected for short terms, with assistants chosen on the basis of political patronage, with no assured tenure, yet charged with wide undefined powers, is ideally adapted to misgovernment.[3]

The suggestion has been made that the prosecutor should be removed from this control of the political machine by providing for

___

[3] Alfred Bettman, "Report on Prosecution," *Natl. Com. on Law Obs. and Enf.*, No. 4, pp. 11-12, 14.

his appointment by the governor from a list nominated by the judicial council and for his removal by the governor on recommendation of the judicial council, but otherwise remaining in office for life. The prosecutors in this case would be assistants of the attorney general of the state.

The prosecutor is tending to become a criminal investigator, also. Several prosecutors have made great reputations by vigorous campaigns for law enforcement, in which they made investigations, secured evidence, and initiated prosecutions. Jerome in New York was an illustration of this and an example for other prosecutors. The police department generally assigns a number of policemen to the prosecutor's office for this work, and the number thus assigned seems to be increasing. Students of the administration of criminal justice have generally opposed this trend toward expansion of the work of the prosecutor, because he already has an enormous task, because it produces friction between police and prosecutor, and because there is no reason to think the prosecutor will be more efficient than the police in making investigations.

INITIATION OF PROSECUTION AND THE GRAND JURY. Prosecution in misdemeanor cases is customarily initiated by complaint of a victim or witness of the offense; very frequently the police officer who makes the arrest is the complaining witness. The complaint and evidence are presented in the inferior court and the whole matter settled there, subject to an occasional appeal.

In felony cases the procedure is much more complicated. The complaint is made by a victim or witness and the prosecutor or his assistant hears the evidence. If he decides that the case should be prosecuted, he must prepare the evidence for presentation before the inferior court where the defendant is arraigned. If the inferior court decides the evidence is sufficient, the prosecutor must in many states present the evidence again to the grand jury. If the grand jury regards the evidence as sufficient, the offender is indicted, and the prosecutor must then present the evidence in the trial court. This involves one informal preliminary hearing of the evidence by the prosecutor and two formal preliminary hearings before the case goes to trial, and this whole procedure is necessary even if the accused person pleads guilty.

The desirability of a grand jury indictment has been questioned for many years. As early as 1825 Jeremy Bentham insisted that the grand jury indictment was unnecessary and was of no value. For almost a century the state of Connecticut has permitted the initiation of prosecutions by information in most felony cases, and the tendency elsewhere has been in this direction. At the present time only twenty-two states require indictments in all felony cases, and in three of these states the accused may waive the grand jury hearing if he desires. Nineteen states permit the use of indictments or information in all felony cases, and seven require indictments in certain felony cases but permit initiation of prosecution by information in other types of felony cases. Those who favor the use of the information claim that the indictment does not protect the accused person, that it encumbers the whole process, that it delays decisions and thus facilitates the acquittal of the accused, that it is generally a perfunctory rubber-stamping of the prosecutor's evidence, and that it is a useless expense. Hall, in an excellent analysis of these criticisms, has shown that their validity is by no means demonstrated. The tendency is toward permissive use of initiation by information, rather than the absolute requirement of an indictment or the absolute prohibition of an indictment. The possibility of the indictment as a check on the prosecutor's information is desirable, even if it is seldom used.[4]

The grand jury also has authority to initiate general investigations, but since the evidence in most cases must be collected and presented by the prosecutor, this work has not been very effective. A severe criticism of the grand jury from this point of view was made by the foreman of the Cuyahoga County Grand Jury, for the autumn term of 1933, in which he showed the helplessness of a grand jury which was anxious to make an investigation of banking practices, racketeering, police corruption, and other serious and organized forms of lawlessness. Because of the inactivity of the prosecutor in regard to these forms of lawlessness, the grand jury was actually confined to minor routine cases of helpless offenders.[5]

THE JUDGE. One of the problems concerning the judge is his relation to politics. Judges are generally elected and their terms

---

[4] Jerome Hall, "Analysis of Criticisms of the Grand Jury," *Jour. Crim. Law and Criminol.*, 22:692–704, January, 1932; A. A. Bruce, "The Judge and the Grand Jury," *Jour. Crim. Law and Criminol.*, 23:10–19, May, 1932; Raymond Moley, *Politics and Criminal Prosecution*, New York, 1929, Ch. 6; Wayne L. Morse, "A Survey of the Grand Jury System," *Ore. Law Rev.*, 10:119–275, 1931; Alfred Bettman, "Report on Prosecution," *Natl. Com. on Law Obs. and Enf.*, No. 4, pp. 34–37, 124–126.

[5] Wm. Feathers, *Grand Jury Report*, Cuyahoga County, Ohio, December 21, 1933.

are relatively short. Opposition to this method of selecting judges is growing. Voters cannot know the qualities which are essential in a good judge, such as personal integrity, adequate legal training, and judicial temperament. Since the voters cannot easily know these things, the judges in many places try to make the voters acquainted with them by disgusting self-advertisement, by attending banquets, weddings, funerals, prize-fights, and lodge entertainments, by sensational behavior on the bench, and in other ways. Some judges ask to be transferred from the civil to the criminal branch of the court shortly before elections because of the better opportunity for publicity in the criminal court. It is reported that one of the judges in New York offered a large sum of money to the district attorney in order to have the Harry Thaw case tried before him, because of the publicity this trial would give him. The bar associations in many cities are trying to assist the voters in the selection of judges by announcing preliminary rating of the candidates by the members of the association. This sometimes has an effect but is likely to be unimportant if the judicial election is held at the same time as a regular election, for it is difficult to induce voters to scratch their tickets. The bar association recommended twenty judges in Chicago in 1933, of whom twelve were running on the Democratic ticket and eight on the Republican. Not one of the candidates on the Republican ticket was elected, although eight of the Democrats who were elected were rated by the bar association as very inferior. A notorious case of this selection of judges by the political machine was revealed by the Seabury investigation in New York City in 1932. The supreme court of the second judicial district needed additional judges. This district was Democratic, and the legislature at the time was Republican. The leaders of the two parties in this district had a conference and entered into a bargain that if the Republican legislature would authorize the election of twelve additional judges, five of the judges would be Republicans and seven would be Democratic.[6]

Appointment of the judges, however, does not solve the problem. In New York the mayor appoints the magistrates of the inferior courts. Judges of high character were appointed when the court was first organized, but the judicial quality deteriorated greatly after the World War. The appointments were made on the basis

[6] Testimony quoted by Norman Thomas and Paul Blanchard, *What's the Matter with New York?* pp. 95–102.

of patronage and by recommendations of the party leaders. It was therefore not surprising that several of these judges were found to be involved in bribery and other crimes, and to be associating and co-operating with racketeers and gangsters.[7]

The Seabury Committee recommended that the magistrates should be appointed by the Appellate Court, the members of which are appointed by the governor of the state. Others believe that the governor should appoint the judges from a list nominated by the judicial council and have authority to remove any judge on recommendation of the judicial council, but otherwise the judges would serve for life.

Efforts have been made in some places to bring public pressure to bear on the judges which will be strong enough to offset the control by the politicians. The judges are then between two fires, and the tendency is to compromise by imposing severe penalties on the helpless offenders and acquitting the criminals who are protected by the politicians.

A study of the judges in state supreme courts and federal district and circuit courts has shown that these judges, at any rate, are better prepared than judges in the same courts thirty years ago. This gives some basis for a conclusion that the quality of the personnel in the higher courts is improving.[8]

A second problem concerning the judge is the explanation of his decisions. Aside from political influences, why does a judge make decisions as he does? His judgment is not purely impersonal but is affected by his experiences and temperament. An attempt has been made at least in one case to analyze the influences that entered into a particular decision,[9] and Judge Cardozo has made a more general analysis of decisions.[10] The statistics regarding dispositions of cases in courts in which judges rotate indicate, at least, that judges vary widely in this respect. Sellin has shown that judicial treatment of the different racial and national groups in this country varies wide-

---

[7] New York Legislature, *Report of the Joint Committee on the Government of the City of New York* (Hofstadter Committee), Vol. II, pp. 30–55. See, also, Raymond Moley, *The Tribunes of the People,* New Haven, 1932; Norman Thomas and Paul Blanchard, *What's the Matter with New York?* Chs. 6–7; E. H. Lavine, *The Third Degree,* Ch. 14.

[8] R. L. Mott, S. D. Albright, and Helen R. Semmerling, "Judicial Personnel," *Annals of Amer. Acad. of Pol. and Social Sci.,* 167:143–155, May, 1933.

[9] T. Schroeder, "Psychologic Study of Judicial Opinions," *Calif. Law Rev.,* 6:89–113, January, 1918.

[10] B. N. Cardozo, *The Nature of the Judicial Process,* New Haven, 1922.

ly. This variation is not due entirely to the prejudices of the judges.[11]

A third problem concerns the function of the judge. At present the judge has two functions: to preside at the trial, enforcing the rules of evidence and declaring the law, and to impose sentences in cases of conviction. The judge is well qualified, in general, to perform the first duty, and his influence in this field should be considerably increased. With his training and ability he should have much more complete control of the trial than he has at present. He should really be in control of an investigation to determine guilt. An approach to the Continental system, in which the judge actually directs the trial, would appear to be desirable. This method has been well developed in the juvenile courts and is being constantly extended in the courts for adults, particularly in the specialized courts.

But the judge is not able to perform in a satisfactory manner the other function of imposing sentences. The evidence presented in court is designed to show merely the fact of guilt or innocence; that is entirely insufficient for the purpose of determining what should be done with the individual who is proved guilty. It is necessary to know the entire character of the offender, and the possible effects of different methods that might be used in dealing with him. The judge must fix penalties by guessing at the character of the person on the basis of his appearance and of incidental information that has come out during the course of the trial. No matter how wise or honest the judge may be, he cannot determine treatment in a satisfactory manner by means of the information which he has. The lack of principle in the sentencing of offenders in Indiana is shown in a study by White.[12] Because judges have no good basis for determining treatment, they vary immensely in their policies. One judge in New York placed 7 per cent of those convicted on probation; another judge dealing with offenders of the same types placed 40 per cent on probation. In Cleveland 6 per cent of the cases before one judge were *nolle prossed,* 43 per cent before another judge; one judge suspended sentences in 31 per cent of the cases before him, another in 6 per cent, and as a result 80 per cent of the defend-

---

[11] Thorsten Sellin, "Race Prejudice in the Administration of Justice," *Amer. Jour. Sociol.,* 41:212–217, September, 1937.

[12] R. Clyde White, "Sentencing and the Treatment of the Criminal," *Soc. Serv. Rev.,* 11:234–246, June, 1937.

ants pleaded guilty before the first, 30 per cent before the second.[13] In New Jersey six judges, rotating among the courts and dealing with the same types of cases, showed similar variation. One judge sentenced 57.7 per cent of the convicted persons to imprisonment, and another judge sentenced only 33.6 per cent to imprisonment; the first judge placed 19.5 per cent on probation, the second 30.4 per cent.[14] Some judges establish a reputation for severity, and criminals secure a change of venue in order to come before another judge who has a reputation for leniency. In addition some judges vary widely from day to day, apparently with temporary moods. Such variations with individual moods and tendencies cannot be avoided unless objective standards and objective information can be supplied. Attempts have been made to assist the judges by field investigations by probation officers, by recommendations of psychiatrists, and in other ways. If judges are to retain the sentencing power, it is clear that they should have assistance of this nature. Many people, however, believe that this function should be transferred entirely to a dispositions board composed of representatives of disciplines regarding human behavior, such as a psychologist, a psychiatrist, a sociologist, a social worker, and an educator.[15]

CLERKS AND ATTENDANTS. The importance of clerks and attendants in the judicial process was not recognized until recently. The crime surveys have shown that these agents, like the prosecutors and judges, are subservient to politicians and are frequently the agents of corrupt bondsmen and fixers. The Seabury investigation made it clear that these clerks and attendants are political appointees and that they assume responsible positions without previous experience or training for their work and frequently hold office for a short time. These clerks make out the complaint forms and frequently manipulate them so that discharges result. Dates for which trials are set are changed by clerks without the knowledge of the complaining witnesses so that the defendants will be discharged for lack of prosecution. Contents of indictments and of other secret papers are revealed to the lawyers for the defense. The

---

[13] R. H. Smith and H. B. Ehrmann, "The Criminal Courts," *Cleveland Survey of Criminal Justice,* Part I, pp. 76–80.

[14] F. J. Gaudet, G. S. Harris, and C. W. St. John, "Individual Differences in the Sentencing Tendencies of Judges," *Jour. Crim. Law and Criminol.,* 23:811–818, January, 1933.

[15] Nathaniel Cantor, "A Dispositions Tribunal," *Jour. Crim. Law and Criminol.,* 29:51–61, May, 1938.

clerks advise the court in many cases, and especially transmit suggestions and instructions from the politicians to the judges. The clerks and bailiffs steer cases to professional bondsmen and to lawyers who will split fees with them. In other ways these agents of the courts have been instrumental in betraying the cause of justice and at the same time do not perform efficiently the clerical duties which they are supposed to perform.

THE LAWYER FOR THE DEFENSE. Legal defense for a person on trial was generally prohibited in early English law but has now become a general right. The defendant may employ his own attorney or, under certain circumstances, the state may provide an attorney for him.

Criminal lawyers are generally in disrepute in the legal profession. A large proportion of criminal cases is in the hands of a small number of professional criminal lawyers. These lawyers are recommended to the accused persons by the police and court attendants. They attempt first to bargain with the prosecutor, but if the case comes to trial without a compromise, they make use of every possible subterfuge and trick to secure acquittal.[16] These include bribery of jurors, intimidation of witnesses, instruction of witnesses in perjury, motions of various kinds for purposes of delay, and emotional appeals. Moreover, these criminal lawyers have been very influential as members of legislatures in preventing the enactment of bills for the reform of criminal procedure and of court organization. Gallison has stated:

The preponderating cause of the failure of American justice is the American lawyer. . . . Any system so constructed that improvement and symmetrical growth are inimical to the material welfare of its personnel is fundamentally unsound. Alone among industrial and business enterprises and the "learned" professions, reform inevitably reacts to the material injury of the legal profession. Every proposal of value means loss of income, loss of power, and loss of position to the lawyer. Simply stated, the lawyer cannot reform the system nor permit others to reform it and survive.[17]

Some improvement has been secured as the result of higher

[16] For illustrations of these tricks by a clever criminal lawyer, see Charles E. Erbstein, *The Show-Up*, Chicago, 1926.

[17] I. P. Gallison, "A Layman Looks at Justice," *Jour. Amer. Jud. Soc.*, 16:176–181, April, 1933.

standards of legal education, and the action of grievance committees of bar associations. But the New York judges who, with much
publicity, were dismissed from their positions have, in general, still
retained their membership in the bar association, which leads one to
conclude that they are too dishonest to be judges but not too dishonest to be lawyers. Moreover, the courts have been extremely
reluctant to disbar lawyers except in cases of the most flagrant
violations.

If the defendant is unable to hire his own lawyer, the court may
assign one. All states make provision for an assigned counsel in
capital cases, thirty-four states make this provision for all felony
cases, and twenty-eight states make the provision for misdemeanor
cases. In practice, however, the person charged with a misdemeanor
seldom has an assigned counsel. A relatively capable attorney is
frequently assigned in capital cases, but in other cases the assigned
counsels are generally capable in a relatively small number of places.
The judge generally selects either a young lawyer who is anxious to
secure experience even though the fee be very small, or a "shyster"
who waits in the courtroom for such business and who uses the
assignment as a means of extorting money from the relatives and
friends of the defendant.

Because of the inefficiency and unfairness of the system of assigned counsels, some states have authorized a special public
defender who devotes his entire time to the defense of poor persons
charged with crimes. The public defender was found in Ancient
Rome, in the fifteenth century in Spain, and in many European
countries in recent decades. In this country it was first adopted in
Los Angeles in 1913 and since that time has been authorized in
seven states (California, Connecticut, Illinois, Minnesota, Nebraska,
Tennessee, and Virginia), although generally confined to the large
cities in those states.

The public defender system is superior to the system of assigned
counsel. Delays are reduced, technical motions seldom made, and
the expense to the state is reduced. At the same time they provide
more efficient protection to the accused than do the assigned counsels. Because of their specialization they can help develop public
opinion and criminal procedure as assigned counsels cannot. The
arguments which have been brought against the public defender
system, in comparison with assigned counsel, are clearly spurious.

Bar associations in some states, while recognizing the inefficiency of assigned counsels, have advocated voluntary defenders paid by the bar association or some other group as preferable to public defenders paid by the state. One of their arguments is that the defender and the prosecutor are likely to be members of the same political party and therefore both are under political control. Since most cases are settled in conference between the prosecutor and the lawyer for the defense, this is an important consideration.

The JURY. The jury was originated as a protection against the despotism of the king and has frequently been acclaimed as the "palladium of our liberties." Recent statistics, however, show that the trial plays a very small part in criminal justice, and the jury plays a very small part in the trial. In thirty states in 1936 77 per cent of those convicted in the trial courts were convicted on plea of guilty, 17 per cent on the finding of a jury, and 6 per cent on the finding of the court. Many states have made legislative provision for waiver of the jury trial and substitution of trial by the judge. Few cases go to trial by jury in some states where this legislation has been in existence for some time. In Maryland, for instance, 4,644 persons were found guilty of felonies in 1930, of whom 2,735 pleaded guilty, 1,677 were found guilty in trials before judges, and only 232 in jury trials. Consequently the problem of the jury is not so important as it was previously regarded.

The jury trial is slower and more cumbersome than trial before a judge. Ninety-one days were required to select a jury in the Calhoun case in San Francisco. In some cases several thousand prospective jurors have been examined before twelve were secured. This procedure is not due to the jury system as such, for Judge Riddell of the Supreme Court of Ontario has stated:

I have never in thirty years' experience seen it take more than half an hour to get a jury, even in a murder case.

The jury is generally selected expeditiously in the federal courts of the United States, also, for there the judge has more authority than in the state courts.

According to legal theory the business of the jury is to determine, on the basis of evidence, a question of fact: Did the accused person commit the crime? It is supposed to be a problem in logic similar to the problem which confronts a scientist in a laboratory. In practice, however, the prosecutor tries to select jurymen who will be antagonistic to the accused, and the attorney for the defense tries to select jurymen who will be sympathetic. One tries to exclude all persons not of the same race, religion, politics, or occupation as the accused, and the other tries to exclude all persons who are of the same race, religion, politics, or occupation. The process is perhaps generally more subtle than this and is thus described by Clarence Darrow:

Jurymen seldom convict a person they like, or acquit one that they dislike. The main work of a trial lawyer is to make a jury like his client, or, at least, to feel sympathy for him; facts regarding the crime are relatively unimportant.

I try to get a jury with little education but with much human emotion. The Irish are always the best jurymen for the defense. I don't want a Scotchman, for he has too little human feeling; I don't want a Scandinavian, for he has too strong a respect for law as law. In general I don't want a religious person, for he believes in sin and punishment. The defendant should avoid rich men who have a high regard for the law, as they make and use it. The smug and ultra-respectable think they are the guardians of society, and they believe the law is for them.

The man who is down on his luck, who has trouble, who is more or less a failure, is much kinder to the poor and unfortunate than are the rich and selfish.[18]

The weight of opinion is distinctly in favor of retaining the jury trial but of facilitating the waiver of the jury. In so far as the jury is retained, it should be improved by giving to the judge increased control of the selection of the jury, and by provision for less than unanimous decisions, and by reduction in the size of the jury.[19]

EVIDENCE AND TESTIMONY. Evidence in a trial is furnished by the witnesses for the two sides. Several problems arise in regard to

---

[18] From a statement made in an anniversary dinner at the Quadrangle Club, Chicago, in 1933; quoted with permission of Mr. Darrow.

[19] Alfred Bettman, "Report on Prosecution," *Natl. Com. on Law Obs. and Enf.*, No. 4, pp. 126–128; "Report on Criminal Procedure," *ibid.*, No. 8, pp. 23–28; Raymond Moley, *Our Criminal Courts*, New York, 1930, Ch. 7; C. T. McCormick, "Functions of Judge and Counsel in the Examination of Jurors," *Jour. Crim. Law and Criminol.*, 22:734–739, January, 1932; K. J. Martin, *The Waiver of Jury Trial in Criminal Cases in Ohio*, Baltimore, 1933; Francois Gorphe, "Reform of the Jury System in European Countries," *Jour. Crim. Law and Criminol.*, 27:17–30, 155–168, 473–479, May–November, 1936.

the evidence. The first is that it is very difficult to induce witnesses to appear in court and give testimony. In certain cases of a serious nature there is much terrorism involved. One of the important reasons for the difficulty of convicting the gangsters who have committed serious crimes is that witnesses are afraid to testify. In other types of cases witnesses are reluctant to attend court because of the great inconvenience involved. They may be required to go to court again and again, at great loss to themselves. Consequently they do not make known to anyone that they have important evidence.

A second problem is the honest mistakes which witnesses frequently make. Memory is a fickle thing. One remembers what he wants to remember in many cases. Also, his memory is a combination of what was actually witnessed and of other things that have been heard or imagined subsequent to the occurrence. Delusions of perception occur, also. Tests given to students regarding accuracy in reporting occurrences show very decided differences on many points, with a very high error under the best conditions. The only checks on mistakes in testimony in court are the testimony and appearance of other witnesses. The psychologists have been working for some time, however, on tests of the comparative accuracy of different groups of persons, of replies to leading questions, and of narrative accounts.[20]

A third problem is dishonesty in testimony. The only official check on dishonesty is the oath and the possibility of prosecution for perjury. In a few famous cases witnesses have not been permitted to testify because they were atheists to whom the oath would have no meaning. In general the oath probably has little significance to a large proportion of the witnesses in courts. Judges and others believe that there is an immense amount of perjury in testimony.[21] Samuel Untermyer states, "Perjury has become so general as to

---

[20] An extensive literature on the psychology of testimony has developed. See Alfred Kuraner, "The Consistency of Testimonial Accuracy," *Jour. Crim. Law and Criminol.*, 22:406–413, September, 1931; D. S. Gardner, "The Perception and Memory of Witnesses," *Cornell Law Quart.*, 8:391–409, April, 1933; H. E. Burtt, *Legal Psychology*, New York, 1931; W. A. Marston, "Studies in Testimony," *Jour. Crim. Law and Criminol.*, 15:5–31, May, 1924–1925; Robert M. Hutchins and Donald Slesinger, "Some Observations on the Law of Evidence (Memory)," *Harv. Law Rev.*, 40:860–873, May, 1928; Donald Slesinger and E. M. Pilpel, "Legal Psychology: A Bibliography and a Suggestion," *Psychol. Bull.*, 26:679–692, December, 1929.

[21] Dorothy D. Bromley, "Perjury Rampant," *Harpers*, 163:37–47, June, 1931; Harry Hibschman, "You Do Solemnly Swear," *Jour. Crim. Law and Criminol.*, 24:901–913, January, 1934.

taint and well nigh paralyze the administration of justice." In Chicago only three persons were sentenced to the penitentiary for perjury in the years 1926–1930. Much of the perjury is due to coaching by lawyers.

Experimental work has been conducted for some time in the effort to develop methods of detecting guilty knowledge. These devices are intended to be substitutes for the testimony of witnesses rather than tests of the accuracy of testimony. The "lie detector" at present has the best standing of any of these methods. This instrument does unquestionably register accurately the emotional changes which occur as the result of questions presented, but the emotional changes are not necessarily due to lies. Probably the "lie detector" is of less value in the direct detection of lies than in the detection of emotional disturbances which may be utilized by the examiner to induce a confession.[22] A drug, known as scopolamin, is being used to some extent for the same purpose. It is reported that this drug induces a state of semi-consciousness in which one will answer truthfully every question presented to him. This method, also, is still in the experimental stage and certainly should not be used as evidence in the courtroom.

Even without the development and use of such methods it is possible to make great improvements in the evidence in courts. The Continental courts and the juvenile court have shown the way, as have some of the specialized commissions, such as the Interstate Commerce Commission. These courts and commissions have agents to secure evidence for them. The ordinary criminal court, on the other hand, uses the method of partisan witnesses even on such items as sanity and character and circumstances of the crime. The greatest agitation has developed for psychiatrists as officers of the court to give evidence on the question of sanity, but there is no good reason why similar evidence should not be secured by officers of the court on any other aspect of the crime or of the personality and character of the defendant.

POLITICS. The trend among students of criminal justice is to ascribe the principal defects of the system to politics. This criticism applies to the judges, prosecutors, clerks, bailiffs, and other agents of the courts. Judge Seabury in 1932 found the same system that was described in the investigation twenty-five years earlier, though

---

[22] J. A. Larson, *Lying and Its Detection*, Chicago, 1932.

many formal changes had been made in the meantime. He speaks of the "hideous caricature which parades as justice in these courts" and states that these courts which were intended to be a great instrument of justice have throughout this period remained

. . . a part of a political system, the purpose of which is to retain and control the jobs and perquisites relating to government. As long as appointments to office in these courts are permitted to rest in the hands of a politically controlled agency, just so long must we expect the appointees to be recruited from the ranks of those whose only claim to appointment is their subservience to their political party, and as long as this remains the yardstick by which candidates for these places are to be measured and elected, there is no justification for expecting any substantial improvement in the administration of these courts. . . . No change which fails to convert the Court from the mere medium for the distribution of political patronage, which it now is, into a seat of justice, presided over and administered by persons selected solely for their character and fitness to perform the high and important duties of their offices, can accomplish the desired and necessary result. Reform of any other character would create only a mirage, or, at best, a structure fostering and nursing a new type of corruption and soon calling for another investigation.[23]

This political subservience of the courts is found especially in the larger cities but is by no means unknown in the smaller cities and the towns. Apparently it is less prevalent in federal than in state and city courts.

FIXING THE CASE. The courts and other agencies of justice find constant pressure upon them by friends of the defendant. Members of the family, church, lodge, trade union, club, business firm, neighborhood, and other groups swear to the good character of the defendant and ask for leniency. This may be based on close personal friendship or may represent a desire to protect the reputation of the group. In any case it represents a personal and sympathetic appeal.

The politician has become a regular practitioner in fixing cases. The alderman takes care of thousands of tickets for traffic violations, as a part of his preparation for the next election. Other political

---

[23] New York Legislature, *Report of the Joint Committee on the Government of the City of New York*, Vol. II, pp. 15, 18.

leaders, from the precinct up, perform similar services either directly or indirectly, and they extend their services to persons charged with murder, burglary, robbery, kidnaping, forgery, picking pockets, and other crimes. All of the agencies of criminal justice are under the control of the political leaders and at some point in the process almost any case can be fixed, either in the sense of having a case dropped entirely, or having a penalty mitigated. Judge Seabury stated with reference to the inferior courts of New York City in 1932:

> It is a by-word in the corridors of the Magistrates' Courts of the City of New York that the intervention of a friend in the district political club is much more potent in the disposition of cases than the merits of the cause or the services of the best lawyer and, unfortunately, the truth of the statement alone prevents it from being a slander upon the good name of the City.[24]

Pressure is most frequently placed upon victims of crimes to induce them to refuse to prosecute and upon the police to induce them to present uncertain and confusing testimony. The prosecutor is unquestionably the most important person in the whole process and he could, in spite of the unwillingness of the victim and the confusing testimony of the policeman, organize the evidence in the case if he cared to do so. The inferior court or the magistrate's court is the place where most of these provisions for fixing operate. One of the Tammany leaders stated, "Give me ten magistrates and you can have the whole supreme court." The judge is seldom "fixed" because his position is too public, but when it is necessary he must bear his share of the responsibility of releasing criminals. He may satisfy the public by a severe lecture and a severe penalty imposed in the courtroom and then satisfy the political machine by mitigating or vacating the penalty in his chambers later. Fifteen years ago a national crime commission and several state and municipal crime commissions were organized. Their program was to watch the courts and to bring pressure to bear upon them by publicity in order to secure certain and severe penalties. This program certainly resulted in the conviction and punishment of some professional criminals, but professional criminals still secure immunity

---

[24] New York Legislature, *Report of the Joint Committee on the Government of the City of New York*, Vol. II, p. 15.

at the command of the politician in many cases, while occasional criminals are given terrific penalties in order that the court may compensate for its failure to punish the professional criminals.

THE "SPORTING THEORY" OF JUSTICE. The essential business of a trial should be to determine a question of fact: Did the accused commit the crime? In the performance of that duty tricks and surprises are no more justifiable than in determining a fact in a laboratory. In practice, however, the criminal trial is regarded as a game between two lawyers. Large audiences were attracted in the past and in some sections of the country the criminal trials still are the principal amusement. Each side tries to win the case and takes advantage of every possible trick, surprise, and technical device. It is not at all unusual for as many as fifteen formal motions to be introduced in a case, each of which involves debate, possible continuances, and decisions by the court. When a case is continued, witnesses disappear and public sentiments weaken, and the chance for conviction decreases. Millar has suggested that each side should be required to submit a list of witnesses who are to be called, with an abstract of the evidence to be presented. This would make it possible to reach a decision without the surprises which are not a part of real justice. Since this suggestion and most other suggestions for the reform of criminal procedure are designed to strengthen the state in the trial, they are opposed by the professional criminal lawyers and have made little progress in the legislatures. Justice operates in accordance with this sporting theory, however, in a small proportion of cases and is perhaps illustrated best in capital trials.

THE "BARGAIN THEORY" OF JUSTICE. Many of the legal conflicts which would have been conducted in the courtroom in earlier days in accordance with the sporting theory of justice are now settled in the office of the prosecutor by a process of bargaining. This, also, involves conflict between the opposed attorneys, but it is not sport for there is no audience. Each side tries to make the best possible bargain. The attorney for the defense will go to trial, with certain exceptions, if he feels certain of acquittal. The attorney for the state, also with certain exceptions, will go to trial if he feels certain of a conviction. In the intermediate cases each is willing to bargain, and this generally takes the form of a plea of guilty of a lesser offense than the one charged. In New York State in 1936 58 per cent of those convicted in trial courts were convicted for the offense charged, 42 per cent for a lesser offense. In 43 counties in Ohio in

1937 these percentages were 86 and 14. This plea of guilty of a lesser offense satisfies the prosecutor, for he has an immense burden of work and cannot go to trial on all cases, and this bargain enables him to settle the case expeditiously. It is probable that he has developed good will for the next election by his leniency, but otherwise no corruption is involved in this type of bargaining. The attorney for the defense is satisfied, also, for his client has escaped a severe penalty which might have been inflicted.

Not all of these bargains, however, are equally honest. There may be a direct purchase by money of a penalty that is less severe than the one which might have been inflicted in court, or there may be bargaining which involves a politician who asks for leniency for the accused. It is not possible, however, to determine what proportion of the reductions of charges involve corruption. Neither is it possible to determine how much corruption is involved in the cases which are dismissed by motion of the prosecutor. Certainly corruption is involved in some of them, but it is equally certain that the prosecutor performs an important public service in sifting out the cases which should not go to trial, either because of the innocence of the accused, the triviality of the offense, or the inadequacy of the evidence.

"CASH REGISTER" JUSTICE. The "sporting theory" of justice and the "bargain theory" of justice, in general, apply to defendants who can afford to employ attorneys to secure justice for them. In other cases the accused are rushed through the court with scant attention, either of the prosecutor or the judge. This type of justice is well known in the traffic courts, where the whole procedure is mechanical. This procedure is perhaps inevitable in view of the large number of cases, but hundreds of thousands of citizens are angry about the impossibility of securing justice there.[25] The poor and uninfluential persons accused of other minor offenses are rushed through the courts in exactly the same manner. More than fifty cases of vagrancy, drunkenness, and disorderly conduct were disposed of in the DesPlaines Street Court in Chicago in less than thirty minutes.[26] It is difficult for a person to retain much respect for the system of justice after he sits in an inferior court for a few sessions and sees the inadequate information on which decisions are

---

[25] R. L. Burgess, "Can You Get a Square Deal in the Traffic Court?" *Amer. Mag.*, 114:11-13, 111-115, October, 1932.
[26] Nels Anderson, *The Hobo*, Chicago, 1923, p. 166.

based. This effect is produced, moreover, on millions of persons each year. In New York City in 1930 a half million persons were arraigned in the magistrates' courts, and each of these cases, characteristically, involved the presence of several complainants, witnesses, and friends. From the standpoint of the number of cases settled and the number of persons affected, these are the "supreme courts"; they are inferior courts only with reference to the character and training of the judges, the efficiency of the machinery, and the type of justice which is secured. At no point, in a very large proportion of cases, is there an opportunity for an adequate consideration of the facts in the case either by the prosecutor or by the court.

THE COURT AS A WELFARE AGENCY. The conventional court system was an expression of a principle of conflict. The theory was that the state had been injured by a crime and in return should injure the offender by punishment, and also that the truth regarding guilt could best be determined by a conflict between opposed lawyers. The juvenile court, on the other hand, has been built on a different principle. Its work proceeds on the hypothesis that the delinquent child and the state have much in common and that the interests of both will be promoted by efforts to help the child rather than injure him. This is believed to be a superior principle of control, so far as it is practicable to use it.

Some branches of the criminal court, also, have adopted the principle that future crime can best be prevented by helping the accused. Probation and psychiatric service are the best illustration of this and both have been adopted in many criminal courts in more or less restricted form. They are to be discussed in a later chapter. The women's court and the boys' court are organized on somewhat the same principle as the juvenile court. A judge of the municipal court in Chicago in 1933 asked to be assigned to the branch of the court in which most of the chronic alcoholics were tried. For some months he studied these offenders and studied the literature regarding drunkenness. He tried by correspondence with relatives, by personal suggestions regarding hospital care, by securing co-operation of social agencies, and by personal advice to assist in the rehabilitation of these drunkards. The fact that he was not successful in many cases does not alter the significance of this attitude in court work. The prosecutor frequently brings together persons who have been quarreling and by conciliation induces them to drop the prosecution. In many other branches of court work where the emotions of anger are not aroused in the public the court is endeavoring to assist in welfare work either in co-operation with social agencies or without such assistance. It is certainly possible that this endeavor may become more prominent in several other branches of court work in the near future.

A specialized feature of this welfare work is the effort to provide indemnification to injured parties for errors of justice. Verdicts are sometimes incorrect and persons are injured as the result. The same arguments may be advanced for indemnification for errors of justice as for indemnification for unjustifiable arrests. The same limitations should be placed upon indemnification of this kind, also. Precedents for indemnification for errors of justice run back at least as far as 1660.

THE AUDIENCE AND PUBLICITY. One of the rights for which the common people fought two centuries ago was the right to a public trial. This right is no longer highly prized by accused persons, but one of the highly prized privileges which a few of the defendants secure is to be tried in the judge's chambers or to have the judge come to the courtroom at an unusual hour so that they may be protected against a public trial. This right to a private trial has been granted in the juvenile court and it would appear wise that restrictions at least as great as those in the juvenile court should be imposed in all trials and that the audience should be confined to those who have a particular and justified interest in the case. The night courts in New York City, dealing principally with persons accused of prostitution, came to be one of the sights of the city. After-theater parties finished the evening by a trip to the night court. Judges tried in vain to restrict and control the audience. Finally one judge walked to the railing and, pointing to the spectators one at a time, asked each what business he had in the courtroom. The audience quickly left the room. Spectators are equally troublesome in many murder cases. Nearly eight thousand persons, according to newspaper reports, tried to get into the courtroom during the first day of the trial of Dr. Wynekoop in Chicago in 1934, although the courtroom had a maximum capacity of two hundred. The bailiff in this courtroom, on the second day of the trial, reserved the seats for his friends. The chief bailiff of the court building, angered because his friends could not get into the trial, withdrew the policemen who were holding the crowd back, the crowd crashed into the courtroom, and the judge was compelled to declare an intermission while the room was cleared. Many accused persons legitimately ask the question: When the state compels me to stand trial what right does the state have to expose me to curiosity seekers? Many of these trials are unquestionably an invasion of the accused person's right to privacy. Probably the most notorious offenders in this respect are the reporters and photographers from the newspapers. In some jurisdictions where the judges have little self-respect and are anxious for publicity, the constant flashing of the photographer's lights interferes seriously with the trial and certainly results in a lowering of the public's respect for the court. Aside from this, the tendency is toward greater privacy, for the courtroom is generally arranged so that the audience hears almost none of the evidence except in jury trials.

Publication of accounts of crime, both before and during the trial, should be restricted, also. An illustration of the lengths to which newspapers go is furnished by the many columns of sordid details printed about the more spectacular crimes. Much less space is given to the most important national and international developments than to any one of these spectacular crimes. The newspapers justify this by the argument that the public demands such stories; but the demand is certainly stimulated and developed by the newspapers, and many people express their disgust at such news. It is significant that English newspapers contain nothing comparable.

POPULAR JUSTICE. One of the characteristics of law, according to legal theory, is the calm and restrained procedure by which it is accomplished. Since human beings are not always calm and restrained, they sometimes take the law into their own hands and act as police, judge, and executioner. This happens most frequently when two groups in close proximity differ widely in culture and in social status. It happens, also, in communities where the law is slow, weak, or corrupt. Out of these situations in modern society have developed vigilance committees, the Ku Klux Klan, lynchings, and other sporadic activities.

The vigilance committees in California and other Western states about the middle of the nineteenth century were not far removed from the orderly procedure of the law, for they were definitely opposed to mob action.[27] Other less permanent vigilance committees did not have the same restraint. The Ku Klux Klan in the recon-

---

[27] H. H. Bancroft, *Popular Tribunals*, Vols. I and II.

struction period after the Civil War was fighting against dangers
that they believed were caused by a corrupt government arbitrarily
forced upon them from outside, while the later Ku Klux Klan was
primarily a form of sport, which developed into terrorism under
the protection of secrecy and organization.[28] The Black Legion in
Michigan in 1936 was an expression of this same interest. Lynching
mobs are more sporadic than these general and somewhat permanent organizations and their behavior is less controlled. Lynchings
have decreased steadily from an average of about 150 per year in
1885–1899 to an average of 11 per year in 1934–1938.[29] A bill was
before Congress in 1938 to make lynching a federal crime. A poll
of public opinion showed that 72 per cent of those interviewed were
in favor of this bill, and that even in the South 57 per cent favored it.

Vigilance committees have been formed in several states, largely
under the stimulation of bankers' associations and for police purposes rather than judicial purposes. In some states, however, they
offered a reward for a bank burglar and a larger reward for a dead
bank burglar. This resulted in a policeman in Texas luring two
Negroes into a bank in 1930, where he shot them and claimed the
reward. The bankers' association became suspicious of the circumstances and the policeman was convicted of murder.[30]

SUGGESTED READINGS

Alexander, Franz, and Staub, Hugo, *The Criminal, the Judge, and
the Public,* New York, 1931.

Baker, N. F., and DeLong, E. H., "The Prosecutor and His Office,"
Jour. Crim. Law and Criminol., 23:770–796, 926–963; 24:1025–
1065; 25:358–400, 884–901; 26:821–846, January, 1933 to March,
1936.

Bettman, Alfred, "Report on Prosecution," *Natl. Com. on Law Obs.
and Enf.,* No. 4, Washington, 1931.

Borchard, E. M., *Convicting the Innocent,* New Haven, 1932.

Burtt, H. E., *Legal Psychology,* New York, 1931.

Cardozo, B. N., *The Nature of the Judicial Process,* New Haven, 1922.

---

[28] John M. Mecklin, *The Ku Klux Klan,* New York, 1924.
[29] P. W. Black, "Lynchings in Iowa," *Iowa Jour. Hist. and Pol.,* 10:151–
254, 1912; J. H. Chadbourn, *Lynchings and the Law,* Chapel Hill, 1933;
Arthur Raper, *The Tragedy of Lynching,* Chapel Hill, 1933; Walter White,
Rope and Faggot, New York, 1929.
[30] E. J. Hopkins, *Our Lawless Police,* New York, 1932, p. 56.

Davis, H. A., "Officers of the Court," *Amer. Mercury*, 12:293–300, November, 1927.

Frankfurter, Felix, "Surveys of Criminal Justice," *Proc. Natl. Conf. Social Work*, 1930, pp. 163–169.

Gallison, I. P., "A Layman Looks at Justice," *Jour. Amer. Jud. Soc.*, 16:176–181, April, 1933.

Haines, C. G., "General Observations on the Effects of Personal, Political and Economic Influences on the Decisions of Judges," *Ill. Law Rev.*, 17:96–116, June, 1922.

Hepbron, J. M., "Local Crime Surveys: Their Origin, Purpose and Accomplishments," *Social Forces*, 24:426–431, May, 1927.

Howard, Pendleton, *Criminal Justice in England*, New York, 1931.

Illinois Association for Criminal Justice, *Illinois Crime Survey*, Chicago, 1929.

Keedy, E. R., "Administration of the Criminal Law," *Yale Law Rev.*, 31:240–262, January, 1922.

Larson, J. A., *Lying and Its Detection*, Chicago, 1932.

Millar, R. W., 'The Modernization of Criminal Procedure," *Jour. Crim. Law and Criminol.*, 11:344–367, November, 1920.

Mishkin, Charles, "The Public Defender," *Jour. Crim. Law and Criminol.*, 22:489–505, November, 1931.

Missouri Association for Criminal Justice, *The Missouri Crime Survey*, New York, 1926.

Moley, Raymond, *Our Criminal Courts*, New York, 1930.

Moley, Raymond, *The Tribunes of the People*, New Haven, 1932.

Moley, Raymond, and Wallace, S. C. (Editors), "Administration of Justice," *Annals of Amer. Acad. of Pol. and Social Sci.*, 167:1–220, May, 1933.

New York Legislature, *Report of the Joint Committee on the Government of the City of New York*, New York, 1932.

Perry, S. H., "Politics and Judicial Administration," *Annals of Amer. Acad. of Pol. and Social Sci.*, 169:75–85, September, 1933.

Pound, Roscoe, *Criminal Justice in America*, New York, 1930.

Rubin, Samuel, "Criminal Justice and the Poor," *Crim. Law and Criminol.*, 22:705–715, January, 1932.

Smith, R. H., *Justice and the Poor*, New York, 1919.

Ulman, Joseph H., *A Judge Takes the Stand*, New York, 1933.

Waite, J. B., *Criminal Law in Action*, New York, 1934.

Zelitch, Judah, *Soviet Administration of Criminal Law*, Philadelphia, 1931.

Chapter Seventeen

THE JUVENILE COURT

DELINQUENT CHILDREN IN THE EARLY COURTS. A century and a half ago children were tried and treated for violations of law in the same ways as adults, with the exception that a child under seven years of age was regarded as not responsible and therefore as incapable of committing a crime, while a child between the ages of seven and fourteen was regarded as having the possibility of such discernment as would make him responsible, and this was to be decided in each case by an examination. A child under seven years of age, therefore, could not be punished by order of the court, while a child between the ages of seven and fourteen could be subjected to all forms of punishment that were suitable for adults. In the course of time the maximum age was raised in some American states from seven to ten or some other age, but it still happens that children under fourteen years of age are arrested, held in jail, tried in court, and punished in the same ways as adult criminals. The state prisons and reformatories in 1936 received from the courts 21 persons fourteen years of age or under.

ORIGIN AND DEVELOPMENT OF THE JUVENILE COURT. The original method of identical treatment for children and adults has been undergoing modifications for at least a century. As early as 1824 a juvenile reformatory was established in New York State so that children, after conviction, would not be confined with adult criminals. The laws of Illinois in 1831 provided that for certain offenses the penalties for minors might differ from those for adults. In 1861 the legislature of Illinois authorized the mayor of Chicago to appoint a commissioner before whom boys between the ages of six and seventeen could be taken on charges of petty offenses; this commissioner had authority to place the boys on probation, to send them to reform schools, and to use other methods of treatment. In 1867 this work was transferred to the regular judges of the courts. Separate hearings for juvenile offenders were required in Boston in 1870 and in all parts of the state of Massachusetts in 1872. In 1877 both Massachusetts and New York State authorized separate sessions with separate dockets and records for juvenile cases. During the last quarter of the nineteenth century cases of truancy and incorrigibility of children were heard in some places by probate courts, without juries or the ordinary legal technicalities and formalities. These policies were combined and were supported by a consistent theory, which had been lacking in the earlier developments, and thus the juvenile court came into existence in 1899 in Chicago. The two significant points about this new court were: First, the age below which a child could not be a criminal was advanced from seven to sixteen years, which was in line with changes that had been made elsewhere. But whereas the previous law had made no provision for those below the age of responsibility, the new law did make provision for all of them under the softer name "delinquents." Second, the work of the court was placed under chancery or equity jurisdiction. For several centuries dependent children had been under chancery jurisdiction; in principle all children were wards of the state if their parents were not willing or able to care for them; in practice the protection of dependent children was confined almost entirely to those who had property. The juvenile court law of Chicago was merely a logical extension of this principle of guardianship by the court of chancery to all children who were in need of the protection and guardianship of the state, and thus was made to include delinquent children.

The juvenile court movement developed rapidly after the Chicago court was authorized. Twenty-two states had somewhat similar laws within ten years. By 1925 all except two states—Maine and Wyoming—had such laws and each of these states had some of the juvenile court methods. In 1932 a federal law authorized the federal courts to divert juvenile cases to the juvenile courts of the several states. The Federal Bureau of Prisons and the Federal Children's Bureau attempted to develop the policy co-operatively, with the hope that most of the federal juvenile cases could be turned over to the states. But in the first two years only 5 per cent of the federal juvenile cases were thus diverted, due principally to the fact that the maximum age jurisdiction of the juvenile courts in most of the states excluded a large proportion of the federal cases and partly to the fact that many of the states did not have adequate facilities for treating federal delinquents. The situation has not changed appreciably since that first effort to divert federal cases to the states.

The juvenile court movement has expanded in other ways, as well as geographically. The age was raised from sixteen to seventeen or eighteen and in some cases even to twenty-one. Adults who commit crimes against children or contribute to the delinquency or dependency of children are included in the jurisdiction of many juvenile courts. Many administrative tasks have been assumed by the juvenile court, including mothers' pensions, recreational work, and even educational work. The juvenile court movement has spread, also, to other continents, and most of the civilized countries now have specialized juvenile courts.[1]

COMPARISON OF JUVENILE COURT AND CRIMINAL COURT. A comparison of the juvenile court with the criminal court is difficult because of the large number of variations in the procedure and organization in each court. The following comparison refers to the conventional criminal court, without its recent modifications, and to the juvenile court in its ideal form.[2]

Criminal Court	Juvenile Court
1. Trial characterized by contentiousness; two partisan groups in conflict.	1. Hearing characterized by scientific methods of investigation.
2. Purpose of trial to determine whether defendant committed the crime with which he is charged.	2. Purpose of hearing to determine the general condition and character of the child.
3. No machinery for securing information regarding the character of the accused.	3. Elaborate machinery for securing information regarding the character of the child.
4. Such information, if secured, may not be introduced as a part of the evidence.	4. Such information is the basis on which a decision is made.
5. Punishment if convicted.	5. Protection and guardianship of the state if the existing conditions show the need.

---

[1] Winifred A. Elkin, *English Juvenile Courts*, London, 1938.

[2] For a more extended comparison, see Pauline V. Young, *Social Treatment in Probation and Delinquency*, New York, 1937, pp. 182–185.

Criminal Court	*Juvenile Court*
6. Treatment in a specific case determined not by the needs of the particular individual but by the legislature, in advance, for all who violate the law in question, with reference primarily to other actual or potential delinquents.	6. Treatment in a specific case determined by the needs of the particular individual without reference to other actual or potential delinquents.

The juvenile court in many places and in many respects is significantly different from this description, and the criminal court in some respects has approached rather closely to the description of the juvenile court. Nevertheless there is, characteristically, a significant difference between them. The ideal of the juvenile courts is that "they are not looking outwardly at the act but, scrutinizing it as a symptom, are looking forward to what the child is to become."[3]

CHARACTERISTICS OF THE JUVENILE COURT. Miss Belden in her survey of the courts hearing children's cases in 1918 gives the following as the characteristics of juvenile courts:[4]

1. Separate hearings for children's cases.
2. Informal or chancery procedure.
3. Regular probation service, both for investigation and supervisory care.
4. Detention separate from adults.
5. Special court records and probation records, both legal and social.
6. Provision for mental and physical examinations.

Of these the first, third, and fifth are stated to be absolutely essential, so that a court without any one of them is not a juvenile court.

The characteristics of the juvenile court, stated in more detail, are as follows: (a) A "blanket" definition of delinquency and de-

---

[3] White House Conference on Child Health and Protection, *The Delinquent Child*, New York, 1932, p. 257. Reprinted by permission of D. Appleton-Century Company, publishers.
[4] Evelina Belden, "Courts in the United States Hearing Children's Cases," *U. S. Children's Bur.*, No. 65, pp. 10–12.

pendency is provided. The following definition of a delinquent child is given in the standard juvenile court law formulated by a committee of the National Probation Association:

The words "delinquent child" include: (a) A child who has violated any law of the state or any ordinance or regulation of a subdivision of the state. (b) A child who by reason of being wayward or habitually disobedient is uncontrolled by his parent, guardian or custodian. (c) A child who is habitually truant from school or home. (d) A child who habitually so deports himself as to injure or endanger the morals or health of himself or others.

This standard law defines the neglected child and the dependent child, also, in general terms. It was no oversight that the juvenile court was given jurisdiction over both delinquent and dependent or neglected children and uses essentially the same procedure for both. In both the purpose is the same—to determine whether the child needs special guardianship by the state. The elements of guilt, responsibility, criminal intent, and punishment are, theoretically at least, eliminated. In New Zealand by act of 1925 a charge of delinquency need not be made or heard. The court may act on the basis of the parentage, history, education, mentality, or other relevant data. It is probable that in more than a majority of cases the child could be brought into the juvenile court in the United States on either a delinquency or dependency petition. On that account the juvenile court law of California made no distinction between them. Miss Belden in 1918 reported that 57 per cent of the cases in courts hearing children's cases were delinquency cases. In 1932 72 per cent of the cases heard in ninety-two courts were delinquency cases.

(b) Jurisdiction over children's cases varies widely from state to state and even from county to county within a state. The juvenile court is sometimes independent, sometimes a specialized part of another court. By 1929 independent juvenile courts had been created in nineteen states and the District of Columbia, but in fifteen of these states the juvenile court was independent only in certain counties. The juvenile court is usually a specialized branch of some other court, generally a county court or a probate court. In thirty-seven of the states and the District of Columbia and in parts of another state the court which hears juvenile cases has exclusive jurisdiction over children's cases, with certain exceptions. In the other states the delinquent child may be taken either to the juvenile court or to a branch of the criminal court. Provision is frequently made in the states in which the juvenile court has exclusive original jurisdiction that the judge may, at his discretion, transfer the cases involving serious crimes to the criminal court. In 1929 in eleven states and parts of another the juvenile court did not have any jurisdiction over juveniles charged with offenses which, if committed by adults, would be punishable by death or by life imprisonment, and similar limitations were made in a few other states for other serious offenses. Good reasons exist for the opinion that the juvenile court should have original, exclusive, and complete jurisdiction over all cases of delinquency of children.

The county seems to be the best territorial unit for a juvenile court system, at present. If the city is taken as a unit, the rural parts of the county in which the city is located are left without provision. If the plan for the organization of courts should be adopted, the juvenile court would be a branch of the county court, with a specialized judge.

(c) Equity or chancery jurisdiction. Equity courts stand for flexibility, guardianship, and protection rather than rigidity and punishment. Consequently the friends of the juvenile court insist that children's cases should fall within the equity jurisdiction rather than the criminal jurisdiction. The supreme courts have approved of this in several decisions. But there is a minority opinion. E. Lindsey, for instance, states that there is no justification for placing the juvenile court under equity jurisdiction, and explains the decisions of the supreme courts as due to the influence of public opinion and the fact that few persons of wealth or influence have fought the question in the courts.[5]

Many courts that try children's cases do not have equity powers. But many of them have, nevertheless, adopted what is, in essence, the equity procedure—informality in the hearing, inquiries regarding character and the general needs of the child, separate hearings, separate records, etc. They are not distinguishable in procedure from the children's courts that operate under equity jurisdiction. From the standpoint of theory, however, the children

---

[5] E. Lindsey, "The Juvenile Court Movement from a Lawyer's Standpoint," *Annals of Amer. Acad. of Pol. and Social Sci.*, 52:140–148, March, 1914.

in such courts are criminals, while in the juvenile courts with equity powers they are not.

Even in the juvenile courts which operate under equity jurisdiction many vestiges of criminal procedure may be found: (1) The right to trial by jury is retained, due to the fear that the supreme court might otherwise find the law unconstitutional. (2) Delinquency, while given a blanket definition by some phrases, is defined by some specific phrases, in imitation of the criminal law. The laws of Alabama and California have lately retained merely the blanket phrases and avoided the term "delinquent." (3) The juvenile courts in their reports frequently classify offenses in terms of the criminal law, such as grand larceny, petty larceny, etc. (4) Some judges use methods that are distinctly those of the criminal court, even of the medieval criminal court, such as whipping, fining, and short term imprisonment. From the point of view of juvenile court theory commitment to an institution is not an infliction of punishment but is a substitute for home training; in practice judges frequently order a delinquent child committed to an institution and then explain that the order will be suspended and the child will be given another chance on probation. Commitment to the institution is held over the child's head as a threat and is regarded as a punishment by the child, his parents, and the judge. The juvenile court is generally regarded, in spite of legal theory, as a place in which bad children are punished. Though it is the purpose of the equity jurisdiction to remove the stigma of crime, much of the stigma, in fact, remains in spite of the law to the contrary and the efforts of the officers of the court to avoid it. In the minds of the child, the parents, the neighbors, and others, juvenile court action is generally equivalent to a criminal process. This feeling is increased and justified by the fact that a very large proportion of the "complaints" against delinquent children are filed by police officers. In 1930 60 per cent of the complaints in the ninety-two courts reporting to the Children's Bureau were thus filed, and frequently much more than that in the larger cities. Moreover, in Chicago in 1926 only 4.4 per cent of the juveniles arrested by the police were referred to the juvenile court. The other 95.6 per cent were held in the police station for a time, warned, and sent home. Thus the police department is the real agency which deals with a large proportion of juvenile delinquents.[6]

---

[6] Illinois Association for Criminal Justice, *Illinois Crime Survey*, p. 646.

(d) Age jurisdiction varies widely from state to state. In 1937 the maximum age for boys in juvenile courts was sixteen years in eleven states, seventeen in eleven states, eighteen in seventeen states, and twenty-one in four states; in the other five states the age varied within the state. The maximum age for girls is higher than for boys in five states. It is difficult to fix a logical dividing line. The Committee on Juvenile Court Standards recommended that the age limit be not lower than eighteen years. In many states a child taken into the juvenile court before he reaches the maximum age of juvenile court jurisdiction remains within the jurisdiction of the juvenile court until a later age, generally until he reaches majority. In practice, however, few cases appear in the juvenile court under this provision.

A special Boys' Court for offenders between the ages of seventeen and twenty-one has been organized in Chicago as a branch of the municipal court. It is not a juvenile court but a regular criminal court with some modifications in procedure. A similar court has been organized in Brooklyn.

(e) Many juvenile courts have jurisdiction over certain adults. Forty-three states have laws which make it possible to deal through the courts with parents or others who contribute to the delinquency or dependency of children, and in thirty-one states and parts of six others the court which has jurisdiction over the children has jurisdiction, also, with limitations in some states, over the adults contributing to their delinquency or dependency. The juvenile court in a few states is given jurisdiction over the following specified groups: adults deserting or failing to support juveniles, adults accused of crimes against children, adults violating the child-labor law, parents failing to comply with the compulsory school law or concealing the birth of a child, adults aiding a child to escape from an institution, adults furnishing children in institutions with tobacco.[7] The justification that is offered for extending the jurisdiction to these adults is that it keeps the child, even as a witness, out of the criminal court, it is easier to deal with the whole problem together, and the judges in the other courts hesitate to use the ordinary criminal procedure in dealing with such offenders, and consequently discharge them with a futile warning. The Supreme Court of the

[7] S. P. Breckinridge and Helen R. Jeter, "A Summary of Juvenile Court Legislation in the United States," *U. S. Children's Bur.*, No. 70, pp. 21–24, 84–85.

District of Columbia, however, in its decision in the Moreland case, held that an indictment by a grand jury was necessary before a person could be sentenced to the workhouse at hard labor for contributing to the delinquency of children.[8] This practically means that the juvenile court there has no jurisdiction over adults, but this decision does not affect the procedure in the states. Much criticism of the decision has been expressed and it is probable that it will not be found to be good law in the long run.[9]

(f) The judge of the juvenile court is elected in certain cities or counties in six states, appointed by the governor in certain cities or counties in five states, and by the President of the United States in the District of Columbia. In most rural counties the judge of the county, circuit, or district court, of which the juvenile court is a part, acts ex-officio as judge of the juvenile court. In the larger cities where the juvenile court is more completely separated from the court of which it is a branch, and one judge gives full time to juvenile court work, the judge of the juvenile court is appointed by his associates in most cases. When the appointment is not made in this way the judges frequently rotate, each one taking one month, or two months, or perhaps a year in the juvenile court. This method of rotation is very unsatisfactory, especially when the terms are short, for it makes specialization impossible. The average length of time the judges have served in the juvenile court of St. Louis since 1903 has been 10.9 months each. In North Carolina the clerk of the county court is the juvenile court judge except in the larger towns and cities; he is a permanent member of the community, while the judges frequently are not.

The North Carolina system raises the question, Should the judge of the juvenile court have a legal training? The Westchester County Children's Association in 1922 recommended that the candidates for judge in the new juvenile court should be persons with knowledge of child care and education rather than persons with legal training. On the other hand the committee appointed to formulate juvenile court standards recommended that the judge should have legal training. Evidently it is desirable for the judge to have both legal training and knowledge of child care; many parts of the pro-

---

[8] 42 *Sup. Ct. Rep.*, 368.
[9] J. H. Wigmore, "Obstructing the Efficiency of the Juvenile Court," *Jour. Crim. Law and Criminol.*, 13:165–167, August, 1922; R. Oppenheimer, "Infamous Crimes and the Moreland Case," *Harv. Law Rev.*, 36:299–320, January, 1922.

cedure of the juvenile court require a knowledge of the law, and it does not seem possible to dispense with this requirement.

It is possible, however, for very much of the work to be done under the supervision of the judge by persons who have not had legal training. Many of the cases are now settled by probation officers who have had no legal training. The legislatures of Colorado, Missouri, New Mexico, North Dakota, and Alabama have given the juvenile court judges authority to appoint referees who may make tentative disposals of cases; and in other states in which the juvenile court has equity jurisdiction the judge has authority without specific legislative enactment to appoint masters or referees for the same purpose. This power to appoint referees makes it possible for the judge to transfer all cases of girls involved in sex delinquency to a woman, who, as referee, will make the decisions to be approved by the judge, if it seems desirable. This power is valuable, also, in extending the court to rural districts that are far from the place where the sessions of the court are held. If no such arrangement is made, offenses are passed over, if the injury is trivial, until it may become too late to modify the behavior of the offender, or the justice of the peace is appealed to for the exercise of his police power, or some other unsatisfactory method is adopted because of the inconvenience of attending the sessions of the juvenile court. This can be avoided by the appointment of several referees to act under the supervision of the judge. The same extension of the juvenile court may be found advantageous in the large cities.

(g) Investigation of complaints is made by probation officers, acting as agents of the court. This investigation involves not merely the question of fact regarding a specified offense, but the whole social situation of the child—especially his home and neighborhood conditions and school and work records. In many places physical, mental, and psychiatric examinations are made, also. The information secured in this way is the basis of decisions and of policies. The juvenile court law generally makes an absolute requirement that these investigations be made before the hearing in court.

(h) Procedure in the juvenile court is generally required, by law, to be "summary" or informal. In many cases the proceedings begin with a petition for a hearing in regard to a certain child. In such cases the child is generally not arrested, but is summoned to appear in court, or his parents are summoned to bring him to court. The general practice is to exercise great care in weighing evidence, but without the same observance of forms as in the criminal courts. It is necessary to prove a specific violation of the law, even of the blanket provisions; that is, it must be proved that the child did violate a specific municipal ordinance or is in a specific way growing up in a career of idleness and crime. This specific proof is the basis of the whole treatment. Attorneys sometimes appear for the child, but not often. Many states permit a jury trial, if demanded by the child or parents; but few of them make such demands, and, as the committee on juvenile court standards stated, jury trials "are inconsistent with both the law and the theory upon which children's codes are founded." In forty states and the District of Columbia special provisions are made in the law for appeals from the decisions of the juvenile court. A study of the appeals from the juvenile courts in Suffolk County, Massachusetts, from 1930 to 1935, showed variations in dispositions in a large proportion of cases. The Superior Court filed, *nol prossed,* or discharged as not delinquent 46.1 per cent of these appeal cases. Of 216 children who had been committed to institutions by the juvenile courts only 9.3 per cent were committed by the Superior Court; this doubtless explains why 34.4 per cent of all juveniles ordered committed by the juvenile courts took appeals. Of five judges in the Superior Court who heard most of these appeal cases during the five-year period, one discharged 11.1 per cent of the cases, while at the other extreme one discharged 71.4 per cent. The reason for these changes from the decisions of the juvenile court is not that the higher court has a better basis for a decision than the juvenile court, but that the judge and the district attorney, struggling with an overload of work, regard the juvenile cases as trivial in comparison with the adult cases on which they are usually engaged, and as not deserving of serious treatment.[10]

The judge may hear the case either in his chambers or in the courtroom, but the courtroom is generally arranged so that spectators are so far removed from the bench or table at which the judge is sitting that they cannot hear the conversation. The records are customarily regarded as confidential, and some states prohibit the publication of information on juvenile court cases or printing a photograph of a child in the juvenile court.

[10] Benedict S. Alper, "Juvenile Justice: A Study of Juvenile Appeals to the Suffolk County Court, Boston, 1930–1935," *Jour. Crim. Law and Criminol.,* 28:349–367, September, 1937.

A great many judges feel that they fail if they do not secure the confidence of the child to such an extent as to get a complete confession and the explanation of the delinquency by the child.[11]

(i) The treatment of the child is determined by the whole investigation, of which the court procedure is a part. In a very large proportion of the cases advice is given to the parents or to others and the case is dismissed; in some places such cases do not get to the judge at all, but are settled by the probation officers. Three methods of treatment for the others are approved in an unqualified manner: continuance, probation, and commitment. The continuance is designed as a trial or test of the offender and his parents without special assistance of the court. Probation is used in a large proportion of the cases in the places where juvenile court methods have been well developed. But in places where the judge has given no special thought to the problems of juvenile delinquency, where there are no trained social workers or psychiatrists, the child is either dismissed or else sent to an institution. Even when a child is placed on probation in such places it generally means almost nothing. The difference between such places and those in which trained probation officers are employed may be illustrated by a comparison of the methods of disposing of cases in the Chicago Juvenile Court and in sixty-two juvenile courts in the rest of the state, which is largely rural and in which the methods are not as well understood or developed.[12] This is shown in Table VI.

TABLE VI

COMPARISON OF THE DISPOSITIONS OF JUVENILE DELINQUENCY CASES IN THE CHICAGO JUVENILE COURT AND 62 RURAL JUVENILE COURTS IN ILLINOIS

	Chicago	Rural Courts in Illinois
Number of cases......................	3,007	974
Dismissed, per cent	6.4	19.0
Probation, per cent	45.6	28.0
Commitment to institution, per cent.....	25.5	46.9
Other treatment, per cent	22.5	6.0

Fines are sometimes used as a method of dealing with juvenile delinquency, but the general weight of opinion is opposed to this.

---

[11] See H. Weiss, "A Great Judge," *Survey*, 48:117, April 22, 1922.
[12] Belden, *op. cit.*, p. 41.

Some judges have maintained that when the delinquent child makes a financial gain without injuring others, as by violating a peddling ordinance, he should suffer a financial loss in the form of a fine. During the period 1906–1911, Judge Baker of the Boston Juvenile Court imposed 715 fines amounting to $2,581; during 1911–1916, he imposed 376 fines amounting to $1,244.[13] The committee on juvenile court standards recommended that "fines should never be imposed in children's cases." Somewhat related to the method of fining is the method of requiring reparation, as in cases of larceny. Miss Belden found that a few courts in thirty-two states used this method. The committee on juvenile court standards recommended that

Restitution or reparation should be required only in cases where they seem to have disciplinary value or to instill respect for property rights.[14]

Some judges use the method of commitment to a detention home for a few days. This is much like the commitment of adults to jails for a few days, and is generally injurious. The committee on juvenile court standards recommended that "the detention home should not be used as a disciplinary institution."[15] Some of the courts, generally in the rural sections, go much further than this in the application of penal methods. The juvenile court in one state is authorized by law to order a delinquent child to be whipped.

In three states the judges referred to whipping as one method of disposition of the cases. One judge said his method of dealing with truants was: "First, lectured; second, ordered whipped by parents; third, turned over to the state board of charities and correction." Among the dispositions listed in the published statement in a report of a state board of charities, whipping was reported for four courts for 121 children, both white and colored. In another state a judge said that in a great many cases where nothing serious has been done the parents of the child or children are required to give them a whipping. . . . Of the children brought before [another] court in the

---

[13] "Harvey Humphrey Baker," *Pub. Judge Baker Foundation,* No. 1, pp. 25, 102–103.

[14] Juvenile Court Standards, "Report of Committee, 1923," *U. S. Children's Bur.,* No. 121, p. 7.

[15] Juvenile Court Standards, *op. cit.,* p. 4.

year for which the report was made, 65 were sent to jail; 40 were placed in a chain gang; 12 were sent to a reformatory and 1 to an orphanage; 156 were fined; 156 were dismissed; judgment was suspended for 25 and only 51 were placed on probation.[16]

Such methods as these would meet with the unqualified disapproval of all intelligent advocates of the juvenile court and are used only in the isolated districts where the movement has not been understood.

EXTENSION OF THE JUVENILE COURT. The statements made above regarding the juvenile court, as most other descriptions of juvenile courts, give an incorrect impression of the present methods of dealing with juvenile delinquents for the reason that the attention is fixed on the well-organized courts in a few large cities. But 90 per cent of the courts that hear children's cases are in counties that have no city of more than 25,000 population. Miss Belden found in 1918 that only 50,000 children's cases out of a total of 175,000 in the United States came before courts adapted to hearing children's cases; only 16 per cent of the courts that heard children's cases had the three absolutely essential characteristics: separate hearings for children, probation service, and records of social information.[17] In the counties containing no city of more than 5,000 population only 1 per cent of the courts had facilities for mental examinations, in those with cities of from 5,000 to 25,000 only 7 per cent, in those with cities of from 25,000 to 100,000 only 28 per cent; 77 per cent of the counties with cities over 100,000 had such facilities. But the percentage of all courts hearing children's cases in the United States that had such facilities was only 7. Only thirteen courts in the United States had clinics working with the court as a part of the court machinery.[18] While the facilities in the juvenile courts outside of the large cities have increased greatly since 1918, the difference between the city and the smaller towns is still very great.

This indicates that the great need of the juvenile court is the extension of its machinery and point of view to the rural sections. Thousands of children are deprived every year of rights which are guaranteed to them by law, the right not to be detained in jails with adult offenders, the right to a separate hearing, the right to be

---

[16] Belden, *op. cit.*, p. 42.
[17] *Ibid.*, pp. 12–15.
[18] *Ibid.*, pp. 63–65.

regarded as the ward of the court in need of protection and help rather than of punishment. The loss of these rights causes little protest because few people speak for such children; if the rights of a professional or other influential class were so denied or abridged, a howl of protest would compel the authorities to obey the law. But the rights of the children must be secured by more gradual and indirect methods. This situation impelled Judge Schoen to urge that all children's cases should be tried by federal courts.[19]

THE SUCCESS OF THE JUVENILE COURT. Someone has said that the juvenile court does more to prevent crime in one year than the criminal court does in ten years. Judge Lindsey said:

One probation officer, earnestly and enthusiastically engaged in his work, will do more in the course of a year to prevent crime than the best District Attorney can do in five years in prosecuting crimes.[20]

On the other hand, distinct antagonism toward the juvenile court may be found in many places.[21] Judge Baker, for some time presiding over the juvenile court of Weld County, Colorado, said:

Juvenile courts are held in suspicion by the layman, in contempt by the lawyer, and regarded with a sense of weakness by the judge. The only conclusion anyone familiar with even the best of them can reach is that in providing machinery for the reformation of incorrigible children, they have failed.[22]

In view of this disagreement, adequate proof by statistical methods is desirable. Several studies have been made of the outcomes of juvenile court procedures in Boston. Of the delinquent children in the Boston Juvenile Court in the first year of each of the periods 1906–1911 and 1911–1916, 34 per cent and 29 per cent respectively were returned to the court during the course of the five-year period. Healy and Bronner report that of 800 boys studied by them in Boston 24.6 per cent appeared subsequently in adult courts, and

[19] Edward Schoen, "The Field of the Juvenile Court," *U. S. Children's Bur.*, No. 97, pp. 37, 40–42.
[20] Denver Juvenile Court, *The Problem of the Children*, Denver, 1904, p. 42.
[21] T. D. Eliot, *The Juvenile Court and the Community*, New York, 1914, pp. ix-x.
[22] H. M. Baker, "The Court and the Delinquent Child," *Amer. Jour. Sociol.*, 26:177, September, 1920. Reprinted by permission of The University of Chicago Press, publishers.

that of 420 boys studied by them in Chicago 61 per cent were failures subsequently, of whom 15 per cent became professional criminals and 5 per cent became murderers. Sheldon Glueck and Eleanor T. Glueck found that of one thousand juvenile delinquents in the Boston juvenile court and the Judge Baker Foundation 88.2 per cent had additional delinquencies during the subsequent five years and that 70 per cent of them had an average of 3.6 arrests each.[23] These cases, however, are not a random sample of the delinquent cases but are largely confined to the more difficult cases which were referred to the Judge Baker Foundation for recommendation. On the other hand, the Boston Court and the Judge Baker Foundation are superior to the average juvenile court according to the standards of case work.

Another method of appraising the value of the juvenile court is by enumerating the offenders in older ages who had been previously in the juvenile court. Of 145 men committed to New York State prisons and reformatories in 1926, 42 per cent had appeared at least once in juvenile courts.[24] Of 847 boys in the Boys' Court in Chicago during 1924–1925 whose records could be located, 46.8 per cent had no previous record of delinquency, 11.1 per cent had a juvenile court record only, 27.9 per cent had a record in other courts only, and 14.3 per cent had both juvenile court and other court records.[25] This shows, therefore, that 25.4 per cent of the boys who appeared in the Boys' Court had appeared previously in the juvenile court.

These statistics are evidently an incomplete measure of the effects of juvenile court work. Many children under the care of the juvenile court commit delinquencies which do not come to the attention of the juvenile court. In fact, in Chicago and probably to an equal extent in most other towns and cities, 95 per cent of the children of juvenile court age who commit delinquencies serious enough to result in arrests are kept in the police station for a short time and then released by the police without reference to the juvenile court. Dozens of boys have written life histories which

[23] "Harvey Humphrey Baker," *Pub. Judge Baker Foundation*, No. 1, pp. 33–34, 105; Wm. Healy and Augusta F. Bronner, *Delinquents and Criminals*, New York, 1926, pp. 245, 253; Richard C. Cabot, "One Thousand Delinquent Boys," *Survey*, 70:38, February, 1934; Sheldon and Eleanor T. Glueck, *One Thousand Juvenile Delinquents*, Harv. Univ. Press, 1934.

[24] New York Crime Commission, *Individual Studies of 145 Offenders*, 1928, p. 22.

[25] Dorothy M. Burke, "Youth and Crime," *U. S. Children's Bur.*, No. 196, pp. 96–102, 1930.

describe scores and a few which describe hundreds of delinquencies prior to the first arrest and equal numbers between the first and second juvenile court appearances.

On the basis of such information as has been presented some of the leaders of the juvenile court movement have stated that the juvenile court is a dismal failure. But, after all, the question is largely a question of comparison. When considered as a substitute for the criminal court, it is regarded as a decided success; when considered in relation to what might conceivably be done, it appears to be a failure. Those who speak most frequently of the failure of the juvenile court would probably not prefer the old criminal court procedure. They are insisting that the juvenile court has failed in order that a still better substitute for the criminal court may be developed.

In so far as the wards of the juvenile court refrain from subsequent delinquency, it is not clear why they do so. The assumption has been that the social work methods used in the juvenile court are the explanation. Serious questions have been raised regarding the validity of the belief that individual case work methods are valuable in a large proportion of cases.[26] These questions are illustrated in the experience of the Cincinnati court, which has had a reputation for unusual success in turning delinquents from their careers. A proposal was made that an intensive study be made of this court because of its success, but a preliminary investigation showed that the court was far inferior to the Boston juvenile court in its standards of case work and facilities for case work but secured at least equally successful results, and consequently that whatever degree of success it might have could not be explained by its case work methods.[27]

The juvenile court has been comparatively free from political corruption, and the character of the personnel has been distinctly higher than in other courts. These courts have been under the almost continuous scrutiny of the Children's Bureau, and many intensive studies of their operations have been made. The probation officers have been trained in social work, and the result has been an

---

[26] Richard C. Cabot, "Treatment in Social Case Work and the Need of Criteria and of Tests of Its Success or Failure," *Proc. Natl. Conf. Social Work,* 1931, pp. 3–24.

[27] W. I. and Dorothy S. Thomas, *The Child in America,* New York, 1928, p. 143.

abundance of data in the records which are not available in any other court, and from which future policies may be developed.

PROPOSALS FOR THE FUTURE. Among the plans suggested for the improvement of the juvenile court, the two most important are: a merger of the juvenile court with a general family court, and a transfer of most or all of the work of the juvenile court to the schools.

The suggestion that the juvenile court be merged with the general family court is made because of the conviction that the various problems of the family are related and should all be handled by one agency. The result when the courts having jurisdiction over family or domestic relations are not unified may be seen in the following description of the procedure in New York in 1919:

Complaint is made to the Charity Commissioner against the negligent husband and father, by the complaining wife. Investigation by the Charity Department follows. If no agreement results there follows requisition to the Domestic Relations Court. There a complaint is again filed, then comes trial in the court, and if the defendant is found guilty another investigation is made by the Probation officer for purposes of judgment, probation, bond, or imprisonment. In these disrupted homes the children are usually found wandering abroad and brought to the Children's Court, charged with juvenile delinquency. Arraignment of the children follows. Again an investigation by the probation officer of the Children's Court is made. If the children are committed to an institution the parent is summoned to the Children's Court to pay institution charges for support of the children. If not paid as ordered, then they are proceeded against in some instances in the Magistrates Court. If found guilty of non-payment, they are held for trial in our Special Sessions Court. All these steps involve separate examinations and investigations.[28]

It is evident that the procedure would be immensely simplified if these cases were all dealt with at one time in one court by one set of witnesses and investigations. In 1937 juvenile cases were heard in such family courts in sixteen states. A very successful court of this kind, dealing with all cases of domestic difficulty—non-sup-

[28] E. J. Cooley, "Report of the Committee on Courts of Domestic Relations," *Proc. Natl. Prob. Assoc.*, 1919, p. 114.

port, desertion, paternity, divorce, alimony, custody of children, guardianship of children, adoption of children, juvenile delinquency and dependency, contributing to the delinquency or dependency of children—has been established in Cincinnati. The National Probation Association and the American Institute of Criminal Law and Criminology have both recommended the amalgamation of juvenile courts with such courts.

It is evident that this procedure, to some extent, is in opposition to the earlier demand for separate hearings for children. The purpose of the separate hearings was not merely to keep the adult audience from the courtroom during the hearing of children's cases, but was rather to produce a complete separation in the mind of the child and the public between juvenile delinquency cases and crimes. When the child is taken into such a unified family court, dealing with many crimes of adults that affect family relations, this separation of juvenile delinquency from crime is not so complete. But, as indicated above, the separation in the juvenile court has been an aspiration rather than an actuality.

The second suggestion for the future is that the work of the juvenile court be confined to the performance of judicial functions, and that all case work functions be transferred to case work agencies. This proposition first took the form of suggestions that much of the work of the court be transferred to the schools. As early as 1903, Aschaffenburg urged that the discipline of children of school age should be transferred to the schools and that they should not be tried at all in courts. In 1912 Professor Hotchkiss, in his report on the Chicago Juvenile Court and in the National Conference of Social Work, urged that the schools do much of the work customarily performed by the juvenile courts. In 1914 Eliot gave a more detailed argument in favor of this transfer. These earlier discussions have been supplemented by many journal articles and conference papers. In recent years the tendency is to suggest that the school should not be regarded as the only agency to do the case work which has been done by the juvenile court, but that other agencies should participate and that it may be co-ordinated by a council for a neighborhood or community.

The argument for these transfers is that the juvenile court is doing an immense amount of administrative work at present which is extra-judicial. This work includes mothers' pensions, recreation, relief, and especially the education and training of children. Probation workers are essentially case workers who use education as their principal method of work. Even the institutions to which some delinquents are committed are essentially educational institutions, but if they do their work effectively they combine case work and class work. Moreover, a large proportion of the cases of juvenile delinquents are settled or handled by probation officers without official court action. As has been indicated, over 90 per cent of the cases which come to the attention of the police are settled by them without reference to the juvenile court, and of those which go to the juvenile court a large proportion are settled by the probation officer without appearing before the judge. The question is therefore asked, Why should not all of this work be centralized in some agency or council of agencies which is devoting its energies to case work? And, why should not the juvenile court be left with the exclusive judicial functions?

As a matter of fact, there is a definite tendency in the direction of care of delinquents or "pre-delinquents" by non-court agencies. Schools are trying to solve their own behavior problems instead of transferring them to the court. Of all new delinquency cases before the juvenile court of St. Louis the proportion initiated by school attendance officers decreased from 3.8 per cent in 1909–1913 to 1.0 per cent in 1916–1920, and has doubtless decreased to practically zero since that time. The schools have established special grades and ungraded classes, vocational training, and individualized attention in special cases. Truant officers of the detective type have been replaced in many places by visiting teachers whose duty is to solve the problems which result in truancy, as well as other problems of maladjustment. The school is in a natural position to secure information, make investigations, make friendly approaches to the family, and assist in the correction of maladjustments of children, especially in their earlier stages. Other agencies than the school are working along the same line, and these efforts are in many places now being co-ordinated in community councils. When all of these agencies are forced to confront their own failures instead of passing them on to the juvenile court, they can modify their procedures so that the maladjustments do not occur.

This argument does not assume that no cases need go to the juvenile court for adjudication and that no delinquents need be committed to institutions. Moreover, it does not assume that the change should be brought about instantaneously. It is an expression of a belief that it is undesirable for a child to appear in a court of any kind, juvenile as well as criminal, and should be obviated as far as possible by the development of extra-court methods of dealing with problem behavior.[29]

EXTENSION OF JUVENILE COURT METHODS TO ADULTS. The problem of the juvenile court may be approached from another standpoint. Why should not the methods now used in juvenile courts be extended to adults? If we do this, does the separate existence of the juvenile court have an adequate justification?

Two principles have been used to justify the trial and treatment of juvenile offenders separately from adults: (a) Juveniles lack responsibility and discernment. Since an essential element in crime, as defined in conventional law, is intent, the child has been regarded as not capable of committing crime because he does not have sufficient intelligence and experience to understand the situation adequately. But the juvenile court has retained the element of intent, to some extent, in the distinction between delinquency and dependency; both terms are defined very broadly, and whether a particular juvenile is treated as one or the other is determined largely by his intent. Moreover, if the child under sixteen or even under eighteen or twenty-one is by law incapable of having criminal intent, it would appear that many persons over the juvenile court age would be similarly incapable. The law admits that those who are insane cannot have criminal intent. But it is just as certain that some persons with subnormal mentality, or with borderline mentality, cannot understand the situation. It might be suggested that mental age, rather than physiological age, should determine the jurisdiction of the juvenile court. But this is inadequate, for many immigrants and Negroes and, also, many normal-minded native-born whites are no more capable of dealing with the complex problems of modern civilization on the basis of their training and experiences than are many of the children within the juvenile court age. Other persons have strong passions or strong emotions, perhaps because of maladjustments in their glands, perhaps because of maladjustments in their training, which make them quite as incapable of responsibility as are the majority of the children under

---

[29] T. D. Eliot, "The Unofficial Treatment of Children Quasi-Delinquent," *Proc. Natl. Prob. Assoc.*, 1922, pp. 68–103; N. H. Hegel, "The Public School as a Little Used Agency for the Prevention of Juvenile Delinquency," *Proc. Natl. Conf. Social Work*, 1921, p. 101; T. D. Eliot, "Case Work Functions and Judicial Functions," *Yearbook Natl. Prob. Assoc.*, 1937, pp. 252–266.

eighteen years of age. No logical method exists of drawing a line between those who have responsibility and those who have not. A juvenile court based on the principle of lack of responsibility is, therefore, either not justified or else it indicates the necessity of similar methods for adults.

(b) Juvenile courts developed because it was felt that criminal courts were based on the assumption of vicious depravity of criminals and on a belief in the efficacy of severe penalties in deterring others from crime. It was insisted that the best policy in dealing with children would be to guard and protect them rather than punish them. But, in theory at least, the criminal law and criminal courts are making efforts to reform, protect, and assist adult criminals. American prisons had reformation as an objective a century and a half ago; they were called penitentiaries because they were designed to produce penitence; the reformatories for adults and the systems of probation and parole show the purpose more clearly. These changes have indicated that the function of the criminal court cannot be stated in terms of punishment; it is attempting to assist criminals to secure a better adjustment. If it be objected that this is only in theory and that in actual practice the object of the law is punishment, it may be replied that in actual practice, also, the object of most institutions for juvenile delinquents is punishment, regardless of what the laws and the supreme courts say about them. Certainly the differences between the criminal courts and the juvenile courts are not so great as they were thirty years ago, and there is no logical justification for the motive that has characterized the criminal court of the past. If it is desirable to adopt a new procedure for children, it is also desirable to adopt the procedure for adults, and the separate existence of the juvenile court will not then be justified when such a modification in the criminal court has developed further.

Evidences of the change in attitudes and of the extension of the juvenile court methods and procedure to the courts for adults are numerous. Judge Lindsey stated that the juvenile court methods should be used in half of the cases in the criminal courts,[30] and the following statements are somewhat to the same effect:

The chief significance of the juvenile court movement is that in

[30] B. B. Lindsey and H. J. O'Higgins, *The Beast,* New York, 1910, p. 149.

breaking away from the old procedure it is preparing the way for a new procedure for adults as well as for children.[31]

We have long believed that the juvenile court methods are destined to become, by expansion, the methods of the future in dealing with certain classes of adult delinquencies.[32]

In addition to such statements certain laws show the same tendency. In 1909, Colorado passed a law called "The Act for the Redemption of Offenders,"[33] which made it possible to place within the equity jurisdiction of the court all those who committed what were previously defined as misdemeanors. Kentucky, also, adopted the same principle in an act of 1908, which put contributory delinquency under equity jurisdiction and removed it from the criminal jurisdiction. The law was repealed in 1910, and Bernard Flexner, who drafted the act, stated that it had not given the results expected.[34] Iowa adopted the same system in 1913. And Dean Wigmore raised the whole question again in 1922 with the query:

Why not, instead of sentencing the lazy parent to a penal farm, decree him to go to work, put him under a recognizance to turn over a share of his wages to support the children, and authorize the garnishee process upon his employer? To reach the obstinate idler, why not declare him to be in contempt of court, for not obeying its order to work, and place him in the workhouse until he is willing to go to work?[35]

Also in many of the specialized courts, such as morals courts, domestic relations courts, or boys' courts, the methods are very similar to those of the juvenile court.

If the essential elements in the juvenile court are considered, all of them seem to be applicable to the criminal court and would

---

[31] From M. Parmelee, *Criminology*, New York, 1918, p. 407. By permission of The Macmillan Company, publishers.

[32] J. H. Wigmore, "Obstructing the Efficiency of the Juvenile Court," *Jour. Crim. Law and Criminol.*, 13:167, August, 1922.

[33] *Colorado Session Laws*, 1909, Ch. 199, pp. 478–483; *Colorado Annotated Statutes,* 1914, section 160.

[34] Quoted by F. E. Wade, "The Prosecution of Parents for the Delinquencies of Their Children," *Proc. Natl. Conf. Char. and Corr.*, 1909, pp. 305–306. Reprinted by permission.

[35] Wigmore, *op. cit.*, pp. 165–167.

probably improve very greatly the work of that organization: definite social investigations, use of summons, reformation as the ideal of treatment, informal procedure, and secret sessions. Of course the two items of separate hearings of children's cases and detention separate from adults would not apply.

One other thing should be considered, however. Delinquency is defined very broadly in the juvenile court laws, so that it includes every child who, because of actual or potential misconduct, is in need of the guardianship of the state. Should the same broad definition be made for adults, if the juvenile court procedure is extended to adults? Some instances of that attitude are evident in the law and decisions. Some states have laws which provide that persons of suspicious character may be bound over; but such a law passed in the District of Columbia in 1892 was declared void. Some states have laws which provide for the punishment of "known thieves"; an Ohio law was held valid in 1881, and explained by the court as follows:

It is a mistake to suppose that offenses must be confined to specific acts of commission or omission. A general course of conduct or mode of life which is prejudicial to the public welfare may likewise be prohibited and punished as an offense.[36]

But Freund maintains that the contrary doctrine is better law and that specific acts must be proved.[37] Aside from existing law, it is clear that it would be dangerous to have a blanket definition of crime for adults, because of the many class conflicts and differences in fundamental beliefs. If a judge were given authority to commit any individual who was an undesirable character to an institution, many strikers or socialists or teachers of the doctrine of evolution would soon be within the walls of the prisons.

The justification of the juvenile court, therefore, in general, is that it is an experiment in methods and procedure. There may be a justification for all future time in separating age groups within the court, but if the results of the juvenile court experiment are recognized and the methods adopted by other courts, the distinction between the juvenile court and the other courts will practically disappear. Jerome Hall suggested that this procedure be adopted in

---

[36] Morgan v. Nolte, 37 Ohio 25.
[37] Ernst Freund, *Police Power*, pp. 95–97.

a special court for thieves,[38] and Harrison and others have urged similar procedures for young adults.[39]

SUGGESTED READINGS

Abbott, Grace, *The Child and the State,* Chicago, 1938, Part II.

Additon, Henrietta, "Should the Schools Take Over the Work of the Children's Courts?" *Proc. Natl. Prob. Assoc.,* 1919, pp. 84–98.

Alper, Benedict S., "Juvenile Justice: A Study of Juvenile Appeals to the Suffolk County Court, Boston, 1930–1935," *Jour. Crim. Law and Criminol.,* 28:340–367, September, 1937.

Belden, Evelina, "Courts in the United States Hearing Children's Cases," *U. S. Children's Bur.,* No. 65, 1920.

Breckinridge, S. P., and Abbott, E., *The Delinquent Child and the Home,* New York, 1912.

Burke, Dorothy M., "Youth and Crime: A Study of the Prevalence and Treatment of Delinquency among Boys of Juvenile Court Age in Chicago," *U. S. Children's Bur.,* No. 196, 1930.

Eliot, T. D., *The Juvenile Court and the Community,* New York, 1914.

Eliot, T. D., "Case Work Functions and Judicial Functions," *Yearbook Natl. Prob. Assoc.,* 1937, pp. 252–266.

Elkind, H. B., and Taylor, M., "The Evaluation of Juvenile Courts and Clinics," *Amer. Jour. Orthopsych.,* 5:217–226, July, 1935.

Flexner, B., and Oppenheimer, R., "The Legal Aspect of the Juvenile Court," *U. S. Children's Bur.,* No. 99, 1922.

Flexner, B., Oppenheimer, R., and Lenroot, Katharine F., "A Study of the Administration of Justice in the Field of Domestic Relations," *U. S. Children's Bur.,* No. 193, 1929.

Gleuck, Sheldon and Eleanor T., *One Thousand Juvenile Delinquents,* Harv. Univ. Press, 1934.

Harrison, Leonard V., and Grant, P. M., *Youth in the Toils,* New York, 1938.

Healy, Wm., and Bronner, Augusta F., *Delinquents and Criminals: Their Making and Unmaking,* New York, 1926.

Hiller, F. H., *Juvenile Court Laws of the United States,* Natl. Prob. Assoc., 1938.

---

[38] Jerome Hall, *Theft, Law and Society,* Boston, 1935.
[39] Leonard V. Harrison and P. M. Grant, *Youth in the Toils,* New York, 1938; Jeannette G. Brill and E. George Payne, *The Adolescent Court and Crime Prevention,* New York, 1938.

Jeter, Helen R., "The Chicago Juvenile Court," *U. S. Children's Bur.*, No. 104, 1922.

Lenroot, Katharine F., "Juvenile Courts at Work: A Study of the Organization and Methods of Ten Courts," *U. S. Children's Bur.*, No. 141, 1925.

Lindsey, B. B., and O'Higgins, H. J., *The Beast*, New York, 1910.

Lindsey, E., "The Juvenile Court Movement from a Lawyer's Standpoint," *Annals of Amer. Acad. of Pol. and Social Sci.*, 52:140–148, March, 1914.

Lou, H. H., *Juvenile Courts in the United States*, Chapel Hill, 1927.

Lyman, Freda R., "Analysis and Tabular Summary of State Laws in Relation to Children's Cases and Cases of Domestic Relations in the United States," *Chart of U. S. Children's Bur.*, No. 17, 1930.

National Probation Association, "A Standard Juvenile Court Law," *Report of Committee*, 1928.

Reckless, W. C., and Smith, M., *Juvenile Delinquency*, New York, 1932.

Rogers, Carl R., *The Clinical Treatment of the Problem Child*, Boston, 1939.

U. S. Children's Bur., *Annual Reports on Juvenile Court Statistics*.

Waite, E. F., "How Far Can Court Procedure be Socialized without Impairing Individual Rights?" *Jour Crim. Law and Criminol.*, 12:339–348, November, 1921.

Waite, E. F., "The Outlook for the Juvenile Court," *Annals of Amer. Acad. of Pol. and Social Sci.*, 105:229–242, January, 1923.

White House Conference on Child Health and Protection, *The Delinquent Child*, New York, 1932.

Young, Pauline V., *Social Treatment in Probation and Delinquency*, New York, 1937.

Chapter Eighteen

ORIGIN AND EVOLUTION OF PUNISHMENT

Two GENERAL PROBLEMS have arisen in regard to punishment. The first is causal, the second utilitarian. The first is concerned with the natural history and psychology of punishment, the second with the values and efficiency of punishment in general and of particular methods of punishment. The natural history of punishment is a prerequisite for the efficient direction of future policies. Thus far this natural history has not been written except in scattered and unorganized form. The present chapter is not such a natural history but supplies some of the data and trends which need consideration in the final development of a natural history. The following chapters are concerned somewhat more with the utilitarian aspects of punishment.

DEFINITION OF PUNISHMENT. Two essential ideas are contained in the concept of punishment as an instrument of public justice. (a) It is inflicted by the group in its corporate capacity upon one who is regarded as a member of the same group. War is not punishment, according to this, for it means suffering inflicted upon foreigners. The loss of reputation which follows crime is not punishment, except in so far as it is administered by the group in its corporate capacity. (b) Punishment means pain or suffering produced by design and justified by some value that the suffering is assumed to have. If the pain is merely incidental, to be avoided if possible, it is not punishment. A surgical operation performed for the purpose of correcting a physical defect that has been instrumental in producing crime should not be considered punishment, for the pain is not regarded as desirable. The confinement of an insane person may involve suffering for him but it is not punishment. Many of the modern methods of dealing with criminals, especially in the juvenile courts, are not punishment. Some authors are attempting to stretch the concept of punishment to include any method that is used by the courts in dealing with criminals, but it seems preferable to limit it to the infliction of suffering when that suffering is regarded as valuable. This is the conventional attitude of the criminal law.

The difficulty of determining when a method of treatment is punishment and when it is not punishment is illustrated in the following statement regarding the Anglo-Saxon period in England:

A detected criminal was either fined, mutilated, or killed, but punishment, as we now understand the term, was seldom inflicted; that is to say, the dominant idea was neither to reform the culprit nor to deter others from following in his footsteps. If a man was killed it was either to satisfy the bloodfeud or to remove him out of the way as a wild beast would be destroyed; if a man was mutilated by having his fore-finger cut off or branded with a red-hot iron on the brow, it was done not so much to give him pain as to make him less expert in his trade of thieving and to put upon him an indelible mark by which all men should know that he was no longer a man to be trusted; if a fine were levied, it was more with a view to the satisfaction of the recipients of the money or cattle or what not, than with the intention of causing discomfort or loss to the offender.[1]

In view of this uncertainty it will be preferable in the long run to abandon the term "punishment" and substitute "treatment" or some other colorless term.

THE ORIGIN OF PUNISHMENT. Many writers have maintained that punishment is the expression of an instinct of vengeance; others have maintained that it is the expression of a desire for vengeance but that this desire is a complex of instincts and other processes. These explanations are unsatisfactory. There is no evidence that a specific instinct of vengeance exists. Undoubtedly some crimes and other acts which are regarded as wrong upset the equilibrium of the society and of its individual members, and various reactions which have the function of restoring this equilibrium take place. There is, however, no evidence that these reactions are directed by a specific instinct of vengeance. Furthermore, vengeance, whether instinctive or not, was not the important factor in the origin of punishment in preliterate life.

[1] W. L. M. Lee, *History of Police in England,* London, 1901, p. 10.

Three types of wrongs may be found in preliterate life, followed by three types of reactions, no one of which is clearly punishment. The first includes the tribal and sacral offenses, such as treason, witchcraft, sacrilege, and poisoning, which were the first crimes. Though such offenses seldom occurred in simple homogeneous groups, when they did occur they were followed by annihilation. The group might annihilate the offender either by death or exile; both rendered the offender non-existent so far as the group was concerned. The tendency to annihilate the offender grew out of three attitudes—war, social hygiene, and sacrifice. The offender was regarded as an enemy and was treated as an enemy. This was war, not public justice. Also, the offender was regarded as polluted and the tribe attempted to get rid of him and of everything connected with him as a social hygiene measure. Thus, in many tribes witchcraft was followed by death and the body of the offender was thrown into the sea, which was supposed to have cleansing power, or was buried on foreign soil and not even his name might be mentioned for fear that it might carry pollution with it. An element of sacrifice appears, also, in the treatment of these offenders; this was designed to please the gods.

The second group of wrongs consisted of injuries to private individuals who were not in the same family (gens, clan, etc.), such as assault, murder, theft. These generally provoked blood feuds between families and involved severe suffering. Doubtless the attitude in these feuds was largely vengeance. But it was a private action, involving two private individuals with their relatives, and the general community was a spectator. This seems to have been the origin of the system of payment of damages in civil courts, but not of punishment by the criminal courts.

The third group of wrongs consisted of injuries to other members of the same family. These were not regarded as crimes or followed by punishment in the ordinary sense of the word. In the family, as in the tribe in general, ridicule was the most powerful method of control and was generally sufficient to secure observance of the rules. Among modern savages who are fairly well segregated from civilization, as among primitive peoples, punishment of children seldom occurs.

In savage life, parents almost never chastise their children.[2]

[2] B. Malinowski, *The Family Among Australian Aborigines*, London, 1913, pp. 238–257.

Travelers everywhere have remarked upon the extreme indulgence toward children. This is very marked among the Eskimos, though perhaps not more so than among the Fuegians of South America. Wherever we have data parents almost never punish or even severely reprove, but such pressure as may be needed is exercised by certain relatives. . . . Chastising the young seems to have been practised in the centres of higher culture, but outside of these limits was practically unknown. . . . In short, the same principles applied to control of the young as to adults, *viz.*, admonition and ridicule. In fact, the whole control of the local group in aboriginal days seems to have been exercised by admonition and mild ridicule instead of by force and punishment.[3]

Even at the present day Fox children are rarely whipped.[4]

The Winnebago Indian had the following precepts: "If you have a child and it is naughty do not strike it. In old times if a child was naughty the parents did not strike it but made it fast. When it is quite hungry it will reflect upon its disobedience. If you hit him you will merely put more naughtiness into him. It is said that mothers should not lecture the children, that they merely make the children bad by admonishing them." [5]

Not only do the preliterate peoples seldom punish their children but they resent it when civilized parents in their midst punish their own children. Krohn tells of a Dyak army officer who murdered his master for punishing a child and who explained his action by the statement: "No grown-up person has the right to strike any child." Radcliffe-Brown states that punishment of adults by the organized society was not found among the Andaman Islanders.

There is no such thing as the punishment of a crime by the society. If one person injured another, it was left to the injured one to seek vengeance if he wished and if he dared. There were probably always some who would side with the criminal, their attachment to him

[3] C. Wissler, *The American Indian*, New York, 1922, pp. 177–178. Reprinted by permission of Oxford University Press, publishers. Stefánsson agrees that Eskimo children are seldom punished and explains that this is due to a belief that children are guarded by the spirits of the deceased. See *My Life with the Eskimo*, New York, 1913, pp. 395–399.
[4] Truman Michelson, "Autobiography of a Fox Indian Woman," *U. S. Bur. of Ethnology*, 40th An. Report, p. 297.
[5] Paul Radin, *Crashing Thunder: The Autobiography of a Winnebago Indian*, New York, 1926, p. 463. Reprinted by permission of D. Appleton-Century Company, publishers.

overcoming their disapproval of his actions. The only painful result of anti-social actions was the loss of the esteem of others. This in itself was a punishment that the Andamanese, with their great personal vanity, would feel keenly, and it was in most instances sufficient to prevent such actions. For the rest, good order depended largely on the influence of the more prominent men and women.[6]

Even if a person killed his father, which was in many groups regarded as a horrible offense, he was not punished by the other members of the family or by the tribe; the members of the family felt that since the family had already been weakened by the loss of one member, it would be foolish to weaken it still more by injuring the offender. They looked upon such acts, however, with great surprise and disgust.

In these primitive groups, therefore, we find certain motives and attitudes that preceded punishment but were not, in themselves, punishment: desire to annihilate the enemy of the group, sacrifice to appease or fend off the wrath of the gods, social hygiene measures to rid the community of pollution, self-redress in cases of private injury, and surprise and disgust at the person who injured his own family.

An explanation of punishment must account not only for the desire to produce suffering, but also for the desire to prevent excessive suffering. Its explanation, though not entirely clear, can apparently be found only in the interactions of people in the more developed and less homogeneous societies. In such societies the individual who violated certain rules aroused the desire for annihilation or injury; but he belonged, also, to other groups and the members of these other groups "took his part" and demanded that he should not be annihilated. The great mass of the population, however, were relatively impartial observers; they instituted proceedings designed to secure a compromise that would satisfy both groups. From this conflict of interests developed the regulation of the earlier spontaneous reactions in the interest of the group as such, and this made it necessary to proceed in such ways as would secure the approval of impartial observers.[7]

---

[6] A. Radcliffe-Brown, *The Andaman Islanders*, Cambridge, 1922, p. 52.

[7] E. Faris, "The Origin of Punishment," *Inter. Jour. Ethics*, 25:54–67, October, 1914. See, also, Max Radin, "Enemies of Society," *Jour. Crim. Law and Criminol.*, 27:328–356, September, 1936; Hans von Hentig, *Punishment*, London, 1937.

DEVELOPMENT OF METHODS OF PUNISHMENT. Four principal methods of punishment have appeared during the history of mankind: financial loss, physical torture, social degradation, and removal from the group; removal from the group has been secured by death, exile, imprisonment, and by more subtle means, such as branding, mutilating, and other methods of degrading the person.

These four methods were invented early in the history of mankind. But it is not clear, for instance, when an offender is put to death, that this is punishment in the strict sense of the word, as defined above. A rather intensive study of the particular circumstances must be made to determine whether it is or is not punishment. Such a study of penal methods has not yet been made and it will, therefore, be necessary to accept the uncritical statements now accessible.

1. *The death penalty.* Death penalties have varied in frequency in different societies. The prevalence of death penalties is not closely correlated with savagery, though death penalties tend to decrease in number and in the ferocity of methods with advancing civilization. Such methods of inflicting death as burning, boiling in oil, breaking at the wheel, the iron coffin, drowning, and impaling have their greatest development, not in the lowest groups or in the highest, but in the society of the medieval period. A sentence was imposed in 1712 in New York upon a Negro slave

". . . to be burned with a slow fire that he may continue in torment for eight or ten hours and continue burning in the said fire until he be dead and consumed to ashes."[8]

Impaling and immuring were prohibited in Switzerland about the year 1400, and death by drowning in 1615. The last case of burning at the stake in Berlin was in 1786, and no similar penalty had been inflicted there for seventy years before this. In Frankfort a. M. the number of executions was 317 in the fifteenth century, 248 in the sixteenth, and only 140 in the seventeenth.[9] In the cantons of Zürich and Schwyz 572 executions occurred in the sixteenth century, 336 in the seventeenth, and only 149 in the eighteenth.[10]

---

[8] Lewis E. Lawes, *Life and Death in Sing Sing*, Garden City, N. Y., 1928, p. 129.
[9] G. L. Kriegk, *Deutsches Bürgerthum im Mittelalters*, Vol. I, pp. 200–201.
[10] Carl L. von Bar, *A History of Continental Criminal Law*, Tr. by T. S. Bell, Boston, 1916, p. 299.

In England, however, the situation is somewhat different, for there were only 17 capital offenses in the early part of the fifteenth century, about 200 in 1820, and then, by 1839, the number was reduced again to about the same as it had been four centuries before. The death penalty was inflicted frequently in the earlier part of this period in England for religious offenses, but most of the later additions were for offenses against property, and many of them for very trivial offenses. In 1814 three boys—aged eight, nine, and eleven—were sentenced to death for stealing a pair of shoes,[11] and this was not unusual. In a time of rapidly shifting standards, the property owners demanded severe penalties as a means of protection. But because the common people were increasing in political and social power these sentences, though imposed, were not executed in a large proportion of the cases, as is shown by the statistics for England and certain counties in England in Table VII.

TABLE VII

CHANGES IN THE PROPORTION OF CAPITAL PENALTIES EXECUTED

Years	Per Cent
1689–1718*	52.6
1755–1784*	28.3
1784–1814*	25.6
1813–1819	10.5
1820–1826	6.9
1827–1833	4.1

*Counties of Essex, Herts, Kent, Surrey, and Sussex only.

During the early part of the modern period the corpse was gibbeted, that is, remained hanging in chains, and was sometimes soaked in tar so that it would remain for a long time as a warning to evil-doers. These objects were seen so frequently that landscape painters considered them an essential part of the scenery and not infrequently introduced them into their landscapes.[12]

Under the leadership of Romilly, Bentham, Peele, McIntosh, Montagu, Cruickshank, and others capital punishment was reduced, as the power of the common people increased. But as late as 1814, Romilly tried in vain to substitute simple hanging for treason in place of the existing penalty of hanging, cutting down alive, disemboweling, cutting off the head, and quartering the body. Though

---

11 "Punishment of Death," *Philanthropist*, 4:190, 1814.
12 W. Andrews, *Old-Time Punishments*, London, 1899, pp. 211–212.

that penalty which the law provided was not actually carried out, the members of Parliament were afraid that treason would be greatly increased if the law was modified.[13]

2. *Physical torture.* Corporal punishment has flourished in most societies as a method of punishment. The following penalty was provided in early Anglo-Saxon England for habitual criminals:

At the second time let there be no other bot if he be foul than that his hands be cut off, or his feet, or both, according as the deed may be, and if then he have wrought yet greater wrong, then let his eyes be put out, or his nose and his ears and the upper lip be cut off; or let him be scalped . . . so that punishment be inflicted and also the soul preserved.[14]

Such penalties, in general, increased and decreased in prevalence with the death penalties. They disappeared from England, just as did the death penalty, because even when the courts imposed the sentences, public sentiment prevented their execution. Bentham made the following statement in the last part of the eighteenth century regarding the penalty of branding:

Burning in the hand, according as the criminal and the executioner can agree, is performed either with a cold or a red-hot iron; and if it be with a red-hot iron, it is only a slice of ham which is burnt; to complete the farce, the criminal screams, whilst it is only the fat which smokes and burns, and the knowing spectators only laugh at this parody of justice.[15]

Similarly as opposition to the policy of quartering the corpse after execution developed the method became more and more symbolic until in 1820 "quartering" consisted merely of scratching two criss-cross lines on the back of the neck of the corpse. Also some of the corporal punishments at present are almost symbolic.

The laws of Delaware provide that the warden must whip certain offenders. The warden explained that "the law doesn't tell me how

---

[13] *Philanthropist*, 3:267–293, 1813.
[14] Thorpe, *Laws of Cnut*, p. 169; quoted by George Ives, *A History of Penal Methods*, London, 1914, p. 8.
[15] Jeremy Bentham, *Principles of Penal Law*, Ch. 9, p. 550.

hard to whip. Here's the way I whip . . . ," slowly, gently almost doubtfully, the warden's right arm swung back and forth, like the pendulum of a clock deciding to cease to work.[16]

3. *Social degradation.* Shame and humiliation have been penalties designed to reduce the social status of the offender, sometimes temporarily, sometimes permanently. Many methods of producing shame have been used, of which some have, and others have not, been connected with physical torture, mutilations, and branding. The ducking stool, the stocks, the pillory, the brank, and other devices were punishments less because of the physical injury than of the public shame. Occasionally, to be sure, the ears of the offender were nailed to the pillory and had to be torn loose by the efforts of the offender. The crowd often pelted the offender in the stocks or pillory with objectionable missiles, and in this way killed several criminals in England. One offender who had stolen cabbages from a neighbor's garden in New York in the seventeenth century was ordered to stand in the pillory with the cabbages on his head, and in addition was banished from the colony for five years.[17] The brank was a device, like a cage, placed over the head and provided with a bar which was thrust into the mouth of the offender, thus holding down the tongue; occasionally this bar had sharp spikes on it to prevent any effort to use the tongue. This brank was regarded as superior to the ducking stool in dealing with scolds, because the scold could talk between ducks. In general these penalties flourished from the beginning of the sixteenth to the end of the seventeenth century, but the ducking stool was a legal penalty for scolds in New Jersey as late as 1890. These penalties were used for the minor offenses, such as scolding, giving short weights, begging, brawling, drunkenness, prostitution, theft, forgery, and blasphemy.[18] These marks of degradation often failed to accomplish their purpose. An English statute of 1698 which provided for branding on the left cheek was repealed after eight years with the explanation that this penalty

. . . had not had its desired effect of deterring offenders from the

---

[16] O. F. Lewis, "Delaware's Prison—A Paradox," *Survey*, 46:465, July 2, 1921. See, also, J. E. Jones, *Pioneer Crimes and Punishments*, pp. 25–26.
[17] Philip Klein, *Prison Methods in New York State*, p. 23.
[18] W. Andrews, *Old-Time Punishments*; Alice M. Earle, *Curious Punishments of Bygone Days.*

further committing crimes and offenses but, on the contrary, such offenders, being rendered thereby unfit to be entrusted in any service or employment to get their livelihood in any honest and lawful way, become the more desperate.[19]

4. *Banishment and transportation.* Outlawry was used frequently in savage society and amounted almost to a death sentence, because of the lack of support and protection by an organized group. In ancient Rome banishment might be either a prohibition against coming into a specified territory, generally the city of Rome, or a prohibition against going outside of a specified territory, such as an island to which the offender had been removed; in either case it might be for life or for a short period. Practically all other societies have used this method more or less. After almost complete abandonment of this method, it was revived in the modern period. In England the first modern legalization of transportation was in 1597, and concerned "rogues, vagabonds and sturdy beggars." With an intermission of forty-six years after 1671, transportation of convicts to American colonies continued until the American Revolution, though it was strenuously opposed by most of the colonies. After a few years of wild proposals and almost as wild experiments, the policy of transportation to Australia was definitely adopted in 1786 and continued until 1867. The total number transported by England during this period was 134,308, but the average number per year from 1787 to 1816 was 474; between 1816 and 1838 it was about 3,000 per year. In England in 1834 the sentence of transportation was imposed on 4,053 persons, death on 480, and imprisonment on 10,716. This shows that at the time transportation, though at its height, was not being used as frequently as imprisonment. But all except 314 of those sentenced to prison had terms of one year or less, which means that imprisonment was used almost entirely for the relatively trivial offenses. While many of the offenses for which the death penalty and transportation might be inflicted were trivial, also, most of the serious offenses were punished by one or the other of those two methods.

Transportation was abandoned by England because it was found not to be a good method of reformation or deterrence, because it was expensive, and primarily because it was strenuously opposed by

[19] Luke O. Pike, *A History of Crime in England,* London, 1873–1876, Vol. II, p. 280.

the Australian colonies. A league against transportation of convicts was formed in New South Wales in 1830, which was sufficiently influential to result in shifting the convicts to Van Dieman's Land in 1840. Within a decade this colony became saturated and England tried in 1848 to shift the convicts back to New South Wales. This aroused such a storm of protest that the government abandoned the policy and sent the convicts, instead, to West Australia. The other colonies then passed stringent laws against immigration of convicts from West Australia and the premier of Victoria suggested that West Australia be boycotted by the other colonies as long as she continued to receive convicts from England. John Mitchel, a convict transported for aiding in the Irish rebellion, described the conditions in Australia in 1851 as follows:

There is but one political question now existing—the transportation system. Most of the decent colonists, having families growing up, and feeling the effects of the moral and social atmosphere that surrounds them, and the ignominy of having no country but a penal colony, no servants, no laborers, few neighbors even, who are not men fairly due to the gallows—ardently desire to use this new Constitution, such as it is, to make vigorous protest against the continuance of the penal system.[20]

Many other countries have made a more or less extensive trial of transportation in the modern period. Portugal in the sixteenth century sent criminals and women of ill-repute to Brazil and later sent criminals to Angola. Spain tried transportation in a limited way in the eighteenth century. Russia has used Siberia as a penal colony since 1823. Since 1865 Italy has transported some convicts to the islands along her coast, and France from 1763 to 1766, in 1824, and from 1851 to the present has used transportation to some extent. Other countries which had no colonial possession which might be used for penal colonies resorted to the policy of banishment. Ontario provided a penalty of life banishment in 1802 and of more limited banishment later, such as leaving the neighborhood or the district for a specified number of months.

5. *Imprisonment.* (a) In ancient and medieval societies. In the primitive and savage societies imprisonment had a very restricted use as a penalty. Among the ancient civilized peoples it was used

[20] John Mitchel, *Jail Journal*, p. 264.

only for small groups. Vinogradoff stated that the penalty of imprisonment was almost never used in Greece.[21] Imprisonment was not used at all as a penalty in the Roman Republic, but was used for minor offenses in the Empire. Von Bar states that "the penalty of imprisonment was almost unknown in France in the later Middle Ages."[22] The last code of laws in France previous to the Revolution was made in 1670 and contained no mention of imprisonment as a penalty. It was sometimes used in France and other countries, however, either as a means of enforcing the payment of fines or as a commutation of death sentences when mitigating circumstances were found. In the first part of the sixteenth century in Frankfort it was ordered that for certain offenses "the criminal shall be imprisoned and forgotten for a time."[23] In the Copenhagen code of 1294, which was in use until about 1500, imprisonment for life was provided for manslaughter.

In England imprisonment was used in a few cases in the Anglo-Saxon period, as in the law of Æthelstan, which provided that a person convicted of murder should be imprisoned for 120 days before he could be redeemed by his kinsmen, and 40 days for theft. Henry II provided a penalty of imprisonment for one year for perjury in a grand assize, and Henry III provided the same penalty for breaches of the forest law. In 1241 some Jews convicted of circumcising a Christian child were ordered either to pay twenty thousand marks "or else be kept perpetual prisoners." But it was in the reign of Edward I in the last half of the thirteenth century that imprisonment came into extensive use in England, though it was used primarily as a "squeezer" or means of securing fines.

The condition of prisons in ancient times was well represented by the cuneiform symbol for prison, which was a combination of the symbols for house and darkness. In general the sanitary conditions were awful; chains were frequently loaded on the prisoners; no work was provided; the prisoners were generally permitted to congregate as they wished within the institution.

Thus, in general, until about the last part of the thirteenth century in England and probably a little later in some of the Continental countries imprisonment as a penalty was used only for very

---

[21] P. Vinogradoff, *Outlines of Historical Jurisprudence*, London, 1920, Vol. II, p. 190.
[22] von Bar, *op. cit.*, p. 191.
[23] Kriegk, *op. cit.*, Vol. I, p. 262.

restricted groups of offenders. It is, therefore, a comparatively modern method of dealing with offenders, though its roots run back to the earliest societies.

(b) Imprisonment by the church. The early church authorities developed imprisonment partly because they were not permitted by law to use the death penalty, partly because they had an appreciation of the value of withdrawal from association with others. In 1283 a certain Brother John had bitten his prior's finger "like a dog" and the bishop gave orders to

Keep the said Brother John in prison under iron chains in which he shall be content with bread, indifferent ale, pottage, and a pittance of meat or fish (which on the sixth day he shall do without) until he is penitent.[24]

Though imprisonment was used by the church as early as the fifth century, it was used most extensively during the Inquisition, when it was the most severe penalty that could be inflicted for any offense on those who professed conversion. In 1229 Gregory IX ordered that all who were converted after arrest because of fear of death should be imprisoned for life; this rule was stated by several councils, also. In the Inquisition of Toulouse from 1246 to 1248, of 192 known sentences all were imprisonment except 43 death penalties imposed on persons who refused to appear; of the 149 prison sentences, 127 were for life, 6 for ten years, and 16 for an indefinite period. Of the 636 sentences imposed by Bernard Gui from 1308 to 1322 (of which 88 were imposed on persons already dead), 300 were imprisonment. Many of these sentences were commuted, however. Of the 300 persons imprisoned by Bernard Gui, 119 were released on commutation. Such releases were necessary in part because of the lack of prisons, but in general the idea of reformation was taken into account. Chrysostom said:

I require not continuance of time, but the correction of your soul; demonstrate your contrition, demonstrate your reformation, and all is done.[25]

This ecclesiastical imprisonment varied from strict confinement in absolute solitude, known as "in pace," to congregate life in the

[24] Quoted by George Ives, *A History of Penal Methods,* London, 1914, p. 43.
[25] Quoted by Ives, *op. cit.,* p. 38.

corridors of the prisons, with occasional retirement to a cell, which was known as *"murus largus."* As a matter of fact there was much association between prisoners in many institutions, some gambling and feasting, and some "grafting" by jailers who kept the money of prisoners or food that had been sent to the prison for them, and ordered supplies for prisoners who had long been dead.

(c) Imprisonment: the galleys. The galleys were used considerably as places of confinement of criminals from about 1500 to the early part of the eighteenth century. This was a revival of the ancient method of forced labor. Galley slavery continued until the large sailing vessels were developed to such an extent as to make the galleys unsuitable for competition. In 1602 Queen Elizabeth appointed a commission to make arrangements for commuting other penalties to galley labor, so that offenders may be

In such sort corrected and punished that even in their punishment they may yeld some profittable service to the Common welth.[26]

In the seventeenth century in France the courts were ordered to refrain from other methods of punishment as much as possible in order to provide crews for galleys. Those who could not work in the galleys, such as women, aged, and infirm, were frequently imprisoned during this period, and when the galleys were abandoned the former slaves were held in hulks on the shores or in arsenals.

(d) Imprisonment: the house of correction.[27] The house of correction appeared in England about the middle of the sixteenth century, when, on the petition of Bishop Ridley of London for help in dealing with the "sturdy vagabonds" of the city, the King gave his palace at Bridewell to be one of the "hospitals of the city," for the "lewd and idle" and a place for the employment of the unemployed and the training of children. By act of 1576 Parliament

---

[26] Ives, *op. cit.*, pp. 103–104.

[27] It is necessary to make a distinction between the house of correction and the workhouse. Technically the workhouse was an institution in which employment was furnished to those able and willing to work, and industrial training was furnished for the young; consequently, it was a part of the poor-relief system. The house of correction, on the other hand, was a part of the penal system, designed to protect the poor-relief funds against encroachments by those able but unwilling to work. Thus, the house of correction was designed to compel "sturdy beggars" to work. But as a matter of fact, the two institutions are hardy distinguishable during the larger part of their history in England and America, and no attempt is made in the present discussion to differentiate them; no attention is paid, however, to the workhouse in its pure form.

provided that a house of correction should be erected in each county, and in 1609 provided penalties for counties failing to erect such institutions. The justices were ordered to make search for "rogues, vagabonds and idle persons" and commit them to institutions; these institutions were to be used, also, for the confinement of "lewd women" with illegitimate children who might become a charge on the community and for men who deserted their families. By the act of 1711 the maximum period of confinement in these houses of correction was fixed at three years, and by subsequent legislation the number of offenses for which persons might be committed was greatly enlarged. Webb states that by the early part of the eighteenth century the house of correction and the common jail were practically the same in discipline and character of inmates.[28] Whipping of the inmates and confinement in irons were customary until the early part of the nineteenth century.

The house of correction developed in much the same way on the Continent. It began a little later, but was used more extensively than in England. Peter Rentzel established a workhouse in Hamburg in 1669 at his own expense because he had observed that thieves and prostitutes were made worse instead of better by the pillory, and he hoped that they might be improved by work and religious instruction in the workhouse.[29] A house of correction was established in Waldheim in 1716 with the lower floor for criminals and the upper floor for paupers and orphans, and with complete separation of the sexes on both floors. On entrance the criminals received a "welcome" of ten lashes; work was compulsory and silence was the rule. The staff of the institution included a chaplain, a teacher, and a physician, which was distinctly noteworthy at that time. During the first century of its history this institution received 13,954 persons, of whom 7,921 were criminals, 4,642 paupers, and 1,391 orphans. Practically half of the criminals were convicted of theft, a fourth of begging and vagrancy, and an eighth of sexual offenses; 270 of them were convicted of homicide, which was generally infanticide.[30] Perhaps the most famous house of correction on the Continent was established in Ghent in 1775

---

[28] Sidney Webb and Beatrice Webb, *English Prisons Under Local Government*, London, 1922, pp. 16–17.

[29] F. H. Wines, *Punishment and Reformation*, New York, 1919, p. 117.

[30] Glauning, "Das Zucht-, Armen-, und Waisenhaus zu Waldheim, wahrend der ersten 100 Jahren seines Bestehens," (1716–1816), *Monats. Krim. Psych. und Strafrechtsreform*, 10:32–43, April, 1913.

under the direction of Viscount Vilain XIV. Wines states that this institution used practically all the essential principles of modern penology.[31]

(e) Imprisonment: early prison reforms. The early prison reform movement culminated in the last part of the eighteenth and the first part of the nineteenth centuries. It should be understood that this was a reform movement in the prison as a place of detention of persons awaiting trial. The movement may be seen best in England. From the middle of the sixteenth century there had been considerable publicity regarding prison evils and various suggestions regarding methods of improvement. Geoffrey Mynshal, committed to prison as an insolvent debtor, while in prison wrote "Certaine Characters and Essays of Prison and Prisoners," which was published in 1618. Wines calls this the first regular treatise on prison abuses; it describes most of the evils of prison life that John Howard found a century and a half later. In 1699 the Society for the Promotion of Christian Knowledge, with a committee on prisons, was formed. This committee, of which Dr. Thomas Bray was chairman, visited many prisons and presented a report in 1702, under the title "Essay towards the Reformation of Newgate and other Prisons in and about London." The following evils are mentioned: the old criminals corrupt the new; swearing, blasphemy, and gambling; unlimited use of intoxicating liquors; personal lewdness of officers and keepers; and the co-operation of officers with the prisoners in their vices. The committee suggested methods of reducing these evils as follows: separate confinement in cells, labor while in prison, regular religious services, abolition of fees, prohibition of liquor in prison, retention of hardened offenders until evidence is furnished that they will secure decent employment when released and until they give security for good behavior, and advertisement to the public of the names of those prisoners who have lived decently in prison with the object of securing the help of good people for these prisoners after their release. During the next century investigations, reports, and discussions continued; a few laws were passed; a few individuals in control of prisons undertook to make improvements as suggested by committees. In 1773 Parliament authorized magistrates to appoint chaplains in their jails. This was the first official recognition of the desirability of attempting to

---

[31] E. C. Wines, *State of Prisons and of Child-saving Institutions in the Civilized World*, Cambridge, 1880, pp. 10-11.

reform the prisoners. But in some institutions as late as 1808 the felons were not permitted to attend the religious services.

The great prison reformer of England was John Howard, who wrote "State of Prisons in England" in 1777, after a personal investigation of practically all the prisons of England. This book contains, after a short summary, a description of each prison, so that it is a mass of concrete details. His general conclusion was:

If it were the wish and aim of magistrates to effect the destruction present and future of young delinquents, they could not devise a more effectual method, than to confine them so long in our prisons, those seats and seminaries . . . of idleness and every vice.[32]

Nothing has exerted so much influence in prison reform as this book. Howard's work was supplemented by other leaders, including several notable justices of the peace and Mrs. Elizabeth Fry. Several societies for prison reform were formed. Substantial improvements were made in the prisons, as may be determined by a comparison of Dixon's account of the prisons in 1850 and Howard's account in 1777. In fact Beaumont in 1821 lamented the fact that prisons had been improved so much that they were no longer a deterrent and that workmen preferred prison life to the life of freedom; he urged a return to the earlier harsh methods.[33] And another author rated the justices of the peace for indulging

in such costly fads as the separation of male prisoners from females, of adults from children, and of the convicted from the unconvicted, whilst altogether disapproving the extravagant cubic space required either for the cellular confinement or for the useful employment of any prisoners.[34]

In general this prison reform movement was the result of two streams of influence—evangelical Christianity, especially of the Quakers, and the utilitarian theory under the leadership of Bentham and others. Both of these groups were interested primarily in re-

---

[32] John Howard, *The State of the Prisons in England and Wales*, 2nd ed., p. 13.

[33] B. Beaumont, "Essay on Criminal Jurisprudence," *Pamphleteer*, 18:73 ff., 1821.

[34] Edward Mullins, *A Treatise on the Magistracy of England*, London (1836); see Sidney Webb and Beatrice Webb, *English Local Government: The Parish and the County*, Vol. I, p. 596.

moving the more brutal methods, but their efforts led, also, to the introduction of constructive methods.

This sketch of imprisonment shows that imprisonment in early society was seldom used for the punishment of criminals, that it was adopted by the church and used extensively, that it was then adopted by the secular authorities in the operation of the galleys because of the value of the labor of criminals, and at about the same time was used extensively in commitment of vagrants and others to houses of correction as a means of making them work; then it was gradually extended in the common jails and special prisons for larger and larger proportions of the criminals until in the early part of the nineteenth century it came to be the principal method of punishing criminals.

6. *Financial penalties.* Financial penalties, either in the form of general confiscation of property or of a fine, have existed in most literate societies. They developed somewhat as follows: When an individual was injured by another he might claim damages, the amount depending on the injury done and the social position of the injured party. Then the king claimed a part of this payment or an additional payment for the participation of the state in the trial and for the injury done to the state by the disturbance of the peace. About the twelfth century the victim's share began to decrease and the exactions of the king to increase, until finally the king took the entire payment. These payments came to be one of the principal sources of revenue. Imprisonment was used largely at this time as a means of compelling the defendant to pay the fine. Fines, therefore, developed out of private damages or civil actions and were in their origin a part of the civil court rather than of the criminal court.[35]

MITIGATION OF PENALTIES. Penalties imposed by the courts have been mitigated in various ways. One of these methods was "securing sanctuary." One might secure sanctuary in a special city or in a special building. In the thirteenth century a person could claim refuge in a church for a period of forty days, at the end of which time he was compelled to leave the realm by a road and port assigned to him. In 1530, instead of leaving the realm he

---

[35] L. T. Hobhouse, G. C. Wheeler, and M. Ginsberg, *The Material Culture and Social Institutions of the Simpler Peoples*, London, 1915, pp. 86–119. These authors show that the fine as a payment to the court was relatively late in its origin.

might be compelled to spend the rest of his life in a place in England assigned to him and was branded on the thumb for identification. This right began to weaken in the last part of the fifteenth century. By 1540 murder, rape, burglary, arson, and a few other offenses no longer gave the right of sanctuary and the whole policy was ended when the monasteries were broken up. A second mitigation of penalties was the "right of clergy." This grew out of the original demand of the church to try its own officers. To be tried by an ecclesiastical court was a distinct privilege, for the church was not permitted to impose the death penalty during a part of the period of its supremacy, and its treatment in general was more merciful except for the offenses of heresy and witchcraft. The "clergy" were defined at first in the strict sense, but came later to include all who had the clerical tonsure, then all who could read, and the reading ability might be merely nominal. The test used in determining whether a person could read was generally the first verse of the fifty-first psalm, and a little coaching would enable almost anyone to pass this test. Finally the peers who could not read received the same benefit of clergy by nature of their position. This was a very interesting device by which those who were culturally similar to the lawmakers were made exempt from the more severe penalties. Those who were responsible for the laws could not inflict severe penalties upon their own members but reserved these punishments for the lower classes. While the number of persons who could claim this right increased, the number of times a person could claim the right and the number of offenses for which this right could be claimed were reduced. Thus penalties came to be more nearly the same for those who had the benefit of clergy and those who did not. The act of 1705 provided that even those who claimed the right of clergy might be punished by the secular authorities at least to the extent of confinement in a house of correction for not less than six months or more than two years. By the end of the eighteenth century the right of clergy meant practically nothing. A third method of mitigation of penalties was the pardon. It was considered to be good policy to make the penalties as severe as possible and then permit the king to relax the severity in individual cases. Finally, the courts were authorized to fix penalties within limits set by the legislature and in this manner to adjust the penalty to the needs of the particular individual.

FACTORS IN THE MODIFICATION OF PENALTIES. The methods of treatment of criminals have varied in content from time to time and place to place. They show a general tendency to be consistent with the culture. Two centuries ago criminals were disemboweled, quartered, hung in chains, branded, pilloried, ducked, and in other ways tortured, mutilated, and shamed. That was a culture in which physical suffering was regarded as the natural lot of mankind and in which the means of preventing pain were not well developed. Today safeguards against physical suffering have been provided in other fields and a policy of physical torture of criminals cannot be harmonized with the general interest in the reduction of suffering. The price system developed during the modern period, and the methods of punishment have developed somewhat consistently with the price system. Just as a price is assumed to bear a constant relation to a commodity, so, it was assumed, the penalty should bear a constant relation to the crime. The classical economists insisted that reward should be commensurate with service; the classical criminologists concluded that punishment should be commensurate with disservice or crime. The ideal of uniformity in the treatment of offenders was stated about the time of the French Revolution when democracy meant the equality of all classes. Democracy has been re-interpreted since that time and the policy of uniform penalties has been similarly modified. Again, uniformity developed at the time when one cure was used by physicians for all kinds of diseases and all kinds of patients. Individualization in medical treatment has developed during the last two centuries and with it individualization in penal treatment. Punishment was emphasized in the home, the church, and the school, and necessarily the treatment of offenders by the state was consistent. Since the penal methods have been generally abandoned by the home, school, and church, it is doubtful whether the state can continue to exercise penal policies successfully. Finally, the penalties tend to be more severe for acts which endanger values which are highly regarded than for acts which endanger less important values. It is for this reason that in several states the minimum penalty for bribing a baseball player is greater than for robbery with a gun.

Somewhat more specifically, two general tendencies appear in the last few centuries and seem to be correlated with each other: imprisonment has been used more frequently, physical torture and death less frequently. The reason for the unwillingness to continue the method of torture and killing and for the willingness to substitute imprisonment is not entirely clear, but certain elements of the explanation stand out.

In the first place, imprisonment on an extensive scale was practically impossible in the earlier period. No institutions sufficiently secure for the imprisonment of large numbers of people had been constructed, and the difficulty of building such institutions made their development impractical. With the constant wars, the changes in control, the lack of police and other guardians, such institutions, even if constructed, would have been relatively useless; it was necessary for social life to become more settled before imprisonment could become a general policy.

Second, a greater appreciation of freedom developed in the modern period. A punishment is a method of depriving a person of some value. During the medieval period with its intense interest in theology no punishment was more severe than excommunication. Similarly during the modern period, with its interest in democracy and freedom, the loss of freedom meant much more than it had previously. In the earlier period when persons were ordinarily kept confined in castles by wars or religious beliefs, imprisonment would not have been significantly different from the life of many persons who had not committed crimes. Many castles of the time were no more pleasant than the prisons; in fact many castles were turned into prisons and then later used as castles again. Because of the increased valuation of freedom, the loss of freedom has come to be regarded as sufficiently punitive for the worst criminals.

In the third place, labor power has been appreciated more highly. Imprisonment developed at about the time of the waning of the system of slave labor. Because of the higher valuation of labor power, it became necessary to conserve it instead of destroying it by death or mutilations.

Finally, the more brutal punishments flourished at a time when the social distance between those who imposed the punishment and those who suffered it was very great. The situation changed in this respect in the modern period by the development of democracy and the means of communication. Democracy was important in this way because it meant that the control was secured by persons who had much the same experiences as the defendants; one was tried by his peers who understood his situation and looked upon him as a human being like themselves. The development of the means of communication was important because it meant an increasing number of contacts between those who committed crimes and others. This enabled a larger part of the population to appreciate the situation of those who committed offenses, so that it was no longer similar to the injury of an animal or a foreign enemy but was the injury of another human being like themselves. With limitations imposed by color of skin and other similar marks, contacts that were frequent and intimate increased, with the result of a better understanding and a keener sympathy.

Penalties at a particular time and place vary with the status of the offender. Discriminations are made because of the sex, age, wealth, education, political prestige, color, nationality, religion, club membership, and other things. Female prisoners are held in prison on the average about two-thirds as long for a specific type of offense as male prisoners. Negroes are often punished more severely than whites. In North Carolina 25.5 per cent of the white persons sentenced to death between 1909 and 1928 were actually electrocuted, while 54.5 per cent of the Negroes sentenced to death were electrocuted; the white offender had twice as many chances as the Negro to escape the execution of the penalty.

PURPOSE OF PUNISHMENT. Attempts have been made to determine the purpose or function of punishment in different groups at different times. Many investigators have insisted that some one motive was *the* motive in punishment. On the one hand, the function of punishment in restoring the solidarity of the group which has been weakened by the crime is emphasized. Thomas and Znaniecki have indicated that among the Polish peasants the punishment of crime is designed primarily to restore the situation which existed before the crime and renew the solidarity of the group, and that revenge is a secondary consideration.[36] From this point of view punishment is concerned primarily with the group and only secondarily with the offender. On the other hand, expiation, deterrence, retribution, reformation, income for the state, and other things have been posited as *the* function of punishment. In the past as at present it is not clear that any one of these is *the* motive; punishments seem to grow from many motives and to perform many functions. This is true both of the individual victims of crimes and of the state. Certainly the laws of the present day are

---

[36] W. I. Thomas and F. Znaniecki, *The Polish Peasant*, Vol. II, pp. 1254-1255.

not consistent in aims or motives; probably the same condition existed in earlier societies. Moreover, no consistent course of development can be discerned.

PUNISHMENT AND RESPONSIBILITY. The question of responsibility was not considered at all in the early period when the offender was annihilated. Not only was the offender annihilated, but his relatives, without any assumption regarding responsibility, were treated in the same way. Though the penalties for accidental violations of law were sometimes less severe than for those that resulted from design, in general no distinction was made between them. This lack of consideration of responsibility can be shown best by the penalties imposed upon inanimate objects, insects, and lower animals. In Athens an axe was tried in the courts for injuring a citizen and, when found guilty, was solemnly taken to the boundary of the city and thrown over, thus being exiled. Until the last century in England a tree which fell on a man or a cart which ran over a man was confiscated and sold for charity. In 1591 the great bell in the Russian town in which the Tzarevitch was fatally stabbed was flogged, deprived of its top ring, and sent to Siberia for three hundred years. And a church bell in La Rochelle was treated in a somewhat similar way in 1685.[37] Corpses were frequently punished. In 1428 the bones of Wycliffe, which had been in the grave for forty-five years, were disinterred and burned. Evans has collected a mass of materials regarding the medieval and modern procedure in punishing animals.[38] They were tried in the courts in the same way as human beings; cases were appealed to the higher courts and decisions sometimes reversed; pardons from the king were sometimes secured for dogs or hogs or cattle. In 1474 a pig was sentenced to be hanged in Lausanne "until death ensueth" for having devoured an infant in its cradle and to remain suspended from the gallows for a certain period as a warning to evil-doers. When animals were charged with crime, they were thrust into the same prisons with human beings and subjected to the same treatment while awaiting trial. The jailer charged the same amount for boarding a pig as for boarding other prisoners. A dog, for the crime of biting the leg of a member of the municipal council in 1712, was sentenced to one year's imprisonment in an iron cage in

[37] Ives, op. cit., p. 252.
[38] E. P. Evans, The Criminal Prosecution and Capital Punishment of Animals, London, 1906, p. 143, 175.

the marketplace. Much doubt, however, has been cast on the authenticity of Evans' account, and it is highly probable that the few cases which may have occurred have no important significance from a theoretical point of view.[39]

In general until the last two centuries, intent was not considered in the treatment of criminals, or was considered only occasionally or incidentally; little interest in the question of responsibility appeared. Intensive studies of particular communities indicate, however, that generalizations of this nature are subject to many exceptions. For instance, in Basel criminal responsibility was emphasized considerably by the beginning of the fourteenth century, and the law took into account youthful age, mental disease, drunkenness, force, accident, and negligence as factors involved in the responsibility.[40]

Schools of penology. Nothing that can be called a school of penology developed until the late modern period. Since that time three schools have been important, particularly in connection with the question of responsibility: the classical, the neo-classical, and the positive or Italian. The classical school, to which Beccaria made one of the first significant contributions and to which Rousseau, Montesquieu, and Voltaire belonged, maintained the doctrine of psychological hedonism, that the individual calculates pleasures and pains in advance of action and regulates his conduct by the results of the calculations. They concluded from this that it was necessary to make undesirable acts painful by attaching punishment to them and to make the amount of pain thus attached entirely definite, so that the prospective criminal could make his calculations on it, and to make it just sufficient so that the pain would exceed the pleasure. Since the punishment must be one that can be calculated, it must be the same for all individuals, regardless of age, mentality, social status, or other condition. Responsibility had nothing to do with it. Bentham tried to work out definite mathematical laws for the infliction of punishment; this was merely an extension of the hedonistic calculus.

The neo-classical school of the French Revolution and the period immediately following maintained that the classical doctrine was correct in general, but that it should be modified in certain details;

---

[39] Sister Mary Liguori, "The Trial and Punishment of Animals," *America*, February 1, 1936, pp. 395–396.
[40] Karl Metzger, *Die Verbrechen und ihre Straffolgen im Basler Recht des späteren Mittelalters*, Basel, 1931.

since children and "lunatics" could not calculate pleasures and pains they should not be regarded as criminals or be punished. They extended this principle to others, also, to some extent by taking into account "mitigating circumstances." By these exceptions they took responsibility into account as of primary importance. This became the basic principle of the judicial and legal system of Western civilization during the last century.

The positive school denied individual responsibility to any criminal. They maintained that a crime, as any other act, is a natural act, just like a cyclone, a flood, a stroke of lightning, or the striking of a snake. Therefore they denied entirely the ethical desirability of punishment. The admitted that, in self-protection, the group must do something about it just as it must take precautions against floods or lightning or snakes. But they maintained that such precautions, even if they involved the death or permanent segregation of the criminal, should not be considered to be punishment, any more than similar methods of dealing with the insane should be considered punishment. They contended, therefore, that those criminals who could be reformed should be reformed, that those who could not be reformed should be segregated or killed, but that it was especially important to modify the conditions which produced the criminal.

In contrast with these three earlier schools of penology, two present-day tendencies are appearing. The first of these is case work, which is based largely on the premises of the positive school, although differing from it as to procedures. The second cannot easily be named, but it involved a belief that crime is an expression of a situation, generally involving a group, and cannot be "treated" effectively by isolating particular persons for case work, but must be treated as a situation or group problem. This might be called group work, but it is different from the group work of the social workers.

SUGGESTED READINGS

Alinsky, Saul D., "The Philosophical Implications of the Individualistic Approach in Criminology," *Proc. Amer. Prison Assoc.*, 1937, pp. 156–171.

Andrews, W., *Old-Time Punishments*, London, 1899.

Bar, Carl L. von, and Others, *A History of Continental Criminal Law*, Tr. by T. S. Bell, Boston, 1916.

Barton, R. F., *Ifugao Law*, Berkeley, 1919.

Durkheim, E., "Deux lois de l'évolution pénale," *L'Anné Sociol.*, 4:65-95, 1900.

Durkheim, E., *Division du travail social*, 2d ed., Paris, 1902, Chs. 4-5.

Earle, Alice M., *Curious Punishments of Bygone Days*, New York, 1922.

Eaton, M., "Punitive Pain and Humiliation," *Jour. Crim. Law and Criminol.*, 6:894-907, March, 1916.

Evans, E. P., *The Criminal Prosecution and Capital Punishment of Animals*, London, 1906.

Faris, E., "The Origin of Punishment," *Inter. Jour. Ethics*, 25:54-67, October, 1914.

Frazer, J. G., *The Golden Bough*, Abridged ed., London, 1923, Chs. 19-22.

Gabel, Leona, "Benefit of Clergy in England in the Later Middle Ages," *Smith Coll. Studies in History*, Vol. XIV, Nos. 1-4, 1928.

Gillespie, J. E., "The Transportation of English Convicts after 1783," *Jour. Crim. Law and Criminol.*, 13:359-381, November, 1922.

Gotein, H., *Primitive Ordeal and Modern Law*.

Gutmann, Bruno, *Das Recht der Dschagga*.

Hartshorne, A., *Hanging in Chains*, New York, 1893.

Helbing, Franz, *Die Tortur*, Berlin, n.d.

Hentig, Hans von, *Punishment*, London, 1937.

Hobhouse, L. T., Wheeler, G. C., and Ginsberg, M., *The Material Culture and Social Institutions of the Simpler Peoples*, London, 1915.

Howard, John, *The State of the Prisons in England and Wales, with Preliminary Observations and an Account of Some Foreign Prisons and Hospitals*, London, 1777.

Innes, A. M., "Love and the Law, A Study of Oriental Justice," *Hibbert Jour.*, 11:273-296, January, 1913.

Ives, George, *A History of Penal Methods*, London, 1914.

Lowie, R. H., *Primitive Society*, New York, 1920, Ch. 20.

MacLeod, W. C., "Aspects of the Earlier Development of Law and Punishment," *Jour. Crim. Law and Criminol.*, 23:169-190, July, 1932.

Malinowski, B., *Crime and Custom in Savage Society*, New York, 1926.

Margolin, A. D., "The Element of Vengeance in Punishment," *Jour. Crim. Law and Criminol.*, 24:755-767, November, 1933.

Mead, G. H., "The Psychology of Punitive Justice," *Amer. Jour. Sociol.*, 23:577–602, March, 1918.

Oppenheimer, H., *The Rationale of Punishment*, London, 1913, pp. 7–175.

Pollock, F., and Maitland, F. W., *The History of English Law Before the Time of Edward I*, 2d ed., Cambridge, 1903.

Radin, Max, "Enemies of Society," *Jour. Crim. Law and Criminol.*, 27:328–356, September, 1936.

Saleilles, R., *The Individualization of Punishment*, Tr. by R. S. Jastrow, Boston, 1911, Chs. 2–5.

Stephen, J. F., *A History of the Criminal Law of England*, 3 Vols., London, 1883.

Swain, John, *The Pleasures of the Torture Chamber*, New York, 1931.

Szerer, M., "La conception sociologique de la peine," *Bibliothèque Sociologique Internationale*, Vol. LI, Paris, 1914.

Tulin, L. A., "The Rôle of Penalties in Criminal Law," *Yale Law Rev.*, 37:1048–1069, June, 1928.

Webb, Sidney, and Webb, Beatrice, *English Prisons Under Local Government*, London, 1922.

Westermarck, E., *The Origin and Development of the Moral Ideas*, 2nd ed., 2 Vols., London, 1912, Vol. I, Chs. 14–16.

Wines, F. H., *Punishment and Reformation*, New York, 1919, Chs. 3–6.

Wood, Ledger, "Responsibility and Punishment," *Jour. Crim. Law and Criminol.*, 28:630–640, January, 1938.

Chapter Nineteen

ETHICS AND ECONOMY OF PUNISHMENT

THE TWO ATTITUDES TOWARD THE CRIMINAL. Two attitudes are taken toward the criminal. One is a hostile attitude, with insistence that the criminal be made to suffer. According to that conception, every law must contain a penalty, and the penalty must be inflicted on everyone convicted of violating the law. The penalty means suffering, which is justified in various ways. The demand for punishment may be merely vengeance, or it may be on the somewhat higher level of retribution, deterrence, or reformation. The second attitude is one of inquiry, desire to secure comprehension of the situation and to work out methods of control based on this comprehension. This represents scientific procedure both from the point of view of understanding and of controlling the situation. Suffering may be necessary in the process of control, but the suffering is incidental, not the direct aim of the process. The second attitude is now evident in the juvenile court procedure and is being extended into the criminal courts, the prisons and reformatories, and the systems of probation and parole.

In the previous chapter we were concerned somewhat with the impulses and conditions which gave rise to punishment and with the natural history of punishment. Here we are concerned with the reasons which men give for punishment or for other methods of treating criminals. Exner has said, "So far as we can look back men have always punished and have never ceased to dispute their reasons for so doing."[1] We shall consider some of the reasons which have been advanced in these disputes.

THE VALUES OF PUNISHMENT. After the early attempt to justify punishment by considerations of a transcendental nature, the

---

[1] Franz Exner, *Gerechtigkeit und Richteramt,* 1922, p. 6.

leaders of thought in this field stated punishment in terms of social utility. That is, they insisted that social utility resulted from punishment and constituted the justification of punishment. But little of this literature frankly faced the issue of punishment *versus* other methods of dealing with criminals. It was assumed without argument that punishment was necessary, and the problem was to formulate an acceptable statement of this necessity. This was largely a controversy between adherents of rival concepts of punishment, not a controversy between the adherents and opponents of punishment. The philosophers were concerned, also, principally with the abstract right of the state to punish for crime. Even if one admits that the state has such a right in general, the further problem remains of determining whether punishment is economical in the larger sense. Moreover, the philosophical discussions have been concerned primarily with the purpose or aim of punishment and with the amount and nature of punishment, not with its value in comparison with other methods of dealing with criminals.

The following values of punishment are indicated by those who insist on the desirability of punishment: (a) Punishment as retribution. It is urged by leaders and is accepted by the general public that the criminal deserves to suffer. This suffering is imposed by the society in its corporate capacity and is the political counterpart of individual revenge. Sir James Stephen stated:

Criminal procedure is to resentment what marriage is to affection: namely, the legal provision for an inevitable impulse of human beings.

This is a statement of the aim or purpose of punishment, and not a justification of punishment in terms of the social utilities produced by it. Dewey states that we are not relieved of the responsibility for the consequences of our procedure by the fact that the offender is guilty.[2] A justification of punishment must be stated in terms of the future effects of the punishment. The future is not often considered by those who insist that the criminal deserves to be punished. It is urged that unless the criminal gets the punishment he deserves, one or both of the following effects will be produced: the victim will seek individual revenge, which may mean lynchlaw if his friends co-operate with him; or the victim will refuse

---

[2] John Dewey, *Human Nature and Conduct,* New York, 1930, pp. 18–19.

to make complaint or offer testimony and the state will therefore
be handicapped in dealing with criminals.

(b) Punishment as a means of reformation. Among those who
advocate punishment because of its social utility, some claim that it
tends to reform criminals and that it may accomplish this either
by creating a fear of repetition of the punishment, by creating a
conviction that crime does not pay, or by breaking habits that
criminals have formed, especially if the penalty is a long period of
imprisonment which gives the habits no opportunity for expression.
Such illustrations as the following are given in support of this
argument: If the bees swarm out of their hive and sting the boy
who molests them, they will not be troubled by him in the future;
if they should fly from the hive on the approach of the boy and
leave their honey at his disposal, they would be troubled again and
again. Moreover, attention is called to the fact that experiments
with animals have shown that animals frequently learn an operation more quickly when they are punished for failure than when
they are not punished.[3] A city attorney, speaking in defense of
punishment, stated:

You must inflict pain to get results. It was that way with me when
I was a boy: I had been misbehaving and my father gave me an
awful "whaling" and he had to do it only once. I had the same experience in dealing with my son. It is the same way with criminals.
You must inflict pain to get results.

(c) Punishment as a deterrent. It is maintained, also, that the
infliction of pain upon those convicted of crime serves to deter
others from crime, and that it has great value for that reason, even
if some individuals are not deterred by the prospect.

Not the crimes punished, but the crimes prevented should measure
the worth of the law. . . . If out of a score of law-abiding persons,
only one obeys the law from fear of its penalties, it does not follow
that the penal system occupies a correspondingly insignificant place
among the supports of social order. For the rules of the social game
are respected by the many good men chiefly because they are forced
upon the few bad. If the one rascal among twenty men might
aggress at will, the higher forms of control would break down, the

[3] M. F. Washburn, *The Animal Mind,* New York, 1917, pp. 323–325.

fair-play instinct would cease to bind, and, between bad example and the impulse of retaliation, man after man would be detached from the honest majority. Thus, the deadly contagion of lawlessness would spread with increasing rapidity till the social order lay in ruins. The law, therefore, however minor its part at a given moment in the actual coercion of citizens, is still the cornerstone of the edifice of order.[4]

When deterrence was regarded as the principal purpose of punishment, penalties were made as public and as brutal as possible—witness the ducking stool, the stocks, the pillory, the public hangings, and the gibbeting of the body so that it might remain as long as possible as an example to the public. The radio has been used in a few recent cases to carry to the public the specific details of the punishment. Whenever the fiction that is known as a "crime-wave" is heralded, a demand for an increase in the severity of the penalties arises, based on the assumption that the more severe the penalty, the more effectively it will deter others from similar crimes.

(d) Punishment and social solidarity. It is asserted, finally, that respect for law grows largely out of opposition to those who violate the law. The public hates the criminal, and this hatred is expressed in the form of punishment. In standing together against the enemy of their values, they develop group solidarity and respect for the orders of the group. Tarde has said that crime will increase if we cease to hate the criminal. This may be so not only because the punishment deters the near-criminals by fear of punishment but also because it is an instrument for the development of ideals and attitudes in the general law-abiding public. Lundstedt maintains that the fear of punishment is not the significant value in punishment but rather the legal sentiments, legal conscience, or moral feeling which have been developed in the general public by the administration of the criminal law during previous generations, and which have become so organized that they regulate behavior spontaneously almost like an instinct.[5] Park has stated in class lectures, "Punishment of crime is a ceremonial affair, from which you get a

---

[4] From E. A. Ross, *Social Control*, New York, 1916, p. 125. By permission of The Macmillan Company, publishers.

[5] A. V. Lundstedt, *Superstition or Rationality in Action for Peace*, London, 1925, pp. 47–49, 190–192.

new and more vigorous definition of the crime and make the public realize its gravity. When you talk of dealing with criminals as medical cases you are treating them not as human beings but as animals."

LIMITATIONS AND EVILS OF PUNISHMENT. Efforts have been made to determine the values of punishment by objective tests and measurements. Experiments are set up for the purpose of measuring the relative values of rewards and punishments in relation to animal learning and performance. Miss Chase made a good summary of these experiments and concluded that the number of studies which showed that punishment was more effective than reward was greater than the number of studies which showed the opposite, but that punishment was not even thus clearly superior in the learning and performances by human beings.[6] The effects of punishment, therefore, even in these experimental situations cannot be stated as a simple proposition. A mild punishment may promote learning but a more severe punishment may cause terror and panic which interfere with the whole learning process.

These experiments, however, have no great significance for purposes of social control. The social situations in which punishments for crime are inflicted are much more complex and involve elements which are lacking in school punishments or punishments in experimental laboratories.[7]

The improvement in order in schools in spite of, or because of, the disappearance of corporal punishment is much more significant than the laboratory experiments. According to Barnard, a Suabian school teacher left an itemized list of 1,423,100 corporal punishments which he had inflicted on school children during his career.[8] The average number of whippings per day in 1845 in a school of about two hundred and fifty pupils near Boston was 65.6. The principal part of the teachers' time in almost all schools of that period was devoted to the maintenance of order and infliction of punishments. In spite of this, nearly four hundred schools in Massachusetts were broken up in the year 1837 because the teacher was unable to maintain discipline. The behavior of school children in modern

---

[6] Lucile Chase, "Motivation of Young Children," Univ. of Iowa Studies, *Studies in Child Welfare*, Vol. V, No. 3, March, 1932.

[7] For an analysis of the complexities in the effects of punishment see Laurence Sears, *Responsibility: Its Development through Punishment and Reward*, New York, 1932, especially Part III, Ch. 1.

[8] Henry Barnard, *English Pedagogy*, Second Series, 1876, p. 327.

schools in which corporal punishment is unknown is unquestionably
much better than in the schools of a century ago where corporal
punishments were extremely frequent.[9] It is evident that the effect
of punishment depends very much on the situation in which the
punishment is inflicted. Consequently while punishment for crimes
does unquestionably produce the desired results in some situations,
it also produces undesired results and it is impossible to determine
what the net effect of punishment is in producing reformation,
deterrence, or group solidarity. At any rate certain types of undesired effects are produced.

(a) Punishment often isolates the individual who is punished and
makes him a confirmed enemy of society, and his influence may
extend to other individuals. Criminals are isolated from law-abiding
groups, and neither understand nor are understood by these groups.
In this respect, it is much like war, which produces a relatively complete isolation and dissociation of warring nations. Hatred of the
criminal by society results in hatred of society by the criminal.
Because he is ostracized the criminal has two alternatives. He may
associate with other criminals among whom he can find recognition,
status, and means of further criminality, or he may become disorganized, psychopathic, and unstable. The illustration of the bees
and the boy would apply to the relations of society and the criminal
only if the social policy were to get rid of the criminal entirely after
his first offense, by policies such as death, banishment, or permanent
segregation in penal institutions. But our actual policy is to permit
almost all of the criminals to return to society, in a physical sense,
but to hold them off, make them keep their distance, segregate them
in the midst of the ordinary community. Thus they are kept as
aliens, outsiders, isolated from the culture of the group. If they are
to be turned into good citizens they must assimilate the culture of
the group, or the group must assimilate them. The only way for the
group to do this is by frequent and intimate contacts with them. If
the bees had to assimilate the boy after stinging him, they would
find their efficiency in assimilation distinctly low. The greatest failure of punishment is that it makes reformation difficult for those
convicted of the more serious crimes, because the hatred of society
produces hatred in the criminal, a demand for revenge, personal
disorganization, isolation, loss of status, and the acquisition of a

---

[9] P. E. Harris, *Changing Conceptions of School Discipline*, New York, 1928.

technique of crime. The following quotations from autobiographies of criminals illustrate the attitudes that are developed by punishment.

I know that degradation and a spirit of revenge, a determination to retaliate, "to get even," is frequently the result. The prisoner is not only deprived of his liberty, but also of his self-respect and whatever innate sense of decency he may possess.[10]

Everywhere I am catalogued as a social outcast, and am lawful prey for any officer of the law. All my relations with society impress me with the fact that I am outside the pale of decency. The language, manners, and acts of those who deal with me are voiced in a single monotonous accusation: "You are a bad man and we hate you." I am slapped on the face by society. I am not human if I fail to hit back.[11]

I left prison with a feeling of bitterness and of hatred in my heart. . . . Almost every man with whom I came in contact while in prison expressed that same feeling. . . . He was "going to get even" and "make somebody pay" for his punishment and suffering. . . . The sense of being shut out by society from all normal lines of activity simply served to intensify these instincts and increase their force.[12]

Professional criminals are admired and emulated by many of the youth of the community. With their attitudes of hatred and revenge, they become the nucleus of an increasing group who develop the same attitudes. Thus the effect of punishment is depreciated and the good effects may be more than balanced by the bad effects.

(b) Punishment develops caution. It is asserted that a painful experience with the bees will make a boy "think twice" before he molests them again. But the "thinking twice" may be a means of securing immunity from the bees while molesting them. At least on the frontier, where the wild bees do not have protection from the father of the boy, the boy soon learns that he can smoke out the bees and get the honey without suffering. He has been made cautious by the previous suffering, but not deterred.

---

[10] D. Lowrie, *My Life in Prison*, New York, 1912, pp. 37–38.

[11] J. P. Alexander, "The Philosophy of Punishment," *Jour. Crim. Law and Criminol.*, 13:240–241, August, 1922, quoting a criminal of international reputation, who had spent twenty-five years in jails and prisons.

[12] Anonymous, *In the Clutch of Circumstances*, New York, 1922, pp. 148 ff. Reprinted by permission of D. Appleton-Century Company, publishers.

The professional and organized criminals who are committing the crimes generally regarded as most serious have skill in the execution of their crimes and in addition take many precautions to provide in advance for immunity in case they are caught. The result is that twenty-five amateur shoplifters who have stolen little articles in stores are likely to be convicted in a court while one professional shoplifter who steals hundreds of times as much as all of these amateurs escapes conviction. The amateur criminal, however, in the course of a few punishments of this nature acquires skill, largely in the penal institutions.

(c) Punishment creates other undesirable attitudes. The prevention of a specific act by means of punishment does not prove that punishment has promoted the social welfare. The good accomplished by preventing that specific act may be more than off-set by general attitudes produced by it.[13] For instance, a child may be deterred from lying by punishment. But the child may, as a result, come to fear the parent who inflicted the punishment, and be estranged or alienated. If the parent is to have great influence over the child, he must keep the confidence of the child, and the relation between them must be very intimate and friendly, especially at the time when the child begins to be away from home many hours a day in school or elsewhere. If a particular delinquency is prevented with a loss of power to control the child in general, it is a doubtful gain. And thus the state frequently creates other attitudes in criminals or in the public even when a particular crime is successfully prevented—lack of respect for law, lack of patriotism, lack of willingness to sacrifice for the state, lack of initiative, and, in general, a sodden and shiftless character. The most serious consequences of punishment is the loss of self-respect. Van Waters has stated that the self-respect of the offender is the basis of all successful efforts for his rehabilitation.[14] Cooley has stated that the community is extremely unwise to take any action that will destroy the self-respect of the offender,[15] and McDougall shows in the following statement how the offender directs his behavior in the effort to retain self-respect:

---

[13] Kurt Lewin, *Die psychologische Situation bei Lohn und Strafe*, Leipzig, 1931 ; Lucile Chase, "Motivation of Young Children," Univ. of Iowa Studies, *Studies in Child Welfare*, Vol. V, No. 3, March, 1932.

[14] Miriam Van Waters, "The Delinquent Attitude," *The Family*, 5:112, July, 1924.

[15] C. H. Cooley, *Life and the Student*, New York, 1927, p. 204.

Physical punishment is effective as a deterrent chiefly because and in so far as it is a mark of the disapprobation of the community. But a man when he has once been convicted and jailed for crime, has lost his social standing and his regard for social approbation and disapprobation. Such self-respect as he retains no longer feeds upon the esteem of the community at large; rather it turns to satisfy its cravings by demonstration of skill, wit, and boldness in defying the law.[16]

Thus, real efficiency in dealing with criminals requires not only the stopping of specific violations of law but the accomplishment of this result without weakening the state in its relations with individuals and without weakening the powers of the individual. Punishment is frequently injurious in that it fails to accomplish these other results.

(d) Punishment sometimes gives an offender status. Many persons find the thing that is dangerous to be especially thrilling, and gain standing because of their courage or skill.

A young boy, thirteen years of age, succeeded in breaking into a store and stealing $1,500 from a safe. While awaiting a hearing of the case in the juvenile court, he remained at home and had a large company of boy admirers visiting him. When a probation officer came to see him the boy opened the conversation with the question, "Did you see where I made the headlines?"

Among criminals one's standing is frequently promoted by punishment. When Donald Lowrie informed a fellow-prisoner in San Quentin prison that his sentence was fifteen years, his status immediately rose, for status is in direct proportion to the seriousness of crimes and the length of sentences.[17]

(e) Reformation must be a constructive process. Punishment may produce fear, but more than fear is required for an alteration of character and personality. Reformation means not only a determination to change one's character, but a constructive process of organizing or reorganizing character. Materials for the construction of character are therefore necessary, and pain does not furnish these materials. One must have stimulations, patterns, suggestions, senti-

---

[16] William McDougall, "Crime in America," *Forum,* 77:523, April, 1927. Reprinted by permission.
[17] D. Lowrie, *My Life in Prison,* New York. 1912, pp. 62–63.

ments, and ideals presented to him. And the individual must develop his definitions and attitudes by practice, generally in a slow and gradual manner, in association with other human beings. One must have an appreciation of the values which are conserved by the law, and this can be produced only by assimilating the culture of the group which passed the law, or, stated otherwise, only if the group which passed the law assimilates the criminal. The negative act of prohibiting a thing is not sufficient because it is not constructive and does not promote assimilation.

(f) Punishment generally stops constructive efforts. If the group, in a spirit of hatred, inflicts punishment upon the offender, it generally sits back, after the penalty is inflicted, with a sigh of relief and with a feeling that the matter is now settled. Especially when a serious crime is committed, the whole community may become incensed, start on a hunt for the criminal, and punish him severely. Something has been done about it and that is a relief. But the situation remains, in general, just as it was before, and in a short time others commit the same crime. The punishment has been a means of releasing the emotions and using up the propelling forces in conduct in a relatively unproductive effort to get even with the particular individual who disturbed the community. It would be more satisfying in the long run to make an intensive effort to determine the psychological and social conditions that led to the atrocious crime, using the interests, emotions, and wishes in a more controlled way to produce an eventual modification in the situation.

In general the argument that punishment reduces crime is based on the assumption of hedonism, that people regulate their behavior by calculations of pleasures and pains. Dewey states the general fallacy in this assumption in the proposition:

Deliberation "no more resembles the casting-up of accounts of profit and loss, pleasures and pains, than an actor engaged in drama resembles a clerk recording debit and credit items in his ledger." [18]

Many criminals never consider the penalty. Sometimes this is because they are psychopathic or feebleminded or acting under the stress of a great emotion. Sometimes the penalty merely makes the prohibited act more alluring. Many prisoners have described their

---

[18] John Dewey, *Human Nature and Conduct*, New York, 1927, p. 199. Reprinted by permission of Henry Holt and Company, publishers.

mental processes in the violation of law, and it appears that few of them give much consideration to the penalty.

Münsterberg sums up the reasons for believing the deterrent power of punishment is limited as follows:

The hope of escaping justice in the concrete case will easily have a stronger feeling tone than the opposing fear of the abstract general law. The strength of the forbidden desire will narrow the circle of association and eliminate the idea of the probable consequences. The stupid mind will not link the correct expectations, the slow mind will bring the check too late, when the deed is done, the vehement mind will overrule the energies of inhibition, the emotional mind will be more moved by the anticipated immediate pleasure than by the thought of a later suffering. And all this will be reinforced if overstrain has destroyed the nervous balance, or if stimulants have smoothed the path of motor discharge. If the severity of cruel punishments has brutalized the mind, the threat will be as ineffective as if the mildness of punishment had reduced its pain. And, worst of all, this fear will be ruled out if the mind develops in an atmosphere of crime where the child hears of the criminal as a hero, and looks at jail as an ordinary affair, troublesome only as most factors in his slum life are troublesome; or if the anarchy of corruption or class justice, of reckless legislation or public indifference to law defeats the inhibiting counter idea of punishment and deprives it of its emotional strength.[19]

(g) In preliterate society a crime upset the equilibrium of the group just as the rape of a white woman by a Negro in a Southern community does now. Each individual acted immediately and spontaneously and they acted together, so that the behavior was collective. The punishment then restored the equilibrium. Punishment seldom has this effect at present. First, the equilibrium of the community is not much disturbed by a crime. Crime is an impersonal event to be read about in the newspapers, and no collective reaction occurs. Second, many persons are protected against crime by insurance. The insurance company is customarily interested primarily in restitution. The shock is taken from the crime in such cases and the burden is distributed over a period of years in the premium paid to the insurance company. Third, even if the victim is not protected by insurance, he is generally willing to drop the

<hr>

19 H. Münsterberg, *On the Witness Stand*, New York, 1908, pp. 258–260.

prosecution if he can secure restitution. The victim is interested only secondarily in the offense against the peace and dignity of the state. Fourth, the law-enforcing agencies do not feel that an organized public opinion is back of them, and the politicians and friends of the offender may be more powerful than the victim and his friends who are disturbed by the crime. The whole community is sometimes disturbed by a high crime rate, but is generally interested in protecting its fair name by concealing the truth rather than by changing the situation. Finally, when punishment is inflicted it has little effect on the community except in the spectacular cases.

MODIFICATIONS IN THE ORTHODOX THEORY OF PUNISHMENT. During the last fifty years, as never before, the orthodox theory of punishment has been compelled to meet questions and criticisms. As a result it has been undergoing decided modifications. Two factors have been especially important in producing this modification: one is the development of a causal explanation of behavior, the other is the introduction of elements of procedure which were in conflict with the orthodox theory but were not realized to be in conflict with it.

In the earlier period the will, assumed to be isolated from all other psychological and social processes and conditions, was given as the explanation of behavior. The Italian school of criminologists undertook to state a mechanistic explanation of crime, thereby denying the doctrine of the freedom of the will. Their explanation was not at all satisfactory, but it resulted in a demand by them that crime should be regarded as any other natural phenomenon and dealt with as such. They denied the validity or efficiency of the hostile attitude that had been expressed in punishments and insisted that crime should be controlled just as are floods or lightning or other natural evils.

To that argument of the Italian school has been added an immense weight of authority in the present generation. By many methods the factors that produce crime are being isolated and investigated. With this development of a natural science point of view in regard to crime, it is logical and "natural" that the same conclusion should be reached regarding control that has been reached and applied in natural science: control by a comprehension of the mechanisms and processes involved rather than by a mere act of will or an emotional reaction. The emphasis on feeblemindedness and psychopathic personality as explanations of crimes in recent years has undoubtedly helped establish the view that the criminal should be understood and helped, or else be segregated, rather than made to suffer as a result of the hostile attitudes of the public.

The actual effect of the development of explanations of crime has, therefore, been to modify procedure in dealing with criminals. It would be logically possible, to be sure, for a person to accept a mechanistic interpretation of crime and still favor the hostile, punishment attitude as a means of control. But since the legal policies have been based on the doctrines of individual responsibility and freedom of the will, the conclusion that those doctrines were not valid, at least for a large portion of the criminal population, has caused the whole super-structure of punishment to topple.

Probably an even more important factor in the modification of the orthodox theory has been the large number of encroachments made on the punitive procedure. A bit at a time, conflicting policies have been introduced—reformatories, education in prisons, probation and parole, juvenile court, specialized courts, and psychopathic laboratories connected with courts. Even while orthodox theorists were loudly advocating the policy of punishment, that policy was, without their knowledge, being supplanted. And as these competing policies have been introduced, it has appeared that some of them are more successful than the punitive procedure of earlier days. In support of the new methods a new theory has been organized. So the development has been as follows: First, modifications in practice, which were not realized to be in conflict either with the previous policies or theories, then the development of a new theory to support these new practices, with a gradual increase in strength until the old theory is now far along the course of disintegration. Probably the juvenile court has been more important than any other modification of practice in producing this result. For it was apparent that if a child sixteen years of age should not be punished but should be guarded and trained, a child seventeen or eighteen years of age similarly should not be punished. And then some states raised the juvenile court age to twenty-one, and most courts have a continuation jurisdiction until the age of twenty-one. If "children" between the ages of eighteen and twenty-one can be dealt with effectively without the punishment attitude, adults between the ages of twenty-one and twenty-five can be treated the same way. And naturally the question arises, Why punish anyone? Why not abandon the punishment attitude?

THE TWO ATTITUDES CANNOT BE COMBINED. Some people admit that punishment brings evils in its train, but insist that punishment should be retained, with the pain inflicted in a spirit of love rather than of hatred; that is, they suggest that the two attitudes be combined. Professor Mead, however, has insisted that such a combination is logically impossible.

The two attitudes, that of control of crime by the hostile procedure of the law, and that of control through comprehension of social and psychological conditions, cannot be combined. To understand is to forgive, and the social procedure seems to deny the very responsibility which the law affirms, and, on the other hand, the pursuit by criminal justice inevitably awakens the hostile attitude in the offender and renders the attitude of mutual comprehension practically impossible.[20]

Devon suggests that the existing procedures are similar to those of a surgeon who, in order to reduce drunkenness, first applied the germs of erysipelas to the scalp wound received by a drunken man and subsequently made the best possible effort to cure the wound.[21] According to this view, the two attitudes are not in harmony and cannot be combined. It is then necessary either to retain the punishment and abandon the effort to understand the crime or else to abandon the punishment attitude and continue the effort to understand the crime.

This view is a corollary of one of the theories of punishment. A different corollary may be derived from another theory. If Lundstedt's theory, for instance, is accepted the conclusion might be as follows: Crime in the generic sense, rather than an individual criminal act, must be understood in order to develop satisfactory policies of control. From this point of view the most important factors in causing or preventing crime are the reactions of other persons toward criminal acts and toward criminals. The reactions which are most effective in preventing crime are expressions of antagonism and hostility, and those which are most effective in causing crime are expressions of appreciation. This can be stated as an hypothesis for scientific work, and an understanding of the

---

[20] G. H. Mead, "Psychology of Punitive Justice," *Amer. Jour. Sociol.*, 23:592, March, 1918. Reprinted by permission of The University of Chicago Press, publishers.

[21] James Devon, *The Criminal and the Community*, London, 1912, p. 175.

genesis of crime may be secured. This theory, if found valid, may then support punitive policies and may, in fact, even direct the expressions of hostility. In that sense, it may be possible to combine the attitude of understanding of crime in general and the attitude of hostility toward crime in general.

ATTRIBUTES OF PUNISHMENT. The classical school argued that if every crime were automatically, by law of Nature, followed immediately by extreme suffering, crime would almost entirely disappear. Their ideal was to make a social policy which would approach as closely as possible to this supposititious law of Nature. The attributes of punishment which they assumed to be desirable were severity, certainty, uniformity, and celerity. The positive school, on the other hand, regarded any method of treatment of criminals with considerable scepticism. They pointed to intoxication which is automatically and rather promptly followed by suffering, but which is continued nevertheless. They maintained that a society has the amount of crime it deserves in view of its economic conditions and its biological composition, and that the policy used in dealing with criminals was relatively unimportant in determining behavior. Prevention rather than treatment was the slogan of the positive school.

Uniformity in the conventional system referred to the similarity of punishment of all persons who violated a particular law. This uniformity was justified on the ground that it was necessary to have a definitely predetermined penalty in order that prospective offenders might take it into their calculations of pleasures and pains which would result from the act. The pride of the system was its impersonality. Theoretically it gave no consideration to social status, wealth, religion, previous behavior, age, sex, or any other element or circumstance of the person. The crime was dealt with as a disembodied act and the effect of the treatment upon the general public was the only consideration. Emphasis on uniformity was, in addition, an expression of the spirit of democracy then strong in European countries. The positive school, on the other hand, insisted that criminals differ and that the offender rather than the offense should be the object of attention. The general trend is toward the individualization which the positive school outlined. This policy of individualization tends to result in uniformity of treatment, but it is a uniformity of treatment of all persons who are similar in type of personality or in situation rather than uniformity based on the crime committed. It is a uniformity like that in medicine. Uniformity, however, has no significance as a deterrent regardless of whether the abstract act or the person is considered as the basis. Absolute uniformity in treatment might exist without the least deterrent influence, for equal rewards might be given to all persons who violate a law or who have a particular personality trait. The content of the treatment rather than the uniformity must be considered in evaluating the deterrent effect of the treatment.

Certainty of treatment refers to the frequency with which violations of law are followed by detection, identification, conviction, and official treatment. Certainty cannot be attained in modern society, especially for robbery and burglary which perhaps cause the greatest concern. The number of arrests for burglary and robbery is probably not more than 10 per cent of the number committed. In spite of the uncertainty of treatment a very small proportion of the population commits serious crimes. Most of the serious crimes are committed by a very small number of persons who violate the same laws persistently. Two young men were caught in a robbery in Minneapolis late one night and confessed that they had committed ten robberies earlier in that same night. Certainty must decrease as society becomes more complex unless phenomenal developments occur in the detection of criminals.

Severity of treatment is a bone of contention among people who write on penology. The positive school generally minimized the significance of severity of penalties, as have most of the American penologists. Tarde, however, concluded that the effect of an increase in severity of penalties upon crimes is somewhat like the effect of an increase of prices upon consumption. Just as an increase of price produces very little effect on the consumption of some articles and a very great effect on the consumption of other articles, so increased severity produces little effect on the frequency of some crimes and great effect on others.[22] The efforts to demonstrate the effect of severity upon crime rates have been inconclusive. A few of the data may, nevertheless, be reported. An interesting attempt was made to prove that crime was not reduced by increased severity by a comparison of the frequency of convictions and severity of penalties by judicial districts in New York State for the period 1846–1850.[23] The statistical reports of Canada show that since 1891

---

[22] G. Tarde, *Penal Philosophy*, Boston, 1912, pp. 482–483; for his evidence regarding the general deterrent effect of penalties, see pp. 473 ff.
[23] New York, *Assembly Documents 20*, 1852, pp. 40 ff.

the severity of penalties for indictable offenses decreased decidedly with no appreciable change in the proportion of recidivists.[24] But the crimes which have been treated with greater severity in Canada have increased less than those which have been treated with less severity.[25] It is often claimed that few murders are committed in England because the death penalty there is swift and certain. But the murder rate in the Southern states is high, though the death penalty is swift and certain there, also. In fact, it seems impossible to isolate the two factors of severity and criminality for specific comparison. It is, however, probably true that severity would be effective if all offenders were punished. But when one offender is punished severely and ninety are not detected in their crimes, the punishment is of little value either in reforming the one who is caught or in deterring others. Moreover, the social life is changing so that the offender gets more support and the state less support in its policy of severe punishment. When the state uses punitive methods it no longer has the support of a punitive culture in the home, the church, and the school, while the offender may always succeed in securing support from a criminal or a law-abiding group.

In general, therefore, dependence upon certainty and severity of treatment seems to be increasingly unwarranted and their attainment in practice increasingly difficult. Moreover, that policy is unable to encourage or utilize the increasing knowledge regarding offenders.

THE SUBSTITUTE FOR PUNISHMENT. The policy that, from the factual point of view, is taking the place of punishment and that, from the ethical point of view, is presented as preferable to punishment is the policy of studying the personality of the offender and the whole social situation in which he becomes a criminal and controlling by means of the knowledge thus secured. This is the procedure of science. No flaring emotion, such as the hatred connected with punishment, appears in the process, but it is, nevertheless, an emotional process, involving curiosity, sympathy, hatred, and other emotions welded into a consistent working method under the general direction of the intelligence.

This policy is based on the conviction that the individual can be

---

[24] Canada, Bureau of Statistics, Judicial Statistics Branch, *Annual Report on Criminal Statistics*, 1920, p. viii.
[25] Canada, Bureau of Statistics, Judicial Statistics Branch, *Annual Report on Criminal Statistics*, 1930, pp. xi and 95–97.

developed in practically any direction desired by the group and can acquire any attitude. If he fails to acquire the socially desirable attitudes, society, to be sure, has the right to protect itself against him, but he, on the other hand, has the right to be made socially useful.

The policy based on the comprehension of the criminal and of his social situations will involve, first, the reformation of the criminal, second, the segregation of those who cannot be reformed, and third, the prevention of crime. It is clear that reformation of offenders up to the present generation has been largely a matter of accident, understood by no one. The experts are perhaps slightly superior to others. In cases in which the recommendations of the Judge Baker Foundation were carried out 17.9 per cent had no further records, while in cases in which the recommendations were not carried out 4.6 per cent had no further records.[26] Doubtless the tendencies of many persons cannot be modified by any known technique, either because of the mental deficiencies of the delinquents (or of those in authority) or because of the rigidity of their habits. No other policy is advocated for them except complete segregation for as long a period as necessary, presumably for life for most of them. This should not be regarded as different in its purpose from the segregation of the feebleminded or insane. During this period of incarceration, efforts should be made by experimental methods to develop a technique of modification of behavior even for such persons. Gland surgery, medical experiments, sociological experiments, and other methods may yield results for the improvement of the technique of modification of attitudes, even for those who are now regarded as hopeless. And it is quite certain that the comprehension of the criminal and his social situation will give a basis for policies that will change the situation and perhaps prevent the birth of such individuals. It is apparent that most criminals could have been kept from undesirable behavior by proper control in the early stages.

The very largest share of delinquency and crime in young people is preventable. . . . With anything like reasonable effort in a reasonably decent community, delinquent tendencies in most individuals can be thwarted. The study of causes shows them to be ascertainable and generally alterable.[27]

[26] Sheldon and Eleanor Glueck, *One Thousand Juvenile Delinquents*, p. 175.
[27] Wm. Healy, "Study of the Individual Child as a Preliminary to Treatment," *U. S. Children's Bur.*, No. 97, p. 30.

Though punishment is one method of building up desirable attitudes in the general public, it is not the only method. The development of habits and attitudes by education, by the spreading of traditions, by the contacts and interactions between those who appreciate the values and those who do not is the thing on which we must depend for the prevention of crime. As we find out more about crime, we shall have a better basis for the determination of specific policies for this purpose. These other policies, if carried out consistently, may be expected to protect society from crime in three ways: First, they would secure a relatively permanent segregation of persons who, because of mental abnormality, anti-authority complexes, or lack of appreciation of conventional values or social situations, constitute the greatest menace to the group. Segregation will probably not reform these offenders but it will protect the group by incapacitating them and to a slight extent by deterring others. Apparently no other policy can be used in the present state of techniques of control for a large proportion of chronic and professional offenders and a considerable number of first offenders. Second, this policy would restore to society without alienating them a large proportion of those who have not definitely broken away from the general culture of organized society. Third, this policy would define the type of personality and the social situations from which crimes are most likely to issue, and would make it possible to deal with such persons in advance of crime and to attack and eliminate those social situations. Thus protection against crime would be secured by modifying those who could be modified by available techniques, segregating those who could not be so modified, and correcting or segregating in advance of crime those who were proved to be most likely to commit crime, and attacking and eliminating the social situations which were most conducive to crime. Such policies would be as much evidence that the organized society disapproved of crime as would punishment, and it is this disapprobation rather than the punishment which tends to deter the large majority of the population from crime.

MEETING OBJECTIONS. The immediate reaction to such a program is often antagonistic. Many people assert that this method would ruin society. In general the objections that are raised against it may all be met by the answer that as a matter of fact we are now using the policy in the juvenile court and to an increasing extent in the courts for adults. The rebuttal that will be made is that we have an increasing amount of crime as the result. But there is no available proof that the change in court and penal methods has anything to do with it, and there is just as much reason to assert that the survival of the punishment attitude, which is quite out of harmony with the other attitudes and policies of the present day, is the reason for the great amount of crime. A more detailed consideration of some of the objections may assist in clarifying the general argument.

(a) It is asserted by those who favor punishment that the general public cannot be prevented from engaging in a general debauch of crime except by the fear of punishment; we must keep punishment in order to deter from crime. To this objection, it may be replied, first, that not all of the unpleasantness and suffering will be removed from crime even if the formal punishment is abandoned. The arrest, the detention and trial, and many of the methods that will be used as substitutes for punishment will cause discomfort, not because the discomfort is regarded as desirable, but because the discomfort cannot easily be eliminated. And because the attitudes of some criminals cannot be modified by any known method, some criminals will be retained in institutions for life. In addition there will always be some stigma connected with crime, regardless of the official treatment of delinquents. And those individuals who are deterred from crime only because of the fear of punishment should probably be segregated anyhow. But the real reason for believing that the substitution of comprehension for hatred would not result in a debauch of crime is that the control, after all, lies in the group pressure, the recognition and response secured by lawful conduct rather than the fear of punishment. Not the fear of legal penalties, but the fear of loss of status in the group is the effective deterrent. But this is not really fear; what really occurs is that the person feels that doing a specified thing in violation of the group standard, which also happens to be in violation of the law, would not be in harmony with his personality, would lower him. It does not occur to him to do such a thing. He would feel uncomfortable in violating such a law and would secure no satisfaction from it. This is the principal method of control whether the conduct is regulated by law or is not. One who would not think of breaking into a jewelry store and robbing a private merchant will smuggle jewelry into his country in violation of the law, or will violate the child-labor law or the tax law, or will engage in a lynching mob or in preventing a

Negro from voting; his group does not regard such violations as beneath the dignity of one of its members. Regardless of the official methods of dealing with criminals we shall retain this method of control by group pressure.

One of the weaknesses of the legal system at present is the dependence on the threat of punishment for the enforcement of the law. It is much better to develop an attitude of appreciation of the values before the law is passed, and then perhaps the law will be unnecessary. It is certainly possible to develop the attitudes of appreciation more effectively than has been done to date. At any rate the threat and infliction of punishments are not the only methods of deterrence from crime.

(b) A second objection is that, if the criminal is not punished, the victim will take the law into his own hand and this will mean either self-redress or lynch-law. This assertion is based on the belief that there is an unalterable demand for vengeance which will be satisfied by illegal means, if not by legal means.

In present society the demand for vengeance is, to be sure, somewhat general. There is probably no one who would not demand vengeance under certain circumstances.[28] But the vengeance attitude is quite certainly the product of social contacts and interactions. The difference between the Italian immigrants of the first and second generations shows this.[29] Even if an instinct of vengeance be admitted, the instinct is certainly not fixed in its method of expression; one may secure revenge by a blow with the fist, by spitting, by calling names, by shooting with a gun, by spreading calumny, by voting, and perhaps even by "heaping coals of fire upon the head" of the opponent. One may secure vengeance against the criminal, for instance, by bringing him to trial and assisting the state to use methods that will reform him. And, after all, the problem is not the attitude of the particular victim but of the state. A very large proportion—probably more than 75 per cent—of the crimes arouse the resentment of no particular individual. And when resentment is aroused, it is generally confined to a very small number of persons, and their resentment is counteracted by the attitudes of other members of the group. To be sure, in offenses involving the

---

[28] F. C. Sharp and M. C. Otto, "A Study of the Popular Attitude toward Retributive Punishment," *Inter. Jour. Ethics*, 20:341–357, 438–453, April, July, 1910.

[29] See p. 128.

relations of white and colored people in the South, in certain horrible sexual offenses, and in offenses involving the relations of different classes, a more general demand for vengeance may arise and the individual who takes the law into his own hand may receive the support of the group. Some who now take the law into their own hands for the purpose of securing vengeance would be content to let the law take its course if they had confidence that the law would deal with the problem in a scientific way rather than muddling through with it as at present.

(c) The third objection against the abolition of the punishment attitude is that the victim would be unwilling to testify or make complaint if he could not see his opponent suffer; he would take the loss and remain silent rather than go to the trouble of court procedure which would yield him no satisfaction. Against this objection the following things may be considered as inducements to produce willingness to testify and make complaint. First, the victim would still secure the satisfaction of seeing his aggressor put to the trouble of a trial, and would secure the satisfaction of a conviction, which would show that the public was on his side; this would vindicate him and perhaps would grant him all the satisfaction he wished. Second, he would secure satisfaction from the methods used in dealing with the offender, which might include permanent segregation. Again, many people are disgusted with the present-day procedure to the extent that they are unwilling to go to the trouble of making complaints or offering testimony because they feel that it will do no good. A man who had suffered a loss by theft recently refused to make complaint for this very reason; when the thief was prosecuted by others who had suffered, he was fined $25, which his parents paid, and confined in the county jail for ten days. The original victim remarked that this penalty was what he had expected and that it would evidently do no good; he expressed willingness to spend much time in an attempt to deal with the offender in a way that would assist him to overcome the difficulty. Fourth, with the present procedure the friends of the criminal are certain to rally to his support in opposition to the hostile procedure of the law. If these friends had any reason to believe that the procedure was designed to improve the offender and would have some efficiency in this respect, they would be more inclined to assist in securing a conviction for his own good. And finally, punishment of approximately 75 per cent of the offenders does not give satisfaction to any witness. For such offenses as drunkenness, prostitution, violations of traffic regulations, and vagrancy the complaint is made by a public officer and the testimony furnished by the same officer and others subpœnaed to appear in court. If we can depend on public prosecutors in such cases, it is reasonable to believe that testimony can be secured in the other offenses in which personal feeling is involved somewhat more.

(d) Another objection is that the solidarity of the group and the respect for the law which are now developed by the hostile attitude toward the criminal would decrease without this support. As a matter of fact group solidarity and respect for law can be developed in a great variety of other ways. If opposition is necessary, it can be found in the problem of comprehending the causes of the crime and controlling by means of the knowledge thus attained. The only thing needed is that something be presented on which the group can act together. War and the pursuit of the criminal appeal to this tendency to stand together in its lowest form; but the interest can be attached to such other things as insect evils, disease germs, bad housing conditions, or anything else that is injurious to social welfare.

(e) A final objection is that the clinical method of treatment of delinquents has not been much more effective in changing delinquents than punishment was. This objection is based either on biological or social determinism, and leads to the conclusion that it is necessary either to practice eugenics or else modify objective conditions in order to reduce delinquency. While there is doubtless much truth in this view, especially the social portion of it, it need not be associated with complete pessimism regarding the value of treatment.[30]

SUMMARY AND CONCLUSION. Modern science has shown that wonderful results can be secured by an understanding of the forces that operate or the mechanisms that are going on, and that an efficient technique of control can be developed only on the basis of such an understanding. This is true in the field of social behavior, as in physical action. The methods of control have not been worked out thoroughly yet, and can be worked out only by an extension of

---

[30] Saul D. Alinsky, "The Philosophical Implications of the Individualistic Approach in Criminology," *Proc. Amer. Prison Assoc.*, 1937, pp. 156–171; Edwin H. Sutherland, "The Person and the Situation in the Treatment of Prisoners," *Proc. Amer. Prison Assoc.*, 1937, pp. 145–150.

the knowledge of causation and by experimentation based on that knowledge. Our knowledge regarding the factors producing human behavior and the mechanisms of this behavior is extending rapidly, and the success in the use of the methods of control is increasing. The control of behavior must come, for the most part, from others than legal authorities, in the prevention of crime, but the authorities can deal much more successfully with those who have committed crimes if the policies are based on such scientific knowledge as has been suggested. The primary method will certainly be educational, in the broader sense of the word. There should be no predetermined exclusion of any method, but it is probable that pain or suffering need not play a large part. The methods of dealing with criminals must always cause them some suffering, but it should be regarded in the same way as pain in connection with the treatment of disease or insanity—to be avoided if possible.

Punishment has evident values, but its values are limited and are off-set by effects not designed, so that it is a relatively inefficient method of dealing with criminals. Because of this inefficiency, regardless of the right of the state to punish or the fact that the criminal may deserve to suffer, it is desirable to substitute the scientific procedure for the emotional procedure.

This method will work only if the general public becomes persuaded of the superiority of this method of punishment. If the attitudes of the public change in that way, no fundamental difficulty that cannot be overcome is apparent. The situation will be for adult criminals then just what the situation now is for juvenile delinquents. Accordingly it is desirable to regard punishment as a thing which has been tending for some time to disappear and be replaced by these other methods, and as a thing which, from the point of view of ethics and economy, it is desirable to get rid of as quickly as the general public can be induced to take the other attitude toward criminals. The proper procedure is, doubtless, the one that has actually been used—an extension of the attitude of control by knowledge of the situation to larger and larger groups of offenders rather than a complete change overnight. Moreover, the trend toward including within the scope of treatment the wider situation is desirable. Non-punitive treatment up to date has been concentrated largely on individuals, regarded as isolated entities. The trend is toward the inclusion of culture and the social situation within the scope of treatment.

SUGGESTED READINGS

Alexander, J. P., "The Philosophy of Punishment," *Jour Crim. Law and Criminol.*, 13:235–250, August, 1922.

Alinsky, Saul D., "The Philosophical Implications of the Individualistic Approach in Criminology," *Proc. Amer. Prison Assoc.*, 1937, pp. 156–171.

Aschaffenburg, G., *Crime and Its Repression*, Tr. by A. Albrecht, Boston, 1913, pp. 241–285.

Bentham, Jeremy, *Principles of Morals and Legislation*, Oxford, 1879, Chs. 13–16.

Cantor, Nathaniel, "Conflicts in Penal Theory," *Jour. Crim. Law and Criminol.*, 26:330–350, September, 1935.

Davenport, C. B., "Heredity, Culpability, Praiseworthiness, Punishment and Reward," *Pop. Sci. Mo.*, 83:33–39, July, 1913.

Devon, James, *The Criminal and the Community*, London, 1912, Ch. 7.

Dewey, John, "Force and Coercion," *Inter. Jour. Ethics*, 26:359–367, April, 1916.

Ferri, E., *Criminal Sociology*, Tr. by J. I. Kelly and John Lisle, Boston, 1917, Part III.

Hamilton, J. A., "Making the Punishment Fit the Crime," *Jour. Crim. Law and Criminol.*, 12:159–177, August, 1921.

Harris, P. E., *Changing Conceptions of School Discipline*, New York, 1928.

Hentig, Hans von, *Punishment*, London, 1937.

Innes, A. M., "Love and the Law: A Study of Oriental Justice," *Hibbert Jour.*, 11:273–296, January, 1913.

Kirchwey, G. W., "Crime and Punishment," *Jour. Crim. Law and Criminol.*, 1:718–734, January, 1911.

Levitt, A., "Some Societal Aspects of the Criminal Law," *Jour. Crim. Law and Criminol.*, 13:90–104, May, 1922.

Lisle, John, "The Justification of Punishment, *Inter. Jour. Ethics*, 25:346–359, April, 1915.

McConnell, R. M., *Criminal Responsibility and Social Constraint*, New York, 1912.

Mead, G. H., "The Psychology of Punitive Justice," *Amer. Jour. Sociol.*, 23:577–602, March, 1918.

Oppenheimer, H., *The Rationale of Punishment*, London, 1913, pp. 184–316.

Ross, E. A., *Social Control*, New York, 1916, Ch. 11.

Saleilles, R., *The Individualization of Punishment,* Tr. by R. S. Jastrow, Boston, 1911, Chs. 6 and 7.

Sharp, F. C., and Otto, M. C., "A Study of the Popular Attitude toward Retributive Punishment," *Inter. Jour. Ethics,* 20:341–357, 438–453, April, July, 1910.

Sutherland, Edwin H., "The Person and the Situation in the Treatment of Prisoners," *Proc. Amer. Prison Assoc.,* 1937, pp. 145–150.

Sutherland, Edwin H., "The Person *versus* the Act in Criminology," *Cornell Law Quart.,* 14:159–167, February, 1929.

Tarde, G., *Penal Philosophy,* Tr. by R. Howell, Boston, 1912, Chs. 3, 4, and 8.

Timasheff, N. S., "The Retributive Structure of Punishment," *Jour. Crim. Law and Criminol.,* 28:396–405, September, 1937.

Webb, Sidney and Beatrice, *English Prisons Under Local Government,* London, 1922, Preface by Bernard Shaw, pp. i-lxxiii.

White, W. A., *Insanity and the Criminal Law,* New York, 1923, Ch. 18.

Wines, F. H., *Punishment and Reformation,* New York, 1919, Chs. 7 and 13.

Chapter Twenty

PROBATION

WE NOW BEGIN the study of the several types of treatment that may be prescribed by the court after an offender has been found guilty. Probation is considered first because of its potential importance among the methods of treatment.

THE NATURE OF PROBATION. Probation is an illustration of the process described at the end of the previous chapter, namely, the development of a non-punitive method of treating offenders within the framework of a system which, in general, is punitive.

From the constitutional point of view probation is the suspension of a sentence during a period of liberty in the community conditional upon good behavior of the convicted offender. The courts have without exception found the constitutional justification of probation in the right of the court to suspend the sentence. The suspension of the sentence may be either a suspension of the imposition of the sentence or the suspension of the execution of the sentence. Some states suspend the imposition, others the execution, and others use both methods. If the judge imposes a sentence and then suspends the execution of the sentence, and if the offender violates the probation, the judge merely orders the execution of the original sentence. If the judge suspends the imposition of the sentence, he will in case of violation of probation have additional information on which to base a decision regarding the sentence which should be imposed.

Whichever method of suspending the sentence is used, it is a method of suspending a penalty so that other methods of treatment may be used. It is thus a substitute for a penalty. It is generally regarded as a substitute for imprisonment, but there is no logical reason why it might not be regarded as a substitute for any other penalty.

Some questions of law have arisen regarding probation. A federal court sentenced an offender to serve two years in a penitentiary and then provided that he be released on probation at the end of six months and kept on probation during the remainder of the two years. The higher court held that this was illegal because the court was really ordering the offender paroled and the court had no jurisdiction in regard to parole. Again, the court may convict an offender on two counts, then commit him to an institution on the first count and place him on probation on the second count. This, apparently, is not illegal, but it is a violation of the social principle of probation, which is to keep offenders out of prison.[1]

Within this constitutional framework probation has developed, but it is from the social point of view one of the important methods of dealing with offenders. It is clearly something different from the mere suspension of a sentence, in that the state attempts to assist the probationer to maintain good conduct. This assistance has come to be the important part of the probation system, and it is for that reason that the person who receives the assistance of the state while he is securing money to pay a fine in installments is regarded as "on probation." A broader definition of probation might be stated as follows: Probation is the status of a convicted offender during a period of suspension of the sentence in which he is given liberty conditioned on his good behavior and in which the state by personal supervision attempts to assist him to maintain good behavior.

Suspension of sentence without supervision, from the theoretical point of view, is not probation. This procedure, nevertheless, is used frequently by many courts. In New York City in 1928, 33 per cent of the sentences imposed in the magistrates courts and the courts of special sessions were suspended, but only 4 per cent of the persons whose sentences were suspended were placed on probation. In Massachusetts 29 per cent of the persons convicted in the lower courts were discharged without supervision, and 21 per cent were placed on probation with supervision. Half of the persons convicted received no penalty, but the number kept under supervision was less than the number on probation.

In practice probation is therefore to be regarded as a substitute for either of two other methods of dealing with convicted offenders:

[1] Sam B. Warner, "Some Legal Problems Raised by Probation," in Sheldon Glueck (Editor), *Probation and Criminal Justice*, New York, 1932, Ch. 2.

imprisonment or discharge without supervision. It is important to judge probation in relation to these two alternatives; it is frequently judged as though it were an alternative to imprisonment alone.

Probation represents a distinct break with the classical theory of criminal law, for it attempts to deal with offenders as individuals rather than as classes or concepts, to select certain offenders who can be assisted while at liberty to form correct habits and attitudes without a penalty, and to use a great variety of methods for this purpose. It represents, also, a distinct break with the retributive theory of punishment. It does not attempt to make the offender suffer; it attempts to prevent him from suffering. Some suffering results from the status, to be sure, but it is not intentional and is avoided as far as possible. Consequently there is no good reason for insisting that probation is punishment, as some authors have in the effort to win approval for the system.

THE ORIGIN AND DEVELOPMENT OF PROBATION. Under the common law the court could suspend a sentence temporarily for various reasons. At an early date the court began to suspend sentences indefinitely, permitting convicted offenders to remain at large on good behavior.[2] Sometimes the offender was compelled to furnish financial guarantee that he would maintain good behavior while the sentence was suspended. The fact that the sentence might be executed any time he failed to behave properly exerted some influence upon him, as did also the possibility of the loss of the financial security. Then volunteers began to assist such offenders during the period of the suspension of the sentence. Among the early volunteers was John Augustus, a shoemaker of Boston, who in 1849 secured the release of a confirmed drunkard from the police court of Boston by acting as surety for him. This offender turned out to be a "sober, industrious citizen" under his care. Then Augustus extended his efforts to others. During the course of seven years he acted as surety for 253 males and 149 females in an amount that totaled $15,320, and it is reported that not one of his charges violated the conditions of his release.[3] Such volunteers became more

---

[2] An early case in America, which became a precedent, is described by F. W. Grinnell, "Probation as an Orthodox Common Law Practice in Massachusetts Prior to the Statutory System," *Mass. Law Quart.*, 2:595, August, 1917.

[3] Ada Eliot, "The American Probation System," *Charities*, 9:279, September 20, 1902.

numerous and were, in effect, probation officers before probation had been authorized by statute.

From 1861 to 1867 Chicago had a commissioner to hear cases of delinquency of boys; he had legal authority to place the boys on probation.[4] In 1869 a state visiting agency in Massachusetts was authorized by the legislature to accept the custody of juvenile offenders, with the right of placing them in private families. This amounted to probation, and 23 per cent of the juvenile offenders convicted in the courts of Boston in the year 1869–1870 were dealt with in this manner.

The first statutory provision for probation with publicly paid officers was the Massachusetts law of 1878, which authorized the Mayor of Boston to appoint and pay a probation officer and authorized the municipal court to place offenders on probation. No restrictions were made, as in many subsequent probation laws, regarding the term of probation, the age, previous record, or other characteristics of the offender. The legislature extended this power to all other mayors of the state in 1880, but few of the mayors took advantage of the authority.

By 1900 six states had authorized probation with paid officers. By 1917 it had been authorized by every state. The states which had the highest percentage of urban population developed probation first and it gradually spread to the more rural states. No general statistics of probation in the United States are available. The number of persons placed on probation in Massachusetts increased from 15,518 in 1910 to 27,817 in 1936, while the number committed to prisons and jails decreased from 31,081 to 12,305. In New York a similar trend occurred. These states are not representative of the entire country, for probation is probably used more generally in these states than in any others. For thirty states in 1936 31.1 per cent of those convicted in courts of general jurisdiction were placed on probation or given suspended sentences; this percentage ranged from 65.8 in Rhode Island to 11.6 in North Dakota. Of those convicted of burglary, 73.5 were placed on probation or suspended sentence in Rhode Island, while at the other extreme only 14.9 were given probation or suspended sentences in Kansas.

The federal courts used probation before 1916 without statutory authority. This was declared illegal in the Killits case. Probation

---

[4] T. H. MacQuery, "Reformation of Juvenile Offenders in Illinois," *Amer. Jour. Sociol.*, 8:647, March, 1903.

was authorized by Congress in 1925 but was not used extensively by the federal courts until 1930. The number of persons on probation on June 30, 1930, was only 4,281 but increased to 25,526 on June 30, 1937. The number of federal probation officers increased from 8 in 1929 to 171 in 1937.

Most of the European nations have provision for the suspension of sentence and many of them have volunteer or philanthropic assistance for persons during the period of suspension of sentence, but few of them have provided for publicly paid probation officers.

SCOPE OF THE PROBATION SYSTEM. Though every state has authorized probation, many states have legal limitations on its use. Probation is limited in thirteen states to juvenile delinquents, in Wyoming to adults. In eight states probation may be granted regardless of the type of crime. In five states it is not available for offenders punishable by capital punishment or by life imprisonment, in three states for offenders punishable by terms of imprisonment of more than ten years, and in sixteen states for certain specified serious offenses. In four states it is limited to misdemeanors, and in two states to specified minor misdemeanors. Furthermore, in some states probation may be used only by courts in cities or counties of specified size, or by courts with specified types of jurisdiction. These statutory restrictions are quite absurd if the probation department and the court do their work efficiently. Persons of all ages, with all kinds of previous records, and with all kinds of charges against them should be eligible for probation. The actual grant of probation should be determined by a study of the particular offender rather than by his age, present crime, or previous record.

A second limitation on the probation system is the failure to appoint and pay probation officers. Less than half of the courts hearing children's cases in 1918 had probation service, and in only eight states was there a recognized probation officer for every court.[5] The rural districts are far behind the urban communities in this respect. Only 25 per cent of the courts in districts that were entirely rural had probation workers for juvenile delinquents.[6] In New York State in 1933 23 per cent of the counties had no paid probation officer and 8 per cent more had paid probation officers for juveniles only. No later statistics on these points are available,

---

[5] Evelina Belden, "Courts in the United States Hearing Children's Cases," *U. S. Children's Bur.*, No. 65, 1920, p. 13.

[6] *Ibid.*, p. 52.

but it is probable that the rural districts have improved during the last twenty years.

The third limitation is the failure of the court to use probation when it is authorized by law and when probation officers are provided. This limitation is due in part to the personal opinions and habits of the judges, and partly to the community standards. In Massachusetts courts of similar jurisdiction vary from less than 1 per cent to 50 per cent in the proportion of convicted offenders placed on probation, though probation officers are available for all the courts. In general probation is used less frequently in rural districts than in urban districts even when probation officers are available. In Minnesota in 1926 only 29 per cent of the juvenile offenders committed to institutions from rural counties had been on probation prior to commitment, while 80 per cent of those committed from the three largest cities had been on probation previously.[7] On the other hand, for specified serious crimes probation was used in rural counties in Ohio in about the same proportion of cases as in the most densely populated counties in 1937.

SELECTION OF PROBATIONERS. The laws of some states require that before an offender be placed on probation an investigation of his character and conditions be made and the results submitted to the judge. This is for the dual purpose of verifying the name and address of the offender and determining the characteristics of the prospective probationer. If no investigation is made, offenders may give fictitious names and addresses and disappear immediately, and in addition many persons may be released on probation who should be kept segregated. As a matter of fact, many judges do not wait for an investigation even when the laws require that they do so. Within recent years only 10 to 15 per cent of the offenders placed on probation by the Boys' Court in Chicago had been officially investigated. In other cases the judge made decisions on the basis of the offender's statement about himself, his personal appearance, the social status of the family, the nature of the offense, or the recommendations of other persons. These are likely to be decidedly inadequate as a basis for policies, and it is largely because of this inadequacy that probation has been brought into ill repute.

When investigations are made, they are generally made by the

---

[7] Edwin H. Sutherland, "Probation in Minnesota," *Proc. Minn. Conf. Social Work,* 1927, pp. 219–229.

regular probation officers. In New York State the probation officers report that they make more than thirty thousand investigations of this nature each year. These investigations in some jurisdictions take so much of the time of probation officers that little is left for correctional work. A study of the magistrates courts in Brooklyn in 1932 showed that about 5 per cent of the working time of probation officers was available for supervising offenders who were placed on probation.[8] In addition, the investigation is distinctly different in some respects from the supervisory work and should be done by specialized officers. Furthermore, the supervisory officer is likely to be handicapped later in dealing with probationers if he makes the investigations, for the investigator will be regarded as a detective.

The person or agency which makes the investigation will need organized and centralized records. The entire official record of previous crimes and delinquencies should be centralized and should include the very valuable information which is now locked up in the files of the juvenile court. The educational record, together with various types of appraisals by teachers, should be centralized and kept on file. The social service records are now centralized in most cities through the confidential exchange. Massachusetts has developed a state system superior to that of any other state in the records which have been built up by the Commission on Probation.

In Massachusetts those arrested for drunkenness need not go to court; the probation officer has the semi-judicial function of releasing such offenders when he thinks it is desirable to do so. In 1909 probation officers released 43 per cent of the persons arrested for drunkenness, in 1919 62 per cent, in 1922 49 per cent, and in 1931 45 per cent. This is probably somewhat better than the release by the police under the Golden Rule policy. The comparatively high proportion of violations of probation among this group in Massachusetts shows the need of more careful selection, but does not show the need of absolute prohibition of probation for this group. The same thing may be said in regard to the feebleminded offenders. The feebleminded offenders have been regarded as poor risks for probation by some persons, but the statistical information indicates that they get along on probation as well as normal persons, and in any case some of them get along so suc-

---

[8] *Survey,* 68:605, November 15, 1932.

cessfully that it is not a question of prohibiting them from probation entirely, but of knowing the combinations of other characteristics and conditions of life which result in violation of probation by the feebleminded.

Probation is used, as explained previously, primarily as a substitute for discharge without supervision and for imprisonment. The principle that should be used in determining whether probation should be substituted for discharge without supervision is, Does this offender need supervision and assistance in adjusting to community conditions, and will he profit by this assistance and supervision? The principle that should be used in determining whether probation should be substituted for imprisonment is essentially the same, but includes also the danger to the community during the period of readjustment. For both groups these questions can be answered best by an analysis of the rates of violation of probation by offenders in the past, in comparison with the behavior of persons dealt with by other methods.

THE TERMS OF PROBATION. The terms of probation are generally fixed jointly by the legislature, the court, and the probation department or staff. The following are generally included: observance of all laws, good habits, keeping good company, regular reports as required, regular work or school attendance, payment of fines or reparation. In Massachusetts these terms must be communicated to the probationer in writing in order that there may be no misunderstanding. Sometimes the probationer is required to live in a specified place. It may be necessary to require the probationer to live at home, not to live at home, or to live in some philanthropic institution, such as Waverly House in New York City, or the Boys' Hotel in Kansas City.

Payment of restitution, fines, or costs is frequently a part of the requirement. Though restitution or reparation is a valuable requirement in many cases, two objections have been made regarding the method by which this is enforced: first, probationers may be required to pay so much that their dependents suffer seriously;[9] second, this frequently interferes with other work of the probation department and makes it primarily a collecting agency. The average probation officer in New York collected about $8,000 in this way in 1938, and this amount was frequently secured in very

---

[9] For cases of this kind see New York, *Report of State Probation Commission,* 1916, p. 35.

small sums. In 1915 the work of collection was transferred in Buffalo to the cashier of the court; this seems to be a desirable method of relieving the probation officers of the work.

The maximum probationary period is generally fixed by law and is the same as the maximum prison sentence for the offense. Within that limit the court may fix the period of probation, and after fixing it once may subsequently alter it. The average period of probation of those convicted of felonies in New York State in 1918 was twenty-one months, of those convicted of misdemeanors fourteen months. In many states the average for all offenders is less than one year. It appears desirable to have absolutely indeterminate probation, with no fixed maximum. Some individuals can get along satisfactorily in the community as long as they have the supervision of a probation officer but fall into crime as soon as this is withdrawn. The following case is an illustration of this.

A man who was a good workman, married, with several children, was involved repeatedly in dishonest transactions. "He was placed on probation for a year. After a few months of temporary jobs, his probation officer got him steady work. From then on he improved, receiving an advance in wage and then the promise of a foremanship. To the delight of his wife, his interest in his children awakened. The man himself said he owed all to the probation officer, who, as he observed, was wonderful in his understanding of men. Unfortunately for this fellow, probation terms end. At last accounts he had disappeared, leaving his children to be supported by charity. While under the supervision of a man of good standards this man could keep straight. Without that brace he went to pieces."[10]

The probation officer has the duty of informing the court if the probationer does not maintain the conditions imposed upon him. The court may then warn the probationer or impose a sentence for the original offense, in which case the time served on probation need not be counted as a part of the prison term. In many states the probationer is automatically taken off probation if he is convicted of a new crime or is arrested for a new crime. The Massachusetts Commission on Probation, however, states the following principle:

[10] Mary E. Richmond, *Social Diagnosis*, New York, 1917, p. 70. Reprinted by permission of Russell Sage Foundation, publishers.

The best practice seems to be to treat any new offense during the term of probation only as an indication of the conduct of the probationer, bearing upon the question of his continuance on probation.[11]

If the probationer maintains the conditions imposed upon him, discharge from probation may come automatically at the end of the probationary period in some states, or the court may discharge him before or at the end of the period in some states, or the probation officer may discharge him without court action in some states. The New York Probation Commission insists that the discharge should always be made by the court, since this tends

to impress the probationer with the authority and clemency of the court and to encourage and fortify him in his efforts to make good.[12]

THE PROBATION OFFICER. One of the first questions that arose regarding the probation officers was, Should they be volunteers or paid officers? In various places volunteers were used exclusively, sometimes with good results at first, as in Indianapolis,[13] sometimes with poor results from the first.[14] Judge S. W. Greene of the Juvenile Court of Louisville stated in 1916, "The men as volunteer probation officers are a dismal failure,"[15] and J. J. Kingsbury, chief probation officer of Buffalo, said in 1914,

I have about fifteen or twenty Polish volunteer probation officers. About four of them are really interested in the work. One of them, when I spoke to him about his laxity, said, "Oh, if I had my way, I would take a club and hit them on the head and get rid of them that way."[16]

The best results from volunteers are probably secured when offenders are placed on probation to organizations. After considerable

---

[11] *Massachusetts Prob. Manual,* 1916, p. 18.
[12] New York, State Probation Commission, *Methods of Supervising Persons on Probation,* Albany, 1918, p. 64.
[13] Lucy C. Bartlett, "The Value of Volunteers in Probation Work," *Charities,* 14:955–957, July 29, 1905.
[14] C. R. Henderson (Editor), *Correction and Prevention,* Vol. IV, *Preventive Treatment of Neglected Children,* by H. H. Hart, pp. 351–352.
[15] S. W. Greene, "Probation in the Juvenile Court," *Proc. Natl. Prob. Assoc.,* 1916, p. 77.
[16] New York, *Report of State Probation Commission,* 1914, p. 152.

experience with volunteer probation officers, the conclusion is fairly unanimous that probation work should be administered by paid officers, who may be assisted in special work or in special circumstances by volunteers working under the direction of the paid officers.

Not many of the paid probation officers have a high degree of efficiency. This is due to the fact that probation work is new, few persons have been trained for the work, the importance of skill is not realized, salaries are small, and the positions are sometimes used as rewards for political service. Few trained probation officers are found outside of large cities, and even in these cities many of the officers have had no training. In small towns the position may be given to the mayor, the sheriff, the chief of the police department or fire department, the widow of a prominent citizen, a cripple, or a superannuated person. The average period of service of probation officers working in Massachusetts in 1922 was nine and nine-tenths years, with 10 per cent having periods of more than twenty years.

NUMBER OF PROBATIONERS PER OFFICER. Fifty probationers is now generally regarded as the maximum number for one officer, provided he has a densely populated territory and can give his entire time to supervision. The number should be less than fifty if he has a rural territory or has work other than supervision. In practice many probation officers have several times that number of probationers under supervision. Intensive supervision then becomes impossible. If offenders do not need supervision they should not be placed on probation; if they do need supervision, the number under the care of one officer should be restricted so that supervision will mean something.

ASSIGNMENT OF PROBATIONERS. Three systems of probation assignments are used: by districts, by sex, race, or religion, and by problems. The first method, which is used most frequently, gives to one officer all probationers living in a particular district. The second method makes assignments of male probationers to male officers, female probationers to female officers, and similarly for race and religion. Flexner and Baldwin state that probation work among Jewish or Polish people is reported to be successful only when the officers speak those languages easily.[17] The specialization

17 B. Flexner and R. N. Baldwin, *Juvenile Courts and Probation*, New York, 1916, p. 145.

of probation work by problems has not developed far. L. N. Robinson, however, stated the ideal thus:

It seems to me that we will unquestionably get away little by little from the practice of assigning probationers to probation officers by districts, or by sex, or by race, or by religion, and assign them according to the function for which the probation officer has been trained. . . . The child needs something more than a good natured friend; he needs skilled direction.[18]

DIAGNOSIS. Present procedure places the work of diagnosis almost entirely upon the probation officer. The probation officer in most jurisdictions knows practically nothing about the probationer who is assigned to him. He secures certain items of information during the course of the probation period and gradually builds up a more or less definite diagnosis of the difficulty. He is not an expert at diagnosis; he knows very little about the methods of determining feeblemindedness, psychopathy, temperament, attitudes, or other traits. And he does not have the time to make the home visits and other visits necessary to supplement the superficial impressions that may be gained from conversation with the probationer.

Evidently the procedure is quite wrong. The diagnosis should be made before the offender is admitted to probation. This is necessary, first, in order to determine whether he should be placed on probation, and, second, in order to determine the policies that should be used by the probation officer. Such a study should be made by experts in diagnosis, who should specialize in that work. Though the method of making such studies has not been definitely standardized and the importance of such studies has not been generally realized, it is clear that probation work would be greatly improved if it could be based on such studies. Until it has such a basis, it cannot be a technical or scientific procedure and must be largely kind-hearted assistance.

CONTACTS BETWEEN PROBATION OFFICER AND PROBATIONER. Contacts between the probation officer and the probationer are generally made either in the office of the probation officer or the home of the probationer. Home visits are regarded as desirable because they enable the probation officer to come into contact with this most

---

[18] L. N. Robinson, "Standards of Child Welfare," *U. S. Children's Bur.*, No. 60, p. 377.

important part of the environment of the offender, thus making possible a better understanding of the offender. In addition, as has been said by a probation officer:

When you undertake to make over the average delinquent your work will be one-fourth reforming him and three-fourths reforming his family.[19]

The New York Probation Commission fixed one home visit every two weeks as the standard; the same standard was accepted by the committee appointed to formulate juvenile court standards. In practice, home visits are much less frequent than this. The average interval between home vistis in New York State in 1928 was seven weeks, and the average length of visits in 1917 was between ten and fifteen minutes. The probation officer who visits a probationer once a month and spends ten minutes at each visit cannot be, from the point of view of the frequency of contacts, a very important influence. He is in contact with the probationer during one 43,200th part of the month, while many of the companions of the probationer are with him almost constantly during the waking hours. In 1928 the average number of visits per year to one probationer ranged from zero in some courts to twenty-nine in others, with a general average of seven and five-tenths for the state. While some officers make visits as frequently as once in two weeks, others never make such visits. One officer in New York State reported that he "never has to visit them," another that he visited "only when in the neighborhood," and another "only when complaints are received." Some officers are opposed to home visits because of the neighborhood gossip or special conditions in the home. The number of home visits to federal probationers, also, is very small. In 1933 the average was 1.6 visits per year with a maximum of 8.4 times.

Most probationers are required by the order of the court to report at regular intervals to the probation officer in his office or some other place selected by him. Sometimes these reports are made once a week, sometimes once a month; at one time in Detroit the probationers who were not working were required to report daily. The New York Probation Commission recommended that, with some exceptions, weekly reports be required in the first part of the pro-

[19] Julia Houston, *Proc. Natl. Prob. Assoc.,* 1916, p. 119.

bation period, and that the frequency of the reports be decreased in the last part of that period.

The procedure in making these reports varies widely. In some places the officer merely checks a card which the probationer hands through a window to him. This was the method used in Buffalo in 1911 when sixteen probationers reported in eight minutes. The average time required in New York State is about ten minutes for one report. In the less perfunctory reports the officer asks the probationer regarding his work, companions, recreations, habits, and other things; he gives advice on many topics—economic, family, legal, habits, reading, self-improvement, etc. The probationers are frequently required to bring written reports, such as school reports, reports from employers, receipts for payment toward the support of the family or for restitution or reparation.

Opinions regarding the value of these reports differ. The New York Probation Commission found that only eight of the 165 probation officers of the State disapproved or had doubt of the method and only one opposed it unequivocally.[20] These office reports were not required in 1920 in five out of fifty-nine principal probation departments in the United States—Seattle Juvenile Court, Louisville Juvenile Court, Chicago Juvenile Court, Boston Municipal Court, and Boston Superior Court. Aside from the very evident facts that such reports are a means of securing information about probationers, that they offer an opportunity for privacy which frequently cannot be secured in the home, and that they enable a probation officer to see a much larger number of probationers in a given period, the principal argument advanced in favor of them is their disciplinary value.

The greatest value of reporting is the discipline involved in it.[21]

Reporting "ordinarily involves some inconvenience to himself and has accordingly distinct disciplinary value."[22]

This argument is not impressive; it is based on the logic of imprisonment rather than of probation. It represents a conviction that

---

[20] New York, State Probation Commission, *Methods of Supervising Persons on Probation*, Albany, 1918, p. 23.

[21] C. L. Chute, "Probation in Children's Courts," *U. S. Children's Bur.*, No. 80, p. 21.

[22] Mabel B. Ellis, *Report of New York State Probation Commission*, 1917, p. 261.

reformation is produced by suffering, inconvenience, and compulsory performance. If offenders can be reformed in that way, they should be sent to prison where they can be compelled to obey rules, be punctual, and suffer inconvenience. In addition, those who favor the method of reporting assert that the courts which have abandoned the formal reports have not increased the frequency of home visits.

Those who oppose the formal reports maintain that such methods of discipline are relatively useless, and that, in fact, they irritate and alienate the probationer, thus reducing the efficiency of other methods; also, that the office report must be checked by outside investigation, since the statements of the probationer cannot be trusted, especially in the early part of the probation period. Again, the system of reports in offices isolates the offender from the situation of which he is a part and attempts to alter him while the rest of the situation remains fixed. This is methodologically unsound. A final objection is that this system results in the assembling of probationers in the places in which they report and this is regarded as conducive to continued delinquency. Some of those who favor the system of office reports deny that this mingling is injurious. Judge Lindsey, for instance, insisted that since the probationers have to meet other offenders in schools and places of employment and of recreation, no injury will result from contacts in the places in which reports are made. The other advocates of this system generally state that the mingling of probationers is undesirable, but can be reduced to a minimum by having district rather than central offices, fixing a definite time at which each probationer should report, having several waiting rooms, or requiring that those in the waiting room sit at least three feet from each other and maintain silence.[23]

In general the office reports appear to be relatively unimportant. Home visits are certainly much more important. It would be preferable to have office reports once in two weeks and home visits once a week rather than reverse the frequencies.

TREATMENT. The word "treatment" refers to the efforts of the probation officer to assist the probationer. The word is unsatisfactory, for most of the efforts are or should be educational, and we do not like to think of education as "treatment." But no better word has been found.

---

[23] New York, *op. cit.*, pp. 19–21.

The important function of the probation officer is to change the attitude of the probationer. Miss Maude Miner has stated the purpose as follows:

The most important work of the probation officer, I take it, is not merely finding work for a probationer or visiting the girl in her home, but it is helping to change the point of view of that young woman so that she is going to look at life in a different way.[24]

A scientific technique for the modification of attitudes has yet to be stated. One prominent judge in the rural part of a Central Western state made a statement in 1926 as follows:

Many children are inclined to become as delinquent as they think they are permitted to go. We adults do not want to commit them to institutions, so we place them on probation. I do not know how it is in the city but in the rural community the way the probation officer produces his results on the probationers is by bluffing and kidding them along. By bluff here I mean make use of the threat of sending them to the institution.

Probably practice is far ahead of any formulated theory. A great deal of information of this kind is "in the heads" of probation officers, but little has found its way into the records or reports or conferences of probation officers. Instead of descriptions of technique we find such statements as the following, "by gaining the confidence and friendship of the young man," "through friendly admonition and encouragement," "by stimulating the probationer's self-respect, ambition and thrift." It is necessary to know just how ambition is stimulated or just how confidence is secured. Unfortunately the New York Probation Commission, in its study of the methods of supervising persons on probation, did not secure any information on these technical processes, but confined its investigation entirely to the machinery of probation.

In the absence of a specific technique for the modification of attitudes, the general principle which is involved may be recalled. The attitudes of the individual are largely a product of social contacts. The contacts that are of the greatest importance in determin-

---

[24] Maude E. Miner, "Probation Work with Girls," *Proc. Natl. Prob. Assoc.,* 1916, p. 104.

ing attitudes are those that are frequent and intimate, as in the play-groups, the family, the neighborhood. Because the offender has been isolated from what is generally regarded as law-abiding society, that group has not had much influence on him. The technique of reformation consists essentially in changing or enlarging the group relations, either by making the probationer feel that the probation officer is one of his intimate associates, or by inducing some other individual (a Big Brother or Big Sister or an ordinary friend) to take the same attitude, or by inducing some club, settlement, church, or other organization to include him in their activities, or by inducing the probationer to read, which is a method of producing contacts with other groups.

Among the methods of getting the probation officer and the probationer into the same group the following may be mentioned:

Be sure you don't talk *at* the boys, or even *to* the boys. Talk *with* the boys. Think their thoughts. Get down . . . to their intellectual perspective. Touch them just where they are in their own words and ideas. Never use your own forms of speech if you can help it. Talk slang. Be a boy. Be one of them.[25]

The best way to reach a girl is to take her to the theater or museum, or invite her to one's home in a social way. More things are told and confided and a better insight obtained than by a dozen "reports."[26]

Up to date the probation officers have secured a good deal of prestige in the eyes of the probationers by material assistance, such as jobs, relief, vocational guidance, etc. Ninety per cent of the probation officers of New York State gave assistance in securing jobs, assisting about a tenth of the probationers in good times, and about two-thirds in very difficult times. Eight probation departments out of fifty-nine studied in the United States tried to maintain regular employment agencies. In Hudson County, New Jersey, two of the probation officers are nurses. The New York City Probation Department at one time maintained a vocational guidance bureau. In many states the probation officers administer relief, either mothers' pension or other relief. In Massachusetts since 1914 probation officers have been authorized to use county funds under

25 Quoted by Chute, *op. cit.* p. 17.
26 *Ibid.*

certain circumstances for the temporary assistance of probationers. Though these efforts at assistance constitute a bond between the probationer and the probation officer, this work should be done by other agencies to which the probation officer has introduced the probationer, such as the schools, departments of health, or employment agencies, rather than by the probation departments.

Probationers are sometimes induced and sometimes compelled to save money. In Los Angeles the judge required the probationer to deposit a specified portion of his earnings in a savings bank. During the war many judges required probationers to purchase thrift stamps. In 1918 about $3,000 worth of thrift stamps were purchased by probationers in Syracuse, New York, and about $2,000 worth in Niagara Falls. But it would be preferable to elicit the interest of the probationer in saving.

Many probation officers give some attention to the direction of the spare-time activities of the probationers. But Thurston found in Cleveland that this attention did not go to the length of an effort to develop an attractive and practical program for the spare-time activities of any delinquent child.[27] The same condition was found to exist in 1923 in Rochester, New York. It is clear that the probation officer should work for an organized direction of recreation for the entire population.

Much of the effective work of the probation officer consists in getting a probationer affiliated with some group.

The individual probation officer is not the agent in himself for bettering a child's condition. The most effective probation work that I have ever come in contact with is the result of tying a probationer up to the constructive forces of the community; for instance, in getting the boy into a club, a girl into a sewing circle, etc.[28]

An attempt to secure the co-operation of such groups was not made in 73 per cent of the cases of probation from the Manhattan Children's Court in 1912–1913. Frequently when an offender is permitted to remain physically in a group he is ostracized socially. It is seldom that the offender can be included in the ordinary

---

[27] H. W. Thurston, *Delinquency and Spare Time*, Cleveland, 1918, p. 121.
[28] New York, *Report of State Probation Commission*, 1912, p. 281; see also, New York, State Probation Commission, *Methods of Supervising Persons on Probation*, Albany, 1918, pp. 36–38.

friendly neighborhood associations or groups. Because of the difficulty of inducing ordinary groups to include the probationers, some
probation officers have attempted to form groups of their own, such
as a boys' club composed of probationers. The following is a
description of such a group in Yonkers, New York, where about
thirty school-boys were required to report to the probation officer
on Friday afternoons:

"There was a mutual exchange of friendly salutations, and after
making their reports the boys lingered in the room to talk and play
games. Often ex-probationers want to continue to come, and boys who
have never been on probation have asked for probation cards in order
that they might join the games." This officer also takes his probationers on walks and joins in their sports. Last summer for two weeks he
had a camp about twenty miles from Yonkers, composed of about
twenty boys who were probationers or ex-probationers.[29]

Though such groups are dangerous in some respects and have
been generally abandoned by the more developed probation departments, it is not impossible to make them distinctly useful.
. One of the essential methods is to work on the web of relations
of the offender. He is what he is because of those relations, and in
order to alter him fundamentally and permanently it is desirable
either to remove him from the relations or to alter the relations.
It is easier to move the individual, but it is more profitable, in the
long run, to alter the situation. The probation officer has an excellent opportunity to alter the home, and can frequently extend his
efforts beyond that to the neighborhood. The most effective work
of the probation officer must be in securing the co-operation of
other agencies interested in altering such situations.
Some probation officers and judges would rely on the fear of
punishment as preferable to the constructive efforts previously described. The following statements, the first by a probation officer
and the second by a judge, illustrate this attitude:

I suppose we have all discovered if the jail were not behind us our
conversation with the probationer might not be as effective as it is.[30]

---

[29] New York, *Report of State Probation Commission,* 1907, p. 78.
[30] *Ibid.,* 1914, p. 187.

The fear of punishment has played a very important part in the production of our present civilization, and I am not one of those who believe that it can be dispensed with. A wholesome fear of the probation officer and of the consequences of disobeying his or her directions is, in my opinion, worth more than a whole lot of advice. . . . Keep your probationer at arm's length.[31]

Some fear of the probation officer and of the prison is inevitable, but the effect of it is to set up social distance between the probationer and the probation officer. The logic of that argument leads to universal imprisonment of offenders. The logic of probation is that it is not the fear of punishment but contacts and assimilation and incorporation of the offender in normal groups that will be most effective in modifying his behavior.

ORGANIZATION OF THE PROBATION DEPARTMENT. Two agencies have been suggested as the proper bodies to control probation work: the court, and an independent administrative body. Characteristically the control of probation work is in the hands of the court. The reason for this is that probation originated in the suspended sentence and hence is regarded as an extension of the judicial function. This has carried with it the decision in some states that probation officers can be appointed by no agency except the court.[32] This method of control is justified, also, by the argument that the politicians would have more difficulty in influencing a probation department organized in this manner. The objections to the method are: First, the work of supervision is essentially administrative, not judicial. There is no more reason for having probation administered by the courts than for having prisons or reformatories so administered. Second, the judge is not able to handle this administrative work efficiently. He has other duties which interfere with his supervision of probation, and the probation department really becomes an independent administrative body. Consequently there has been a trend toward the other method of appointment and supervision of probation officers. In Utah, Rhode Island, Vermont, and Wisconsin adult probation officers are appointed by a state board which controls probation, in Michigan by the governor on recommendation of the judges, and in Maine upon recommendation of the council. Six states require competitive examinations for

---

[31] New York, *Report of State Probation Commission,* 1911, p. 283.
[32] Witter v. Cook County Commissioners, 256 Ill. 616.

the appointment of probation officers and other states, by agreement with the court, have the same requirement.

A second question regarding the organization of probation work is the relation of the state to the locality. Should probation be controlled by municipality, county, or state? Should the state administer or merely inspect probation work? Approximately half of the states have a state board which either administers probation or supervises it. The theory of probation workers is that the administration of probation should be a function of the state. In 1932 the state had complete control of probation supervision in four states— Rhode Island, Utah, Vermont, and Wisconsin; in seventeen states a state department had supervision over the local probation officers, while six other states had restricted powers of requiring reports of various kinds. Rhode Island first developed state supervision in 1899; five states had state supervision by 1910, nine by 1920, and twenty-seven by 1931. In the states which have a strongly centralized system the greatest progress has been made in probation. The State Probation Commission of New York carries on campaigns for the extension of the probation system, makes investigations of the work of the local probation officers, secures publicity for such reports, and develops standards. The agents of the Commission secure monthly reports from all probation officers, and make visits at least once a year to the important probation offices. It has published a manual for the guidance of probation officers. It holds two conferences annually, one for probation officers and one for the judges of the inferior courts. By such efforts the probation work of the state is being raised to the level of the best methods known. While the probation work in some communities in New York amounts to almost nothing, the methods in rural districts of that state in general are decidedly superior to those in states that have no such state department. If the control is to be retained, as at present, by local organizations, each state should have a probation department that would at least do as much as has been done in New York. In the long run, however, it would appear to be preferable to place complete control over the probation work of the state in the hands of a state department.

The probation departments in the different states should co-operate to produce greater uniformity and progress. Such co-operation is now secured to some extent by means of the National Probation Association. In addition, some specific agreements have been made.

An instance is the agreement dating from 1917 that the probation departments in the principal cities will supervise probationers moving into their cities from other districts. In 1937 twenty-five states entered into interstate compacts for supervision of probationers and parolees from other states.

A third problem of the organization of probation work is the unofficial work. Should probation officers be permitted or encouraged to take cases which are not transmitted to them by court action? As a matter of fact, many probation officers do an immense amount of this unofficial work. As soon as parents and others know that a person is a probation officer they go directly to him for consultation and advice regarding problems such as the control of children, non-support, and tendencies toward immorality.

RECORDS AND REPORTS. Proper case records are of great value both for the control of procedure in a particular case and for research and more general control.[33] Yet all investigations show that the records of the probation officers are inadequate in a considerable proportion of the courts. The technique of case-recording has not yet been perfected, but it is evident that the records must contain much information regarding the attitudes of the probationers, even if this is stated only in unprecise and unstandardized terms.

All probation officers of the state should be required to send regular reports to a state board or commission, which should publish annual reports of the work of the entire state. These annual reports should contain the facts that are more easily standardized, such as the number of probationers per officer, the number of home visits per probationer, and the general outcome in each case.

SUCCESSES AND FAILURES ON PROBATION. Probation departments generally report that about 75 per cent of their probationers succeed on probation and only 25 per cent commit new crimes or disappear. This percentage is, of course, a very rough average of the reports of many departments in many different years. Even in this sense it is inadequate in at least three respects. First, the number reported to be failures is incomplete because the probation officer is not in sufficiently close contact with his probationers to know how many of them become delinquent, and also because the identification records of police departments are so restricted that they do not adequately supplement the knowledge of the probation officer. Frequent reports are made of probationers who without the

---

[33] Ada E. Sheffield, *The Social Case History*, New York, 1920.

knowledge of the probation officer are arrested or even who serve short terms in institutions while on probation for another offense. These inadequacies in the official records are being corrected in some jurisdictions. In general the departments which have the reputation of doing the best probation work show the smallest proportion of successes, due to the fact that they have more complete information regarding the behavior of their probationers than do the departments which are doing their work in a less satisfactory manner.

Second, the value of probation should be determined by comparing it with the alternative methods of dealing with offenders. Probation is generally a substitute either for discharge without supervision, or else for imprisonment. A few efforts have been made to measure the results of probation by comparing subsequent behavior of persons placed on probation and those committed to institutions. It was found in Baltimore, for instance, that 29 per cent of the offenders placed on probation had subsequent convictions, as compared with 31 per cent of those who were committed to institutions.[34] This shows no significant difference between the results of probation and of imprisonment, but the method of selection of cases and the methods used in the study are not defined with complete clarity. Similar studies are needed before a conclusion is reached.

Third, the statistics of probation departments are confined to behavior during the period of probation and do not include the behavior subsequent to release from probation. Several studies have been made for the purpose of supplying this information. A study of 200 former probationers in Erie County, New York, in 1920, showed that 72 per cent of those who had been reported as successful during probation remained successful during the subsequent period.[35] A study of 383 adult probationers in Massachusetts who had been convicted in 1915 of "general offenses" (that is, all offenses except drunkenness, vagrancy, and non-support), showed that by 1923 12 per cent had been committed to institutions, and an additional 23 per cent had court records without commitments to institutions. Of those who had not been committed during the period of probation, 97 per cent had no subsequent commitments

[34] J. M. Hepbron, "Probation and Penal Treatment in Baltimore," *Jour. Crim. Law and Criminol.*, 19:64–74, May, 1928.
[35] New York, *Report of State Probation Commission*, 1920, p. 31.

and 76 per cent had no subsequent court records.[36] Among those placed on probation in 1915 for drunkenness, 60 per cent had subsequent court records. Among the juvenile probationers 43 per cent had subsequent records within seven years. These studies show that the number of failures is not greatly increased after the end of the probation period. It may be indicated that the outcomes of probationers could be determined much more reliably if a universal fingerprint system were adopted in the United States, so that every arrest of a person on probation or subsequent to release from probation could be known.

Conclusions regarding the value of probation are sometimes erroneously based on the number of ex-probationers committed to penal or reformatory institutions. In 1923 43 per cent of the admissions to institutions for juvenile delinquents had been preceded by probation; this percentage varied from 88 in Rhode Island, 73 in Michigan, and 66 in Massachusetts to 6 in Illinois and 1 in Nebraska. This does not justify a conclusion that probation is a comparative failure in Rhode Island, Michigan, and Massachusetts and a comparative success in Illinois and Nebraska, for it shows nothing whatever regarding the number of probationers who did not appear subsequently in institutions.

That extensive use of probation does not in itself result in an immense increase of serious crimes is shown by the fact that the number of burglaries and robberies known to the police in Massachusetts and New York, where probation is used extensively, is much lower per 100,000 population than in other parts of the United States.

CONDITIONS OF SUCCESS AND FAILURE ON PROBATION. Almost everyone admits that probation should be used to some extent. The important question, therefore, is not whether probation in general is a success or a failure, but what types of offenders succeed on probation and under what conditions probationers succeed. Three intensive studies on this point contain organized information, and in addition scattered bits of information are contained in many other studies.[37] These studies agree in the conclusion that the high-

---

[36] Massachusetts, Commission on Probation, *Report on an Inquiry into the Permanent Results of Probation*. Mass. Sen. Doc. 431, 1924.

[37] Massachusetts, Commission on Probation, *Report on an Inquiry into the Permanent Results of Probation*, 1924; E. D. Monachesi, *Prediction Factors in Probation*, Hanover, N. H., 1932; C. H. Young, *Prediction in Probation in the Boys' Court in Chicago*. (Mss.)

est rates of violation of probation are found among the probationers who had previous criminal records, previous records of irregular work, low economic status, low occupational level, residence in deteriorated neighborhoods, families with records of crime or vice, immoral associates, great mobility in residences, and few or irregular contacts with schools and churches. Young, for instance, found that among the probationers from the Boys' Court in Chicago 50.3 per cent of those who resided in the areas with the highest delinquency rates violated probation, as compared with 31.2 per cent of those who resided in the areas of lowest delinquency rates.

These studies make specific the general proposition that the probationers who have better previous records and better social backgrounds violate probation least frequently. This specific information is being organized in statistical form in order that the court may have a basis of information on which to determine whether an offender should be placed on probation, and in order that the probation officer may have a basis of information on which to determine probation policies. This information, furthermore, should be of value to the legislature in deciding what types of offenders should be eligible for probation. Studies of this nature have been carried somewhat further in regard to parole than in regard to probation, and the method is actually being used by the parole board of Illinois at the present time. Plans are being developed for the use of such actuarial methods in probation in the Recorder's Court in Detroit. It is evident that the information regarding probation is not adequate at present from the point of view of reliability, classifications, or significance, but these defects can be corrected.

ADVANTAGES OF PROBATION. The advocates of probation do not insist that all offenders should be placed on probation, but rather that certain types of offenders will get along better and do less injury to society if they are placed on probation than if they are imprisoned or are dismissed without supervision. The probation policy enables these offenders to remain in the general society, which is the best situation in which to develop character, and at the same time to receive assistance in adapting themselves to the conditions of life, so that they will not be so impotent in struggling against the conditions which produced the delinquency.

Probation, furthermore, has the advantage that the probationer, being at liberty, has a better opportunity to make payments toward the support of his family or toward reparation or restitution. In 1931 probationers in Massachusetts paid, through the probation officers, $1,517,151 toward the support of their families, and $148,374 in reparation and restitution, and in New York in 1932 they paid over $3,500,000 directly or through the probation officers in family support, fines, and restitution.

Probation officers, while assisting their charges, attempt to modify the family or neighborhood situations that are producing delinquency. Thus, by their own efforts, the co-operation of other agencies, and the public opinion which they develop, they are instruments for the prevention of crime. In this way, as well as by producing reformation in the probationers, probation should be regarded as one of the deterrent agencies in modern society. Orthodox theory assumed that the only way to prevent crime was by severe punishment of those convicted, but other methods also may be useful in this respect. Moreover, probation not only represents a change but is producing a further change in the attitude of vengeance. The more the group, through its agents, uses the method of constructive assistance, the more rapidly will the desire for vengeance be dissipated. One of the values of probation, therefore, is its purifying effect on the group.

Probation, as now operated, is very much cheaper than imprisonment. In New York the current cost of imprisonment is eighteen times as much as probation per offender dealt with under each system, and in Massachusetts ten times as much. Probation would cost more if it were properly administered and might be quite as expensive, in financial costs, as imprisonment. The value of the system, therefore, is its effect on personality rather than its effect on financial expenditures.

OBJECTIONS TO PROBATION. Certain objections have been raised against probation, of which the most important are the following: (a) probation decreases the average penalty for crime and therefore tends to increase crime; (b) probation is a method by which crimes are "fixed" and therefore is an encouragement to criminals; (c) probation replaces the offender in the environment which produced him and is not likely to modify his behavior; (d) probation does not satisfy the desire for revenge and therefore tends to eliminate the incentive for prosecution.

The first and second of these objections are found most frequently in the newspapers and probably represent public suspicions to some extent. They are, however, less serious objections than the other two. The first objection is a reflection of the classical theory of crime which, as has been shown previously, has little basis in fact. The second objection undoubtedly describes a practice which is used occasionally; this practice, however, is not widespread, for if the offender has money or political influence and is dealing with officials who are corrupt, the case can be fixed more easily and with less publicity before it reaches the court. It is at these earlier stages that most cases are "fixed."

The argument that probation does not alter the environment of the offender is a sound argument and is presented primarily by those who insist that case work must be expanded to include the larger community if it is to be effective. It is not an argument against probation, but against the specific methods of probationary work. While it is not possible to place a neighborhood on probation by order of the court, the procedure demanded by these persons would be indicated by the type of work required if a neighborhood could be so placed on probation.

The last of these objections requires additional comment. Professor Kocourek advances that argument as follows: Support for prosecution must ordinarily be secured from the injured party and this support is given because of the desire for revenge. As probation increases, the number of injured persons who will be willing to go to the trouble of prosecuting offenders will decrease, because they will secure so little satisfaction from it. Though restitution may be made by probationers, this does not serve as a sufficient incentive to the injured party, since civil process is a much more certain means of securing restitution.[38]

But it is quite fallacious to assume that the desire for revenge is the only or the most important reason for prosecution. The general motive is to prevent a repetition of the offense. And many injured persons now refrain from prosecution because they feel that imprisonment will make a hardened and confirmed criminal of one who might be turned into a good citizen if constructive rather than punitive efforts were made; they would be much more willing to prosecute if they thought it would change the behavior of the offender. Moreover, if the courts can be speeded up and organized

[38] Albert Kocourek, "An Unconsidered Element in the Probation of First Offenders," *Jour. Crim. Law and Criminol.*, 6:9–17, May, 1915.

in a better way and the technicalities reduced, the number of persons, whether motivated by revenge or something else, who will be willing to appear in criminal trials will be greatly increased.

In so far as the motive is revenge, the method of probation has some advantages. In the first place, probation is a substitute for dismissal without oversight, as well as for imprisonment, and probation gives more satisfaction than dismissal. Secondly, the victim does not know in advance of the prosecution whether the offender will be placed on probation or committed to an institution. Also, he will secure some satisfaction even if the offender is placed on probation, for the desire for revenge is, to some extent, a desire to "show up" the offender in public and thus to vindicate himself. The amount of injury that must be inflicted in order to satisfy this desire for revenge is a distinct variable; a few centuries ago nothing except death of the offender would satisfy, at present imprisonment will generally satisfy, and there is no reason for doubting that a smaller amount of suffering would serve just as well.

Moreover, resort to civil courts will not generally serve the purpose of the victim. For, though the judgment of the court may be more certain if the process is civil, most of the offenders are impecunious and the judgment is worthless to the victim. The criminal court, with its combination of probation and restitution, is a more effective means of securing financial compensation for injury than the civil court in a large proportion of cases.

If all of these considerations amount to nothing, there is still the possibility of organizing the courts on the basis of social welfare rather than of revenge. In fact, a large proportion of criminal cases involve no particular injured party and in those cases the criminal court has already been organized on the basis of public welfare. The juvenile court, however, is much more completely organized in that way, for it is seldom that anyone appears in the juvenile court to "prosecute" the child. We may expect that the same development will occur in the courts for adults.

SUGGESTED READINGS

Beard, Belle B., *Juvenile Probation*, New York, 1934.

Belden, Evelina, "Courts in the United States Hearing Children's Cases," *U. S. Children's Bur.*, No. 65, Washington, D. C., 1920.

Bruce, A. A., "The Power to Suspend a Criminal Sentence for an Indefinite Period During Good Behavior," *Minn. Law Rev.*, 6:341–362, April, 1922.

Chute, C. L., "State Supervision of Probation Work," *Jour. Crim. Law and Criminol.*, 8:823–828, March, 1918.

Cooley, Edwin J., *Probation and Delinquency*, New York, 1927.

Flexner, B., and Baldwin, R. N., *Juvenile Courts and Probation*, New York, 1916.

Glueck, Sheldon (Editor), *Probation and Criminal Justice*, New York, 1932.

Grinnell, F. W., "Probation as an Orthodox Common-Law Practice in Massachusetts Prior to the Statutory System," *Mass. Law Quart.*, 2:591–639, August, 1917.

Halpern, I. W., *A Decade of Probation*, Court of General Sessions, New York, 1938.

Hart, H. H., and Others, "Report on Penal Institutions, Probation, and Parole," *Natl. Com. on Law Obs. and Enf.*, No. 9, 1931, pp. 146–169, 184–207.

Hiller, F. H., "Adult Probation Laws of the United States," *Natl. Prob. Assoc.*, New York, 1933.

Hiller, F. H., "Probation in Wisconsin," *Natl. Prob. Assoc.*, New York, 1926.

Hughes, Charles E., Jr., "Probation Progress," *Jour. Crim. Law and Criminol.*, 23:915–925, March, 1933.

Illinois, State Probation Office, *Probation Manual*, Springfield, 1932.

Indiana, Division of Probation, *Indiana Probation Handbook*, Indianapolis, 1936.

Johnson, Fred R., *Probation for Juveniles and Adults*, New York, 1928.

Kerr, J. M., "Judicial Parole against Sound Public Policy," *Amer. Law Rev.*, 55:512–528, July, 1921.

Kocourek, A., "An Unconsidered Element in the Probation of First Offenders," *Jour. Crim. Law and Criminol.*, 6:9–17, May, 1915.

MacBrayne, L. E., and Ramsay, J. P., *One More Chance*, Boston, 1916.

Massachusetts, Commission on Probation, *Report on an Inquiry into the Permanent Results of Probation*, Mass. Sen. Doc. 431, 1924.

Mead, B., "Evaluating the Results of Probation," *Jour. Crim. Law and Criminol.*, 23:631–638, November, 1932.

Monachesi, E. D., *Prediction Factors in Probation*, Hanover, N. H., 1932.

Moore, Joel R., "The United States Probation System," *Jour. Crim. Law and Criminol.*, 23:638–648, November, 1932.

National Commission on Law Observance and Enforcement, *Report on Penal Institutions, Probation, and Parole*, Washington, D. C., 1931.

National Probation Association, *Yearbook*.

New York, Commission to Investigate Prison Administration, *Probation in New York State*, Albany, 1933.

New York, State Probation Commission, *Manual for Probation Officers*, 1926.

New York, State Probation Commission, *Methods of Supervising Persons on Probation*, Albany, 1918.

Sutherland, Edwin H., "Probation in Minnesota," *Proc. Minn. Conf. Social Work*, 1927, pp. 219–229.

Trought, T. W., *Probation in Europe*, Oxford, 1927.

Williamson, Margaretta A., *The Social Worker in the Prevention and Treatment of Delinquency*, New York, 1935.

Young, Pauline V., *Social Treatment in Probation and Delinquency*, New York, 1937.

Chapter Twenty-One

HISTORY AND TRENDS OF PRISONS IN AMERICA

WE HAVE CONSIDERED previously the development of imprisonment until it became an established and generally used policy in England about the beginning of the nineteenth century. The present chapter continues this discussion with reference to the development of prisons in the United States, especially after the beginning of the nineteenth century.

EARLY AMERICAN PRISONS. Jails and houses of correction were established in the American colonies soon after settlement. The jail was designed originally for the retention of persons awaiting trial. It soon came to be used as a place of punishment after conviction. This change occurred primarily because of increasing opposition to the use of corporal punishments. Convicted drunkards and vagrants, especially, were confined in these institutions. The house of correction began as an institution for vagrants but before long was not different except in name from many of the jails. In Connecticut by an act of 1730 prisoners on life sentences were confined in the workhouse rather than in jails.[1] The number of persons confined either in jails or workhouses after conviction was very small. It was not until 1788 in New York State that a general law was passed for the use of jails or workhouses as places of punishment. Previously commitments to those institutions were made only by a special law in each case.[2]

The conditions in these jails and houses of correction were generally horrible. The prisoners spent their time in association, without labor, depending on charity for their maintenance. Drunkenness and vice generally prevailed in these institutions, as had been

---

[1] E. W. Capen, *The Historical Development of the Poor Law of Connecticut*, New York, 1905, p. 64.
[2] P. Klein, *Prison Methods in New York State*, New York, 1920, pp. 25–26.

411

customary in England. The following description of the Walnut Street (county) jail in Philadelphia at the end of the Revolutionary War could be duplicated with regard to many other institutions of the time.

It is represented as a scene of promiscuous and unrestricted intercourse, and universal riot and debauchery. There was no labor, no separation of those accused, but yet untried, nor even of those confined for debt only, from convicts sentenced for the foulest crimes; no separation of color, age or sex, by day or by night; the prisoners lying promiscuously on the floor, most of them without anything like bed or bedding. As soon as the sexes were placed in different wings, which was the first reform made in the prison, of thirty or forty women then confined there, all but four or five immediately left it; it having been a common practice, it is said, for women to cause themselves to be arrested for fictitious debts, that they might share in the orgies of the place. Intoxicating liquors abounded, and indeed were freely sold at a bar kept by one of the officers of the prison. Intercourse between the convicts and persons without was hardly restricted. Prisoners tried and acquitted were still detained till they should pay jail fees to the keeper; and the custom of garnish was established and unquestioned; that is, the custom of stripping every newcomer of his outer clothing, to be sold for liquor, unless redeemed by the payment of a sum of money to be applied to the same object. It need hardly be added, that there was no attempt to give any kind of instruction, and no religious service whatsoever.[3]

The Quakers of Philadelphia made decided efforts to improve these prisons. In 1776 Richard Wistar at his own expense provided soup for some of the prisoners in the county jail, when it became known that some of them had died of starvation. Others became interested in his efforts, and in that year the Philadelphia Society for Alleviating Distressed Prisoners was formed. Its activities were

---

[3] F. C. Gray, *Prison Discipline in America*, pp. 15–16. It has been reported frequently that when the first attempt was made to preach to the prisoners in this Walnut Street jail, the prison authorities remonstrated and opposed it for fear of an outbreak by the prisoners, but finally agreed on condition that the preacher leave all of his valuables outside and that a loaded cannon be placed facing the prisoners, with a man standing ready with a lighted fuse to touch it off. It seems probable that this was merely a device of the keeper of the prison to frighten the preacher rather than the prisoners. J. T. Scharf and T. Westcott, *History of Philadelphia*, Vol. I, pp. 444–445, note.

stopped by the war. It was revived in 1787 with the name Philadelphia Society for Alleviating the Miseries of Public Prisons. About half of its members were Quakers. It had the primary purpose of relieving the physical suffering of prisoners, but soon attempted, in addition, to reduce the number of capital penalties and substitute imprisonment in solitary confinement for the death penalty.

THE ORIGIN OF THE STATE PRISON. During the colonial period no institutions similar to the present state prison were established until, in 1773, Connecticut purchased an old mine near Simsbury and turned it into a prison. This was used by the state as a prison until 1827. Though it was the first state prison, the state has never taken great pride in it. The prisoners were fastened during the night by heavy chains attached to their necks at one end and the heavy beams above them at the other; in addition heavy iron bars were fixed to their feet. In 1785 Massachusetts provided that persons sentenced to solitary confinement and hard labor should serve the sentence in Castle Island, a military post in Boston harbor, instead of in the county jails and houses of correction, most of which were insecure. Massachusetts authorized a new state prison in 1803. The movement spread rapidly during the last part of the eighteenth and the first part of the nineteenth centuries. New York erected a state prison in 1796, New Jersey in 1798, Virginia in 1800, Vermont in 1808, Maryland in 1812, New Hampshire in 1812, and Ohio in 1816. The following inscription was placed over the door of the New Jersey state prison:

Labor, silence, penitence. 1797. That those who are feared for their crimes may learn to fear the laws and be useful. *Hic labor, hoc opus.*

The immediate motive for the erection of state prisons, as contrasted with county or other local prisons, was to obtain greater security for those sentenced to long terms of imprisonment. The number of prisoners with long sentences was increasing because of the development of opposition to the death penalty. Zephaniah Swift states that Connecticut authorized a state prison because of opposition to the death penalty and because no other substitute than long-term imprisonment could be found for the death penalty.[4]

---

[4] *A System of Laws of the State of Connecticut*, 1796, Vol. II, p. 295; L. N. Robinson, *Penology in the United States*, p. 69.

This motive stands out more clearly in Pennsylvania than in any other state. The constitution of that state in 1776 directed that imprisonment at hard labor be substituted for capital punishment. Immediately after the war, under the direction of Benjamin Rush, Benjamin Franklin, William Bradford, Caleb Lownes, and others, a plan was prepared, which was made law in 1786 and amended several times during the next decade. By these laws capital punishment was abolished for all crimes except murder, corporal punishment was abolished, and fines and imprisonments were the only penalties left. It was directed that imprisonment should be "with hard labor, public and disgracefully imposed." At first this resulted in gang labor on the streets with the prisoners restrained by ball-and-chain, dressed in a distinctive garb, and with heads shaved. They were soon returned to the prison because street labor was unsatisfactory. At this time the state had no prison of its own and therefore made an arrangement that the state prisoners be kept in the county jails; a part of the expenses of these institutions was paid from state funds. An unsuccessful attempt was made in 1803 to secure an institution exclusively for state prisoners, but it was not until 1818 that the effort succeeded.

In addition to this desire to obtain more secure places of confinement for long term prisoners, the hope that these prisoners, because they were confined for long periods, might be able to pay the expenses of the institution by their labor was instrumental in the development of the state prison. Doubtless, also, the growing state consciousness had something to do with it.

THE PENITENTIARY. About the time the state became interested in the maintenance of prisons of its own, a new conception of prison discipline appeared, which resulted in calling these institutions penitentiaries. The word "penitentiary" had a significance at that time which it has generally lost at the present, *viz.*, an institution to produce penitence or penitentiary reformation. There is no doubt that the medieval prisons under the control of the Church had this ideal and the same purpose was reflected in the law of England passed in 1778, authorizing a penitentiary. The purpose of this institution was stated by the law to be:

By sobriety, cleanliness, and medical assistance, by a regular series of labour, by solitary confinement during the intervals of work, and by due religious instruction to preserve and amend the health of the unhappy offenders, to inure them to habits of industry, to guard them from pernicious company, to accustom them to serious reflection and to teach them both the principles and practice of every Christian and moral duty.

This law was framed by Blackstone, Eden, and Howard. Howard stated:

The term penitentiary clearly shows that Parliament had chiefly in view the reformation and amendment of those to be committed to such places of confinement.

This institution was not erected, but the law undoubtedly influenced the Quakers of Pennsylvania. They developed not only a state prison, but also a new conception of prison discipline which made their institution and others modeled on it penitentiaries. These innovators looked upon imprisonment as, in itself, a sufficiently severe penalty, though many persons of the time did not so regard it. Judge Walworth, in declaring whipping in prison a proper punishment, in 1826 stated:

That confinement with labor merely had no terrors for the guilty; that the labor which the human body was capable of performing without endangering its health was but little more than many of the virtuous laboring class of the community daily and voluntarily perform, for the support and maintenance of their families; that to produce reformation in the guilty or to restrain the vicious from the perpetration of crime by the terrors of punishment, it was absolutely necessary that the convict should feel his degraded situation . . . ; that the system of discipline adopted by the inspectors under the sanction of the laws was well calculated to have the desired effect of reforming the less vicious offenders and of deterring others from the commission of crime . . . ; that it was, however, through terror of bodily suffering alone that the proper effect upon the mind of the convict was produced.[5]

THE PENNSYLVANIA SYSTEM. The prison leaders in Pennsylvania contended that the association of all types of criminals in prisons was disastrous. They suggested, as had been suggested fre-

[5] Quoted by Klein, *op. cit.*, p. 206.

quently for several centuries, that prisoners should be kept in solitary confinement. Arrangements for this were made in the Walnut Street jail, in which the state prisoners were confined. Solitary confinement, it was contended, not only prevented the disastrous association of criminals, but also had the positive virtue of forcing the prisoners to reflect on their crimes and therefore of producing reformation. During a part of the history of the system of solitary confinement the prisoners were not permitted to work at anything, and when they were permitted to work, the work was made subordinate to reflection. The authorities were afraid that work might prevent reflection. It was realized that this solitude would be injurious if too long continued, and provision was therefore made for association with the following official visitors: the governor of the state, the members of the state legislature, the judges of all courts, the mayors of Philadelphia, Pittsburgh, and Lancaster, the county commissioners and sheriffs, and a committee of the Philadelphia Society for Alleviating the Miseries of Public Prisons. The relation between the prisoners and these official visitors could not have been very intimate. The Committee of the Society did very well to average four and a half hours a year per prisoner, and their conversation was confined largely to theological exhortations. The solitude was not frequently broken, therefore. But it was argued that the effect of this solitude was to cause an appreciation of these good men when they did come.

The physical conditions in the old Walnut Street jail were very bad. The new prison erected in 1818 was decidedly superior in this respect to most of the other prisons of the country.

THE AUBURN SYSTEM. On the demand of Governor John Jay for the improvement of the criminal law of New York State, a commission was sent to Pennsylvania in 1794 to study the new system. After the report of this commission in 1796 a law was passed in New York, reducing the capital offenses to two, and substituting imprisonment for the death penalty and for corporal punishment. Two prisons were authorized, of which only one was built, and that one in New York City in 1797. This did not provide for solitary confinement. This institution proved to be inadequate and in 1816 another prison at Auburn was authorized, a part of which should be used for solitary confinement. By act of 1821 the prisoners in Auburn were divided into three classes: the first class, composed of the "oldest and most heinous offenders," were to be kept in solitary confinement continuously; those in the second class were to be kept in their cells three days a week; and the others one day a week. The cells were small and dark and no provision was made for work in the cells. This experiment with solitary confinement proved to be a great failure; of eighty prisoners who had been in solitary confinement continuously all except two were out of the prison within two years, as the result of death, insanity, or pardon. A legislative commission which investigated the policy in 1824 recommended that it be abandoned at once and this recommendation was adopted. Being now thoroughly opposed to the method of solitary confinement, which had not, however, been tried under as favorable conditions as in Pennsylvania, the Auburn authorities provided for work by the prisoners in association but in silence during the day and solitary confinement during the night. This has been known as the Auburn system, in contrast with the Pennsylvania system, which was solitary confinement by day and night.

THE CONTROVERSY BETWEEN THE AUBURN AND PENNSYLVANIA SYSTEMS. The literature of criminology during the forty years subsequent to the establishment of the Auburn system is devoted almost entirely to a hot controversy between these two systems. It was carried on largely by two prison reform associations: The Philadelphia Society, mentioned above, which supported the Pennsylvania system, and the Boston Society for the Improvement of Prison Discipline and for the Reformation of Juvenile Offenders, organized in 1815, which supported the Auburn system. Both societies were intensely interested in the reformation of offenders, both were convinced of the merits of their method and the demerits of the other method, and both were entirely unscrupulous in their use of statistics to prove their arguments. When Dickens, after a visit to America, wrote his American Notes, he included a severe arraignment of the Pennsylvania system, which still further increased the antagonism between the two parties in America.

The Pennsylvania system was tried in a number of the states, but was generally abandoned in favor of the Auburn system after a short trial. Probably the principal advantage, if not the only one, of the Auburn system was that it made possible a better utilization of the labor of the prisoners. European visitors, however, generally secured and carried away an impression that the Pennsylvania system was superior. In 1835 commissioners were sent from England,

France, Prussia, and Belgium to examine the American prison systems; they made their visits together and presented practically identical reports to their home governments in favor of the Pennsylvania system. These reports produced a great effect in Europe and most of the European countries adopted the Pennsylvania system in a modified form.

It seems clear at the present time that both systems were inefficient methods of realizing their objectives. The complete isolation of prisoners does not produce reformation, but the incomplete isolation which prevailed under the Auburn system is probably not much, if any, better.

The controversy between these two systems, after raging for more than half a century, was ended by the importation of a new system from Europe and Australia. This system was started in an organized manner in the Australian convict camps by Captain Maconochie. His methods were imported into Ireland and England and under the name of the Irish system became known to and were discussed by American leaders shortly before the Civil War. The Irish system consisted of the indeterminate sentence, the mark system as a method of measuring good behavior in prison, and parole. The first institution based on these methods was the Elmira Reformatory in New York, created by law in 1869 but not opened until 1876. Emphasis was placed on education, productive labor, the mark system, the indeterminate sentence, and parole. It is not correct to think of this as the first reformatory, for the penitentiaries three-quarters of a century earlier were designed to produce reformation. The reformatories had the same aim as the penitentiaries but differed in methods. The reformatory policy spread rather quickly to state prisons, so that it is now difficult to draw a line between state prisons and state reformatories so far as methods are concerned. Some state prisons use more definitely reformatory methods than some reformatories do.

JUVENILE REFORMATORIES AND INDUSTRIAL SCHOOLS. The first American institution for juvenile delinquents was opened in New York City in 1825 after more than a generation of discussion. It was under the control of a private society called the New York Association for the Prevention of Pauperism, but the state made annual grants for its maintenance. A similar institution under private control was started in Philadelphia in 1826. The first institution of this type under state control was started in Massachusetts in 1847. Even this institution received assistance from private funds. Seven institutions had been opened by 1850, thirty-two more by 1875, and sixty-six more by 1900. Though these institutions started and made their best progress in the early period under private control, the private institutions at present show no clear superiority to the public institutions. Several institutions have changed from private to public management though none has changed from public to private management.

From the first it was contended that these institutions were not penal institutions or prisons, but schools. The contention was supported by the courts, especially by the Supreme Court in a decision regarding the institution in Philadelphia in 1828. In certain respects they were distinctly different from the prisons; they had self-government, religious teaching, academic teaching, indeterminate sentence, release on good behavior, which was similar to parole, and many efforts were made to reform the delinquents by methods other than solitary confinement. In the second year of the New York House of Refuge the president of the board made the following statement which was quite opposed to the prevailing sentiment regarding penal institutions:

A child may be made quiet and industrious by beating, but it seldom happens, I believe, that kindheartedness, morality, and intelligence are induced by whipping.[6]

Some of these policies were only temporary, and in some respects from the time of their origin these institutions were practically prisons.

The earliest institutions for juvenile delinquents were organized under the dominance of the prison idea. . . . In all regards this was true; the establishments were distinctly prison enclosures, the dormitories were blocks of cells, the dining-rooms were chambers of silence, with only the meagerest provision of the rudest table furniture; the earning capacity of those confined was exploited to the highest possible figure, and education in letters was only provided for during such hours as could not be profitably employed in work; and the greatest

---

[6] B. K. Peirce, *A Half Century with Juvenile Delinquents, or the New York House of Refuge and Its Times*, New York, 1869, p. 120.

ambition and strongest claim for popular approval was a low per capita cost of maintenance.[7]

It seems probable, therefore, that, with temporary exceptions in regard to certain policies, these institutions were during the first half century of their history primarily prisons, and their principal value was that they removed juvenile prisoners from association with adult prisoners. Though it may properly be argued that these institutions have changed very much since that time and therefore are not prisons now, at least, it is clear that the ideal of the prison for adults has changed, also, and that in practice there is more that is penal in some institutions for juvenile delinquents than in some institutions for adult criminals.

One of the important developments in juvenile reformatories was the cottage system of architecture, in place of the old cell-block structure. The first example of the cottage system in America, which was copied from European systems, was the Ohio School for Boys at Lancaster, opened in 1865. This system won general approval and most of the state institutions have adopted a similar plan because of the more homelike surroundings and the greater ease of classification.

NUMBER AND SIZE OF PENAL AND REFORMATORY INSTITUTIONS. The exact number of penal and reformatory institutions cannot be determined, in part because no complete list of them has been made, in part because the several types of institutions cannot be differentiated. The approximate numbers are as follows: (a) 2,500 county jails, workhouses, farms, and chain gangs for offenders convicted of misdemeanors; (b) 1,500 municipal jails, workhouses, farms, and stockades for offenders convicted of misdemeanors; (c) 109 state prisons, state farms, and state chain gangs used primarily for persons convicted of felonies; (d) 25 state reformatories for young adult offenders convicted of felonies or serious misdemeanors; (e) 16 federal prisons, reformatories, and camps under the direction of the Bureau of Prisons, and 3 federal prisons under the direction of the Army and Navy; (f) 150 juvenile reformatories, of which 2 are federal, 93 state, 30 county or municipal, and 25 private. This makes a total of about 4,300 penal and reformatory institutions.

---

[7] F. H. Nibecker, "Education of Juvenile Delinquents," *Annals of Amer. Acad. of Pol. and Social Sci.*, 23:483, May, 1904.

The distribution of the inmates of these institutions (not including the army and navy prison, the private institutions for juveniles, and most of the city lockups) is shown for 1933, the date of the last report of all types of prisons, in Table VIII.

TABLE VIII
PRISONERS IN INSTITUTIONS IN 1933

CLASS OF INSTITUTION	PRESENT JAN. I		COMMITTED DURING 1933	
	Number	Per Cent	Number	Per Cent
Total	233,631	100.0	693,988	100.0
Federal prisons and camps.......	12,276	5.2	8,333	1.2
State prisons and reformatories....	137,721	59.0	59,204	8.5
County and city jails............	51,436	22.0	608,484	87.7
Juvenile reformatories	32,198	13.8	17,967	2.6

The average number of prisoners on January 1, 1933, was about 12 per county or municipal prison, 1,000 per state prison or reformatory, 1,000 per federal prison, and 210 per juvenile reformatory. The average period of incarceration was about five weeks in county and municipal prisons, two and a third years in state prisons and reformatories, eighteen months in federal prisons, and twenty-two months in juvenile reformatories. About 64 per cent of the prisoners serving sentences in institutions at a particular time are in state or federal institutions for felons, and about 88 per cent of the inmates committed on sentences during a year are committed to municipal or county institutions for misdemeanants. On January 1, 1936, 14,762 prisoners were present in federal prisons and reformatories and about 140,000 in state prisons and reformatories. During the year 1936 11,459 prisoners were received in federal prisons and reformatories from the courts, and about 54,000 in state prisons and reformatories. The figures for state prisons and reformatories are incomplete because of the failure of Georgia, Alabama, and Mississippi to make returns.

PRISON TRENDS: SPECIALIZATION. One of the evident trends in the history of American prisons is toward specialization of prisons. The jail was the first penal institution. Various groups of prisoners have been withdrawn from the jail for incarceration in specialized institutions. Vagrants were first withdrawn and placed in houses of correction. This proved to be abortive and the houses of correction have now either been abandoned or become identical with the jail except in name. Then state prisons, with differing names, were established for juvenile delinquents, for insane criminals, for young adults, for women, for Negroes, for defective delinquents, for misdemeanants, for the sick, and for other groups of criminals. In the development of these specialized institutions, the principles which have been used in the selection of offenders have included the governing unit, the seriousness of the crime, the age, color, sex, and mental or physical condition of the offenders. The motives for specialization have included two principles: the prevention of contamination of one type of offenders by another, and the adaptation of methods of work and of facilities to the characteristics of the special groups of offenders.

This trend toward specialization is clearly desirable. The principles which have been used in specialization, however, are not beyond question. The most important principle of specialization is the seriousness of the particular offense of which the prisoner was convicted; the state institutions generally care for felons, the county and municipal institutions for misdemeanants. This differentiation of prisoners is not satisfactory, for the particular offense is not a suitable index of the character, danger, or needs of the offender. The misdemeanant generally violates a law of the state as well as of the municipality, and the state would therefore be justified in taking charge of the prisoner rather than transferring this work to the local community. Moreover, the number of offenders in the typical county jail is so small that adequate facilities and personnel cannot be afforded. The average number serving sentences in a county jail on a particular day is about fifteen. In 1923 one-third of the county jails had no sentenced prisoners during the entire year. In the jail the males should be segregated from the females, the adults from the juveniles, the sick from the well, and each of these classes subdivided. Thus there should be a department for sick adult male prisoners, and a separate department for sick adult female prisoners. It is evidently impossible to provide this classification except in the larger institutions.

The local prisons of England were taken over by the central government and have been thus operated for more than half a century with improvement in efficiency and great decrease in expense. Several states in America have established state farms for misdemeanants which, to some extent, take the place of county jails. Indiana established a state farm for misdemeanants in 1915. The law provides that male misdemeanants are to be sent to this state farm unless their sentences are thirty days or less, in which case they may be retained in the county jail or sent to the state farm at the discretion of the judge. The expenses of transportation are paid by the county, the expenses of maintenance by the state. The average population of the state farm in recent years has been about twelve hundred, of the county jails (including only convicted prisoners) about four hundred. This shows that most of the convicted misdemeanants have been removed to the state farm. Bane made the following statement regarding the jails of Virginia:

> For ten or fifteen years we attempted to regulate the jails in Virginia. We went from jail to jail in an effort to improve the conditions. We have just about given up this effort. We have come to the conclusion that the local jail, as at present maintained, cannot be materially improved, and that the only thing to do with it is to abolish it; to do away with the local jail as a penal institution, in which people serve time after conviction, because the average county in a rural state is not able, from a financial standpoint, to erect or maintain an institution suitably equipped and suitably manned to handle all types of delinquency.[8]

The state farm for misdemeanants is decidedly superior to the county jail for misdemeanants, but an institution which specializes by types of offenders is still better. Many of the misdemeanants, for instance, are chronic alcoholics who make almost continuous rounds of jails, saloons, police stations, and jails again. Special institutions are desirable for this group, for they present a problem which is unique and which requires a uniform method of treatment. This includes a very large part of the jail population, to be sure, but the remainder of the jail population resembles the state prison population more than the chronic alcoholic population.

Specialization of institutions by sex of inmates is characteristic of all types of prisons—jails, houses of correction, reformatories, and state prisons. There are, for instance, fifty-one state prisons for male offenders only, nineteen for female offenders only, and thirty-two for both sexes. The states in which both sexes are in the same institution are with a few exceptions either the Western sparsely populated states or else the Southern states with large Negro populations.

[8] Frank Bane, "How Virginia Is Solving the Jail Problem," *Report of Natl. Com. on Prisons and Prison Labor*, 1929, pp. 13–14.

When both sexes are confined in one institution, the two departments are separated almost as completely as though they were different institutions. This separation of the sexes, whether in different
institutions or in the same institution, is regarded as necessary because of the administrative difficulties which would arise if the
sexes were not kept completely separate. A few persons have suggested coeducation in correctional institutions, but this suggestion
has not been taken seriously.

Another principle of specialization is by age. The desirability of
special institutions for juveniles, if they are to be kept in institutions
at all, is beyond question. The state reformatory for young adults
is not clearly justified. It was established on the theory that it
would serve younger, less criminal, and more easily reformable men.
As a matter of fact, 64 per cent of the men committed to state
reformatories in 1930 had previous commitments to correctional
institutions, and only 54 per cent of those committed to state prisons.
Also, there is considerable overlapping in age; of offenders committed to reformatories in 1923 74.5 per cent were under twenty-
five years of age, while of those admitted to state prisons 31.1
per cent were under that age. Thus the distinction between the
state prison and the state reformatory is not at all clear and is constantly tending to disappear. It has never been drawn as clearly
for women as for men offenders, and at present practically every
institution for women offenders might be called a reformatory.

Still another principle of specialization is by the traits of offenders.
Some special institutions have been established for vagrants, some
for insane criminals, some for defective delinquents, some for
alcoholics, and some for drug addicts. This is an approach to specialization on the basis of character and personality but it could be carried much further and become the principal basis of separation of
offenders. Eight of these are for insane criminals or defective delinquents. The development of special institutions for defective
delinquents is unquestionably desirable.

PRISON TRENDS: CLASSIFICATION AND INDIVIDUALIZATION. A
second trend in prisons has been toward classification of prisoners
within an institution and individualization of treatment within
these classes. The original prison evil against which reformers in-
veighed was the association of all types in a conglomerate group.
In the Pennsylvania system this evil was eliminated by solitary confinement. In the Auburn system, which was more generally adopted,

classification was suggested as the solution. Characteristics of prisoners have been taken into account in the assignment to cells, to work, to health services, to educational classes, to recreations, and to other activities and services. The policy of classification has not gone far and in most institutions the requirements of the institutions rather than the needs of the prisoners determine the assignments. The state of New Jersey probably has the best development of classification. Each inmate is examined on entrance, and by consultation between the various departments a labor program, an educational program, and other programs are worked out for and with him. His record is studied periodically and re-assignments may be made on the basis of these findings. This record is taken into account, also, when application is made for parole.[9] Similar methods of classification have been made in many of the states, as well as in the federal institutions. In fact the development of classification in prisons is the most significant trend in penology during the last twenty years.

The procedures involved in classification work generally involve three types. First, the prisoner's case history is taken and his personality studied. This is ordinarily done by a staff of professionally trained workers, such as psychologists, social workers, sociologists, and psychiatrists. In the ordinary case any one of these workers can take the case history and perform the routine tests as well as any other one, regardless of his training. But each of them can make some contributions to the interpretations which are unique and which grow out of the background of knowledge of the discipline represented. The contribution of the sociologist is as different from that of the social worker, as is the contribution of the psychologist different from that of the psychiatrist.

Second, the information regarding the prisoner is presented to a classification committee which ordinarily consists of the superintendent of the institution, the educational director, the superintendent of industry or trades, the chaplain, and the professionally trained staff. In this committee decisions are reached regarding assignments and treatment policies.

The third step in procedure is the application of the treatment policies. It is at this point that classification work has generally broken down. In the average institution in which classification has developed, the work of diagnosis and interpretation results in the

<hr />

[9] E. A. Doll, "Some Principles of Correctional Treatment," *Jour. Crim. Law and Criminol.* 18:197–206, August, 1927.

assignment of a prisoner to a workshop, to a cell block, and to an educational grade, and practically stops with that assignment. The theory on which classification is based is in conflict with the theory of the prison management, in a large proportion of the institutions in which classification work has developed. There is a developing program for technical training of guards, and this is likely to result in an integration of the two kinds of work.[10] It takes some time for the two groups of workers to come to an understanding of each other and to develop a co-ordinated program. Some attempts are made to deal with the problems of the particular prisoner. Such attempts had been made previously, of course, by certain wardens, guards, and chaplains, but perhaps nowhere as effectively by these persons as by other prisoners. With the development of classification more efforts are made to deal with these individual problems. The following is a simple illustration of this work.

An Italian prisoner in a state prison had been causing many disturbances, getting into fights, being sullen, irritable, tense, and disobedient. He was asked about these acts and an attempt was made to determine what was the trouble. He replied, "All the time I'm home," by which he meant that he kept thinking of home constantly and was troubled by his thoughts. The suggestion was made that he occupy his spare time making toys for his children for Christmas. For several weeks he spent his evenings in a workhouse in the prison, and was perfectly contented as he contemplated the pleasures his children would derive from the toys he was making. During the two months following he caused no trouble whatever.

It would be instructive to know whether recidivism is decreased in prisons in which case-work methods develop, and also whether the crime rate in the community decreases. The statistics on this are inadequate, but indicate that the methods thus far developed have not been attended by very significant changes in either recidivism or crime rates.

PRISON TRENDS: CENTRALIZATION OF ADMINISTRATION. More

---

[10] Thorsten Sellin, "Historical Glimpses of Training for Prison Service," *Jour. Crim. Law and Criminol.*, 25:594–600, November, 1934; Joseph Roucek, "Sociology of the Prison Guard," *Sociol. and Soc. Res.*, 20:145–151, November, 1935; Joseph Roucek, "Social Attitudes of the Prison Warden," *Sociol. and Soc. Res.*, 21:170–174, November, 1936; W. M. Wallack, *The Training of Prison Guards in New York State*, New York, 1938.

than sixty years ago England placed all her penal institutions in one department. A similar development in the United States is impeded by the division of authority between the federal government and the states. Within the state, however, the tendency toward centralization may be seen in three respects. First, a few states have assumed control of a part of the penal treatment of misdemeanants. Second, all of the state penal and correctional institutions in several states have been placed under the control of a central department of correction, whereas previously each institution had its own board of control. Sometimes the unified department of correction is given authority over the entire process of treatment of felons subsequent to conviction. A third tendency toward centralization is found in the increased power of the state to regulate the county and municipal institutions. This power is generally confined to inspection and publicity, but in some states the inspecting board also has authority to close institutions which do not measure up to the standards.

Two objections to centralization have been made. First, it is said to facilitate political interference with the administration of an institution. Second, a central administrative body tends to develop mechanical uniformity in methods, though the specialized groups need special methods. A local board can familiarize itself with the needs of the particular institution, take a personal interest in it, and therefore exercise more intelligent control. On the other hand, the advantages claimed for centralized control are that it is more economical, makes possible a more efficient personnel, impedes local graft, and raises all the institutions of the state to a relatively high level of efficiency, while under local control some are likely to be extremely inefficient.

PRISON TRENDS: REDUCTION OF HORRORS. Unquestionably the horrors of prison life have been reduced. Improvements have been made in diet, cleanliness, ventilation, lighting, and methods of discipline; also, the monotony of prison life has been reduced. In most institutions the marks of degradation, such as the shaving of the head, the lock-step, striped clothing, and the ball-and-chain, have been eliminated. Provisions have been made for medical examination and treatment, but, according to a recent survey,[11] the staff and equipment are still generally inadequate, and in five state prisons routine physical examinations of all incoming prisoners are

[11] F. L. Rector, *Health and Medical Service in American Prisons and Reformatories*, New York, 1929.

not made. Very high rates of tuberculosis are reported in some institutions. It is clear that certain institutions, due to the types of
prisoners received, should be primarily infirmaries. In the New York
City Penitentiary on Welfare Island in 1930 60 per cent of the
incoming prisoners were physically or mentally incapable of work,
and a large proportion of them could not be made capable of work.
More than half of the incapable group were sots, bums, drug addicts, and similar types for whom hospital facilities were the primary
requirement. In general, in spite of the improvement in prisons,
several European visitors have been shocked by the conditions in
American prisons. Dr. Liepmann reported:

Not sentimentality but, to the mind of the European, an often
shocking brutality is characteristic of American criminal procedure
and of American prisons.[12]

PRISON TRENDS: THE INDUSTRIAL FARM.   During the last generation several prisons of the industrial-farm type have been established. These prisons are used principally for offenders who are least
likely to escape. The location of the institution on a farm makes
possible a life of relative freedom which would be impossible in a
city prison. The problem of prison labor is solved more easily there
than in a city prison where prison labor must be confined to factory
work, which arouses the antagonism of trade unions and employers.
The cost of construction of the institution is low, because the land
is cheap, expensive walls are unnecessary, and most of the work
of construction can be done by the prisoners. Since the danger of
escape is reduced, the guard can devote most of his time to constructive social policies.

PRISON TRENDS: SOCIAL LIFE IN PRISON.   The solitary confinement of the early Pennsylvania system has been generally abandoned in the United States except as punishment for infraction of
prison regulations and is rapidly being abandoned in most of the
European countries which adopted it. Even the rule of silence
which was substituted for this has been abandoned in many institutions or has been greatly modified. Entertainments have been provided, athletics and other recreations developed, libraries and
educational classes provided, and self-government in a complete or

[12] M. Liepmann, *Amerikanische Gefängnisse und Erziehungsanstalten,*
Mannheim, 1927.

modified form established in many institutions. These are efforts both to promote contacts among the inmates and between the inmates and the outside world. They are based in part on the conviction that open contacts between prisoners are better than secret contacts which prevail in spite of a formal policy of isolation, in part on the conviction that reformation is a process of assimilation of culture of the outside world and that assimilation of culture is promoted by contact with that culture rather than isolation from it. While the prison in its general plan is a means of isolating offenders from social life, these logically contradictory methods are introduced in the effort to facilitate the reformation of the inmates by breaking down the isolation to some extent. Warden Lawes states that prisoners seldom talk about crime,[13] and Barnes has pointed out that training for a life of freedom can be secured only in an institution in which prisoners have freedom and responsibility.[14]

Several significant experiments have been made in the development of social life in institutions. El Retiro in California, the State Penal Colony in Massachusetts, the English Borstal Institutions, the Thüringian prisons in Germany, and several prisons in the Soviet Union have received publicity because of their developments of social life. For instance, in the English Borstal institution each lad on reception is placed in a group or club of ten or twelve, which has a name, such as Lions or Invincibles. This group has a room assigned to it as headquarters, which is something like a club headquarters. The group eats together, may constitute an athletic team for competition, and in other ways forms a social unit.

In some juvenile reformatories contacts are maintained with the outside world through the Big Brothers, Big Sisters, or similar organizations. Several states have reported successful policies of this nature, but in general the work of these volunteers deteriorates when the novelty wears off.

Very little is known, even by the prison management and guards, of the social life of the prisoners. Studies of the prison as a community are now being made and it is likely that these studies may

---

[13] Lewis E. Lawes, *Life and Death in Sing Sing*, Garden City, N. Y., 1928, p. 75.

[14] H. E. Barnes, *The Evolution of Penology in Pennsylvania*, Indianapolis, 1927, p. 400.

result in distinct developments in the organization of the prison from this point of view.[15]

Another method of promoting contacts between prisoners and outsiders has developed in a few places. In Canada an extra-mural system has been provided for certain prisoners who are not eligible for parole; they may receive permits to work in regular establishments outside of the prison and return to the prison at night, or their time may be distributed in other ways between the prison and the outside world. Formerly in certain Russian and German prisons selected prisoners were permitted to spend the week-end at home or to work in the prison by day and stay at home at night, or work in an outside establishment by day and spend the night in prison, or spend other specified periods outside the prison. This policy is justified by its advocates as a means of keeping prisoners in contact with the general society, and thus of fitting them for more complete liberty, in part as a means of meeting the problem of sex deprivation, in part as a means of keeping up morale within the institution. Clearly it must be used with discrimination and perhaps confined principally to misdemeanants.

PRISON CONFERENCES. In 1846 the first international congress for prison reform was held in Frankfort with 196 delegates from fourteen countries. A second congress was held in Brussels in 1847, a third in Brussels in 1856, a fourth in London in 1872, and others at five-year intervals since that time. At present delegates are sent by more than fifty governments. The early congresses were concerned largely with technical questions of prison architecture and administration. The more recent congresses have been more concerned with the study of the personality of the criminal and his social background.[16] In addition to these international congresses, national congresses or conferences have been developed in several countries, of which one of the most important is that held by the American Prison Association, organized in 1870. One of the best statements of prison theory that has been made was formulated by this association in 1870 and since that time has been reprinted in each issue of the annual report of the association. This organization has been extremely important in the dissemination of ideals and standards

---

[15] Hans Riemer, "Socialization in the Prison Community," *Proc. Amer. Prison Assoc.*, 1937, pp. 151–155; Donald Clemmer, "Leadership Phenomena in a Prison Community," *Jour. Crim. Law and Criminol.*, 28:861–872, March, 1938.

[16] E. Ferri, "Questions penitentiaries," *Revue Inter. de Soc.*, 35:1–23, 1927.

among prison authorities. The Conference of Charities and Correction, established in 1874, is another organization of importance. It has been concerned with juvenile reformatories, juvenile courts, and probation more than with other problems of criminology. Because its primary interest is social work its name has been changed to the National Conference of Social Work.

GRAFT AND POLITICS IN PRISONS. The prisons, like the police departments and the courts, have frequently been extremely corrupt. Positions in many institutions are filled on the principle of political patronage, and this almost inevitably means a corrupt and inefficient personnel. In one community the superintendent of the house of correction has built up and maintained his popularity in his own district by distributing at Christmas and Thanksgiving baskets filled with supplies from the institution. When a prisoner is admitted on a definite sentence he may, if he can make a sufficient payment to an officer and his case has not been too prominent, be released immediately, although his name is carried on the books until the end of his sentence. Prisoners who have been convicted of false entries on the books of a bank may be assigned to bookkeeping work in the prison and be required to falsify the prison records in order to cover the supplies which the prison officers have appropriated for their own use. Contracts with concerns which furnish supplies to the institution frequently yield graft for the superintendent or other officers. When MacCormick became commissioner of correction in New York City in 1934 he made a raid on the house of correction, where he found narcotic drugs, hypodermic needles, knives, male prostitutes, a "politicians' row" in which politically important prisoners secured unusual privileges, and many other abuses which had been permitted by the thoroughly corrupt administration. Similar conditions could undoubtedly be discovered by similar raids on dozens of other prisons. In view of these conditions it is not surprising that imprisonment frequently fails to reform prisoners.

SUGGESTED READINGS

Barnes, H. E., "The Progress of American Penology as Exemplified by the Experience of the State of Pennsylvania, 1830–1920," *Jour. Crim. Law and Criminol.*, 13:170–227, August, 1922.

Beaumont, G. de, and Tocqueville, A. de, *On the Penitentiary System in the United States*, Tr. by F. Lieber, Philadelphia, 1833.

Bowler, Alida C., and Bloodgood, R. C., *Institutional Treatment of Delinquent Boys,* Washington, 1936.

Brockway, Z. F., *Fifty Years of Prison Service,* New York, 1912.

Burns, Robert E., *I Am a Fugitive from a Georgia Chain Gang,* New York, 1932.

Commons, J. R., "The Junior Republic," *Amer. Jour. Sociol.,* 3:281–296, 433–448, 1897.

Hoffer, F. W., Mann, D. M., and House, F. N., *The Jails of Virginia,* New York, 1933.

Klein, P., *Prison Methods in New York State,* New York, 1920.

Lekkerkerker, Eugenia C., *Reformatories for Women in the United States,* The Hague, 1931.

Lewis, O. F., *The Development of American Prisons and Prison Customs, 1776–1845,* Albany, 1922.

McKelway, Blake, *American Prisons,* New York, 1936.

Nalder, F. F., "The American State Reformatory," *Univ. of Calif. Pub., Education,* Vol. V, No. 3, 1920.

National Society for Penal Information, *Handbooks of American Prisons,* 1926, 1929, 1934, 1938–1939.

New Jersey, *Report of Prison Inquiry Commission,* 2 Vols., Trenton, 1917.

New York, *Report of Prison Survey Committee,* Albany, 1920.

Peirce, B. K., *A Half Century with Juvenile Delinquents, or the New York House of Refuge and Its Times,* New York, 1869.

Reeves, Margaret, *Training Schools for Delinquent Girls,* New York, 1929.

Riemer, Hans, "Socialization in the Prison Community," *Proc. Amer. Prison Assoc.,* 1937, pp. 151–155.

Robinson, L. N., "Defective Delinquents," *Jour. Crim. Law and Criminol.,* 23:352–399, July, 1933.

Sellin, Thorsten, "Prison Tendencies in Europe," *Jour. Crim. Law and Criminol.,* 21:485–498, February, 1931.

Snedden, D. S., *Administration and Educational Work of American Juvenile Reform Schools,* New York, 1907.

Sutherland, Edwin H., and Sellin, Thorsten, "Prisons of Tomorrow," *Annals of Amer. Acad. of Pol. and Social Sci.,* Vol. CLVII, September, 1931.

U. S. Bureau of Education, *Industrial Schools for Delinquents, 1917–1918,* Bulletin, No. 52, 1919.

Van Waters, Miriam, "Where Girls Go Right," *Survey,* 48:362–376, May 27, 1922. See, also, "Begun in Idealism—Ended in Politics," *Survey,* 59:83–84, October 15, 1927.

Wallack, W. M., *The Training of Prison Guards in New York State,* New York, 1938.

Williams, E. H., *The Walled City: A Story of the Criminal Insane,* New York, 1913.

Wilson, Walter, "Chain Gangs and Profit," *Harpers,* 166:532–543, April, 1933.

Wines, E. C., *The State of Prisons and of Child-Saving Institutions in the Civilized World,* Cambridge, 1880.

Wines, E. C., and Dwight, T. W., "Report on Prisons and Reformatories of the United States and Canada," *New York Assembly Doc.,* No. 35, 1867.

Chapter *Twenty–Two*

PRISONS: FAILURE AND FUNCTION

THE FUNCTION OF THE PRISON. The primary business of the prison, according to conventional opinion, is to confine criminals. Security against escape takes precedence over everything else, and all policies may be limited by considerations of the danger of escape. The prisons perform this function of confinement efficiently, in the sense that very few escapes occur. Since the policy of imprisonment is adopted as a means of protecting society from crime, the further problem arises, How does security against escape from prison protect society from crime? The justification for imprisonment, in this sense, is that it keeps criminals from committing crimes during their period of incarceration, that it deters the general public from crimes which might result in imprisonment, and that it reforms some criminals. These justifications are called incapacitation, deterrence, and reformation. These objectives are not completely harmonious with each other or with freedom from escape. Especially, the conditions which are most conducive to reformation may be more or less in conflict with conditions which produce the minimum number of escapes, and the maximum incapacitation and deterrence.

As a means of incapacitation, imprisonment has a relatively high efficiency. Very few crimes against the general society are committed by prisoners during the period of incarceration. Though cases have been reported of prisoners coining and issuing counterfeit money and of practicing confidence games, these are so few that they are negligible. The crimes of prisoners are committed principally against prison guards and other officers, against prison property, and against other prisoners. Such crimes within prison communities are very frequent. The prison guard has an extremely hazardous occupation. Prison property is seldom safe from theft. Prisoners frequently commit crimes against each other in the form of theft, assault, and murder. Perverted sex practices and the use of narcotic drugs flourish in many prisons and exist to some extent in most prisons. Intra-mural crimes, as well as extra-mural crimes, vary in frequency in different prisons and are affected by the prison policies. Probably the strict isolation of the original Pennsylvania system was more effective than any other prison policy in incapacitating prisoners. This does not justify a conclusion that the Pennsylvania system is in general most efficient, for other values must be considered.

The success of the prison in deterring the general public from crime is probably much less than its success in incapacitating criminals. It certainly has some deterrent effect, but it is difficult to compare the deterrent effects of different prison policies or to isolate the effect of any prison policy from the effect of the whole process of arrest and conviction. Perhaps the deterrent effect of imprisonment increases slightly with the horrors of prison life, though this is likely to be off-set by the difficulty of securing convictions if the public feels that the horrors of imprisonment are greater than the horrors of the crimes. Perhaps the fact of incarceration, regardless of conditions within prisons, is the most important factor in deterrence.

The success of imprisonment as a means of reformation is very slight, although this, also, is difficult to determine accurately. In 1936 56.5 per cent of the persons committed to state or federal prisons and reformatories had previous records of commitments to penal or reformatory institutions, and this record is certainly incomplete. Glueck found that 63.7 per cent of 510 young men released consecutively from the Massachusetts State Reformatory committed serious offenses either during the parole period or a five-year post-parole period, that an additional 20.8 per cent committed minor offenses either in the parole or post-parole period, and that only 15.5 per cent had no record of serious or minor offenses subsequent to release.[1] This perhaps exaggerates somewhat the number of serious crimes as ordinarily understood, especially because among the serious post-parole crimes are included "escape or rescue, fugitive from justice, desertion or dishonorable discharge from the army and navy, and serious automobile offenses" and these constitute 23 per cent of the serious post-parole crimes. Larceny, burglary, and robbery

---

[1] Sheldon and Eleanor T. Glueck, *Five Hundred Criminal Careers*, New York, 1930, pp. 167–169, 182–192.

constitute 80 per cent of the offenses for which offenders were committed to the reformatory and only 60 per cent of the serious postparole offenses. The high failure rate should not be regarded as the responsibility of the last institution which dealt with these offenders. No institution, receiving the failures of the rest of society, should be expected to reform a very large proportion of them. Also, the reformatory cannot properly be given the credit for those who do reform after imprisonment.

A study of 623 delinquents who had been in institutions for juvenile delinquents in five different states about ten years earlier resulted in the finding that 66 per cent had been arrested after release and 42 per cent been committed again to institutions.[2]

Persistence in crime and desistence from crime are affected by other conditions than the institutional policies. In 1933 300 boys from Chicago who had been in confinement in the Illinois School for Boys during 1925–1930 were located as follows: 187 in prisons and reformatories, 8 shot and killed, 2 electrocuted for murder, 1 died with a criminal record, 18 on probation, 1 a fugitive from justice, 12 in hospitals for the mentally defective, 4 in the army, 18 good citizens with no subsequent criminality, and 47 whereabouts unknown; only 6 per cent were known to have a good record after confinement in the institution. On the other hand, of the boys confined in the same institution who came from rural counties about half were reported to be successful subsequently. The whole situation enters into the success or failure of those who have been imprisoned.

In the absence of objective criteria and measures of the reformative value of penal and reformatory institutions, we can learn something of their value by a study of the opinions of persons who have been in contact with them. The evidence of this nature, also, is not conclusive proof.

ATTITUDES OF PRISONERS TOWARD THE PRISON. Many prisoners have expressed their opinions regarding prisons. These statements have been made regarding all types of penal and reformatory institutions, in different generations, by persons of each sex, and regarding institutions in different sections of America and of other countries.

---

[2] Alida C. Bowler and R. C. Bloodgood, *Institutional Treatment of Delinquent Boys,* Washington, 1936, Part II, p. 98.

In the fifteen years I spent in different prisons I found nothing in the official system which was of any benefit to me, nothing which tended to make me better, and to fit me to earn an honest livelihood.[3]

Prison obstructs or altogether closes every door to genuine moral reform in prisoners.[4]

There is not a single indisputable case of a reformed character in the whole history of Sing Sing that can be placed to the credit of the agencies directly aimed to that end. The wardens will tell you that, and the oldest officers of the widest experience will endorse it with a grin when you speak to them about reform in prison. There is no such thing; and, except in a tentative way, even the means used that are classed as reformative, are only in deference to the public belief that such attempts should be made, and are without hope of results.[5]

There was nothing that could possibly be construed as reformatory or constructive in my prison experience; nothing that would help one to meet the terrific problem of facing life later and earning a livelihood. . . . After what I have seen of the medieval methods of treating the prisoner, and since I know something of the difficulties of life after one has left prison, I wonder that the percentage [of recidivism] is not one hundred. . . .[6]

When I first went to the Chicago Parental School I had rosy cheeks and had a happy-go-lucky spirit. When I came out I weighed more but my spirit was broken. The place changed me but did not reform me. I felt revengeful, spiteful, and dulled. I had more fears of the police and decided to be more careful in the future. I didn't trust anyone when I came out.[7]

I was sent to a juvenile institution at the age of eleven, and returned at about fifteen as a good pickpocket. I went to a reformatory at seventeen and returned as a burglar, with all that implies in one's life

[3] *In the Clutch of Circumstances,* New York, 1922, pp. 259–260. Reprinted by permission of D. Appleton-Century Company, publishers.
[4] Julian Hawthorne, *The Subterranean Brotherhood,* New York, 1914, p. 105. Reprinted by permission of Robert M. McBride & Company, publishers.
[5] *Life in Sing Sing,* by Convict 1500, Indianapolis, 1904, p. 46.
[6] Alice Thornton, "The Pound of Flesh," *Atlantic Mo.,* 135:436–437, April, 1925. Reprinted by permission.
[7] Clifford R. Shaw, *Delinquency Areas,* p. 39. Reprinted by permission of The University of Chicago Press, publishers.

and habits. As a burglar, I went to a state institution, where I acquired all the professional characteristics of the criminal, and have since committed all the crimes, I suppose, which most criminals commit, and expect to end my life as a criminal.[8]

These statements are an adequate illustration of the views of prisoners who have written autobiographies. They are unanimous in condemning prisons as injurious from the point of view of the prisoner's reformation, or at least as not valuable. It is probable that these published autobiographies do not fairly represent the views of prisoners who have been helped by the institutions. Glueck found in his study of prisoners who had been released from the Massachusetts reformatory that 68.2 per cent made some favorable statements about the effects of imprisonment upon them, and of these favorable statements 37.1 per cent were made by prisoners who were total failures in their post-parole period, 22.4 per cent by those who were partial failures, and 37.7 by those who were successes; of those who made unfavorable statements about the effect of the imprisonment 76.9 per cent were total failures, 12.3 per cent were partial failures, and 10.8 per cent successes. This indicates that the prisoners are by no means unanimous in their total condemnation of the effect of imprisonment, though this does not show accurately what the effect actually was, or even what the opinions of prisoners were regarding the net effect of imprisonment.

ATTITUDES OF PRISON AUTHORITIES AND OTHERS IN CONTACT WITH PRISONS. Prisoners are not the only ones who criticize prisons. One may find many caustic criticisms by prison authorities or others who are officially in contact with prisons.

If absolutely innocent individuals were put under prison conditions they would tend to develop anti-social conceptions of conduct.[9]

Prisons and reformatories are a makeshift, good only until a more enlightened method can be found for the treatment of prisoners.[10]

---

[8] Quoted by F. Tannenbaum, *Wall Shadows*, pp. 70–71. Reprinted by permission of G. P. Putnam's Sons, publishers. See, also, C. D. Souder, "The State Industrial School as I Lived Through It," *Survey*, 31:715–718, March 7, 1914.

[9] Wm. Healy, *Individual Delinquent*, Boston, 1915, p. 315. Reprinted by permission of Little, Brown & Company, publishers.

[10] Jessie D. Hodder, "Indenture of Prisoners," *Jour. Crim. Law and Criminol.*, 11:32, May, 1920.

If he is reformable . . . he should not be sent to a reformatory. It is liable to ruin him.[11]

If the system had a good effect on any prisoners, I failed to mark it. I have no shadow of doubt of its power to demoralize, or of its cruelty. It appears to me not to belong to this time or civilization at all. My main argument here is that we not only do not deter, but that we actually make over our criminal to crime. . . . It may appear that . . . I have no good word to say for our prison system. I have not. I think it creates a criminal class, and directly fosters recidivism, that our method is dead and done with, and in need of decent cremation.[12]

The discipline of these institutions has, in most cases, had the effect of degrading those committed to them, and of plunging them further into vice and crime.[13]

It would be possible to secure many such statements regarding the county and municipal jails, the state prisons, the state reformatories, and the juvenile reformatories.

A few statements have been made on the other side, either in the form of denial that prisons should be expected to reform prisoners, or in the form of a general defense of the prisons, or in the form of particular cases of reformations.[14]

ATTITUDES OF SOME OTHERS. Other persons, some in public life, some students of the penal system but not in public life, have expressed dissatisfaction with the prison system, and from such expressions the following are selected as representative.

In an address in Parliament, John Bright stated that if the institutions that controlled behavior were reckoned at 100, the criminal courts and penal institutions would not rate higher than 5.[15]

---

[11] Carrie W. Smith, "The Elimination of the Reformatory," *Proc. Natl. Conf. Social Work*, 1921, pp. 127–132. Reprinted by permission.

[12] Mary Gordon, *Penal Discipline*, London, 1922, pp. xl–xli and 206.

[13] G. W. Kirchwey, "The Future of the Criminal Law," *Proc. Natl. Conf. Social Work*, 1921, pp. 144. Reprinted by permission.

[14] For a statement regarding persons who have become successful after imprisonment, see Lewis E. Lawes, *Life and Death in Sing Sing*, pp. 132–133.

[15] C. W. Hoffman, "Probation as a Juridical Policy," *Proc. Natl. Prob. Assoc.*, 1919, p. 21.

The only persons we save nowadays are those we do not send to prison.[16]

Imprisonment as it exists today . . . is a worse crime than any of those committed by its victims.[17]

Every person who understands penal institutions—no matter how well such places are managed—knows that a thousand are injured or utterly destroyed by service in prison, where one is helped.[18]

It is a fact which is only too well understood that the prison makes the individual worse on his departure than when he entered. But it has another consequence, namely, that in most cases it places the person who has suffered this punishment in a position more difficult than the one in which he was before his conviction.[19]

Like the older forms of punishment which it superseded, imprisonment too has proved a failure, so far at least as the newer aim of punishment, the reformation of the wrong-doer, is concerned. And we are coming to see that the protection which society enjoys through the imprisonment for a few months or years of a small proportion of the criminal class is dearly purchased by a system which returns the offender to society less fitted than before to cope with the conditions of a life of freedom.[20]

Let me add in all seriousness that the managers of my own shops and factories make a more efficient and intelligent sorting and reclamation of scrap metal than the laws have generally made of the living men and women that have been thrown upon the scrap heap of our jails and prisons.[21]

---

[16] Judge Edgar J. Sherman, quoted by L. E. MacBrayne and J. P. Ramsay, *One More Chance*, Boston, 1916, p. 337.

[17] G. B. Shaw, in Introduction to S. and B. Webb, *English Prisons under Local Government*, p. vii. Reprinted by permission of Longmans, Green & Co., publishers.

[18] C. Darrow, *Crime: Its Causes and Treatment*, New York, 1922. Reprinted by permission of Thomas Y. Crowell Company, publishers.

[19] E. Desprez, *De l'abolition de l'emprisonnement*, pp. 54–55

[20] "Report of Pennsylvania Commission to Investigate Penal Systems," *Penn. Jour. Prison Discipline*, 58:39, 1919.

[21] E. N. Foss, "The Ideal Prison System," *Proc. Amer. Prison Assoc.*, 1913, pp. 120–121.

Of all methods of penalizing culprits, the one most usual in our days, imprisonment, appears to be the most unsatisfactory. There is nothing to recommend it but the ease of its application to large numbers of delinquents. It has been described by all competent observers as an active incitement to further wrong-doing.[22]

GENERAL NATURE OF THE OBJECTIVES AND CONDITIONS OF IMPRISONMENT. The view which is accepted by many prison leaders is that the prison should make every possible effort to reform prisoners, within the framework of a system of security. The reason for the emphasis on reformation is that practically all of the prisoners return to free society sooner or later and for that reason it is desirable that these prisoners should be changed by the prison experience so that they will desist from crime. At the same time the prison system contains many evils which impede and perhaps render futile the efforts at reformation. Some of these prison conditions are easily modifiable, while others are rooted in the attitudes of the general public and in the relations between criminals and the general public. The small, unhealthy cells, the bad odors, the vermin, the idleness, the brutality, for instance, could be almost entirely eliminated by the employment of efficient prison administrators and have been eliminated in many institutions. On the other hand, some of the conditions in prisons are not so superficial. The following analysis is intended as an interpretation of prison conditions in terms of these general and fundamental attitudes.

INEFFICIENT PRISON OFFICIALS. Efficient administration of prisons is generally lacking. It is very difficult to secure efficiency, for the personnel is selected on the basis of political patronage, and the officers consequently are seldom well equipped for the exceedingly difficult task of reconstructing personality. Regarding the officers of institutions for juvenile delinquents, who are probably as efficient as officers in any type of institutions, Dr. Adler asserted:

The officials who preside over these institutions are usually as ill equipped for constructive and scientific work as the domestics and window-washers of a hospital to carry out the medical and surgical measures of relief. . . . Is there a single institution in this country which has provided for its wards the same grade of personnel, the

---

[22] P. Vinogradoff, *Outlines of Historical Jurisprudence,* New York, 1920, Vol. I, p. 59. Reprinted by permission of Oxford University Press, publishers.

same training and expertness, that we find in a good, general hospital?[23]

Even if an institution secures well-trained personnel the overload of work and the inadequate facilities and equipment generally restrict accomplishments. Both the inefficient personnel and the inadequate facilities are due to the apathy of the public. The public is not sufficiently interested in efficient administration of prisons to be willing to pay taxes or insist on appointments on the basis of efficiency rather than of political service. Occasionally, as in Massachusetts and New Jersey and the federal prison system, capable leaders have been able to secure appointments on the basis of efficiency, but these leaders are constantly engaged in conflict to keep their prison systems from falling back into the hands of politicians. The inefficiency of prison administration in the typical state is rooted in this apathy of the public and cannot be changed without extraordinary leadership.

GOVERNMENT BY RIGID DISCIPLINE. Prison discipline means, conventionally, the regulation or attempt at regulation of all the details of the life of the prisoner by means of rules. The prisoner is permitted to do nothing except under direction of the officers of the prison. This means denial of the possibility of making choices on any activities whatever. Miss Doty, after first-hand experience with prison conditions, concluded:

The worst feature of the prison system [was] . . . the brutal officialdom that treated human beings as though they were not human, as though they were cogs in a machine.[24]

Two effects follow from this régime: (a) Some prisoners adapt to it, obeying all the rules. The prisoners who secure this adaptation drift into dreaming, a general condition of apathy, a vegetablelike existence.

Leaving the prisoner practically no opportunity for the exercise of choice even in the smallest things of life, prison discipline tends to

---

[23] H. M. Adler, "Medical Science and Criminal Justice," Part V of *The Cleveland Foundation Survey of Criminal Justice,* Cleveland, 1921, p. 6. Reprinted by permission.

[24] Madeleine Z. Doty, "Maggie Martin, 933," *Century Mag.,* 88:843, October, 1914.

reduce him to a merely passive machine, incapable of deliberation, forethought, or intelligent self-direction. Once the decision has been made to accept the routine and to obey all orders, no further demand is made upon the will. This condition of purely passive obedience is the dominant characteristic of the "good prisoner," and it is upon the ability to forego the satisfactions which proceed from the exercise of will that adaptation to prison conditions largely depends. After a long term of imprisonment, passive obedience and dependence upon authority have become habitual, and the prisoner finds himself, when he at last faces the tasks of normal life, without decision, without initiative, and lacking in self-control.[25]

Testimony from prisoners shows clearly that many prisoners tend to fall into this mechanical routine, to become automata.[26] Dr. Sieverts collected a large number of prisoners' autobiographies and concluded from an analysis of them that the prisoner loses his ability to concentrate, loses strength of memory, loses determination and emotional balance, and develops phantasies, daydreams, and illusions. These changes occur because of the monotony of prison life, from which all extraordinary events are eliminated, and because of the compulsory nature of much of the overt behavior.[27] Victor Nelson describes the mental product of this life as follows:

One cannot rest. One can merely escape from the existing drabness. One can merely lie down on the bed and drift off into the dream world; into memories of the past, visions of the future; neither of which is satisfactory except in retrospect or anticipation. One lies in a stupor, shutting out the undignified, unappetizing dullness; deliberately or unconsciously running away from life. This is a bad habit to get into, this flying from reality; but it is a habit into which practically all of us get, mildly or terribly, depending entirely on the length of our sentences, our ages, our intensities of awareness. . . . Day after day we find that prosyness, inertia, stolidity, weariness and dejection are the prevailing qualities of our lives. The escapes and murders—

---

[25] S. Hobhouse and A. F. Brockway, *English Prisons Today, Being the Report of the Prison System Enquiry Committee*, London, 1922, p. 573. Reprinted by permission of Longmans, Green & Co., publishers.

[26] Hobhouse and Brockway, *op. cit.*, pp. 485–500.

[27] Rudolf Sieverts, "Die Wirkungen der Freiheitsstrafe und Untersuchungshaft auf die Psyche der Gefängenen," *Hamburgische Schriften zur gesamten Strafrechtswissenschaft*, herausgegeben von Dr. M. Liepmann, Heft 14, Mannheim, 1929.

the exciting things—are so infrequent as to be practically non-existent. Every minute of the day, all the year round, the most dominant note is one of monotony.[28]

These two facts are the underlying causes of prison stupor—the habit of day-dreaming, of escaping from reality—which is the worst effect of imprisonment. First indulged in at night, in the cell, the habit is carried over into the drowsy morning hours, then to the drowsy noon hour, until finally it takes full possession of the man, so that he spends most of his waking moments in a species of hypnosis, nearly or utterly incapable of reacting to the normal emergencies of life.[29]

(b) Some prisoners rebel and continue to rebel in spite of or because of the rules and punishments. Lane, speaking of the prisoners in the federal prison at Alcatraz, and Tannenbaum, speaking of the general conditions in state prisons, say:

They violate the rules all the time.[30]

The breaking of the rules is constant, discovery frequent, and punishment follows discovery. To the warden discovery spells lack of discipline, lack of isolation, danger of collusion. . . . So the rules are made more numerous, the discipline stricter, and the punishment more severe upon each discovery of a new violation. . . . This simply means that the more rules there are, the more violations there are bound to be; and the greater the number of violations, the more numerous the rules. The greater the number of violations, the more brutal the punishments.[31]

When the prisoners break the rules, punishment follows as a matter of course. In the earlier days punishment practically always meant some form of bodily suffering. At present punishment much

---

[28] Victor Nelson, *Prison Days and Nights*, Boston, 1933, pp. 14–15. Reprinted by permission of Little, Brown & Company, publishers.
[29] Victor Nelson, *op. cit.*, p. 197. Reprinted by permission of Little, Brown & Company, publishers.
[30] W. D. Lane, "Alcatraz," *Survey*, 44:471, July 3, 1920.
[31] Tannenbaum, *op. cit.*, p. 19. Reprinted by permission of G. P. Putnam's Sons, publishers. See, also, Victor Nelson, *Prison Days and Nights*, pp. 219–242.

more frequently consists of loss of privileges, such as picture shows, or, especially, parole or advantage of the good-time laws.

Thus either reaction to the system of rigid discipline tends to become something very much like insanity—either apathy, listlessness, vagaries, or else irritability, hatred, and nervous instability. No statistics are available for the United States that show how many prisoners, judged sane on entrance, become insane while in prison. English statistics show that among those judged to be mentally sound at the time of reception insanity increased steadily with the length of imprisonment, being forty times as high at the end of twelve months as at the end of one month, and nine times as high at the end of five years as at the end of one year.[32]

The question remains, Can this system of rigid discipline be modified or eliminated? An optimistic assurance that it can be modified or a pessimistic assurance that it cannot be modified would be inadequate; it is necessary to consider the possibility of modification with reference to the causes that have produced it. Four principal attitudes or conditions enter into the production of the system: the ideal of reformation by denial of choice, the attitude of dominance by prison officers, the attitude of retaliation by the prison officers, and the danger of escape.

(a) The earlier psychology of reformation was based on the assumption that a habit formed by compulsion would be retained after the compulsion was removed. It was felt that since the prisoner had failed to make the proper choices before his entrance into the prison he should be given no opportunity to make choices afterward, but that all of his acts should be imposed upon him from without. Brockway stated this ideal as follows:

In order to train criminals for social life they must have a strict régime and learn quick and accurate self-adjustment to a uniform requirement, habituation to the yoke of established custom. Exactness of observance is of the greatest importance . . . so that the newly formed habit of precision calls up the instinctive impulse to social orderliness quite independent of conscious volition.[33]

It is clear that this theory is incorrect and the policy based on it has already been changed to a great extent. As an ideal of reforma-

---

[32] Hobhouse and Brockway, op. cit., pp. 538–539.
[33] Z. R. Brockway, Fifty Years of Prison Service, New York, 1912, p. 355.

tion this denial of choices is not inherent in the system of discipline.

(b) Prison officers are shut off from ordinary society by their work and are not able to associate with the prisoners on a normal basis. Consequently they have only one general social relation, that of dominance. This is made easier by the helplessness of the prisoners and the general assumption of a great moral difference between prisoners and other people. Dominance is the relation, then, in which the officers must secure their social satisfactions. That means they must show their authority, and the making and enforcing of rules and the infliction of punishment are methods of showing this dominance.[34] This attitude is not absolutely fixed; it can be modified to some extent by giving the prisoners more authority or by giving the prison officers more social contacts with others than prisoners. Some prison officers certainly have other attitudes and it seems possible that all of them could, by proper training, develop a scientific attitude toward the prisoners that would supplant this attitude of dominance.

(c) The prison officers frequently have an attitude of retaliation toward the prisoners. In an investigation of the discipline of the Preston School of Industry in California, the superintendent found that the officers demanded retaliatory punishment. He added:

It is doubtful whether such an institution could be administered without letting its officers have the satisfaction of knowing that offenders receive what seems to be an adequate return in punishment for the trouble they have occasioned. . . . It is to be hoped that the time is coming when we can ignore the officer's instinct for Mosaic justice.[35]

This is true because the prison officers reflect the attitude of the general public toward offenders or toward certain types of offenders. The general law of outside society is, "If a person breaks a rule, punish him." The attitude of the prison officers is therefore due to a tradition carried into the institution from the outside life. It is possible by proper training to modify this attitude. A rule was passed in Preston which was instrumental in modifying the methods of discipline to a considerable extent: A single officer was made responsible for all discipline; in that way every issue was given a hearing before a third party; and in addition a record had to be

---

[34] Tannenbaum, *op. cit.*, pp. 25–29.
[35] California, *Report of Preston School of Industry*, 1916–1918, p. 39.

kept of all punishments, which tended to restrict hasty and ill-considered punishments.

(d) The great danger in prisons, which is perhaps the principal source of the rigid discipline, is escapes. While some prisoners have become so adapted to institutional life that they do not wish to escape, the great majority would attempt to escape from a prison which was as delightful as some of the newspapers picture the actual prisons. The fundamental reason why people are opposed to confinement is the fact of confinement, and the most delightful entertainments, recreations, and food would not make such a place desirable. It has been found that women and children seldom escape from penal or reformatory institutions that have no walls. And notable cases of refusal to escape under the honor system and self-government are reported. But in general it is not safe to permit prisoners to work in the open without walls or guards. Doubtless the proper selection of prisoners for the outside tasks and the development of the proper morale in the group would prevent most of the escapes; the example of some institutions proves that it is not impossible. But there seems to be an inherent conflict between prisoners and prison officers; it is the business of the officers to keep the prisoners from escaping, and the ardent desire of the prisoners is to escape. Because of this antagonism, it will be extremely difficult to develop morale. While it would be absurd to contend that the antagonism cannot possibly be eliminated, it appears to be inherent in the prison system in a way that the vermin or lack of work are not.

This does not, however, make it impossible to eliminate most of the rigid discipline. The rule of silence, for instance, has been abandoned in many places with no increase in escapes. In certain institutions for the less dangerous classes of offenders a great deal of liberty is granted without unfavorable results. In certain institutions for the more dangerous classes of offenders the disciplinary punishments have decreased immensely with changes in personnel or in policies. In the hospitals for the insane, where, also, there is danger of escape, the disciplinary system is seldom as rigid as in prisons. In general, therefore, the system of rigid discipline, which is an important source of many of the more injurious effects of imprisonment, is to a considerable extent modifiable.

PUBLIC OPINION IN THE PRISON. The essential life of the prisoner is determined by his fellow inmates. Though the prison officers may control his overt behavior, they may not be able to control his feelings and thinking. In many essential respects the prisoners inevitably and always control the prison life. The prisoner must be orthodox in his statements and in behavior, from the point of view of the public opinion of the prisoners. Orthodoxy is more important in prisons than in outside life because in outside life a person has freedom of mobility but does not in prisons.[36] This public opinion of the prison is usually conducive to the retention and development of criminal attitudes. This is the result of three types of factors: the personal traits of the prisoners acquired prior to imprisonment, the suggestion of crime which results from the massing of criminals in one institution, and the opposition between the prisoners and authorities. It is not merely or primarily the contamination of one prisoner by another. It is rather the collective development of attitudes and opinions favorable to crime, and the collective repression of attitudes and opinions favorable to reformation. The group in that way becomes self-conscious, with crime as the common interest.

Welded together in the heat of kinship born of similarity of misfortune, these men cling to one another with a group loyalty not excelled in purity and inviolability by those fine emotions which animate and consolidate groups of human beings in any . . . relationship. . . . Every inmate talks freely only with some other inmate. Each knows the other's crime. There is no reticence over the discussion of crime. Everyone feels unashamed where everyone else has the same cause of shame. No matter how diverse the crimes may be, they are cast into a common pool of shamelessness because there is nobody except the hated official to inspire compunction. And this hardening of the conscience, which has its origin in the atmosphere free from shame, soon grows worse until we finally find it in a popular boasting of crimes committed and a brazen bragging of new crimes planned for the first opportunity of freedom.[37]

The tougher you are in prison, the more you are held in respect by the average prisoner.[38]

---

[36] Victor Nelson, *op. cit.*, pp. 18–19.
[37] L. A. Higgins, "Prison Education," *Mass. Prison Assoc. Leaflet*, No. 67, pp. 9–11.
[38] Victor Nelson, *op. cit.*, p. 150. Reprinted by permission of Little, Brown & Company, publishers.

A mother whose son was in a reformatory made this statement regarding him after a visit: "Last visiting day his looks frightened me. He'd brushed his hair down to his eyes. He looked sullen and ugly. At home he wears his hair straight back. Then he has a sweet face. I says 'Oh, son, don't wear your hair like that' and he answered gruffly 'I can't help it, mother. It don't do to look good. They get after you. You've got to look hard here to live.' " [39]

Thus public opinion is a very powerful factor in the prison, as in any other community. By means of it the prisoners support each other and secure admiration and status in proportion to the immensity of the crime or the cleverness of the technique or the length of the prison sentence. Riemer secured a prison commitment for the purpose of studying this public opinion and spent about four months in a state prison without the knowledge of any prisoner or administrative officer that he was not a bona fide offender. He has published a brief analysis of the process by which the in-coming prisoner assimilates the culture of the prison and in this sense becomes socialized.[40] The prisoner who does not have the support of this culture is indeed miserable. A dishonest detective was imprisoned in Sing Sing; the prisoners would have nothing to do with him, not because he had been a detective, but because he had demanded more than the contractual share of the loot from the criminals whom he permitted to work under his protection. The other convicts hissed him, scoffed at him, ridiculed him, and no prisoner in the institution was more uncomfortable.

If the prison is to be efficient as an institution for reformation, this public opinion must be controlled and directed either by the prison authorities or by the prisoners themselves under their natural leaders. Wines maintains that the successful prison administrators have learned how to control this public opinion.

Wherever there is a society, no matter what sort, there must of necessity be a public opinion, a general sentiment, an *esprit de corps.*
. . . The pre-eminent success of Wichern at the Rauhe Haus, of Demetz at Mettray, of Crofton in Ireland, of Charles Lucas at Val

[39] Madeleine Z. Doty, *Society's Misfits,* New York, 1916, p. 129. Reprinted by permission of D. Appleton-Century Company, publishers.
[40] Hans Riemer, "Socialization in the Prison Community," *Proc. Amer. Prison Assoc.,* 1937, pp. 151–155.

d'Yevre, of Obermaier at Munich, of Maconochie at Norfolk Island, of Guillaume at Neuchatel, of Sollohub at Mascos, of Petersen at Christiana, and of Brockway at Detroit was and is mainly secured through this potent agency. . . . It is to the formation of a sound, strong, controlling public opinion among his prisoners that a prison-governor must above all and before all direct his attention and bend his efforts—a public opinion, an *esprit de corps,* which will lend itself to the maintenance of a just, wise and effective reformatory discipline.[41]

To facilitate this control of the opinion of the prison, Wines and others have suggested that the population of the institution should always be small—not more than four hundred inmates. Not much other information is accessible regarding the methods by which prison administrators may secure such control. A few individuals have been able to do this, but this does not help the individual who is not able and wants to become able. It is a difficult task for the prison authorities, with the opposition and antagonism of the prisoners, to develop or control the opinion in its nature or content. There is little reason to hope that efforts by such authorities can ever be generally successful.

In addition there is little reason to think that the prisoners themselves will generally develop an opinion favorable to reformation. The leaders of the prison population look upon themselves as enemies of society, and on society as an enemy of the prisoners. They are not to be induced in ordinary circumstances to shift their attitudes, and even if one group of prisoners should make this shift the changing personnel would make it extremely difficult to keep up the tradition. This public opinion, therefore, seems to be an evil inherent in the prison system which can be modified only slightly or not at all.

ISOLATION OF PRISONERS. During the period of imprisonment the criminals are isolated from ordinary society. Isolation in prison is not similar to moving from one town to another, for the general social influences of the two towns would be much alike. But the prison is a very unnatural environment. One aspect of this is the separation of the sexes. Except in the George Junior Republic it is practically universal that the sexes are kept completely separate,

---

[41] E. C. Wines, *The State of Prisons and of Child-saving Institutions,* Cambridge, 1880, pp. 104–105.

by being confined either in separate institutions or in separate wards or cottages. This contributes, though it is not the sole cause, to the great frequency of sex perversions; these are found in all types of institutions, being one of the most difficult problems even in the institutions for juvenile delinquents.[42] A uni-sexual group, in prison or elsewhere, is strikingly different from ordinary society.

In addition the prisoner is shut off from contacts with situations in which he must spend his life after release. Visits from friends or relatives, writing and receiving letters, and similar methods of contact are restricted. No good reason for such restrictions exists, for these influences are undoubtedly the most humanizing influences that could be brought to bear upon many prisoners. Censorship, however, would be necessary in order to prevent the smuggling of drugs or means of escape.

It has been recognized since the time of Maconochie, at least, that the offender should be trained for society in society. Imprisonment seldom operates on this principle. Devon stated that the longer a person is in prison the less fit he is to return to social life,[43] and Osborne stated that a person might as well train for a race by remaining in bed for months as train in prison for a return to social life.[44] The person who is isolated from ordinary society cannot assimilate the culture of that society. The isolation can be reduced to some extent by greater freedom of association within the institution and by unlimited communication in person or by letter with friends or relatives, subject to censorship, by a general provision of newspapers, books and magazines, by lectures and picture shows. But there are evident limitations on the possibility of establishing ordinary social life within the prison. Consequently the reformative influences of the prison are distinctly limited in ways that cannot be modified.

LOSS OF STATUS FROM IMPRISONMENT. The prisoner suffers a loss of status and does not regain it when he returns to the community. In the prison he is customarily treated as a machine, with a number. In the Missouri state prison at one time a prisoner was not permitted to address another prisoner as "Mister"; probably the

---

[42] A. Berkman, *Prison Memoirs of an Anarchist*, New York, 1912, pp. 316 ff; Hobhouse and Brockway, *op. cit.*, pp. 586–589; Kate R. O'Hare, *In Prison*, New York, 1923, pp. 112–113; K. Plättner, *Eros im Zuchthaus*, Berlin, 1929; Victor Nelson, *Prison Days and Nights*, pp. 140–169, 191–197.

[43] J. Devon, *The Criminal and the Community*, London, 1912, p. 270.

[44] Introduction to F. Tannenbaum, *Wall Shadows*, p. xii.

same rule exists in most American prisons today. When he returns to society he is suspected, scorned, called an "ex-convict." The difficulty of securing employment, the danger of marrying and rearing children, the difficulty of accomplishing anything are well known. If the prisoner returns to his own community where his record is known, he has a desirable status only in the criminal group and with a few philanthropic individuals. The same thing is true if he goes to a new community and makes known his record; while if he conceals his record he is in constant fear that someone else will reveal it. It is customary, therefore, for a large number of criminals to feel that they have an insuperable difficulty and that the effort is not worth while. Consequently many of them seek recognition in the only way they can find it—by the development of an efficient technique of crime and an attitude of hatred toward society. These win the approval of a certain group, in which they secure a desirable status. In that way the feeling of set-apartness which comes with imprisonment is to some extent overcome. But no feeling of obligation to society or ambition to reform comes in connection with this.

The prison authorities are relatively powerless to alter this condition. The attitudes of the public are being modified somewhat, especially in connection with the probation system. But the evil is deeply rooted and makes reformation especially hopeless.

In general, it would be absurd to prophesy that these evils can never be removed from imprisonment. Almost any attitude may conceivably be developed in the general public toward prisons and prisoners. Kirchwey made the statement a few years ago that "the time would come when a degree from Sing Sing Prison would be worth as much as a degree from Harvard University." Both institutions are, to be sure, designed to provide training for people, but the present attitudes toward the two institutions are still so distinctly different that one suspects the time will be very distant. There is more reason, probably, to agree with Webb:

We suspect that it passes the art of man to contrive a prison which shall not be greatly injurious to the minds of the vast majority of the prisoners, if not also to their bodies.[45]

---

[45] S. and B. Webb, *English Prisons under Local Government*, p. 248. **Reprinted by permission of Longmans, Green & Co., publishers.**

DEMANDS FOR THE ABOLITION OF IMPRISONMENT. Fundamental and relatively inherent difficulties, as have been shown, accompany imprisonment. The prison must necessarily have a very low degree of efficiency in reformation. Certain leaders have become convinced that imprisonment as a principal policy in dealing with criminals should be regarded as undesirable and other methods substituted for it as rapidly as possible. The first thorough-going argument against imprisonment was stated by Desprez in 1868;[46] he demanded the substitution of agricultural colonies at home and abroad, with the conditions of life as much as possible like those of ordinary society. But this, after all, is imprisonment. The general tendency in the last generation has been to substitute probation for imprisonment; in Massachusetts at the present time probation is used for more offenders than imprisonment, though thirty-five years ago the ratio was about one to ten. Judge Hoffman reports that he has practically abandoned the policy of committing juvenile delinquents to institutions.

The old theory that to conserve law and order it is necessary to punish children by imprisonment is now practically obsolete. By means of thorough physical, mental and neurological examinations and careful supervision by a probation officer, it has become unnecessary to institutionalize any normal child. . . . It has been possible to reduce the number of delinquent boys now in the Industrial School at Lancaster from Hamilton County to fourteen.[47]

The better-trained judges in juvenile courts send relatively few children to institutions; the judges in rural districts, without the same point of view or assistance from trained probation officers, send a much larger proportion.

SELF-GOVERNMENT BY PRISONERS. It is often asserted that the solution of most of the problems of prison discipline and the best method of reformation of prisoners is self-government. It is necessary, therefore, to consider the history and nature of self-government in detail in order to determine its values for this purpose. As early as 1793 a modified system of self-government was used in the Walnut Street jail in Philadelphia. In the institutions for juvenile

---

[46] E. Desprez, *De l'abolition de l'emprisonnement.*
[47] C. W. Hoffman, "The Extension of Probation to Adult Cases," *Jour. Crim. Law and Criminol.,* 12:569, February, 1922.

delinquents in New York and Boston in the first few years of their history the delinquents had a self-governing court and voting participation in the election of some of the officers. In the Massachusetts state prison about 1845 the prisoners were organized into a society for improvement and mutual aid, primarily by discussion of topics of interest to the prisoners; the warden was president of the organization and it was clearly not spontaneous but was imposed upon the prisoners.[48] Brockway organized a system in the Detroit House of Correction in the decade of the sixties which he described as "almost complete self-government."[49] In 1895 William George founded the George Junior Republic at Freeville, New York, with the principle of self-government very prominent. Apparently it is this institution rather than the earlier precedents which has been important in the development of self-government in the last two generations, for one of the directors of this Republic was Osborne, who has been the chief propagandist for self-government.

Self-government has been developed during the last generation or two in institutions for juvenile delinquents, in county prisons, in state prisons and state reformatories, and in the naval prison at Portsmouth, New Hampshire. One of the best illustrations is the Iwahig Penal Colony in the Philippine Islands, which has had a long history and has been less dependent on the personality of the warden.

Lane gives a very good statement of the theory of self-government, as follows:

Self-government in penal institutions "is simply an application of the educational principle that people learn by doing. . . . . Its method is to establish on a small scale a society in which he can form the habits, accustom himself to the responsibilities and gradually acquire the wholesome mental attitudes that make normal life attainable. . . . It is an effort to train persons in the art of living in concert. . . . The traditional fealty of the law-breaker is first to himself and then to his 'pal.' Often this fealty to his 'pal' is the most inspiring thing in his life, his greatest spiritual achievement. The new fealty is loyalty

---

[48] O. F. Lewis, *The Development of American Prisons and Prison Customs, 1776–1845*, pp. 169–170.
[49] Z. R. Brockway, *Fifty Years of Prison Service*, p. 97.

to the whole body of prisoners. By its very operation, self-government identifies each inmate with all of his fellow-inmates." [50]

Many incidents are related to show the results of self-government. Under the system of self-government in Auburn prison the inmates were permitted one night, for the first time in the history of the institution, to attend a concert in the chapel; as they were on their way, the lights went out, leaving them in complete darkness so that any prisoner could easily have made a break and scaled the wall; the line halted automatically and remained absolutely quiet until the lights came on again.[51] The whole population of the Preston State School was permitted to attend the state fair; the president of the self-government organization, a boy eighteen years of age, assumed the entire responsibility for the return of the group and not one of the five hundred boys escaped. The previous year, before self-government started, the boys were taken to the state fair with one guard for each eight boys and thirteen boys escaped. Twenty prisoners from Auburn prison constituted an honor camp (with self-government in the prison and in this camp) about eighteen miles from the prison and remained there for three months with only one guard and for one week with no guard at all, though the average term of these prisoners was eleven years, though they had been convicted of serious crimes—burglary, robbery, murder, and manslaughter—and though only one of the twenty had less than a year to serve.[52] Osborne took nine cars of prisoners from Auburn, New York, to a town in New Hampshire to give a play; on the return the cars became separated in the darkness, some of them went astray, and Osborne returned with only two cars; the rest kept straggling in until they had all returned by ten o'clock in the morning. One of the prisoners who was on life sentence was asked why he did not try to get away and he replied:

Why the idea of running away never came into my head. I was sent to participate in a play and help raise some money for the boys. . . . I went because they sent me and if I had not come back they would have suffered the consequences.

[50] W. D. Lane, "Democracy for Law Breakers," *New Rep.*, 18:173, March 8, 1919. Reprinted by permission.
[51] T. M. Osborne, *Society and Prisons*, New Haven, 1916, pp. 169–171.
[52] Osborne, *op. cit.*, pp. 36–37.

And another one of the group explained:

There we were, all convicts, doing from two years to life, and free to run away, and yet no one did. What is more, I am sure if anyone had tried to do it, the others would have prevented him. .... Probably, too, there was also in our minds the knowledge that the rest would suffer if we failed them, and you know, there isn't a single one of us who regrets having come back. We feel that this experience has made the life of every one of us richer. I guess that we all came back because we were expected to and because everyone was sure that we would.[53]

When the system of self-government started in Sing Sing under Osborne the number of fights decreased, the number of escapes decreased, and the amount of work increased. Frederick A. Dormer, former principal keeper of Sing Sing and a prison officer under the old system for twenty years, after two years' experience with self-government, stated:

When the new system was inaugurated, I had little faith in it, but it has stood the test and I am convinced that the men are better under it, the officers are happier under it, and the officers' families are grateful for it.

Moyer, also, was opposed to this system when it started in Sing Sing, but he became an enthusiastic supporter. When he was warden at Sing Sing later he used self-government, and when he went as warden to the state prison of Kentucky he introduced it there also.

In spite of these glowing accounts of the accomplishments of a system of self-government in some places and the theoretical value of a system which develops self-control, many conscientious students of the prison system have grave doubts regarding it. The principal objections are, first, that shrewd prisoners get in control of the system and manipulate it for their own advantage, and second, that prisoners do not have a scientific attitude or technique for dealing with violations of their regulations and are likely to be more cruel and less scientific in their treatment of refractory prisoners than

---

[53] Tannenbaum, *op. cit.*, pp. 49–53. Reprinted by permission of G. P. Putnam's Sons, publishers.

are the prison officers. In the Deer Island House of Correction in Boston it resulted in frequent escapes; the officers of the league were arrogant toward the prison officials and lorded it over the inmates, locking up more in solitary confinement than had ever been locked up under the control of the prison officials. The prisoners finally pleaded to have it abolished. After a trial of self-government for about a year the inmates of the New Jersey State Reformatory at Rahway abandoned it by a vote that was practically unanimous; ward politics had developed, cliques were formed, the shrewd prisoners were elected to offices, and prisoners against whom grudges were held were punished. Preston abandoned the system after a short trial. Similarly the Connecticut State School for Boys found that disastrous political methods were used by the more clever boys; there, also, it was voted out unanimously. The New York State Prison for Women abandoned it after a short trial by vote of the inmates after the matron had made herself president of the league.[54] In fact the system has been abandoned in almost all places in which it was started two or three decades ago.

This experience with self-government does not furnish absolute proof that it must fail. It has been opposed by prison guards and keepers who were trained in the old school; it has been opposed by politicians outside of prison and by the prison contractors. In addition, the system has been introduced frequently without a proper appreciation by the prisoners of what it means. Osborne stated that the first reaction of some of the prisoners in Auburn was distrust. And Bowers stated:

I have found that the vast majority of convicts do not even care to attempt self-government. They distrust themselves as well as one another.[55]

Osborne reported, also, that it was very difficult to get this work started in Auburn because so few prisoners were trained to take responsibility and so many had lost the initiative they had on entrance into the prison. If self-government is not built upon educational work and a developed appreciation, it necessarily fails. If

[54] Madeleine Z. Doty, "Maggie Martin's Friends," *Century Mag.*, 89:880–883, April, 1915.
[55] P. E. Bowers, "Treatment of Criminals," *Jour. Delinq.*, 5:159, September, 1920.

self-government is to be used at all, it should probably be used after the prisoners have been divided into more homogeneous groups, and then they should be given control of their activities in different degrees.

THE HONOR SYSTEM. Osborne differentiates the honor system and the self-government system very sharply, as follows: The honor system means rewards granted by the warden for good behavior and loyalty to him; the self-government system means loyalty to the other prisoners and responsibility based on that. But it is doubtful if there is much difference either in principle or practice. Certainly the honor system involves loyalty to the other prisoners, because the prisoner who is given privileges or rewards does not want the other prisoners to suffer in case he fails. Consequently the same miraculous returns of prisoners who could easily have escaped, the same groups in camps without guards, the same improvement in morale and behavior may be found in the honor system. There is real merit in the system as it is worked in some places for the reason that it places responsibility on the prisoner and gives him an opportunity to make choices. But the honor system, as the self-governing system, finds its principal difficulty in dealing with the defective and psychopathic types. As Bowers states:

Mentally abnormal prisoners cannot be converted into men of honor by merely saying, "From henceforth I am going to trust you.[56]

The honor system has generally failed unless restricted to a very small number of selected prisoners. It does not seem, therefore, to be the solution of the general problem of prison discipline or the proper principle for reformation of prisoners as a group.

CONCLUSION. Finally, the suggestion has been made that the prison population should be divided into relatively homogeneous groups and policies adapted to these special groups. Those who are least dangerous and desperate should be housed in minimum security prisons, which have among other things the advantage of costing much less than the bastile type of prisons. In these institutions in which there would be least danger of escape and least antagonism between prisoners and officers, the program could include a large measure of freedom of choice, relative absence of rigid discipline,

---

[56] P. E. Bowers, "Treatment of Criminals," *Jour. Delinq.*, 5: 159, September, 1920.

variety of activities, frequent contacts with outside society, and other conditions which would largely eliminate the bad effects which have been characteristic of prisons in general.

At the other extreme the bastile type of prison building would still be needed for those who are most desperate and most danger-ous. Many of these offenders should, perhaps, be kept in confine-ment for life, though this should be determined with reference to the individual and his progress toward a life of freedom. The super-intendent of the unwalled farm located about ten miles from the state prison of Indiana, when asked what types of offenders got along best on the farm, replied, "Give me the murderers first of all, then the bank robbers, and the rapists. I don't want confidence men, pickpockets, and petty thieves." This suggests that it is not possible to select persons for minimum security institutions on the basis of crime alone. Whatever groups are found to be most dan-gerous should be retained in the maximum security institution. This would then be primarily a custodial institution, but would to some extent endeavor to provide agencies for reformation. It is probable that the reformative agencies here would be least successful. Pre-sumably progress from this institution to a life of complete freedom should be by degrees and by promotion to some of the intermediate institutions.

The prison should be a research and experiment station, however, as well as a place of custody. The authorities should have a thoroughly scientific knowledge of the principles of human behavior and should use all possible means of understanding the prisoners. There has been practically no development in the understanding and control of insanity that has not been largely influenced by the research work that has been done in the institutions for the insane. In the same way the prisons should be research stations. There will be many opportunities for experimentation of a psychological, sociological, or physiological nature and such work should yield results for control of the prisoners in confinement and of human behavior in general. The following experiment with a group of difficult young men in Elmira Reformatory illustrates what may be done. The superintendent found—

That there were certain boys in his institution who either would not or could not conform to its discipline, who fought among them-selves, broke the reformatory rules, were impertinent to officers and who made no progress in their studies or in their work. He sorted out these boys and placed them in separate quarters for eating, sleeping and working. He fed them a more generous and a more varied meal than that served ordinarily in the institution. He placed this class in charge of a young man with instructions to teach the boys how to play. . . . The instructor started games and the name of the winner in these games was conspicuously placed in the class room so that the boys always had before their eyes that John Jones was the best jumper or that Bill Smith was the best quoit thrower. By this means a spirit of emulation and a desire to excel was stimulated among these boys. School lessons especially prepared and adapted to the mentality (for all of these boys were mentally defective) were prepared and simple carpentry work was added. The result was astonishing. The play and the special lessons seemed to start every boy anew, for after being in the class an average of six months the boys could be returned to the regular life of the reformatory, adapting themselves to it, keeping up with their book class and their work in the industrial schools. This success with what had heretofore been "incorrigibles" shows what ought to be done in every institution.[57]

This policy would not, however, require the abandonment of the educational and reformatory work in prisons. There is no prospect that such a policy as suggested will be adopted immediately. The punishment attitude is still too strong, the other agencies that should be used as substitutes for the prisons are not sufficiently developed, and the prisons are not ready for the research work that should be carried on in them. It is not suggested, therefore, that the change should be made over night, even if public opinion would sanction it. In addition, those who should be committed to these institutions are those *judged* to be beyond reformation. This judgment may be incorrect. The judgment will certainly be made in relation to the reformative abilities of those dealing with offenders and these abilities are notoriously poor and undeveloped. Consequently it will be desirable to continue to improve the system of prison labor, of education, and of administration, as much as possible.

---

[57] New York, *Report of Department of Efficiency and Economy*, 1915, Vol. IV, p. 827.

SUGGESTED READINGS

Adler, H. M., "The Function of the Correctional Institution," *Mental Hygiene*, 5:778–783, October, 1921.

"Background of Prison Cruelty, by Number 13," *Atlantic Mo.*, 126:214–221, August, 1920.

Bates, Sanford, "Have Our Prisons Failed?" *Jour. Crim. Law and Criminol.*, 23:562–574, November, 1932.

Bates, Sanford, "Honor System for Inmates of Prisons and Reformatories," *Jour. Crim. Law and Criminol.*, 13:109–116, May, 1922.

Berkman, A., *Prison Memoirs of an Anarchist*, New York, 1912.

Bowler, Alida C., and Bloodgood, R. C., *Institutional Treatment of Delinquent Boys*, Washington, 1936.

Carter, J. M. (pseud.), "Prison Life as I Found It," *Century Mag.*, 80:752–758, September, 1910.

"Concerning Imprisonment, by One Who Has Suffered It," *Hibbert Jour.*, 8:582–602, April, 1910.

Debs, E. V., "Behind Prison Walls," *Century Mag.*, 104:362–372, July, 1922.

Derrick, C., "Segregation, Self-government, and State Control," *Proc. Amer. Prison Assoc.*, 1916, pp. 77–94.

Doty, Madeleine Z., *Society's Misfits*, New York, 1916.

Field, Henry E., and Winslow, R. S., "Constructive Factors in the Life of the Prisoner," *Jour. Crim. Law and Criminol.*, 23:205–230, July, 1932.

George, W. R., and Stowe, L. B., *Citizens Made and Remade*, New York, 1912.

Harrison, Leonard V., and Grant, P. N., *Youth in the Toils*, New York, 1938, Ch. 6.

Hart, H. H., and Others, "Report on Penal Institutions, Probation, and Parole," *Natl. Com. on Law Obs. and Enf.*, No. 9, 1931.

Hawthorne, Julian, *Confessions of a Convict*, Philadelphia, 1893.

Hawthorne, Julian, *The Subterranean Brotherhood*, New York, 1914.

Hobhouse, S., and Brockway, A. F., *English Prisons Today, Being the Report of the Prison System Enquiry Committee*, London, 1922, Part I, Ch. 23; Part II, Chs. 1–9; Appendix I.

In the Clutch of Circumstances, My Own Story, by a Burglar, New York, 1922.

Jennings, Al, *Through the Shadows with O. Henry,* New York, 1921.

Johnson, C. H., "Administrative Management of Institutions, from the Standpoint of the Inmate," *Proc. Amer. Prison Assoc.,* 1919, pp. 367–386.

Kirchwey, G. W., "The Human Element in Prison Discipline," *Proc. Amer. Prison Assoc.,* 1919, pp. 83–96.

Klein, P., *Prison Methods in New York State,* New York, 1920, Chs. 7 and 13.

Liepmann, Clara, *Die Selbstverwaltung der Gefängenen* 1927.

Lowrie, Donald, *My Life in Prison,* New York, 1912.

Nelson, Victor, *Prison Days and Nights,* Boston, 1933.

New York, *Report of Prison Survey Committee,* Albany, 1920, Ch. 11.

O'Hare, Kate R., *In Prison,* New York, 1923.

Osborne, T. M., *Society and Prisons,* New Haven, 1916.

Osborne, T. M., *Within Prison Walls,* New York, 1914.

Shaw, Clifford R., *The Jack Roller,* Chicago, 1930.

Shaw, Clifford R., *The Natural History of a Delinquent Career,* Chicago, 1931.

Simpson, R. M., "Why Prisons Fail," *Jour. Crim. Law and Criminol.,* 25:601–606, November, 1934.

Smith, Carrie W., "The Elimination of the Reformatory," *Proc. Natl. Conf. Social Work,* 1921, pp. 127–132.

Souder, C. D., "The State Industrial School as I Lived Through It," *Survey,* 31:715–718, March 7, 1914.

Sutherland, Edwin H., and Sellin, Thorsten, "Prisons of Tomorrow," *Annals of Amer. Acad. of Pol. and Social Sci.,* Vol. CLVII, September, 1931.

Tannenbaum, F., *Osborne of Sing Sing,* Chapel Hill, 1933.

Tannenbaum, F., "Southern Prisons," *Century Mag.,* 106:387–398, July, 1923.

Tannenbaum, F., *Wall Shadows,* New York, 1922.

Tasker, R. J., *Grimhaven,* New York, 1928.

Chapter Twenty – Three

PRISONS: LABOR

FOUR METHODS of occupying the time of prisoners are found in penal and reformatory institutions: idleness, punitive labor, productive labor, and training.

IDLENESS IN PRISONS. As early as the sixteenth century several European countries decided that it was good policy to require prisoners to work. In 1682 Pennsylvania provided that "all prisons should be workhouses." This tendency was to some extent off-set by the theory that labor interfered with meditation which was essential for penitence. At present no one defends idleness as a prison régime on any ground, and the recognition of the injurious personal and social effects is general. In spite of this, idleness in prisons is increasingly prevalent. More prisoners have learned that time and labor are of no value in prison than have learned the opposite. The proportion of prisoners who are engaged in productive labor has been steadily decreasing since the beginning of statistical reports on this topic in 1885. In that year 75 per cent of the inmates of state and federal prisons were engaged in productive labor, in 1932 only 52 per cent. Moreover, the number now engaged in productive labor is padded by over-assignment and probably at least two-thirds of the prisoners are in fact idle on an average day. In almost all of the prisons for misdemeanants, except in Southern states, the prisoners are idle all the time.

PUNITIVE LABOR. When labor was introduced into the prisons, it was regarded primarily as a means of punishment. In some places it was entirely punitive, consisting of such methods as the shot-drill—carrying a cannon ball back and forth in a long hall—or tread-mills or cranks, which were sometimes attached to pumps or other instruments so that the work was useful, but were frequently attached merely to a meter to measure the number of units of work performed. The laws required that the labor should be "hard and servile" or "publicly and disgracefully imposed." This punitive element in labor is still retained in many institutions by reason of the regulations, the methods of employment, or personal attitudes.

SYSTEMS OF PRODUCTIVE LABOR. Prison labor has been used, also, for the production of wealth. As such, it may be either public or private with reference to three items: the maintenance and discipline of the prisoners, the control of the employment, and the control of the sale of the products. The lease system gives a private individual or firm control over all three of these. The contract system gives a private individual control over the employment and the sale of the products, while the public retains control over the maintenance and discipline. The piece price system gives a private individual control over the sale of the products, but not over the employment or the maintenance and discipline. The public retains control over all three of these in the public account, state use, and public works and ways systems.

The three public systems differ from each other in the extent of the market. In the public account system the market is entirely unrestricted. In the state use system the market is restricted to the public institutions in the state in which the goods are produced. In the public works and ways system the market is restricted to the state, and in addition to the "sale" of public buildings or roads. The last system, therefore, is merely a specialized form of the state use system.

DEVELOPMENT OF THE SYSTEMS OF CONVICT LABOR. The first system of convict labor in America was the public works and ways system. After several temporary experiments with this system during the seventeenth and eighteenth centuries, it was practically abandoned until late in the nineteenth century. The earlier experiments were entirely forgotten. When the mechanics of St. Louis suggested in 1844 that the convicts in the state prison of Missouri be employed on road work the legislative committee appointed to investigate the proposition reported that the plan was absurd and unheard of.

The direction the memorialists propose should be given to the labor of the convicts is so novel and unusual in its character that the committee were rather at a loss to know whether the memorialists were serious in making the suggestion. . . . The utter impracticability of employing one hundred and seventy or eighty desperate men, felons and murderers, in working on the highways of the country, must be apparent to every reflecting mind.[1]

It was not until 1880 when the advent of the bicycle helped create a demand for good roads that the general use of convict labor for such purposes was resumed; this was stimulated still more by the development of the automobile.

A second form of convict labor in this country was the indenture system which appeared in Massachusetts as early as 1695. It was used in other colonies, also, and was generally a substitute for a fine. In 1804 Louisiana passed a law providing that if an offender could not pay his fine he might be bound out for a period not longer than seven years to any person who would pay his fine and that he might be restrained by chains. Missouri retained an indenture law until 1897. Massachusetts, after a long period of disuse, started about 1920 to use indenture again as a preliminary to parole, with a careful selection of cases.[2]

A third form of labor developed in Massachusetts when relatives or masters were permitted to furnish tools and materials on which prisoners might work; the products were turned over to these outsiders for sale or use.

A fourth system was the public account system. This was used generally in the early state prisons and even in county and municipal jails and houses of correction. The officers of the prisons were made responsible for the labor of the prisoners and the sale of the products; sometimes they were given commissions on the sales. The state expected to secure a profit from the institutions in this way. In general the system prevailed in the houses of correction in an irregular way, and in state prisons from about 1800 to 1825. It failed because of the inadequate equipment, capital, transportation facilities, and demand for prison-made goods, and because of the consequent inability to keep the prisoners steadily employed, and the introduction of machinery in outside industries which resulted in lower prices with which the prison products could not compete. After the failure of the system in this early period it was resumed

---

[1] Missouri General Assembly, 1844–1845, *House Journal*, Appendix, p. 242.
[2] Jessie D. Hodder, "Indenture of Prisoners," *Jour. Crim. Law and Criminol.*, 11:29–32, May, 1920.

in the decade of the eighties as a substitute for contract labor and has been more or less flourishing since that time.

A fifth system in order of appearance was the contract system, which had been authorized as early as 1798 in Massachusetts and was actually used there in 1807 but did not get well started until the decade of the twenties. Up to this time there had been no organization that could use prison labor to advantage and there was no market for prison products; the keeper could not use the labor of the prisoners and no master could. In the decade of the twenties the merchant-capitalist appeared, seeking for cheap labor which he found, in part, in the prisons. He could use this labor profitably and could enable the institution to make a profit on the prison labor. Thus he supplied the element which had been lacking in the public account system.[3] After that the contract system was the principal method of employing prison labor for a period of half a century, when great agitation arose against it. In later decades it has been steadily decaying.

A sixth system was the piece price system, which is similar to the contract system except that the state directs the labor of the convicts, turning over the finished product to a contractor at a specified price per piece. This system was used in the prisons of Pennsylvania in the beginning of the nineteenth century and in New Jersey from 1798 to 1838 in connection with the public account system. Except for a few such temporary trials it had its greatest development in the decade of the eighties and nineties, when the agitation against the contract system broke out. The piece price system was merely a subterfuge—really the contract system under a different name and in a somewhat preferable form.

A seventh system was the lease system, which was authorized in Massachusetts in 1798, in Kentucky in 1825, and in a few other states about the same time as in Kentucky. It was used in Missouri in 1839, the state prison being turned over entirely to the lessee, who had control of the maintenance, discipline, and employment of the inmates. The same system prevailed in the state prison of Illinois from 1839 to 1867. It had its greatest development in the South after the Civil War, where the states had no prisons and were financially unable to construct them. Consequently the convicts were leased to private parties who used their labor in lumber

---

[3] J. R. Commons, *History of Labor in the United States*, New York, 1918, Vol. I, pp. 153–155.

camps, turpentine camps, or other camps far from civilization. There they were completely under the control of the lessee, though nominally subject to inspection by the state. The greatest atrocities occurred in such camps. This produced opposition which drove this system out of all state prisons. It is still authorized by law and used somewhat in the county prisons of several Southern states.

The state use system came into prominence in the decade of the eighties. It had, to be sure, been used somewhat during the Civil War in the production of army shoes, guns, and other necessities of war. It became one of the principal substitutes for the contract system during the last two decades of the nineteenth century and developed rapidly. By 1899 it had been authorized by twenty-four states.

TRENDS IN PRISON SYSTEMS. The previous survey shows a distinct tendency to substitute public systems of prison labor for private systems. In 1885 only 26 per cent of the inmates of state prisons who were engaged in productive labor were employed in public systems, in 1905 47 per cent, in 1914 64 per cent, in 1923 81 per cent, and in 1932 84 per cent. Although the number of prisoners employed in private systems was comparatively small in 1932, twenty-two states used some of their prisoners in this manner, and of these nine used the contract system to some extent. In four states the number of prisoners employed under the contract system was greater than under any other system; in eleven states the number employed under the piece price system was the greatest.

This trend toward public systems has been still further strengthened since 1932, largely as a result of the Hawes-Cooper Bill, which was enacted in 1929 to go into effect in 1934. This is a federal law which enables the states to regulate the sale within their boundaries of commodities made in the prisons of other states. This act divests prison-made goods of their interstate character upon arrival in the state of their destination, so that their sale may be regulated without interfering with interstate commerce. By 1938 38 states had regulations which in different ways restricted the sale of imported convict-made goods. Consequently a manufacturer who makes goods in prisons is finding a constantly restricting market, and this form of manufacture is proving to be unprofitable. Of the prisoners engaged in productive labor in the prisons and reformatories of thirteen states, 47.9 per cent were working under contract or piece price systems in 1923, 30.8 per cent in 1932, and 18 per cent in 1936; 29.2 per cent were working under state use or public works and ways systems in 1923, 39.1 per cent in 1932, and 60.5 per cent in 1936. The public account system remained practically constant. The contract and piece price systems produced 81.1 per cent of the values of prison-made goods in 1923, 56.8 per cent in 1932, and 27.4 per cent in 1936; while the state use and public works and ways systems produced 12.7 per cent in 1923, 36.1 per cent in 1932, and 57.3 per cent in 1936.[4] This shows that the private systems are doomed to disappear if the present trend continues.

Another trend which is regarded by many students as very serious is the increasing idleness in prisons. In the states included in the study just described, 70.5 per cent of the prisoners were engaged in productive labor in 1923, 56.9 per cent in 1932, and 44.6 per cent in 1936. The value of the commodities produced in prison decreased from $1,850 per prisoner in 1923 to $650 in 1936. This decrease in the number productively employed is the principal reason for the decrease in the values produced.

COMPARATIVE VALUES OF THE SYSTEMS. The systems of prison labor should be appraised not only by the trends which they show but by the effects which they produce, especially with reference to the following points: the immediate welfare of the prisoners (health, satisfaction, etc.), training and reformation of prisoners, financial returns to the state, ease of efficient administration, and competition with free labor. It is impossible to weigh these factors accurately, but the reformation of prisoners must be regarded as of primary importance as long as penal and reformatory institutions continue to receive large numbers of prisoners who are turned back into the community after a relatively brief period of incarceration. Each of these factors will be considered with reference to the principal types of prison labor.

IMMEDIATE WELFARE OF THE PRISONERS. The immediate welfare of the prisoners is at the zero point in the lease system, with its private control of the maintenance and discipline of prisoners. The long hours of drudgery, the frequent and cruel punishments, the poor food, and the unsanitary conditions which almost always prevail in lease camps outweigh all the advantages this system may have. In one of the lease camps of Alabama, for instance, in the

---

[4] E. P. Sanford, "Prison Labor in 1936," *Monthly Lab. Rev.*, 47:251–268, August, 1938.

month of June, 1916, there were 103 convicts and 280 cases of punishment recorded; most of the punishments were whippings; one prisoner received 105 lashes.[5]

The contract system has frequently been almost as injurious as the lease system. The control is nominally in the hands of the prison authorities, but in many places the prison authorities have been merely agents of the contractors. An illustration of some of the worst features of the contract system, which might be found duplicated in many other places, came from the state penitentiary of Maryland for 1909. The records show for that year 3,067 punishments, of which 736 were cases of "cuffing up" (hands stretched up above the head and fastened in iron cuffs, and the weight either lifted off the heels or entirely off the feet). Almost invariably these punishments were recorded as due to "failure to get work," or "indifferent to work." The prisoners were punished because their work did not satisfy the private contractor.[6] An investigating commission found, in addition, that the prison was decidedly lacking in sanitary and medical facilities, that many undesirable transactions were being made between prisoners and private employees of the contracting company, that the prisoners hated the warden bitterly, and that the warden had been using his influence in suspicious and underhanded ways to prevent the passage of legislation which would end the contract system. The contractors, however, have been chastened in most states by opposition to their system, and at the present time the contract system has few of the earlier abuses.

Little difference can be found among the several public systems in their effects on the immediate welfare of the prisoners. The public works and ways system, in so far as it consists of road work, has the advantage of being outdoor work, away from the hated walls, and the disadvantage of inadequate facilities for bathing, medical care, recreation, and other necessities.

TRAINING AND REFORMATION. The following points related to the value of a system of prison labor in training and reforming prisoners should be considered: selection of the work for which the prisoner is best fitted, interest of the prisoner in the work, the contribution of the work to the economic and moral development

---

[5] Alabama, "Report of Legislative Investigating Committee on Convicts and Highways," 1919, *Legis. Doc. 6*, pp. 8–9. See, also, Isadore Shapiro, "The Prison Problem in Alabama," *Proc. Amer. Prison Assoc.*, 1917, pp. 90–94.

[6] Maryland, *Report of Penitentiary Penal Commission*, 1913, pp. 84, 127.

of the prisoner, continuing the work after release, and the possibility of paying a wage that will increase the interest and efficiency of the prisoner. Some people have limited their attention to the first of these and have maintained that because a large proportion of the prisoners (approximately 70 per cent for the United States in general) are unskilled workers, generally engaged in outdoor work, prior to imprisonment, they should be employed in outdoor and relatively unskilled work during imprisonment. The conclusion does not necessarily follow; the fact of criminality may indicate that just the opposite training should be given. It is necessary to take all of these factors into account.

The importance of continuation after release of the work learned in prison is sometimes minimized, also. It is asserted that the prisoner does not wish to tell where he learned the trade, he wishes to throw off everything that reminds him of his prison career, and, in practice, he seldom learns a trade sufficiently well to pursue it efficiently after his release. The argument is pertinent, but, nevertheless, if other things are equal it is preferable for a prisoner to learn a trade that he can pursue after release rather than one he cannot possibly pursue.

In order that prisoners may have the work best fitted to them and most interesting to them and that can be pursued after release it is necessary that the prison industries be diversified. The objection to all of the private systems, the public account system, and the public works and ways system, is that the work is not diversified, and there is little opportunity to adapt the work to the requirements of the individual prisoner. The state use system has a decided advantage over all of the other systems in this respect. In order to supply the requirements of the institutions of the state a great many occupations are introduced into the prison. In New York State, for instance, more than 700 articles for the institutions of the state are produced in prisons. In Minnesota, on the other hand, with the public account system, the prisoners engaged in productive labor are practically all employed in making twine and farm machinery. The prison has such a monopoly in this field that it would be necessary for a prisoner after release to cross several states in order to find similar work outside of the prison.

The possibility of paying a wage to the prisoner is limited to the public systems, though bonuses for extra work may be paid under the private systems. The public systems are about equal in respect to the possibility of wages, except that the one which is financially most profitable will be best able to pay the wage.

FINANCIAL RETURNS TO THE STATE. The lease system has proved to be the most profitable to the state of all of the systems. There is almost no cost to the state and a relatively large return. The contract system, also, often yields a big profit. In Maryland all of the expenses of the prison were paid from the earnings of the prisoners, and in addition a net profit of half a million dollars was secured from 1888 to 1912. But it is doubtful if this gain should count for much in comparison with the effects of these systems on the prisoners. In the early history of prisons the Pillsburys were the most efficient prison administrators from the point of view of financial profits, but Amos Pillsbury, shortly before his death, expressed his regret that he had not reserved the earnings of his prisons for the benefit of the prisoners.[7]

Some prisons have made profits under each of the public systems. Even local institutions with a fluctuating personnel, such as the Chicago House of Correction, have made a profit. There are also examples of losses under each of the systems. The equipment has frequently been so poor, the methods of management so inefficient, the initial appropriation so inadequate, that no method of control could yield profits. It is probable that with good management and sufficient capital the public account system stands to make the greatest gain. The state prison of Minnesota has made a very spectacular showing with the public account system. It started to produce binding twine in 1891, added farm machinery in 1907, and has used nothing except the public account system since 1909. During the first seven years the prison suffered a net loss from its productive industries, but made profits each year thereafter until 1929, except in 1921 when a deficit of $93,000 was reported. The institution accumulated from its industries a revolving fund for productive purposes which amounts to about $4,000,000.[8] Though Minnesota has a large profit on its industries, several other states which tried to produce binding twine either sustained a loss or made a very small profit.

The state use system, theoretically, has the advantage of an assured market, especially if the institutions of the state are com-

[7] Z. R. Brockway, *Fifty Years of Prison Service*, p. 33.
[8] Only the maintenance costs are included in determining profit and loss in most of the reports. The state legislature of Minnesota appropriated about $3,000,000 for the state prison from 1905 to 1921.

pelled by law to purchase their supplies from the penal institutions in so far as their requirements can be met there. The state use system, therefore, stands a better change of avoiding disastrous losses than does the public account system. In practice, however, the prisons under the state use system probably have a larger proportion of their inmates idle than prisons under any other system, due primarily to the opposition of private industries to any competition from prison labor.

EASE OF EFFICIENT MANAGEMENT. The private systems are the easiest for the state to manage, since the state does not sell the products. The public account system is the most difficult of the public systems from this point of view, since it sells prison products on the open market in competition with private industry. The state use system, with its preferred market, is in this respect most easily managed. Even this system, as any other big business, cannot be successful without efficient administration. Public works and ways systems have two disadvantages from the standpoint of administration: difficulty of preventing escapes, and difficulty of sanitation in temporary camps.

COMPETITION WITH FREE LABOR. The consideration that has in the past been most important in determining the system of prison labor is competition with free industry. From early times employers and employees have objected to prison labor on the ground that it was unfair competition. It has been assumed frequently that the objections came entirely from the trade unions, but this is decidedly fallacious.[9] One illustration of the opposition by manufacturers or entrepreneurs is furnished by the efforts of the association of vehicle and implement manufacturers and dealers to ruin or prevent the development of the manufacture of binding twine and farm machinery in the state prison of Minnesota.[10] A garment manufacturing association reported that it had spent $200,000 in an advertising campaign to combat the competition of prison-made goods. Since the origin of prison labor in the United States efforts have been made by employers and employees to restrict the com-

---

[9] For cases of objection by employers see U. S. Commissioner of Labor, *Report on Convict Labor*, 1905, pp. 49–172; Michigan, *Report of Bur. of Labor and Industrial Statistics*, 1887, pp. 115–118, and 123; A. M. Edwards, "Labor Legislation of Connecticut," *Pub. Amer. Econ. Assoc.*, 1907, 3rd series, Vol. VIII, p. 247; H. S. Riddle, "State Use System of Ohio," *Natl. Com. on Prisons and Prison Labor*, Leaflet, 1919, No. 45, pp. 21–23.

[10] U. S. Department of Commerce, Bureau of Corporations, *Report on Farm-machinery Trade Associations*, 1915, pp. 107–110.

petition by such methods as stamping the goods "prison made," diversification of prison industries, prohibition of the use of power machinery in prison industries, restriction of interstate marketing of prison-made goods, exportation of prison-made goods, reduction of hours of labor of prisoners, requirement that prison-made goods be sold at a price not less than the market price, and various other laws or projects.

Are managers and wage-earners justified in the contention that prison products are unfair competition? And are the systems different in their effects on free labor? It should be recognized that any system of prison labor will cause competition with outside labor. If a prison makes brooms and sells them exclusively to state institutions, so much work is taken from free industries which previously supplied the brooms. If the convicts make roads, so much work is taken from outside contractors and laborers, though it is true that some of the work might not have been done at the same time under private management. The competition, in this general sense, is very small. About one-tenth of 1 per cent of the productive laborers are in prisons, and many of the prisoners would be more or less efficiently employed if they were not in prison. This makes the total competition of prison labor insignificant.

This is not the only thing to be considered. A system in which the market price is directly affected by the competition of prison goods, sometimes called price competition, is distinctly different from a system in which the price is affected less directly, sometimes called quantity competition. In the long run the two systems do not differ materially, but in their immediate effects they do differ. Prison-made goods which are not sold in the general market influence prices only through the quantity produced, while those that are sold in the general market influence prices in addition by entering into the bargaining processes, resulting in price cutting that may be temporarily disastrous. Quantity competition and price competition would not differ if prices were fixed in a purely automatic way, but prices are not actually fixed in that way.

The system of prison labor which produces the smallest number of units per prisoner per day causes the least competition, when considered only as a quantity matter. The Commissioner of Labor in 1905 reported that the state use system was the least efficient.[11]

11 U. S. Commissioner of Labor, *Convict Labor*, 20th An. Report, 1905, p. 35.

The reports on prison labor show that the average prisoner produces a smaller value under the state use system than under any other system. The inferiority of the state use system in this respect was less in 1932 than in other years, probably because the state market was affected less by the depression in 1932 than were other markets.

The effect of prison industry on free industry would be negligible if goods were produced in prisons in the same proportion and with the same diversity as outside and were sold in the same market. But this is not the case. Prison goods have a practical monopoly in certain fields and are in effective competition in several fields. The total value of prison-made goods sold on the open market in 1923 was $45,000,000 and of this amount $18,500,000 was in the form of garments. About 5 per cent of the shirts made in the United States were made in prisons, but almost all of the prison-made shirts were workshirts and within that part of the garment industry the competition was very severe. Prisons make 6.5 per cent of the rope and twine manufactured in the United States, but the prison-made commodity is almost always in the form of binding twine and in that particular part of the industry, again, the competition is serious. The various systems differ in respect to this concentration of work. The private systems concentrate on a small number of commodities. The same is true, to a limited extent, of the public works and ways, and the public account systems. On the other hand, the state use system tends to diversification, because the demands of the institutions of the state are diversified.

Competition, in general, is less harmful if spread over a wide territory. The private systems generally produce commodities that enter the general commerce of the nation, as do, also, the public account and the contract systems. In 1932 88 per cent of the goods produced under the contract and piece price systems were sold outside of the states in which produced, and 32 per cent of the goods produced under the public account system were so sold. The goods produced under the state use or public works and ways are necessarily confined to the state in which they are produced, and this results in restricting the competition geographically.

The constancy of the competition is, likewise, important. Even though prison labor might compete injuriously with outside industry, a readjustment could be made so that the injury would be temporary. But if the commodities produced in prison change from one administration to another, the necessity for readjustment becomes continuous and the injury is therefore continuous. Consequently it is desirable that the system of prison labor should remain fairly constant from year to year in the types of commodities produced. From this point of view the lease, the contract, and the piece price systems are objectionable. The great danger of competition is that prison-made goods will be sold in the general market below the market price. This is made possible under any system with an unrestricted market, because the government may subsidize the system. Frequently contracts have been granted that enabled manufacturers to sell prison-made goods far below the market price. This may occur, also, under the public systems. For instance, in the public account system in Connecticut, school desks which were produced in prison at a cost of $15 were sold at first at a price of $18.75; but a supply was accumulated and could not be sold; the price was finally reduced to $7.50 and then to $1.21.[12] Because of the connection between the contract system and politics there has been more danger of a subsidy under that system than any other. The same thing may happen under the public account system. In 1925 when the management of the Missouri penitentiary changed, a surplus stock of overalls, valued at $1,300,000 was dumped on the market in a period of three months at a price about 75 per cent as high as the cost of production in free factories. Private manufacturers asserted that this dumping broke the market and upset the prices for a year and a half. The state use and public works and ways systems are decidedly superior in this respect.

In general, the state use system is less injurious to free industries than any other system. This is the system which the outside industries have advocated as preferable to any other system. But the enactment of an exclusive state use system has by no means satisfied the manufacturers. The cotton manufacturers, for instance, are in favor of a state use system but object strenuously if prison labor is used to produce cotton goods for state use; the furniture industry is in favor of state use, but objects to prison labor in the manufacture of furniture for state purposes. And so on for each other industry. Probably no other system has resulted in such strenuous efforts to keep the prisoners out of particular industries as has the state use system. There is in this respect a surprisingly different

---

[12] A. M. Edwards, "The Labor Legislation of Connecticut," *Pub. Amer. Econ. Assoc.*, 3rd series, Vol. VIII, 1907, pp. 250–251.

behavior of business men in European countries, where almost no difficulties are raised on this point.

GENERAL SUMMARY REGARDING THE COMPARATIVE VALUES. The lease system, contract system, and piece price system are distinctly undesirable because of the difficulty under any private system of controlling the work and life of the prisoners in the interest of their reformation rather than in the interest of the contractor or lessee, and also because these systems have generally resulted in collusions with politicians and a division of the spoils, which has disrupted the prison administration and turned it over to the mercies of the political employees. These systems have, however, had the merit of providing steady employment for practically all able-bodied prisoners.

On the other hand, each of the public systems has merits, though the state use system is probably superior to the public works and ways and to the public account systems, as a general basis of prison employment. The primary defect of the public systems, and specifically of the state use system, is the idleness of an increasing proportion of prisoners under this system. This is due, on the one hand, to the legislative or administrative restrictions on occupations, resulting from the constant pressure of each industry to keep out prison competition, and on the other hand to the superiority of private salesmanship, including the bribery of purchasing agents for the public institutions. In view of this, the time has not yet arrived for an exclusive state use system. It is desirable, especially, to retain a public account system, so that if the state becomes unable because of the opposition of free industries to sell its products to the public institutions, it can then sell the surplus on the open market. This sale of the surplus on the open market is more likely to injure the free industry than is the sale to public institutions. This will tend to restrain private industries from unfair practices in preventing the sale of prison-made commodities to public institutions. Unless some alternative is retained prison labor will be eliminated entirely in many states. Gill reaches the following conclusion:

Considering the circumstances in every state, it is doubtful if any one system of production or marketing may yet be selected as universally applicable. Experience has indicated that the lease system is intolerable and that the exclusive contract or piece-price system is not expedient. It has not yet demonstrated that the exclusive state-use system is desirable. Perhaps in ten or twenty years New Jersey, Pennsylvania, Ohio, or New York [which have exclusively state-use systems] may demonstrate it. The best that can be said at present is that a variety of systems has proved most successful, all things considered. With one group of states experimenting with exclusive state use, another experimenting with state use and public account, and a third trying contract, state use, and public account, another twenty years may develop the ideal system.[13]

It may be noted that there is practically no idleness in European prisons and also that there is practically no opposition to the use of prison labor for the production of articles for state use.

ADMINISTRATIVE PROBLEMS. Several problems confront the administrative officers of a prison with reference to the employment of prisoners, even after the system of labor is settled. One of the problems is the assignment of prisoners to their tasks. No state has developed this as satisfactorily as has New Jersey. A beginning of job analysis and personnel work has been made there. The different classes of jobs are studied and the kinds and numbers of laborers required are determined. Each prisoner is studied on entrance to determine the kind of labor he is equipped to do. The prisoner's preferences are noted and he is given the occupation he wishes if it is possible to do so in view of his capacities and the institutional opportunities.[14]

A second problem is the institutional work, such as cleaning and cooking. It is generally agreed that this work should be performed by prisoners. If a sufficiently profitable system of productive labor could be devised, it would not be objectionable to hire free laborers to perform such parts of the institutional work as are not desired by the prisoners. In the meantime it will be necessary for the prisoners to do this work. The same method should be used in assigning prisoners to this work as to other tasks—job analysis and personnel study—so that the prisoner will be fitted as well as possible for his task and his preferences will be considered.

A third problem is the organization of working time so that interference with work will be reduced to a minimum, consistent

---

[13] Howard B. Gill, "The Prison Labor Problem," *Annals of Amer. Acad. of Pol. and Social Sci.*, 157:96–97, September, 1931.

[14] New Jersey, *Report of State Prison*, 1920–1921, pp. 95–100, 112–120.

with the performance of other necessary activities. Two questions are involved in this: The first is merely a question of organization, involving no essential principle. On May 18, 1920, 729 men were working in the Auburn prison shops; on that day 620 of these were called from work for school, band practice, self-government league work, work in other shops, repair work, doctor, or discipline; five were called from work to practice baseball; altogether this involved 1,039 hours of lost time that day, an average of 1.4 hours per inmate. It frequently happens that when one prisoner is called from work, a process on which eight or ten other prisoners are engaged is interrupted. Most of these interruptions could be prevented by a proper distribution and organization of prison activities.[15] The second question involves a more difficult principle. It is: Which should take priority in the prison—work or formal education? Should the school work be done in the daytime, which would mean interference with work, or at night, which would mean that the prisoner would get a smaller benefit from the school because of his fatigue? It is possible, of course, to have school half of the day and work half of the day. But should the time be divided equally between education and labor? Some prison authorities decide that the division should be equal, but the general practice is to give very much less than half of the time to education. No one really knows the comparative values of work and of formal education for purposes of reformation. It will doubtless vary from one individual to another and can be determined for each prisoner only by a thorough acquaintance with his personal traits and attitudes. It is not necessary to use the same policy in all prisons or in all wards of a prison. The prisoners should be classified, and the group that can profit by education should be given much education and little labor.

VOCATIONAL TRAINING. According to the special committee of the American Prison Association 70 per cent of the prisons do not teach trades.[16] Some have explained or justified this by the argument that prisoners cannot be taught trades that they will follow after release from prison.

It is manifestly impossible to teach men a trade while confined in prison. The experience at Elmira confirms this. A most complete sys-

---

[15] New York, *Report of State Commissioner of Prisons,* 1920, p. 60.
[16] F. Moore (Chairman), "Report of Special Committee on Prison Labor," *Proc. Amer. Prison Assoc.,* 1919, p. 122.

tem of trade schools, well-equipped with the necessary machinery and supplies and taught by practical instructors has been long established in Elmira. The prisoners committed to Elmira are young men, much more able to learn than the elder prisoners committed to State prisons. If trades could be taught in prisons, certainly Elmira should be able to demonstrate it, yet with eighteen months daily instruction of two and one-half hours, and frequently for the whole day, where both theory and practice are conjoined, all that Elmira can do for its men, is to make them practically advanced apprentices and nothing more. The parole records of Elmira show that not ten per cent of the men released from Elmira under parole follow the trade taught them in that institution.[17]

The experience of Elmira is not conclusive; the inmates, as a rule, have not had the privilege of selecting their own trades, and the training there is not adequate in all respects.[18] The New York Prison Survey Committee, after making the most thorough study of the question that has been made, concluded that vocational training should be continued and presented an outline of the prerequisites for a suitable system of vocational training. In general everyone agrees that it is desirable to have vocational training in the institutions for juvenile delinquents. The difficulties are much greater in the institutions for adults and the results not so apparent. But at this point, again, classification of the prisoners and a policy of vocational education or training for some of the classes and not for others appears to be the solution.

WAGE PAYMENTS TO PRISONERS. Payment of wages to prisoners is not a new device. As early as 1700 Massachusetts provided that inmates of the houses of correction should receive eight pence out of every shilling they made, under a system in which masters or relatives furnished tools and materials. In the county prisons of Pennsylvania in 1790, in the state prison of New York in 1796, of New Jersey in 1798, Massachusetts in 1800, and Maryland in 1811, the wardens were instructed by the laws of the state to put the prisoners at hard labor and give them wages as an incentive to work. It was expected that the sale of the products would produce a profit for the institution from which the wages could be

[17] New York, *Report of Department of Efficiency and Economy*, 1915, Vol. IV, pp. 791–794.
[18] *Ibid.*, pp. 923–925.

paid, and that the prisoners would pay for their maintenance out of the wages. But no profits were secured, no wages could be paid, and the prisoners had to be maintained at the expense of the state. For a time prisoners were held until they paid for their maintenance, but the prisons soon became congested and the system was modified. After this general failure of the wage system in prisons, it disappeared almost entirely. But in 1852 the Eastern Penitentiary of Pennsylvania began to pay small wages to prisoners. Other states gradually adopted the same policy. In 1932 66 of the state institutions and 5 of the 12 federal prisons paid wages to prisoners. Wages generally range from 2 to 15 cents per day.

Various reasons have been given for paying wages to prisoners: to increase the efficiency, to increase the interest in work, to prevent prison-made goods from selling below market prices, to make provision for the dependents of prisoners, and to secure abstract justice. A real wage would tend to make the prisoner more interested in his work, more contented, less hostile toward the state. It would give him an opportunity to make choices in disposing of his money, thus introducing an element of foresight which is sadly lacking in the conventional system. These things will help change the attitudes of prisoners.

It has been our experience in Michigan that the compensation of prisoners has not only made for better prison discipline, but has tended toward reformation, and has enabled men to feel more like men.[19]

It is desirable that the prisoner should continue to maintain his family, not only for the sake of the dependents, but also because this gives him an attitude while he is in prison that is helpful in the modification of his behavior, and it will lead to a more kindly reception by the family when he is released. He can go back to them with the feeling that they have not been pauperized, that he has been supporting them, and that they will welcome him.

The argument is raised, however, that the prisoner has no right to a wage because he has forfeited his right to the products of his labor. The Attorney General of Texas in 1913 held that a law authorizing the payment of wages to prisoners was unconstitutional on the ground that when an offender is convicted he loses not only his freedom but also his right to the products of his labor, and that

---

[19] Eamann, *Jour. Crim. Law and Criminol.*, 6:519, November, 1915.

the sentence makes him both a prisoner and a slave. The state constitutions, with two exceptions, provide that slavery is illegal except for conviction of crime. This, however, does not mean that the prisoner must necessarily be a slave. The argument for a wage may rest, therefore, either on the right of the prisoner to a wage or on expediency. After all these amount to the same thing, for one has no rights except those which, from the point of view of the group, it is expedient that he should have.

It is asserted by some, in a specious way, that this amounts to paying a person to commit crime. But, of course, it is a payment for work during incarceration, not for the crime.

Some maintain that money in the hands of a criminal is likely to be dangerous, that the prisoner will go on a spree as soon as released, refrain from work until all his money has been spent, and then drift into crime again. But it probably affects as many in the opposite way. Ex-prisoners drift into crime because they find it difficult to get work and their money does not last until they secure their first wages. If a satisfactory system of gradual release under the supervision of a parole officer is developed, it will be unnecessary for either of these after-careers to be frequent.

Again, some maintain that reward for work should consist in the reduction of the period of imprisonment rather than in money. This is an unsatisfactory method of determining the time of release; though regularity and efficiency of work should be taken into account in determining the fitness of the prisoner for release, these should not be the sole determinants, as would be necessary if a person were paid for his work by a reduction in the time of imprisonment.

If a wage is to be paid, it should be determined primarily by the efficiency of the prisoner. As a matter of fact prison wages are dependent on a variety of other things, according to the statutes or regulations of prison boards, such as good conduct, the number of children in the prisoner's family, and especially on the profits of the institution. It is theoretically unfair, assuming that a wage is to be paid, to make it dependent on the profit of the institution for the reason that the institution may fail to make a profit because of conditions over which the prisoner has no control, such as inadequate working capital, poor location of prison, poor choice of industries, poor salesmanship, or poor organization of the work. Galvanized garbage cans are made in one of the state prisons of New York; this prison is quite distant from New York City, where most of the cans are sold and, as a result of the high cost of transportation, the industry suffers a net loss. If these cans were made in one of the penal institutions near New York City and the difference in freight saved, the industry would show a net profit. The state prison of Minnesota and some of the workhouses, such as the ones in Chicago and Detroit, have been able to make profits. If other penal institutions fail to make profits it is presumably not due to the inefficiency of the prisoners, but to the poor organization of work, the inadequate equipment, or the inefficient salesmanship. Many of the institutions in New York State have made no profits, due to the idleness of a large part of the prison population. This idleness is due to the fact that the prisons do not get orders for a sufficient quantity of goods to keep the prisoners busy. Since, under the state use system, the prison goods have a preferred market in all of the institutions of the states and actually produce only 5 per cent of the goods used in these institutions, the failure is in salesmanship rather than in industrial efficiency. For such conditions the prisoners are not responsible and the refusal of wage payments for the failure to make profits in the prison industries is theoretically unjustified.

It is preferable to base the wage on a comparison of the efficiency of free labor and of prison labor, taking into account the physical equipment and the organization of work. This should determine the wage scale for the prison, and wages should be paid whether the prison makes a profit or suffers a loss. Prisoners should be paid even when idle, if their idleness is due to no fault of their own. In view of the popular attitude toward prison labor, this theoretical principle is not likely to be used.

Some prisons undertake to assist the dependents of prisoners from funds separate from the wages of the prisoners. The Detroit House of Correction and the Minnesota State Prison are examples of such systems. This policy is of doubtful value. It would be preferable to support the dependents, if necessary, by mothers' pensions because a great deal of supervision and personal service is generally needed for these families and the prison authorities cannot do this work. It is possible, however, for the prison to make a payment from its earnings into the fund of the mothers' pension department, sufficient for its share of the support of dependent families.

INDUSTRIAL ACCIDENTS AND DISEASE IN PRISON. An explosion in the convict mines of Alabama in 1911 killed 123 prisoners.

A great deal of tuberculosis among the prisoners of Alabama is due to the nature of their prison work. About 50 per cent of the prisoners work in coal mines and only the strongest are selected for this work; but 80 per cent of the patients admitted to the tuberculosis hospital for prisoners came from the coal mines.[20] Lowrie stated that the cog machines in San Quentin prison had no shields, and that in 1909 19 amputations occurred for which no compensation was available.[21]

In the earlier period many states passed special laws for the compensation of injured prisoners. Thus, in 1872 the Assembly of Missouri provided that Henry Dillard be paid seventy cents a day in provisions and clothing because, though inexperienced at blasting, he had been compelled to do this work and had been injured so that he lost one hand and both eyes and suffered other injuries that rendered him permanently incapable of work.[22] At the present time most states make practically no provision for injured prisoners. If the state should compel private establishments to maintain safe and sanitary places of employment, it should certainly have similar standards for its prison workshops. Prison industries should, therefore, be subjected to all of the laws that govern private establishments, and when prisoners are injured, they or their dependents should be compensated just as in private industry. Alabama has a fund for compensation of injured prisoners and their families. In 1927 Wisconsin and Maryland passed laws which extended the benefits of workmen's compensation acts to prisoners, and in the same year California passed an act which excluded prisoners engaged in road work from the workmen's compensation acts.

LABOR IN INSTITUTIONS FOR WOMEN AND CHILDREN. The problems of prison labor have been discussed primarily from the standpoint of the adult male convict. But the problems are essentially the same for all kinds of institutions for delinquents. There is no difference between institutions in the desirability of work rather than of idleness, the desirability of public rather than private control of employment, the desirability of careful administrative selection of occupations and assignment of prisoners, of payment of wages, and of compensation for accidents.

A good deal of outdoor work is desirable for women delinquents,

---

[20] Alabama, "Report of Legislative Investigating Committee on Convicts and Highways," 1919, *Legis. Doc. 6*, p. 11.
[21] D. Lowrie, *My Life in Prison*, p. 138.
[22] Missouri, 26th General Assembly, *Appendix to Laws*, 1871–1872, p. 21.

and they are active and enthusiastic in this work.[23] This aptitude should certainly be considered in determining the occupations of delinquent women, and similar occupations should be secured for them after release, if possible. The labor of juvenile delinquents in the earlier history of juvenile institutions was let out on contracts in making cane-seats for chairs, making brushes, cigars, or shoes. Later it was used largely for housework with some incidental trade training. Many of the institutions are now established in rural districts and the juvenile delinquents are employed in farm work. It is probable that a larger proportion of the children in institutions should be given vocational training than in the institutions for adults, but otherwise the problems are very much alike.

LABOR IN JAILS. Prisoners in a large proportion of local jails are completely idle, except for maintenance of the institution. In 1932 29.6 per cent of the prisoners serving sentences in county jails were engaged in productive work, and these were almost exclusively in the Southern states, where the chain gang flourishes. In the workhouses in cities of more than one hundred thousand population 31.8 per cent of the convicted prisoners were engaged in productive labor, but in about a third of the workhouses no productive labor was provided. It is difficult to furnish steady employment in many of the jails, with their shifting personnel and small numbers. This is one of the important reasons for the belief that the jail should be abolished. If the jail were abolished, the employment problem would be divided as follows. Those convicted of misdemeanors which would now result in jail sentences should, if committed at all, be held in state institutions which had a sufficiently large and stable population to justify facilities for employment of all inmates capable of work. Those who are now held in jail awaiting trial would be almost entirely removed by the measures previously described, and those who remain would be held in institutions under the control of the state. These institutions, also, should serve a sufficiently large population to justify them in providing facilities for the inmates who care to work for wages. Under the constitution the labor could not be made compulsory, but most prisoners prefer to work if given an opportunity.

---

[23] Jean Weidensall *The Mentality of the Criminal Woman*, Baltimore, 1916, p. 285.

SUGGESTED READINGS

Barnes, H. E., "Economics of American Penology, State of Pennsylvania," *Jour. Pol. Econ.*, 29:617–642, October, 1921.

Bloodgood, Ruth S., "Welfare of Prisoners' Families in Kentucky," *U. S. Children's Bur.*, No. 182, 1928.

Cable, G. W., "The Convict Lease System in the Southern States," *Proc. Natl. Char. and Corr.*, 1883, pp. 265–301.

Gill, Howard B., "The Prison Labor Problem," *Annals of Amer. Acad. of Pol. and Social Sci.*, 157:83–101, September, 1931.

Gill, Howard B., "The Future of Prison Employment," *Proc. Amer. Prison Assoc.*, 1935, pp. 178–185.

Illinois, *Report of Bureau of Labor Statistics*, 1886, pp. 5–142.

Jackson, H. T., "Prison Labor," *Jour. Crim. Law and Criminol.*, 18:218–268, August, 1927.

Klein, P., *Prison Methods in New York State*, New York, 1920, Chs. 8–9.

Maryland, *Report of Penitentiary Penal Commission*, 1913, pp. 78–102, and 269–282.

McKelway, Blake, "The Prison Labor Problem, 1875–1900," *Jour. Crim. Law and Criminol.*, 25:254–270, July, 1934.

Michigan, *Report of Bureau of Labor and Industrial Statistics*, 1887, pp. 1–233.

Mohler, H. C., "Convict Labor Policies," *Jour. Crim. Law and Criminol.* 15:530–597, February, 1925.

New Jersey, *Report of Prison Inquiry Commission*, 2 Vols., Trenton, 1917.

New York, *Report of Department of Efficiency and Economy*, 4 Vols., Albany, 1915, Vol. IV, Chs. 11 and 15.

New York, *Report of Prison Survey Committee*, Albany, 1920, Chs. 3–11.

Pennypacker, J. E., Fairbanks, H. S., and Draper, W. F., "Convict Labor for Road Work," *Bull. of U. S. Dept. of Agri.*, No. 414, 1916.

Robinson, L. N., *Should Prisoners Work?* New York, 1931.

Sanford, E. P., "Prison Labor in 1936," *Monthly Lab. Rev.*, 47:251–268, August, 1938.

U. S. Commissioner of Labor, *Convict Labor*, 20th An. Report, 1905.

U. S. Department of Commerce, *Prison Industries,* Domestic Commerce Series, No. 27, 1929.

U. S. Department of Labor, Bureau of Labor Statistics, *Laws Relating to Prison Labor in the United States as of July 1, 1933,* Bull. No. 596, 1933.

U. S. Department of Labor, Bureau of Labor Statistics, *Prison Labor in the United States,* Bull. No. 595, 1932.

Weyand, L. D., *A Study of Wage Payments to Prisoners as a Penal Method,* Chicago, 1920.

Whitin, E. S., *Penal Servitude,* New York, 1912.

Whitin, E. S., "The Prisoner: Public Servant," *Survey,* 51:69–71, October 15, 1923.

Chapter Twenty-Four

PRISONS: EDUCATION

MEANING OF PRISON EDUCATION. Education, as popularly understood, means the process or product of training in schools or classrooms. The word is sometimes used to include more than that, and is so used here to include, in addition to the academic or school work, the vocational training, the religious exercises, the lectures, the library, the recreations, the self-government activities, the entertainments, and the productive labor, in so far as these are related to the training of the prisoner.

HISTORY OF PRISON EDUCATION. The chuch has been interested in the conversion of prisoners since the origin of imprisonment. During the medieval and early modern periods preachers and priests visited the prisons more or less regularly and conversed with prisoners in congregate or separate meetings. Many of the suggestions for prison reforms in England before the time of John Howard came as the result of these contacts between prisoners and preachers. Some of the early houses of correction had resident chaplains who, in addition to holding regular religious services, attempted to teach the elementary subjects, especially to the children confined in these institutions. The first recorded instance of regular visitation of prisoners in America was by the Quakers of Philadelphia just prior to the Revolutionary War. These laymen, as the preachers after this time, distributed Bibles and theological tracts and conversed with the prisoners in the cells. Prior to 1845 few prisons had regular resident chaplains, and these were poorly paid and were, in general, inefficient.

The development of secular educational work in prisons resulted directly from the effort to teach prisoners to read the Bible and the tracts. This effort to introduce secular education met with some resistance. The warden of Auburn prison in 1824 successfully opposed an attempt to teach the younger convicts to read and write. His opposition was based on the "increased danger to society of the educated convict." It was regarded as especially dangerous to teach convicts to write, for, it was asserted, this could easily result in forgery. The same fear was expressed in England about this time.[1]

The first organized educational work in America started in the New York House of Refuge. Provision was made there for two hours a day for each child; one hour of this consisted of learning to read the New Testament, the other of lectures and talks by the superintendent. The following year the school period was increased to four hours a day, and the work consisted of the three R's, geography, and bookkeeping. At about the same time an effort was made in Auburn prison to determine what proportion of the prisoners were unable to read and write. As a result of this investigation the chaplain in 1826 organized the prisoners into small groups to learn to read and write, with the assistance of theological students; within a few years 31 such classes were formed and 160 prisoners were attending them.[2] As late as 1845 very few institutions taught even the three R's, and these few gave a very small amount of time to formal educational work, though systematic efforts were made about the middle of the century to introduce this elementary educational work into all penal and reformatory institutions.

In practically all institutions for adults up to the middle of the nineteenth century the prisoners were not permitted to meet in groups and the school work was practically always done at night. Lewis describes the typical prison school at that time as consisting of

the chaplain standing in the semi-dark corridor, before the cell-door, with a dingy lantern hanging to the grated bars, and teaching to the wretched convict in the darkness beyond the grated door the rudiments of reading or of numbers.[3]

The first legal recognition of academic education as desirable in penal or reformatory institutions was in 1847 when the legislature of

---

[1] O. F. Lewis, *The Development of American Prisons and Prison Customs, 1776–1845*, Albany, 1922, p. 95; Sidney and Beatrice Webb, *English Prisons under Local Government*, London, 1922, p. 157.

[2] P. Klein, *Prison Methods in New York State*, New York, 1920, pp. 308 and 311.

[3] Lewis, *op. cit.*, p. 341.

New York State provided for the appointment of two teachers for each of the state prisons to give instruction in English for not less than an hour and a half a day (except Sunday) in the evening between six and nine o'clock. The salary for the instructor was $150 a year. Within a comparatively short time many of the prisons in other states made similar provisions. In most places the educational work continued to be confined to the evening and no congregate groups were permitted. This continued, in fact, in some institutions to the present generation; it was not legal to have congregate classes in the Eastern Penitentiary of Pennsylvania until 1913.

After the Civil War the importance of academic education in prisons was much more generally recognized. Brockway's description of the changes in his own attitudes during the last half of the nineteenth century may be taken as an illustration of the changes in public opinion. He stated that he had at first placed his dependence on regular labor with the expectation that it would form habits that would persist after release; then he was converted in a religious meeting and for a time had great faith in the power of religion to modify the behavior of the prisoners; by 1885 he had developed a greatly enhanced estimation of the reformative value of rational education.[4] By rational education he meant vocational education and the teaching of ethics, as well as the ordinary academic course.

EARLY HISTORY OF THE PRISON LIBRARY.   The state prison of Kentucky had a small library as early as 1802. Most of the prisons made no effort to secure libraries until about 1840. They depended entirely on Bibles and tracts that were distributed by preachers. Lewis describes the situation as it existed in 1845 as follows:

Only the better organized prisons maintained libraries. Connecticut had a small library; each prisoner was furnished also with a weekly temperance paper, and a religious paper. Massachusetts had a library of several hundred volumes, initiated by a donation of $50 "sent by a mother of a life prisoner to her son, to furnish him with proper reading." The prisoners in the Massachusetts prison made frequent donations for the library out of their earnings. The State appropriated, in the early forties, $100 annually for the increase and greater variety of books. Books were distributed at intervals of several weeks

---

[4] Z. R. Brockway, *Fifty Years of Prison Service*, p. 279.

in prisons possessing libraries, at the discretion of the warden and chaplain.[5]

It is probable, however, that practically all of the books in these libraries were theological and were intended to compel prisoners to contemplate the eternal sufferings to which they would be subjected if they did not repent. As late as 1853 the moral instructor in the Eastern Penitentiary of Pennsylvania complained because books that were not "of a strictly religious kind" were being placed in the library, resulting in an "alarming decrease in the call for religious books."[6] The chaplain of the women's prison in Sing Sing made public charges against the matron because of her interference with the religious education of the prisoners, charging her, among other things, with supplying the prisoners with such morally destructive literature as Dicken's *Nicholas Nickleby*.[7] After the prison library movement started, about the middle of the nineteenth century, it grew much more rapidly than did the school work.

EXTENT OF PRISON SCHOOL WORK. About one-fifth of the state prisons have no schools of any kind, about three-fifths have schools which are so restricted in hours and in attendance that they have little significance, and about one-fifth have fairly extensive training. In most of the prisons which provide academic training the work is restricted either to the first three grades or the first five grades, and the time spent in the classroom is generally not more than five or six hours per week.

The school work in reformatories for young adults is more extensive than in the state prisons, but it also is decidedly restricted in the time allotted to it and in the proportion of the inmates in attendance.

Practically every institution for juvenile delinquents has provision for school training, but not all of the inmates attend the schools. In 1927 only 77 per cent of the inmates were attending classes, and this was practically the same as the proportion in 1900.[8] In 8 per cent of the institutions less than 70 per cent of the inmates were attending school in 1927. It is doubtful if there is one juvenile

---

[5] Lewis, *op. cit.*, pp. 341–342.
[6] H. E. Barnes, "The Progress of American Penology," *Jour. Crim. Law and Criminol.*, 13:206–207, August, 1922.
[7] Klein, *op. cit.*, p. 309.
[8] U. S. Bur. of Educ., *Biennial Survey of Education*, 1926–1928, pp. 1181 ff.

reformatory in which the children spend as much time in school as normal children do.

Formal educational work in jails and workhouses is almost entirely lacking. The period of confinement of the average prisoner is so short that attempts to teach him anything are frequently believed to be futile. This indicates not only the uselessness of educational work in these institutions, but also the uselessness of these institutions as a whole.

THE PROBLEM OF PRISON EDUCATION. The problem of prison education is essentially a problem in socialization. This means, first, a modification of the general attitude, and, second, a sublimation of special interests and attitudes. The modification of the general attitude means a conversion, a transference of allegiance from one group to another. To produce this conversion it is essential that the prisoners be put in contact with the ideals, sentiments, and traditions of ordinary society. This means not merely an intellectual comprehension of these traditions, though that is an important part of education, but such contacts with them as those who have assimilated the traditions have had. Little specific knowledge has been acquired regarding the exact technique of producing this conversion, this identification of self with the normal group. But a few steps, at least, are certain. They must be immersed in these traditions. Probably the best way to accomplish this would be by frequent and intimate contacts with the people who have the traditions; this is limited, from the point of view of practicability. Reading and writing assist in producing the contacts, but contacts can be produced also by picture shows, lectures, classroom instruction, sermons. This conversion, however, need not be cataclysmic or abrupt. It may be and generally is gradual and unnoticed. It consists principally in enlarging the interests of the group to which the prisoner belongs until he feels himself identified with the larger group. Consequently it is undesirable to start by attacking the group to which the prisoner belongs, for this generally results in rallying the members of the group to its support and increasing their loyalty.

Furthermore, the process of socialization consists in building up concrete attitudes and interests. In fact, the general attitude discussed above will be modified largely, if not entirely, as the result of modification of concrete attitudes. The process of building up these attitudes is essentially a process of sublimation. This means redirecting the tendencies from paths that have proved to be in conflict with the laws to paths that are in accordance with the laws. For instance, many crimes are the result of a wish for excitement and new experience. The wish is legitimate, the path taken by the criminal to satisfy the wish ends in crime. The problem is to assist the prisoner to secure excitement and new experience without violating laws. Crime is certainly not the only interesting activity. The number of objects or activities that may be made interesting and exciting is almost unlimited. Recreational activities, for instance, may be substituted, but it is necessary to find recreational activities that are really exciting to the prisoner and that will remain so in ordinary society, not merely in the monotonous life of the prison. What will be thrilling to him will be determined by his other attitudes and the definition he has made of the situation in which he finds himself. Consequently an intensive study of the attitudes and interests of each prisoner must be made and a great deal of experimentation carried on in many cases before it will be possible to develop a sublimated activity that will give him the same excitement that he previously secured in crime. This method is being used for juvenile delinquents by the Institute for Juvenile Research in Chicago.[9] Doubtless many prisoners have attitudes so fixed or limited that no substitute can be found, but the procedure at any rate is fairly certain.

Vocational training is an essential part of this process of socialization. It has significance, first, in that it gives the offender an opportunity to meet the economic requirements after his release and to associate with persons of law-abiding characteristics; second, it gives the offender a conception of himself as a productive citizen that is of great value in the modification of his attitudes.

Other parts of the prison system can be made a part of the educational system. These include the religion, the entertainments, the library, the self-government groups, and the productive labor. In fact, every part of prison life can become a part of this process of training.

METHODS AND AIMS OF PRISON EDUCATION. MacCormick states that prison education should be individualized, adultized, made

---

[9] Claudia Wannamaker, "Problems in Recreation at Institute for Juvenile Research," *Institution Quart.*, 14:46–51, June, 1923; Claudia Wannamaker, "Methods of Recreational Adjustment as a Form of Social Case Treatment," *Mental Hygiene*, 7:744–754, October, 1923.

broadly inclusive in its offerings, and sparing in its use of compulsion. This procedure is based on the general philosophy of considering

the prisoner as primarily an adult in need of education and only secondarily as a criminal in need of reform. Its aim is to extend to prisoners as individuals every type of educational opportunity that experience or sound reasoning shows may be of benefit or of interest to them, in the hope that they may thereby be fitted to live more competently, satisfyingly, and co-operatively as members of society.[10]

This means that the prison education should include the fundamental academic training, vocational training, health education, cultural education, and social education.

HINDRANCES TO EDUCATIONAL WORK. Among the hindrances to educational work in prisons is the conception that these institutions are primarily places of punishment, in which the prisoners are to serve a more or less definite time to produce a specified amount of suffering. The walls and bars needed to prevent escapes keep this aspect of the prison continually before the attention of the inmates. Prisoners conventionally react by a hostile attitude toward the institution and all its activities; the régime of the prison tends to provoke and develop this attitude. The educational, recreational, religious, and other activities constantly struggle against this attitude and generally with little success. Prisoners cannot be expected to appreciate efforts to help them when the institution as a whole is designed to injure them and make them suffer. Those who are most susceptible to modifying influences are fixed in their hostile attitudes, therefore, because of the penal aspect of the institution. Probably this difficulty is so great that the institution should not be expected to modify behavior or attitudes very greatly. As long as individuals are sent to such institutions for comparatively short terms, and then permitted to return to ordinary society, every effort should be made to counteract the influence of the institution as a whole by education and other constructive policies.

A second hindrance to educational work is the inadequate equipment and organization of this work. In certain places no room is provided for education except the mess-hall. In some institutions

10 A. H. MacCormick, *Education of Adult Prisoners,* Natl. Soc. of Penal Information, New York, 1931, pp. 11–12. Reprinted by permission of the author.

children's school desks are used for adult prisoners. The textbooks are frequently those used in the public schools for children. Some years ago, according to reports, a class of prisoners was engaged in copying from the blackboard a sentence which read, "How swiftly and pleasantly the hours fly by." The New York Prison Survey Committee in 1920 reported regarding the conditions in the institutions of that state as follows:

Every condition which should make prison education stagnant, uninspired, unprogressive, exists today.[11]

The following conditions in penal institutions were reported recently:

History taught from texts that were published before the World War, and reading from primers published as far back as 1868; seventy-five men of all ages crammed into the only classroom in the prison, seated on backless benches without desks, taught under the district school method by an earnest but untrained chaplain, and searched by guards on entering and leaving the classroom; sixty reformatory inmates in a single room, taught by an untrained inmate under twenty years of age, with a sleepy, stupid-looking guard on a high stool in the front of the classroom to keep order; guards conducting classes with hickory clubs lying on their desks; guard-teachers, after a hard day's work in the school, "swinging the club" over their erstwhile pupils in the cell houses and mess hall; a $130-a-month guard in charge of the education work in a 3,000-man penitentiary; men studying in the prison of one of the wealthiest states in the country by the light of fifteen-watt bulbs; rules forbidding prisoners attending school to have writing material of any kind in their cells; educational "systems" which consist of allowing prisoners, without guidance, to purchase correspondence courses far beyond their ability and to follow them without assistance; schools that are nothing but dumping grounds for the industries, places of temporary sojourn for men who have not yet been assigned to work, or convenient roosting places for yard gangs that are called on occasionally to unload cars of coal and other supplies; libraries in which there are not more than a dozen

---

[11] New York, *Report of Prison Survey Committee*, Albany, 1920, p. 216.

up-to-date books possessing educational value; and so on almost endlessly.[12]

A third hindrance to educational work is the productive industry of the institution. This involves a difficult problem in the comparative importance of labor and of formal education. The school authorities generally insist that the work should not interfere with school; the warden, interested in the financial status of the institution, insists that the school should not interfere with the productive work. Consequently we find the condition described by the Prison Survey Committee of New York.

If an inmate is very much needed in the shops, he is not expected to attend school. On the other hand, if he is no good anywhere else around the prison, he is sent to school.[13]

In general the school activities are organized so that they interfere as little as possible with the productive labor. This is justified by the argument that it is necessary that the institution pay as large a part of its expenses as possible. This should be done, it is asserted, not merely in order to save money for the taxpayers, but in order that the institution may have a surplus from which to pay wages to the prisoners. Wages must be paid in order to make productive labor educational. Stated otherwise, the argument is: The most important education prisoners can receive is the training in regular labor. But they must have an incentive or they will look upon their work as slave labor, to be avoided whenever possible, and the relationship between effort and reward will be lost. The best incentive is a wage for labor, but if school activities interfere with production, the expenses of the institution are not met from its products and there can be no surplus from which to pay wages and the educational value of the labor will be lost.

On the other hand, it is asserted that the wage system does not make labor interesting or educational outside of prison and that after the newness wears off, it will not make labor attractive inside the prison. The whole modern system of production is at fault and wages cannot remedy the defect. In addition, the criminal needs

---

[12] MacMormick, *op. cit.*, pp. 42–43. Reprinted by permission of the author.

[13] New York, *Report of Prison Survey Committee*, 1920, p. 216.

a fundamental modification of attitudes unless he is to be retained in the institution all his life. Even if labor is valuable for this purpose, many other methods must be used, also, and these other methods are, in general, included in the educational system.

As a matter of fact existing school work and existing labor are both of slight value for the purpose of modification of attitudes. But the improvement of both systems will leave the controversy unsettled.

The difficulty is that each side is trying to give a general prescription for the entire prison population. It is not necessary that all prisoners should spend the same amount of time at labor and at school work. A policy should be adopted for each individual, based on his capacities, needs, and interests. It will be found that many prisoners are somewhat similar, so that they can be classified; much school work can be required of some of these groups, and little or no school work of others.

THE NEW YORK STUDIES AND EXPERIMENTS. Several commissions in New York State have been appointed within the last fifteen years and each has made recommendations regarding the educational system. The Prison Survey Committee in 1920, the Commission to Investigate Prison Administration and Construction in 1933, and the Commission for the Study of the Educational Problems of Penal Institutions for Youth in 1937 have made significant reports on this subject. Experimental work in education began in Elmira Reformatory in 1933 as a result of the second commission, and has been developed in several other institutions as a result of the efforts of the last commission. The report of the last commission, in itself, is a guide that may be used for any penal or reformatory institution.[14] It was developed co-operatively by educational authorities, prison authorities, and others. Through contributions from private sources somewhat extensive experiments are being made that should give further guidance to other institutions.

THE TEACHER. Investigations have shown that the teachers in penal and reformatory institutions, with some exceptions, are poorly paid and are not prepared for the exceedingly difficult task of teaching prisoners. These teachers have no conferences in most states and generally have to bear their own expenses if they attend general conferences of teachers. In New York State special confer-

---

[14] New York, *Report of the Commission for the Study of the Educational Problems of Penal Institutions for Youth,* Legis. Doc. No. 71, 1937.

ences of prison teachers have been organized and these are assisting to develop a technique and an *esprit de corps* among the teachers.

The general practice in the state prisons is to have one civilian teacher or superintendent, and inmate assistants. Most of the inmate teachers are poorly equipped for the work. The situation in the state prisons of New York in 1920 was described by the Prison Survey Committee as follows:

One paid teacher only is provided for each prison. This teacher has as assistants only inmates, who are often assigned to him because there is no other work open to them. Not one of the present inmate teachers is a trained teacher, not one even thought of teaching until he was assigned to the job, and not one ever intends to teach after discharge. The best of the men from the newcomers are given office jobs, and he is offered discards. For example, the only inmate previously trained as a teacher, now in Auburn, has been "promoted" to be a butler.[15]

The average length of the experience of the inmate teachers in Sing Sing in 1922 was seven months; that is, the inmate teachers beginning with no experience do not continue this work long enough to acquire a good technique. In some places the head teacher has organized a normal class for the inmate teachers.

Aside from the fact that few prisoners are able to do this work efficiently, the principal objection is that the most important function of the teacher is to serve as an example, and a convict is not a good example. The objection against inmate teachers would be decreased considerably if it could be certain that the "natural leaders" among the prisoners were selected as teachers. It is necessary to change the whole public opinion of the prison, and the leaders among the prisoners could exert considerable influence in doing this if they had the ability to act as teachers. In general, however, it is distinctly preferable to have teachers who represent ordinary society, who have had sufficient experience with delinquents to be able to understand them and to present the school work in ways that appeal to the prisoners.

In the reformatories and especially in the institutions for juvenile delinquents it is customary to have the teaching force composed entirely of civilians. In some places the reformatory school is a

[15] New York, *Report of Department of Efficiency and Economy*, 1915, Vol. IV, p. 771.

branch of the regular public school, with types of teachers, curricula, and procedures identical with those of the public school. This is a doubtful policy, however. The delinquents are a special group and need special procedure and policies adapted to them.

CURRICULUM. In most state prisons the curriculum is confined to reading and writing. In New York a few years ago the course consisted of the study of one thousand words selected by the teachers. The prisoners were taught to pronounce, spell, and write these words. About nine-tenths of the formal educational work in prisons is nothing more than this. Of the other subjects that are included, generally for a very small number of advanced prisoners, the ones given most frequently are bookkeeping, drawing, stenography, and civics. Comparatively few institutions give courses in any of the social sciences other than civics, though it is evident that the social sciences should make a great contribution to the modification of the attitudes of the prisoners, by developing an appreciation of the traditions of organized society. It is evident that the curriculum must be greatly enlarged and it is not necessary that reading and writing should be prerequisites to all of the advanced work. The citizenship courses in the Army proved that even illiterates can acquire an appreciation of the standards and ideals of American society.

CLASSIFICATION AND ASSIGNMENT OF PRISONERS. Illiterates in prison are assigned to the equivalent of the first grade of the public schools. Those who have completed some of the grades in the public schools are customarily classified in prison schools so that they will continue their school work from the point where it was dropped. If they have already finished the regular courses offered by the prison school, arrangements are sometimes made for advanced courses, but most of the prisoners have no opportunity or incentive to take advanced work. If certain prisoners cannot learn readily, they are dropped from the school.

Many prisons are making efforts now to classify prisoners in a more careful way than this. In many institutions mental tests are used as a means of classifying prisoners according to mental ages. A few institutions give standardized educational tests and assign the prisoners to school work according to their abilities as thus measured. When this method is used, it is necessary to have ungraded classes, since one prisoner will be found retarded in arithmetic and advanced in composition, and another prisoner will be the reverse.

In Preston School all the juvenile delinquents who work at one trade are assigned to the same class in school, regardless of mental age or educational development. This is justified by the argument that the common interest in one trade will serve as a basis of education for the group, and that other methods have failed because the prisoners lack a common interest in the school work.

Whether this Preston plan will succeed better than the others will depend on the method of assigning the prisoners to trades. It is clear that there should be something more than the mere fact of similarity of trades to regulate the assignment to school work. The classification should be based on a thorough study of each prisoner, in which the trade to be followed would be merely one item. The combination of attitudes and abilities should determine both the assignment to trades and to school work.

VOCATIONAL AND TRADE TRAINING. As a result of his survey in 1927 MacCormick reported:

No prison in the country has a program of vocational education worthy of the name and in no prison is the industrial and maintenance work definitely organized to provide vocational training. . . . Only a few American reformatories have succeeded in establishing well-balanced and effective vocational training programs.[16]

The New York Prison Survey Committee reported:

The examination of what was being accomplished [in state prisons] in vocational training was quickly dismissed for the reason that there was no such training in evidence in any prison.[17]

The state prison of New Jersey has made a good beginning by the careful study of prisoners on entrance, determining their capacities and interests and assigning them to work in accordance with the findings. This examination of the prisoner was preceded by an analysis of the different kinds of work provided in the institution. Thus it is possible to make a more satisfactory assignment of the prisoners to tasks, and this furnishes the basis for training in specified forms of work. The training, however, has not been developed in proportion to the method of assignment.

A great deal of attention has been devoted to the desirability of

---

[16] MacCormick, op. cit., pp. 10–11. Reprinted by permission of the author.
[17] New York, Report of Prison Survey Committee, 1920, p. 162.

teaching agriculture to prisoners, and the general tendency in the last generation has been to establish institutions in the country so that agriculture can be carried on. It is maintained that this has the advantage of solving the convict labor problem, of breaking the monotony of prison life, of helping supply the demand for farm labor, and of training the prisoner for an occupation in which the temptations and pressures after his release will be less severe. But the disadvantages of this are evident. In most parts of the United States not much farm work can be done in winter, farmers are unwilling to hire ex-convicts, and many prisoners come from the cities and are unwilling to live on farms. It is as unwise to attempt to fit all prisoners for agriculture as for the barber's trade or the automobile industry. Unquestionably agriculture is desirable as an occupation for some prisoners and they should be trained in it. Whether a particular prisoner should be trained in agriculture or some other occupation should be determined by his attitudes, experiences, and abilities.

The vocational training in reformatories for young adults is not much better, on the whole, than in the state prisons. After a careful survey of fifteen state reformatories, Nalder concluded that the industrial training in those institutions was not successful, that modern industry requires many unskilled workmen, and that it would be preferable to devote the time to developing right attitudes.[18] He found that about 18.5 per cent of the 9,251 inmates of these reformatories were being taught trades in trade classes; the others acquired merely a smattering of knowledge from the institutional and productive work. The greatest difficulty is that the inmates either stay in the institution for too short a time to acquire a trade or else shift from one trade to another. A most admirable system was devised for Elmira, based on the courses given in a private trade school. But very few of the inmates completed any of the courses. In the year 1921 instruction in trades was given to 1,462 inmates, of whom only 26 graduated from their trades; the highest proportion of graduates was in typewriting and stenography, in which 35 were enrolled and 4 graduated; none of the 130 who took instruction in bricklaying graduated; of 87 who took barbering only 1 graduated.[19]

---

[18] F. F. Nalder, "The American State Reformatory," *Univ. of Calif. Pub., Educ.*, Vol. V, No. 3, 1920, p. 420.
[19] New York, *Report of Elmira Reformatory*, 1922, p. 105.

The institutions for juvenile delinquents have attempted to give trade training, but they are handicapped by the fact that most of the inmates are young and remain in the institution for a short time. Even if they develop vocational skill, they cannot acquire positions when they are released. The best training in the House of Refuge was in telegraphy, but when the boys with some skill in telegraphy applied after release for jobs, they became messenger boys for the telegraph companies. The number trained in vocations in the institutions for juveniles did not increase appreciably from 1900 to 1918.[20]

It is hardly necessary to mention the fact that the jails and work-houses characteristically have no vocational training. In the small number of these institutions that have any labor some skill may be acquired in connection with the maintenance work for the institution or the productive labor.

CORRESPONDENCE COURSES. Hill reported that in 1913 eight prisons had made arrangements for correspondence courses for the prisoners. Such courses have increased in number since that time. Arrangements were made by the Y. M. C. A. and the Welfare League for the prisoners in the state prisons of New York to take correspondence courses, but some wardens are still doubtful about such work. The prisoners in Kansas may take correspondence courses from the University of Kansas, on payment of a fee of $1.00; the courses include soils, farm drainage, stock breeding, shop mathematics, and other vocational courses. Similar arrangements exist in Pennsylvania with Penn State College, but in 1917 only sixty-eight out of fourteen hundred prisoners were taking advantage of this opportunity. The institution in which the greatest amount of correspondence work is done at present is San Quentin, California. Approximately 45 per cent of the inmates of this prison in 1932 were engaged in educational study. Each of these, on the average, took one class course and one correspondence course from the University of California. The papers in elementary correspondence courses are graded by inmates who are appointed as assistant readers, while the papers in the advanced courses are read by the extension staff of the University. This work is entirely voluntary. Correspondence cources are developed similarly, though less extensively, in the prisons of Wisconsin. The Illinois State Prison

---

[20] U. S. Bur. of Educ., *Biennial Survey*, 1916–1918, Vol. IV, p. 759.

at Stateville has an intra-mural correspondence course, which to some degree is extended to the other penal institutions of that State. This makes possible much more individualization in training and many more advanced courses than are available in the other institutions. In 1937 404 prisoners were registered for these courses. Eighty courses, generally on the high school level, were available. The number of courses completed in the year was 225, as compared with 77 in 1935.

THE PRISON LIBRARY. Almost all the penal and reformatory institutions, except some of the jails and workhouses, have libraries. The library is generally in charge of the chaplain. Few of these chaplains are able to do the library work efficiently. Perhaps the extreme in inefficiency was the chaplain in the Maryland House of Correction who recommended that the library be abandoned for the following reason:

> The men earn a good deal of money and for the most part spend it. If they want reading matter they can supply their wants for themselves by subscribing to the various magazines.[21]

The funds for purchase of books are seldom more than nominal, and most libraries consist of gifts of unwanted books from other libraries. For that and other reasons the selection of books is seldom suitable. Most of the books are trash, and the number of books that would be educational, inspiring, or even interesting is not large. Fiction is generally the strongest department of the library, and as might be expected, the fiction has the largest circulation.[22] For instance, the prison library in Folsom, California, contains 4,027 volumes, of which 75 per cent are fiction; and 91 per cent of the circulation in 1922 was fiction.

The state prison in Joliet, Illinois, had until the prison riot and fire in 1931 the largest library of any prison, but the average book there was issued only 1.8 times in the year 1916, while the average book in Clinton Prison, New York, was issued 28.5 times. The average prisoner in Iowa state prison withdraws about five times as many books a year as the average prisoner in Joliet.[23] This is prob-

---

[21] Maryland, *Report of State Board of Control*, 1922, p. 90.

[22] Florence R. Curtis, "What the Convict Reads," *Survey*, 29:323–325, December 14, 1912.

[23] Florence R. Curtis, "The Libraries of the American State and National Institutions for Defectives, Dependents and Delinquents," *Univ. of Minn. Studies in The Social Sciences*, No. 13, p. 26, September, 1918.

ably due to the prison regulations governing the library privileges, different selection of books in the library, and different definitions of "book" in the reports.

The instituitons for juvenile delinquents do not have as satisfactory libraries as the institutions for adults. Of thirty-one juvenile reformatories studied in 1916, nine had no libraries and of the others fifteen had made no book purchases during the year, one of these none in nine years.[24]

If the library is to play an important part in the formation of new attitudes and a new point of view, the books must be selected carefully and the reading should be supervised. Library authorities have made a few experiments in placing selected libraries in penal and reformatory institutions, and some of these have met with considerable success. Even in these experiments particular books have not been selected for particular prisoners on the basis of a comprehensive knowledge of the personality of the prisoners.

The State Library Commission of Wisconsin has developed an unusual service for the inmates of the state prisons. Prisoners are supplied with any book available on request and in addition are supplied with reading lists on any subject they may select.

The American Library Association in co-operation with the American Prison Association has published a *Prison Library Handbook* to be used by prison librarians. The federal Bureau of Prisons has mimeographed lists of books that are most valuable for prison libraries. These activities are tending to improve the library facilities of the prisons.

ENTERTAINMENTS. Many institutions have frequent entertainments in the form of music, plays, picture shows, lectures, or recitals. Eight of the eighteen state reformatories own and use moving-picture machines. Some institutions secure films from the companies at very low rates, either by showing the films that have been practically worn out in commercial houses, or by showing in the forenoons the films that are shown in the commercial houses of the town during the afternoons and evenings. Other institutions are decidedly handicapped and sometimes for trivial reasons. The State Department of Education of New York offered to loan a balopticon to the state prison so that visual education could be developed, but the balopticon could not be used because the window shades in the assembly

---

[24] *Ibid.*, p. 22.

room of the prison would not keep out the light and new shades could not be secured.

Most institutions have bands or orchestras or both, and most of them have choirs or choruses. Such activities are decidedly beneficial from the standpoint of the development of morale and socialization. The ones in which the prisoners participate are probably most valuable. But the procedure is too mechanical and not sufficiently adjusted to the needs of particular prisoners to be of the greatest value.

ETHICAL TRAINING. Methods of formal ethical training have been suggested and need to be considered. Much attention was attracted by a class in ethics which Brockway established in Elmira. Of this class Brockway said:

> The practical purpose of the class was not, as might at first thought be supposed, directly to inculcate moral maxims in expectation that the prisoners would unconsciously adopt the maxims, and afterwards shape their conduct in accordance therewith, but rather to create in their minds a habit of qualitative moral discrimination.[25]

The class was in charge of Charles A. Collins, a practicing attorney, who later became a teacher of law in Cornell University. He described the procedure as follows:

> Ethical study calls for a keen, critical, dissecting spirit, and it is thereby precisely adapted to receive the immediate attention of a prison audience. Not merely learning moral maxims nor listening to good advice is meant, but the culture of that temper of mind and soul designated by the great modern teacher, Arnold of Rugby, as "moral thoughtfulness." Answering back their arguments firmly and sharply the audience will be curious to see what one of their members will say. Their interest will be transferred to the replies of the teacher. Men who say nothing will begin to think what they might say. . . . To have attracted interested attention is more than half the battle. . . . However it may be with religion, there is no such thing as a sudden conversion to morality. Morality means firmly set habits acquired by long practice and severe discipline. Men cannot be kept steadily thinking with a genuine interest on higher and better things, with reference to better ends, without acquiring better habits of thought.[26]

[25] Brockway, *op. cit.*, pp. 246 ff.
[26] Brockway, *op. cit.*, pp. 249–250, 256.

The prisoners entered into the discussion very freely. Professor J. W. Jenks of Cornell, who attended some of the classes, stated that the general level of the discussion was about that of the senior classes in the University.

Many of the reformatories have established military drill and urge its value as a means of teaching self-control, obedience, and respect for authority. While some individuals may be modified in that way, as a general method of reformation it is a vain hope. If anything is certain about reformation it is that the method of forcing persons through a rigid and mechanical scheme of external conformity is practically useless. As soon as the external compulsion is removed, the behavior is just as it was before.

It is sometimes asserted that the system of grades, with greater privileges for those in the advanced grades, teaches prisoners to obey the rules and control their conduct in order to secure the rewards. This is probably better than the system of penalties for failure to obey the rules, but is, like the military method, too mechanical and does not carry with it a real modification of attitudes and interests.

THE HONOR SYSTEM AND SELF-GOVERNMENT IN RELATION TO PRISON EDUCATION. The honor system and self-government are frequently advocated for their educational value to the prisoners. Opinion regarding the effects of self-government on the regular school system is divided. Hill reports that "this notion wrecked the school in Sing Sing for a long time,"[27] while Klein gives the other side as follows:

A real impetus has been given to education in the state prisons as a result of the work of the Mutual Welfare League at Sing Sing Prison. . . . The prisoners succeeded in organizing a school with varied branches of instruction in which pupils worked with a will. Compared with the stagnant deadly routine instruction in the official school of the prison, the work of the Mutual Welfare School has been like an educational revolution. . . . In the field of industrial or vocational training, as in the field of education, the most promising start has been made in Sing Sing under its inmate organization. Classes in commercial subjects, in machine construction, in mechanical drawing, and the like, were organized, and successfully conducted by the committee on education of the Mutual Welfare League. They have had

[27] New York, *Report of Prison Survey Committee,* 1920, p. 235.

the co-operation from time to time of experts from the state education department and others.[28]

The school work of the self-government league has not continued to be as satisfactory as it was in the beginning, but this may not be the fault of self-government. It is clearly desirable to have the prisoners take an active part in the educational work of the prison; whether this is done through the self-government organization or otherwise is not important.

In some places the prisoners are given control over the entertainments and group organizations. In Preston School in California, for instance, a department of social work, under the control of the inmates, has charge of the organization of clubs, study classes, band, games, and athletics. It is clearly desirable that the prisoners should participate in the control of such activities.

The argument for self-government is that it gives the prisoners an opportunity to make choices, to discuss, to co-operate with others. Tannenbaum tells of one of the "toughs" from New York City who reported, after some experience with self-government in prison, that he had learned to argue with people; previously a disagreement had been the occasion for a fight.[29] Self-government is valuable, also, from the educational point of view in that it tends to affect the public opinion of the prison and thus develop and direct the opinion of the group as a whole toward the systematic and orderly life of the community. It seems clear that it has this advantage and that it is very valuable. But, as indicated above, the disadvantages and difficulties of self-government make it impossible as a general and unrestricted method of control.

RELATION TO THE STATE DEPARTMENT OF EDUCATION. The state department of education should be intimately related to the educational work of the penal and reformatory institutions. Two suggestions have been made regarding this. One is that the control and administration of these institutions should be placed in the department of education, on the ground that these institutions are essentially educational institutions. This suggestion seems to be impractical and undesirable. The second suggestion is that the state department of education should co-operate with the prison authorities in the educational work of the institutions, including, at this

---

[28] Klein, *op. cit.*, pp. 315 and 324.
[29] F. Tannenbaum, *Wall Shadows*, p. 55.

point, only the literary and vocational training. This suggestion is not entirely specific and no definite plan has been formulated. Sometimes it appears that this is intended to mean a division of the control, with statutory regulations regarding the educational work of such institutions, and with authority vested in the department of education to carry out these regulations. It is highly undesirable to have such a division of authority. But it is possible to have co-operation without this division of authority. The state department of education can take an interest in and give advice regarding the educational work of prisons. Such assistance is already given in some states and should be generally extended to all states and all institutions.

SUGGESTED READINGS

Ames, E. S., "The Moral Education of the Training School Inmate," *Proc. Natl. Conf. Social Work,* 1919, pp. 125–129.

Barnes, H. E., "A History of the Penal, Reformatory and Correctional Institutions of the State of New Jersey," *Report of Prison Inquiry Committee,* Trenton, 1917, Vol. II.

Barnes, H. E., "The Progress of American Penology," *Jour. Crim. Law and Criminol.,* 13:170–227, August, 1922.

Brockway, Z. R., *Fifty Years of Prison Service,* New York, 1912, Chs. 7 and 16.

California, *Report of Preston School of Industry,* 1916–1918, pp. 69–86.

Curtis, Florence R., "The Libraries of the American State and National Institutions for Defectives, Dependents and Delinquents," *Univ. of Minn. Studies in the Social Sciences,* No. 13, 1918.

Doll, E. A., "Classification of Prisoners for Purposes of Training, Work and Parole," *Jour. Crim. Law and Criminol.,* 14:110–116, May, 1923.

Doll, E. A., "Education of Juvenile Delinquents," *Jour. Delinq.,* 6:331–346, March, 1921.

"Facing the Issue," by Two Prison Chaplains, *Atlantic Mo.,* 130:35–39, July, 1922.

Freden, G., and Robins, C. L., "The Prison School," *School and Soc.,* 25:77–82, May 14, 1927.

Halbert, L. A., "The Moral Clinic as an Auxiliary to the Court," *Proc. Natl. Prob. Assoc.,* 1918, pp. 77–89.

Henderson, C. R. (Editor), *Correction and Prevention,* 4 Vols., New York, 1910; Vol. II, *Penal and Reformatory Institutions,* Ch. 11.

Higgins, H. A., "Prison Education: The Experiment at Deer Island House of Correction," *Boston, Mass., Prison Assoc. Leaflet,* No. 67, Boston, n.d. (1920?).

Hill, A. C., "Prison Schools," *U. S. Bur. of Educ.,* 1913, No. 27.

Hobhouse, S., and Brockway, A. F., *English Prisons Today, Being the Report of the Prison System Enquiry Committee,* London, 1922, Part 1, Chs. 9–12.

Klein, P., *Prison Methods in New York State,* NewYork, 1920, Ch. 10.

Lewis, O. F., *The Development of American Prisons and Prison Customs, 1776–1845,* Albany, 1922.

MacCormick, A. H., *Education of Adult Prisoners,* Natl. Soc. of Penal Information, New York, 1931.

Nalder, F. F., "The American State Reformatory," *Univ. of Calif. Pub., Educ.,* Vol. V, No. 3, 1920, pp. 371–436.

New York, Commission to Investigate Prison Administration and Construction, *An Educational Program for New York's State Penal System,* Albany, 1932.

NewYork, *Report of the Commission for the Study of the Educational Problems of Penal Institutions for Youth,* Legis. Doc. No. 71, Albany, 1937.

New York, *Report of Prison Survey Committee,* Albany, 1920, Chs. 12–14.

Snedden, D. S., *Administration and Educational Work of American Juvenile Reform Schools,* New York, 1907.

Wines, E. C., and Dwight, T. W., "Report on the Prisons and Reformatories of the United States and Canada," *New York Assembly Doc. No. 35,* 1867, Vol. II, pp. 184–220.

Chapter Twenty-Five

RELEASE FROM PRISON

THE EXITS FROM PRISON are more numerous than the entrances into prison. Entrance into prison on sentence must always be by way of the court, generally in accordance with conditions fixed by the legislature. But one may be released from prison by completion of the full term imposed by the court, or before the end of the full term by an executive who grants a pardon or commutation, or an administrative board that grants a parole or a release on good time. That is, acting by authority of the constitution or statutes, the legislature, the court, an executive, or an administrative board may determine the time of release of a prisoner.

I. PARDON

PARDON AND RELATED CONCEPTS. The modification of penalties by the executive may take the form of pardon, commutation, or amnesty. A pardon is an act of mercy or clemency, ordinarily by an executive, by which a criminal is excused from a penalty which has been imposed upon him. It has been held in many decisions that the pardon wipes away guilt and makes the person who committed the crime as innocent as though he had not committed it. Pardon may be either conditional or absolute. The conditional pardon is one in which the guilt is wiped away on condition that the offender perform certain acts or refrain from certain acts specified by the pardoning power, such as leaving the country or abstaining from intoxicating liquors. If a person who has received a conditional pardon fails to perform the required acts, the pardon becomes void and he may be returned to prison for the remainder of his original term.

Commutation of sentence is a reduction of the penalty by executive order. A sentence is frequently commuted so that it expires at once. Commutation differs from conditional pardon in that it does not wipe away guilt in the eyes of the law, and consequently does not restore civil rights as does a pardon. Amnesty is a pardon applied to a group of criminals, as, for instance, all who have violated a specific law. The King of Italy in 1930 on the eve of a royal wedding granted amnesty to six thousand convicts. Amnesty has now been almost entirely abandoned in America. A reprieve or respite is a temporary postponement of the execution of a sentence, generally for the purpose of further investigation of the guilt of the prisoner. It is used in connection with the death penalty rather than with sentences of imprisonment.

HISTORY OF PARDONS. From very early times the executive had authority, more or less restricted, to grant pardons. In the American colonies the pardoning power was generally vested in the executive, but in some cases in the assembly. After the Revolution, because of the fear of executives, the pardoning power was generally retained by the legislative assembly. A tendency soon appeared to increase the power of the governor in this field, generally as an expression of the doctrine of separation of powers. Recently the responsibility of the governor has been limited by the development of pardon boards.

LAWS REGARDING PARDON. In twenty-one states in 1933 the governor shared the power to pardon with a board or council, and had no more power than any other member of the board in eight of these states. In twenty-seven states the governor had the sole and complete power to pardon except in impeachment cases. In seventeen of these states in which the governor had final authority, a pardon board or other assistants were appointed for advisory purposes. An advisory pardon board in practice may have complete control of the pardons because in those cases the governor always adopts the recommendations of the board. On the other hand the recommendation of an advisory pardon board in some states is seldom accepted. In South Carolina the governor is required to report to the legislature his reasons if he rejects the recommendation of the board. In thirty-one states the governor or board of pardons is required to report each case to the legislature at the next regular session.

The President of the United States is authorized to grant pardons to those who violate federal laws, except in cases of impeachment. Ordinarily pardons are granted only to those who are recommended by the pardon attorney, but not all of the persons recommended receive pardons. Out of 1,081 applications for federal pardons acted upon in 1937, 653 were thrown out by adverse reports of the attorney; of the 428 on which favorable reports were made, pardons or commutations were granted to 291, or 68 per cent. Of the 291 pardons granted 187 were merely restoration of civil rights, 37 were commutations, 3 were respites, 59 were remittances of fines, and only 5 were remission of guilt as usually understood.

Mayors are given authority, with restrictions, in a few states to grant pardons to those who violate municipal ordinances. This power has been greatly abused in a few cities.[1]

CRITICISMS OF THE PARDON SYSTEM.   The pardoning system has been assailed by many people and many have demanded that it be completely abolished.   The arguments most frequently advanced for abolishing it are as follows: It is a device by which criminals who have political influence or other influence escape a penalty. It produces an unfavorable effect on prisoners in that they try to secure a pardon rather than reform. It makes the court careless in imposing sentences or enables judges to impose very heavy penalties at a time of public frenzy and later recommend clemency. The principal criticism of the ordinary method of granting pardons is that the governor, upon whom the responsibility rests, does not have time to determine whether the pardons should be granted. A governor of New York State asserted that the state should have two governors, one to attend to pardon matters and another to attend to the rest of the business of the state. Because the governor does not have reliable information on which to base a decision, he is susceptible to pressure or clamor. Consequently many pardons are granted for reasons that are entirely inadequate. One governor gave as his reason for pardoning criminals that "he could deny Carrie [his wife] nothing and she could refuse nothing to anyone else." Another governor, when a friend sought the pardon of two criminals, offered him his choice of the two but refused to pardon both "because that county's quota is exhausted." In the earlier period many prisoners were pardoned to make room for newcomers;[2] in 1813 pardons were granted to 134 prisoners in the state prison at Greenwich Village, New York, and 198 new prisoners were admitted; it was necessary

---

[1] R. M. Story, *The American Municipal Executive*, Urbana, 1918, pp. 107–108.

[2] O. F. Lewis, *The Development of American Prisons and Prison Customs, 1776–1845*, Albany, 1922.

to pardon the others in order to admit the new prisoners. The following are some of the recorded reasons for granting pardons: the offender has been adequately punished, the ends of justice have been met sufficiently, the age (either very young or very old) of the offender, sickness of the offender, injury of the prisoner, dependents need his help, relatives or others are able to care for him, the crime was committed under the influence of liquor, has rendered service in convicting others, meritorious service in prisons (such as saving the life of a prison official or helping extinguish a fire), or serving his country in the war.

DECREASE IN PARDONS. As a matter of fact pardons are constantly decreasing in frequency. In 1905–1909 3.0 per cent of those released from federal prisons were released by pardon. This percentage had decreased to 0.009 per cent in 1936. The same decrease is found in many states. Table IX shows this decrease in a few

TABLE IX

PER CENT OF THOSE DISCHARGED FROM STATE PRISONS WHO WERE
PARDONED IN SPECIFIC STATES BY DECADES

Decade	New Jersey	New Hampshire	Pennsylvania [1]	Missouri	Michigan [2]
1800–09	14.3	...	...	...	...
1810–19	25.5	9.2	...	...	...
1820–29	25.7	20.1	21.4	...	...
1830–39	38.1	50.8	19.0	78.6 [3]	...
1840–49	22.4	43.4	21.1	25.2	24.6
1850–59	40.9	41.2	13.4	40.3	23.3
1860–69	31.0	37.7	16.2	50.0	10.0
1870–79	10.0	24.0	8.4	11.1	5.9
1880–89	10.5	13.9	2.9	6.2	4.5
1890–99	5.2	10.5	3.7	5.9	3.9
1900–09	0.6	7.6	3.1	3.8	3.5
1910–19	0.2	2.8 [4]	...	0.9	0.1 [5]

[1] Decades are 1826–1835, etc., the last ending in 1915.
[2] Decades are 1841–1850, etc.
[3] For the years 1836–1839 only.
[4] For the years 1910–1912 only.
[5] For the years 1910–1916 only.

states for which statistics are available over a long period. These states are not representative of the entire United States for they are, with one exception, Northern states, and the pardon rate is at present about eight times as high in the Southern states as in the Northern. The trend has been equally pronounced, however, in the Southern states in recent years.

The general law of pardons is that the more serious the crime and the more severe the sentence, the more probable is release by pardon.[3] Wines and Dwight presented statistics of the state prison of Massachusetts from 1828 to 1866, showing that pardons were granted to 20.5 per cent of those on terms of five to ten years, 32 per cent of those on terms of ten years or more but not including life, and 50 per cent of those on life sentences.[4] At present the same tendency is found. Of those released in 1936 from state and federal prisons and reformatories 5 per cent were by pardon for those on homicide charges, 1.6 per cent for those on robbery charges, 1.1 per cent for those on burglary charges, and 0.2 per cent for those on auto theft charges. Of those released after serving ten years or more 6.0 per cent were released by pardon, of those who had served five but less than ten years 1.6 per cent, and of those who had served less than five years 1.2 per cent. This law, of course, does not express a physiological necessity. Things other than severity of sentence affect the frequency of pardons. The gentlemen thieves, like the embezzlers, are pardoned more frequently than other thieves.

VALUE OF THE PARDONING POWER. Pardons are regarded as justifiable because of errors of justice which call for some method of review of the evidence. These errors of justice are of two types. The first is the conviction in which doubt regarding guilt arises. The second is the conviction in which doubt regarding the justice of the penalty arises. In Massachusetts prior to 1871 life imprisonment was the only legal penalty for burglary. When less severe penalties were authorized in that year, many of those who had been sentenced previously applied for pardons. In Illinois the minimum sentence for robbery with a gun was raised from one year to ten years, and subsequently reduced again to one year. Many prisoners who had been sentenced with a minimum term of ten years during this interim applied for pardons. In some states many children are sentenced to state prisons for long terms. In 1917 Governor Bickett of North Carolina pardoned six children between the ages of eleven and thirteen years who had been sentenced for terms ranging from fifteen years to life.[5] A Colorado judge, not in sympathy with the indeterminate sentence law, fixed a minimum penalty of nine years

---

[3] This law was stated by Henry Cabot Lodge, "Naval Courts-Martial and the Pardoning Power," *Atlantic Mo.,* 50:43–50, July, 1882.

[4] E. C. Wines and T. W. Dwight, "Report on the Prisons and Reformatories of the United States and Canada," *New York Assembly Doc.,* No. 35, 1867, Vol. II, pp. 297–298.

[5] W. T. S. Culp, "A Social Tragedy," *Survey,* 39:368, December 29, 1917.

and a maximum penalty of ten years for a certain offender; the governor of the state commuted the sentence to "from five to ten years," thus carrying out the intent of the legislature in such cases. Because of these and similar changes in legislation or decisions of courts or because of changes in the spirit of the times, some method of modifying the actions of the courts should be available. If prison sentences were completely indeterminate, few pardons would be needed, for the occasions for pardons are found principally in connection with penalties which are regarded as unjustified. Much has been said about the abuse of the pardoning power, but it is probably true, as Tedrow said before the American Prison Association in 1911, that "For one abuse of the pardon power there are a thousand abuses of the convicting power."

Aside from the pardons above mentioned, many pardons are granted in some states after the period of imprisonment has ended and for the sole purpose of restoring the civil rights of the offenders. The automatic restoration of civil rights at the time of release from prison, or at least at the time of release from parole, would probably be a much better social policy.

II. GOOD TIME LAWS

As early as 1817 a good time law was passed in New York State, which provided that first-term prisoners on sentences of five years or less could abridge their sentences by one-fourth for good behavior. Apparently the law was not used. The method was adopted in several other places; Connecticut passed a law of this kind in 1821 relating to inmates of workhouses; Tennessee passed a good time law in 1833 and Ohio in 1856; Maconochie put it into general use in 1842 in the convict colonies in Australia; and Marsangy advocated this method in France in 1846. In spite of the earlier precedents in the United States, the method became generally known just after the Civil War when the news regarding the famous Irish system spread.[6] By 1868 as many as twenty-four states had made provision for reduction of the period of imprisonment for good behavior.

The general principle of the good time laws was that the prison board was authorized to release the prisoner in less time than the sentence imposed by the court, if, in their opinion, the prisoner main-

---

[6] E. C. Wines, "Commutation Laws in the United States," *Report of Prison Assoc. of New York*, 1868, pp. 154–170.

tained good conduct in prison. The prison board was the administrative authority and could determine whether the prisoner had earned the reduction in sentence or had not, but the legislature made the schedule of reductions in time.

The purpose of these laws was complex. It was at the same time an attempt to mitigate the severity of the laws, to solve the problem of prison discipline, to get good work from the prisoners and thereby increase the profits of the contractors, and to assist in the reformation of the prisoners.

The principal objection to the good time laws is that they tend to become mechanical. A clerical force automatically advances the maximum amount of good time to each convict unless his record is especially bad. It takes a definite sentence as a basis and no one knows how long this definite sentence should be in a particular case, because no one has made an intensive study of the particular criminal. In general this method of release does about as much injury as good.

III. THE INDETERMINATE SENTENCE

MEANING OF THE INDETERMINATE SENTENCE. The exact time of release of a prisoner may be determined by the legislature, which fixes a definite sentence for the offense, by the court, which receives authority from the legislature to fix definite penalties within the limits set by the legislature, or by an administrative board, which receives from the legislature authority to fix the definite penalty within the limits fixed by the legislature or by the court. When the time of release is determined by the administrative board and the court merely imposes minimum and maximum limits of the penalty, the sentence is known as an indeterminate sentence. Strictly speaking, the sentence is not indeterminate if the limits are fixed by the court or by the legislature, and it should be called indefinite rather than indeterminate. No state has sentences that are completely indeterminate and the general practice is to call these indefinite sentences indeterminate.

The administrative board which fixes the penalties is called a parole board, but there is no necessary connection between parole and the indeterminate sentence. The "indeterminate sentence" refers to the fact that the exact period of custody is not fixed before the custody begins, while the term "parole" refers to the fact that a portion of the period of custody may be spent outside the institution.

Either may be used independently of the other. The federal government has a parole system but no indeterminate sentences; it would be possible to have indeterminate sentences with complete and final release without supervision. Parole is the status of the prisoner after release from the walls of the institution, while still under the special guardianship of the state. It may be granted either to the prisoner on a definite sentence, though this is generally restricted to the period of freedom granted by the good time allowance, or the prisoner on an indeterminate sentence. A person on an indeterminate sentence may be released either conditionally on parole or unconditionally and completely without parole. The two methods, though distinct in principle, are generally combined in practice and must be combined for the greatest efficiency of either system.

HISTORY OF THE INDETERMINATE SENTENCE. As early as the Inquisition the indeterminate sentence was used, for criminals were sometimes sentenced to prison "for such time as seems expedient to the Church." In some of the early workhouses in the first part of the eighteenth century, commitment might be for an indeterminate period, especially for minors. In 1769 the colony of Connecticut provided that all rogues, vagabonds, sturdy beggars, and other lewd, idle, dissolute, profane, and disorderly persons without settlement in the colony might be confined in the workhouse at hard labor "until released by order of law." The indeterminate sentence has been used in the institutions for juvenile delinquents since their origin, the maximum period of confinement being the minority of the delinquent.

These developments of the indeterminate sentence in the workhouses and houses of refuge did not, however, carry to the public an implication that it should be extended to the state prisons. Occasional arguments to that effect were presented, to be sure, from the time Dr. Benjamin Rush urged it in 1787 to the Civil War. But the system really became known to the United States shortly after the Civil War, when there was a flood of information regarding the Irish system, which had, in imitation of Maconochie's example in the convict colonies of Australia, included an indeterminate sentence. Largely under the influence of this information Wines and Dwight in a report to the state legislature of New York in 1867 urged that sentences should be indeterminate for certain types of offenders. In its present form the indeterminate sentence law was passed in Michigan in 1869 and was known as the Three Years'

Law, but it was soon declared unconstitutional. Indeterminate sentences were an essential part of the program of Elmira Reformatory, which was authorized in 1869. Probably the most important influence in America in forming a favorable opinion regarding this system was a paper by Brockway on "The Ideal Prison System" before the National Prison Association in 1870, in which he stated the essential reasons for the indeterminate sentence as clearly as they have ever been stated.

It was not until 1889 that a general indeterminate sentence law was secured, this being in New York State. The law gave the court authority to sentence a convicted person to an indefinite term of imprisonment, within the limits fixed by law for the offense. This law was not mandatory and during the twelve years after its passage it was applied in only 115 cases out of about 13,000 in which it might have been used. In 1901 a law was passed in New York State, requiring the court to impose an indeterminate sentence on first offenders, with a minimum of not less than one year and a maximum as fixed for each crime by the laws of the state.

Indeterminate sentence laws had been enacted in five states by 1900. The number increased to thirty-one by 1915. Seven additional states enacted such laws by 1925 and none between 1915 and 1933. In the period 1925–1930 three states—New Jersey, South Carolina, and Montana—repealed their indeterminate sentence laws so far as concerned state prisons, and in addition many other states placed limitations on the laws in the period 1917–1927. The federal government has not enacted an indeterminate sentence law.

The use of the indeterminate sentence increased until shortly after the war, and thereafter tended to decrease slightly. Of commitments to federal and state prisons and reformatories in 1910 37 per cent were on indeterminate sentences, in 1926 55 per cent, and in 1936 54 per cent.

RESTRICTIONS ON THE INDETERMINATE SENTENCE. Not all prisoners in the states that have adopted this system are held on indeterminate sentences. The method is often applied only to restricted classes of offenders and the restrictions vary from state to state. It generally does not apply at all to misdemeanors or to the most serious felonies. In various states kidnapers, train-wreckers, train-robbers, dynamiters, defaulting notaries public, bank or homestead officials who misuse the funds of depositors, persons guilty of arson and crimes against nature, and tramps are excluded from the provisions of the law in various states. In South Dakota "criminals with abnormal tendencies" are not eligible for indeterminate sentences. It is sometimes restricted to those below a specified age or above a specified age. In general such restrictions are quite unjustified, and the general tendency has been to extend the indeterminate sentence system to all offenders.

THE MINIMUM AND MAXIMUM LIMITS. Originally the legislature fixed a definite penalty for each offense. The trend has been for the legislature to transfer to other agencies the authority to fix definite penalties within limits set by the legislature for each offense or class of offenses. It transferred this authority first to the court and then to the parole board. When the court was given authority to fix limits within the limits fixed by the legislature some judges who were opposed to indeterminate sentences abused their authority by making the minimum almost identical with the maximum. The following are illustrations of such sentences: two years and nine months to two years and ten months; nineteen years and six months to twenty years; thirty to thirty-one years; thirty-eight to forty years; one hundred and fifty to one hundred and sixty years. The legislature tried at first to correct these abuses by providing that the minimum set by the court must be not more than one-half, or some other specified fraction, of the maximum. More frequently the legislatures have deprived the courts of the authority to fix any limits within those set by the legislature and have given authority to the parole boards to fix the penalty within the limits set by the legislatures. In that case the court has authority merely to impose the minimum and maximum penalties provided in the law.

The question arises, Why should either the court or the legislature fix the limits? Why should not the sentences be completely indeterminate and the parole board have complete and unlimited authority to determine the time of release? As a matter of fact the sentences of about 1 per cent of the prisoners committed to state and federal prisons and reformatories in 1936 were completely indeterminate. In addition, 20 per cent of the indeterminate sentences had no minimum limit and 5 per cent either had no stated maximum or had a maximum of life. The problem of the minimum limit is somewhat different from the problem of the maximum limit, and the problems will be considered separately.

The principal argument for the minimum limit is that it is needed as a check on the parole board, so that at least a minimum punishment be provided in case the board should become sentimental or corrupt. In some states a large proportion of those on indeterminate sentences are released as soon as the minimum sentence is served. This is taken as proof that many prisoners would not be punished at all unless the legislature or the court imposed a minimum penalty. As a matter of fact the few states in which the minimum limit has been removed have witnessed no wholesale prison deliveries. If the administrative board is given authority to determine whether a prisoner should be held one year or five years it should be trusted to decide whether the prisoner should be held six months or ten months. It is probable that the very existence of the minimum sentence serves as a convenient time of release of all offenders against whom no bad behavior in prison has been recorded. If no minimum were provided, a decision on the merits of each case would be necessary.

Sometimes the assertion is made that a minimum period is necessary in order to give the parole board time to study the prisoner and to determine how long he should be retained. But if the sentence were absolutely indeterminate the board would still have authority to hold the prisoner as long as necessary and would also have authority to release a prisoner within a very short time if a clear-cut diagnosis could be made in a very short time.

The absolute maximum penalty probably results in more injury to society than does the minimum. It is perfectly clear to anyone acquainted with certain types of offenders that they will repeat their offenses as soon as released. The law requires the authorities to release them nevertheless when the maximum period of imprisonment has been served. In a few days or months, after society has been injured again by their crimes, they return to the prison. The International Prison Congress in 1910, in its resolution favoring the indeterminate sentence, insisted that:

It is advisable to fix the maximum duration of the sentence only during such a period as it may be necessary because of the novelty of the institution and lack of experience with it.

The reason for the general existence of the legal maximum is a fear that the administrative board will make mistakes and keep some prisoners confined for life who would be perfectly safe in society. The administrative board is not omniscient, to be sure, and will make just such mistakes, but the same thing is true of the court and legislature. There is less reason to expect that mistakes will be made when a decision is reached by a board that is intimately acquainted, as a result of long study, with the particular prisoner, than when a decision is reached by the legislature which is not acquainted with the individual at all and attempts to prescribe limits for the entire class, or by the court which has a superficial knowledge of a particular offender.

It may be urged that juries will not convict offenders if they may be held in prison for life for comparatively trivial offenses. This argument might, to be sure, be supported by the experience with the "habitual criminal act." If the sentences were absolutely indeterminate the jury would not know whether a particular offender would be held for one year or for life; it would know only that the administrative board would hold the offender for as long a time as he needed to be held for the protection of society. That would tend to make the jury more willing rather than less willing to convict.

It would not be desirable, however, to remove these limits if everything else were to be left just as at present. The administrative board must be able to do much more efficient work than at present before it should be trusted with authority of this nature. Assuming some improvement in the personnel and in the methods of the boards, it would be preferable to give them complete control over the period of imprisonment.

DETERMINING THE TIME OF RELEASE. The American Parole Association adopted a Declaration of Principles in 1933, in which the following paragraph states the principles which should be used in determining the time at which a particular offender should be released from prison:

Has the institution accomplished all that it can for him; is the offender's state of mind and attitude toward his own difficulties and problems such that further residence will be harmful or beneficial; does a suitable environment await him on the outside; can the beneficial effect already accomplished be retained if he is held longer to allow a more suitable environment to be developed?[7]

Nominally, at least, parole boards generally attempt to use this principle of fitness for limited freedom in determining the time of

[7] *Jour. Crim. Law and Criminol.* 24:791, November, 1933.

release. Actually they depart from this principle in many respects. In New York for several years over 95 per cent of the inmates of state prisons were released as soon as they were eligible for parole, which meant at the completion of the minimum term. Moreover, this procedure was defended[8] and there is no final proof that it is not as good a method as any. Several studies of successes on parole indicate that the prisoners who remain longer violate parole more often than those who remain a shorter time in prison. This may result either from the imposition of longer terms upon prisoners who are least fit for life in society or from the decrease in fitness for life in society with the length of the period of isolation from society.

Releases are frequently determined by pressures of various kinds. On the one side, attorneys, relatives and friends, politicians, and others frequently make an organized attack on the parole board to secure the early release of a prisoner. Sometimes this pressure is accompanied by bribery of one or more members of the parole board, though, in general, parole boards have been less influenced by bribery than have the police forces and the courts. On the other side, the policies of the parole board are frequently determined primarily by the pressure of newspapers, crime commissions, and other agencies which believe that long periods of imprisonment should be made uniform.

In some institutions fitness for release has been determined by a marking or credit system, designed to measure the behavior of the prisoner while in the institution. The credit systems differ considerably from one institution to another, but the essential points in most of the systems are as follows: (a) Release on parole is granted only to those who have secured a specified number of credits, just as graduation from an educational institution is dependent upon securing a specified number of units or hours of credit. (b) Credits are secured by good conduct and lost by bad conduct. The prisoner generally secures a uniform credit per day or per month unless reports have been made against him for bad conduct, negligence, or laziness. (c) The prisoner is promoted to a higher grade when he has secured a specified number of credits. He has additional privileges in that grade and is able to earn credits at a more rapid rate than in the lower grade. The number of such grades varies in different institutions from three to fourteen. He is not eligible for

---

[8] New York, *Report of Superintendent of State Prisons*, 1919, p. 412.

parole until he reaches the highest grade. (d) A bonus in addition to the regular credits may be granted for especially meritorious acts, such as reporting an attempt to escape, and an additional demerit may be given for especially bad conduct. In one of the New York institutions three thousand credits, which were equivalent to good conduct for six months, were given for catching a runaway inmate. (e) In some institutions these credits are stated merely as credits, in others as units of time, in others as money, which may have real value or may be token-money. An experiment in using real money was tried in Westchester County, New York, and the prisoner was released when he had earned a specified amount of money. (f) Some institutions have offered an opportunity to earn group credits. Extra credits were given in Westchester County Penitentiary to the inmates of a corridor for good behavior in the corridor during a week. The group as a whole must maintain good conduct in order to earn this extra credit and this makes the group self-disciplining.

The credit system is a doubtful method of measuring the goodness of conduct. It tends to produce mediocrity, for there is no incentive to extraordinarily good work except in the form of preventing escapes and similar acts against their associates. It places too much power in the hands of guards; an act that would be permitted by one guard would be reported as a minor offense by a second guard and as a major offense by a third. A specific act might be reported as disobedience, causing a loss of ten credits, or disrespect, causing a loss of one hundred credits, or insubordination, causing a loss of two hundred credits. Moreover, it is difficult to secure the proper relation in this system between flexibility and rigidity. In some institutions the inmate secures parole automatically when he has earned the required number of credits.

Aside from the question of the credit system, there is the larger question whether fitness for release can be determined by behavior in the institution. Three types of prisoners behave well in prisons: those who attempt to secure an early release by good behavior in order to return more quickly to crime, those who reach their highest level under the careful control of others, and those who really profit by the experience and the training. The good behavior of the last group alone indicates fitness for release. On the other hand some prisoners who behave badly under the surveillance of prison guards get along satisfactorily in the general community. The behavior in the institution is significant but is not in itself an adequate test of fitness for freedom.

In a number of institutions a "progressive merit system" has been tried. By this method the liberty of the prisoner is increased gradually, as an experiment or test, before he is released entirely from the institution. In Montana the prisoners have been placed outside the walls of the institution, on their honor, for six months before they are released. During this time they do road work, construction work, and other tasks. The Preston School of Industry permitted some boys who had earned about two-thirds of the credits necessary for parole to work outside of the institution, living either in the School, in camps, or on a ranch belonging to the institution. This gave more freedom than the institution afforded and the boys were permitted to earn money for their work. The Industrial School for Girls in Massachusetts established a "parole cottage" in which the girls were given greater freedom and choice of work, so that they had a better opportunity than girls in the regular institution for expression of individuality, personality, and self-reliance. In the state prison at Joliet several years ago the prisoners passed through the following stages: confinement in the prison with little personal responsibility, increased opportunity, positions of trust in the prison, life in cottages outside the walls but under the supervision of prison officials, work on the prison farm without guards, and parole.

It seems evident that everything that has demonstrable significance should be taken into account in determining the time of release of a particular prisoner, and that this information should be organized and tested. In the following chapter a description of the methods of prediction of behavior on parole, in relation to this organized and tested information, will be presented.

It is clear that a parole board cannot be an independent autocracy. It must conform more or less to the wishes of the public. If the public insists on long terms for certain types of offenders, the parole board may not insist on short terms. This raises a difficult question, for it is necessary to differentiate between the demands of a local community which has been affected by a particular crime and the demands of the entire state. A particular community in which an embezzlement has ruined a bank and thus has injured hundreds of depositors may insist that the embezzler be retained in prison for the maximum term. Some newspapers and crime commissions exert pressure in the same direction. The friends of the prisoner, including many of the prison guards, point to his excellent character and the certainty that he will commit no crimes in the future. The people of the state in general show no concern. The parole board feels the necessity of consistency and does not want to hold an embezzler of excellent character longer than a professional burglar. It is therefore generally forced into compromises by the pressure of these influences and considerations.

HAS THE INDETERMINATE SENTENCE DECREASED PENALTIES? Many accusations have been made that the indeterminate sentence has resulted in a decrease in the average period of imprisonment and therefore has tended to increase crime. The evidence, on the contrary, indicates that the average sentences have increased under the indeterminate sentence system.

At the state prison [of Indiana], the last 304 men sentenced under the definite sentence law served an average of two years and two months each. A study has been made at three different dates (1900, 1906, and 1910), of the same number of commitments under indeterminate sentence, and it has been found that the first group served an average of six months, twenty-three days longer; the second group one year, two months, five days longer; the third group eight months, ten days longer. A similar study of four groups of commitments to the Indiana Reformatory discloses that the last 300 men sentenced to that institution for a definite time served an average of one year, eight months, and twenty-two days, while the first group of 300 men committed under the indeterminate sentence law served an average of seven months, fourteen days longer; the second group one year, two months, fourteen days longer; the third group six months, twenty-two days longer.[9]

The same thing is shown in Table X, which is a comparison of the average time served by prisoners in Joliet prison, Illinois, in the last five years under the definite system (1890 to 1894) with two recent years under the indeterminate system (1932 to 1933) for certain types of offenses and offenders.[10] Similar evidence has been published regarding at least six other states. The average time served in the New Jersey State Prison increased from 31 months in 1860

[9] W. T. McCray, "Indiana and Her Crime Problem," *Ind. Conf. on Delinquency*, Indianapolis, 1922, pp. 3–4.

[10] See, for similar comparison of 1890–1894 and 1916–1920, Illinois Department of Public Welfare, *The Illinois Parole Law*, 1920, p. 8.

to 51 months in 1920 for robbery, from 23 to 30 for burglary, from 15 to 29 for assault, and from 18 to 20 for larceny.[11]

TABLE X

COMPARISON OF THE AVERAGE TIME SERVED UNDER THE DETERMINATE
AND INDETERMINATE SENTENCE SYSTEMS, ILLINOIS

TYPE OF OFFENSE OR OFFENDER	DETERMINATE SENTENCE 1890–1894		INDETERMINATE SENTENCE 1932–1933	
	Number Discharged	Average Time Served; Years	Number Discharged	Average Time Served; Years
Burglary	1483	1.64	263	2.55
Larceny	776	1.36	307	2.35
Robbery	286	1.77	349	5.39
Second term	392	2.08	204	5.04
Third or more terms.	131	2.56	90	5.20

These statistics need to be interpreted. They do not prove that a particular prisoner receives a longer period of imprisonment under the indeterminate sentence system than he would have received under the earlier system of definite sentences. It is possible that the majority of the offenders may have shorter sentences, but the average for the entire group be increased by very long sentences for a minority. This does not appear to be the case in Illinois at least, for during the last five years of the definite system only 17 prisoners were sentenced to Joliet for the maximum terms on conviction of burglary, robbery, and larceny, and the average term actually served was 6.63 years, while during the five years 1916-1920 of the indeterminate sentence system (the latest years for which information on this point is available), 162 were held for these crimes to the end of the maximum term and the average term actually served by them was 8.18 years.[12] A second interpretation that should be made is that probation has been developed since the indeterminate sentence system started. A large proportion of offenders who would have been held in prison a generation ago for short terms are now placed on probation, and only the ones judged to be most dangerous are imprisoned at all. The evidence given previously compares the sentences of all offenders with a selected group of offenders, after the best have been eliminated by probation.

[11] Emil Frankel, "One Hundred Years of Prison Sentencing in New Jersey," *Proc. Amer. Prison Assoc.*, 1936, pp. 22–23.
[12] Illinois Department of Public Welfare, *The Illinois Parole Law*, 1920, p. 8.

The current reports of the Bureau of the Census on prisoners show that the average time actually served is slightly longer for those released on parole than for those released at the expiration of definite sentences. This is true for all offenses combined, and for approximately half of the specific offenses, while for the other offenses the time served by those discharged on parole is slightly less than for those discharged at the expiration of the sentence. These differences, however, are so small that the only conclusion that can be reached is that is makes practically no difference in the length of time served in an institution whether the offender is sentenced on a definite or an indeterminate term; the court, which imposes the definite sentence, and the administrative board, which determines the time of release under the indeterminate sentence, act in practically identical ways on the average.

ARGUMENTS PRO AND CON. The arguments against this system most frequently presented are as follows: (a) The indeterminate sentence takes into account nothing except the reformation of the prisoner, while other things, especially the deterrence of potential criminals, should be considered. This general theory has been considered already and it is sufficient here to point out that, if deterrence should be considered, the parole board can take that into account; and that the average penalties under the indeterminate system seem to be longer and therefore, if the length of sentence determines the deterrent effect of the treatment, this system will be preferable for that reason. (b) No satisfactory method of determining when a prisoner has reformed has been developed; his prison record is generally used, but this is unsatisfactory for the reason that a good prisoner is frequently a poor citizen. Other sources of information are now used in some places and nothing would tend to develop methods of determining reformation as rapidly as the extension of the system. Even as the methods stand, they are more dependable than the advance judgments of courts. And they can be safeguarded by gradually increasing the liberty of the prisoner and supervising him while on parole. (c) It is possible that a prisoner may be held in the institution for a very long period because he has antagonized a guard, for release depends largely on the reports of prison guards. This is a very real danger, but the same danger exists if the decision is left to a judge. The remedy is to secure better guards and better supervision of guards, and a system of discipline in which the present antagonism between guards and prisoners will be reduced. (d) It tends to produce sycophancy in prisoners, making them work to get good reports from the guards rather than work to modify their behavior. This danger, also, exists but it can be minimized by the development of better guards and better methods of measuring reformation and attitudes. It exists, also, in the system in which judges determine penalties. (e) No adequate supply of suitable administrative officers for such work is available and it is certain that many who are not suitable will be appointed; the judges are the most trustworthy public officers we have and they should therefore retain this power rather than transfer it to others who will be less efficient and trustworthy. This, also, is a real difficulty, but the judge has a task that no human being, however honest and trustworthy, can perform efficiently, for no one can tell in advance how long the prisoner should be retained. Moreover, it is evident that administrative boards must do a great deal of the governmental work in modern society, and the solution of the difficulty is not the reduction of the power of such boards, but an increase of their power so that they will become sufficiently important to attract the interest of the citizens and create a demand for greater efficiency. (f) Uncertainty regarding the time of release causes much anxiety for prisoners. Some prisoners have stated that they prefer a longer term fixed in advance to a shorter term with its early period of worry and anxiety while they await a decision or "setting" by the parole board. This is one of the difficulties in the indeterminate sentence system which cannot easily be overcome. The following statement by an ex-prisoner illustrates the effect.

I was sentenced to San Quentin on an indefinite term. The prisoner there has no notion during the entire first year regarding the term the parole board will set for him to do. At the end of that year the parole board fixes his maximum, and may later reduce it. That first year is a perfect hell for the prisoner. He keeps asking others who were convicted of a similar offense about the details of their crimes and of their maximum sentences. One man committed the same crime I did and he received a sentence of nine years but he had a long previous record and he was armed. Another man who was a first offender and was not armed got four years. I was a first offender and was armed. Consequently I figured that I will get between four and nine years. But I keep thinking and worrying about it, for every year in prison makes a big difference. My worry interferes with my work, and I get sent to the "hole" for inefficiency in work. That looks bad on my record and I wonder whether it will increase my maximum sentence. This worry drives a person mad. As soon as the sentence is fixed the prisoner can settle down to serve his time, and it is a great relief to have it settled.

(g) The prisoners suspect that differences in the terms of prisoners who are convicted of the same offense are due to favoritism or graft. The standard of justice of the prisoners is the customary or average penalty, and variations from this average arouse suspicion. Since the length of the imprisonment is determined by the character of the offender under the indeterminate sentence system, this difficulty is inevitable but it may be possible to develop an understanding of the new principle involved. The following statement was made by an ex-prisoner.

Parole is the worst thing that can happen in a prison. The prisoner learns that some other prisoner is paroled. The other prisoner committed the same offense and has no more children, no better friends, and the same previous record. This causes suspicion of graft or politics. It makes the prisoner resentful of the entire system. He is willing to pay a regular penalty for a certain crime and regards that as proper and just. When he commits a crime he knows he is likely to get caught and he expects to pay the regular penalty if he does get caught. The underworld has the penalties all figured out, so much for this offense and so much for that, and it is a consistent and definite system. They regard the indeterminate sentence and parole as mere camouflage. When a particular prisoner get out sooner than this system of thought provides, it is graft; when he is held longer, it is a grudge. This disrupts the prison.

The general public, as well as the criminals, have in mind a system of fixed penalties adjusted to the seriousness of the crime. They have not appreciated the principle of the indeterminate sentence. Doubtless on that account the parole boards in several states have tended to fix the penalty almost entirely by the type of crime committed. This surrenders the principle of the indeterminate sentence. If the penalty is to be determined by the nature of the crime, the court can fix it as satisfactorily as the parole board.

(h) The constitutionality of the indeterminate sentence has been questioned. This doubt is probably justified in some states but can generally be overcome by re-wording the law. The grounds on which the constitutionality of the indeterminate sentence are questioned are, first, that it is a grant of power to an administrative board which belongs to the court, and second, that it is an interference with the executive's right of pardon. If necessary, the constitution may be amended.

The prisoner must be released by some agency unless he is to be held for life. No one can determine in advance how long the prisoner should be held, and there is no apparent possibility of developing a scientific prediction regarding the length of time imprisonment should continue. The method can be more scientific if the length of imprisonment is determined by observation of the prisoner during the time of his incarceration, in connection with his previous record and situation, and the technique can improve with experience. Release should therefore be under the control of an administrative board. The principles on which this system is based were stated in 1897 by Spalding.

That punishment should be made to fit the criminal rather than the crime; that character, and not actions, should be the ground of treatment; that a criminal act furnishes little proof regarding the real character of criminality of the offender; that the criminal has forfeited his right to liberty, not for a definite term, fixed in advance, as the penalty for a single act, but until such time as he shall cease to have a criminal character; that this cannot be ascertained before the convict begins his imprisonment; that it is unfair to the community to release an unreformed criminal.[13]

In addition, when the sentence is definite the criminal feels and is given a right to feel that when he has finished that term he has paid the penalty and balanced the account. This is a dangerous doctrine for the criminal or others to hold. There is no such account. Moreover, when the criminal is on an indeterminate sentence he knows that his release will depend on his efforts to reform and will make a decided attempt in that direction. His desire for an early release will make him more favorably inclined toward efforts to produce reformation for himself and others in the institution.

---

[13] W. F. Spalding, "The Indeterminate Sentence," *Proc. Natl. Conf. Char. and Corr.*, 1897, pp. 50–51.

THE PAROLE BOARD. The parole board has the duty of determining when a prisoner shall be released. Parole boards are of three principal types, with various combinations of these types: first, a special parole board limited to one institution, which is sometimes composed of the staff of the institution, and at other times merely includes the warden of the institution as one member of the board; second, a general state parole board which is located in the state department of correction and which has authority to release from any state institution; third, a general state parole board which is located outside of the department of correction and has authority to release from any state institution. The parole board of the first type is generally dominated by the prison staff. In New Jersey, for instance, the classification committee which supervises and directs the activities of the prisoners also determines when they shall be released. In this respect it acts in a manner analogous to the staff of a hospital. At the other extreme is the parole board which is entirely independent of the department of correction. This parole board, at least in some states, is concerned less with the progress of the prisoner and more with the possible reactions of the public toward parole. The argument for the centralization of parole authority has generally been that experts are required for this work and that experts can be secured only if the board is composed of full-time salaried members. Only six states have full-time salaried boards and these have developed recently, beginning with the Illinois board in 1927. Furthermore, in a system like that of New Jersey the parole board of a particular institution is composed of persons who are experts in their particular fields and who devote full time to the study and direction of the particular prisoners whose prison terms are determined by them. The trend during the last two decades has been toward centralization of parole authority and toward removal of the parole board from the department of correction. While this has been supported by the prison staff in many cases on the ground that it relieves them of a troublesome responsibility which interferes with their efficiency in the institutional work, it has been criticized by others on the ground that the prison staff knows better than any other agency when a prisoner should be released.

JUDICIAL REVIEW OF SENTENCES. Some persons who admit the weakness of the system of definite sentences argue that re-entrance of the offender into society should be under the control of the court rather than of an administrative body. By periodic judicial review of sentences, the court could release those prisoners who seemed to be fit for release and retain in prison those who should be retained. This suggestion is based on a belief that the court has a superior personnel and is more completely free from political and other extraneous considerations than the parole board.

The difficulty in the judicial review of sentences is to convince the court that the earlier sentence was a mistake. The presumption in favor of the earlier definite sentence would be difficult to overcome. Judicial courtesy and self-confidence would tend to make the sentences in review the same as the original, no matter how inadequate the basis for the penalty in the earlier case might have been. The judges in reviewing the penalties would depend for their information on the reports of the administrative officers and would therefore rubber-stamp their reports. Also, the superiority of the judges in personal character, if it exists at all under present conditions, is to some extent off-set by the fact that they are more imbued than administrative officers with the orthodox notion of retaliation and fitting punishments to crimes and are less able to confine their attention to the personality of the criminal. Finally, training in law includes practically nothing in penology, while it is possible for persons trained in psychology, sociology, and psychiatry to become members of parole boards.

HABITUAL CRIMINAL LAWS. For more than a century laws have made provision for increasing the severity of penalties for offenders who have earlier criminal records. Massachusetts enacted an habitual criminal law in 1817, and before 1900 similar laws were passed by nine other states. Twenty-three states have passed habitual criminal laws since 1900, of which three were passed during the first decade of the century, four during the second, and sixteen during the third. Thus in 1933 thirty-three states had habitual criminal laws. In general these laws permit increased penalties for habitual offenders, but the increased severity is not mandatory. Seven states, however, make a life sentence mandatory on conviction of a third felony and nine make a life sentence mandatory on conviction of a fourth felony.

These habitual criminal laws of the mandatory type developed after the World War as a result of pressure of various crime commissions. They had the purpose of depriving courts and parole boards of the authority to fix penalties in these cases. The legislative assembly made the pronouncement that no one who had the specified number of previous convictions should be granted freedom by any authority other than a governor.

Those who advocated these habitual criminal laws believed they would practically eliminate serious crimes. At present their effects cannot be determined accurately. Within a short time after the laws were enacted claims were made that crimes had decreased decidedly. No statistical evidence of this decrease can be secured. On the other hand, these laws did increase the proportion of charges which were reduced to minor offenses. In the year 1927 28.6 per cent of the charges under the fourth offender act in New York were reduced to misdemeanors, while only 16.1 per cent of all felony charges were thus reduced. Furthermore, it is probable that the professional criminals for whom this law was designed were not much affected by it, and that the occasional criminals were the principal victims of the law. Finally, prison riots have often been ascribed to the presence of a large number of these habitual offenders sentenced to prison for life.

The previous criminal record is unquestionably an important consideration in determining the treatment a criminal should receive. It should not be the only consideration.

SUGGESTED READINGS

Barnett, J. D., "The Grounds of Pardon," *Jour. Crim. Law and Criminol.*, 17:490–530, February, 1927.

California, *Report of Crime Commission,* 1931, pp. 11–15, 81–97.

Disque, B. P., "Prison Progress: A Warden's Programme," *Atlantic Mo.,* 129:330–337, March, 1922.

Goodrich, J. P., "The Use and Abuse of the Power to Pardon," *Jour. Crim. Law and Criminol.,* 11:334–342, November, 1920.

Hallheimer, J., "Justice by Formula," *Century Mag.,* 117:232–240, December, 1928.

"Indeterminate Sentence, by a Prisoner," *Atlantic Mo.,* 108:330–332, September, 1911.

Jensen, C., *The Pardoning Power in the United States,* Chicago, 1922.

Lewis, B. G., *The Offender,* New York, 1917, Ch. 7.

Lindsey, E., "What Should Be the Form of the Indeterminate Sentence and What Should Be the Provisions as to Maximum and Minimum Terms, If Any?" *Jour. Crim. Law and Criminol.,* 12:534–542, February, 1922.

Neal, Ann, and Hager, Beatrice, "Summary of the Provisions of the Constitutions and Statutes of the Several States Relating to Pardons," *Jour. Crim. Law and Criminol.*, 20:364–395, November, 1929.

New York, *Report of Crime Commission*, 1931, pp. 41–43.

New York, *Report of Prison Survey Committee*, Albany, 1920, Ch. 15.

Pennsylvania, *Report of Pennsylvania State Parole Commission*, Philadelphia, 1927.

Posner, H. R., "Prior Conviction—Baumes Laws," *Jour. Crim. Law and Criminol.*, 21:612–615, February, 1931.

Rice, W. G., "The Power of Pardon," *Wis. State Bar Assoc. Proc.*, 1927, pp. 36–55.

Wines, E. C., "Commutation Laws in the United States," *Report of Prison Assoc. of New York*, 1868, pp. 154–170; 1869, pp. 284–290.

Chapter Twenty-Six

PAROLE

NATURE OF PAROLE. Parole is the act of releasing or the status of being released from a penal or reformatory institution in which one has served a part of his maximum sentence, on condition of maintaining good behavior and remaining in the custody and under the supervision of the institution or some other agency approved by the state until a final discharge is granted. The term "parole" is used in analogous manner with reference to institutions for insane and feebleminded persons.

Parole is related to but should be distinguished from probation. Parole is preceded by a part of a sentence served in a penal or reformatory institution, while no formal penalty is imposed in probation or, if imposed, is not executed. Probation is granted by a court, parole by an administrative board or an executive. A conditional pardon is similar to parole in that both are liberation from an institution on conditions, with restoration of the original penalty if the conditions of liberation are violated. They differ in that conditional pardon carries with it the remission of guilt, and parole does not; parole refers to imprisonment only, while conditional pardon may refer to other penalties also; and they generally differ in administrative details, such as the degree of supervision, which is generally greater in parole than in the conditional pardon.

HISTORY OF PAROLE. Parole is a combination and extension of practices that had existed previously for a long time. The first trace of parole was the system of indenturing prisoners. By this means prisoners were removed from institutions and placed under the supervision of masters or employers and could be returned to the institution if they did not behave properly. This method was used for juvenile delinquents from the time of the origin of the houses of refuge. Later the supervision was extended by the appointment of a state visiting agent with the special function of protecting the wards of the institution against imposition. This constituted a rather fully developed parole system for juveniles. Several other experiments and influences were combined with this before a parole system for adults was formed. One of these was the after-care of discharged convicts. At first philanthropic societies, beginning as early as 1776 but working most energetically during the decades of the forties and fifties, attempted to assist ex-prisoners to adjust themselves to social life.[1] Later the state made efforts in the same direction. Massachusetts was the first state to do this, by the appointment in 1845 of a state agent for discharged convicts, who had public funds at his disposal with which to assist ex-prisoners to secure employment, tools, clothing, and transportation to places of employment. Other states appointed similar agents, and these agents began to realize the necessity of continuing the custody over the ex-prisoners. The agent for discharged convicts in New York pointed out in his reports that his work could be greatly improved if the state retained custody over prisoners for some time after their release; he suggested that the good-time allowance should be merely a release from the institution, but not from custody.

As early as 1820 the English convict colonies developed a parole system, with little supervision after release, under the name of ticket-of-leave. This was later made a part of the Irish system and in that form became known to the American leaders. When the Massachusetts Prison Board made a plea for a parole system in 1865 it called it "the English ticket-of-leave system." The English Prevention of Crimes Act of 1871 also helped create a demand for a parole system in the United States. That act provided for surveillance by the police for a period of seven years after release from prison of all except those on their first terms and a central register of all such ex-prisoners. The Massachusetts Prison Board called attention to this act repeatedly and urged the adoption of a similar law.

Parole in its developed form was first adopted by New York State in the law of 1869 authorizing the Elmira Reformatory. It was hailed at the time as a great invention and Brockway sincerely felt that he was the inventor. But it is evident that the system had existed for over fifty years in European countries and in its essential

---

[1] For a history of such societies, see H. H. Hart, "Prisoners' Aid Societies," *Proc. Natl. Prison Assoc.*, 1889, pp. 270–287.

features had as long a history in the United States. The parole method was first extended to state prisons by Ohio in 1884. After that the system developed rapidly, being adopted in twenty-five states by 1898. In 1933 parole laws had been passed by forty-six states. In practice the other states, also, used parole methods for juvenile delinquents even if not authorized to do so by the legislatures. The federal government, also, has a parole system.

Of the states that have authorized parole, many make extensive use and others make little use of it. Of prisoners discharged from state prisons and reformatories in 1936 more than 80 per cent were released on parole in Maine, Vermont, New Hampshire, New York, New Jersey, Pennsylvania, Ohio, Indiana, Illinois, Michigan, Colorado, Nevada, and Washington, while less than 20 per cent were paroled in seven of the thirteen Southern states on which reports were made.

In 1929 nine of the states had authorized parole for inmates of institutions for misdemeanants. This, however, is generally a farce in most states and amounts to little more than "floating." The Board of Public Welfare of Kansas City, which had control of paroles from the city prison for misdemeanants, described the method in use in 1912, which is still in use in many cities:

> This class of men, when sobered, are given a parole, told to get a shipment away from the city and not to return.[2]

ELIGIBILITY FOR PAROLE. The essential question regarding eligibility for parole is, Should any prisoner be released absolutely without supervision? The answer which is made by parole authorities is that if a prisoner is to be released at all he should be released under supervision. Probably even the prisoners who are released by pardon after proof of innocence should receive the assistance which parole officers are able to provide. Some thoughtful and sincere criminals have opposed this policy. One criminal of this nature made the following statement:

> The criminal does not feel that he has been treated unjustly if he is forced to pay the penalty for his crime, but when he gets out of prison he wants to regard it as finished. Parole means that the state

---

[2] Kansas City, Mo., *Report of Board of Public Welfare,* 1912–1913, pp. 52–53.

still regards him with suspicion, keeps snooping around, and is unwilling to give him a fair chance to get along as an ordinary individual. Consequently it has a bad effect psychologically upon the prisoner who is paroled.

The statutes exclude certain types of criminals from parole. These are generally the prisoners convicted of the most serious offenses, who are above all others most in need of the supervision which is afforded in efficient parole work. The exclusion of the prisoners who are most in need of parole is due to the mistaken notion that parole is a form of leniency. This notion should have been corrected before this time by the comparison of time served by those paroled and by those released without parole.

Two specific prerequisites of parole are frequently made. One is that the prisoner have no "detainer" against him. This requirement is made partly out of courtesy to the jurisdiction which "wants" the prisoner for a former crime, and partly because success on parole is unlikely if the prisoner goes immediately into another trial or another prison. The second specific requirement is a guarantee of employment. Four objections have been made to this requirement. First, many of the positions which are guaranteed are fictitious. Second, many prisoners who have reached the point where they are best prepared to go out are detained in prison because no jobs are available. In December, 1933, newspapers reported that nearly one hundred men were being held in the Eastern Penitentiary of Pennsylvania for the sole reason that jobs could not be guaranteed for them. Third, the paroled man is exploited because the employer must be notified of the prison record. Fourth, parole officers spend much time in locating positions which the offenders should find for themselves.

Everyone agrees that the prisoner should have employment into which he can go immediately after release. However, the first position is generally temporary, either because it is fictitious, or because the employer tries to exploit the prisoner or because the parolee wants to "get a reference behind him" so that he can go to another position where his criminal record will not be known, or because of his personal characteristics. Glueck reported that 60 per cent of the parolees studied by him held their first jobs one month or less.[3] Much of the work of securing employment is, in fact, done

---

[3] Sheldon and Eleanor T. Glueck, *Five Hundred Criminal Careers*, p. 171.

by friends and relatives of the prisoner, and in the future most of this may be done by public employment offices. In the meantime the provision of a job assists in establishing a friendly relationship between parolee and parole officer.

CONDITIONS ON PAROLE. Parole is "conditional liberation," that is, liberation on condition that the prisoner live in accordance with specified rules. The conditions are sometimes fixed by law, sometimes by the parole board, and sometimes by other agencies. These conditions may include: leading a law-abiding life, abstaining from intoxicating liquors and drugs, keeping free from bad associates, spending evenings at home, refraining from gambling and other vicious habits, supporting legal dependents, remaining in a specified territory, not changing residence or employment without permission (sometimes merely without reporting the change), attending church at least once each Sunday, not marrying without permission, not becoming dependent on charity, making reparation or restitution for the crime, and making written or personal reports as required.

ORGANIZATION OF SUPERVISION. The board which has authority to grant paroles generally has supervision over the parolees, but sometimes the parole supervision is under the direction of an independent board. On the principle that imprisonment and parole should constitute a continuous series of efforts to prepare for a life of complete freedom, there is a theoretical superiority in a parole system in which the board which controls the institution also determines the time of release and supervises the parolees from that institution. This has the disadvantage of duplication of efforts in supervision, for an officer from each of the institutions of the state must work in the same territory. Therefore, in the interest of economy, parole supervision which is more than nominal is generally organized on a territorial rather than an institutional basis, and one officer supervises all parolees who reside in his territory, regardless of the institutions from which they were released.

Parole supervision is little more than nominal in most states. Only eight states have a sufficient number of officers to make adequate supervision possible. In Massachusetts where the work of supervision is better than in the average state, 12.2 per cent of 400 parolees from the reformatory had no supervision, and 71.2 per cent had one parole visit in six months or more.[4] In 1936 82 per cent of the

---

[4] Glueck and Glueck, *op. cit.*, p. 265.

prisoners released on parole from federal and state prisons and reformatories were under the supervision of parole officers, 6 per cent
were under the supervision of other public officials or of private
individuals, while 8 per cent merely made written reports.

The real work of supervision in many states is left largely to
philanthropic organizations, such as the Catholic Church, a Prison
Association, the Salvation Army, a Jewish welfare society. It has
generally been found that supervision by philanthropic agencies
is very inadequate, though the co-operation of these societies is unquestionably beneficial. Probation officers are used in some places
for purposes of supervision. In the federal system the officer has
supervision both of probationers and parolees. Attempts have been
made to use policemen, sheriffs, and other officers of the law as
supervisors of paroled prisoners. In some states this has been required by law. Brockway stated that this method was used at first
reluctantly for those paroled from Elmira Reformatory, but that it
grew in favor with him.[5] The Committee on Prisons and Police
Administration of the National Prison Association in 1907 stated:

> The police is the logical department for the supervision of criminals,
> and prisoners should be paroled to their custody. Having such super-
> vision, I believe that their attitude would so change toward the crim-
> inal that they would perform their functions judiciously.[6]

These early experiences with supervision by the police were generally
unfavorable. After policemen had been used as parole officers for
twenty years in Canada, the Superintendent of Prisons urged that
the method be abandoned. If the attitude of the police can be
changed as it has been in some places, the police should be able to
do effective work in this line.

PRINCIPLES AND METHODS OF SUPERVISION. One view regarding supervision places the emphasis on detective work; another view
places the emphasis on friendly assistance. The first view is illustrated by the following quotations:

> In Oklahoma we do not parole a man until we feel that he is able
> to make good alone, without being nursed or coddled along.[7]

---

[5] Z. R. Brockway, *Proc. Natl. Prison Assoc.*, 1898, pp. 312–315.
[6] "Report of the Committee on Prisons and Police Administration," *Proc.
Natl. Prison Assoc.*, 1907, p. 91.
[7] Quoted in *Jour. of Crim. Law and Criminol.*, 6:290, July, 1915.

It is thought that too strict prison surveillance over a man after he is released is not wholly in accord with the humane principle of the system. Such should be exercised only when necessitated by the conduct of the paroled man, who must understand that he must depend upon his own initiative.[8]

It has been the experience of the Board that an excessive amount of official routine supervision is more harmful to the paroled man than a system which gives him every opportunity for advice and counsel, and which looks after his family in an intelligent manner.[9]

This system provides sufficient supervision of a proper type to insure rather accurate knowledge concerning the activities of the boy. At the same time the supervision is not so close as to destroy initiative or the boy's confidence in himself; rather it tends to create the feeling that those who have him under observation consider him sufficiently trustworthy to manage his own affairs.[10]

This conception is based on the assumption that reformation is practically complete at the time of the release of the prisoner and that the function of the parole officer is to watch him to determine whether he is maintaining the conditions fixed for his parole. The other conception is illustrated by the following quotations:

The man on parole needs help. He needs it often. He needs strong help. He needs it many times even more than he needs it while in confinement. If he does not get it all the good which has been done for him before his release is lost. Our efforts and our money are squandered because of the pettiness and the penuriousness with which our parole system is supported.[11]

To obtain successful results, parole must cease to be a mechanical operation of law and rules, and must become a vital creative force to preserve human material for itself and for society, which might otherwise become wreckage and waste.[12]

---

[8] New York, *Report of Superintendent of State Prisons,* 1918, p. 439.
[9] *Ibid.,* 1920, p. 417.
[10] California, *Report of Preston School of Industry,* 1916–1918, p. 100.
[11] F. Moore, "A Few of Our Failures," *Proc. Amer. Prison Assoc.,* 1914, pp. 170–171.
[12] Edith M. Burleigh, "The Future of Parole," *Proc. Amer. Prison Assoc.,* 1919, p. 423.

The ideal which the trustees try to have them [the parole officers or visitors] attain is to treat each boy as if he were the visitor's own child, and to counsel with him, to guide him and struggle with him with a fatherly interest.[13]

This conception is based on the belief that essential work of adjustment has to be done after release from the institution, and that this requires assistance, not to prevent the person from exercising his own initiative but to assist him in exercising it correctly, so that crimes will not be repeated.

Both of these types of work are needed, but it is difficult for one officer to do both types of work. The suggestion has been made that parole officers should be of two classes, one to do detective work, the other to render friendly assistance. The objection has been made that we already have the police to do the detective work and that parole officers should confine themselves to the second.

Even for the work of friendly assistance specialization is desirable, and some experiments in this specialization have been made, especially for juveniles. The parole officers of the Massachusetts Industrial School for Girls in 1915 specialized as follows: one gave her entire time to the investigation of homes, heredity, and history of the girls before they were paroled; a second specialized on placing girls in foster homes; a third had charge of the supervision of girls attending public schools; a fourth had charge of all mother-and-baby cases. These different kinds of work require different training, personalities, and techniques; one who specializes in a particular field acquires an ability that could not be secured by an officer who dealt with all kinds of problems.

In order that the parole officer may be of real assistance to the person on parole it is necessary that he should have in advance an intimate acquaintance with the personality of the offender. This information must be secured before it can be determined what method should be used in dealing with the offender. The information secured through the original investigation and the institutional career of the offender should be accessible to the parole officer. In addition the parole officer must have an intimate knowledge of the family and other personal groups into which the individual will go, and should attempt to prepare these groups for his return before the parole begins. The parole officer must form intimate contacts

---

[13] Massachusetts, *Report of Training Schools,* 1919, p. 13.

with those under his supervision. This part of the work has been done most successfully for those on parole from institutions for juvenile delinquents. A case is reported from the Massachusetts Training School for Girls of a girl who was

sensitive, proud, moody, stubborn, distrustful and secretive. Her visitor first overcame her distrust by playing with her—taking her to the theatre for instance. The visitor, having won her confidence, learned her warped ideas of life, which she was able gradually to combat and overcome. . . . Her whole attitude towards life is so changed she bids fair to become a well-poised woman.[14]

The parole officer cannot, however, continue to do the entire work, for the period of parole must end sooner or later. One of the most important things for the parole agent to do is to assist the person on parole to secure friends and contacts of his own; such friends may be clergymen, settlement workers, or other institutional representatives, but when possible should include others with whom the paroled person will be in more intimate relations. Miss Weidensall reports that appreciation of some person who has been an ideal is a part of the explanation of the success of women on parole.[15]

In one place a club was formed by the persons on parole from the New York State reformatories; they have club rooms, with easy chairs, reading matter, a billiard room, and a pianola; they have monthly meetings with speakers and informal association every evening. One boy said, regarding this club,

When a man comes down here he has a place to go, and somebody to shake his hand. You don't know the lost feeling a fellow has when he finds himself free. There is nobody he can turn to, and small inducement to keep straight. I, for one, could never have made good if it had not been for this place and the people who stand behind it.[16]

This club also acts as an employment agency for its members and in other ways exerts considerable pressure to prevent violations of parole.

---

[14] Massachusetts, *Report of Training Schools*, 1915, p. 112.
[15] Jean Weidensall, *The Mentality of the Criminal Woman*, Baltimore, 1916, p. 285.
[16] New York, *Report of State Board of Managers of Reformatories*, 1917, pp. 97–98.

An appeal to group influence in a somewhat different manner was made by the Preston School of Industry. Each month the School published a list of persons on parole, grouped as "honor-roll," "failure to report," and "parole violators." In addition, the school published a monthly bulletin which was mailed to all the boys on parole; this contained accounts of the notable accomplishments of those on parole.

In every way possible the person on parole should be made to feel that he is a part of society. While in the institution he has the feeling that he has been set apart from society and is ostracized. Contacts must be developed so that the individual will not feel isolated. The larger the number of associations that can be formed between the person on parole and the normal social groups, the more likely he is to become and remain a law-abiding person.

VIOLATION OF PAROLE. The law generally states that any violation of the conditions imposed upon the person on parole constitutes a violation of parole, and that for a violation of parole the person is to be returned to the institution. In practice the supervising authority generally uses discretion and permits some technical violations without formally pronouncing them violations of parole. When a formal declaration of violation of parole is made a warrant for the arrest of the person is issued and served if the parole violator can be located. Very few parole violators are returned if they have left the state. Some parole boards grant paroles to prisoners to go out of the state, knowing that their return will be very difficult in case of violation. Such boards are primarily interested in getting rid of the prisoners. Similarly if a parolee violates the conditions of his parole and leaves the state, the state makes little or no effort to secure his return.

When a parole violator is arrested, a trial in court is not needed, for the decision of the supervising authority is final. He may be required to serve the remainder of his unexpired term if he was on a definite sentence, or the remainder of the maximum term if he was on an indeterminate sentence. This, however, is left to the parole board which has control of the releases.

In a few states the prisoner may be returned to the prison without a violation of parole. This may occur in several ways. He may desire to return because he cannot find work outside, or because he wishes to complete a course in trade training. He may be returned by action of the supervisor because the supervisor believes the parolee needs additional training or needs medical care or for other reasons which do not involve a formal violation of the conditions of parole. An appreciable number of returns of this nature is reported in New Jersey, where the program of training within the institutions is somewhat closely integrated with the parole program.

DISCHARGE FROM PAROLE. According to usual court decisions a person may not be kept on parole beyond the end of his maximum sentence to prison. In some states he cannot be released from parole before the end of that maximum period; in others he can be released when he has served on parole a shorter period specified by law or by the regulations of the parole board; and in others the parole board has complete authority to determine, within the limits of the maximum sentence, how long supervision shall continue. Vold reports that in Minnesota the period in the institution and the period on parole together equal the maximum sentence in 25 per cent of the state prison cases, are not more than one year less than the maximum in 63.4 per cent, and are four or more years less than the maximum in only 14.7 per cent.

The suggestion has been made that the maximum limit on the period of supervision should be eliminated, on the ground that some persons behave satisfactorily only as long as they are under supervision, and that it is preferable to continue the supervision indefinitely rather than have these persons rotating between crime and imprisonment or even spending all their time in prison under habitual criminal acts. Furthermore, the provision would make it possible to hold for a longer period some of the offenders who are paroled from juvenile institutions for the period of minority.

The assertion has been made that violations of parole are concentrated in the early period of parole. The evidence on this point is not conclusive. In California in 1918-1920 64 per cent of the violations of parole occurred within six months of release from prison, and only 11 per cent after one year. Glueck found in Massachusetts a slight concentration of violations in the early months of the parole period,[17] while Vold found little concentration in a similar group.[18] Supervision should certainly continue beyond the period of concentration of violations, but the limits of that period have not been made definite.

---

[17] Glueck and Glueck, *op. cit.*, p. 169.
[18] G. B. Vold, *Prediction Methods and Parole*, Hanover, 1931, p. 53.

Parole is either ended automatically at the expiration of the maximum sentence or else by order of the parole board, sometimes with the approval of the governor of the state.

RESTORATION OF CIVIL RIGHTS. Civil rights, which are lost in most states on conviction of certain types of crimes, are restored in some states automatically when parole is granted; in others they are restored only when one is discharged from parole; and in others they are restored, if at all, only by a pardon by the governor. By act of 1919 California authorized the parole board to restore civil rights to persons on parole at such time and to such a degree as they saw fit, except that they could not restore the right to be an elector, hold public office, or act as trustee.

The deprivation of civil rights is undesirable at any time, but if the prisoner is released to the community he should be made to feel, as much as possible, that he is a member of that community. Consequently civil rights should be restored automatically at the beginning of the parole period.

SUCCESS OR FAILURE ON PAROLE. The attempts to determine what proportions of the persons on parole get along satisfactorily have yielded percentages ranging from 50 to 85, with an average of about 75.[19] These percentages include only the violations known to the parole officers and, in general, are restricted to the relatively serious violations for which paroles are revoked. In many states the parole force is not sufficient in numbers or activities to have reliable or complete information regarding the conduct of the parolees and on that account considerable scepticism regarding these figures has developed. In the states in which the parole work is more complete the percentages of successes are generally lower than in the states where the parole supervision is less complete. Glueck made an intensive study of the after-careers of 510 inmates of the Massachusetts Reformatory. Of 474 who were paroled, 262 or 55.3 per cent were officially known to have committed serious violations of parole.[20] To this number of violators Glueck added

---

[19] W. W. Clark, "Success Records of Prisoners and Delinquents," *Jour. Delinq.*, 6:443–452, July, 1921. This reports a general average of 72 per cent of successes among those paroled from nineteen institutions. Gault in 1915 reported 84 per cent successful, in a study of 38,593 on parole in sixteen states. See R. H. Gault, "The Parole System a Means of Protection," *Jour. Crim. Law and Criminol.*, 5:801, March, 1915.

[20] Glueck and Glueck, *op. cit.*, p. 169.

by intensive search only 25, making a total of 60.3 per cent of the parolees who committed serious breaches of parole.[21]

In addition, since statistics of success refer only to the conduct of persons during the period of parole, it is of interest to learn how the conduct after release from parole compares with this. One of the first studies of this kind was made by Brockway in 1888 to determine the careers of all who had been inmates of, and paroled from, Elmira up to that date. Inquiry was made of the persons themselves, their relatives and neighbors, and in all the prisons of the United States. The general conclusion was that 78.5 per cent of them were at the time leading law-abiding lives and were self-supporting.[22] One of the most accurate studies was made of 301 juvenile delinquents on parole from Whittier State School. A first study was made in 1918 at least two years after any one of the number had

TABLE XI

CONDUCT OF JUVENILE DELINQUENTS RELEASED ON PAROLE FROM WHITTIER STATE SCHOOL, PERCENTAGES

Conduct	1918	1920
Doing well	42.7	44.0
Doing fairly well	30.2	24.6
Doing poorly	27.1	31.4

left the institution and in some cases as much as seven years after release from the institution. A second study of the same group was made in 1920. The conduct of the groups at the two dates is shown in Table XI.[23] This might be stated as 73 per cent successful in 1918 and 69 per cent successful in 1920. This shows a comparatively small decrease in the proportion successful. Glueck found that 77 per cent of the parolees from the Masachusetts Reformatory who were total failures during the parole period were also total failures during the five-year post-parole period, and that 75 per cent of

---

[21] *Ibid.* The number of violators discovered by additional investigations is not large. For purposes of predicting success and failure, as described on pages 549 ff., the violators known to the parole board would be adequate. At least a relatively small part of the errors in prediction would be due to the failure to discover violators not known to the parole officers. Also, it is highly probable that the Gluecks did not discover all of the violators and that no other investigator could discover all of them.

[22] Z. R. Brockway, *Fifty Years of Prison Service*, p. 297.

[23] Clark, *ibid.*, p. 446; California, *Report of Whittier State School*, 1916–1918, pp. 96–114. The percentages in Table XI are based on 258 cases in 1918, and 252 in 1920, regarding which the information was definite.

those who were total failures during the post-parole period had been total failures also during the parole period. This shows a relatively high correlation between behavior on parole and behavior during the post-parole period, so far as serious offenses are concerned.[24]

Success or failure on parole cannot be measured completely by the criminal record, for a person may fail in other respects even though he commits no crimes. The studies which have been made indicate, however, that failure in respect to crime has a high correlation with failure in other respects. Glueck found that 78.1 per cent of those who had crimes recorded against them during the post-parole period had failed in respect to industrial activities, economic obligations, family relationships, or use of leisure time, and that 72.2 per cent of those who failed in one or more of these non-criminal activities had failed, also, from the point of view of crime.[25]

Glueck's general conclusion was that only 20 per cent of the releases from the Massachusetts Reformatory were successful during the parole and post-parole periods. This finding, of course, cannot be used as a measure of the value of the reformatory or of the parole system, because the failures are the result of a complex of situational and of previous and present personal factors. It would be desirable to compare the subsequent careers of a group of prisoners released on parole with the subsequent careers of a similar group of prisoners released unconditionally without parole. No study of this nature has been made. Statistics from certain states indicate that those released on parole are returned for new crimes less frequently than those released at the termination of their sentences. This difference, however, may be due to the selection of the less hardened criminals for parole, while the professional criminals remain in prison until the end of the maximum sentence.

CONDITIONS AFFECTING SUCCESS OR FAILURE ON PAROLE. Positive information regarding the types of offenders who fail on parole and the conditions under which they fail is being secured and organized in statistical form.[26] Most of these studies have taken

---

[24] Glueck and Glueck, *op. cit.*, p. 266.

[25] *Ibid.*, p. 222.

[26] The following studies furnish the most complete information of this nature: A. A. Bruce, E. W. Burgess, and A. J. Harno, *The Workings of the Indeterminate Sentence Law and the Parole System in Illinois*, Springfield, 1928, Ch. 28 ; Glueck and Glueck, *op. cit.*, Chs. 16–17; G. B. Vold, *op. cit.*, Ch. 4. In addition, many scattered studies may be found in journals and in reports of

as a criterion of failure a recorded violation of parole, either in the form of new crimes or of other violations. Moreover, a considerable part of the information regarding the "factors" in success or failure has been taken from the unverified statements of inmates. In the study by Sheldon Glueck and Eleanor Glueck a more complete field investigation was made, the after-careers were followed beyond the termination of parole, and in other respects the methods justify more confidence. However, so far as the topics agree, there is little difference between the conclusions reached on this point by the Gluecks and those reached in other studies.

These studies show, with certain exceptions, that the largest proportion of failures in parole occur in the classes which have previous criminal records, records of irregular work before admission to the institution, records of disciplinary punishments within the institutions, residence in cities and in the deteriorated neighborhoods of cities, no marital ties, marital relations of incompatible kinds, no associates in the particular crimes for which committed, recorded habits of alcoholism, drug addiction, and sexual immorality. In general, also, the proportion of failures increased as these factors are combined in individual cases. The failures increase inversely as the age of first delinquency, and directly as the number of previous arrests, the irregularity of previous work habits, the frequency of institutional punishments, and the size of the community in which the offender resided. The older offenders in general succeed on parole better than younger, the foreign-born better than the native-born of native parents, the native-born of foreign parents better than the native-born of native parents, the whites better than the Negroes, the sex offenders and murderers better than those engaged in crimes against property.

The several studies either show no consistent relation or a very slight relation between failures on parole and intelligence, height and weight, psychiatric classification, conditions in the parental

institutions. Among these the following contain important information: W. W. Clark, "Success Records of Delinquent Boys in Relation to Intelligence," *Jour. Delinq.*, 5:177–181, September, 1920; W. W. Clark, "Success Records of Prisoners and Delinquents," *Jour. Delinq.*, 6:450–451, July, 1921; W. W. Clark, "Supervised Conduct-Response of Delinquent Boys," *Jour. Delinq.*, 6:387–401, May, 1921; F. L. Heacox, "A Study of One Year's Parole Violators Returned to Auburn Prison," *Jour. Crim. Law and Criminol.*, 8:253–258, July, 1917; S. B. Warner, "Factors Determining Parole from the Massachusetts Reformatory," *Jour. Crim. Law and Criminol.*, 14:172–207, August, 1923; Helen M. Witmer, "Some Factors in Success or Failure on Parole," *Jour. Crim. Law and Criminol.*, 18:384–403, November, 1927.

home, religion, occupational classes, and work habits in the institution. This lack of significant relationship may be due either to the inadequacy of the information, the inadequacy of classifications, or to the absence of significance. Glueck found no significant association between failure on parole and the economic, educational, and criminal records of parents. This negative finding may be due to the difficulties even in an intensive study of securing accurate information regarding the records of the parents in this respect.

These studies show a close association between success on parole and various conditions and types of behavior during parole, such as constructive use of leisure time, regular church attendance, regular work habits, good associates, good family situation, dependents, and constructive neighborhood influences.

PREDICTION OF SUCCESS ON PAROLE.   The studies of the successes and failures on parole have shown also that the psychiatrists, the classification committees, the superintendents of institutions, and the judges and attorneys have some efficiency in picking the successes. Those who are recommended by these groups succeed on parole more frequently than those who are not recommended for parole. On the other hand, these groups frequently make mistakes both in choosing successes and in choosing failures. This has raised the question whether it may not be possible to develop a more adequate system of predicting the behavior of parolees.

The studies by Burgess, Glueck, and Vold organize in statistical form the information which has been secured and use this as a basis for prediction. Burgess, for instance, found that those who had more than fifteen unfavorable factors, such as poor work record, previous criminal career, institutional punishments, and residence in a deteriorated neighborhood, violated parole in 98.5 per cent of the cases, while those who had less than five unfavorable factors violated parole in only 24.0 per cent of the cases. On the basis of this experience in the past it is possible to predict that a person who has more than fifteen unfavorable factors is almost certain to violate parole, and that a person who has less than five unfavorable factors has three chances out of four of success on parole. Glueck and Vold use methods that are different in certain respects from the method used by Burgess but they involve the same principle of predicting behavior on the basis of past experience. The reliability of the original data, the methods of classification, and the statistical methods of organizing the information are being improved by additional studies.[27] Some of the classes can be further divided, with the result of gaining more significant information. For example, the studies have generally shown that married men succeed on parole more frequently than single men, but Glueck showed, in addition, that those who are married but have incompatible relations succeed on parole less frequently than single men. As these improvements are made, the method of prediction may become more and more precise. Most of this precision must be developed in the practical application of the method. The State of Illinois, in the summer of 1933, employed three persons to assist the parole board by studies of this nature. These actuarial sociologists prepare for the parole board a prediction of success or failure of each person who comes before the board. This gives the board organized information which may be or may not be used as the basis of a decision. Subsequent comparisons of the predictions with the actual violation rates show that offenders predicted to be the poorest risks violate parole in six times as large a proportion of cases as those predicted to be the best risks.[28]

Two principal criticisms have been made of this prediction technique as a method of selecting persons for parole. The first is that it does not provide a standard for selecting parolees. Should the parole board grant parole to those who have fifty chances out of a hundred or only to those who have seventy-five or ninety chances out of a hundred? The prediction technique, if adequately developed, may be able to give information regarding the chances of success but it cannot provide a standard. Moreover, the question recurs, Should prisoners who have no chance of success on parole be held to the end of the maximum sentence and then released without supervision or should they be released on parole anyhow, since the studies show that the longer an offender is held in prison the greater is the chance that he will violate parole? It is clear that the prediction technique cannot provide the standards, but they may assist the parole board in defining the standards.

The second criticism is that this technique largely neglects the

[27] Clark Tibbitts, "Reliability of Factors Used in Predicting Success or Failure on Parole," *Jour. Crim. Law and Criminol.*, 22:844–853, March, 1932; S. A. Stouffer and Clark Tibbitts, "Tests of Significance in Applying Westergaard's Method of Expected Cases to Sociological Data," *Jour. Amer. Stat. Assoc.*, 28:293–302, September, 1933.
[28] E. W. Burgess, "Parole and the Indeterminate Sentence," *Illinois Depart. Pub. Welf., Annual Report*, 1937, p. 692.

fact that every prisoner reaches a point where he is a better risk on parole than at any other time. If he is held a shorter time or a longer time than this he is more likely to violate parole. This time is determined by the attitudes of the prisoner. The prediction technique, however, is concerned principally with events and characteristics which preceded the period of imprisonment, only to a slight extent with behavior while in prison, and not at all with the changing attitudes of the prisoner while in prison. Laune and others have attempted to take these changing attitudes into account and to base predictions on them.[29]

FINANCIAL SAVING BY PAROLE. The direct cost of the parole system to the state is very small. Brown made a survey of the costs in various states in 1915 and found that they varied from $0.48 per person on parole in New Jersey to $66 in North Dakota, with a mean cost of about $15.[30] The cost of the state prison system of California in 1922 was about $240 per inmate; the cost of the parole system was about $30 per person on parole that year. One writer has attempted to estimate the financial value to the state of Brockway's "invention" of the Elmira reformatory and parole system and concluded that New York State alone saved over $16,000,-000 by it between 1876 and 1900.[31] One may easily believe that few mechanical inventions have been more profitable. Brown concluded that parole has produced better results at less than two-fifths the cost of prison methods.

The financial saving, however, is not the principal value of the parole system. In fact, if the parole system is operated properly, it may cost as much as the present prison methods. Efficient parole work must be expensive. Expensive experts will be required to determine fitness for parole and to supervise those on parole. A great deal of intensive work must be done. The value of the parole system, therefore, will not be in the financial saving, but in the saving in personality.

APPRAISAL OF PAROLE. The antagonism toward parole is probably greater than toward any other penal policy. This is surprising,

---

[29] F. F. Laune, *Predicting Criminality; Forecasting Behavior on Parole,* Northwestern Univ. Stud. in the Soc. Sciences, No. 1, Evanston, 1936; F. F. Laune, "The Application of Attitude Tests in the Field of Parole Prediction," *Amer. Sociol. Rev.,* 1:781–796, October, 1936.

[30] B. W. Brown, "Parole an Institution of the Future," *Jour. Crim. Law and Criminol.,* 6:69, May, 1915.

[31] H. M. Boies, *The Science of Penology,* New York, 1901, pp. 135–137.

for there is no well-known student of penology who is not whole-heartedly in favor of the principle of parole, and who does not insist that parole in practice is better than any available alternative in practice. These students insist, first, that parole should be evaluated not as an abstract principle but in comparison with the only available alternative, which is the determination in court at the time of the trial of the definite date of release, and the complete release at that time without subsequent supervision. They insist, second, that those who are released on parole serve at least as long inside prison walls for a specific type of crime as do those sentenced on definite terms, and in addition remain under supervision outside the prison for periods which generally range from one to three years, and that parole therefore is not leniency but on the contrary is more severe and is a better method of protecting society against crime than the alternative method. They insist, third, that persons released from prison on parole do not commit more crimes than persons released at the expiration of sentences without supervision, for the same offences. It has been reported that only 0.7 per cent of the persons whose arrests were recorded by the Federal Bureau of Investigation were on parole at the time of arrest. J. Edgar Hoover has questioned the adequacy of his statistics on this point and has claimed that at least 30 per cent of the "mad dogs" listed in the Bureau of Investigation "had been paroled by lenient or foolish parole boards." Since approximately half of the releases are by parole and these mad dogs are defined as confirmed criminals, who have therefore probably been in prison previously, it means that 70 per cent had been released at the expiration of sentences without supervision. From this one might conclude that those released at the expiration of the sentence without parole are more than twice as likely to get into the list of most dangerous criminals as those released on parole. These statistics, to be sure, are not adequate to justify a certain conclusion, but whatever conclusion they do justify is favorable to parole. Finally, the advocates of parole insist that the number of cases of political bribery and fixing of cases in order to secure releases on parole is relatively small; those who have political or financial influence and who can find public officials susceptible to that influence keep out of prison entirely, by operating upon the police departments and the courts. Though there is undoubtedly some corruption in parole boards, it is infinitesimal in comparison with the police and the courts.

In spite of this clear-cut justification for parole in comparison with its alternative, many improvements need to be made in the parole system. These improvements are needed at three points: first, better personnel on parole boards; second, more adequate information on which parole boards can base their decisions; and third, more adequate supervision of those on parole.

SUGGESTED READINGS

Argow, W. W., "A Criminal-Liability Index for Predicting Possibility of Rehabilitation," *Jour. Crim. Law and Criminol.*, 26:651–577, November, 1935.

Bruce, A. A., Burgess, E. W., and Harno, A. J., *The Workings of the Indeterminate Sentence Law and the Parole System in Illinois*, Springfield, 1928, Ch. 28.

Burgess, E. W., "Protecting the Public by Parole and by Parole Prediction," *Jour. Crim. Law and Criminol.*, 27:491–502, November, 1936.

"Declaration of Principles of Parole," *Jour. Crim. Law and Criminol.*, 24:788–793, November, 1933.

Glueck, Sheldon and Eleanor T., *Five Hundred Criminal Careers*, New York, 1930.

Glueck, Sheldon and Eleanor T., *One Thousand Juvenile Delinquents*, Cambridge, 1934.

Glueck, Sheldon and Eleanor T., *Five Hundred Delinquent Women*, New York, 1934.

Hart, Hornell, "Predicting Parole Success," *Jour. Crim. Law and Criminol.*, 14:405–413, November, 1923.

Hawthorne, Julian, *The Subterranean Brotherhood*, New York, 1914, Ch. 14.

Huff, R. L., "Is Parole Prediction a Science?" *Jour. Crim. Law and Criminol.*, 27:207–218, July, 1936.

Kite, St. Alban, "Developments in the New Jersey Parole System," *Proc. Amer. Prison Assoc.*, 1931, pp. 277–282.

Kolakoski, L. W., and Broecker, T. W., "The Pennsylvania Parole System," *Jour. Crim. Law and Criminol.*, 23:427–438, September, 1932.

Lane, Winthrop D., "A New Day Opens for Parole," *Jour. Crim. Law and Criminol.*, 24:88–108, May, 1933.

Lane, Winthrop D., "Parole in a Community Welfare Program," *Proc. Natl. Conf. Social Work,* 1933, pp. 179–185.

Lanne, W. F., "Parole Prediction," *Jour. Crim. Law and Criminol.,* 26:377–400, September, 1935.

Laune, F. F., *Predicting Criminality: Forecasting Behavior on Parole,* Evanston, 1936.

Lowrie, Donald, *My Life Out of Prison,* New York, 1915.

Marsangy, Bonneville de, "Preparatory Liberation," *Report of Prison Assoc. of New York,* 1867, pp. 165–178.

Pennsylvania, *Report of Pennsylvania State Parole Commission,* Philadelphia, 1927.

Rice, S. A., "Some Inherent Difficulties in the Method of Prediction by Classification," *Social Forces,* 7:554–558, June, 1929.

Sanders, B. S., "Testing Parole Prediction," *Proc. Natl. Prison Assoc.,* 1935, pp. 222–233.

Stouffer, S. A., and Tibbitts, Clark, "Tests of Significance in Applying Westergaard's Method of Expected Cases to Sociological Data," *Jour. Amer. Stat. Assoc.,* 28:293–302, September, 1933.

Tibbitts, Clark, "Reliability of Factors Used in Predicting Success or Failure in Parole," *Jour. Crim. Law and Criminol.,* 22:844–853, March, 1932.

Tibbitts, Clark, "Success or Failure on Parole Can Be Predicted," *Jour. Crim. Law and Criminol.,* 22:11–50, May, 1931.

Van Vechten, C. C., "Parole Violation Rates," *Jour. Crim. Law and Criminol.,* 27:638–640, January, 1937.

Vold, G. B., "Do Parole Prediction Tables Work in Practice?" *Pub. Amer. Sociol. Soc.,* 25:136–138, May, 1931.

Vold, G. B., *Prediction Methods and Parole,* Hanover, 1931.

Vold, G. B., "Prediction Methods Applied to Problems of Classification within Institutions," *Jour. Crim. Law and Criminol.,* 26:202–209, July, 1935.

Warner, S. B., "Factors Determining Parole from the Massachusetts Reformatory," *Jour. Crim. Law and Criminol.,* 14:172–207, August, 1923.

Wilcox, Clair, "Parole: Principles and Practice," *Jour. Crim. Law and Criminol.,* 20:345–354, November, 1929.

Witmer, Helen M., "Some Factors in Success or Failure on Parole," *Jour. Crim. Law and Criminol.,* 18:384–403, November, 1927.

Witmer, Helen M., "The History, Theory, and Results of Parole," *Jour. Crim. Law and Criminol.,* 18:24–64, May, 1927.

Chapter Twenty – Seven

PUNISHMENT: MISCELLANEOUS METHODS

TRANSPORTATION AND FLOATING. The transportation of criminals still has some advocates. As late as 1895 the International Prison Congress, which met in Paris, voted in favor of transportation, with some restrictions, and this resolution was readopted at a congress in Lisbon in 1897. Considerable publicity was given in 1933 to a suggestion that the United States should establish a penal colony. The arguments advanced in favor of it are that it gives the criminal a new start away from the old environment, that normal family life may be permitted there while it cannot be permitted in a prison, and that the transported criminals can be entirely self-supporting. Ives, though in general opposed to transportation, states that persons who were in Australia and in a position to judge believed that

Many convicts were really reclaimed through the new life transportation afforded them, and that occasionally they earned such good reputations as to be placed on the magisterial bench.[1]

In general, however, the experiences of various countries have shown that it is a distinct failure. The only penal colony that could be called even moderately successful is the one maintained since 1857 by India on Andaman Island in the Bay of Bengal. The experience of the past may be expected to continue in the future. It will always be opposed by the inhabitants of the country selected for the penal colony. If an uninhabited country is selected, the emancipated convicts who desire to remain there and rear families will object to the continuation of transportation. The country soon

[1] G. Ives, *A History of Penal Methods*, London, 1914, p. 140.

555

becomes saturated with criminals; three-fourths of the adult population of New South Wales in 1836 were either convicts or emancipated convicts. It is not possible to have a normal life in such a place. Association will be almost entirely with criminals. Though a man may be permitted to take his wife to the colony, it is not conceivable that it would be good policy to permit them to rear children in this environment. Moreover, the transported convicts have never been self-supporting. And even if they were, this method does not solve the problem of crime; it merely removes it out of the boundaries of the country. What should be done with those who commit crime in the penal colony? Should they be transported to another place? In the past those who committed crimes in the penal colonies were treated with the greatest brutality, which was made possible by lack of publicity and was encouraged by the feeling of danger to those in control. Unofficial reports indicate that about half of the convicts sent to French Guiana die during their first year of residence there. Sexual perversions flourish in the penal colonies even more than in prisons.[2] As a result of such experiences it is almost inconceivable that penal colonies will be regarded as an efficient method of dealing with the problem of crime.

Banishment, which is somewhat related to transportation, is a penalty in certain types of crimes. The law of the United States requires that every criminal alien who has been in the United States less than five years be deported. In 1937 1,603 alien criminals were deported; in addition 443 were deported as narcotic addicts, as anarchists, or because they were immoral. The Department of Labor, which has the responsibility in this matter, has explained that this policy is not used with greater frequency, because the appropriation has been insufficient to pay the expenses of deportation, governors of states frequently pardon criminal aliens who, then, cannot be deported, many countries refuse to receive their nationals when deported from the United States for crimes, and it is difficult to prevent deported criminals from returning to the United States.

---

[2] For descriptions of modern penal colonies see J. L. Gillin, *Taming the Criminal,* New York, 1931; R. Heindl, *Meine Reise nach den Strafkolonien,* Berlin, 1913; Carl Bartz, *The Horrors of Cayenne,* New York, 1930; W. E. Allison-Booth, *Hell's Outpost,* New York, 1930; Blair Niles, *Condemned to Devil's Island: The Biography of an Unknown Convict,* New York, 1928; Frank Schoonmaker, "Lipari—the New Devil's Island," *New York Herald Tribune,* March 23, 1930. A somewhat similar autobiography for the earlier period is: *Adventures of an Outlaw: Memoirs of Ralph Rashleigh, a Penal Exile in Australia, 1825-44,* New York, 1929.

On the other hand, the procedure used in deporting aliens, whether criminal or non-criminal, has been criticized frequently.[3]

The deported offenders are often left in a helpless condition. The National Committee on Prisons and Prison Labor has been trying to assist criminals deported from the United States to Canada or from Canada to the United States, especially in securing positions. Immigration societies have made occasional efforts to assist criminals who were being deported to get established in their home countries. International agreements regarding the policy of deportation and care of deported criminals should be developed.

A modified form of banishment is used constantly in the United States at present. It consists of giving a person accused or convicted of an offense a specified number of hours in which to leave the county, town, or state. This method is used frequently in dealing with tramps or "floaters" and hence is called "floating." Out of a total of 2,300 persons arrested in four counties in California 2,200 were "floated."[4] The method is not confined to floaters, however. In November, 1933, a boy seventeen years of age was permitted to leave the state of Maryland because of destruction of school property, as an alternative to prosecution. It is frequently used by the courts, also, either before or after conviction. In 1933 the judge and prosecutor in a Chicago court agreed to *nolle pros* a charge of vagrancy against one of the "public enemies" on his promise that he would go to Florida. A man convicted in Mississippi in 1927 of shooting another man was permitted to choose between seven years in prison and exile from the state for life, and he chose exile. A man convicted in Michigan in 1932 of repeated violations of the prohibition law was permitted to choose between a prison sentence of seven and a half to fifteen years and permanent exile from the county in which he had been living, and he chose exile. A man convicted in Urbana, Illinois, of using a feebleminded girl for immoral purposes was released upon his promise to leave the county in which he had been living with his family as a county charge for two years.

This policy of banishment from a locality is justified by the authorities on the ground of economy for the local community. In the long run a community receives as many offenders by this policy

---

[3] Reuben Oppenheimer, "Report on the Administration of the Deportation Laws of the United States," *Natl. Com. on Law Obs. and Enf.*, No. 5, 1931; Jane P. Clark, *Deportation of Aliens from the United States to Europe*, New York, 1931.

[4] S. A. Queen, *The Passing of the County Jail*, Menasha, Wis., 1920, p. 7.

as it sends to other communities and no progress is made toward a solution of the problem by any community. This method would probably cease almost entirely if the expense of dealing with these offenders were transferred to the state by the provision of a state penal farm for misdemeanants.

WHIPPING. The medieval and early modern periods had a great variety of corporal punishments. Whipping is the only one of these which has been retained in Western civilization and the trend of opinion is so much against it that a discussion of the penalty is needed only because agitation for the restoration of the penalty is occasionally resumed. This penalty is authorized in Maryland for wife-beating but is practically never used. It is authorized in Delaware for several serious offenses and is probably used frequently, though no official reports regarding it are published. According to newspaper reports 170 whippings were administered in the New-castle Workhouse in Wilmington in 1929–1934, of which 80 per cent were to Negroes, and 20 per cent to white persons; more whippings are administered for petty larceny than for any other offense, and two-thirds of the penalties involve ten lashes each.[5] In 1924 Virginia enacted a law authorizing the juvenile court to order this penalty imposed upon juvenile delinquents by their parents or by other persons. Canada has used this penalty since its settlement and during the last two decades has increased the number of offenses for which it may be imposed. In Great Britain it is a legal penalty for certain adult crimes and juvenile delinquencies. It is seldom imposed upon adults except for robbery, and its use both for adults and juveniles has decreased decidedly. Whippings were 4.4 per cent of the penalties imposed upon adult and juvenile offenders for indictable offenses in 1904, and 0.2 per cent in 1930. In Leeds whippings were 15 per cent of all penalties for juvenile offenders in 1917, and only 0.8 per cent in 1920.

Agitation for the authorization of the penalty of whipping developed in several states subsequent to the World War, but the bills all failed. One of the more extreme bills was introduced in Minnesota in 1925. It provided for whipping as a mandatory penalty, in combination with imprisonment or fine, for twelve offenses, ranging from murder to drunken driving. However, the bills introduced in the Delaware legislature to abolish this penalty have failed

---

[5] *Chicago Tribune,* December 6, 1934.

by large majorities, and in fact in 1920 the number of offenses for which whipping might be used was increased. Denmark made a trial of this law in 1905 and abandoned it after a few years.

The arguments presented in favor of whipping are that it prevents the recidivism of those upon whom it is inflicted more effectively than any other penalty, that it deters potential offenders, and that the humiliation destroys the criminal's prestige so that he is no longer regarded as a conquering hero. The argument that whipping prevents recidivism does not seem to be substantiated by the data. Of ninety-nine boys who were whipped in Shoreditch in 1915–1916 35.3 per cent had been birched previously, and in one of the English towns where whipping was used frequently 25 per cent of those whipped were re-charged within one month and 80.3 per cent within two years.[6] No recent statistics for Delaware are available, but in 1904 461 offenders were whipped, of whom 16 per cent had been whipped previously, and 4 per cent had been whipped two or more times previously. Jack Black reports that after he was whipped in a Canadian prison he returned to crime in Canada with more determination than before he was whipped. This evidence, to be sure, is not conclusive, in part because the penalty of whipping is likely to be used principally for delinquents who are regarded as most vicious and for whom all other methods of treatment generally fail.

The evidence that whipping is an effective deterrent of the potential criminals is similarly inconclusive. The history of the garroter gang in England about 1860 is often cited as evidence of the value of whipping. It has been claimed that whole cities were terrorized but that when Parliament authorized whipping for this offense and the penalty had been inflicted twenty or thirty times the crime was not repeated for more than sixty years. The historical accuracy of this argument has been questioned and the more accurate account is that crimes of this nature were being committed by a very small band of criminals, that garroting had been almost completely stopped by the regular method of imprisonment before whipping was authorized, and that it was the breaking up of the gang by imprisonment rather than the whippings which eliminated this crime. It has been claimed that when robbery became punishable by whipping in Delaware that offense almost ceased. The com-

---

[6] A. F. Brockway, *A New Way with Crime*, pp. 63–65.

mitment rate to prisons, which is a totally inadequate index of crime but the only index available, was lower in Delaware in 1936 than in the adjacent states for robbery but it was higher for burglary, for which, also, whipping may be imposed. Occasionally the newspapers report that an offender in one of the jurisdictions in which whipping is authorized requests that whipping be substituted for imprisonment. Statements of officials in Delaware, as well as in Canada, are frequently quoted as evidence of the deterrent value of this penalty, but the statement of one official can be balanced by a conflicting statement of another official.

On the other hand, it is claimed that this penalty is a relic of barbarism, an expression of a sadistic tendency which assists in the development of that tendency, that it bestializes the man who is whipped, and that it debauches the community which tolerates it. Warden Meserve of Wilmington, Delaware, Workhouse, stated: "Men who have been whipped are never as good prisoners as before." Others have claimed that the official who must flog the prisoner is brutalized, and this makes two brutes where one brute was before. The assertion is made, in addition, that because the public and the officials are unwilling to enforce this penalty offenders are acquitted, and that it is used only in cases of helpless prisoners, especially Negroes.

The value of this penalty in reducing crime is probably not the most significant value concerned. In most communities the penalty would probably not be in favor with the public even if they were certain that it was more effective than any other penalty in reducing crime. A decision in regard to it is made on the basis of sentiments rather than of rational evaluations. This penalty is, in that sense, a point at which conflicting theories meet, and the public is not willing to consider whipping solely on its merits as a means of reducing crime.

THE DEATH PENALTY. During the course of the last century a very distinct trend away from the death penalty occurred. Twenty-four countries abolished it entirely, and in other countries the offenses for which it may be imposed have been generally limited to murder. In the United States in 1939 five states have a mandatory death penalty for certain offenses (Connecticut, Massachusetts, Vermont, North Carolina, and New Mexico), thirty-seven states have a permissive death penalty, and six states do not permit the death penalty. The states which do not permit the death penalty are clustered in the north central part of the United States (Michigan, Wisconsin, Minnesota, North Dakota) and in New England (Maine and Rhode Island).

Several trends may be observed in the death penalty in the United States during the recent period. The first is a slight and fluctuating tendency to abolish it. Between 1847, when the first state abolished the death penalty, and 1876 four states prohibited capital punishment; one addition to this list was made in 1907 and another in 1911. From 1913 to 1918 seven other states were added, but five of them restored the penalty after an average experience of two and a half years. Kansas abolished its capital punishment law in 1887; in 1935 the law was reinstated and one death sentence was imposed in 1936, the first in sixty-four years. South Dakota in 1939 restored the death penalty which had been repealed in 1915. A second and more pronounced tendency has been to substitute a permissive death penalty for the mandatory penalty. In 1918 the death penalty was mandatory on conviction of capital crimes in twelve states, in 1938 in only five states. A third trend, appearing in the earlier period, was to reduce the number of capital crimes. The number was generally twelve in the colonies; now only one crime is punishable by death in eight states, two in five states, and only four have as many as six capital crimes. The number of capital crimes has been increased during the last decade by the addition in several states of kidnaping as a capital crime. A fourth trend, regarding which the evidence is not conclusive, is to reduce the total number of executions as the result of the changes previously mentioned and of other changes. In some states the number of executions has decreased decidedly, while in Pennsylvania and some other states there has been no decided trend. During the last few years there has been an upward trend in the United States in general; the number of executions increased from 140 in 1932 to 194 in 1936. Table XII shows that in Ohio the number of death sentences decreased very greatly in proportion to the number of admissions to prison for first degree murder, while the per cent of the death sentences which were actually executed decreased from 1900 to 1915, increased decidedly until 1925, and then a decrease again developed. Fifth, executions have been closed to the public. Sixth, the method of execution has been made as swift and painless as possible in a large proportion of the states. Considerable opposition developed against the method of hanging because of evidence that

TABLE XII

ADMISSIONS TO OHIO STATE PRISON FOR FIRST DEGREE MURDER, PER CENT
OF THESE WITH DEATH SENTENCES, AND PER CENT OF DEATH
SENTENCES EXECUTED BY FIVE-YEAR PERIODS, 1896–1930[7]

Years	Number of Admissions for First Degree Murder	Per Cent of First Degree Murder Admissions with Death Sentences	Per Cent of Death Sentences Which Where Executed
1896–1900	33	58	58
1901–05	44	43	74
1906–10	55	40	59
1911–15	43	21	45
1916–20	118	27	59
1921–25	151	41	82
1926–30	197	26	69

the neck was frequently not dislocated and that death was due to slow suffocation. It was reported from Arizona in 1936 that an offender writhed and groaned on the gallows for thirty-three minutes before death resulted. Electrocution was adopted by New York State in 1888 and, by 1938, by twenty-one other states out of the forty-two which permit the death penalty. Eight states now provide for execution by lethal gas. In any case the principal distress is due to the anticipation of death rather than to the actual execution of the penalty.

In 1936 194 executions occurred in the United States, of which 180 were for murder, 10 for rape, and 4 for kidnaping. Of the executed persons 92 were white, 100 were Negroes, and 2 were other races. None was under eighteen years of age, 51 were between eighteen and twenty-four years of age, and 143 were twenty-five years or over. One hundred twenty-eight occurred in Southern states, 40 in Northern states, and 26 in the West. All except one were male.

The importance of the death penalty lies not so much in the number of persons upon whom it is inflicted as in the emotions aroused in those who discuss it. It has become a point at which conflicting theories of penology have met. The voluminous literature on the subject is devoted largely to arguments pro and con. The arguments have been essentially the same during the last century, and the evidence on one side makes little impression upon the other side.

---

[7] Compiled by The Ohio Institute from the records of the Ohio State Prison.

The most important arguments in favor of the death penalty are: it is more effective than any other penalty in deterring from murder; it is more economical than imprisonment; it is necessary in order to prevent the public from lynching criminals; it rids society of defectives; it is the only certain penalty, for murderers who are sentenced to life imprisonment frequently secure pardons. On the other hand, those who oppose the death penalty argue that the death penalty is not more effective than imprisonment as a deterrent, that the abolition of the death penalty does not promote lynchings, that it reduces the certainty and speed of punishment, that it is completely inadequate as a method of dealing with defective criminals, that by breaking down respect for human life it tends to promote murder, that errors of justice are irreparable, and that it has a very bad effect on the prisoners and the staff in institutions in which it is inflicted. Of these arguments, the one in regard to the deterrent effect of the death penalty is by far the most important.

1. *The death penalty as a deterrent.* The usual method of testing the deterrent effect of the death penalty is to compare the homicide rate in states which have abolished the death penalty with states which retain the death penalty. If the homicide rate in states which authorize the death penalty is compared with the homicide rate in states which have abolished the death penalty, it is found that the former states have a homicide rate approximately twice as great as the latter. This comparison, however, is evidently unfair because the death penalty is retained in all of the Southern states, and the Southern states have the highest homicide rate. A more justifiable comparison is between states in a particular section of the United States. In this comparison the states which have abolished the death penalty are generally found to have slightly lower homicide rates than the adjoining states which have retained the death penalty. The significant difference is not between states which have the death penalty and those which do not, but between the different sections of the country, regardless of whether the states have or do not have the death penalty. The composition of the population and the general culture of the section is much more important than the presence or absence of the death penalty in determining homicide rates. Similar differences are found within states. Vold has found[8] that the homicide rate in Iowa in 1920 and 1925 combined

8 G. B. Vold, "Can the Death Penalty Prevent Crime?" *The Prison Jour.*, October, 1932.

was 2.4 per 100,000 population, in Missouri 10.4. Since both states have the death penalty the difference in rates cannot be explained in that manner. He found, also, that the average homicide rate in the southern tier of ten Iowa counties was 3.9 and in the northern tier of eight Missouri counties was 3.5, but in the southern tier of twelve Missouri counties was 10.5. The northern tier of Missouri counties is very similar to the southern tier of Iowa counties in culture and composition of the population, but the southern tier of Missouri counties is significantly different. Thus the difference in the rate of homicides is due to things other than the death penalty.

The data on which the preceding analysis is based are the best available at present, but it should be indicated that they are not completely adequate. In the first place the homicide rate is very different from a murder rate. First degree murders, for which the death penalty may customarily be imposed, probably constitute not more than 10 per cent of the homicides. Massachusetts, which has the death penalty, has more homicides than Maine, which does not have the death penalty. But it is not certain that Massachusetts has more first degree murders than Maine. It is highly probable, on *a priori* grounds, that the refinement of the homicide rate by eliminating the less serious homicides would not alter the results of the comparisons previously presented, but this refinement is not possible at present and therefore the conclusion is somewhat questionable. Secondly, if the death penalty has any deterrent value it presumably lies in its actual execution rather than in the legal possibility of execution. Sections in which murders are actually executed should be compared with sections in which the law prohibits such executions. Moreover, the sections should be sufficiently small (say, counties), so that an execution will produce some influence on potential murderers in that section. This method has been used to compare in a particular locality the homicide rate prior to an execution with the homicide rate subsequent to the execution. No significant difference was found in this respect in a study of rates prior and subsequent to five executions in Philadelphia.[9]

The results of the relatively crude comparisons in the United States are re-enforced by comparisons in European countries. On

---

[9] Robert H. Dann, "The Deterrent Effect of Capital Punishment," *Friends' Social Service Series*, Bull. No. 29, 1935.

the average the European states which have abolished the death penalty have lower homicide rates (which generally means lower murder rates in Europe) than states which retain the death penalty. The Scandinavian countries, which have abolished the death penalty, have homicide rates about one-half as high as England, which has retained the death penalty.

A second method of testing the deterrent value of the death penalty is by comparing, in the states which have abolished the death penalty, the homicide rates before and after the abolition. The general conclusion from this comparison is that the states which abolished the death penalty had no unusual increase in the homicide rates. Some of these states restored the death penalty after a few years, on the ground that the murder rate had increased greatly after the abolition. The statistics show, however, that the changes in homicide rates were almost exactly parallel in other states which made no changes in their laws regarding the death penalty. For instance, Missouri abolished the death penalty in 1917 and restored it in 1919 on the ground that murders had increased greatly. But the changes in the homicide rate in Missouri from 1910 to 1924 were almost exactly the same in direction and amount as in Ohio, which retained the death penalty throughout this whole period, and were very much like the changes in the United States in general. The legislature of Illinois in 1917 passed a bill abolishing the death penalty, but the governor vetoed the bill and it did not become a law. Murders increased very greatly in that state after 1917. If the bill had become a law doubtless many persons and newspapers would have presented the figures as absolute proof that the abolition of the death penalty increased the murder rate.[10]

The statistics available do not justify an absolute conclusion regarding the value of the death penalty as a deterrent. The evidence, such as it is, shows a relatively unimportant relation between the murder rate and the death penalty. The argument of the advocates of the death penalty that it is the most effective deterrent is, at least, not substantiated by the data available. It is based on preconceptions rather than on data, and the preconceptions are taken from the hedonistic psychology which assumes that the psychological processes are much less complex than they are in fact. Even pre-

---

[10] Edith Abbott, "Recent Statistics Relating to Crime in Chicago," *Jour. Crim. Law and Criminol.*, 13:354, November, 1922.

meditated murders are generally committed under the stress of a great emotion and the penalty is seldom considered.

2. *The certainty of the penalty.* The argument is made that juries are less willing to convict and witnesses less willing to testify when the penalty is death than when it is a less irreparable penalty, and that therefore the death penalty reduces the certainty of the penalty. Calvert quotes a petition of English bankers in 1830 that the death penalty for forgery be abolished on the ground that convictions could not be secured because of the severity of the penalty, and that a less severe penalty be authorized in order that their property might be protected more adequately.[11] Bye found that a slightly larger proportion of convictions was secured in murder cases in states which had abolished the death penalty than in states which retain it.[12] The advocates of the death penalty argue that the death penalty is more certain than imprisonment, because imprisonment is frequently terminated by escape, pardon, or parole. The time actually served in prison for homicide is about six years, but homicide in this sense included a large proportion of offenders for whom the death penalty was never contemplated as an alternative to imprisonment. Of 1,628 persons convicted of homicide in twenty-nine states in 1936, only 4 per cent were sentenced to death, while 63 per cent were sentenced to state prisons or reformatories, 18 per cent to local jails, 13 per cent were placed on probation, and 2 per cent were fined. Homicide is a very inclusive term, and perhaps not more than one-tenth of the persons committed to prison for homicide have been found guilty of premeditated murder. When the terms served by this miscellaneous group are found to average about six years, it should in no sense be regarded as a self-evident condemnation of the parole board, the pardon board, or the courts. Of 50 cases sentenced to Sing Sing for execution after conviction of murder in the first degree, 54 per cent were executed, 38 per cent were commuted to life imprisonment, and 8 per cent received new trials on appeal. While it is clear that imprisonment is not a completely certain penalty, it is clear, also, that the death penalty is not a certain penalty

[11] E. R. Calvert, *Capital Punishment in the Twentieth Century,* London, 1927, p. 15.

[12] R. T. Bye, *Capital Punishment in the United States,* Philadelphia, 1919, pp. 47 ff.

[13] Amos T. Baker, "A Clinical Study of Inmates Sentenced to Sing Sing Prison for Murder First Degree," *Amer. Jour. Psychiatry,* 91:783–790, January, 1935.

until it is actually executed. It is more probable in a given case that a pardon will be granted to a person under sentence of death than to a person on a life term, though the pardon in this case generally means commutation to a long term of imprisonment. Advocates of the death penalty generally speak of the certainty of the death penalty in England and Canada with much appreciation, but as a matter of fact less than 50 per cent of the death sentences in England and Canada are executed, and in England less than 10 per cent of the known murders result in executions.[14]

3. *The death penalty and speed of punishment.* It is asserted that the delays in court procedure are due largely to the fact that human life is at stake, that the defenses made necessary for that reason extend to other less serious cases, and that justice in murder cases especially and in all other cases to some degree would be more speedy if the death penalty were abolished. As an illustration it is shown that in the Hickman case in California, which has the death penalty, more than nine months intervened between the arrest of the defendant and the final sentence, while in the somewhat similar Hotelling case in Michigan, which does not have the death penalty, only two days intervened. More general data on this point have not been organized and a final conclusion is not justified.

4. *The death penalty and lynchings.* The argument has been made that the public is so insistent upon the death penalty for certain types of offenses that if the state does not execute a death penalty legally the public will execute it illegally by lynching. The experience of Colorado has been cited as evidence. The annual number of lynchings between 1891 and 1897, when the state had capital punishment, was 0.30; between 1897 and 1901, when it did not have the death penalty, the number increased to 0.75; and between 1901 and 1917, when it had the death penalty, the number was reduced to 0.05. It is probable that even in Colorado the lynchings in 1897–1901 were the result of unusual disturbances and that the presence or absence of the death penalty had nothing to do with them.[15] In addition, the number of lynchings decreased in Washington, Oregon, North Dakota, and Arizona after the abolition of the death penalty. The states where lynchings are most frequent are states which have the death penalty. Widespread use

[14] J. W. Hall, "Some Aspects of Capital Punishment," *Howard Jour.*, 1:237, April, 1925.
[15] Bye, *op. cit.*, p. 66.

of legal executions has not abolished lynchings in the Southern states. Lynchings and capital punishments are expressions of the same underlying attitude and where one flourishes the other is likely to be prevalent.

5. *The death penalty in relation to prisoners and staff.* Several prisoners in their autobiographies have testified to the terrific strain produced in prison by an execution. Some prisoners relieve themselves by screaming and beating the bars, others by sexual orgies. Prison authorities have recognized this and generally keep the prisoners confined in the cells during the execution. An execution in a Colorado prison was postponed because of fear that a prison riot would be produced. Hobhouse and Brockway report that intense emotional excitement is found in English prisons at the time of executions. Similar effects are produced on prison officers, especially on the executioners. Several executioners have committed suicide. An English prison warden stated:

For many nights before and after the execution I cannot sleep. Before it comes, every time I see the man or think of him, the thought of what I shall have to do at the execution strikes me. I see him hanging there, whilst I hastily undo the buttons of his jacket and pull open his shirt for the doctor to listen to his heart. After it has taken place I cannot shake the memory of the scene from me. You see, I have sometimes been in daily contact with the man a month or more, and often he has bared his soul to me. Many of these men have occupied quite a warm place in my heart.[16]

Calvert maintains that the difficulty of securing efficient wardens is increased because of the connection with the death penalty.[17]

6. *The death penalty and the public.* The argument has been made that executions arouse and furnish occasions for the expression of sadistic emotions. The following excerpts and abstracts illustrate this view:

The London Times on August 14, 1888, just after the prohibition of public executions in England, contains this statement: "We shall not in future have to read how the night before an execution thou-

---

[16] Hobhouse and Brockway, *English Prisons Today; Being the Report of the Prison System Enquiry Com.,* p. 248. Reprinted by permission of Longmans, Green & Co., publishers.

[17] Calvert, *op. cit.,* p. 103.

sands of the worst characters in England, abandoned women and brutal men, met beneath the gallows to pass the night in drinking and buffoonery, in ruffianly swagger and obscene jests; how they hooted the hangman or cheered the criminal; how at the very foot of the gallows, they committed with impunity deeds of lawless violence, scarcely less reprehensible than the crime of which they had come to witness the expiation."[18]

A report of an execution in North Carolina described the large number crowded outside the prison who could not secure admission, although in the death chamber people were packed so tightly that the doors could not be closed and that when one of the women spectators fainted she could not fall to the floor.[19]

Similarly Lawes has described the crowding of the vicinity of Sing Sing prison at the times of the commitment and of the execution of Mrs. Snyder,[20] and has stated that more than seven hundred persons applied for the position when the former executioner resigned.[21]

So long as capital punishment exists, a neurasthenic, emotional, erotic and sadistic tinge will inevitably color the attitude of those who prosecute murderers and those who read about them. . . . Consider the case of Gerald Chapman, of late hanged for the murder of a Connecticut policeman. . . . Had there been no question of official killing in the Chapman case, the tabloid (and the respectable) press would have been deprived of its sadistic romanticism, the community would have been spared the spectacle of a state officer wheedling and pleading with twelve simple men for the destruction of a human life, resorting to cute tricks and rhetorical devices, and all of us would have been relieved of the necessity of reading—as of course we all did—the ghoulishly vivid accounts of Chapman's end, accounts designed, consciously or unconsciously, to play upon the secondary sexual instincts of the Under Man. Had it not been for capital punishment, the Chapman trial would have been disposed of scientifically, expeditiously, dispassionately, without affronting the consciences of an increasing body of humane people, and with no more furore than

[18] E. R. Calvert, *Capital Punishment in the Twentieth Century*, London, 1927, p. 96, note. Reprinted by permission of G. P. Putnam's Sons, publishers.
[19] N. C. Board of Charities and Public Welfare, *Capital Punishment in North Carolina*, Special Bulletin, No. 10, 1929, pp. 43–44.
[20] Lewis E. Lawes, *Life and Death in Sing Sing*, p. 241.
[21] *Ibid.*, p. 189.

attends an operation for the removal of adenoids. . . . Abolish capital punishment and it will be no longer possible for judges and prosecutors to exhibit their sadistic proclivities to the world under guise of superior moral vigor. Abolish capital punishment and you will take away half the fun in the tabloid method of treating crime—along with the debauching consequences upon public opinion. . . . Before the human mind had been very deeply plumbed we could disguise sadism as moral indignation or public spirit. These matters are better understood now and, as science slowly but surely overtakes our criminal practice, jurists who now seek applause and satisfy erotic stirrings by advocating more whippings and higher hangings will be forced to take their pleasure in slaughter houses and in esoteric flagellation.[22]

Since the public has been barred from executions, the newspapers, with a few exceptions, have competed with each other in efforts to describe the executions as realistically as possible. Many people, however, wish neither to witness nor read about such events and feel that their sentiments are injured by the display. The advocates of the death penalty argue that this means more regard for the life of the criminal than for the life of the victim. The argument is not pertinent. If a murder has occurred, the victim is not restored to life by the execution of the criminal, and the evidence does not show that other persons are deterred more successfully by an execution than by other penalties.

7. *The death penalty and selectivity.* One of the objections to the death penalty is that it, like other severe penalties, is not imposed equitably upon all offenders and that those who have money or status escape it. Only 25.5 per cent of the white and 54.4 per cent of the Negro offenders committed on death sentences to the state prison of North Carolina in the period 1909–1928 were actually executed. The significant point is that the proportion of convicted Negroes executed was more than twice as great as the proportion of whites. This shows a discrimination against the Negroes, but when the specific descriptions of the white prisoners are considered it is found that most of the white persons executed were helpless, also. For instance, 43 per cent of the white offenders sentenced to death were illiterate.

8. *The irreparability of the death penalty.* The life of a con-

---

[22] Editorial, *New Rep.*, 46: 263–265, April 21, 1926. Reprinted by permission.

victed person is wasted by imprisonment, but the damages done by imprisonment may to some extent be repaired if the penalty is later found to be unjustified. No reparation can be made for the damage done by an unjust death penalty. Errors of justice of this nature are irreparable. Though most mistakes are prevented by the judicial system or by executive clemency, some occur, due to the pressure of public opinion, the decisions of judges, the personnel of the jury, the laws of evidence, the unreliability of testimony, and even by confessions of the accused. Again and again persons have been convicted, and have been on the verge of an execution when new evidence not only saved them from the execution but from any penalty whatever. Also, persons have been sentenced to prison for murder and after several years have been released when new evidence proved their innocence. Though such errors of justice in murder cases are not frequent, they are an important factor in the problem. Of 415 persons committed to Sing Sing for execution in 1889–1927, 30 were acquitted on appeal and 18 others convicted of a less serious crime for which the death penalty could not be used.

9. *The death penalty and financial economy.* The immediate financial cost of an execution is less than the financial cost of life imprisonment. The per capita cost of imprisonment is perhaps $400 per year, and the life term may amount on the average to twenty years, making a total of about $8,000. This is perhaps the only definite argument in favor of the death penalty but it would apply equally well to the non-criminal insane and feebleminded and to criminals who have committed offenses less serious than murder.

In general the arguments and the available data are not in favor of the retention of the death penalty. Very few persons who have made a careful study of the data advocate the death penalty. It is probable, however, that the trend away from the death penalty during the last century is due less to rationalistic considerations than to the humanitarian sentiments and the respect for human life. Certainly it is desirable to abandon the mandatory death penalty and leave the imposition of the sentence to the discretion of the court or jury.

It is generally suggested that life imprisonment should be the alternative to the death penalty. No good reason exists for insisting on life imprisonment as the sole substitute. Those convicted of capital offenses should be treated on the same principle as other criminals, namely, careful study of personality and social situation.

This may mean life imprisonment but certainly does not mean this in all cases.

FINES. Fines are imposed much more frequently than all other penalties combined. Probably more than 75 per cent of all penalties imposed are fines. This is because they are used in the great mass of the relatively trivial offenses. Moreover, fines in the United States and in the principal European countries have increased in ratio to other penalties. This is, in part, due to the increase in trivial offenses growing out of the increased number of technical regulations, in part due to the substitution of fines for other penalties.

The court is generally given authority to fix fines within maximum and minimum limits set by the legislature. Sometimes only the maximum limit is fixed, sometimes only the minimum. The constitutions of the several states provide that fines shall not be excessive. Even so, fines are occasionally very large, as is shown by the fact that a man in Boston was fined $2,350 in 1931 for illegal parking, having been found guilty on forty-seven counts.

At common law fines were enforced by executions against property.[23] At present an offender is generally imprisoned in a jail or house of correction in default of payment of the fine. About 80 per cent of the persons committed to the Chicago House of Correction in 1930 were committed for non-payment of fines. In 1933 31 per cent of the persons committed to jails on sentences were committed in default of payment of fines. Of those thus committed 60 per cent had fines of less than $20, and 22 per cent had fines of less than $10. These offenders "lie out" the fine at some specified rate, such as $0.50 a day. This brings in practically no income and is a very considerable expense. From 1907 to 1921 the Chicago courts assessed $8,764,790 in fines, of which two-thirds was not collected; most of that amount was "laid out" in the workhouse at the rate of $0.50 a day, and at a cost to the city of about $0.40 a day per prisoner. This means that the city not only did not secure the $6,000,-000 in fines, but also spent approximately $5,000,000 more to support the prisoners who could not pay their fines.

When a fine is imposed, it is tantamount to a declaration that neither the safety of the community nor the welfare of the offender requires the imprisonment of the offender. Imprisonment is there-

---

[23] In colonial New York corporal punishment was inflicted as an alternative for non-payment of fines. P. Klein, *Prison Methods in New York State,* New York, 1920, p. 25.

fore only a means of collecting a debt to the state. It is evidently a very expensive method. From early times efforts have been made to avoid this difficulty. In New Jersey in 1775 the offender who could not pay his fine might be sold for a term not to exceed five years to any person willing to pay the fine,[24] and a similar provision was made in 1804 in Louisiana. In Connecticut as early as 1841 provision was made that an offender sentenced to pay a fine might, if unable to pay the fine, be released on his note.[25] An English law of 1905 authorized the courts to permit installment payment of fines without imprisonment unless the installments were defaulted. Little use was made of this law, however, and in 1914 it was made mandatory for the court to accept installment payments of fines with certain exceptions. Largely as a result of this the number of persons imprisoned in default of fine decreased from 107,555 in 1904 to 12,497 in 1930, and England closed many of her local prisons. In 1904 20 per cent of all persons who were fined were imprisoned in default of payment, in 1930 only 2 per cent. Several states in America have authorized the installment method of paying fines, and it is used somewhat extensively in connection with probation. The fines collected by probation officers in New York State increased from $1,583 in 1910 to $32,069 in 1920 and $32,095 in 1930, while in Massachusetts the amounts increased from $17,125 in 1910 to $83,911 in 1920 and $326,892 in 1930. But no state has developed this method to the extent that England has.

The question of the method of paying fines may be waived and the question still remains, Why have fines at all? The arguments pro and con are generally given as follows: First, the fine is the most easily and thoroughly remissible of any of the penalties; capital punishment, whipping, or imprisonment once administered cannot be remitted effectively, but a fine that has been paid can be repaid. Second, the fine is a most economical penalty; it costs the state practically nothing when used without imprisonment for default. Third, the fine is easily divisible and can be adjusted to the enormity of the offense, the character and wealth of the offender, the state of public opinion, and other conditions more easily than any other penalty. Fourth, it does not carry with it the public

[24] New Jersey, *Report of Prison Inquiry Commission,* 1917, Vol. II, p. 37.
[25] E. W. Capen, *The Historical Development of the Poor Law of Connecticut,* New York, 1905, pp. 225–226.

stigma and disgrace that imprisonment does, and therefore does not hamper readjustment of the offender. Fifth, it affects one of the most general interests of mankind and causes a kind of suffering that is universal; therefore it is efficacious in dealing with the great majority of mankind. Finally, it provides an income for the state, county, or city.

On the other hand, opponents of the system of fines urge: First, the fines, in practice, are adjusted to the offense and therefore bear unequally on the rich and poor. It is a much greater penalty for a poor man to pay a fine of $10 than for a rich man to do so. It was suggested long ago that a fine, instead of being an absolute amount, should be a specified part of a man's income.[26] Finland passed a law in 1921 authorizing the court to fine an offender by an amount equal to his average income for not less than one day and not more than three hundred days.[27] Second, fines are not effective as a reformative agency in many types of cases in which they are customarily used. Many offenses are committed under the influence of drugs, alcohol, or of fixed habits. A fine seldom changes these elements in the situation. Again, the fine is generally not sufficient to balance the financial gain from the offense. Prostitutes, gamblers, and professional thieves, for instance, seldom abandon their criminal activities because of fines. The mentally defective offender is not made more capable by paying money to the state. Koren made a study of 140 persons committed to Deer Island, each of whom had a total of fifteen or more commitments. Most of these commitments had been for drunkenness and inability to pay fines; one man had been committed 125 times, of which 96 were for inability to pay fines; one man was committed 16 times in one year.[28] Several cities have practically or completely ceased to use fines for prostitutes; of the prostitutes convicted between January 1 and June 30, 1920, none was fined in New York City, 0.1 per cent were fined in Philadelphia, 5.6 per cent in Boston. With these cities should be contrasted Chicago where 62 per cent were fined.[29] And finally,

[26] B. Beaumont, "Essay on Criminal Jurisprudence," *Pamphleteer*, 18:412, 1821.
[27] A. P. Arvelo, "Om Dagsbotssystemet i Finland," *Nordisk Tidsskrift for Strafferet*, 16:12–22, 1928.
[28] J. Koren, "Some Statistics of Recidivism among Misdemeanants in Boston," *Proc. Amer. Stat. Assoc.*, 7:277 ff., June, 1901.
[29] G. E. Worthington and Ruth Topping, "Summary and Comparative Study of the Special Courts in Chicago, Philadelphia, Boston, and New York," *Social Hygiene*, 9:350, June, 1923.

parents, other relatives, or friends are frequently compelled to pay the fines and thereby the hardship is imposed upon them rather than upon the offender. Perhaps, however, it would be an even greater hardship for them if the offender were sent to prison.

In view of these arguments, it would be desirable to abandon entirely the practice of fining the habitual offenders, such as prostitutes, drunkards, or "dope fiends." In case an offender has committed an offense repeatedly, he should be studied carefully in order to find the source of his repeated deviations in behavior, and appropriate policies should be based on these findings. This should be done no matter how trivial the offense. For others whose offenses are not habitual, it is probable that official warnings or remonstrances or some task that will tend to change the attitude of the person or counteract the effect of the offense would be preferable to fines. Fines can be retained to advantage for some of the minor offenses of a purely technical nature. In so far as they are retained they should be payable in installments when they cannot be paid in a lump sum, and a person should never be committed to a penal institution because of inability to pay a fine. If his character or reputation are such as to make him untrustworthy, he should be committed, without fine, to an institution while policies are being developed to modify his characteristics. For certain types of offenders, it is possible that the fine should be indeterminate, just as a prison sentence may be. A person guilty of speeding, for instance, might be sentenced to pay $10 a month for such a period as the court or some administrative agency felt necessary, keeping him under observation to determine the necessity of requiring additional payments.

Fines may be remitted by executive or judicial acts. In general the governor alone has power to remit fines in state cases, but some variations are found. During the biennium 1917–1918 the governor of Iowa remitted fines amounting to $9,227 in twenty-one cases. A practice has developed, in some courts, of imposing a fine and then, in chambers, allowing motions in mitigation, by which the fines are reduced. This was a favorite method in Cleveland, especially in liquor cases, of securing publicity by imposing very heavy fines, and also securing friends by secretly reducing the fines. Of 131 fines involving over $200 each in liquor cases originating in January, 1921, motions in mitigations were allowed in 85, for a total reduction of $39,150, or 52 per cent of the amount of the fines.[30]

RESTITUTION AND REPARATION. In the previous discussion of the origin of fines, it was explained that the fine appeared in a clear-cut form when the state appropriated all of the payment made by the offender; what had previously been a combination of civil and criminal procedures became thereby distinctly a criminal procedure. The offense came to be regarded as an offense against the state alone; the victim was sent to the civil court to recover damages for the injury done to him.

It was found in practice, however, that the injured party had very little success in securing damages because of the insolvent condition of the ordinary criminal and the opportunity to hide or transfer his property before sentence. Consequently the victim generally made no effort to recover by civil process, but resorted to the criminal court, and this caused an additional financial loss.

For nearly a century opinion has been developing in favor of reparation or restitution by order of the criminal court. Several of the American states at the beginning of the nineteenth century had laws which provided that a person convicted of larceny should return to the owner twice the value of the property stolen. Bonneville de Marsangy outlined a definite plan of reparation in 1847. Later Garofalo became the foremost advocate of this method, seconded by Ferri, Fioretti and others. It is urged in favor of this method that, first, it would enable the injured party to recover, which is now almost impossible. It is rather absurd that the state undertakes to protect the public against crime and then, when a loss occurs, takes the entire payment and offers no effective remedy to the individual victim. One of the prevalent methods used by professional thieves when they are arrested is to suggest to the victim that the property will be restored if the victim refuses to prosecute. This results in release in a large proportion of cases, for most victims are more interested in regaining their stolen property than in "seeing justice done." Second, it would have a much better reformative effect on many offenders than would other methods, because the result of the offenses would be more clearly recognized and no stigma would be attached to make reformation difficult. Third, it would relieve the state of the great burden of supporting in penal or reformatory institutions those guilty of minor offenses;

---

[30] R. H. Smith and H. B. Ehrmann, "The Criminal Courts," *Cleveland Survey of Criminal Justice*, Part I, p. 58.

because of the reduction in the number of the inmates, individualized methods could be used to better advantage for those committed to these institutions.

The plan presented by Garofalo and others for enforcing reparation or restitution is as follows: If the offender is solvent, his property should be attached at the time proceedings are started, so that he can be compelled by order of the court to make restitution. If he is insolvent, he can be compelled to devote a part of his income to restitution. It is proposed that the amount to be paid in this way should never be greater than the total amount of the injury (including the cost to the state for arrest and prosecution) and never be so great as to cause undue injury to the offender or his dependents. If the offender fails or refuses to pay the assessment or if he is not dependable, the plan is to make him a state workman, to receive wages for his work; a part of the wage would be retained by the state and paid into the compensation fund.

It is not proposed that restitution or reparation should be used for all offenders. It must necessarily be confined to those who have committed minor offenses for which they need not be held in confinement. The confirmed murderer, for instance, could not be permitted to work at large for the purpose of making restitution to the victims or the dependents of his victims. The Swedish Parliament, however, in 1926 enacted a law which provided that the murderer pay damages to the dependents. In so far as restitution and reparation are used, they should probably be used in connection with probation, and the method is actually developing in that manner in the United States. The probation department of New York State collects about $200,000 a year from probationers for restitution. In Massachusetts a man who had discharged a rifle within the city limits, resulting in the loss of an eye of a boy, was placed on probation for five years and ordered to make weekly payments of damages to the boy during that period and, if at the end of the five years, the damages had not been adequately satisfied, to be continued on probation for a longer period with a continuation of payments.

LOSS OF CIVIL AND OTHER RIGHTS. For many centuries certain crimes have been known as infamous crimes, and for these crimes to which infamy attached and for certain other crimes rights of various kinds have been lost. Roman lawyers made a distinction between infamy due to the nature of the crime and infamy due

to the nature of the punishment—*infamia facti* and *infamia juris.*
In the Roman Republic infamy as the result of the conviction of
crime meant loss of the right to vote, to hold office, to represent
another in the courts, to be a witness, to manage the affairs of
another, and the abridging of the right to marry. During the early
modern period, also, certain crimes resulted in infamy. This infamy
was produced to some extent merely by the publicity of the trial,
but also by the subsequent loss of rights of citizenship. In addition,
offenders were branded or mutilated, so that everyone might know
that they had been guilty of crimes and thus would suffer infamy.
Loss of rank, mutilation of the body after death, and other methods
were used to produce a greater infamy than the public would naturally or ordinarily attribute to the offender. During the feudal
period, by bills of attainer, persons convicted of treason or felony
might be deprived of their real and personal property, their right
to inherit or transmit property, and all rights in the courts. This
was known as civil death.

The Constitution of the United States prohibits bills of attainer.
Some states, nevertheless, declare that the person convicted of an
infamous crime is civilly dead, but it is quite certain that the criminal does not lose all of his legal rights in any state.

Two principal questions are asked regarding infamy and infamous
crimes: Does infamy attach to the crime, as such, or to the punishment? What is the degree or kind of punishment that makes a
crime infamous?

The general weight of opinion seems to be that infamy attaches
only to the punishment, not to the crime as such. But Professor
Schofield, in an acute essay on the origin and development of the
concept of infamy, has shown that this opinion is incorrect and
that in some jurisdictions, at least, and for some deprivations the
infamy is due to the nature of the crime, not to the nature of the
punishment. If the infamy attached to the punishment, it could
be wiped out by a pardon; but Professor Schofield shows that many
civil rights may be lost by infamous crimes and not restored by
pardons. A lawyer who has embezzled the funds of a client may
be sentenced to the state prison, and then be pardoned; but even
after receiving a pardon he may be debarred and prevented from
acting as a lawyer. A person convicted of a felony may lose his
right to vote and in some jurisdictions a pardon does not restore
this right. The loss of rights in such cases is not a part of the pun-

ishment; it is rather a part of a general social policy of determining
who may practice law or medicine, or who may vote; until recently
women, illiterates, and those convicted of felonies, for instance,
were prohibited from voting, not as a punishment, but as a part
of the policy to promote the welfare of the country. This seems
to show that the infamy attaches to the crime, and not merely to
the punishment. The decisions and laws, however, are very confusing and there is good reason to believe that the infamy attaches
to both the crime and the punishment. For instance, the disabilities
are not imposed if the offender is proved guilty but is not sentenced;
this would indicate that the infamy attaches to the punishment.[31]

The second question has to do with the nature of the punishment
which produces infamy, and is important because the decision on
this point determines the conditions under which the offender loses
his rights. Originally any corporal punishment, including capital
punishment, flogging, and the pillory, rendered the offender
infamous. Later imprisonment at hard labor was included as an
infamous punishment, presumably because hard labor was regarded
as a corporal punishment. By implication, then, imprisonment in
a state prison, in which hard labor was generally required, came
to be regarded as an infamous punishment, while imprisonment in
a local workhouse or jail, in which hard labor was seldom required,
was not an infamous punishment, even though the particular institution to which commitment was made did require hard labor of
all its inmates who were able to work. It was decided, however,
in the Moreland case that it is the hard labor which makes the
punishment infamous, and that commitment to a workhouse at
hard labor is an infamous punishment.[32]

The whole set of decisions is in confusion. It is absurd to use
either of the two criteria that are now declared by the courts; the
performance of hard labor should not be regarded as a good reason
for depriving one of his rights; neither should the person committed to a state penal farm be regarded as having suffered a more
infamous punishment than those held in idleness in the unsanitary
county jail. Spalding has shown that commitment to the state prison
of Massachusetts has been determined largely by the comparative

---

[31] Henry Schofield, *Essays on Constitutional Law and Equity*, Boston, 1921,
Vol. I, pp. 421–456.
[32] Reuben Oppenheimer, "Infamous Crimes and the Moreland Case," *Harv.
Law Rev.*, 36:299–320, January, 1923.

crowding of the prison and the county jails, not by the infamy that should attach to crimes.[33] It would probably be preferable to abandon the whole concept of infamy rather than try to improve it.

The following are the principal rights that may be lost by the crimes that are decided to be infamous: (a) The right of suffrage is lost by conviction of an infamous crime in all of the states except five—Arizona, Michigan, New Hampshire, Pennsylvania, and Vermont. (b) The right to hold public office is lost in most of the states. Public offices are generally restricted to electors and therefore the loss of suffrage carries with it the loss of the right to hold office. In addition certain other restrictions are specified in some states, such as incapacity to serve on a jury, to hold any military office, or to act as a guardian or administrator. (c) The common law assumed that a person who committed a heinous crime had such a depraved character that he would be insensible to the obligations of an oath and therefore his testimony in court would be unreliable. This deprivation has been generally abandoned by American legislatures, but in practice it is still possible to present facts regarding the criminal career of a witness as pertinent to the credibility of the witness. (d) The right to practice certain professions or occupations is denied to those convicted of infamous crimes. Many states prohibit an attorney who has been guilty of embezzling the funds of his clients forever from practicing law. Liquor licenses might be refused to those convicted of infamous crimes. In some states persons convicted of infamous crimes cannot practice medicine. (e) Rights in court and prison are lost or curtailed. The presumption of innocence and eligibility for parole or probation, for instance, may be lost if the offender has been convicted previously of an infamous crime; and the sentence may, according to law, be more severe for such persons. (f) Certain marital rights are lost. Conviction of crime is a ground for divorce in all of the states except New Mexico, Maryland, North Carolina, South Carolina, and Florida. But the states differ in the restrictions placed on divorce under such circumstances; in some states the crime must be a felony, in others the period of imprisonment must exceed a specified number of years, in others the divorce cannot be granted within a specified time after the conviction. In Maine the bonds of matri-

---

[33] W. F. Spalding, "The Legislative History of a 'State Prison' Sentence as a Test of 'Felony' and 'Infamous Punishment' and the Practical Results in Massachusetts," *Mass. Law Quart.*, 7:91–108, January, 1922.

mony are automatically severed by a sentence of life imprisonment. Less than 1 per cent of the divorces granted in the United States are on the ground of conviction of felony. The right to propagate, also, is abridged or denied to those convicted of certain crimes. A law which provides for sterilization has been passed in twenty-eight states, but it is designed primarily as a protection against defectives rather than as a penal measure in all except two of these states; it is practically never used against criminals. (g) The right to an ordinary burial may be lost. In all states except Wyoming, the body of a person who dies in prison, if not claimed within a specified time by friends or relatives, may be turned over to a scientific society, medical college, or other institution for scientific purposes. It will be given an ordinary burial if not claimed for scientific purposes. (h) An infamous crime committed by a foreigner prevents him from being naturalized, in some states, unless he is pardoned. (i) Loss of the right to migrate to a foreign land or liability to deportation result, in some jurisdictions, for certain crimes.

Two restrictions or interpretations should be added. Civil disability is generally restricted to the state in which the offender is convicted; rights in other states are not lost. A crime is infamous and the rights are lost not because an infamous punishment has been imposed in a particular case, but because an infamous punishment may be imposed for crimes of the class of which one has been convicted.

The disabilities produced as the result of infamy are terminated automatically in some states when the sentence has been served; in other states they are terminated if the person is not indicted or convicted of another crime within a specified time after the completion of his sentence. In most states the disabilities are removed only by pardon, and some of them not even by pardon. Some are removed only if specifically mentioned in the pardon. Many pardons are granted for the purpose of restoring the civil rights of voting, naturalization, residence, and professions. In New York State in 1932 seventy-eight pardons were granted for these purposes and none for the purpose of release from imprisonment.

The original purpose of infamous punishments was to isolate the offender. It was a form of banishment; at least it was designed to produce the same result that banishment did, namely, place social distance between the offender and the law-abiding citizen. In later society an evident desire to protect the social and political institutions plays a part, and the suffering of the offender from the loss of the rights may be merely incidental.

Both from the standpoint of the punishment of offenders and the qualifications for participation in our institutions such deprivations are undesirable, as they now stand. While the offender is in prison, he probably should not be permitted to vote, hold office, or exercise some of the other rights. His rights should be automatically restored as soon as he is placed in the outside community, even on parole. The purpose of the restoration to the community is that the group may assimilate him. Assimilation will not be promoted by this device for maintaining social distance. The group cannot assimilate him by driving him out of the group in the social sense. Participation in the social institutions, on the other hand, should be decided in each case by the particular personality and circumstances. For instance, while conviction of crime should be one of the reasons for which divorce may be granted, the character of the individual and the nature of the home need to be considered in connection with this.

Somewhat related to the loss of civil rights is the deprivation of a license which is required for many activities at the present time. A person convicted of violation of traffic regulations may be deprived of his driver's license. A person convicted in Michigan of violating the game law may be deprived of the right to secure another hunting license within three years.

REMONSTRANCE AND ADMONITION. It was an established principle in Roman jurisprudence that the law should warn before it struck. In the French code of 1670 admonition was recognized as one method that might be used, while the Canon law provided that the offender should be thrice admonished. Courts are using this method much more frequently now than formerly, probably because of a recognition of the futility of short sentences in prison or jail. In many cases such official remonstrances serve to express to the offender the opposition of the group to his behavior. When this remonstrance is counteracted by the general practice of the group to which the offender belongs, it will probably be ineffective. The moralizing of the judge is not likely to produce a decided modification of behavior in many cases and it is evidently applicable as a method only to a small number of offenses. As a method of badgering and pestering it may do some good and is likely to do much harm. In most cases it would probably be preferable for the judge to make an explanation in his chambers rather than hector the offender in public.

SUGGESTED READINGS

Brearley, H. C., *Homicide in the United States*, Chapel Hill, 1932, Ch. 7.

Bye, R. T., *Capital Punishment in the United States*, Philadelphia, 1919.

Calvert, E. R., *Capital Punishment in the Twentieth Century*, London, 1927.

Cantor, N. F., "The Prisoner and the Law," *Annals of Amer. Acad. of Pol. and Social Sci.*, 157:23–32, September, 1931.

"Corporal Punishment," *Encyc. of Soc. Sciences*.

Dann, Robert H., "The Deterrent Effect of Capital Punishment," *Friends' Social Service Series*, Bull. No. 29, 1935.

Garofalo, R., *Criminology*, Tr. by R. W. Millar, Boston, 1914, pp. 419–435.

Great Britain, *Report from Select Committee on Capital Punishment*, 1931.

Harley, H., "Segregation versus Hanging," *Jour. Crim. Law and Criminol.*, 11:512–527, February, 1921.

Hobhouse, S., and Brockway, A. F., *English Prisons Today, Being the Report of the Prison System Enquiry Com.*, London, 1922, Part I, Ch. 15.

Ives, G., *A History of Penal Methods*, London, 1914.

Kane, R., Vogt, O., and Campanelli, V., "From the Death House," *Forum*, 53:627–628, May, 1915.

Koren, J., "Some Statistics of Recidivism among Misdemeanants in Boston," *Jour. Amer. Stat. Assoc.*, 7:269–309, June, 1901.

Lawes, Lewis E., *Man's Judgment of Death*, New York, 1924.

North Carolina, "Capital Punishment in North Carolina," *State Board of Charities and Public Welfare, Special Bulletin*, No. 10, 1929.

Oppenheimer, Reuben, "Infamous Crimes and the Moreland Case," *Harv. Law Rev.*, 36:299–320, January, 1923.

Orchard, J. E., *The Fine System*, Philadelphia, 1917.

Phelps, H. A., "Effectiveness of Life Imprisonment as a Repressive Measure against Murder in Rhode Island," *Jour. Amer. Stat. Assoc.*, Suppl., 23:174–181, March, 1928.

Potter, Z., "Fines and Community Protection in Illinois," *Jour. Crim. Law and Criminol.*, 6:675–683, January, 1916.

Queen, S. A., *The Passing of the County Jail*, Menasha, Wis., 1920, Ch. 1.

Schofield, Henry, *Essays on Constitutional Law and Equity*, 2 Vols., Boston, 1921, Vol. 1, pp. 421–456.

Spalding, W. F., "The Legislative History of a 'State Prison' Sentence as a Test of 'Felony' and 'Infamous Punishment' and the Practical Results in Massachusetts," *Mass. Law Quart.*, 7:91–108, January, 1922.

Stern, Max, "Imprisonment for Non-Payment of Fines in Chicago," *Social Serv. Rev.*, 5:459–467, September, 1931.

Sutherland, Edwin H., "The Decreasing Prison Population of England," *Jour. Crim. Law and Criminol.*, 24:880–900, January, 1934.

Thompson, J. J., "Early Corporal Punishments," *Ill. Law Quart.*, 6:37–49, December, 1923.

Vold, G. B., "Can the Death Penalty Prevent Crime?" *The Prison Jour.*, October, 1932.

Whitin, E. S., "The Caged Man," *Proc. Acad. Pol. Sci.*, Vol. III, 1912, Ch. 8.

Chapter Twenty-Eight

RECIDIVISM AND REFORMATION

THE IMPORTANCE OF RECIDIVISM. A large proportion of the offenders under the care of any agency are recidivists. Of the offenders committed to jails, prisons, and reformatories in 1933, 48 per cent had been committed previously to such institutions. This is far from a complete enumeration of the recidivists in these institutions, for methods of identification are not much used in the jails or in the institutions for juveniles. In states where the local organization of the methods of identification is more complete, the percentage known to be recidivists goes above 60. About 65 per cent of the offenders admitted to all types of correctional institutions in Massachusetts in 1936 had been in such institutions previously, and the average number of previous commitments for the recidivist was 5.6; 2 per cent of the recidivists had more than 30 commitments each.

This high rate of recidivism is extremely important in relation to crime. A large proportion of the crimes can be attributed to recidivists. A large part of the work of the police, the courts, the penal and reformatory institutions is concentrated on recidivists. They provide more than their share of the failures on probation and parole, and more than their share of the disciplinary problems in the institutions. Massive walls and other devices to prevent escapes are needed principally for recidivists.

REASONS FOR RECIDIVISM. The persistence of criminals in their crimes may be explained either in terms of the characteristics and conditions of the offenders or in terms of the inadequacy of agencies of reformation. The first involves a social psychology of the recidivist, the second an analysis of the techniques of reformation. The Gluecks emphasized the second of these in their *Five Hundred Criminal Careers,* the first in their *Later Criminal Careers.*

SOCIAL PSYCHOLOGY OF RECIDIVISM. One of the findings of the prediction studies is that, with some exceptions, the personal characteristics and social situations which are conducive to criminality in the first place are also conducive to persistence in crime. Persons who live in good residential areas, are reared in wholesome homes, have occupations on the higher levels, and a comfortable standard of living are least likely to return to crime after any method of treatment. They, like persons with minor physical ailments, probably cure themselves. Those who fail most frequently on probation and parole were reared in deteriorated areas, in homes where destitution, vice and criminality were usual, in isolation from the constructive agencies of the community. Negroes have a higher rate of recidivism than whites, and boys have a higher rate of recidivism than girls.[1] Various explanations have been suggested for this persistence in crime in such situations.

One of the explanations of persistence in crime is habit formation; persistence in crime is merely persistence of habits. Some of the habits were formed prior to the official treatment, others during the course of the treatment. Drug addiction and drunkenness are illustrations of offenses which persist after punishment as the result of habit formation. It is doubtful, however, whether the term "habit formation" is an adequate explanation of the persistence even of drug addiction or drunkenness. This concept implies physiological mechanisms and leaves the situational factors in obscurity. The process at any rate is much more complex than is ordinarily conceived when explained in terms of habit formation. The offender is rather necessarily confined in his group membership by his occupational skill, his table manners, his methods of conversation, his manners in dancing and in wearing his clothes. By these manners, skills, and other traits he is confined to certain social classes and for that reason he must remain in the situations in which his criminality developed. If he gets out of these social classes, he will do so slowly. Furthermore, this involves a complex of emotions, sentiments, codes, and social situations, in which many kinds of mechanisms are involved, so that the term "habit formation" is likely to be misleading.

Isolation from law-abiding society has been suggested as another explanation of recidivism. This occurs more frequently after

---

[1] Robert M. Woodbury, "The Juvenile Delinquent Population and the Rates of Recidivism," *Soc. Serv. Rev.*, 11:623–633, December, 1937.

imprisonment than after other methods of punishment but exists to some extent in connection with every method. The following is an illustration of this effect.

After I got out of the Chicago Parental School I couldn't, to save my soul, get used to the freedom and ease of the outside schoolroom. I felt out of place among the boys on the outside. I kind of felt strange and inferior about having come out of such a place. People distrusted me; I couldn't convince my folks that I wanted to go straight, attend high school and finally go to college. Everybody expected me to steal again. I had extreme trouble in finding something to talk about to my fellow students. I felt ashamed and then didn't know anything that was going on to talk about. Conversation had not been permitted in the Chicago Parental School except out in the yard. In the cottage and school you were compelled to keep absolute silence. I hardly ever had a heart to heart conversation with anyone while I was there. The Chicago Parental School kind of made a clam out of me and put a sort of inferiority and shameful feeling in me. I have never since been able to rid myself wholly of the feeling. I kind of felt unpopular with everybody, that people were afraid of me and distrusted me.[2]

Ordinarily the offender acquires no facility in the manners of the law-abiding group and has no opportunity to come in contact with them after or during his punishment. If he lived previously in a law-abiding group he is likely to be ostracized, while if he lived previously in a criminal group he may acquire status by his punishment.

Another explanation of the persistence of the criminal is found in the criminality and near-criminality in the general society. Albert Nock has pointed out that a person would secure no satisfaction from smoking in church because a church is not a suitable situation. Similarly an offender can feel comfortable in committing crimes only in a situation where that behavior has become customary. Shaw has shown that the areas with high rates of juvenile delinquency are also areas with high rates of recidivism in juvenile delinquency. Patterns of dishonesty, however, are prevalent outside

---

[2] Clifford R. Shaw, *Delinquency Areas*, p. 41. Reprinted by permission of The University of Chicago Press, publishers. The boy who wrote this statement was later committed to two other juvenile reformatories and then to the state prison on a sentence of twenty-three years.

of these deteriorated areas. Advertisements of toothpaste, cigarettes, and hundreds of other commodities are notoriously fraudulent in their claims and suggestions. The bribery of purchasing agents by business concerns is almost universal in many trades. Sharp practices have become customary in many lines of business. Ruthlessness in making money has become an important part of the business code. Trade unions have become involved in racketeering. Political graft and corruption are widespread. Thus lying, cheating, fraud, exploitation, and graft are prevalent in the general society. The offender who remains reformed must be superior to the society in which he lives. Certainly the reformation of the offender would be very much easier if the general society contained fewer persons of criminal and near-criminal type.

Again, the criminal by reason of his crime and the methods of dealing with his crime, forms associations, loyalties, and attitudes which tend to persist. The offender who manifests a desire to reform is called "yellow," "rat," or "stool-pigeon." He is then ostracized from the delinquent society, but is not on that account accepted by law-abiding society. Violence and threats of violence may be used to keep him a criminal. Opportunities for crime are placed in his way. One offender while on parole stated that he had at least forty opportunities for crime suggested to him in a month but not a single opportunity for legitimate work. Probably more important than any of these is his feeling of obligation to assist those who have assisted him in the past. Jack Black describes his difficulties when he attempted to desist from crime, thus:

The more strictly a criminal adheres to the underworld code, the greater will be his handicap if, and when, he decides to mend his ways. This adherence makes him friends and he is proud of it; but these very friends help to anchor him in that life. . . . Many former associates had a right to expect and demand help from me, and of course they did demand it. In the fifteen years that I have been playing Society's game, I have many times had one foot in a jail as the result of trying to reconcile the underworld and upperworld codes. I have been asked to send pistols and explosives and narcotics into jails by men who had a right to demand them because they had done favors for me in the past. . . . Many ex-prisoners who try to go straight become involved with the law in an effort to discharge their obligations. The underworld is always reaching out to them, and the more help they are in a position to give, the greater the demands upon them will be.[3]

Finally, persistence in criminal behavior has been explained as due to personality traits, most frequently as due to pathological traits of personality, such as mental defectiveness, emotional instability, mental conflicts, egocentrism, and psychosis. The Gluecks' explanation of persistence in crime beyond the age of forty is almost entirely in terms of mental deviations which are not corrected by the natural maturation of the individual.[4] In contrast with this, Thompson reports that of 1,380 repeaters in the clinic of the Court of General Sessions in 1935, the mental defectives, psychotics, and psychopathic personalities were 8.8 per cent of all repeaters and were approximately the same proportion in all clinic cases; the defectives practically disappear from among the repeaters after the age of 30, and the psychopathic personalities appear among the repeaters above the age of 45 in the same proportion as in the repeaters below that age.[5] Nevertheless, personality characteristics, whether pathological or not, tend to persist in spite of the treatment in any of the penal processes. Since the situation subsequent to the treatment remains essentially the same as prior to the treatment, and the personality traits remain the same, the old behavior almost inevitably persists.

RECIDIVISM DUE TO INSTITUTIONAL FAILURES. The second explanation of recidivism is that the methods of reformation are inadequate. If the offender were reformed when the first agency had supervision over him, the problem of crime would largely be solved. As a matter of fact, every policy that has been tried has resulted in a large proportion of failures. This is true of penal measures and of case-work measures; it is true of prisons, probation, parole, and fines. The failure of reformative policies was recognized two generations ago, and it was explained that it is necessary to start when offenders are young. When the juvenile court failed to reduce crime rates, the measures were pushed further back into childhood, and child guidance clinics were estab-

---

[3] Jack Black, "A Burglar Looks at Laws and Codes," *Harpers*, 160:308–310, February, 1930. Reprinted by permission.
[4] Sheldon and Eleanor T. Glueck, *Later Criminal Careers*, New York, 1937.
[5] Charles B. Thompson, "A Psychiatric Study of Recidivists," *Amer. Jour. Psychiat.*, 94:591–604, November, 1937.

lished. Even these agencies have had a relatively low degree of success in modifying behavior and personality.

In the subsequent analysis of the failure of agencies we shall be concerned with technical policies rather than with personnel and facilities. The policies divide somewhat sharply into the conventional penal policies and a group of newer policies concentrated more specifically on reformation. The conventional penal policies, with which the new policies are in disagreement, had three characteristics. First, the conventional policies aimed at uniformity in punishment for all who violated a specific law, with a slight development of methods of reformation which were similarly uniform and mechanical in their procedures. This general policy was the product of the classical school of criminal law, and was an expression of religious, legal, and social beliefs and conditions. In contrast with this the newer policy is individualization, directed specifically at reformation of the individual.

A second characteristic of the conventional system was the isolation of criminals. This was most apparent in the methods of transportation and imprisonment, but was evident also in the methods of mutilation, social stigma, and deprivation of civil rights, which were all designed to put social distance between the offenders and law-abiding people. Isolation of offenders was regarded as desirable as a method of producing suffering, of protecting the law-abiding from contamination by the lawless, and of protecting the law-abiding from the assaults of the lawless. In contrast, the new policy attempts to reform by socialization, and this calls for contacts with, rather than isolation from, the law-abiding culture.

A third characteristic of the conventional system was the dispersion of control, with resulting disunity and disorganization. The federal government, the state, the county, the municipality, and the township all dealt with criminals, without co-ordination or organization of efforts. Legislature, police, court, prison, probation department, parole board, and pardon board acted independently without much consideration for one other. Separation of powers and local self-government were the pride of the system. In contrast, the newer system is making an attempt to organize and co-ordinate the various policies and agencies.

These contrasting characteristics of the policies will be taken up for more detailed analysis.

THE CONVENTIONAL METHODS OF REFORMATION.   Although the conventional system was interested primarily in punishing the offender in order to deter others from crime, some applications of the theory to reformation were made. All of the reformative efforts in the conventional system were mass methods designed to modify the person in some mechanical manner.

Chief reliance was placed on the suffering of the offender. The theory was that an offender would reform if he learned that he suffered a sufficient amount of pain for his crimes. This was a strictly hedonistic theory, and it is still held by considerable numbers in the general public. It has generally been discarded by psychologists. Pain undoubtedly has some value in the control of behavior, but the value is more or less completely balanced by the antagonism, isolation, and group loyalties which it produces. Furthermore, the infliction of punishment upon the offender does not change the situation which produced the criminality.   In some cases there is not much more justification for punishing a criminal than for punishing a person with tuberculosis or smallpox.   Adler, speaking especially with reference to the psychopathic delinquent, states:

To punish such an individual . . . is to increase his defeat rather than to strengthen his defenses. It is like administering alcohol to the patient suffering from delirium tremens.[6]

A second method designed to produce reformation was meditation, generally enforced by isolation from all or almost all other persons. The theory was that crime was due to a failure to think, and that meditation would develop remorse and repentance. Early in the nineteenth century Mease made a clear-cut statement of this method of producing reformation. He maintained that repentance was produced by:

(1) A tiresome state of mind from idle seclusion; (2) self-condemnation arising from deep, long-continued and poignant reflections upon a guilty life. All our endeavors, therefore, ought to be directed to the production of that state of mind, which will cause a convict to concentrate his thoughts upon his forlorn condition, to abstract himself from the world, and to think of nothing except the suffering and the

---

[6] H. M. Adler, "A Psychiatric Contribution to the Study of Delinquency," *Jour. Crim. Law and Criminol.*, 8:67, May, 1917.

privations he endures, the result of his crimes. Such a state of mind is totally incompatible with the least mechanical operation, but is only to be brought about, if ever, by complete mental and bodily isolation.[7]

Some prisoners have testified that during the period of solitude they were compelled to think over their careers and that this did result in decisions to desist from crime. In general, this procedure does not seem to be effective. Saleilles has well said:

The constant thought of remorse and, still more, of shame, becomes the greatest hindrance to individual regeneration.[8]

The offender has little except his crimes to think about and the concentration on crime prevents him from developing new interests. Hobhouse and Brockway accumulated considerable documentary evidence that isolation results in deterioration and degradation.[9]

A third method, used in earlier and in later times, was moralizing. By tracts, sermons, and personal exhortations, in the name of God, mother, and country, appeals were made to the offenders. These exhortations generally produce antagonism in prisoners. Exhortation is an extremely important method of social control when it is used by members of a group upon other members of the same group. It is seldom effective when used by one group upon another group.

A fourth method is by inducing the offender to sign a pledge or make resolutions in some other form. The futility of this method is abundantly illustrated every New Year's Day. Dr. Fernald has defined the process of reformation as follows:

1. To really regret the damage done to one's life and other lives by the mistakes made.
2. To intend to do better.
3. To make a plan by which one might live day and evening for a

---

[7] Mease, *Penitentiary System*, p. 73; quoted by F. C. Gray, *Prison Discipline in America*, p. 30. For further discussion of the advantages and disadvantages of isolation by the penologists of the early nineteenth century, see New Jersey, *Report of Prison Inquiry Commission*, 1917, Vol. II.

[8] R. Saleilles, *The Individualization of Punishment*, Boston, 1911, p. 195, Tr. by R. S. Jastrow. Reprinted by permission of Little, Brown & Company, publishers.

[9] Hobhouse and Brockway, *English Prisons Today*, pp. 476–589.

long time (four or five years) while one is practicing his good intentions.

4. To decide whether to adopt the plan or give it up, and if the former, then to determine to be a stayer.

5. To live this plan for the time set by practicing it.[10]

The difficulties about this conception of reformation are, first, that it regards the process of reformation as going on entirely within the mind of the individual and as accomplished merely by making up his mind, and, second, that the reaction upon the individual when he breaks the resolution, as is almost certain to be the case if the reformation involves nothing more than the resolution, is very injurious.

A fifth method of reformation is mechanical habituation, produced by various compulsory methods. The constant surveillance of the offender, which was made possible by Bentham's panopticon type of prisons, was justified by him as resulting in the formation of good habits.

If you prevent men from doing mischief, almost anything will suffice as a motive to induce them to do good. The pain of being idle is a never failing impulse. Restrain it from operating in a wrong direction; the gentlest means will be sufficient to turn it into a direction that is good.

To render a man totally unable to do mischief, you have only to keep him constantly in sight, after depriving him of such offensive instruments as would render him dangerous to you. Place a man by himself, in an iron cage, for example, and keep him every hour and every minute of his life in sight, and it is evident you can prevent him from doing mischief, whether by making his escape to prey again upon society, or by exerting his powers to any pernicious effect where you have him confined.

To place criminals then under perpetual inspection is the object, the all-powerful object, which it is required to accomplish. If this can be done, without loading society with exorbitant expense, the problem respecting a better disposal of criminals than killing them is already resolved.[11]

---

[10] Massachusetts, *Report of Commissioner of Correction,* 1927, p. 44.
[11] "On Houses of Safe-Custody and Industry," *Philanthropist,* 1:229, 1811.

The panopticon prison was constructed in circular form with a central guard tower, from which one guard could look into all the cells and thus keep all the prisoners under constant surveillance. When this prison architecture was used in the Joliet prison it was found that the construction which enabled the guard to watch all of the prisoners also enabled any prisoner to watch the guard and therefore any prisoner could do whatever mischief he pleased while the guard's back was turned. In addition the constant surveillance produced antagonisms in the prisoners. Hard work in prison was another device from which results were expected. The following statement was made by the superintendent of a boys' reformatory:

Every boy should have something to do every waking hour. What this effort is, is not important. . . . It may be drudgery, but is it part of the price he must pay for better things. That every day has its work, and every hour of every day its task must be well understood by the young malefactor, and the habit of doing what comes to his lot must become a fixed habit. In time a spirit of pride in doing well even the uninviting task will become a stimulus to greater skill.[12]

Brockway seemed to have the same mechanical psychology during a part of his career, though he did not state it in this crude form. Some mental defectives, perhaps, can be trained in that way, and the habits once formed remain fixed. But habits shift very quickly in ordinary individuals as soon as the situation changes, unless the habits are thoroughly in harmony with the rest of the personality. Unless interest in labor is developed, the habit of mechanical exertion will be quite unavailing to produce a law-abiding character or continuance of hard work after release.

These methods are examples of the efforts to produce reformation in the past. They show the necessity of understanding the principles of human behavior better than they were understood in the last century.

ISOLATION VERSUS ASSOCIATION. The mechanical methods of reform were generally applied to the offender while he was isolated from the law-abiding culture. The newer methods consist essentially of contacts with the law-abiding culture, and are implicitly in conflict with the fundamental policy of isolation. As early as

---

[12] H. W. Charles, "The Problem of the Reform School," *Proc. Child Conference for Research and Welfare,* 1910, p. 88.

1868 Desprez stated the argument against isolation, with special reference to isolation of prisoners from each other and from the public.

> All isolation, even if voluntary, is bad. There is no idea more fallacious than that isolation from the world by prolonged imprisonment will produce moral meditations in the culprit which will be the source of his reformation. It is not sufficient to place a person between four walls in order to improve him. . . . How is it possible to hope or believe for a single moment that gross natures, uncultured and degraded, can find in themselves the force to condemn and sincerely detest their faults, and maintain a firm resolution during the years of detention, in the midst of all the elements of corruption, if the imprisonment is in common, or in apathy and despair, if the imprisonment is in cells?[13]

The essential reason why persons become criminals is that they have been isolated from the culture of the law-abiding group, by reason of their residence, employment, codes, native incapacity, or something else, or else have been in contact with a rival criminal culture. Consequently they are lacking in the experiences, feelings, ideas, and attitudes out of which to construct a life organization that the law-abiding public will regard as desirable. Poverty of ideas and of feelings about people, social relations, codes, and the effect of one's conduct upon others is the difficulty that must be overcome. Criminality, which is the product of this isolation from culture, will not be overcome by more isolation. Assimilation of the culture will come only by contact. Consequently the policies are including more and more provision for contact—probation, which permits or assists the offender to come in contact with society instead of isolating him behind prison walls; education and self-government in prison, which are attempts to develop social interaction even while the prisoners are physically isolated; classification of similar offenders within prisons; parole, which acts in the same way as probation, though it begins after a period of imprisonment; and various other efforts to assist the offender after release from prison to gain or regain contacts with normal groups.

This method of producing reformation by contact with the law-abiding culture is important, but it has two shortcomings. First,

---

[13] E. Desprez, *De l'abolition de l'emprisonnement,* pp. 18–19.

the presence of a cultural pattern does not necessarily result in its adoption. Acculturation comes only as the result of contact, but contact does not necessarily result in acculturation. All persons are in contact with law-abiding culture, and all persons are in contact with criminal culture. Something more than contact is needed. The anthropologists have shown that cultural patterns are diffused among preliterate groups, not radially from a center as the result of spatial proximity, but in selected paths as the result of receptivity to the new patterns. Long-continued contact with a culture produces assimilation but it accomplishes this by affecting a large variety of elements of the culture. Immediate results in the reformation of an offender require not only that the cultural pattern be present but also that the offender be receptive to it. Second, offenders frequently find great difficulty in securing intimate contacts with law-abiding groups. A boy who has been in a reformatory may not feel at home in a club, and the other members of the club do not feel comfortable in his presence. Employees in a factory often threaten to strike if an ex-convict is not dismissed.

INDIVIDUALIZATION. Fixed penalties were based on the assumption that they produce the same effect on all individuals. This assumption is fundamentally fallacious. [14] In contrast, individualization is the adjustment of the methods of treatment to the requirements of the individual offender. It is the adjustment of the treatment to the offender rather than to the offense. The argument for individualization in the treatment of offenders has been stated as analogous to the individualization of methods in medicine. Two or three centuries ago diseases were not differentiated from each other or explained as natural products. Blood-letting was almost the only treatment, varying in amount with the seriousness of the ailment. In the meantime the germ theory of disease and experimental methods have produced a great variety of methods of treatment adapted to particular diseases. Crime almost until the present generation was treated as sickness was two centuries ago, and the methods of dealing with criminals consisted of depriving them of freedom for a longer or shorter period of time or depriving them of larger or smaller amounts of money. The study of the origin of criminality and the adjustment of methods of treatment to the

---

[14] For a general analysis of this fallacy see Thomas and Znaniecki, *op. cit.*, 1927, Vol. I, p. 12.

nature of the processes by which the criminality develops is just beginning.[15]

Individualization means, first, an intensive study of the individual offender for the purpose of learning the specific conditions, circumstances, processes, and mechanisms involved in the criminality, and second, a policy determined by that knowledge regarding the offender, in connection with knowledge previously secured regarding the methods of dealing with such cases. It will not mean an entirely different policy for each individual, any more than scientific treatment of diseases means an entirely different policy for each patient. In many cases individualization need not mean pain or suffering, and when it does mean suffering the degree and kind of suffering should be regulated in reformable cases by the effect on the individual offender rather than by the effect on other people.

In the classical system the character of the offender was not included among the pertinent facts of the case. Later the judge attempted by a consideration of the appearance of the offender and the testimony regarding him to form a conception of his character and personality. This was very unsatisfactory, because looks are frequently deceiving and because the testimony in court is concerned with the facts of guilt, not of personality or character. More recently the judge is being assisted in his attempts to understand the offender; this development appeared first in the juvenile court and later in many courts for adults. Much of this assistance consists of nothing more than mental and psychiatric tests and is therefore quite inadequate. Similarly in the probation system and in prisons until recent times little effort was made to understand the individual offender or adapt methods to him. The following description of the method used in the New Jersey State Home for Boys in 1921 illustrates the development of a policy of individualization.

First: We make a definite study of each boy when he enters the institution. This study extends over a period of several weeks and is conducted by trained people (psychiatrist, psychologist, director of

---

[15] See J. H. Wigmore (Chairman), "General Introduction to the Modern Criminal Science Series," in R. Saleilles, *The Individualization of Punishment*, Tr. by R. S. Jastrow, Boston, 1911, pp. vi-xii.; V. C. Branham, "The Individualization of the Prisoner: Report of the Committee on Case Work and Treatment for Prisoners," *Proc. Amer. Prison Assoc.*, 1932, pp. 147-186.

education, etc.) . . . During the period of these examinations we secure from the Central Parole Bureau, probation officers and other sources, all the information possible about the ward's earlier history, his home and community relations and other vital facts.

Second: Once a week all of the people concerned with the examinations named in the last paragraph meet with the Superintendent for the purpose of comparing reports and consulting as to the best means of promoting the welfare of the ward while in the institution, —this is called our Classification Meeting.

Third: We make a definite plan for the development and training of the boy. This plan, or parts of it, at least, are discussed with the boy. We try to secure his co-operation with us for his own development, with a definite purpose in his mind and ours of preparing him for a successful parole. Every boy's case is reconsidered by the Classification Committee within three months, and if the case presents unusual factors, it may be reconsidered several times.

Fourth: As time for his parole approaches, each boy's case is taken up for pre-parole investigation. . . . Home investigations are made, employment and friendly counselors are secured; and the family prepared for the return of the boy. Sometimes the Central Parole Bureau has to prepare the neighborhood or move the family to a new locality, in order to further the interests of the boy.[16]

Certain objections have been raised against this policy of individualization. These have been stated most clearly by Parmelee[17] and answered most satisfactorily by Queen.[18] The following discussion follows Queen's argument very closely. The first objection is that individualization, except to a limited degree, is financially impractical. This objection is based on the assumption that individualization means a separate caretaker and a separate room for each offender. This is, of course, incorrect. It is probable that a policy of individualization would have a higher initial cost than a policy of indiscriminate lumping of offenders. But this greater initial cost would be off-set by the reduction in recidivism and the consequent reduction in crime. And in addition the cost of indi-

---

[16] New Jersey, *Report of State Home for Boys*, 1921, pp. 19–20.

[17] M. Parmelee, *Criminology*, New York, 1918, pp. 394–397. Parmelee is not opposed to individualization, but believes it has practical limitations.

[18] S. A. Queen, *The Passing of the County Jail*, Menasha, Wis., 1920, pp. 142–153.

vidualization could be materially reduced by unifying and centralizing the system.

A second objection is that individualization would endanger personal rights. As a matter of fact, this policy has been used in the courts of equity and in the juvenile courts without endangering personal rights. The criminal has no personal right to receive a fixed penalty, regardless of his character and personality. Rather he has a right to receive such assistance, regardless of his crime, as will enable him to adapt himself to the group, if this is possible. Fixed penalties are largely futile in producing this adaptation. Moreover, as has been shown, individualization promotes social welfare and that is the conclusive answer to the objection. It is true, of course, that abuses may be found in the system of individualization, but this is true, also, when penalties are fixed in advance. In its practical operation, the system of individualization has quite as many safeguards against abuses as the system of fixed penalties.

The third objection to individualization is that criminal justice will be discredited in the eyes of the public because of the inequalities of penalties. But the public does not have much confidence in the administration of justice now. Such confidence as does exist is largely a hold-over from the time when courts were supposed to have some connection with divinity. Real confidence must be based on a belief in the scientific efficiency of the courts. It is logically impossible to adjust penalties to crimes; therefore a system based on fixed penalties never can be made scientifically efficient. There is at least a possibility that criminal justice can be made scientifically efficient if it is adjusted to the individual offender, by a policy of individualization; thus this system stands a chance of gaining the confidence of the public. The public has more confidence at present in the juvenile court and the specialized courts in which the nearest approach to individualization may be found than in other types of courts. Moreover, it is not true that the public does demand fixed penalties; at least, the public is inconsistent in its demands, sometimes clamoring for fixed penalties, sometimes for individualization in treatment.

A fourth objection is that criminals would feel that they were treated unjustly; one offender would be placed on probation for burglary, another would be held in prison for life. But the criminals now feel that just such discriminations are made. Since no well-organized method of adapting treatment to character and personality is being used, they have difficulty in appreciating the policy of individualization. The criminals can understand and appreciate such a policy and can be made to see the fallacy of fixed penalties.

Professionally trained persons in the field of treatment of offenders generally emphasize individualization and speak disparagingly of mass methods of reformation. This contrast is unnecessary and unwarranted, and is avoided in practice if not in discussion. It is obvious that treatment policies cannot be applied to a person in a vacuum, and that larger units must be modified if the individual offender is to be reformed. Probably the person and the family are too small units for effective work. Tendencies are apparent, at any rate, to develop neighborhood organization, group work, local co-ordinating councils, the prison community, and other larger units. Queen long ago stated this idea in terms of individualization and socialization,[19] but perhaps the contrast can be stated better in terms of individual and group.

THE TECHNIQUE OF REFORM. In the effort to develop the policies of individualization, some attention has been paid to the theory of reformation and to the specific methods and elements which may be regarded as constituting the technique. Knowledge of the technique of reformation is very scanty. Some of the fundamental principles are fairly certain and the details are being filled in.

1. Reformation can be produced in two general ways: first, by suppressing tendencies toward delinquency either by not furnishing the stimulations that will draw out these tendencies or by furnishing the stimulations that will draw out the opposite tendencies; second, by sublimation of the tendencies, which consists in directing them so that they produce desirable instead of undesirable results.[20] The loyalty of a criminal to his fellows is frequently instrumental in producing crime; that loyalty may be suppressed, leaving the criminal without loyalty to any group, or it may be transferred to a larger group, and thus sublimated. Both methods have values, but sublimation is the more useful because it conserves the tendency.

2. Both processes really consist in the modification of habits. Dewey has made the best statement of the method of modification of habits.

---

[19] Queen, op. cit.
[20] This general statement of methods of reformation is explained in W. I. Thomas and F. Znaniecki, The Polish Peasant, Vol. II, pp. 1863 ff.

To change the "working character" or will of another, we have to alter objective conditions which enter into his habits. Our own schemes of judgment, of assigning blame and praise, of awarding punishment and honor are part of these conditions. . . . We cannot change habit directly: that notion is magic. But we can change it indirectly by modifying conditions, by an intelligent selecting and weighing of the objects which engage attention and which influence the fulfillment of desires.[21]

The offender cannot change these habits *merely* by making up his mind, for unless the situation changes he does not make up his mind in a different way. It is not even necessary for him to feel remorse and repent and resolve to do right. So far as the processes are concerned, there is no essential difference between abandoning crime and backsliding in church. Without prior determination to bring about the change, the behavior is modified by changes in objective conditions. This change is sometimes very rapid, sometimes gradual; the old notion that a modification of habit must be very slow is now known to be incorrect.

3. The offender is generally assisted in reformation by understanding the situation. This understanding includes both the psychological and social mechanisms involved in the conduct and the reasons for the prohibitions. Especially in the mental conflicts which produce some of the extremely difficult problems of delinquency it is valuable for the offender to understand the situation. An understanding of the conflict may get rid of it entirely and as a result the behavior may be altered. Sometimes an understanding of the situation can be secured only if the offender's process of rationalization, by which he justifies and defends himself, is broken down. Consequently one of the important steps in reformation, even in securing an understanding of the situation, is for the offender to tell the truth. It is not necessary in order to accomplish this to destroy the offender's pride or self-approval. Again, an understanding of the situation may involve factors of a kind illustrated in the following case.

A woman was arrested for selling fish in the streets without covering it to keep out flies and dust, thus violating the law. She was fined $2,

---

[21] John Dewey, *Human Nature and Conduct*, pp. 19–20. Reprinted by permission of Henry Holt and Company, publishers.

and because she could not pay, was compelled to spend twenty-four hours in jail. A son, fifteen years of age, wrote an abusive and threatening letter to the judge who tried the case. The letter was turned over to the judge of the juvenile court and the boy was summoned to appear in court. The judge told the boy of the seriousness of the offense of writing such a letter, but explained that he understood the boy's attitude and praised him for it. The boy admitted that the food law should be enforced, showed deep appreciation of the sympathy and understanding of the judge, promised to apologize, and did so.[22]

This boy became a "recruit for law and order" in this way; probably his mother could have been made a "recruit" by the same method.

4. The technique of suppression or sublimation of tendencies consists in the direction of the wishes. The social worker dealing with offenders must learn to appeal to the wishes with as much skill as the salesman uses in appealing to customers, and to produce an effect that will be much more permanent than that produced by the salesman. MacBrayne and Ramsay, for instance, appealed to the desire of criminals for security by arguing that crime did not pay and could not, in the long run, be made to pay.[23] They contend that a criminal is really never reformed until he is convinced that crime does not yield financial returns. This is doubtless an exaggeration both in that many criminals do reform without reaching that conviction, and also in that many professional criminals are convinced that crime does not pay, but continue their crimes, nevertheless. Marriage has frequently proved to be the means of reformation of the woman of damaged reputation, and this is based principally on the security which results.

The wish for new experience must be used, especially in dealing with juvenile delinquents. Many of the delinquencies of children are the result of a search for adventure and excitement. Organized recreation, camping expeditions, Boy Scout activities can be substituted rather easily and with considerable advantage to the community and the individual.[24]

---

[22] F. C. Hoyt, *Quicksands of Youth,* New York, 1921, pp. 35 ff.
[23] L. E. MacBrayne and J. P. Ramsay, *One More Chance, Boston,* 1916, pp. 80, 291–292.
[24] MacBrayne and Ramsay, *op. cit.,* pp. 92–93; D. Lowrie, *My Life in Prison,* New York, 1912, pp. 287–289.

The wish for response from intimate associates is fundamental in reformation. Opinions on this are illustrated by the following statement of a person connected with institutions for delinquents.

The only enduring reformations are those achieved through the influence of a dominant personality upon those who need guidance and strength.[25]

The Home for Jewish Children in Boston makes considerable use of this method by appointing one of the older children as a monitor for each newcomer. The newcomer takes his troubles to this monitor, and the monitor, even when not consulted, tries to direct and protect the newcomer. The method is probably of more value in reforming the monitor than his charge.

The wish for recognition or status must be appealed to and satisfied. An offender has an opinion of his status and of behavior that is fitting under the circumstances. Modification of behavior often consists, therefore, in giving the offender recognition for something else. A judge in New York State sent a criminal who had shown remarkable organizing ability in the field of crime to oversee the reclamation of large tracts of abandoned farm land. The criminal came to think of himself as a useful member of society. He acquired status in the community by this method, and his opinion of the behavior that was fitting no longer included crime. Judge Lindsey said that "praise is the most powerful factor in reforming a boy" and he used this method on every possible occasion in dealing with juvenile delinquents. This is merely another method of gratifying the wish for recognition. The successful performance of a task produces status both in the eyes of the public and of the individual concerned.

In a reformatory, one of the girls had determined to be a "hell-cat." She did everything possible to get demerit marks. But the matron understood the girl because she herself had a similar desire when a girl. She thwarted the girl at every effort by intentionally misinterpreting the act so that it resulted in merit marks rather than demerit marks. In spite of herself the girl was given the status of a "good girl," and came to think herself as such.[26]

---

[25] Katherine B. Davis, quoted in *Survey*, 46:48, April 9, 1921 ; see, also Hobhouse and Brockway, *op. cit.*, p. 514, note; James Devon, *The Criminal and the Community*, London, 1912, p. 307.

[26] Beatrice P. Hunzicker, "The Hell-cat," *Survey*, 49:628, February 15, 1923.

The professional criminal who has developed a pride in his technique is difficult to reform; he has an almost irresistible desire to use his technique, just as does a skilled craftsman, a skilled hunter, or golf player. If the offender can be taken early in life every attitude apparently can be directed into socially desirable channels.

5. The offender needs to develop a different conception of himself, and he may do this by the methods previously described and also by other methods. The following statement by Jack Black illustrates the manner in which an influence of this nature was introduced into his experience.

For the past fifteen years I have been feeding and clothing myself instead of letting the taxpayers do it, because, at the time of my life when I least deserved it, I met trust and judicial leniency, which gave me hope. The judge who sentenced me to a year when he might have locked me up for life and thrown the key away, took a greater chance on me than I ever took on anything. He stopped my stealing as effectively as a hangman's rope. He gave me my life and I couldn't doublecross him any more than I could doublecross the friend who once cut the bars in a jail window and gave me my liberty. Loyalty is the only virtue of the underworld, and the judge appealed to that. He put me in a hole where I had to stop stealing and fall into the lock-step of society. Such reformation as I have achieved in life is due, initially, to the act of the judge who said, when he sentenced me to a year instead of to life, "I believe you have sufficient character to build a new life. I will give you that chance." The records are full of the cases of men, notorious for their violence, who reformed when their loyalty was challenged.[27]

6. The policy should be adjusted to the attitudes of the offender and should change, therefore, as these attitudes change. It may well happen that one policy should be used one month and the opposite policy the next month. The method should be constantly controlled with reference to this adaptation to the offender as he is at that particular time.

7. Material services are of value in changing the attitudes of offenders and in assisting offenders to secure conditions of life which are conducive to reformation. This procedure is quite in con-

[27] Jack Black, "What's Wrong with the Right People?" *Harpers*, 159:77, June, 1929. Reprinted by permission.

flict with the old penology which attempted to compel submission and to secure co-operation by doing injury to the offender. The old penology was based on the conception that the offender had done an injury to the state and the state should react by doing an injury to the criminal. Naturally the criminal may react by doing a new injury to the state, and thus the process continues. The new method of rendering material services is based on the conception that the desperado complex can be prevented or can be destroyed by rendering a service to the offender on the expectation that this will call out a tendency to render a service in return. No one knows the conditions under which a blow produces submission rather than more conflict, or a service produces another service rather than renewed conflict. Both processes are well known and both are quantitatively important. Unquestionably the rendering of material services has a place in the method of reformation.

8. The court officials, probation officers, prison officers, or other official guardians or assistants need not do all the work of reformation. They cannot do all the thinking or lay out the program in an arbitrary way. To some extent, to be sure, they can modify objective conditions without bringing the offender into the conference at all, but the undertaking must be essentially co-operative. The offender must subsequently participate in overcoming his difficulties, and it is preferable that he should be given as large a share of the control in the present crisis as possible.

9. It may be taken as a matter of course that the whole policy of reformation should be based on a physical examination and the correction of physical defects whenever possible. While there is no evidence that this will go far in producing reformation in most cases, it is important in a few cases and is socially desirable in all cases, even if it is not connected with reformation. It is still more important to make a complete examination from the standpoint of psychopathology, and to make such corrections for defects or pathological conditions as are possible.

PROFESSIONAL SERVICES. The courts and the correctional institutions are adding professionally-trained persons to the staff to assist in the diagnosis and treatment of offenders. This work is recent in origin and the professional training for the work is nowhere adequate.

The social worker has acquired in a training school a theory of interviewing and experience in interviewing. No other branch of professional training gives any skill whatever in this respect. Moreover, the social worker has acquired a theory regarding the collection, verification, and application of social data. The social worker customarily makes the greatest contribution of any of the professionally trained persons when cases are discussed in conferences. But the social worker is seldom trained specifically in the field of crime and delinquency, and has no specific knowledge of the processes which lead to delinquency. Furthermore, the social worker is generally individualistic in his approach and is lacking in a group point of view.

The psychologist is generally trained to give tests in a clinic, including mental tests and personality tests. Almost anyone can be trained in a very short time to give these tests in a routine manner. The contribution of the psychologist, in comparison with others who may acquire the ability to give these tests in a routine manner, is found in the background of knowledge regarding psychology, by reason of which he can make interpretations of test results and of incidents which occur during the testing process. The psychologist, like the social worker, generally has had no acquaintance with the field of criminology prior to employment in correctional work.

The psychiatrist has generally been trained in a medical school; during most of his training he has been compelled to confine his efforts to the study of the organism and has given relatively little attention to behavior problems. In so far as he gets specialized courses in behavior problems, he becomes acquainted with the major psychoses. He has practically no opportunity to become acquainted with the body of knowledge in criminology or with criminals in person. Psychiatrists have shown a tendency, which apparently is on the wane, to interpret all crime as due to psychopathology. Some psychiatrists have maintained that they are the experts in this field, and insist that the results of interviews and examinations by the other members of the professional group be referred to them for interpretation. There is no logical or practical justification for this. Also, some have claimed that they are the experts in the treatment of offenders. The inadequacy of expert methods of treatment is illustrated by Dr. Cabot in a review of a book on *The Healthy Mind*, which is a symposium by psychiatrists. The therapeutic prescriptions presented in the book are as follows:

Dr. Thom: We need a little more effort and encouragement and a different attitude on the part of teachers, parents and others.

Dr. Walsh: Contemplate beauty in nature and art. Have religion.

Dr. Bowman: Face problems of daily life frankly. Don't evade them. Keep interested and occupied in worthwhile activities, so that one has no time to devote to worry or unpleasant emotions.

Dr. Moore: When you've done wrong take the blame and avoid praiseworthy excuses. Work hard, criticize yourself honestly and make personal sacrifices.

Dr. Myerson: Avoid fatigue, linger in the fields, pick flowers, talk to the farmers. Don't build your purposes too far beyond your abilities. Don't be finicky.

Dr. Anderson: Form habits that insure satisfaction and pleasure in the effective performance of your job.

Dr. Richards: Get a job that is not beyond your intelligence quotient. Live in a harmonious family.

Dr. Jastrow: Relax, control your muscles. Avoid anger, fear, and internal conflicts.[28]

These techniques are common to all investigators who have a scientific approach, whether they be social workers, sociologists, psychologists, educational directors, occupational directors, recreational directors, or others; and the psychiatrist, like these others, has very little in the way of verified therapeutic policies.

The sociologist is the only member of the professional group who ordinarily has an academic training in criminology and penology, for academic work in this field is confined almost entirely to departments of sociology. On the other hand, he has had no training in clinical methods; he has been concerned with research work and general interpretations of crime rather than with the diagnosis and treatment of the individual offender. At the same time he has a background knowledge of society, of groups, and of culture which is indispensable for an understanding of individual offenders.[29]

Experience in clinics indicates that almost anyone can secure the case histories and give the tests in a large proportion of the cases, and that disagreements occur principally in the interpreta-

---

[28] Richard C. Cabot, Review of H. B. Elkind (Editor), "The Healthy Mind," *Survey*, 63:596, February 15, 1930. Reprinted by permission.

[29] Saul D. Alinsky, "A Sociological Technique in Clinical Criminology," *Proc. Amer. Prison Assoc.*, 1934, pp. 167–178.

tions of certain types of cases. Consequently every clinic should have at least the four types of professionally trained persons to participate in diagnoses and in treatment programs.[30]

MEASURES OF SOCIAL SECURITY. Since a large number of offenders are not reformed by the methods which are used, and some of them are regarded as quite unreformable by any methods available, various suggestions have been made regarding the protection of society against further crimes by such persons. In the European countries these suggestions have been formulated under the name "measures of social security." These have been directed either at persons who have long records of crimes, regardless of mental characteristics, or else at persons who are diagnosed as lacking in responsibility. Within one year 846 persons were received twice in the penitentiary of New York City, 173 three times, 40 four times, 7 five times, 2 six times, and 1 seven times. Out of 190,257 cases in the Allegheny Workhouses, 498 had been sentenced fifty times or more. Most of these workhouse cases involve drunkenness, vagrancy, and disorderly conduct, but these offenses are frequently committed by persons who at other times commit more serious offenses. The following is an illustration of a persistent criminal. Before the age of fourteen he had been on probation twice and had been detained in reformatories for two years and three months. During the twenty-four years between the ages of fourteen and thirty-eight he had records of arrests in nine cities located in five states on twenty-one charges. He served during this time twenty-two years and nine months in penal and reformatory institutions. He was sent to juvenile reformatories twice, to a state reformatory once, to state prisons of two states, and to workhouses ten times. By transfers he was received in two state hospitals for the criminal insane. Among his convictions were two for assault and battery, and three for carrying concealed weapons. Finally, at the age of thirty-eight, he was committed on a life sentence to a state prison for murder.

When the measures for social defense are restricted to offenders who are lacking in responsibility, such as the feebleminded, psychotic, and psychopathic, they are generally interpreted as nonpunitive; the procedure is not intended as punishment for the

---

[30] For a general discussion of clinical methods and point of view see Carl R. Rogers, *The Clinical Treatment of the Problem Child*, Boston, 1939; C. M. Louttit, *Clinical Psychology*, New York, 1936.

offender but entirely as a means of protecting society against dangerous persons. Consequently provision is sometimes made for the detention of persons of these types even when they have no criminal record. The institutions for defective delinquents in the United States are essentially the same as the measures for social security in several of the European countries. On the other hand, when these measures are based merely on the criminal record they are generally regarded as punitive. The multiple-offender laws, for instance, generally include an increased penalty for a second felony, a still longer penalty for a third felony, and in some states mandatory life imprisonment for a fourth felony. The preventive detention prison in England is somewhat similar to the multiple offender laws of the United States.

UNITY AND ORGANIZATION. The conventional system of police, courts, prisons, probation, and parole is distinctly lacking in unity. The need of unity is apparent, first, because of the difficulty of securing expert services in the large number of agencies in rural districts, each of which deals with a small number of offenders. It is impossible to conceive of a method by which adequate investigations, understanding and control can be developed as long as these local judicial and penal institutions are entirely separate from each other and from the state institutions. The only apparent solution of the difficulty is to abolish the outworn distinction between misdemeanors and felonies and deal with all offenders in one set of courts and one set of penal or reformatory institutions, all of which should be under the control of the state rather than of the local community. The demands for such unification of the courts are numerous and some progress in that direction has already been made. The demand for unification of the penal institutions may be illustrated by the fact that in 1921 the Republican party in Massachusetts included in its platform a project for the state control of all penal institutions. Governor Cox in his inaugural address in 1922 demanded state control of the entire system. Though the counties won in that election, the trend toward centralization is apparent in many states.

A second evidence of the need of unity is furnished by the fact that policies at present are not consistent. Each court makes decisions based on its own preconceptions and impressions; each probation department differs in its policies from other probation departments and from courts; each prison differs from other prisons and from probation departments and courts. An offender is dealt with by one court in a particular manner, while another offender with similar traits is dealt with very differently by another court. The same offender is dealt with successively with no consistent plan. Koren found by a study of recidivists in Boston that for 89 per cent the last sentence was not so severe, usually not by one-half, as the maximum penalty previously imposed on the same person for the same offense.[31] This inconsistency can be eliminated only by some agency that will secure a scientific comprehension of the characteristics of offenders, and on the basis of this comprehension control the policies of all courts, all probation departments, all prisons, all parole boards within the state.

RECORDS. Little specific and detailed information is now accessible regarding the methods of producing reformation. Accurate and complete records are the only means of securing such information. The conventional policy of penal and reformatory institutions is to give publicity to the successes and conceal the failures; the policy of the newspapers is to conceal the successes and give publicity to the failures. The public institutions are less effective in this than the newspapers, for the newspapers present their evidence dramatically, as personal cases of failures, while the institutions must conceal the identity of their successful clients and give the public practically nothing except impersonal and colorless statistical information. The assumption of both is that those who are not reformed are incorrigible. In truth, all that can be said is that the methods used did not reform those who were not reformed. It is evident from many statements of those intimately acquainted with even the worst criminals that they have many good qualities[32] and probably most of them can be made safe for society by proper methods.

The records must show those who do not reform as well as those who do. While medical journals are quite frank in the acknowledgment of failures, few penal or reformatory institutions are as honest. This is due, perhaps, to the necessity of defending themselves against the attacks of political opponents in part, but also to the desire for recognition. From the scientific point of view, as much knowledge

---

[31] John Koren, "Some Statistics of Recidivism among Misdemeanants in Boston," *Proc. Amer. Stat. Assoc.*, 7:15, June, 1901.

[32] Jean Weidensall, *The Mentality of the Criminal Woman*, p. 285; H. J. B. Montgomery, "An Ex-Prisoner on Professional Criminals," *Nineteenth Cent.*, 55:282, February, 1904; F. Boyd, "Some Factors in Prison Reform," *Delinquent*, 7:9, February, 1917.

can be secured by a consideration of what policies do not work or of the circumstances in which a certain policy does not work, as of the ones that do work.

An essential part of the plan to measure the success of policies is the fingerprint system. If all police departments and courts would co-operate with the federal bureau of identification by sending fingerprints of arrested or convicted offenders, the general value of policies such as probation, parole, fines, imprisonment, and particular policies within prison could be determined; also the types of offenders for whom a policy that was, in general, good would not work successfully. By this method the state would be enabled to pursue a consistent policy in the treatment of offenders and to measure the results of the policy.

SUGGESTED READINGS

Bingham, Anne T., "Clearing Houses as Aids to Court Work, Probation and Parole," *New York City Conf. Char. and Corr.*, 1917, pp. 174–184.

Branham, V. C., "The Individualization of the Prisoner: Report of the Committee on Case Work and Treatment for Prisoners," *Proc. Amer. Prison Assoc.*, 1932, pp. 147–186.

Brockway, Z. R., *Fifty Years of Prison Service*, New York, 1912, Ch. 19.

Charlton, T. J., "What Are the Proper Incentives to Reform?" *Proc. Conf. Char. and Corr.*, 1898, pp. 379–384.

Colcord, J. C., *Broken Homes: A Study of Family Desertion and Its Social Treatment*, New York, 1919.

Davis, Katherine B., "Some Institutional Problems in Dealing with Psychopathic Delinquents," *Jour. Crim. Law and Criminol.*, 10:385–408, November, 1919.

Dewey, John, *Human Nature and Conduct*, New York, 1922.

Drucker, S., and Hexter, M. B., *Children Astray*, Cambridge, 1923.

Fernald, G. G., "Character Study in Criminology," *Jour. Crim. Law and Criminol.*, 1:107–112, May, 1912.

Fernald, G. G., "Current Misconceptions Regarding Reformation," *Mental Hygiene*, 3:646–649, October, 1919.

Fernald, G. G., "The Psychopathic Laboratories in Criminology," *Jour. Crim. Law and Criminol.*, 9:413–419, November, 1918.

Fernald, Mabel R., "Practical Applications of Psychology to the Problems of a Clearing House," *Jour. Crim. Law and Criminol.*, 7:722–731, January, 1917.

Fernald, Mabel R., "The Work of the Laboratory of Social Hygiene at Bedford Hills," *Proc. Amer. Prison Assoc.*, 1916, pp. 287–292.

Fetter, F. A., "State Supervision and Administration," *Proc. Natl. Conf. Char. and Corr.*, 1909, pp. 397–413.

Glueck, B., "Clearing Houses and Classification of Institutions as Aids to Institutional Work," *New York City Conf. Char. and Corr.*, 1917, pp. 158–166.

Glueck, Sheldon (Editor), *Probation and Criminal Justice*, New York, 1932.

Healy, William, "Study of the Case Preliminary to Treatment," *Jour. Crim. Law and Criminol.*, 13:74–81, May, 1922.

Healy, William, Bronner, Augusta F., and Bowers, Anna Mae, *The Structure and Meaning of Psychoanalysis as Related to Personality and Behavior*, New York, 1930.

Louttit, C. M., *Clinical Psychology*, New York, 1936.

Otto, M. G., "The Moral Education of Youth," *Inter. Jour. Ethics*, 32:52–67, October, 1921.

Peabody, R. R., "Psychotherapeutic Procedure in the Treatment of Chronic Alcoholism," *Mental Hygiene*, 14:109–128, January, 1930.

Rogers, Carl R., *The Clinical Treatment of the Problem Child*, Boston, 1939.

Saleilles, R., *The Individualization of Punishment*, Tr. by R. S. Jastrow, Boston, 1911.

Stanger, Francis A., "The Importance of Classification as a Guide to the Sentencing Judge," *Proc. Amer. Prison Assoc.*, 1933, pp. 35–44.

Taft, Jessie, *The Dynamics of Therapy in a Controlled Relationship*, New York, 1933.

Thomas, W. I., and Znaniecki, F., *The Polish Peasant*, New York, 1927.

Wannamaker, Claudia, "Methods of Recreational Adjustment as a Form of Social Case Treatment," *Mental Hygiene*, 7:744–754, October, 1923.

Chapter Twenty – Nine

PREVENTION OF CRIME

THE PROBLEM OF PREVENTION. Two methods of reducing the frequency of crimes have been suggested and tried. One is the method of treatment, the other is the method of prevention. The conventional policy has been to punish those who are convicted of crimes, on the hypothesis that this both reforms those who are punished and deters others from crimes in the future. Also, according to this hypothesis, crime rates can be reduced by increasing the severity, certainty, and speed of punishment. Commissions appointed to make suggestions for a reduction of crime rates generally confine their recommendations to measures designed to increase severity, certainty, and speed of punishment. These measures have generally been somewhat effective during short periods of emotional crime drives, but seldom produce permanent effects.

Methods of reformation have been suggested and tried, also. These have been in the form of probation, educational work in prisons, and parole supervision. These methods, like the methods of punishment, have not been notably successful in reducing crime rates. They have failed most frequently in reforming offenders who have been reared in the situations where crime flourishes most. They are less effective in reforming city criminals than rural criminals, less effective in reforming criminals who have lived in deteriorated areas than those who have lived in good residential areas, and less effective in reforming those reared in demoralized families than those reared in integrated families. Thus these agencies have been least effective in dealing with the offenders who come from the crime-breeding situations, from which a considerable proportion of all the criminals who are dealt with by official methods do come.

The policy of permanent segregation of offenders who are least reformable has been suggested and tried, especially in the form of habitual criminal laws. But the courts have generally been unwilling to enforce these laws, and the offenders who have been caught by the laws are in many cases the relatively unskilled amateur criminals, while the skilled professional criminals have escaped.

Moreover, a very small proportion of those who commit crimes receive official treatment for those crimes. Perhaps 10 per cent of the serious crimes result in arrests, and certainly a much smaller percentage result in official treatment. This is especially true of fraud, bribery, and similar crimes which flourish in the business world and the political world, and which almost never result in arrest, although they do great injury to property and to institutions in modern society.

For these reasons it is highly desirable that the policy of prevention should be emphasized much more than it has been heretofore. Most criminals in their earlier stages are probably much like the person who is dishonest in reporting his personal property to the assessor. This man would be willing to make an honest report if others made honest reports. Each individual is driven to dishonesty by the fact that dishonesty is prevalent. In that sense most criminals probably do not need to be reformed, at least in their earlier stages of criminality. This is especially true of the persons who practice fraud and bribery.

Prevention is a logical policy to use in dealing with crime. Punishment and other methods of treatment are, at best, methods of defense. It is futile to take individual after individual out of the situations which produce criminals and permit the situations to remain as they were. A case of delinquency is more than a physiological act of an individual. It involves a whole network of social relations. If we deal with his set of social relations we shall be working to prevent crime. It has become a commonplace in medicine that prevention is better than cure. The same superiority exists in the field of crime.

The superiority of prevention may be illustrated in the problem of school discipline. Two generations ago corporal punishment was used with great frequency in the schools and disorder was generally prevalent in spite of the punishment. Orderly behavior did not develop by increasing the severity and frequency of punishment. Rather the improvement in the behavior of school children came as the result of improvement in the teachers and the curricula, and in the gradual development of a tradition of orderly behavior, together with liberality in the criteria of good behavior. The school system was adjusted to the needs of the children much better than it had been previously. It is probable that analogous changes must be made in the social organization before great reductions can be made in crime rates.

GENERAL PROGRAMS OF PREVENTION. Many general programs of crime prevention have been outlined. Bentham in the last part of the eighteenth century made a comprehensive outline of the "indirect methods" (that is, methods other than punishment) which might be used to prevent crime. He included such things as taking away the physical power of injury, diverting the course of dangerous desires, decreasing susceptibility to temptations, general education, a code of morals similar to a code of laws, and other things. He maintained that if his system were inaugurated, the result would be as follows:

> By good laws all crimes may be reduced to acts which may be repaired by a simple pecuniary compensation; . . . when this is the case, the evil arising from crimes may be made almost entirely to cease.[1]

Ferri, a member of the Italian school, in the last part of the nineteenth century paid considerable attention to the prevention of crime. He had a doctrine of criminal saturation, namely, that a group has the crimes it deserves in view of the type of people and the conditions of the group, and that as long as the type of people and the conditions remain constant, crime will remain constant regardless of methods of punishment. Consequently he insisted that penal substitutes, or methods of modifying the conditions and traits of people, should be used. He outlined a long list of these, including free trade, reduction in consumption of alcohol, metal (instead of paper) money, street lights, reduction in hours of labor, lower interest on public securities, local political autonomy, and many other things.[2]

Other elaborate programs for the prevention of crime have been developed and these programs have included practically every reform that has been suggested by anyone. The programs tend to be

---

[1] Jeremy Bentham, *Principles of Penal Law*, Part 3, pp. 533–580.
[2] E. Ferri, *Criminal Sociology*, Tr. by J. I. Kelly and John Lisle, Boston, 1917, pp. 209–287.

somewhat utopian, principally because the knowledge of the causation of crime has not been sufficiently precise to isolate the conditions and traits which need attention in programs of prevention. Almost everything in the universe is found to be associated in some direct or indirect manner with criminality. These multiple factors have not been reduced to a clear-cut system, with immediate and remote relationships designated. No universals have been discovered; until they are discovered, programs of prevention as well as programs of punishment and other methods of treatment operate on the principle of trial and error. No one can show in advance that crime will be reduced if the whole program of prevention is adopted. If reliable information on which to base programs of prevention could be secured and disseminated, the public would soon become sufficiently educated to insist that they be put into practice.

In the meantime, some situations are clearly undesirable, and could be changed to advantage. For instance, in three generations of a criminal family, all of the children who were removed from the home before the age of six turned out satisfactorily, while all of the other children had long criminal records.[3] Other changes involve much more fundamental modifications, and vested interests and unwillingness to pay taxes stand in the way of these modifications. The elimination of the demoralizing features of motion picture shows, theaters, and other commercial recreations, and of newspapers, the improvement in conditions of labor, improvement in housing, restriction of sale of small arms, restrictions on sale of intoxicating drinks, and similar policies are immediately opposed by those who would suffer financial losses by the modifications. During 1933, when efforts were made to use federal funds for the demolition of houses in certain slum areas and for rebuilding decent houses, vociferous opposition was expressed by real estate dealers who had homes to rent. The effort to restrict the sale of small arms, which are a necessary and usual part of the equipment of the professional criminals, has been strenuously resisted by the manufacturers of arms. Almost every other suggested modification designed to reduce crime injures someone who therefore tries to maintain the *status quo*.

Taxes would be increased by many of the crime prevention policies, such as vocational education, vocational guidance, organ-

---

[3] S. Dahlstrom, "Is the Young Criminal a Continuation of the Neglected Child?" *Jour. Delinq.*, 12:97–121, June, 1928.

ized public recreation, child guidance clinics, and visiting teachers. The general public is opposed to crime, to be sure, but it is opposed, also, to high taxes and apparently would prefer to make emotional gestures in regard to crime rather than pay taxes to get rid of crime.

The policies suggested for the prevention of crime in general are closely related to the theories of causation of crime. Those who believe that crime is due to innate defects advocate a policy of sterilization. Those who believe that it is due to acquired personal defects believe in the development of agencies for education, and of reorganization of many of the social institutions affecting these particular individuals; they are likely to place the emphasis especially on the family. Those who believe that delinquency is due largely to the immediate neighborhood situation have been interested in developing community organization. Those who believe that it is due to the more general and more public standards and relationships believe that a more general social reorganization is needed.

The principal policies advocated at present for the prevention of delinquency may be classified as follows: (a) sterilization of the unfit, on the assumption that the unfit will produce future delinquents; (b) case work with delinquents or near-delinquents who are not at the time under the jurisdiction of the agencies of justice; (c) group work with delinquents or near-delinquents who are not at the time under the jurisdiction of the agencies of justice; (d) community organization in areas of high delinquency rates; (e) adaptation of general social institutions to the needs of constituents; and (f) general social re-organization. These policies may be re-classified into three groups: sterilization, reforming individuals or groups who are already delinquent, and re-forming groups and institutions.

The statement is sometimes made that preventive work must be individualized, directed specifically at persons or conditions, and that all proposed mass methods of prevention can be disregarded. This is a fallacious differentiation, as will be shown in the discussion of some of the programs, and it is obvious that institutional and community modifications should be regarded as extremely important methods of prevention.

STERILIZATION OF UNDESIRABLE TYPES. One policy of prevention that is being urged at present is the sterilization of certain types of people, either on the ground that criminality is inherited, or that certain traits are inherited which predispose to criminality and to many other kinds of maladjustments. It is believed that by preventing the reproduction of these types crimes will be reduced in subsequent generations, even if not at present. Sterilization laws have been passed in twenty-eight states, and 16,066 persons sterilized under these laws up to January 1, 1933. About one-third of these were sterilized in the years 1930–1932. More than half of the operations were performed on persons in California.

This policy of sterilization may be desirable on general grounds, but there is no clear-cut evidence that it will affect crime rates. Criminality as such cannot be inherited. If any trait is inherited which inevitably predisposes to crime, we do not know what it is. Even in the case of the feebleminded and insane, it is not clear that the abnormalities are inherited, in the strict sense of the word. In addition, it is not clear that people with such abnormalities have an appreciably higher crime rate than other people. Consequently it is not demonstrated that the universal application of sterilization laws to the feebleminded and insane would result in appreciable reduction in crime rates, although these laws might have other advantages.[4]

The transportation of criminals from England to Australia during a period of three-quarters of a century did not seem to affect materially the frequency of crimes in England, or, after the initial period, in Australia. If England did not change the character of her population or that of Australia by this method, there is little reason to believe that a policy of sterilization of criminals would affect materially the criminality of future generations. The experiment, to be sure, is not entirely adequate, for the comparative crime rates of the two countries cannot be measured precisely, and even if Australia were found to have higher rates, this might be explained by the precedents and customs established by the transported convicts or by the lack of established customs due to the newness of the country.

CASE WORK WITH NEAR-DELINQUENTS. Certain children have been called potential delinquents or predelinquents. These terms, from the etymological point of view, are misleading, for every child is a potential delinquent, every child in earlier years is a predelinquent, and every able-bodied person who has passed the earlier years of childhood commits delinquencies more or less frequently.

---

[4] For a review of the sterilization movement in general, see J. H. Landman, *Human Sterilization,* New York, 1932.

The term is used, however, to refer to the children who are believed to be extraordinarily likely to become confirmed delinquents. These predelinquents have not been definitely identified, but are believed by certain psychiatrists to be the children who manifest emotional problems such as enuresis, temper tantrums, sullenness, timidity, and in later years difficulties in school and with companions. It is believed that if these problems can be corrected in early childhood by appropriate procedures, the child will develop into a more wholesome and less delinquent adult.

Two principal agencies have developed in the attempt to turn these near-delinquents away from their trend toward delinquency, namely, child guidance clinics and visiting teachers. The Commonwealth Fund started child guidance clinics in several cities, as demonstrations of what might be accomplished.[5] These clinics were maintained in many communities after support was withdrawn from outside, and many others have been started. Some of the clinics have been operated by the public schools, some by public welfare departments, some by private welfare agencies, some by state hospitals, and some by independent agencies organized for this purpose. Problem children are referred to the clinic by parents who are anxious about their children, by kindergartens and schools, by welfare societies and by other agencies and persons. Some of them are referred because they have been delinquent, some because they have deviations in their personal characteristics, and some because of disturbing behavior which is not in violation of the law, such as temper tantrums, enuresis, or bashfulness. These children are sometimes divided into behavior problems and personality problems.

These clinics have had undoubted value in some cases. A study was made of changes in behavior of groups in the schools of Berkeley, California, over a two-year period, with a comparison of three groups matched for sex and age. The behavior scores of 68 problem children treated in the school clinic decreased from 247 to 185, while the scores of problem children not treated decreased only from 213 to 205, and the scores of non-problem children increased from 81 to 107.[6] The studies in child guidance clinics

---

[5] On the child guidance clinic in general, see George S. Stevenson and Geddes Smith, *Child Guidance Clinics*, New York, 1934.

[6] Else H. Martens and Helen Rudd, "Adjustment of Behavior Problems of School Children," *U. S. Dept. of Interior, Office of Education*, Bull. No. 18, 1932.

in general indicate that from a fourth to a third continue to be problems, and that approximately a third manifest no further difficulties. One of the situations in which modification of the behavior is most difficult is the family in which the parent-child relations are unsatisfactory; almost no improvement in the child results from treatment in that situation, and also almost no modification of the parents results.

In general, the child guidance clinic seems to be only slightly more successful in dealing with its problems than do the institutions for delinquents and criminals. Doubtless this failure is due to the fact that the problem is not confined to the organism of the child, but involves wider social relationships in the family, the neighborhood, the institutions, and the general culture.

Somewhat related to the child guidance clinic is the visiting teacher movement. The visiting teacher, who is the extension agent of the school in problem cases, first appeared in New York, Boston, and Hartford, about 1906, as the result of pressure from persons outside of the school system. In 1923 fifty cities in twenty-six states had a total of about 140 visiting teachers, and the Commonwealth Fund enlarged that number for purposes of demonstration. In 1937 200 visiting teachers in 22 states were members of their national association. The justification of the visiting teacher is that about 88 per cent of the time of the child during the first eight years of school is spent outside of the school building. An educational system that is concerned with only 12 per cent of the time of the child will be relatively ineffective in preparing the child for life.

The visiting teacher receives reports from the regular school teacher regarding attendance, scholarship, misbehavior in school, and other difficulties. On the basis of these reports the visiting teacher makes an investigation of the home and neighborhood situation, with the purpose of tracing the difficulty to its source. The following case is an illustration of one type of work done by such agents.

---

[7] Helen M. Witmer and students, "The Outcome of Treatment in a Child Guidance Clinic," *Smith Coll. Studies in Social Work*, 3:341–399, June, 1933; Helen M. Witmer and students, "The Later Social Adjustments of Problem Children: A Report of Thirteen Follow-up Investigations," *Smith Coll. Studies in Social Work*, 6:3–98, September, 1935; Pearl Lodgen, "Some Criteria for the Treatability of Mothers and Children in a Child Guidance Clinic," *Smith Coll. Studies in Social Work*, 7:302–324, June, 1937; William Healy and A. F. Bronner, *New Light on Delinquency and Its Treatment*, New Haven, 1936, p. 156.

In a congested part of the city, Lucy, aged eleven, was losing her interest in lessons and coming late to the afternoon sessions, offering as excuse that "mother was sick," but her classmates whispered that she was talking to boys on the street. The visiting teacher went to the home, and learned from the bed-ridden mother that Lucy had changed since coming under the influence of a playmate and neighbor, Elsie. Lucy's father was insane, and her brother, an invalid home from the war. Lucy escaped at three P.M. from this dreary home atmosphere to go, no one knew where, till she was sought and brought home at eleven P.M. The visiting teacher saw the necessity of getting acquainted with Elsie, and went to her school. Elsie had an unenviable record for repeating grades, half-day absences and poor conduct. The visiting teacher took this record to her home and questioned the parents. They were aware that Elsie had been left back and that there were days when she had not been at home as well as absent from school. But they had been unable to find out where she spent her time. The visiting teacher was not content with her explanation that she went "no place" and finally, by careful probing, based on a study of the record card, showing at what date the child began to go wrong, got the information she was seeking. . . . Within a few hours they had put under arrest a man who had been teaching immoral practices to Elsie and a score of her friends. The man was convicted and sent to jail. The visiting teacher took the children under her care and looked out for their recreation and companionship as well as for their lessons. Lucy became at once, when the friendship with Elsie was broken, a better student at school. Her mother lived to see her become again her faithful nurse and housekeeper. Elsie, because her habits of delinquency were stronger, needed careful supervision at school and at home, but the home co-operation was secured, . . . her interest in school was aroused so that she is now making normal progress. Her character is slowly developing, good points long dormant showing in her changed attitude.[8]

The visiting teachers can make the investigations and can deal with some of the difficulties, but just as probation officers, they must depend for much of the constructive work on the other community institutions. Unquestionably every school system should have a force of visiting teachers sufficient to deal adequately with the difficulties

---

[8] "National Association of Visiting Teachers," *The Visiting Teacher in the United States,* pp. 44-45.

that the school children present. It is doubtful, however, whether they will be very successful in dealing with the children who reside in deteriorated areas and in demoralized homes.

In several cities special schools have been established for the problem children. In these schools the methods are adapted to the interests and abilities of the children much more than in the other schools. These schools have shown a high degree of success in dealing with problem children, as compared with the regular schools, but, like all other agencies, they fail in proportion to the delinquency rates in the areas in which children live.

The psychoanalysts, also, have attempted to extend their theories and procedures to school teachers. They believe that many of the maladjustments of adults begin in early childhood and that these problems can be recognized and solved to some extent by the teachers.

GROUP WORK WITH NEAR-DELINQUENTS. One of the significant developments in social work during the last decade is group work. This development is to some extent based on the desirability of extending case work beyond the person and his family to groups of approximately the same age as the delinquent with whom they are dealing. Group work with delinquents may be regarded as falling into two types. First, an individual delinquent is induced to become a member of a group which is judged to be generally wholesome, as a means of satisfying his needs as a person. While in this group, the person is given particular attention to aid him in adjusting to that group and to overcome tendencies which seem to be conducive to delinquency. This type of group work is individualistic, being concentrated on problems of particular individuals; it is based on the same general philosophy and theory as individual case work.[9]

A second type of group work consists in re-directing the activities of a group of persons, all or nearly all of whom are delinquent. One of the interesting applications of this procedure was made by Keltner in St. Louis under the sponsorship of the Y. M. C. A. In one of the very deteriorated sections of St. Louis, which had been the headquarters of a notorious adult gang, Keltner attempted to re-direct the boys' gangs so that they would be assets to the community. After a period of fifteen years forty of these gangs, now

[9] S. R. Slavson, *Creative Group Education*, New York, 1937.

turned into boys' clubs, are carrying on their activities in this section, with an average membership of about 25 members. They
provide recreation, and educational activities. Keltner claims that
the members have seldom been in difficulties with the police, that
the older members are assisting in developing similar groups for
their younger brothers, and that the business men of the district
are wholeheartedly co-operating with the movement.[10]

Somewhat similar policies have been used in many other places,
with varying degrees of success. The essential characteristics of
this policy, as differentiated from other policies, is that some person
attempts to enter into friendly participation with a gang which is
actually delinquent, at least in minor ways, and turn them into
a law-abiding group, not as separate individuals, but as a group.

THE BOYS' CLUB. The boys' club cannot be completely differentiated from group work with near-delinquents. It differs principally
in the fact that its facilities are offered to all boys in a given area,
of whom some may be delinquent and others not at all inclined
toward delinquency. In actual operation, group work with near-
delinquents is likely to be quite indistinguishable from boys'
club work.

One of the theories of the origin of delinquency is that it is an
expression of a desire for excitement and adventure, and is merely
one of the recreational activities of boys. Stealing by boys in the
deteriorated areas frequently has no economic motive but is a form
of play. Consequently in some communities efforts have been made
to provide facilities for recreation which might compete with delinquency for the satisfaction of this desire. Many small parks and
playgrounds were established in Chicago early in the present century and for a short time seemed to have definite success in reducing
delinquency. Before long the politicians secured control, the park
funds were looted by grafters, and the positions were filled by ward
heelers. In some cases these play places became sources of infection
for delinquency and in general they have not realized the expectations, though delinquencies would probably be more frequent than
at present if such facilities were not available.

In several deteriorated districts in Chicago efforts have been made
to enlist a large proportion of the boys in organized athletics. Base-

---

[10] Harold S. Keltner, "Crime Prevention Program of the Y. M. C. A.,
St. Louis," in Sheldon and Eleanor Glueck (editors), *Preventing Crime*, New
York, 1936, Ch. 24.

ball and football leagues are formed, facilities provided, public playgrounds and vacant lots utilized, and medals awarded. These are regarded as useful, not merely because they occupy the leisure time of the boys, but also because they are a common interest which may unite the neighborhood and be a part of an integrated neighborhood activity.

Boys' clubs have been established by social settlements, churches, and other organizations as a means of occupying the leisure time of the boys. Some of these clubs have reading rooms, swimming pools, vocational work, and many games. Claims have been made that delinquency rates have been greatly reduced in the neighborhood by these clubs.[11] Healy makes the following statement regarding the South End of Boston.

This is a district in which there has been no marked change of population and in which police attitudes toward delinquency have not altered. In this district three main settlement houses have built up a preventive program, school people have co-operated and churches of several denominations have entered into the spirit of the project by organizing boys' clubs and scout groups. The probation officer of long experience in this district states that the former tendency toward delinquent gang formation is practically overcome. Many of the more difficult cases which we ourselves were accustomed to study came from this part of the city, but we have noted a great decrease of these cases. Ten years ago this probation officer carried in this district a case load regularly of about eighty to ninety offenders, many of them serious. The number has gradually gone down until at the present time he has only twenty-two and asserts that none of them is what he would call a serious offender. Another proof of the value of this preventive program is shown by the fact that while there has been a special effort to draw in the younger potential delinquents, it was possible to hold their interest for years in a constructive program. Many of them now twenty-two or twenty-three years old continue their club activities. The spirit has spread so that there is an overwhelming number of applicants at the various centers.[12]

---

[11] *Survey*, 48:120, April 22, 1922; *Boys' Club Round Table*, 7:18–19, March, 1930.

[12] Wm. Healy, "Prevention of Delinquency," *Jour. Crim. Law and Criminol.*, 24:74–77, May, 1933.

The most careful and intensive study of the effect of a boys' club on delinquency has been made by Thrasher. He studied the Boys' Club of New York City and its results during the period 1927–1931. He found that boys who were members of the club had a larger number of delinquencies than boys in the same neighborhood who were not members; that boys who belonged to the club for four years had more delinquencies than those who belonged for one year; that they had more delinquencies while members of the club than prior to or subsequent to that membership.[13] While it is true that this club attracted boys of the underprivileged classes more than other boys and was therefore likely to have boys with more delinquencies, it does not seem possible to explain these findings except by the proposition that the club was directly or indirectly promoting delinquency, probably through the association of boys who were inclined to delinquency. It does not necessarily follow that all clubs must have the same effects.

COMMUNITY ORGANIZATION. In the isolated village delinquency is kept at a minimum by the informal pressure of an integrated group. The deteriorated area in the city has little integration, either formal or informal. In these areas there are no parent-teachers associations, and no other community associations. Some people maintain that our impersonal and secondary relationships in the modern city are too weak to maintain an organized society and that we must return to the earlier social organization. This seems to be impossible, for present-day society is based on large scale commerce and communication. Apparently the solution of the problem of modern community disorganization must be found in the development of methods of communication and interaction rather than by a return to the small village. Three methods of accomplishing this result have been suggested.

The first is the development of a city plan in which residential areas will be bounded by through streets and crossed only by curving and indirect streets; and with community institutions, such as schools, playgrounds, churches, in the center of this district. This method of construction provides a physical setting for a homogeneous and integrated group. Because of the similarity of the houses within an area of this nature, the inhabitants would be homogeneous in regard to rent-paying ability. Because of the centralization of

<hr />

[13] Frederic M. Thrasher, "The Boys' Club and Juvenile Delinquency," *Amer. Jour. Sociol.*, 42:66–80, July, 1936.

social institutions, they would be brought in contact with each other. It would, on that account, tend to resemble somewhat the small village, and would probably be superior to the present city neighborhood in respect to the degree of control it could exercise over its residents. Residential areas with this physical plan are found in Minneapolis; some of them are quite free from delinquency, while others are very delinquent. The physical plan, by itself, certainly does not prevent delinquency.

A second method of securing organization in a community is by the development of what have been called co-ordinating councils. This is a method of co-ordinating the agencies which deal with behavior problems rather than of co-ordinating the residents of a community. The co-ordinating council is composed of representatives of the juvenile court, the probation department, the school, the police department and sheriff's department, and the social welfare agencies. It has the function of forming policies and promoting organization for the carrying out of policies. It attempts to advise, through a case study committee, regarding policies in individual cases, to develop home standards for the treatment of children, to build up and co-ordinate constructive community agencies, and to eliminate the community influences which lead to delinquency. The Los Angeles Council indicates that the number of juvenile petitions filed in the juvenile court decreased from 5,371 in 1929 to 3,546 in 1932, but does not claim that this is all due to the efforts of the council or that it is an adequate measure of the number of delinquencies committed. It was reported in 1936 that 146 cities were found in which co-ordinating councils had developed, and that the total number of the councils in these cities was over 250. Many of these councils have been short-lived, finding little result from the co-ordinating efforts, perhaps because nothing was accomplished by the efforts when not co-ordinated. Some doubts have been raised regarding the claims of co-ordinating councils which have been reported to be most successful. But there is probably a residue of substantial achievement from the co-ordination of agencies which are independently working effectively.[14]

---

[14] B. L. Coulter, "Prevention of Crime," *Proc. Amer. Prison Assoc.*, 1932, pp. 15–31; "The Community Approach to Delinquency Prevention," *Yearbook Natl. Prob. Assoc.*, 1936, pp. 1–55; Martin H. Neumeyer, "Coördinating Councils," *Sociol. and Soc. Research*, 19:460–471, May, 1935; "Proceedings of the Northeastern Conference on Community Organization," *Jour. Educ. Sociol.*, 11:65–121, October, 1937; Kenyon J. Scudder, "Social Aspects of

A third method of promoting community organization for the reduction of delinquency is by stimulating the ordinary citizens of the community to organize for the solution of their common problems. While the functionaries in the agencies in the community need not be completely excluded, they will not play as prominent a part as in the co-ordinating councils. The "natural leaders" of the community will be expected to act in their own way, with a little stimulation and guidance from behind the scenes. This method has been attempted in several areas in Chicago, under the name of "Area Projects." The active programs of these projects have been concentrated somewhat on recreation, but even in this the parents have been stimulated to take the initiative in the development of the programs.[15]

INSTITUTIONAL RE-ORGANIZATION. Another element in the program for the prevention of delinquency is re-organization of the institutions of modern society. The prevention of delinquency is regarded as a by-product of this re-organization, the primary objective being the increased efficiency of the institutions for all persons affected by them.

The public schools have been criticized frequently both by those interested in the development of a better educated public and those interested in the prevention of delinquency. In many places the schools are being re-organized to promote their efficiency. The attempts to adapt the school to the needs of the pupils may be illustrated by the procedure used in Detroit. All children are given psychological examinations in the first grade, and on several subsequent occasions. They are divided into a middle group of about 60 per cent, an upper fifth and a lower fifth, and about 2 per cent who are suffering from definite handicaps. For each of these groups special courses are organized, being simplified for the lower fifth, and enriched for the upper fifth. Special methods and special materials are developed for each group, in view of the special

---

Crime Prevention," *U. S. Attorney General's Crime Conference,* 1934, pp. 413–424; Henry W. Waltz, "Coördinating Councils for the Prevention and Treatment of Delinquency," *Proc. Amer. Prison Assoc.,* 1935, pp. 92–102; "Why Have Delinquents?" *Los Angeles County Plan of Coördinating Councils,* Los Angeles, 1933; Erle F. Young, "The Coördinating Council Plan in Los Angeles County," *Jour. Crim. Law and Criminol.,* 26:34–40, May, 1935.

[15] E. W. Burgess, J. D. Lohman, and Clifford R. Shaw, "The Chicago Area Project," *Yearbook Natl. Prob. Assoc.,* 1937, pp. 8–28; Clifford R. Shaw, "The Chicago Area Project," *Illinois Dept. Pub. Welf.,* 20th An. Rept., 1937, pp. 716–721.

abilities or disabilities of the group. Special studies are made of the behavior problems in the behavior clinic, and special schools are organized for those problem children who need this. It is expected that these adaptations will result in an attachment of the child to the school, contentment with the status which is secured, and adjustment to social life in later years, instead of rebellion in the form of delinquency, if the needs are not met.[16]

The development of the school for this purpose must be based on intensive research of needs and methods. The traits or characteristics that are required in modern life should be determined and the curriculum organized for the definite purpose of producing these traits. In the primitive group and in the isolated communities in modern times the standards are well understood, generally accepted, and easily taught to the youth. In England, two centuries ago, the teacher had a very definite conception of the type he was trying to produce, and knew that he must apply three pressures to produce the type: classical culture, the society of gentlemen, and the Established Church. By these pressures he produced the Christian-gentleman-scholar as in a mold. Thus the teacher knew exactly what he was trying to produce and how to produce it. To some extent the teachers in the Catholic Schools have a definite conception of the product they are trying to turn out, but almost everywhere else the conception is vague and indefinite. No one has a definite pattern that should be used.

It is probable, however, that the social studies will become the backbone of the curriculum of the school, to which mathematics, language, and other studies will be articulated. At present about one-thirtieth of the units submitted as entrance credits to universities are in the social studies (not counting history), and much of the work in the social studies has not been well organized. Moreover, it is necessary that the social studies begin in the lower grades, as does mathematics, and that it be continued after leaving the public school, in the form of adult education. The newspapers, which are now the principal source of information for the adult population, are completely inadequate as agencies for adult education.

Government and politics, also, need to be reorganized in the interest of the general population, as well as for the prevention of delinquency. In modern life government has little prestige. Some

---

[16] Harry J. Baker, "The Diagnosis and Treatment of Maladjusted Children in the Detroit Public Schools," in Sheldon and Eleanor Glueck (editors), *Preventing Crime,* New York, 1936, pp. 155–175.

people try to revive faith in government by appeals to symbols like the flag or the "Star Spangled Banner," but these efforts are futile unless there is a firm basis for the sentiments. Apparently nothing except science can be substituted for divinity as a reason for faith in government. Government must stand on scientific efficiency or it cannot stand at all.

Freund shows that lawmaking is carried on under the three following conditions: lack of responsibility, lack of expert advice, and lack of principle.[17] The work of making laws is left entirely to a large political body, which possesses no particular qualifications for its work. Any legislator can introduce a bill, in contrast with many of the European countries in which the government introduces the important bills and stands responsible for them. There is practically no expert advice in lawmaking, except in a few places where legislative reference bureaus have been developed. Consequently there is no consistent and permanent principle governing the making of laws or the adjustment of means to ends. We depend on the supreme court for restraint on unwise legislation. But legislation must become a science before the public will respect legislators or their acts. The development of a science of lawmaking should give to the law the prestige which it now lacks, and should also produce a preventive justice to supplement the punitive justice which has previously developed. Pound has predicted that the development of preventive justice will be epoch making.[18]

The police and the courts, similarly, have lost prestige. They are under the control of politicians who are more dangerous to society than are the professional criminals, and who are often closely allied with the professional criminals. Until the concerns which support these politicians become convinced that the special privileges which they can gain from the politicians are less important than the crime and graft which is thereby produced, the police and the courts will remain inefficient agents for the protection of society against crime.

One part of the work of the police which should become important is the preventive work. Fosdick states that this should become as important as the detective work or the work of the uniformed police.[19] Arthur Woods, as commissioner of police in New York

[17] E. Freund, "The Problem of Intelligent Legislation," *Proc. Amer. Pol. Sci. Assoc.*, 4:72, 1907.

[18] Roscoe Pound, *Criminal Justice in America*, New York, 1930, p. 35.

[19] R. B. Fosdick, *American Police Systems*, New York, 1920, p. 378.

City, August Vollmer in Berkeley, and others elsewhere have shown specific ways in which this preventive work can be developed by the police. In addition many police authorities maintain that in the highly mobile society of the present day, America must develop a system of registration or a universal fingerprint system as a basis for control.

Similar efforts are being made to improve the other major institutions and to adapt them to the needs of people in modern life. These programs are too indefinite and the results too diffuse to make possible a measurement of results in the prevention of delinquency, but it cannot be denied that they are potentially important.

REDUCING SOCIAL DISORGANIZATION. The programs for the prevention of delinquency seldom include consideration of the reorganization of the broader culture, but the effect on crime rates of changes in this broader culture are important. Many policies have been suggested by one group or another to reduce social disorganization and develop consistent and harmonious standards of behavior. At least two of these are clearly unsatisfactory. The first is to shut our eyes to certain truths, to enforce adherence to certain doctrines that existed before the modern disorganization developed, to restore the formalism of the medieval period. This policy would stop the teaching of the doctrine of evolution and other doctrines that have affected modern culture very profoundly. If a rigid formalism could be arbitrarily enforced on a group, it would reduce disorganization—for the time being. China is proof of that. But in the long run the disorganization would break through. And it is quite certain that in the United States at present it is impossible to produce anything except more disorganization by attempting to force people to believe things which they do not believe, or disbelieve things that they do not disbelieve. We have disorganization because adjustments and adaptations have not been sufficiently facilitated. Formalism and disorganization are, therefore, closely related in that disorganization often follows formalism.[20]

A second suggestion is that social organization can be secured in modern society, as in early society, by compulsion. Bagehot pointed out that arbitrary control was needed in early societies until a cake of custom had been formed.[21] In Italy and Germany the governments have been under the control of organized groups, which

---

[20] C. H. Cooley, *Social Organization,* New York, 1909, pp. 342–355.
[21] B. Bagehot, *Physics and Politics.*

have also exercised ruthless control over the press, the schools, and the other agencies of communication. This has produced unity in action, but the unity has been based, at first, on ignorance and on fear of opposition. Enthusiastic integration may be the final product, but possibly more disorganization will develop whenever the restrictions on the means of communication are removed so that intellectual honesty becomes possible.

A third suggestion is the substitution of communism for the individualistic economic system. The system of individualism is based on the theory that social welfare is secured by competition which is motivated by self-interest. Competitors, motivated by self-interest, are irritated and thwarted by restrictions. They then, if sufficiently powerful, modify these restrictions to suit their own purposes or they violate the restrictions, unless prevented by an outside and impartial authority. Wealthy persons generally have more than average control over the government, the press, and other means of communication, while the poor people have no other alternative than to violate the restrictions. In that situation, many of the powerful groups use methods that are distinctly injurious to the society but are not illegal. The communists maintain that the whole policy must be changed so that the fundamental activities of life be directed by considerations of social welfare, and that competition be in the form of strife for contributions to the social welfare. The development of the policies of the Soviet Union are likely to be of unusual importance from the point of view of the prevention of crime, and they should provide evidence regarding the comparative value of these two fundamental systems for this purpose. The Soviet policy, however, is an experiment at present and may produce disasters which are greater than the criminality of the individualistic societies.

The significant thing about the Soviet system is probably not communism but the common purpose and enthusiasm about communism. It has resolved the conflict between self-interest and social welfare for a considerable number of people, and it has developed a social organization in which integration rather than disintegration is the characteristic thing. Frankwood E. Williams, a psychiatrist trained in and devoted to clinical procedure prior to his visit to Russia, made the following analysis:

"In Russia one lives—not in a communistic state—but in a state in the process of building a civilization based upon communism where the individual is important, but as a part of a group, and the group is important but only in the sense that it is made up of individuals. The two are the same thing. I am an individual but I am the group; I am the group but I am an individual. There is only one loyalty—to the group, but that is myself; or to myself, but that is the group. One has a loyalty here not to a group but to many groups and as the interests of these various groups often come into conflict, conflict arises within us."[22] The number of registered prostitutes in Moscow decreased from twenty-five thousand before the Revolution to an estimated number of three thousand in 1928 and to four or five hundred in 1932. This has been made possible in part by the laws in regard to sex and marriage but in part by the methods used in the Prophylactorium for Prostitution. The method there doesn't consist in psychological and psychiatric examinations or case studies, in our sense. It consists in teaching the girl that she has a place in the scheme of things; that she is the only one who feels that she is un-important and no-good; that she not only has a place but that she is wanted, in fact, needed in that place; that friendship, marriage, children, study if she is interested, leadership, are all possible for her if she will but take her place. (And this is no hoax, it is actually true.) To that end she must learn to read and write and become a 'qualified worker,' that is, one trained in some pursuit. Qualified, she must work, at present seven hours a day, four days in five. The institution is prepared to give her the necessary instruction; during her period of learning she will receive all necessary medical care, food, and lodging and a small amount of money. She will be trained to use the modern machines that she will find when she leaves the institution and enters the factory as a 'qualified worker.' The mental hygiene in all this—the best in the world—is security, present and future; purpose, sense of belonging, sense of being needed, sense of personal worth and value as a human being; confidence in herself, in others and in the joint activity; consciousness of opportunity, freedom from fear. . . . With all the trained personnel and clinical equipment that we could conceivably bring together could we by our method in our social organization attain as much?"[23] "We have a right to be appreciative of such organizations as child-guidance clinics. They are

22 Frankwood E. Williams, "Those Crazy Russians," *Survey,* 67:345, January 1, 1932. Reprinted by permission.
23 Frankwood E. Williams, "Russia—A Nation of Adolescents," *Survey,* 68:14, 57, April 1, 1932. Reprinted by permission.

a partial salvation for individuals but they are not even the beginning of social salvation. Individual, clinical methods as a method of social prophylaxis will go with its civilization. Only a hygiene of society will meet the situation."[24]

The method of reformation is effective in that situation for the same reason the tendency toward crime is weak, because of the social organization. As long as the social organization is one of aggression, conflict, disregard for the welfare of others, we may expect criminality to flourish and we may expect all of the methods of reformation to fail in a large proportion of cases.

The modern problem of social control is due to the fact that we have developed a material civilization based on a science of physics and chemistry far in advance of our knowledge of human nature and social interactions. We know immensely more than Aristotle did regarding the methods of production and distribution of wealth, but little more than he knew regarding the methods of social control. The problems of life are becoming continually more complex because the development of physics and chemistry proceeds so much more rapidly than the ability of human beings to adjust to each other. It has been suggested by a professor of physics that the research work in physics and chemistry should be arbitrarily stopped for a generation until the knowledge of social relations can catch up. This is impracticable, of course, but would probably produce progress in the long run if it could be done. In the meantime, the only way out of the difficulty is by developing with the greatest speed possible a technique and science of social research that will enable us to have as satisfactory knowledge regarding human nature and social interactions as can be secured. Only in that way will it be possible to deal effectively with the problem of crime or any other social problem.

In general, social disorganization can be reduced intelligently only by facilitating adaptations and transition by an increase and spread of knowledge based on sociological research. This knowledge and publicity are desirable because of the direct effect they produce on the attitudes, standards, and codes of people rather than because of the assistance they give in securing the passage of laws. Knowledge is in itself a desirable form of pressure and makes law relatively un-

[24] Frankwood E. Williams, "Out from Confusion," *Survey*, 68:253, June 1, 1932. Reprinted by permission.

necessary. Ultimately the process of making laws must reach an end. The law against contributing to the delinquency of children, for instance, has been a means of preventing some children from being developed into criminals, but it raised the problem, How can we modify the parents and others so that they will not contribute to the delinquency of children? The prohibition law was an attempt to reduce alcoholism, but it raised the problem, How can we modify the conditions which cause people to violate the prohibition laws? If we start in the direction of passing laws in order to keep people from violating laws, we have an endless road ahead of us. And we must finally come back to a modification of the attitudes of the average citizen. Consequently it is desirable to educate and train the youth with that in view, rather than with legislation in view.

SUGGESTED READINGS

Alinsky, Saul D., "The Basis in the Social Sciences for the Social Treatment of the Adult Offender," *Proc. Natl. Conf. Soc. Work,* 1938, pp. 714–724.

Branham, V. C., "A Summary of Some of the Crime Prevention Work Being Done in New York State at the Present Time," *Proc. Amer. Prison Assoc.,* 1932, pp. 301–308.

Burgess, E. W., Lohman, J. D., and Shaw, C. R., "The Chicago Area Project," *Yearbook Natl. Prob. Assoc.,* 1937, pp. 8–29.

"Community Approach to Delinquency Prevention," *Yearbook Natl. Prob. Assoc.,* 1936, pp. 1–155.

Cooley, C. H., *Social Organization,* New York, 1909, Chs. 34–36.

Cooley, C. H., *Social Process,* New York, 1918, Chs. 29–35.

Correvont, Ann M. and E. H., "Prevention of Delinquency from the Community Approach," *Jour. Juv. Res.,* 17:54–61, January, 1933.

Coulter, B. L., "Prevention of Crime," *Proc. Amer. Prison Assoc.,* 1932, pp. 15–31.

"Crime Prevention and the Schools," *Bull. of Research Division of Natl. Educ. Assoc.,* Vol. X, No. 4, 1932.

Ferri, E., *Criminal Sociology,* Tr. by J. I. Kelly and John Lisle, Boston, 1917, Part II, Chs. 4–6.

Freund, E., "Prolegomena to a Science of Legislation," *Ill. Law Rev.,* 13:264–292, October, 1918.

Glueck, Sheldon and Eleanor, *Preventing Crime,* New York, 1936.

Landman, J. H., *Human Sterilization,* New York, 1932.

Neumeyer, Martin H., "Coördinating Councils," *Sociol. and Soc. Research,* 19:460–471, May, 1935.

Perry, Clarence A., "Can the City Be Adapted to the New Leisure?" *Proc. Natl. Conf. Social Work,* 1933, pp. 387–397.

Pettit, M. L., "Rehabilitating the Delinquent Gang," *Proc. Amer. Prison Assoc.,* 1930, pp. 70–78.

"Proceedings of the Northeastern Conference on Community Organization," *Jour. Educ. Sociol.,* 11:65–121, October, 1937.

Rogers, Carl R., *The Clinical Treatment of the Problem Child,* Boston, 1939.

Shaw, Clifford R., "The Chicago Area Project," *Illinois Dept. Pub. Welf.,* 20th An. Rept., 1937, pp. 716–721.

Slavson, S. R., *Creative Group Education,* New York, 1937.

Stevenson, George S., and Smith, Geddes, *Child Guidance Clinics,* New York, 1934.

Thomas, W. I. and Dorothy, *The Child in America,* New York, 1928.

Thrasher, Frederic M., "The Boys' Club and Juvenile Delinquency," *Amer. Jour. Sociol.,* 42:66–80, July, 1936.

Thrasher, Frederic M., "Juvenile Delinquency and Crime Prevention," *Jour. Educ. Sociol.,* 6:500–509, April, 1933.

Waltz, Henry W., "Coördinating Councils for the Prevention and Treatment of Delinquency," *Proc. Amer. Prison Assoc.,* 1935, pp. 92–102.

Witmer, Helen M., and students, "The Outcome of Treatment in a Child Guidance Clinic," *Smith Coll. Studies in Social Work,* 3:341–399, June, 1933.

Witmer, Helen M., and students, "The Later Social Adjustments of Problem Children: A Report of Thirteen Follow-up Investigations," *Smith Coll. Studies in Social Work,* 6:3–98, September, 1935.

Young, Erle F., "The Coördinating Council Plan in Los Angeles County," *Jour. Crim. Law and Criminol.,* 26:34–40, May, 1935.

Indexes

INDEX OF NAMES